THE LIFE AND WRITING OF
FRAY ANGÉLICO CHÁVEZ

Pasó por Aquí Series on the
Nuevomexicano Literary Heritage

Edited by
Genaro M. Padilla,
Erlinda Gonzales-Berry,
and A. Gabriel Meléndez

THE LIFE AND WRITING OF
FRAY ANGÉLICO CHÁVEZ

A New Mexico Renaissance Man

ELLEN McCRACKEN

University of New Mexico Press
Albuquerque

© 2009 by the University of New Mexico Press
All rights reserved. Published 2009
Printed in the United States of America

First paperback printing, 2018
Paperback ISBN: 978-0-8263-4761-9

Library of Congress Cataloging-in-Publication Data

McCracken, Ellen (Ellen Marie)
The life and writing of Fray Angélico Chávez : a New Mexico Renaissance man / Ellen McCracken.
       p. cm. — (Pasó por aquí series on the Nuevomexicano literary heritage)
Includes bibliographical references and index.
ISBN 978-0-8263-4760-2 (cloth : alk. paper)
  1. Chavez, Angelico, 1910– 2. Mexican American authors—20th century—Biography. 3. New Mexico—In literature. I. Title.
ps3505.h625z78 2009
818'.52—dc22
[B]
                              2009025765

For Giuliana and Carlo, whose involuntary long hours in archives and interviews helped to make this book possible. I hope a part of New Mexico always remains with them.

Contents

Illustrations	viii
Acknowledgments	x
Introduction	1
Chapter One: A Life's Trajectory	7
Chapter Two: Hybrid Identity in the Early Cultural Production	65
Chapter Three: The Young Mission Padre and the Kaleidoscope of Culture	110
Chapter Four: Padre in the Pacific: Art in the Face of Death in World War II and Beyond	167
Chapter Five: Re-envisioning History: Hispano-Franciscan Identity, Documentary Recovery, and the Creative Impulse	200
Chapter Six: Hispano Genealogy, La Conquistadora, and the Penitentes: Revisionist History	232
Chapter Seven: The Historian's Return to Art and Literature	265
Chapter Eight: The Renaissance Man as Public Intellectual	311
Chapter Nine: Twilight of the Historian: Vindicating Hispano Clergy	358
Notes	400
Note on Sources	454
Index	456

Illustrations

Fig. 1.1	Manuel Chávez in gaucho costume	8
Fig. 1.2	Manuel Chávez, age three	11
Fig. 1.3	Manuel Chávez and his sister Martha	13
Fig. 1.4	Manuel Chávez, St. Gertrudis Church	14
Fig. 1.5	Manuel Chávez, St. Francis Seminary	17
Fig. 1.6	Manuel Chávez, siblings, and mother	18
Fig. 1.7	*By East García*	19
Fig. 1.8	*On Acequia Madre*	20
Fig. 1.9	Friar Angélico Chávez after tonsure	21
Fig. 1.10	Fray Angélico Chávez, 1937	23
Fig. 1.11	Fray Angélico Chávez in archbishop's garden	26
Fig. 1.12	Fray Angélico Chávez, chaplain major	30
Fig. 1.13	Fray Angélico Chávez with Laura Gilpin	39
Fig. 1.14	Fray Angélico Chávez and Paul Horgan	44
Fig. 1.15	Fabián and María Nicolasa Chávez	47
Fig. 1.16	Fray Angélico Chávez leaving the Palace Restaurant	59
Fig. 1.17	Fray Angélico Chávez and friends	61
Fig. 2.1	Manuel Chávez, St. Francis Seminary	69
Fig. 2.2	Manuel Chávez and seminarians	71
Fig. 2.3	Fray Angélico Chávez, pen-and-ink drawing of Zuni Mission	73
Fig. 2.4	Fray Angélico Chávez, illustration for "Notch Twenty-One"	74
Fig. 2.5	Ordination class, 1937	83
Fig. 3.1	Ordination card	112

Fig. 3.2	*The Stigmata of St. Francis*	114
Fig. 3.3	Poets' Roundup of 1938	118
Fig. 3.4	*Brother Juniper, Francis and Masseo, Francis*	132
Fig. 3.5	Frontispiece, *New Mexico Triptych*	132
Fig. 3.6	Chapel of Santa Dorotea, Domingo Station	140
Fig. 3.7	Chapel of Santa Dorotea after renovation	140
Fig. 3.8	Fray Angélico Chávez before crucifixion triptych	145
Fig. 3.9	Fray Angélico Chávez at north transept door	149
Fig. 3.10	Front exterior of Our Lady of Guadalupe Church	150
Fig. 4.1	Chaplain Angélico Chávez in World War II	177
Fig. 4.2	Fray Angélico Chávez, 1946	192
Fig. 5.1	La Conquistadora procession	213
Fig. 5.2	Fray Angélico Chávez in the History Library	216
Fig. 6.1	Fray Angélico Chávez with prizefighters, Fort Bliss	235
Fig. 6.2	Soldiers bearing La Conquistadora	257
Fig. 7.1	Hymn "Salve Sancte Pater"	267
Fig. 7.2	Illustration, "To a Fly (On an Old Friar's Head)"	268
Fig. 7.3	Fray Angélico Chávez addressing the Catholic Poetry Society of America	269
Fig. 7.4	Chapel of San Francisco, Golden	289
Fig. 7.5	Chapel of San Francisco, Golden, after renovation	292
Fig. 8.1	Fray Angélico Chávez's Silver Jubilee	312
Fig. 8.2	Fray Angélico Chávez, 1979	336
Fig. 9.1	Fray Angélico Chávez's immediate family	382
Fig. 9.2	Fray Angélico Chávez, 1984	394
Fig. 9.3	Fray Angélico Chávez and José Ramón Remacha	395

Acknowledgments

I WISH TO THANK THE many people and institutions that helped to make this study possible. The National Endowment for the Humanities awarded a year's fellowship for writing chapters of the book. Sabbatical leaves from the University of California, Santa Barbara, and research grants from the Academic Senate and the Chicano Studies Institute funded travel to archives, transcription of interviews, and writing.

I thank acquiring editor Lisa Pacheco at the University of New Mexico Press for her patient reading of the manuscript and her enthusiasm for the project. Her energy, verve, and intelligence have made it a pleasure to work with her. Editor Sarah E. Soliz astutely and carefully line-edited the manuscript. I appreciate the careful reading, helpful comments, and support of the manuscript by the anonymous reader and Professor Rose Marie Beebe of Santa Clara University. Professors Ramón Saldívar and Norma Cantú provided crucial early support for this project.

I am especially grateful to the talented archivists whose knowledge, patience, and generosity made this strongly archival-based project possible. Orlando Romero and Tomas Jaehn, the former and current directors of the Fray Angélico Chávez History Library in Santa Fe, aided me immensely in retrieving thousands of documents in the collection on Fray Angélico Chávez. Thomas Chávez, former director of the Palace of the Governors, often assisted in making this material available, as did Charles Bennett, Hazel Romero, and Diana Ortega DeSantis. Daniel Kosharek, photo archivist at the Palace of the Governors, generously made available a treasure trove of uncataloged photographs that I had been waiting years to see. He kindly assigned numbers to those I wished to use and facilitated their reproduction. Barry Drucker, archivist at the New Mexico State Records Center and Archives, efficiently facilitated the granting of permission for reprinting photographs in the collection. Marina Ochoa, head of the Archives of the Archdiocese of Santa Fe, made documents and photographs available and provided information on Fray Angélico's contribution to the formation of the archives and to the cathedral renovation. The late Fr. Virgilio Biasol, O.F.M., allowed me to do extensive research in the Santa Barbara Mission Archive Library on Franciscan documents and publications and borrow material for photocopying.

In Cincinnati, Fr. Dan Anderson, O.F.M., former archivist of St. John the Baptist Province, made hundreds of documents available, allowed me to work long hours in the archives, arranged interviews, reproduced photographs, sent information and photocopies by mail, and shared his knowledge of the Franciscan community with me. I am extremely grateful for his patience, entertaining humor, and kindness. Fr. Jack Wintz, O.F.M., of *St. Anthony Messenger* generously allowed me to photocopy documents in the magazine's offices after hours. Franciscan fathers Murray Bodo, Jovian Weigel, and Bernard Gerbus provided generous hospitality along with informative and entertaining conversation and interviews that helped shape this book. Fr. Marcan Hetteberg and Brother Dan Rewers aided me in retrieving documents and learning Franciscan Southwest history while I worked in the Cincinnati Archives. Provincial archivist Brother Allan Schmitz, O.F.M., kindly gave permission to reproduce photographs for this book.

Former UCSB graduate students Magdalena Torres, Laura Weingarten, and Gabriela Sánchez provided invaluable research assistance in retrieving Chávez's widely dispersed publications. Maura Jess at UCSB digitized several photos for the book. Shirley Ayn Linder worked many hours transcribing interviews for this study. Fr. Jack Clark Robinson, O.F.M., generously advised me on Franciscan issues, shared research material he had gathered, and provided me with a copy of the Peña Blanca House Chronicle and a transcript of his interview with Robert F. Sánchez. Frs. Juan Romero, Francis Smith, S.J., and Michael McCarthy, S.J., provided help with Latin translation, and Viola Miglio helped in a translation from the Italian. I thank Félix D. Almaráz Jr. for making available his well-organized collection of the correspondence between Chávez and José Cisneros, 1951–91. Marc Simmons kindly shared his substantial collection of material on Chávez. I am extremely grateful to Phyllis Morgan for compiling her invaluable bibliography of Chávez's writing and the helpful material she shared with me in interviews.

I wish to thank the generosity of numerous people who knew Fray Angélico Chávez who made time for interviews or provided written testimonies about his life and work to Mario García and me: Rudolfo Anaya, Fr. Salvador Aragón, O.F.M., Darlene Ortiz Armijo, Lorenzo Armijo, Bertille Baca, Carlota Baca, Erlinda Baca, Jaime Baca, Alice Ann Biggerstaff, Fr. Godfrey Blank, O.F.M., Mathilde Bird, Tim Burch, Fr. Crispin Butz, O.F.M., Charlie Carrillo, Judge Antonio Chávez, Bernice Chávez, Consuelo Chávez, Fabián Chávez Jr., Francisco Chávez, José Chávez, Mary Chávez, Nora Chávez, Teresa Chávez, Tom Chávez, José Cisneros, Saul Cohen, María Dean, Roz Eisenberg, Jody Ellis, Fr. Bernard Gerbus, O.F.M., Fred Grillo, Cynthia Farah Haines, Richard Halford, E. B. and Jane Hall, Connie Hernández, Emily Hughes, John Kessel, Clark Kimball, Fr. Otto Krische, O.F.M., John Pen La Farge, Kate McGraw, Doris Maiorano, Robert Martin, Jim Maryol, N. Scott Momaday, Adela Montoya, Phyllis Morgan, Marcia Muth, Ambassador Frank V. Ortiz Jr., Concha Ortiz del Pino y Kleven, Carlos Félix Pacheco, Bessie Enriqueta Pacheco, Donna Quasthoff, Pedro Ribera-Ortega, Fr. Guadalupe Rivera, Fr. Jack Clark Robinson, O.F.M., Fr. Cándido Rodríguez, Eliseo Rodríguez, Fr. Juan Romero, Fr. Bill Sánchez, Fr. Gilbert Schneider, O.F.M., Dr. Randolph Seligman, Julia Silva, Marc Simmons, Mónica Sosaya Halford, Fr. Thomas Steele, S.J., Stewart Udall, Sabine Ulibarrí, Anna Mae Vigil, Federico Vigil, Jim Walsh, R. C. "Doc" Weaver, and Malcolm Withers.

I am especially grateful for my family's love and support during this long project, especially the patience of my children Giuliana and Carlo who spent long hours in archives and at interviews in New Mexico instead of enjoying normal summer vacations. Mario García's intellectual support and insights about the project have been invaluable, as was his teamwork in the many hours of interviews. There is no better family!

Introduction

As I was preparing to travel to New Mexico in the summer of 1995 to research the tradition of santos for my study of popular religiosity in the work of U.S. Latina writers, I looked more closely and with utter fascination at Fray Angélico Chávez's fiction about the santos and other Hispano religious traditions. Once in Santa Fe, I tried to arrange a meeting with this formidable intellectual, but the staff at the cathedral said he was not in good health and no longer seeing people. As soon as I returned to California, I began to organize a special session on his work for an academic conference to be held in Santa Fe in March 1996. When I arrived for the conference, I learned the sad news that he had died two days earlier. The local newspapers were filled with articles and pictures of this crucial contributor to New Mexico life and letters, and I called the *New York Times* to inform the obituary department of his death. As we had lunch with his nephew Tom Chávez in one of Fray Angélico's favorite haunts, the San Francisco Street Bar and Grill, people stopped to offer their condolences to Tom. During our walk back, his colorful front-page picture greeted us from every newsstand. Later that afternoon, a large audience attended our conference panel on Fray Angélico's work to hear presentations by Fr. Thomas Steele, Mario García, and Thomas Chávez, along with mine. Unexpectedly, the academic session had become a site of mourning and tribute to this dearly missed figure. That evening I laid eyes on Fray Angélico Chávez for the first time at the wake, and the next morning I participated with hundreds of others in the Mass of the Resurrection in the cathedral that he had contributed so much to aesthetically throughout his life. I will always remember the long procession of Franciscans singing the "Ultima" at the funeral and the "Adiós, Madre del Cielo" sung at the cemetery on that crisp, sunny morning.

Later that day, Tom Chávez, director of the Palace of the Governors, showed Mario García and me the extensive collection of his uncle's materials at the History Library. The historian in Mario quickly came out as he excitedly remarked, "There's a biography here!" Very soon thereafter, we decided to undertake the project, and there began our many trips to New Mexico to research Fray Angélico's life and work and interview dozens of the people who knew him. Each trip began with the happy anticipation of new discoveries and ended with the rich fulfillment of unexpected paths and new friendships. As a literary scholar, I was especially interested in Fray Angélico's creative writing and painting, but as I was drawn into the details of his life in researching the biography, I realized how inseparable the elements of that life were from the vast writing and culture he produced. I conceived the present project as way to do justice to both by analyzing the trajectory of his intellectual and cultural contributions in the context of key elements of his life story. This book does not replace the full-fledged biography, but rather integrates elements of it to explain and illuminate the vast intellectual production of Chávez's nearly seven-decade career. It is an homage and tribute to this great man of letters at the centenary of his birth in 2010.

The analysis here moves chronologically through his work, which includes fiction, poetry, plays, essays, spiritual tracts, sermons, historical writing, translation, genealogy, painting, church renovation, journalism, and other work as a public intellectual. His vast oeuvre includes twenty-four books and nearly six hundred shorter writings. By grouping his works chronologically, I show their interconnection with his life events and the intersections of related themes and techniques at various periods in his life. I focus on Chávez's complex identity as an ethnic, American, and religious subject who was at the same time a historian and artist, a creative writer and preservationist. The first native New Mexican ordained a Franciscan priest in the centuries of Franciscan presence in the area, Chávez's religious identity was imbued with his sense of the importance of the history of Hispanos in New Mexico.

Rather than examining his work genre by genre, which certainly would have provided an important understanding of his development in various fields, I chose to focus on his closely interconnected contributions in several genres at each stage of his career. How is his work in any given period "all of a piece," as John Gould Fletcher termed it? How did his triptych series of large paintings of the Stations of the Cross in the church at Peña Blanca in 1939 interact with his decision at that very time to cast a book of stories about New Mexico as a literary and visual triptych? And later, precisely as he worked on designing a new altar screen for the Conquistadora Chapel in St. Francis Cathedral, he revised and assembled together seven of his short stories as figurative panels on an altar screen, each centering on a different visually present santo. As he hand-painted a photograph of the Castrense altar screen dedicated to Our Lady of Light for his cotranslation of a key eighteenth-century text, he integrated images from the huge stone reredos into his current book of fiction. How did his discoveries in bundles of unorganized Church documents shape not only his historical and creative writing but also his re-dressing of La Conquistadora and the revival of the statue's *cofradía*? And most importantly, how did his extensive detective work on the early Franciscan missionaries in New Mexico shape his identity and career as a friar, as he performed again, relived, and transcended their work now in the twentieth-century context as a missionary who also renovated churches, faithfully documented his myriad activities, wrote and preserved records of contemporary friars, and published history for both scholars and the larger public? Although his multifaceted identity involved diverse activities at every stage of his life, he is above all a writer. To narrate his life apart from a detailed understanding of his writing and creative activity would leave much of that life unrevealed.

To set the stage, chapter 1 offers a biographical overview of Chávez's life and career as a Franciscan priest, creative writer, artist, historian, and public intellectual. I argue that Chávez's life and work are marked by a hybrid and admixed identity, in which he emphasizes his unique ethnicity despite the melting-pot ideology predominant in the United States until the late 1960s. Finding himself in a semi-exile from the Southwest as the only Hispano in the Franciscan seminary in Cincinnati, Chávez immediately reterritorializes himself as an ethnic subject through artistic and literary work, publishing numerous stories, poems, plays, and drawings, as chapter 2 examines. He connects with the writers' and artists' groups in Santa Fe on summer visits home, fertilizing his creative work. The chapter analyzes all of his creative work in this period, including his first novel serialized in 1931–32 and a 1931 play.

Chapter 3 is an in-depth study of Chávez's prolific literary and artistic production during his first assignment after ordination at Peña Blanca, a rich kaleidoscope of creativity. In this five-year period, he helped to mediate the dispute between the Church and the Santo Domingo Pueblo, which had been placed under interdict; ministered in several pueblos and at the Peña Blanca church and school; undertook the extensive repair and restoration of two village churches; painted two large series of murals; spent time with the Santa Fe writers' and artists' colony; wrote dozens of stories, poems, and essays; and published his first two books, *Clothed with the Sun* and *New Mexico Triptych*.

Chapter 4 studies Chávez's varied writing as a chaplain in the Pacific during World War II, including his literary, autobiographical, epistolary, reportorial, and testimonial writing. These cultural traces of the cataclysmic war not only tell the story of an Hispano chaplain and the troops he served, but suggest the key role that art, spirituality, contact with other cultures, and everyday routine play in periods of extreme social upheaval. The chapter focuses on the battle between Eros and Thanatos and the key role of writing—poetry, reports, essays, and letters—in a period of severe degradation, destruction, and violent death.

Back in Santa Fe after the life-changing historical war, Chávez immerses himself in his new passion—the research and writing of history—the focus of chapter 5. He begins to organize and research the treasure trove of colonial Church records of the archdiocese that had remained in loose bundles over the years. In addition to a number of scholarly articles on colonial New Mexico history, he researches, writes, illustrates, and designs several small books on St. Francis Cathedral, the Archdiocese of Santa Fe, and the Church in New Mexico. Squeezing in time for instruction on paleography in Albuquerque, he plunges into this new work despite the pressures of a heavy schedule of preaching missions throughout the state to Spanish-speaking Catholics.

After returning from his second unexpected tour of military duty in 1952, Fray Angélico produces revisionist historical writing on Hispano genealogy, colonial churches, the Penitentes, and the statue of La Conquistadora, the focus of chapter 6. He completes *Origins of New Mexico Families*, tracing in detail the ancestry of New Mexico Hispanos back to colonial times, and the innovative, hybrid text *La Conquistadora: Autobiography of an Ancient Statue*. He takes the statue on a three-month pilgrimage throughout New Mexico in 1954 and renovates the Conquistadora Chapel in St. Francis Cathedral. As he has throughout his priestly ministry, he experiences tremendous time pressures because he does all of this work while a full-time priest at Jemez, also serving as the postmaster there.

Chapter 7, "The Historian's Return to Art and Literature," notes that even as Chávez continues his prolific historical writing in the late 1950s and 1960s, he also publishes fiction, poetry, and a historical novel with his own illustrations. At this time he receives international recognition for *The Virgin of Port Lligat*, a long poem with commentary inspired by a painting by Salvador Dalí. In addition to scholarly and popular articles on history, he also publishes *Archives of the Archdiocese of Santa Fe, 1678–1900*, finishes *Coronado's Friars*, and begins the translation and annotation of the *Oroz Relación*. When assigned as pastor of St. Joseph Church in Cerrillos in 1959, he immediately begins to renovate the deteriorating chapel at Golden, creating a stunning "sermon in stone" for passersby on the new highway to witness.

The Renaissance man becomes a more prolific public intellectual after leaving active priestly ministry in June 1971 and devoting himself full time to writing, the subject of chapter 8. He makes new friends and enjoys an active social life in Santa Fe, living first with his sister and then in apartments. To support himself, he publishes extensively in *New Mexico* magazine, where he also serves as book review editor. The record of his articles and numerous book reviews is a barometer of his ideas in this period of widespread social change. He shines as a public intellectual in this journalism. After entering secular life, he publishes his extraordinary *My Penitente Land*, in which he freely questions received ideas on history and Catholicism in New Mexico. He publishes an illustrated biography of St. Francis for young adults and accepts the paying job of translating *The Domínguez-Escalante Journal*.

Chapter 9, "Twilight of the Historian: Vindicating Hispano Clergy" examines Chávez's biographies of key nineteenth-century Hispano priests—Padres Martínez of Taos, Gallegos of Albuquerque, and Ortiz of Santa Fe. The first incarnation of the three books was an eight-hundred-page manuscript entitled *Truth Stalks the Archbishop* in which Chávez played on the title of Cather's novel to alert readers that her characters, Lamy and Machebeuf, had not been truthful in their accounts of the native clergy of New Mexico. Chávez also aimed to counter and correct his friend Paul Horgan's 1975 *Lamy of Santa Fe*. These three books (the third completed and published posthumously) attempt to vindicate the Hispano priests and redefine their key role in New Mexico history. We can trace his own sense of the Church's lack of appreciation for his work as an Hispano priest, what he termed "ecclesiastical colonialism," in these biographies. His decades-long research on Hispano genealogy in New Mexico culminated with his final book, a detailed study of his ancestors, *Chávez: A Distinctive American Clan of New Mexico* (1989). In this period he returns to live in the cathedral friary, suffers health problems, but continues to frequent local restaurants and serve as a key twentieth-century public intellectual of New Mexico.

The life and work of Fray Angélico Chávez broaden standard conceptualizations of American culture and its central Hispano component. Chávez's complex and changing identity throughout his life and writing marks his uniqueness as an American intellectual, proud of his people's legacy. His literary, artistic, and historical contributions reinsert the Hispano presence in New Mexico into the master narratives of American history and culture. As we celebrate the centenary of his birth in 2010, an understanding of his vast interdisciplinary intellectual contributions that are harmoniously "all of a piece" is a fitting tribute.

CHAPTER ONE

A Life's Trajectory

*Tell the truth. If you have a hero,
tell his faults too.*

—Fray Angélico Chávez, 1990[1]

IN THE SUMMER OF 1928, a young Hispano from northern New Mexico who aspired to be a writer donned a gaucho costume that won first prize in the annual fiesta in Santa Fe. There he met Witter Bynner and other American poets of the Santa Fe Writers Group who included him in their raucous get-togethers, poetry "roundups," and innovative publication ventures. Unlike other members of the avant-garde group, the young Hispano was studying to become a Franciscan priest—the first native New Mexican to be ordained in the order in the four hundred years since the Spanish conquest of the area. Fray Angélico Chávez would ultimately become one of New Mexico's foremost twentieth-century intellectuals, writing twenty-four books and over six hundred shorter works, making aesthetic and scholarly contributions in the fields of painting, poetry, fiction, history, biography, journalism, genealogy, philology, and architectural renovation. How do such diverse elements as a gaucho costume, an association with a group of American poets, Franciscan priesthood, and contributions in this plethora of fields serve as indicators of the

FIG. 1.1. Manuel Chávez in gaucho costume, Santa Fe, New Mexico, 1926, courtesy the Archives of the Franciscan Province of St. John the Baptist of Cincinnati.

complex sense of identity, self, and community that mark this figure's prolific work?

Coherent notions of identity were central to the movements for ethnic and racial equality that began to change American history in the mid-1960s. Contesting the predominant concept of the melting pot that prescribed the integration of immigrants and racial groups into a harmonious yet fictive whole, minority groups substituted relatively stable, new formations of identity based on pride, community, and political change. By the late 1980s and 1990s more nuanced notions of identity were theorized, based on plural, hybrid, and gendered formations of the self. Singular categories such as "black" or "Chicano" were no longer entirely adequate delineators of selfhood, notwithstanding their usefulness a generation earlier. Unidimensional and stable self-definition gave way to a developing, admixed, and multiply conceived identity.

Here I focus this new optic, in both its literal and metaphoric senses, backward in history to an earlier period of American letters, in order to understand the intellectual and artistic contributions of a pre–Chicano Movement Hispano American whose complex self-definition is evident in a prolific career. As the first comprehensive study of the vast oeuvre of Fray Angélico Chávez (1910–96), this book focuses on the multifaceted formation of identity that literally and metaphorically marks his work, the interplay of the verbal and the visual at nearly every intersection, and the refusal of traditional boundaries in the thought and work of this talented intellectual. While some Chicano scholars have classified him as a kind of forefather who was shaped by the more traditional concerns of his generation, I will argue that his life and work are better understood as marked by the hybridity and complexity with which we currently understand identity, the aesthetic, and border crossing. While he came of age before the post-1960 Chicano Renaissance, his profoundly innovative work represents another sort of cultural renaissance, making him one of the most important U.S. Latino intellectuals of the twentieth century.

Distinct elements such as the gaucho costume; the association with American writers such as Bynner, Thornton Wilder, Paul Horgan, and John Gould Fletcher; work as a Franciscan missionary; and the recovery of the history, architecture, and traditions of Spain in the Southwest emblematize a few of the traces of complex identity formation in Chávez's life and work. Decades before the Chicano Movement, in non-melting-pot fashion, he became part of the American writers' group as an ethnic subject, proudly displaying himself as a Latino Other in writing, painting, and even attire. Both his Hispanic and Franciscan identities, and his work in multiple artistic, literary, and scholarly fields, nuanced his American identity. Although he is quite different from his contemporary Américo Paredes, whom Ramón Saldívar classifies as a "proto-Chicano,"[2] the elements of identity visible in Chávez's prolific work involve the sense of self as an ethnic, American, and religious subject who was also a painter, a poet, and intellectual. I will metaphorically extend the notion of the multiply conceived identity of ethnic subjects to the complexities of the visual/verbal and cross-generic aesthetic and intellectual work of Fray Angélico Chávez. First, however, an overview of the trajectory of his life must be sketched.

Round-Trip Journeys

Born April 10, 1910, in the small northern New Mexico village of Wagon Mound, Manuel Ezequiel Chávez was the first of ten children of Fabián Chávez and María Nicolasa Roybal de Chávez. His parents were the grandchildren of the founders of Wagon Mound. His paternal grandfather, Eugenio Chávez, son of Encarnación Luna, was brought as a child from Belén, and the Roybals on his mother's side were from the Jacona district. His mother's father, Romualdo Roybal, came as a child to the Wagon Mound area.[3] The story has come down through the family that Nicolasa's parents did not like Fabián's, so he proposed to her crossing a street on horseback and gave her the ring this way. They then waited until after her parents died to get married in 1909 when she was twenty-five and he was thirty.[4] Nicolasa's father sent her and her sister to New Mexico Normal School in Las Vegas to study with the nuns and insisted that the girls take music. Nicolasa continued with music, taught piano, played the organ in church, and taught school for one year. Manuel's father learned the carpentry trade from his father, Eugenio, who was also a rancher, and Don Fabián worked repairing and building houses in town. He was adept at cabinet making. The year of Manuel's birth, in 1910, he built the pews for the new church of Santa Clara and during World War II did carpentry work at Los Alamos. Fabián Chávez was also a cantor for the Penitentes, and sang the *alabados* (Penitente hymns) around his house. One son remembers that he loved to chant the alabados from his rocking chair and knew the words to the hymns well.[5]

When Manuel was eleven months old, the family, including baby Martha, moved to San Diego, California, for three and a half years where his father and uncle were hired to help build the Panama-California Exposition that opened in 1915. His father worked on the U.S. Grant Hotel and the first buildings of the San Diego Zoo.[6] The family recounts that the young Manuel was very precocious and one day ran away down the streets of San Diego, fascinated by reading the successive street signs.[7] Two aspects of Manuel's years in San Diego

FIG. 1.2. Manuel Chávez, age three, San Diego, California, 1913, courtesy Palace of the Governors Photo Archives (NMHM/DCA), frontispiece, *Cantares*.

became key factors in his life. Chávez recounts that he spoke primarily English in San Diego because they lived among Anglos: "Because my parents were speaking English with the neighbors, they used English on me."[8] Thus, when he returned to Wagon Mound for kindergarten and first grade, he was ahead of other Hispano children in English skills. He joked, "I knew more English than my teacher!"[9] Secondly, he was introduced to the key role of Franciscanism in the history of the Southwest. His parents took him to see Mission San Diego de Alcalá, the first of the California missions, founded in 1769 near Balboa Park where the exhibition was being constructed. He learned for the first time about Fray Junípero Serra and Franciscanism.

Although Chávez returned to New Mexico at the end of 1914, before the exposition officially opened, he and his family perhaps saw some of the buildings and exhibits as they were being constructed, among them various artistic representations of the history of

Catholicism in New Mexico and the New World. Besides the monument to Serra erected at the exposition, Chávez perhaps saw the buildings in the New Mexico exhibit: the reproduction of the 1629 Franciscan mission at Acoma and the Taos Pueblo building. He might have seen the artist Carlos Vierra painting two of the large murals in the Mayan Cities cycle on-site in San Diego.[10] Perhaps he saw some of the paintings being mounted at the exhibit, including scenes of Santa Fe by Vierra and Chapman, and fourteen oil paintings of the missions of New Mexico by Vierra. Artist Gerald Cassidy also received a commission with Vierra to paint murals for the Science of Man exhibit in the California Building, for which Cassidy won the gold medal.[11] In 1930 Cassidy agreed to do the illustrations for a serialized novel Fray Angélico wrote, *Guitars and Adobes*, a romance of old Santa Fe during the Archbishop Lamy period. Chávez later cited Cassidy as one of the artists who influenced his own painting, remembering the painter (who died in 1934) doing figures in La Fonda hotel.[12] Material representations at the exhibit conceivably made an impression on the young Chávez. In effect, these simulacra selected to represent New Mexico in the exhibition may have offered the child a glimpse of New Mexico's history and its central connection to the churches established by Franciscan missionaries. One of Chávez's first encounters with his people's history, then, probably involved aesthetic constructs, and this experience perhaps sowed the seeds for his future intellectual and cultural production.

Fabián Chávez was successful in San Diego and promoted to foreman, but he decided to return to Wagon Mound because he was homesick and his father was very old.[13] The family returned in late 1914, and twins Nicanora (Nora) and Romualdo (Cuate) were born one year later. Manuel's father was elected county clerk of Mora County in 1916 as a Democrat in a heavily Republican area, and in January 1917 the family moved to Mora where they lived until 1923. Although he had already started his second-grade year in Wagon Mound and had excellent reading skills, the Sisters of Loretto who ran the public grammar school put him back in the first grade because of his small size. Chávez remembers the extremely cold winters in Mora, the scarcity of food, and the difficulty of drawing water from the well and using the outhouse in that season. "Growing up like that taught me a lot about the Spanish people who had settled the land originally. They were truly a *penitente* people. They lived in a *penitente* land, and

FIG. 1.3. Manuel Chávez and his sister Martha, ca. 1917, Mora, New Mexico, courtesy Palace of the Governors Photo Archives (NMHM/DCA), Neg. No. PA-MU-082.05.

hardships were a way of life." In contrast, summers were like paradise, with trout fishing and hunting with slingshots with his friends.[14]

During his elementary school years in Mora, Manuel read his family's volumes of the *Columbia Encyclopedia* from cover to cover, his parents' Spanish primers, copies of the newspaper *El Nuevo Mexicano*, Grimms' fairy tales, Greek mythologies, and the tales of King Arthur. He played with a boy across the street, the son of Dr. Hoag, and

FIG. 1.4. Manuel Chávez, St. Gertrudis Church, Mora, New Mexico, courtesy Palace of the Governors Photo Archives (NMHM/DCA), Neg. No. PA-MU-082.02.

especially enjoyed reading the Hoags' copies of *National Geographic*.[15] Chávez also mentions having read *Collier's* magazine as a boy.[16] In *My Penitente Land* (1974) he recounted one of his youthful transgressions at age ten: he and a friend sang an insulting parody about Penitentes to the town cobbler and barber, who was a member of the brotherhood. His mother's reprimand and her explanation about the goodness of these men made an indelible mark on the young Manuel. His mother gave piano lessons at home and was the organist and church choir director. His sister Nora remembers that her mother held rehearsals for the choir in their house and that she and Manuel sometimes heard Latin hymns as they fell asleep.[17] In those years, he also drew and painted, making caricatures of the political enemies of one town politician whom he met at the courthouse. Fabián Chávez was first county clerk and then assessor of Mora for successive two-year terms until 1921. Then he found work building the new public high school in Mora. When no further work was available in 1923, the family moved to Albuquerque to build a house for a friend, although Manuel stayed behind in Mora to finish school, living across from the courthouse with Doña Felicitas Gallegos, the daughter of Ceran St. Vrain.[18]

A key element in Manuel Chávez's developing identity in this period was his visits to Santa Fe where he stayed with his aunt Victoria Sosaya. He rode with the mail carrier to the train station in Las Vegas, where he took the train to Lamy and then to Santa Fe. His aunt, whose husband, Agustín (Gus), had earlier encouraged Manuel's father to move to San Diego, built a number of houses in Santa Fe, including one for his family on Sosaya Lane. Manuel became enchanted with the new style of architecture developing in Santa Fe, epitomized by the construction of the new Museum of Fine Arts in 1917, modeled on the New Mexico Building at the San Diego exhibition. He experienced Santa Fe's excitement about the dedication of the new museum building, a combination of the church and *convento* of Acoma and the church of Laguna.[19] The *Santa Fe New Mexican* termed the museum a "noble structure that commemorates the martyrdom of the Franciscans in New Mexico."[20] The new museum did not simply represent support for artists in New Mexico and a new style of architecture, but was intimately connected to the history of Franciscanism in New Mexico. The mural cycle in St. Francis Auditorium of the museum would later become the model for Chávez's murals in the church at Peña Blanca. In addition, from 1919 to 1922, La Fonda hotel was rebuilt in Pueblo revival style, designed by architect Isaac Hamilton Rapp. During these visits in Santa Fe, Manuel witnessed the return of the Franciscans to New Mexico and to St. Francis Cathedral beginning in 1920 shortly after Franciscan friar Albert Daeger was named archbishop of the diocese in May 1919. Chávez described the influence of seeing the Franciscans on his incipient vocation: "So when I used to come to Mass and I'd see [the friars] dressed like that, I'd say, 'Oh, here they are.' But I didn't say anything to them until I was ready to go."[21] His visits to Santa Fe helped to shape his developing ethnic, artistic, and religious identity in these early years.

During Lent of 1924 when Manuel was in the eighth grade at the public school in Mora, he met the charismatic Franciscan father Jerome Hesse who had come to Santa Gertrudis Parish to give a mission. He spoke to the visiting priest about his desire to become a Franciscan, cultivated by his early experience in San Diego, the return of the Franciscans to Santa Fe, and his reading about the history of the Franciscans in New Mexico. Fr. Jerome invited him to spend the summer at the friary in Peña Blanca to learn more. Some in Peña Blanca remember the young Manuel that summer playing in front of the rectory, constructing models of Franciscan adobe churches and missions out of dirt. He guarded them and got angry if anyone tried to knock them down.[22] Although on one level a boy's play, this pastime prefigures the renovation and restoration of churches he would undertake after his ordination, and points to his developing sense of himself as part of Franciscan missionary history in New Mexico even before entering the seminary.

In September 1924, fourteen-year-old Manuel Chávez took the train to Cincinnati, accompanied by Archbishop Daeger who was traveling to St. Francis Seraphic Seminary High School to dedicate the new building. A conscientious and strong student, Chávez also developed his artistic talent, finding time to paint, draw, and write poetry, fiction, plays, essays, and spiritual pieces. The rector, Fr. Urban Freundt, gave him paints to encourage his hobby and nicknamed him Angelico (after the medieval painter Fra Angelico da Fiesole), the religious name he was later formally given when he entered the novitiate in August 1929.[23] Manuel received permission to paint a mural of St. Francis feeding the birds on a white wall in the seminary. In 1928 he was allowed to repaint the portrait of St. Anthony preaching to the fishes in the study hall of the seminary. The painting disappeared for a week, and when it was returned, students and faculty saw that Manuel had playfully replaced the saint's face with the image of the popular Mexican movie star Dolores del Río. On a brick wall of the basement of the novitiate at Mt. Airy, where Fray Angélico spent the 1929–30 academic year, he painted a mural of the local archbishop.[24] He did smaller paintings for friends and relatives and illustrated several of his own articles, stories, and poems. He published numerous essays and creative work in the school newspaper, the *Brown and White*, and served as editor in his senior year. In these five years, he would come home to Santa Fe only three times because of the expense, and after entering the novitiate in 1929, spent eight years away.[25]

A Life's Trajectory 17

FIG. 1.5 Manuel Chávez, St. Francis Seminary, Cincinnati, Ohio, courtesy the Archives of the Franciscan Province of St. John the Baptist of Cincinnati.

When he left for the seminary, his family lived across from the Santuario de Guadalupe in the house that later became La Tertulia restaurant. The family had moved to Santa Fe from Albuquerque in June 1924 (on the Sunday of the annual Conquistadora procession) and were allowed to live in the property on Agua Fria Street that the *santuario* had recently purchased for a future convent. Chávez's

FIG. 1.6. "From Me down to Tony (José does not yet exist)," Manuel Chávez, siblings, and mother in front of new family home at 712 Acequia Madre, 1928, courtesy Palace of the Governors Photo Archives (NMHM/DCA), Neg. No. PA-MU-082.10.

mother became the choir director and played the organ. Manuel had stayed in the house after his summer in Peña Blanca only a short time before he left for the seminary in 1924. A baby boy was born August 31, just before Manuel's departure, and he suggested that infant be named for their father, Fabián.[26] In 1928 his father built the family a house on Acequia Madre Street that became their permanent home. Manuel's younger brother Francisco remembers the seminarian carrying him on his shoulders to see the new house.[27]

The young Manuel was already beginning to assemble key elements of his ethnic and artistic identity with which he would project a visual self-image of Hispano Southwestern ethnicity. About this time, on a trip home, he painted a beautiful canvas, *By East García*, depicting the chapel "El Delirio" at the Amelia White estate, now the School for Advanced Research. He gave the painting to his aunt Aurelia Roybal King in appreciation of her sending him spending money at the seminary. A similar work, *On Acequia Madre*, was passed down in his brother's family and is now owned by his niece Mary Chávez,

FIG. 1.7. *By East García,* by Manuel E. Chávez, courtesy Palace of the Governors Photo Archives (NMHM/DCA), Neg. No. 191310.

who had been named after him (María Angélica Chávez). He also painted a scene of two burros as a gift to the seminary, visually transmitting an aesthetically pleasing image of New Mexico to those in the seminary who were unfamiliar with it. At this time as well, he dressed as a gaucho for the Santa Fe Fiesta, winning first prize and making the acquaintance of Witter Bynner and others in the Santa Fe Writers Group. He had taken up smoking at fifteen (although he later claimed that he never inhaled)[28] and appears in the gaucho-costume picture with a cigarette in his mouth. As Chávez described meeting Bynner: "I was 19 and home for the summer and I dressed as a gaucho for Fiestas and won the costume prize. . . . Through him I met Thornton Wilder, John Sloan, Gerald Cassidy, Will Shuster, all those guys."[29] He also attended the 1929 premier of Bynner's play *Cake* and remembers exchanging flirtatious glances with the sister of "Peaches" Mayer during the performance. He says he later told her,

FIG. 1.8. *On Acequia Madre*, by Manuel E. Chávez, courtesy Mary Chávez.

"I always knew I would become a Franciscan, but your beautiful eyes just nearly tempted me out of it."[30]

On August 15, 1929, he became a novice, was given the Franciscan habit and his religious name, and began a rigorous year in the novitiate at Mt. Airy in Cincinnati. His mother traveled to Ohio for the ceremony, where the local families of the other seminarians were kind to her, inviting her to stay with them and to dinners and parties in their homes.[31] One year later he moved to Detroit to the newly built Duns Scotus College for studies in philosophy and other college subjects. He engaged in many creative projects while at Duns Scotus, among them writing the play *The Beloved* to commemorate the seven hundredth anniversary of St. Anthony's death, and himself playing the part of St. Anthony in the public performances.[32] In 1933 he made his solemn vows and moved to Oldenburg, Indiana, for four years of study of theology.

FIG. 1.9. Friar Angélico Chávez after tonsure, August 1929, courtesy Palace of the Governors Photo Archives (NMHM/DCA), Neg. No. PA-MU-082.13.

Sadly, during the Depression, his family lost their house on Acequia Madre Street and moved to 343 Alameda Street. Unable to make payments on their taxes and the mortgages they had taken out in 1927 and 1928 to build the house, they were foreclosed upon by the bank in 1932. Under a program President Roosevelt later introduced, families were able to repurchase their houses, and the Chávezes were able to get their home back. After the election of Governor Seligman, whom Fabián Chávez knew from his days as county clerk in Mora, the governor appointed him capitol custodian, a position he held for many years. Fray Angélico notes that his mother never mentioned the family's hard times in her letters but let him know how happy she was when the job came through for his father.[33]

Finally, after thirteen years away from home, Chávez was ordained in St. Francis Cathedral in Santa Fe on May 6, 1937, by Archbishop Rudolph Gerken, after being granted special permission to return home for his ordination. His sister Nora Chávez, who sang the "Panis Angelicus" at the Mass, was impressed to see him coming out from the sacristy for the ordination with his hands bound, before they would be blessed to consecrate the Eucharist. His six-year-old cousin Mónica Sosaya, dressed in a long white gown and veil, carried a white satin pillow on which Fray Angélico had painted an image of a gold monstrance with the Eucharist. She remembers him giving his mother a small white pillow in the ceremony, which according to the tradition, was placed in her coffin after her death in 1969.[34]

Throughout his years of advanced study, Chávez excelled academically and continued his creative work, painting, writing, and performing in plays. In 1933 when he professed his solemn vows, he collected typescripts of his many poems and had them bound in a volume he entitled *Cantares: Canticles and Poems of Youth—1925–1932*. He dedicated it to his parents "como señal de mi amor y devoción" (as a sign of my love and devotion) and gave the single copy to them for them to keep privately.[35] While most of his writing during his years away was published in small private venues such as the seminary newspaper, several works appeared in the national Catholic magazine *St. Anthony Messenger*. When he returned to New Mexico in 1937 as a full-time Franciscan missionary, he entered an especially prolific period of artistic and literary creativity that brought him great public renown.

Fray Angélico sent a jubilant telegram to his parents in July 1937 announcing that he had been assigned to Our Lady of Guadalupe Church in Peña Blanca. His appointment included ministry at six nearby missions: San Felipe, Santo Domingo, San Buenaventura at Cochiti, Santa Dorotea at Domingo Station, San Miguel at La Bajada, and Santa Bárbara at Sile. By mid-September he had convinced the people of nearby Domingo Station to renovate their small chapel of Santa Dorotea.[36] Fray Angélico worked on this project with the help

FIG. 1.10. Fray Angélico Chávez, 1937, courtesy the Archives of the Franciscan Province of St. John the Baptist of Cincinnati.

of a few retired men from the town. On the front he painted murals of St. Jerome and St. Albert with the faces of his Franciscan mentors Fr. Jerome Hesse and Archbishop Albert Daeger. In 1938 he began painting the walls of the friar's refectory and the church sacristy at Peña Blanca with murals of the story of St. Francis. Fray Angélico then remodeled the sanctuary of the church at Peña Blanca in late summer and early fall of 1938. One year later, from June to November 1939, he painted the famous life-size murals of the Stations of the Cross in the church at Peña Blanca, using the townspeople as his models. The spectacular paintings received widespread recognition and acclaim. Then in 1940–41 he took on the immense job of redesigning and rebuilding the facade of the 1869 church to remedy the problems of previous repairs. In August 1941, he asked his uncle Agustín Sosaya to make new doors for the church, and Fray Angélico carved a series of images and words on the panels.

This architectural renovation and mural painting represented extra work he took on during his first years of full-time ministry in Peña Blanca and the surrounding communities. It was also an exciting period of literary creativity for Chávez, as he continued to be involved with the Santa Fe Writers Group and to publish poetry, fiction, journalism, and his first historical articles. Since meeting Witter Bynner at the Santa Fe Fiesta when home from the seminary, he corresponded with him and attended parties and social events at Bynner's house. Chávez's sister Nora remarked that he insisted that she accompany him to these social gatherings when he was in the seminary,[37] and Chávez later noted that his superiors were concerned that he was spending time with the homosexual poet and his partner. In 1930 Alice Corbin Henderson and other members of the Santa Fe Writers Group had begun public readings, called Poets' Roundups, to raise money for Pueblo Indian causes. The motif was that of a rodeo in which the invited writers would be the horses that were roped in to read their works. Haniel Long invited Fray Angélico to participate in the August 1938 roundup, where he read his poems along with Long, Thornton Wilder, Peggy Pond Church, Alice Corbin Henderson, Will Shuster, Witter Bynner, and others. The Writers Group also helped Fray Angélico to publish his first book in November 1939. Bynner, Long, Corbin, and John Gould Fletcher selected the poems to be included in *Clothed with the Sun*, and their writers' collective financed the publication. Chávez remarked that he spent a good deal of time at cultural events in Santa Fe in the first years after his ordination.[38]

From 1937 on, Chávez published poems such as "Singing Cowboy" and "Sandoval Sunset" in *New Mexico* magazine, in keeping with the local-color themes that many poets in the Santa Fe Writers Group were reciting and publishing at the time.[39] In a similar vein, in January 1940, Fray Angélico sorted through some manuscripts and saw that two published stories on New Mexico traditions fitted well with a third that was "breaking out in [his] mind"—"The Penitente Thief" (*St. Anthony Messenger*, April 1938) and "Mana Seda" (*Missionary*

Catechist, May 1939). He then wrote the third story and "drew some hurried sketches."[40] In February 1940, one week after the ceremony to consecrate his Stations of the Cross in the Peña Blanca church, he asked the provincial for permission to seek a publisher for the stories, arguing that they would be of special interest for the celebration of the Coronado Cuarto-Centennial later that year: "I have three short stories that will appeal—last year both Macmillan and Sheed & Ward wanted to publish one of them *if* I had others like it to make up a small volume. . . . By now I have written two more of the same caliber, and the three fit nicely into a perfect trilogy or triptych. I intend to call it *NEW MEXICO TRIPTYCH*, as the three are like pictures in an altar-piece, depicting Christmas, Holy Week, and the May devotions in pioneer times."[41] This first book of fiction integrated motifs from the milieu of the literary and artistic community in northern New Mexico at the time and the visual genres in which he was then painting, especially the triptychs of the Stations of the Cross in the church, and the St. Francis cycle in the refectory and sacristy.

In these early years of ministry at Peña Blanca, Chávez published dozens of poems, essays, and fictional pieces in national venues, including his homage to Thornton Wilder, "Peña Blanca," in the *New York Herald Tribune* and "Prisoner" in the *New York Times*, for which Wilder served as intermediary. After Chávez and Wilder met in Santa Fe in 1938, the playwright asked for his comments on the manuscript of his new play *Our Town*, which had not yet been produced. Chávez then wrote his poem "Peña Blanca" in response and sent it to Wilder. Later, Wilder gave him an autographed copy of the play at the time it won the Pulitzer Prize.[42]

His Herculean accomplishments from 1937 to 1943 also included full-time religious ministry, which he performed tirelessly. He would stay up writing well into the night and rise at five thirty for Mass. He helped the archbishop to broker a peace with Santo Domingo Pueblo, which had been placed under an interdict that forbade Catholic religious services on the pueblo since 1935.[43] On Saturdays he would give religious instruction and talk with the people of Santo Domingo. He asked for permission to renovate the church of St. Bonaventure at Cochiti Pueblo but was apparently not able to raise funds to do so. He said Mass at Sile on Sundays and First Fridays. Julia Rivera Silva remembers Fray Angélico celebrating First Friday Mass in the village and coming to her family's house afterward for *almuerzo*.

FIG. 1.11. Fray Angélico Chávez in archbishop's garden with Archbishop Gerken and Cochiti Indians, Santa Fe Fiesta, 1939, courtesy the Archives of the Franciscan Province of St. John the Baptist of Cincinnati.

Fray Angélico would help her mother prepare the meal, especially the eggs and potatoes. He also put on boxing gloves and boxed with her brothers, Guadalupe, George, and Pedro.[44] Chávez encouraged the vocations of talented boys, including Guadalupe Rivera of Sile, Guadalupe Fuentes of Mora, Antonio Chávez of Peñasco, and his own brother, Francisco Chávez. May Sarton has written about Christmas Eve ceremonies in 1940 at San Felipe Pueblo with Fray Angélico saying the Mass.[45] He himself wrote about the Christmas dances there in a 1943 article in *Indian Sentinel*. He taught himself phrases in Keres and included them in his sermons.

Despite his tremendous accomplishments, Chávez was somewhat discouraged after his first five years of service, an early foretaste of what lay ahead in his sometimes-troubled relations with the Franciscan Order. He was assigned to the Mission Band in summer 1942 and worried about how he would find time to travel to give missions in addition to his regular duties in Peña Blanca. Despite Chávez's request for clarification about who would say his Masses while he was away, the provincial vaguely replied that someone at Peña Blanca would do it. On August 12, 1942, he warned Provincial Rolfes that he might no longer be able to recruit seminarians because of shortages of manpower at Peña Blanca to help with their preparation. That same day he wrote a disturbing letter to Fr. Robert Kalt, pastor of Peña Blanca, who was away:

> This is to tell you that I am going crazy here in P.B. I don't know the real reason, for there could be several. Regarding the Missions, Fr. Provincial and Fr. Honorius were very nice, but who is going to [do] my missions [Masses at the missions] then? . . . Titus will not be able to go out in my place.
>
> Then, certain things have happened long before, and right before, chapter, which have taken all the wind out of me. I feel like the first five years of my priesthood have been a failure in the eyes of my superiors, and [I] am considered incompetent . . . and the proofs are several, like being supplanted by alcoholism, secret letters to and from headquarters, etc. I should be humble and forget, and I do forget completely when I am away from here, but as soon as I return to Peña Blanca, the sight of everything makes me sad and mad at the same time.[46]

He tells his superior that he has decided not to proceed with publishing *The Single Rose* manuscript and that the house at Peña Blanca gives him "a spirit of despair and futility." Perhaps this discouragement played a role in his decision to enlist as army chaplain a few months later.

In 1942, after the fall of Bataan, Fray Angélico served as a member of the Draft Board and helped the boys from his area fill out their draft forms. General Charlton, the head of Selective Service in New Mexico, encouraged Fray Angélico to join the army as a chaplain to serve the Spanish-speaking soldiers, and Chávez finally agreed to enlist in December 1942. He doubted that he would pass the physical because of his small size. But during the exam at the Santa Fe Armory, the chief medic added a few pounds to Chávez's weight on the medical form. In April 1943 his story about Bataan, "The Colonel and the Lady," won the first prize of the Catholic Press Association, but he still had not heard if he would be inducted. On April 17 he received official notification that he was appointed army chaplain, and he began training at Harvard on May 3. From June 8, 1943, to February 10, 1944, he was stationed with tank regiments in the 16th Armored Division at Camp Chaffee, Arkansas, a new division that was being built from the ground up. While there, he saw his friend John Gould Fletcher, whom he had met in Santa Fe in the Writers Group and with whom he exchanged letters about the ethics of writing literary texts while Fascism was devastating Europe and the Japanese had drawn the United States into the war. Surprised that his assignment seemed to contradict the recruiter's pitch that the army needed his Spanish-language skills, Chávez brushed up on German and Italian, hoping to be assigned to Europe. But orders came for him to go to Pittsburg, California, "which meant the dreaded Pacific."[47]

Chávez stopped in Santa Fe on his way to California to visit family and friends. He did so without authorization, but believed that chaplains had certain leeway in such matters. He especially remembered two events during the short time there. He ran into a friend, Francisco García, from Santo Domingo Pueblo who embraced him in tears, having heard that Fray Angélico had died in the service. He also stopped into a restaurant to say good-bye to the woman who ran it. She brought him into the back room where her non-Catholic husband lay dying. Fray Angélico prayed and talked to him for fifteen minutes, after which he asked to be baptized and receive Extreme Unction. Fray Angélico marveled at the turn of events, since he had stopped in Santa Fe on an impulse.[48]

Chávez proceeded to Camp Stoneman in Pittsburg, California, and visited some friends from Peña Blanca working in the shipyards near there. On February 16, 1944, he was notified of his promotion to captain, and the next day he traveled all night by train from Oakland to Port Hueneme near Ventura where he shipped out to Hawaii. He was stationed at Sand Island in Honolulu harbor and assigned to a battalion of black troops, although there were only a dozen Catholics in the group. "I said Mass in the white area and had a Philadelphia Negro serve always, since the General, a Texan, had decreed that there was to be no mixing of races in theaters or religious services." After six weeks, he was transferred to the white area but had the black man continue to serve his Masses.[49] Early on, we see Chávez's rebelliousness, ethics, and principled positions. His sister Consuelo, a navy nurse, was also stationed on the island, and sometimes they would spend the day together. Without having much to do except visiting a few hospitals where he ministered to the Spanish-speaking, he asked to be sent to the war front.

In July 1944 he was assigned to the 77th Infantry "Statue of Liberty" Division from New York and set sail from Honolulu for Guam. Before the treacherous landing began on July 21, Fray Angélico heard many soldiers' confessions, and there were large numbers of Communions at morning Mass. After the 305th Regiment and the marines carried out the first assault, the rest of the division went ashore from July 23 to 25. Because of coral reefs, Fray Angélico had to wade seven hundred yards with the water up to his neck. For the first few days it rained continuously, and the men suffered from wetness and cold in the foxholes. The island was retaken from the Japanese by August 10—Chávez's division lost 248 men and 663 were wounded.[50] Besides ministering to the soldiers, Fray Angélico performed liturgies for Catholic native islanders, with attendance at the eleven Masses he said in August numbering 12,450.[51]

On November 3 the 77th departed Guam for rehabilitation in New Caledonia and November 17 left Manus Island for Leyte in the Philippines, arriving November 23. They worked on beach defense and patrolling until December 5 and on December 6 loaded for the amphibious landing near Ormoc on the west coast of Leyte. On December 7, three years to the day after Pearl Harbor, they engaged in a two-hour landing behind enemy lines at the beach near Ipil. Fray Angélico noted in his December chaplain's report: "Mass on the Feast of the Immaculate Conception made impossible by Hirohito."[52] On December 10, the division engaged in a bitter, house-to-house battle to capture the city of Ormoc, Japanese headquarters. The struggle to take Leyte continued for two months until the 77th's participation ended on February 9, 1945. Chávez notes that although MacArthur declared Leyte secure by December 25, "there was plenty of dying before that and long after."[53] After the old Spanish church at Ormoc was blown up because the Japanese stored ammunition there, Fray Angélico managed to save an ancient statue of the Blessed Virgin from the burning church, walking over live coals into the baptistery to do so. He gave the statue to his mother when he returned and later sent it back to the Philippines.[54] The detailed descriptions of the suffering in the battles, which Fray Angélico sent home, record the extreme

FIG. 1.12. Fray Angélico Chávez, chaplain major, 1946, courtesy Palace of the Governors Photo Archives (NMHM/DCA), Neg. No. 132818.

hardships he and the troops endured. By early January 1945, Fray Angélico hinted to his religious superiors in Cincinnati that he would like to return home.

In February, Fray Angélico's weight was down to 104 pounds, and while the division prepared to go to Okinawa, he was allowed bed rest at a base hospital, where he regained 10 pounds in two weeks. He was told that his battalion was allowed to send one officer and three enlisted men home for a thirty-day leave, and the colonel chose Fray Angélico as the officer. On March 3, 1945, on the beach waiting for his departure, he received a commendation for landing with the troops at Deposito, Leyte. During his two-week wait to depart and on the long three-week trip home, he wrote chapters of a novel that he had begun while on Leyte. On April 8, 1945, he saw the Golden Gate Bridge: "It looked like Heaven as the sun, that day for once, shone on the white city of San Francisco—the first intact civilized group of houses I had seen since the preceding July."[55] He arrived in Santa Fe on April 14 to begin a forty-nine-day leave.

Happy to be home, Fray Angélico gathered a number of his poems for the volume *Eleven Lady-Lyrics*, which was published in November that year. He reported to Fort Bliss on June 2 "with duffle bag loaded with Mass wine bottles filled with Scotch and bourbon for my pals over there who hadn't seen any."[56] To his surprise he learned that all overseas men in the United States were "frozen" indefinitely. Unaware of the plans to drop the atomic bomb (the Trinity explosion was July 16, 1945), the men who were kept from returning were angry, according to Chávez. He was sent to San Antonio, Dallas, and back to Fort Bliss, where he served until his release on February 29, 1946, after trying every conceivable way to speed up his discharge.[57] He was promoted to major and given sixty days' paid leave, during which he traveled across the country, visiting his sister in Los Angeles, Mission Santa Barbara, and friends from Peña Blanca near Oakland. He then took the train to Detroit to visit his sister Consuelo Gorski, who had married a dentist in Hawaii, and his alma mater Duns Scotus College. Finally he went to Cincinnati and New York City to see another sister and friends from the army. He gave a sermon at a Pontifical Mass at St. Patrick's Cathedral at the opening of the Congress of the Catholic Poetry Society of America, April 28, 1946, his last day of service.

The Postwar Years: Santa Fe and Peña Blanca

Chávez's first writing project once back in Santa Fe was three weeks of work in May 1946 on the thirty-six-page booklet *The Old Faith and Old Glory*, which recounted the history of the Church in New Mexico in the century since the American occupation, a book strongly shaped by his own wartime experiences. Fray Angélico wrote to the provincial requesting that he not be assigned to the Mission Band at the cathedral, but this was exactly the assignment he was given in July. He began working on Spanish and English translations of St. Leonard's *Stations of the Cross*. In August he asked for permission to establish Confraternities of the Third Order of St. Francis, noting, "One big aim is to get all the Penitentes cleaned up and established as Fraternities of the III Order. This will take a long time."[58] That fall, he began work on another booklet for the archdiocese, documenting the history of the cathedral, which has been updated and is still widely circulated. He became friends with photographer Robert Martin, who took several of the pictures for the cathedral booklet. Chávez sent the manuscript of *The Single Rose*, which he had finished before the war, to Cincinnati for "censorship" and then to prospective publishers.

At this time Fray Angélico began serious historical research, examining sources from 1538 to 1680 in the museum library in Santa Fe for information on the Franciscan martyrs in New Mexico. He wished to establish the motives for the Pueblo Revolt: "Were the friars killed in odium fidei or in odium Hispanorum [hatred of the faith or hatred of the Spanish]? How did the friars themselves at different periods treat the Indians?" He planned to write the history of old Spanish times in New Mexico from the friars' point of view, to see if the martyrdoms could officially be called such canonically.[59] With difficulty, Fr. Cletus, rector of the cathedral, got him a typewriter during the postwar shortages, and Fray Angélico used every spare moment to work on the history of the Franciscans martyrs. He expanded the project to all the Franciscans of the Custody of the Conversion of St. Paul in New Mexico from 1539 to 1925, examining old parish registers and documents in the archbishop's archives. Excited about his new project, in February he asked to be released from giving missions in his next assignment and to be stationed at a place within easy reach of the various archives. One letter suggests that during the 1947 visitation, Fray Angélico asked Provincial Mollaun for permission to study at the University of New Mexico, but the provincial discouraged this, arguing that "with McCarthy in the way it may prove an obstacle."[60] Apparently, during the hysteria of the Red Scare, the provincial and other Church authorities were worried about exposing priests to radical ideas that were feared to have permeated secular universities. Chávez was awarded an honorary M.A. degree from the University of Albuquerque, a Catholic institution, in June that year.

At this juncture, Fray Angélico began to devote himself much less to literary writing and focused almost exclusively on history. Noting the difficulty in finding publishers for books of poetry, he asked his superiors for $150 to split the cost of publishing *The Single Rose* with the owner of Los Santos Bookshop. The request was granted, and the book was published in early 1948. While some of his future historical writing would have a literary cast, he continued to make his primary intellectual mark as a historian in the next four decades. He proposed that he be appointed archivist of the archdiocese to allow him time for research, but his Franciscan provincial did not agree. Increasingly, the strenuous work of traveling to give missions and preaching for several days in a row took its toll, and his frustration at not being able to do research on these trips contributed to his feelings of depression. His fall 1947 schedule, for example, included a mission at Sapello October 19–November 3, a retreat at St. Michael's College November 5–7, a mission in Armijo November 16–23, and another at Atrisco November 30–December 7. In late December 1947 he wrote about his depression to the provincial, attributing his state perhaps to a delayed reaction from the war, but also noting that he felt none of this when researching historical documents. By early March 1948 he was hospitalized, having become ill after hearing nine hundred "heavy" confessions in four days while giving a mission. His weight was down to 103 pounds, and the doctors ordered two weeks of bed rest. He quite firmly insisted that he could not do even one more mission. So great was his interest in history and the new documents he had discovered that when told he could not be archivist, he asked if he could at least organize and classify the material when time permitted and publish an index of them on his own.[61] Fray Angélico was finally able to publish *Archives of the Archdiocese of Santa Fe, 1678–1900* in 1957.

In July of 1948 he was reassigned to Peña Blanca with responsibility for Cochiti and Sile. He asked unsuccessfully to be allowed to live full time with the Indians at Cochiti. At the urging of archeologist Sylvanus Griswold Morley, Chávez revised into a book his two groundbreaking articles on La Conquistadora in *New Mexico Historical Review*. As he made new discoveries in his research on La Conquistadora while stationed at the cathedral after the war, he shared them with the parishioners and helped to revive the devotion to the Virgin, the renewal of La Cofradía, and the annual processions to and from Rosario Chapel in June. His new friend Robert Martin photographed the processions for Chávez's book *Our Lady of the Conquest*, published in August 1948, with cover art by Jean Charlot.

This book produced an additional accomplishment for Fray Angélico. In a September 1948 letter, Chávez wrote that one spiritual result of the book was "the conversion of Dr. Morley, one of the greatest archeologists in the world." The two became intimate friends and talked a great deal about religion. Shortly before entering the hospital, he told Fray Angélico that he wanted to become a Catholic, and Fray Angélico encouraged and instructed him. After he was hospitalized, one morning at four he became fully conscious and called for the archbishop, who baptized him. Fray Angélico objected to the diocesan paper saying, "His Excellency converted Dr. Morley."[62]

September 1948 also marked another key event in Fray Angélico's career as a historian. After Dr. Morley's funeral, the new president of the University of New Mexico (UNM) and the well-known historian of the Southwest France V. Scholes, who was academic vice-president of the university, invited Chávez to lunch at La Fonda. They asked him to translate and annotate the famous document Scholes had discovered in 1928 in Mexico, Fray Francisco Atanasio Domínguez's *Missions of New Mexico, 1776*. Chávez received the 423-page manuscript on September 9 but told his superior he was unsure he could take on the task because of his workload at Peña Blanca. He used the occasion to complain to the provincial about the constant interruptions at the friary and his being asked to teach catechism in the school, to fix engines and the pump, and even to type letters for Fr. Jerome. Nonetheless, at this time Fray Angélico began meeting regularly with Dr. Scholes in his home in Albuquerque to receive valuable training in paleography. Chávez worked all winter on translating the manuscript: "It has cost me a lot of eye and finger-strain. But historically it is a rare and valuable thing."[63]

In January 1950, Fray Angélico traveled to California for a month of research at the Huntington and Bancroft libraries. Having planned the trip since November, he also agreed to join a group from Santa Fe that was entering a float representing New Mexico in the Rose Bowl Parade. On January 1 he appeared in his Franciscan habit on the New Mexico float, which won the National Trophy. He attended the football game and rooted for Ohio State, and he also visited family and friends in the area. On the trip from Los Angeles to Berkeley, he stopped at the Santa Barbara Mission, consulted with Fr. Maynard Geiger, and found valuable documents in the archives relating to New Mexico. At the Bancroft, he worked with the famous historian H. E. Bolton. In three weeks of library work, he examined several hundred manuscripts, two hundred of which had once been in Santa Fe. The

Museum of New Mexico then ordered microfilm of the documents. Chávez notes that he regained his appetite on the trip and came home feeling wonderful.[64] On February 18 he officiated at the wedding of his friend Robert Martin and cousin Mela Ortiz y Pino.

Besides his meticulous work translating the Domínguez manuscript in the fall and winter of 1948–49, Fray Angélico also researched and wrote *Lamy Memorial*, an illustrated history for the Santa Fe Archdiocesan Centennial. He complained that the archbishop had "dumped" this big job on him and that he was unenthusiastic about it because it prevented him from working on his other historical projects. He also felt treated like a flunky, a dog who could do tricks. Disappointed that the archdiocese did not send him a copy of the book in October when it was published, Fray Angélico was grateful when his friend Fr. Cletus brought him one. He noted, however, "In general, a handsome publication, but not done exactly as I conceived and planned it. So I'm glad my name was left out as its author."[65] Chávez felt unappreciated for taking on the book at the expense of his other research and, as always, set high standards for aesthetic coherence and design. Echoing his disappointment after his first five years at Peña Blanca, this sense of lack of support and his desire for uninterrupted time for historical research would contribute to his decision to leave active ministry two decades later.

Reluctant Second Tour of Duty

Fr. Cletus did not go to Peña Blanca to bring Chávez the book on the centennial, but rather drove seven hours to Fort Bliss in El Paso on that October Sunday in 1950. In late 1946, a few months after Chávez's military discharge, the state chaplain and the staff general asked Fray Angélico to join the Army Reserves so that he would be eligible to run for state chaplain "to keep a Protestant from getting the position."[66] The provincial immediately granted him permission. Two years later in July 1948, he was notified that he had been elected state chaplain of the American Legion and only had to attend the annual convention.[67] In February 1950 General Sage called Chávez asking him to transfer to the New Mexico National Guard because they needed a New Mexican and a Catholic. Chávez agreed because he believed he would be able to serve the New Mexican boys by doing so. Shortly after his appointment became official, Fray Angélico was shocked to read in the newspaper on July 24, 1950, that two battalions of the New Mexico National Guard had been called to report for active duty August 14. He commented later that General Sage had not been forthright with him that the reserves were soon to be activated for the Korean War. "He didn't tell me; he tricked me. So I gave him permission. . . . All of a sudden I got orders to go down to Fort Bliss with the National Guard."[68]

The provincial's reply probably unintentionally exacerbated Fray Angélico's sense of shock and betrayal. Also expressing his alarm at the activation, Provincial Mollaun told Chávez that he had just learned that their province's Fr. Herman Felhoelter had been killed in Korea attending the wounded. "The present affair looks more serious to me than the papers play it up. . . . We'll have to do some special praying now."[69] Chávez was inducted into the 726th Battalion of the New Mexico National Guard and reported to Fort Bliss on August 27. He requested a car early on because there were long distances to cover on the base. Fr. Cletus generously offered to let him have the new black Chevrolet he had just gotten, and he drove it down to Fort Bliss one Sunday in early October. Grateful for the car, Fray Angélico moved into Roger Bacon friary near the base and became friends with the guardian, Fr. Alonso Cerezo from Mexico. He enjoyed living there and hoped to do a little writing on history from the files he brought with him.[70]

Although happy to be with fellow New Mexicans, within a few months Fray Angélico had an unpleasant experience with the post chaplain, who wanted him to take on additional duties. So upset that he wanted to resign, Fray Angélico took his complaint to the brigadier general, and within a month the post chaplain was transferred. Chávez was asked to take his place and for a while did the new job along with his other duties at his battalion. In early February he officiated at his brother José's marriage to Bernice Hesch in the Santa Fe Cathedral, which the archbishop also attended.[71] José Chávez, the youngest in the family, was also stationed at Fort Bliss, and Bernice Chávez recounts that when she visited the base, Fray Angélico would impishly try to shock his friends by introducing her with the phrase, "This is Mrs. Chávez."[72]

Even though the former post chaplain was gone, and Fray Angélico was enjoying the change in lifestyle away from his concentrated historical research and writing in New Mexico, he told his provincial in

February that the University of New Mexico was working through Senator Anderson to obtain a discharge for him so that he could finish an important Franciscan document the university wanted to publish.[73] In July, however, Chávez was alarmed to receive embarkation orders for the Far East Command. He immediately sent a strongly argued formal letter to the chief of chaplains in Washington. Among other points, he notes that his former overseas commanding officer was disturbed when he saw the new orders: "For he remembered what those lands did to me, even though he nor the medics knew I was coughing up blood, or that I was feverish with dengue when I went on a beach landing."[74] As a result of this letter and numerous people's interventions on his behalf, he was instead assigned to Germany.

On September 11, Fray Angélico sailed from Camp Kilmer, New Jersey, to Bremerhaven, Germany, and then to Heidelberg. He participated in two weeks of difficult training maneuvers in which he had to sleep outside in cold forests. While waiting several weeks for his permanent assignment, he traveled to Konnersreuth, Bavaria, where he had a meeting with the stigmatic Theresa Neumann, and he took the train to Rome through Switzerland for a week's visit October 22–29. There he said daily Mass in St. Peter's Basilica, met with the Franciscan minister general, and saw many famous places and artifacts. In an October 15 letter, he asked the provincial for money to buy a car to enable him to travel between army installations. In November he was assigned to Kaiserlautern to army installations that were far apart and joined by narrow, winding roads. He termed his assignment "a pill," noting that it was a result of his refusal to agree to extend his service beyond July 1952, despite the army's strong efforts to convince him to stay longer. On December 17, he traveled 150 miles on icy and foggy roads to Stuttgart to visit the brother of his mentor, Fr. Jerome Hesse, who was happy to meet him.

In January 1952, Fray Angélico visited a vestment factory in Speyer, Germany. Modeled on the Roman chasubles he saw in Rome, he designed "a true Roman chasuble" that was neither Gothic nor medieval, but the simple, graceful Roman design. "Maybe we can start a 'Fra Angelico' design," he wrote humorously to the provincial.[75] He also had a dress and mantle of gold cloth made for La Conquistadora: "My direct ancestors are recorded as having donated precious dresses to the image in times of trouble since 1625, and so I want to top them all and offer this ex voto in these days of greater danger."[76] Although not engaged in combat, Fray Angélico and others feared that war might break out with the increased buildup of troops in the area. He told his superior that the army was not a good place for a priest in an order. "I don't regret my first three years together with my combat experience. But this second hitch is too much for me as a friar."[77]

When spring finally came to "Kaisers-latrine," as he termed it, and his release seemed closer, Fray Angélico was happier.[78] He sent his father a silver cigar box and a copper cigarette case as gifts, and in an April 10 letter to his parents, noted that he hadn't been able to celebrate his birthday very much because of Holy Week duties. In April he agreed to the provincial's suggestion that he serve at Jemez Pueblo when he returned, but he was surprised (and most likely hurt) to hear that Archbishop Byrne asked that he not be assigned to Santa Fe. He saved leave time so that he could travel in June to Spain and Portugal before coming home. Among other important historical and ancestral sites, he visited the church in Extremadura with the original small statue of the black Virgin of Guadalupe. With a Leica camera he bought shortly after arriving in Germany, he took photos of many scenes in Spain. One he captioned "Cerro de Wagon Mound entre Granada y Anteguerra," noting the similar geography of Spain and New Mexico.[79]

The Jemez Years

Chávez reported to his new assignment in Jemez on August 13, 1952. He was placed in charge of two of the Spanish missions, San Antonio in Ranchitos and Santo Toribio in Vallecitos, and later took on a third. He also assumed the job of postmaster of Jemez Pueblo, a position the Franciscan superiors wished to retain for the order because of the small income it provided. Chávez had to pass a civil service exam, and Provincial Kroger wrote to Fr. Patrick MacCauley, pastor of Jemez: "If Angelico was beat out in the examination by the Indian, he would never live that down."[80] Fray Angélico, however, did not share this attitude toward the Indians, as evidenced in many of his statements, speeches, and publications, and as many Native Americans to whom he ministered over the years testify. N. Scott Momaday, for example, remembers growing up in Jemez, where his parents were teachers and Fray Angélico was postmaster. He recounts that he talked on many occasions with Fray Angélico about literature and Momaday's own

FIG. 1.13. Fray Angélico Chávez with Laura Gilpin, "Did My Picture with La Conquistadora," courtesy Palace of the Governors Photo Archives (NMHM/DCA), Neg. No. PA-MU-082.06.

creative writing. Terming him "a selfless and sensitive human being," Momaday notes, "I remember with pleasure that as a boy I used to go to the Post Office to visit Fray Angelico. . . . (I usually found him reading or writing.) I was a budding poet, and he was a formidable presence to me, a literary giant. He guided me with sound advice and infinite kindness. We formed a friendship that lasted until his death."[81]

When Provincial Kroger visited Santa Fe in summer 1953, Fray Angélico gave him the manuscript of *La Conquistadora: The Autobiography of an Ancient Statue* for approval. Kroger conveyed his great enthusiasm for the "fascinating and enticing" manuscript: "I marveled how you had the statue speaking in truly feminine fashion about her appearance and her wardrobe."[82] On September 9 he gave the Imprimi Potest for this manuscript and also for *The Origins of*

New Mexico Families, which Fray Angélico had sent him August 23. Chávez recounted the story of obtaining Laura Gilpin's color photo for the book cover of La Conquistadora, which had originally appeared in *New Mexico Sun Trails*: "I was with Paul Horgan, the author, when I picked up the issue in Santa Fe. Horgan immediately said that it ought to be used with my book, so he called up the publisher long-distance (they're friends), and asked him for the use of the plates.... Looks like our B. Mother wants her story to be a humdinger in every way."[83] St. Anthony Guild published the book on La Conquistadora in early 1954, but Fray Angélico had more difficulty with the second manuscript. The Museum of New Mexico wanted to publish the volume but lacked the funds. With approval from Cincinnati, he, his friends, and family raised two thousand dollars by gathering four hundred subscriptions to cover the cost of printing.

On May 2, 1954, Archbishop Byrne offered a Solemn Pontifical Mass in honor of La Conquistadora in Zimmerman Stadium at the University of New Mexico, with fifteen thousand people in attendance. It was the first stop of a strenuous pilgrimage Fray Angélico began with the statue of La Conquistadora throughout New Mexico, visiting ninety-five churches, giving eighty-five sermons, and walking in eighty-two processions through August 31.[84] On weekends he returned to Jemez to say Masses, and in any spare time on the road, he worked on the final details of the manuscript that he prepared with Eleanor B. Adams, *The Missions of New Mexico, 1776*. His pilgrimage ended with the Episcopal coronation of La Conquistadora by Cardinal Francis Spellman of New York on September 5 at St. Francis Cathedral. Chávez described the details of the eleven-thousand-mile pilgrimage in an article for the *Provincial Chronicle* signed "Fr. Angélico, C.C.C.C.C." standing for "Chávez, Concionator, Chauffeur, Couturier Conquistadorae." Describing his fatigue during the three months spent traveling with the statue, he noted humorously, "I became so tired toward the end that in my trips I used to converse with Our Lady in the back seat. A psychiatrist would have had a field day if he had heard me. (There was no audible backseat driving.)"[85]

In October 1954 Fray Angélico told the provincial of his unhappiness with running the post office because it impeded his research. "What little research I did was done in a rush, not wishing to absent myself from Jemez for more than half a day for fear of postal inspection.... A trip to Santa Fe or Albuquerque, with only a couple of hours at the libraries and archives, then a rush back home that same afternoon, have been pretty tough on the constitution."[86] He announced that he would take more time off from the post office job and take his chances with the inspectors. He accepted an invitation from his friend Bishop Metzger to bring La Conquistadora to El Paso October 30 for the close of the Marian Year. As the date approached, he expressed concern about having to give sermons in Spanish, worried that the many native speakers from Mexico in attendance would judge his Spanish abilities harshly. In December he reported an agreement he had made with Archbishop Byrne to arrange and classify the archives of the archdiocese and publish a detailed catalogue of the holdings.[87]

Origins of New Mexico Families was published shortly before Christmas in 1954, and Fray Angélico was quite disturbed by the harsh review in the *Provincial Chronicle*. He was disappointed at the lack of support even in Franciscan venues and expressed concern that *St. Anthony Messenger* did not mention the latter book when advertising other Catholic books for sale. In response, Fr. Casey apologized.[88]

On June 19, 1955, at Peña Blanca, Fray Angélico preached at the first solemn Mass of one of his protégés, Fr. Salvador Aragón who had attended grade school in Peña Blanca in the 1930s and studied at St. Francis Seminary in Cincinnati in the 1940s. The strong presence of the Franciscans in Peña Blanca when Fr. Aragón was growing up, including the large annual summer retreat for Franciscan priests, made this order seem synonymous with the priesthood for Aragón and other boys. Not only did he serve 6:00 a.m. daily Mass as an altar boy for Fray Angélico, but he and others were busy during the summer retreats when the large number of priests each had to say their obligatory daily Masses at the side altars.[89] It was an important homecoming for Fr. Aragón in June 1955, and Fray Angélico, one of his early mentors, came from Jemez to preach the sermon at Peña Blanca.

A few months later in early September, Fray Angélico wrote letters to refute rumors that were circulating among some Franciscans that he intended to secularize (leave the order). "Feeling depressed for the past month because of defection of my life-long friend, our Father VK; the marriage of a brother of mine to a divorced woman; some happenings here that I don't consider quite Franciscan, and [health issues]. But secularization has not been thought of or even uttered as a threat."[90] He similarly wrote to Fr. Casey, "There is a rumor among some friar-gossips out here that I am about to secularize! Such crap. I suppose that they would like to see me do it to prove their own theory that 'Mexicans are no good' and 'that writers of books are unstable.' I'm not sorry but glad to say that they'll be awfully disappointed until kingdom come."[91]

Fray Angélico celebrated the New Year in 1956 with the release of *The Missions of New Mexico, 1776*. In the fall of 1948, France Scholes had given Chávez the manuscript of Fray Francisco Atanasio Domínguez to translate and annotate, forgetting that he had several years earlier given it to his research associate Eleanor B. Adams for the same purpose. When Chávez and Adams discovered that each had done the work of translating and annotating the manuscript separately, they agreed to coauthor the book, which, as historian Marc Simmons notes, produced "a volume far superior to what either one could have done independently, since each brought unique qualifications and different background material to the effort."[92] Fray Angélico's artistic and historical talents, for example, produced the hand-painted frontispiece that attempts to reproduce the original colors of the stone reredos installed in the Castrense around 1760 as it may have looked in Domínguez's time. Even in the final stages of the book, Chávez discovered useful documentary material to add to the book while cataloguing the archdiocesan archives.[93]

Also in early 1956, a familiar pattern reappeared in which Fray Angélico strongly desired to move elsewhere in order to have more time for research and writing and developed physical ailments that demonstrated the difficulties of his current assignment. In a January 23 letter he requested "to be taken out of Jemez this summer," a transfer he had wanted for more than two years. A few days later he wrote, "I'll go anywhere you want . . . anyone could take my place in the Post Office."[94] Meanwhile, the pastor of Jemez, Fr. Patrick MacCauley, wrote to the provincial with mounting complaints about Fray Angélico, for example, that Chávez had been called to the cathedral in Santa Fe twice in one week to work on the renovations. Fray Angélico continued with the busy schedule, however, agreeing to give an eight-day retreat for the Sisters of St. Charles Convent in Albuquerque May 27 to June 3, launching the Conquistadora Society in Santa Fe on June 10, and preaching both Spanish and English sermons on July 8 at the Field Pontifical Mass for Albuquerque's 250th anniversary celebration. Archbishop Byrne wrote him that "the sermon was magnificent."[95] Paul Horgan asked Fray Angélico in March if he would "race through" his book manuscript of *The Centuries of Santa Fe* to check for errors and offered to sponsor Chávez's book of stories with his publisher Farrar, Straus & Cudahy.[96] His poem "The Virgin of Port Lligat" appeared in May in *Spirit*, its first venue. By early June, Fray Angélico told Provincial Kroger that he wanted to go to California for a complete physical examination at the clinic where his sister worked, fearing he had tuberculosis and noting that his weight had dropped to 103 pounds. In late June he had a checkup in Albuquerque where doctors told him that he was "starved and undernourished."[97] Repeating a gesture he had carried out in Fort Bliss when he experienced difficulty getting released from the service, in September he sent a picture of himself to the provincial with the inscription, "This is a more suitable portrait for the death card," half-joking, no doubt, yet wishing to make a point. He was released from heading the post office at Jemez on June 30, 1956.

Fray Angélico got his wish to travel to California, and on August 26, 1956, he appeared with Pulitzer Prize–winning author Paul Horgan on the nationally broadcast program *The Catholic Hour* at NBC TV studios in Burbank. The theme of the program was Southwestern Catholic Literature. The two authors first discussed the uncanny coincidences and real-life connections of Horgan's postwar story "To the Castle," in which he modeled the character of the heroic chaplain on Fray Angélico. The last wish of the ill-fated chaplain in the story was that something of him remain permanently in Rome, and in a mysterious coincidence, Fray Angélico himself first read the story in Rome in 1951 in an issue of the *Saturday Evening Post* at the USO. As the program continued, Fr. Angélico dialogued with Horgan about his prize-winning book, *Great River: The Rio Grande in North American History* (1954), which Horgan had asked him read and correct in the manuscript stage. Then Horgan interviewed Fray Angélico about his recent book *La Conquistadora* and his discovery through copious archival research that the Chávez family's ancestors had brought the statue to New Mexico in 1625. Chávez compared his work on the ancient statue to Horgan's on the great role in history of the Rio Grande. He spoke proudly of his own historical role in the preservation of the great tradition of the statue: "I found out I was carrying the tradition,—a member of the same family doing her

FIG. 1.14. Fray Angélico Chávez and Paul Horgan speaking on *The Catholic Hour*, August 26, 1956, NBC-TV studios, Burbank, California, courtesy the Archives of the Franciscan Province of St. John the Baptist of Cincinnati.

history." Unfortunately, reception of the program in Albuquerque was blacked out because of an electrical storm over the Sandia Mountains.[98]

Fray Angélico was invited to preach the sermon at Cardinal Spellman's Pontifical Mass at St. Patrick's Cathedral in New York City at the Catholic Poetry Society of America's twenty-fifth anniversary celebration on October 21, 1956. Fr. Daniel Berrigan, S.J., served as deacon. However, the cathedral rector had already arranged for a special preacher because it was Mission Sunday, so Chávez's sermon was transferred to the luncheon at the Waldorf Astoria. The master of ceremonies incorrectly introduced Chávez as being from Jemez Springs (where troubled priests were sent to the Villa Coeli Center), not Jemez. Fray Angélico quietly joked to the cardinal in Italian that while not yet at Jemez Springs, "he was stationed *alla porta di Via Coeli.*"[99] The day before, Chávez read one of his own poems at the Poets Forum held at Hunter College.

Excited about opportunities to travel and do work related to his historical research, Fray Angélico spent several weeks in January 1957 in Washington, D.C., at the American Academy of Franciscan History finishing his forthcoming volume on the Archives of the Archdiocese of Santa Fe. After long days and nights preparing the manuscript for the printer, he traveled to New York to consult with his publishers. He was asked to make major revisions on a study of St. Francis to make it a book for young people. On his way home he stopped at Santa Fe to leave the manuscript on the archives for imprimatur at the chancery and to check on the progress of the Conquistadora Chapel.[100] He continued his work on the renovation and redesign of the chapel in the ensuing months. In late June, however, he wrote to Fr. Edgar Casey that due to disagreements with the many parties involved in the decisions about the renovations, he had removed himself from the final stages of the project.[101] Nonetheless, Fray Angélico was responsible for the majority of the historic redesign and work on the chapel, including the new altar screen constructed from two side altars in the cathedral.

Fray Angélico went to El Paso February 14–16, 1957, to attend the decoration of Archbishop Metzger by the Spanish ambassador. While there, he worked with artist José Cisneros designing illustrations for the title page and end papers of the archives book. Chávez insisted that the escutcheon of the Archdiocese of Santa Fe with the Franciscan arms have an enlarged image of the crossed arms of Our Lord and St. Francis, "as if proclaiming: 'This is a diocesan archive, but the matter, the history, the region, are all Franciscan.'" On several occasions, Chávez felt he had to justify to his Franciscan superior that the scholarly work of organizing the diocesan archives was an important part of Franciscan history. In March he sent the provincial a display with pieces of the three-hundred-year-old blue fabric of the old Franciscan habits that he had preserved during the renovation of the cathedral.[102]

On July 2 he delivered a lecture at the University of California, Santa Barbara, in a Spanish colonial seminar taught by Professor Phillip Powell of the History Department. His topic was "The Influence of the

Franciscans in Southwestern Culture," and he subsequently wrote that the trip was a very pleasant break and his lecture was well received.[103] Significantly, he missed the elaborate ceremonies for the dedication of the Conquistadora Chapel on July 7 by choosing to stay in California after the lecture. In August he traveled to Washington, D.C., to make a Spanish soundtrack for catechetical films for the National Council of Catholic Men. He was extremely pleased that his friend and classmate Fr. Leo Pfeiffer had arrived at Jemez as pastor. "[This] has been a most welcome boon, and I'm sure the coming year will be a happy and fruitful one."[104]

A small controversy arose in late 1957 when Chávez sought permission to publish *The Virgin of Port Lligat*. The provincial sent the manuscript to Fr. Gabriel Buescher in Oldenburg, who approved the poem and Chávez's commentary, but told the provincial orally that *Madonna of Port Lligat*, the painting by Salvador Dalí that had inspired the poem, was "certainly and positively not according to Catholic tradition" and should not be published. Kroger asked Chávez to exclude the reproduction, but he adamantly refused, so key was the image to the book. Chávez argued that while the Sacred Congregation of Rites might condemn the painting for use as devotional art, it would not condemn it as a work of art, in which capacity he wished to use it in his book. "Since the painting is necessary for an understanding of the poem, I will not publish the poem without the painting." Most likely knowing that the Pope had approved of Dalí's painting, Chávez wrote immediately for an opinion to Archbishop Cicognani, the apostolic delegate in Washington, who saw no problem with publishing the image. Chávez also sent a copy of an ad from a recent issue of the Jesuit magazine *America* that reproduced Dalí's image and sold prints of it. Although another high-ranking Franciscan, Fr. Roger Huser, also thought the image should be excluded, the provincial gave permission on December 9, citing the apostolic delegate's letter.[105] Fray Angélico was so proud of the book with his poem, notes, and Dalí's image that he dedicated it to his parents in honor of their fiftieth wedding anniversary.

In January 1958, Fray Angélico once again proposed an elaborate plan to establish a new mission station at Algodones, which the province had previously rejected. He was devastated by the provincial's reply, which although supportive, informed him that a committee of Southwest friars had previously rejected the plan. Chávez complained

FIG. 1.15. Fray Angélico's parents, Fabián and María Nicolasa Chávez, in Acequia Madre home, fiftieth wedding anniversary celebration, July 11, 1959, courtesy Palace of the Governors Photo Archives (NMHM/DCA), Neg. No. 131451.

that the committee had not consulted him: "What makes my heart sink... is the fact that policies on these missions are formed by committees that exclude a native friar twenty years ordained and thirty-eight years in the habit. Now I feel quite cheap, Father."[106] Fray Angélico again pressed his desire for more time for research in a January 1959 letter to the provincial who replied supportively, but noted the problem of manpower in the province. In April, Fray Angélico was also hurt that only two members of the province bought subscriptions for the deluxe edition of *The Virgin of Port Lligat* to help launch the trade edition. On the positive side, however, both Cardinal Spellman and Archbishop Ritter wrote him enthusiastic letters about the book.[107]

Throughout this period at Jemez, he continued to publish articles and creative writing in academic journals and magazines. The major books he published in this period attest to his insatiable intellectual curiosity, drive, and perseverance: *La Conquistadora: The Autobiography of an Ancient Statue* (1954), *Origins of New Mexico Families in the Spanish Colonial Period* (1954), *Missions of New Mexico, 1776* (translator and annotator, 1956), *Archives of the Archdiocese of Santa Fe, 1678–1900* (1957), *From an Altar Screen: El Retablo: Tales from New Mexico* (1957), and *The Virgin of Port Lligat* (1959). The books of history involved thousands of hours of research, writing, editing, and proofreading. He noted that the book on the archdiocesan archives took him two years off and on to file and catalogue the documents covering two and a half centuries. The final manuscript was 509 pages, plus the introduction and index.[108] He experienced highs and lows—from the publication of his book of stories in 1957 with the major New York house Farrar, Straus & Cudahy and a letter from T. S. Eliot praising his poem "The Virgin of Port Lligat," to continuing physical ailments including pneumonia in January 1959. But on July 6 of that year he was finally transferred from Jemez to become pastor of the small parish of St. Joseph in Cerrillos.

The Last Decade of Ministry

Fray Angélico accepted two assignments in the early 1960s before returning once again to the village in which he started his ministry, Peña Blanca. The 1959 assignment to Cerrillos, where there were about three hundred Catholics, also included ministry at Galisteo, Lamy, and Golden. Shortly after arriving at St. Joseph's, he began to renovate the rectory and church, using his carpentry skills to construct a library/den, building a new carport to replace the deteriorated adobe garage, and having the friary and church converted to gas heating.[109] On March 31, 1960, a whirlwind tore off the roof of the nearby chapel of San Francisco in Golden, exactly one year after it had been replaced. That year, State Highway 10 was widened and paved, making the chapel visible to many more passersby. Chávez decided to completely renovate the old chapel, last altered in 1918 by

Fr. Jerome Hesse. While workers replaced the roof according to Fray Angélico's specifications, he built the front pediment with a new niche for a statue of St. Francis. He constructed a new bell tower in mission style with the help of one man from Cerrillos who mixed the cement and hoisted up the material. His brother Fabián Chávez helped him obtain an old brass railroad bell for the tower, which gleamed in the sunlight. A local woman obtained the wooden pews from Madrid for the Golden chapel. Chávez recruited E. Boyd of the Museum of New Mexico to restore the old five-foot statue of San Francisco that he found in the chapel, and in 1986 he arranged for it to be returned to the cathedral in Santa Fe where it originally had been housed. Invoking Shakespeare and a poem he himself had written in the seminary, Fray Angélico termed the stunning new chapel "a sermon in stone" for the highway travelers to see.[110] (See figure 7.5.)

In spring 1961, Fray Angélico began to renovate the sanctuary of St. Joseph Church in Cerrillos. Behind the altar he installed a nine-by-seven window that he constructed from ornamental cement blocks and small panes of blue, violet, and red glass. He moved a large crucifix from the rear of the church to hang in front of the new window and designed a canopy for above the altar. He painted the sanctuary walls with fleurs-de-lis and raised the steps to make the new altar he designed more visible. On November 11, 1961, he invited priests, friends, and family to a special Mass to inaugurate the new interior of the church.[111]

At this time, Fray Angélico organized the first reunion of the Chávez clan in New Mexico. He invited Frs. Alberto and Arturo Chávez of Taos and Santa Fe to join him to celebrate the feast of San Fernando Rey, the patron of the Chávez family in Spain, on Memorial Day, May 30, 1961. Although he intended only the three Chávez families to attend, many other Chávezes from Santa Fe and Albuquerque also came. At the luncheon after Mass in the Tiffany Restaurant, Judge David Chávez, brother of Senator Dennis Chávez, suggested that a Chávez society of San Fernando Rey be formed to celebrate his feast each year. The society grew and continued to celebrate every year in June.[112]

In 1957 Fray Angélico had finished the manuscript of *The Lady from Toledo*, a novel in which he claimed to tell "the true story of some of [the] southwestern Franciscan martyrs."[113] Finally in early 1960, the Academy Guild accepted it for publication, and Fray Angélico worked on revising the manuscript in Cerrillos before sending it in late February to the provincial for approval. Earlier, in April 1959, he published a companion article, "Nuestra Señora de la Macana," in *New Mexico Historical Review*, documenting the historical basis for the legend about this old statue of the Virgin. The companion novel is a hybrid text that joins the visual and the verbal by including Chávez's illustrations and merges history and the novel. The Academy Guild's reissue of his classic *New Mexico Triptych* in December 1959 perhaps inspired him again to engage in visual-verbal hybridity by making similar drawings for *The Lady from Toledo*. In Cerrillos, serving in the small-town parish and its missions, he returned to the kind of work he began in his first ministry in 1937 in Peña Blanca—church restoration, an illustrated literary text, and dedicated pastoral work.

Fray Angélico continued to have an enjoyable social life during this period as throughout most of his life. He frequented the Tiffany Saloon in Cerrillos where large numbers of people from Albuquerque and elsewhere came to dine on weekends. He was a friend of the owners, who let him drink and eat whatever he wanted and never charged him. Historian and resident of Cerrillos Marc Simmons remembers seeing Fray Angélico one Sunday at noon at the saloon in his black clerical trousers and a wild Hawaiian shirt, enjoying a drink. Chávez later told Simmons that the two women who owned the saloon were non-Catholic but came to Mass every Sunday and put a folded ten-dollar bill in the collection. Chávez knew the donation was from them, because the other parishioners only contributed small change. Chávez also continued his friendship with Witter Bynner during this period and attended the publication event for Bynner's *New Poems, 1960* on September 19 that year. Bynner autographed a numbered copy of the limited edition book for Chávez, "To Fray Angelico with Hal's fond admiration of Manuel through many years."[114]

The year 1962 was special for Fray Angélico, his twenty-fifth anniversary as a Franciscan. On January 1 his friend and protégé Fr. Michael Baca came to Cerrillos to give a mission and stayed through January 13. Fray Angélico no doubt enjoyed the time with his fellow Franciscan, having preached the sermon at Baca's first Mass.[115] Fr. Baca in turn delivered the sermon at Fray Angélico's Silver Jubilee Mass on June 13, the feast of San Antonio de Padua, patron of the Franciscans. Instead of his own words, however, Fr. Baca read a bilingual text Fray Angélico had written for the occasion, "A Canticle of Gratitude."

Chávez's classmate Fr. Aelred Knittles was the deacon; Fr. Salvador Aragón, his former altar boy from Peña Blanca, the subdeacon; and the reception was held afterward at La Fonda.[116] Fray Angélico reprinted the beautiful Mass card for the occasion memorializing his ordination and first Mass May 6 and 9, 1937, picturing himself celebrating Mass surrounded by colonial Spanish families with a large image of the Spanish coat of arms displayed before the altar.

On February 26, 1963, Fray Angélico received the Brotherhood Award from the Albuquerque chapter of the National Conference of Christians and Jews. His humorous acceptance speech noted, "I was born a *goy* and a pagan, but I became a Christian when I was baptized; I also became somewhat of a Jew, for the name given me was *Emmanuel*, and so my boyhood pals called me 'Mannie Chavez,' whence the name of the famous Kosher wine. I suppose that is the reason for this award. I thank you!"[117] Two years before the papal encyclical on ecumenism, Fray Angélico was practicing it. On May 30 he received an Honorary Doctor of Literature from the College of St. Joseph in Albuquerque, the first native New Mexican to receive the college's honorary degree. During the first half of June he traveled to Southern California, where the cold weather brought little relief for his incipient emphysema. He wrote that he didn't feel like doing much on his return but had promised to give lectures on June 22 and 24 and another in August: "Instead of being elated, I feel a burden just thinking about preparing those papers. I think it's the lung ailment that saps my strength & ambition."[118]

A large new friary and church was being built in Atrisco in south Albuquerque at this time. On Tuesday, October 15, 1963, Fray Angélico and fifty-two other friars attended the formal blessing of the new rectory of Holy Family in Atrisco. The church building was solemnly blessed a year later on January 12, 1964, the Feast of the Holy Family, with ninety priests and brothers attending. A few months later, on May 19, 1964, Fray Angélico was assigned to Holy Family friary and the new church "in order for you to pursue your activity in the areas of writing, research, and lecturing," according to the typed letter sent to him. Added in handwriting was the phrase, "and to help in the parish when available."[119] This arrangement may have caused some hard feelings at the friary.

Fray Angélico reported for duty June 24 and within a few months wrote a desperate letter to the provincial:

> Sorry to bother you, but I have to write this letter begging you to let me move to Peña Blanca.... Honestly, Father, I feel like just taking off into the wild blue yonder and the heck with everything.
>
> The Superior flared up anew, and without provocation. It is human to do so once in a while, and a fellow can take it ordinarily. But in this case it is a system of underlying hatred or disdain, perhaps racial. And the manner in which he lays at me is that used on a menial, as though my many more years in religion and in the priesthood don't count.
>
> ... I must go. When I see such arbitrariness ... oh, well.[120]

Within a week, in midyear, Fray Angélico was assigned to Peña Blanca where his work was to remain the same: research, writing, lecturing, and helping out with services when needed. At Christmas Fray Angélico sent a handwritten card to the provincial telling him how happy he was at Peña Blanca. His classmates Frs. Otto and Aelred prepared the best room for him upstairs, setting up bookcases to help him in his work. He praised the always-charitable conversations among the friars there. He reported that he had finished his article on the two seventeenth-century friars buried at the cathedral and had finally been able to get long-needed dental work done. The day after Christmas he wrote again to the provincial reporting how happy he was and that he heard four hours of confessions and said midnight Mass at San Felipe Pueblo without discomfort or coughing. He requested to be allowed to stay at Peña Blanca indefinitely.[121]

In the six years that followed at Peña Blanca, Fray Angélico completed several scholarly projects. Between February and July 1965 he wrote at the request of the Seraphic Curia in Rome a résumé of the Franciscan missions in New Mexico, Texas, and Arizona (1539–1965).[122] He planned to write two books on the early Franciscan martyrs: one on those who came with the Coronado Expedition (1540–42) and a second on the "Blue Martyrs of New Mexico" (1581–1696). The first volume, *Coronado's Friars*, was published in 1968. He also undertook the translation and editing of the 1583 Oroz Manuscript from Tulane University, with the completed manuscript totaling 763 typewritten pages; although finished in 1968, it was not published until 1972. In 1967 one of his most controversial articles appeared, "Pohé-Yemo's Representative and the Pueblo Revolt of 1680," in which he argued that a black man led the Pueblo Indians in the famous revolt. In 1969 he published what he termed his "swan song" of poetry, *Selected Poems, with an Apologia*. He made research trips to California and Washington, D.C., and gave a guest lecture in one of the first Chicano Studies courses in the country in March 1970 at the University of Colorado at Boulder, at the invitation of Professor Juan Bruce-Novoa. Also in 1970 he participated in the meetings of the newly formed organization of Hispano priests, PADRES.

Fray Angélico continued to suffer health problems during this period, the deaths of loved ones, the effects of institutional changes, and other disillusions. Archbishop Byrne had died in July 1963 after having attended the initial sessions of the Second Vatican Council. Replacing him in 1964, Archbishop Davis moved the archives of the archdiocese to Albuquerque and began substantial renovations on the cathedral to facilitate the liturgical changes made official by Vatican II. Fray Angélico wrote that the extensive remodeling and enlarging of the sanctuary "necessitated the unfortunate destruction in 1966 of the hidden 1717 adobe apse . . . as well as the just as old sacristy next to it. Also torn down was the 1806 south chapel of San José. . . . The only original section spared . . . was the north chapel of La Conquistadora. . . . [S]ad to say, this entire renovation, which was in undisguised modern steel-and-concrete construction, clashed entirely with the soft Romanesque look of Archbishop Lamy's original building."[123] Changes such as these and the relocation of the archdiocesan archives to Albuquerque were especially difficult to accept for a scholar and friar such as Fray Angélico whose life and work were so greatly immersed in the material historical legacy of the Catholic Church and Franciscanism in New Mexico.

Although other Hispano priests at the time supported and validated him, especially members of the organization PADRES, sometimes these gestures served only to remind Chávez of the lack of support he felt from his diocesan and Franciscan superiors. Monsignor Tito Meléndez, pastor of Our Lady of Guadalupe and member of PADRES, wrote to Msgr. Francis Tournier, dean of the archdiocese on March 26, 1971, to nominate Fray Angélico to become the first pastoral vicar of the diocese. He sent copies to Archbishop Davis, the deanery pastors, and Frs. Ramón Aragón and Rafael Ruiz, and he listed numerous reasons for his recommendation: that Fray Angélico was a Chicano and had the backing of PADRES;[124] that he was sympathetic to post–Vatican II renewal; that he would unify the Franciscans, the seculars, and the Chicanos; that he had national and international respect; and that he deserved recognition in the face of "neglect (to say the least) by his own and ecclesiastical superiors."[125] On Easter Sunday that year, still in pain from having had two teeth extracted, Fray Angélico wrote to Archbishop Davis after seeing the letter from Meléndez for the first time on the bulletin board of the friary. Although sure that nothing would come of the nomination, he felt compelled to write that he would never accept such an appointment. He alluded to previous campaigns to make him auxiliary bishop and even archbishop and insisted he had no desire to serve in these offices. When Archbishop Ritter had written to him about one such nomination, Fray Angélico had quipped that "dioceses were not run on poetry."[126]

On March 31, 1966, Fray Angélico's father, Fabián Chávez Sr., died, and shortly thereafter in December his beloved second father figure, Fr. Jerome Hesse, died on the feast of St. Nicholas. About three years later, on January 4, 1969, Fray Angélico's mother, Nicolasa Chávez, died. His family recounts that his voice broke when he delivered the sermon at the funeral Mass for his mother. The deaths of these three key figures in his life, the turbulent times we term the sixties, Chávez's mounting frustration with his treatment by some in the Franciscan Order and the archdiocese, and what he termed a crisis of faith spurred him to make a radical change in his life in mid-1971.

Secular Life in Santa Fe

On the morning of June 30, 1971, Fray Angélico put a note on the bulletin board of the Peña Blanca friary announcing that he was leaving the order and the Church, mailed letters of resignation to the provincial and the archbishop, and left for his family's home in Santa Fe where his sister and niece lived. Everyone was taken by surprise, although his superior at Peña Blanca reported to the provincial that a few weeks earlier Chávez had said "he would be gone in about a month."[127] In his letter of resignation Fray Angélico insisted that his departure had nothing to do with frustration, lack of prayer, or a desire to marry as is usually assumed. Rather, he offered scriptural and moral reasons. First, he was upset by Rome's condemnation of the Dutch Catechism that, he argued, was "the closest approach to the only Scriptural evidence of faith." He believed that the bishops and the Catholic press had reverted to "the old non-Scriptural mentality, . . . wrangling about peripheral matters like celibacy, etc.," and after realizing this on May 16, 1969, he "suffered grave mental and spiritual anguish," but tried to hang on for two years. His second reason for leaving involved a moral issue—the Church and the clergy's treatment of the people of his ethnic minority as inferior. He termed this conduct "real ecclesiastical colonialism" and noted that his extensive historical research reveals that "they have looked on us as inferior people" and that he had experienced this personally throughout his thirty-four years in the order. This realization had tested his faith: "Can one be blamed for doubting that the Holy Spirit of Love has been operating? Or, if we are actually an inferior race to deserve such serf treatment from the Church—may God forgive me for questioning His judgment and providence."[128]

In letters a few weeks later, Fray Angélico noted that he left to "avoid a split personality, as one cannot think one way and act another without damage" and that he was "disgusted and confused by the reactionary spirit of the Church since Vatican II, and more so by the confusion in our Order and Province regarding Franciscanism." In August he wrote to a former fellow seminarian, "I am feeling fine and much at peace. Basically, I left to save my sanity, and thus far I think I did the right thing for that end."[129] Provincial Huser gave him permission to reside outside a friary and sent him several hundred dollars for more dental work.

Documents show that the Franciscan superiors were unsure how to deal with Chávez's departure and treaded lightly and kindly at first, hoping to coax him to return to the order. One superior tried to convince him to assume a position with the American Academy of Franciscan History in Washington, D.C., while still living in Santa Fe. After one year of living with his sister, Chávez requested that the provincial consider him completely separated from the order and the province, questioning the role of authority in the Church from his position as a minority:

> My long and deep attachment to the Franciscan life and sacerdotal ministry, which were my whole love and life for so long, is now dead. The cause of it is difficult to express in a few words. Let us say it is a broken heart, and perhaps also

a broken mind, brought on by an ecclesiastical paternalism long practiced on certain poor peoples, and by a subsequent conviction that the so-called magisterium is not as solid as it claims. (Those who belong to the master races and whose faith is unquestioned acceptance of everything cannot begin to understand what this all means.)[130]

At this point, Provincial Huser began to pressure Fray Angélico to request official laicization from Rome, which Chávez repeatedly and firmly refused. The Franciscans and the archbishop were concerned that Fray Angélico's unsettled status would be the source of scandal for the order and the Church. In late June 1972 Chávez asked the provincial for one thousand to two thousand dollars because "things have changed rather drastically" and he had to move out of his sister's home. The provincial sent him five hundred dollars. Chávez did not leave the Acequia Madre house at that time, however, and subsequent documents help to explain his urgent sense that he had to leave.

On February 9, 1973, Provincial Huser, who was in Santa Fe conducting visitation, wrote a report on new developments in the Chávez case that troubled him. He had heard that Fray Angélico was planning to marry Anne Montgomery, a woman in her midtwenties from El Paso whose parents Fray Angélico knew when he was stationed at Fort Bliss. Huser noted that the Chávez family was very disturbed and that his sister would like him to leave her home. Fr. Dennet Jung told him that on a recent visit to the Chávez home, Fray Angélico introduced him to Anne Montgomery and later asked his niece Consuelo if he had shocked Fr. Dennet with his girlfriend. At breakfast in St. Francis friary on February 9, however, Fr. Dennet reported to the provincial that Consuelo had just told him that Ms. Montgomery had canceled the wedding. Fr. Michael Baca commented, "This is his second rejection, for I know he previously wanted to marry some woman here in Santa Fe, and she very definitively would have nothing to do with him."[131] Fray Angélico's short-lived relationships with women after his departure from the Peña Blanca friary deeply disturbed Church officials and some of his family.

Despite repeated pressure from Provincial Huser, Fray Angélico refused to formally petition to Rome for laicization. Chávez noted that "legal decrees per se [do not] make everything all right in internal matters." Nonetheless, in August 1974 Huser sent an official request with supporting documentation to the Franciscan minister general in Rome petitioning that Chávez be officially dispensed from his vows and laicized. On February 20, 1975, the Sacred Congregation of the Doctrine of the Faith denied the petition, citing lack of evidence for dispensation.[132]

When he left Peña Blanca in 1971, Fray Angélico had moved into the back room of his family's home on Acequia Madre with its own entrance, and he spent much of his time writing, hoping to begin to earn a meager living and continue his research. When he became book editor of *New Mexico* magazine with the November–December issue in 1970, he was most likely anticipating his upcoming need to support himself. He sold sixteen articles to the magazine in the next seven years in addition to the hundreds of book reviews he wrote until he resigned as book editor in February 1978. In January 1972 he wrote in low spirits to a friend that the articles he sent out were rejected and that if it weren't for the reviews and articles accepted in *New Mexico* magazine, he "would be curled up at the bottom of the barrel."[133] One year after leaving Peña Blanca, he was awarded a grant from the University of Albuquerque to lecture one week a month and use the rest of his time to write a book on the Hispanic people of New Mexico. He believed this would keep him solvent for a while.[134] Friends and family also gave him money from time to time. In July 1974 he moved into an apartment of his own at 214 C McKenzie Street. He wrote to friends in Connecticut, "On the Fourth of July I declared my Independence and found me a little pad on a back street near the Santa Fe Plaza."[135] This move became possible because Fr. Robert Sánchez was shortly to become archbishop and had offered Fray Angélico a part-time paying job to organize the archdiocesan archives.

While living with his sister Nora, he walked to town frequently, met new friends, and socialized with a different crowd. He met artist Judy Graese at an arts festival at the plaza and became fascinated with her and her work. In November 1971 he requested a copy of his 1964 story of St. Francis, "The Bird of Perfect Joy," from *St. Anthony Messenger*. He wished to revise it for publication as a short book and arranged with Graese to do the accompanying illustrations. In February 1972 he joked to a friend that he might use a gift of postage stamps to write to matrimonial bureaus: "If I do make a rich catch thereby, I shall attribute it to your postage! Or maybe I would put the blame on you when the catch turned out to be a witch!" In the next paragraph he wrote about Graese and the book illustrations. In April he flew to Boulder to deliver two lectures and checked on the progress of the artwork in Denver; he was disappointed that the drawings had not yet been started. In January Northland Press in Flagstaff, Arizona, became interested in publishing the book, but Chávez did not want to send them the manuscript until the illustrations were ready.[136]

Frederick Grillo, a book collector from Connecticut interested in the Southwest, read an article about Fray Angélico in *New Mexico* magazine and wrote to him in November 1970 asking how to obtain copies of his books. A long-lasting friendship developed between Fray Angélico and the Grillos, who later moved permanently to Santa Fe. In the early 1970s they often kept his spirits up by sending small gifts, stamps, and books for him to sign, writing to *New Mexico* magazine to praise his work, recommending his manuscript on St. Francis to Northland Press, and trying to nominate him for the Bancroft and Pulitzer prizes. Fray Angélico sent them humorous as well as serious notes: "Thank you for the Lincoln portrait," he wrote on February 19, 1974, "and I like the Hebrew seal very much as 'Manny Chevitz.' P.S. We've been having snows and sleets too! But the gasoline business is not too bad—yet!" Two months later he thanked them for "money for 'gasoline car fuel.' Got four different *fifths* of scotch as birthday presents to fuel the *driver*." He wrote to them about his ups and downs, for example being rejected for a Guggenheim fellowship in March 1972, despite supporting letters from such stellar figures as France Scholes, Paul Horgan, and Richard Greenleaf. He remarked that he hoped the editor of *New Mexico* magazine would not want him to recast an article he had written about the Santa Fe Trail for the August 1972 issue: "But one has to submit and try again because of the needed Kudos involved. While in the friary, I used to tell such editors to go to hell, and now in the unholy world I am so humble!"[137] He wrote that on reaching his sixty-second birthday, he felt as if he was only forty-two and described how the waitresses at the Palace brought him a little cake with a sparkler and insisted on paying for his lunch.[138] He celebrated other birthdays and enjoyed many social events with his fun-loving group of friends including Malcolm and Arnold Withers, María Hesch, E. B. and Jane Hall, María Orlinda Coriz of Santo Domingo Pueblo, Alice Anne Biggerstaff, and Tim Burch. He frequented local restaurants such as Tía Sophia's, the San Francisco Bar and Grill, and the Palace. He enjoyed many Friday dinners with

FIG. 1.16. Fray Angélico Chávez leaving the Palace Restaurant, Santa Fe, New Mexico, courtesy Palace of the Governors Photo Archives (NMHM/DCA), Neg. No. PA-MU-082.15.

friends Jim and Emily Hughes, and after Jim's death in 1976, he continued a rich friendship with Emily until his death.[139]

Fray Angélico's most groundbreaking accomplishment in the immediate period after leaving full-time ministry was the 1974 masterwork *My Penitente Land: Reflections on Spanish New Mexico*. The radical changes in his life fomented this masterful historical and literary text in which he brought together decades of research and thought on the history and religion of the Hispanic people of New Mexico. On the copy of his Guggenheim application in his records, he wrote,

"Denied! Wrote *My Penitente Land* without any such fellowships!"[140] Later, in the years completely dedicated to writing, he began work on three books on important Hispano priests of New Mexico whose contributions had been undervalued and misrepresented in previous historical accounts. His pioneering revisionist books on Padre Antonio José Martínez of Taos, Padre José Manuel Gallegos of Albuquerque, and the draft he completed of the third volume on Vicar Don Juan Felipe Ortiz vindicate the three priests who were suspended through the machinations of Archbishop Lamy's vicar, Joseph P. Machebeuf. Chávez challenges the legends unquestioned in the works of Willa Cather and even his friend Paul Horgan, that Lamy and Machebeuf were victims of a corrupt Hispanic clergy. Although Chávez denied any parallels between himself and the three unconventional priests, his own sense of being misunderstood and underappreciated by his superiors informed his accounts of his nineteenth-century predecessors. Several of his earlier books were republished in this period, and he was hired to do a new translation of the 1776 *Domínguez-Escalante Journal*. He documented the ancestral roots in Spain and the New World of the Chávezes in his 1989 book *Chávez: A Distinctive American Clan of New Mexico*.

After a trip to Los Angeles in October 1976, he went to Las Cruces to receive the Governor's Award for Achievement in the Arts. On Christmas Eve that year, many were touched to see him return to the altar of St. Francis Cathedral to concelebrate midnight Mass with Archbishop Robert Sánchez. The following July, Franciscan provincial Andrew Fox reported to the rector of the cathedral, Fr. Reynaldo Rivera, "Father Angélico is now in good standing as a priest. He is not in active ministry but he is in good standing. However, as you know from the Constitutions, Father Angélico is no longer a formal member of the Franciscan Order. But he will always remain a Franciscan at heart." He noted that Archbishop Sánchez led Chávez to reconciliation with the Church.[141] Fray Angélico continued to live on his own for several more years, researching, writing, and socializing with friends and family.

In the summer of 1981 he met former secretary of the interior Stewart Udall who was spending a month in Santa Fe researching a book. Two years later, Udall took Jacqueline Kennedy Onassis on a tour of the Coronado Trail and invited Fray Angélico to join them in Santa Fe for dinner at La Casa Sena. Fray Angélico recounted the

FIG. 1.17. Left to right: Archbishop Robert Sánchez, Stewart Udall (back to camera), Fray Angélico Chávez, and Fabián Chávez, Santa Fe, New Mexico, courtesy Palace of the Governors Photo Archives (NMHM/DCA), Neg. No. 180541.

history of Hispanos in New Mexico and gave her a tour of the plaza. Mrs. Onassis wrote him letters of appreciation about his books in subsequent years. Udall attempted to organize a public dinner for Fray Angélico's eightieth birthday and to launch a campaign to name a library after him, but Chávez politely refused both. He noted that St. Francis had been his model for sixty-five years. Like Francis, he was happy with having been a "mission padre among the lowly." He wished to be remembered for his poetry and historical research, not his person. "My one joy and satisfaction is being greeted by persons of every sort as an old padre of St. Francis, especially by the older Indians of Santo Domingo selling their goods around La Fonda."[142]

In the mid-1980s he served on the committee to remodel St. Francis Cathedral, pleased that changes were finally being made to Archbishop Davis' renovations that he disliked. Chávez made noteworthy contributions to the remodeling, such as the return of the old statue of St. Francis, the design of the massive reredos with fourteen panels portraying the saints of the Americas, and the design of the new cathedral doors with sixteen bronze plaques depicting the history of the Church in New Mexico since 1539.

While the Catholic Church was extensively remodeling one of its treasured buildings, however, it was tearing down another, which devastated Fray Angélico. Water had seeped behind the nave of Our Lady of Guadalupe Church in Peña Blanca, causing the wall to collapse. Fortunately, Fray Angélico's magnificent Stations of the Cross were not damaged, and Church officials got a very high estimate for repairs from an Albuquerque company. Thomas Chávez, Fray Angélico's nephew and director of the Palace of the Governors in Santa Fe, the oldest adobe building in the state, arranged for the architect who had overseen similar repairs at the Palace to give Church officials a lower estimate. Thomas Chávez also offered to raise funds to pay for the repairs. Within weeks of the meeting, however, the church at Peña Blanca was razed. An archdiocesan official, Fr. Jerome Martínez, was quoted as saying one month before the demolition, "Those murals at Peña Blanca have no artistic merit whatsoever." Fr. Gilbert Schneider, provincial of the Franciscans, said that the people of the parish wanted a new church rather than to repair the old one. Albuquerque deacon Jaime Baca who was born in Peña Blanca recounts that some parishioners wanted to preserve the old church as a chapel and construct the new church on available land behind it. A number of people in the small village were tremendously saddened that the murals depicting their parents and grandparents were destroyed.[143]

While some of those near him did not always valorize Chávez's work, it received international recognition on several occasions. On September 29, 1987, for example, he was honored to make a special presentation on La Conquistadora to King Juan Carlos and Queen Sofía of Spain during their visit to Santa Fe. In 1992 King Juan Carlos awarded him the medal of the Orden de Isabel la Católica, a recognition rarely granted to those who were not citizens of Spain.

In December 1989, Fray Angélico's family became concerned about his health and his ability to continue living alone because he had fallen in his apartment at Casa Loma. His niece Consuelo spoke to Fr. Crispin Butz, rector of the cathedral, and to Archbishop Sánchez about these worries. Very shortly, Fr. Crispin called Fray Angélico to invite him to live in the cathedral friary. Chávez accepted the next day, and members of his family suspected that he had simply been waiting to be asked to come back. He moved into the friary and joined the new Southwest Franciscan Province of Our Lady of Guadalupe. Having lived frugally on Social Security benefits, his small salary as archdiocesan archivist, book royalties, and generous gifts from friends, he turned over fifty thousand dollars in savings to the province. He told the friars that all he needed was his García y Vega cigars and Scotch. The other members of the friary were extremely generous and patient with his cantankerous personality in these last years, allowing him his choice of television programs and putting up with his occasional bursts of temper. He continued to frequent his favorite restaurants and bars around the plaza. In 1993 he blacked out in front of La Fonda, and doctors discovered that he had a brain tumor and an aneurysm that might burst at any time; these conditions perhaps contributed to his sometimes stormy personality. He began to suffer memory loss and had difficulty recognizing people he knew around town. Fellow Franciscan friar Jack Clark Robinson interviewed him in March 1993, noting that he occupied the small, south-facing, first-floor room near the dining room in the friary and that his clothes and papers were strewn all over the room. He had only two personal photographs displayed, one of his parents in the yard of his sister's house in Los Angeles in the mid-1960s, the last picture of the two of them together, and the other of the King and Queen of Spain, autographed to him.[144]

On February 22, 1996, Fray Angélico did not appear for supper, and when the friars checked his room, they found him on the floor, having suffered a stroke. He was hospitalized at St. Vincent's and later moved to Horizons nursing home. Members of his family stayed with him every day, and his sister Nora remembered that he had stopped eating just as her mother had shortly before her death. Provincial Gilbert Schneider, who had become Fray Angélico's confessor when he affiliated with the Guadalupe province, visited him after the stroke and remembers him trying to pull the tubes out, saying he was ready to die. Following Fray Angélico's wishes that he not be kept alive artificially, he was not given a feeding tube. Fr. Salvador Aragón, the young boy who was his altar server on his first priestly assignment in Peña Blanca, gave him the last rites on the Sunday before he died. His brother Gene (Francisco Eugenio) recounts that although Fray Angélico was in and out of consciousness, on one occasion he woke up and said, "Quiero cigar" (I want a cigar). On March 18, Nora

Chávez noticed that her brother was breathing heavily and brought it to the staff's attention. She left around four in the afternoon when her brother Gene arrived. Gene recounts that Fray Angélico had an especially high fever and that he wiped his face with a wet cloth. Fray Angélico squeezed his hand, and later Gene felt the hand go cold. He then sang the Franciscan hymn "Ultima" to his brother. When Nora and her daughter Consuelo returned after dinner shortly after seven, they were told that Fray Angélico had just died.[145]

Many people gave testimony to Fray Angélico at the vespers service in the cathedral on March 20. Fr. Jack Clark Robinson expressively read Fray Angélico's poem "L'Envoi." At the funeral March 21, the cathedral was filled to capacity as dozens of Franciscans walked in procession, and Archbishop Michael Sheehan concelebrated the Mass of Resurrection. After the service, Fray Angélico was buried in the Franciscan plot at Rosario Cemetery.

CHAPTER TWO

Hybrid Identity in the Early Cultural Production

THE SMALL-TOWN BOY FROM REMOTE northern New Mexico was not entirely inexperienced when he left his nurturing family at age fourteen for the regimented, foreign environment of the eastern seminary. Manuel Chávez had witnessed the construction of a large international exhibition in the important border city of San Diego and spent time in the state capital Santa Fe, where architectural transformation and aesthetic revival were under way. He had avidly read *National Geographic* and the *Columbia Encyclopedia* in his formative years and excelled under the rigorous traditional education of the Sisters of Loretto. He learned about politics firsthand from his father who held civic office and even became involved in a bit of political maneuvering himself when as a boy he drew caricatures of one politician's rivals.

The changing milieu in Santa Fe was especially important in his formation. The small town of seven thousand had unpaved streets, with burros carrying firewood for heating and cooking. The staff of the newly established Museum of New Mexico directed the initial development of Santa Fe–style architecture for the Museum of

Fine Arts. In the early 1920s a number of writers and artists came to Santa Fe, some seeking a cure for tuberculosis and other illnesses at Sunmount Sanatorium, and others to join friends who moved to northern New Mexico. Alice Corbin, coeditor of *Poetry* magazine, came from Chicago in 1916 with her husband, artist William Penhallow Henderson. In 1922 Witter Bynner came to visit her and then moved permanently to Santa Fe. He bought artist Paul Burlin's house at 342 Buena Vista Street and in September 1922 Frieda and D. H. Lawrence were his houseguests. Mary Austin visited Santa Fe in 1918, took up residence in 1924, and with the advice of neighbor Frank Applegate, built an adobe at 439 Camino del Monte Sol in 1925. Among the many writers who spent time in Santa Fe in this period were Lawrence, Willa Cather, Thornton Wilder, Edna St. Vincent Millay, Carl Sandburg, Vachel Lindsay, May Sarton, Robert Frost, John Gould Fletcher, Haniel Long, Walter Willard (Spud) Johnson, and Lynn Riggs. Themes of the Southwest began to appear in their work. Alice Corbin published *Red Earth* (1920), *The Sun Turns West* (1933), and *Brothers of Light* (1937). In 1928 she edited *The Turquoise Trail* with contributions from dozens of poets writing about New Mexico. Among Mary Austin's books on the Southwest were *Land of Journeys' Ending* (1924), *Taos Pueblo* (1930), and *Earth Horizon* (1932). Witter Bynner's included the play *Cake: An Indulgence* (1926), *Indian Earth* (1930) and *Guest Book* (1935). In 1925 poets Corbin Henderson, Bynner, Long, Spud Johnson, and Lynn Riggs formed "The Rabble" (named after their often Rabelaisian mood), which met weekly at the Hendersons' for poetry discussions.[1]

Santa Fe culture in Chávez's youth was also shaped by the many visual artists who took up residence at the time, especially Los Cinco Pintores. Before the emergence of Los Cinco in the 1920s, several important artists who settled in Santa Fe painted ethnic and indigenous subjects, including Carlos Vierra, who worked on the design of the new art museum and built one of the first Santa Fe–style houses for his family. Sheldon Parsons lived in the former Padre Gallegos house after his arrival in 1914. Other key artists at the time included Gerald Cassidy, William Penhallow Henderson, John Sloan, Frank Applegate, Randall Davey, Gustave Baumann, and B. J. O. Nordfeldt.[2]

Los Cinco Pintores, who banded together in 1921 to help each other survive and make an aesthetic mark, presented new visions of the Southwest. They engaged in experimental modernism and therefore had difficulties in arranging exhibitions and sales. Fremont Ellis, Walter Mruk, and Josef Bakos came to Santa Fe in 1919 and 1920. Will Schuster, ill from exposure to gas during his World War I military service, was given only a year to live when he came to Santa Fe in March 1920. Feeling so bad that he decided to hasten his death by vigorous exercise, he instead saw his health improve. The fifth member of the group, Willard Nash, came from Detroit also for health reasons in 1921. Their first group exhibition was in November 1921, and in the ensuing years they became a mainstay of the Santa Fe social scene, performing ingenious skits at parties and organizing elaborate costume events. They are especially remembered for their role in reviving the annual Santa Fe Fiesta by organizing new events such as the Historical-Hysterical Parade and the annual burning of the giant paper puppet Zozobra, or Old Man Gloom, designed by Shuster in 1926.[3]

Witter Bynner describes the ambiance of the artists' and writers' early get-togethers at Alice Corbin Henderson's house:

> It was a small, pleasant, primitive adobe house, with an outdoor privy and with horses corralled alongside. . . . Visitors would come across distances which now demand motoring; but we came on horseback then by day or at night on foot with lanterns and would kick snow off our overshoes in the welcoming glow of the room with its corner adobe fireplace. Painters from near-by houses on the [Camino del Monte Sol] would be there, Applegate, Bakos, Shuster, Nash, sometimes Sloan and Davey from streets farther away . . . occasionally a visiting writer, Lindsay with his chants, Sandburg with his guitar, Frost with his wit, Lummis with a red bandanna around his gray temples.[4]

He also notes that Manuel Chávez came to the gatherings but was not yet called Fray Angélico.

Also active at this time in Santa Fe and other areas of New Mexico was the architect and preservationist John Gaw Meem who came to Sunmount in 1920 with tuberculosis. He attended poetry readings at the sanatorium organized by Alice Corbin Henderson and Witter Bynner and became friends with Vierra, Applegate, Shuster, and Austin. He became involved with Vierra and other members of a preservation group that restored several churches; they raised funds to purchase the chapel at Chimayó and to build the church of Cristo Rey in Santa Fe. Meem played a major role in the restoration of the mission at Acoma, the chapels at Las Trampas and Chimayó, and the design of Cristo Rey Church.[5] The dedicated, generous work of this group of artists, writers, and architects succeeded in preserving, renovating, and even building from scratch great historical treasures in New Mexico.

The young Manuel Chávez was profoundly influenced by these diverse elements of the vibrant culture centered in Santa Fe in the 1920s and 1930s. The multiple representations of Southwest culture that these writers, artists, and preservationists elaborated imbued the environment in which Chávez came of age with an aesthetic sense of his own Hispano ethnicity and difference. These literary, artistic, architectural, and historical images of New Mexico contributed to Chávez's developing sense of personal and communal identity as an Hispano and as part of a distinct region of the United States in which diverse cultures had been preserved for centuries. When he traveled to the unfamiliar Germanic environment of the Franciscan seminary in Cincinnati, Chávez's ethnic and cultural difference stood out in relief.[6] His occasional summer trips home to Santa Fe nourished and developed his Hispano ethnicity. In the exciting environment fomented by the writers' and artists' groups, Chávez's sense of self as an Hispano writer and artist from New Mexico grew. In his writing, art, and self-presentation in the period from 1924 to his ordination in 1937, a striking sense of ethnicity combines with other cultural elements to publicly display his unique hybrid identity.

Chávez's displacement at age fourteen from the small northern New Mexico town of Mora to the strict seminary environment of Mount Healthy outside Cincinnati placed him in a kind of exile. How does the self re-create itself, negotiate the present space and the nostalgia for the homeland to redefine self and identity? The only Hispano in his class of primarily Midwestern boys in a religious order run by German friars, he learned to conform by studying diligently and receiving good grades, yet refusing to give up his ethnicity. Feeling self-conscious about his command of English, he imitated classic authors: "I found myself at St. Francis Seminary in Cincinnati, a thin lad, very conscious of his broken English and backwoods manner. I think my early self-training in reading, plus an ambition to compete with my

FIG. 2.1. Manuel Chávez studying in St. Francis Seminary, Cincinnati, Ohio, courtesy the Archives of the Franciscan Province of St. John the Baptist of Cincinnati.

fellow students in the use of their language turned my interests to literature, when I began imitating the classic authors of English."7 While his exile might be understood as a semi-deterritorialization because he returned to Santa Fe during some summers and after thirteen years of study came back to live and work in New Mexico, for long periods he was deprived of nearly all contact with his home. Especially during these periods of separation, he reterritorialized his identity as an ethnic subject through literary and artistic self-presentation. He learned to negotiate the strict religious environment by engaging in only minor transgressions and ultimately aligning himself through his writing and art with the new cultural movement bourgeoning in Santa Fe as a native expert on Hispano ethnicity.

Like the artists' groups in Santa Fe and Taos, he painted scenes of the Southwest in his early seminary years and illustrated many of his literary pieces with his drawings of New Mexico culture and landscape. In 1928 he inserted ethnicity and crossed gender borders by superimposing the image of popular Mexican movie star Dolores del Río on the face of St. Anthony in a large painting in the study hall. Ethnic, gender, and religious transgression marked the new hybrid signifier, as Manuel playfully engaged in a variation of Michel de Certeau's *la perruque*.[8] He attempted to gain semiotic control over the institution's orthodox religious image by proudly inserting an idealized signifier of his ethnicity. He altered the image of St. Anthony, a key signifier of Franciscanism, to reterritorialize himself as a complex subject precisely as the seminary insisted that he make his religious vocation his primary identity. This small rebellion through public visual signifiers might be connected to his initial involvement with the Santa Fe Writers Group. For example, his superiors worried about him socializing at gay poet Witter Bynner's raucous get-togethers, so he always brought his sister along. Chávez told an interviewer much later that his superiors thought his friendship with Bynner might indicate that he himself was gay, but he was in fact not.[9]

Home from the seminary in summer 1928, Manuel dressed as a gaucho for the fiesta, met Witter Bynner, and won first prize.[10] (See figure 1.1.) He presented himself as a Hispanic subject through sartorial signifiers as well as through writing that included ethnic themes. His association with the Santa Fe Writers Group was overcoded with his ethnic identity as a native New Mexican who included Southwestern themes in his work. He corresponded with Bynner in his remaining years of study and was included in events and parties of the group after his ordination. He performed at the 1938 and 1939 Poets' Roundups in his brown Franciscan robes, the same attire he wore on the 1950 float designed by Will Shuster to represent New Mexico in the Rose Bowl Parade.

Chávez presented himself as an ethnic subject influenced by the Santa Fe Writers Group in short notes in the *Brown and White* newspaper on the graduating class:

Manuel E. Chavez, Santa Fe, New Mexico—"Enamel"; hot-air (traditional). Editor of the Brown and White; has a decidedly Latin complexion; pseudo-poet and author and a synthetic artist; always needs a haircut; speeks hees Eengleesh very wail; will write a history of the Kaiser dynasty; reads Tennyson, Thompson, Millay, and Bynner, and asks St. Anthony to get their books for him; he is a direct descendant of the great Don Quixote, at least in actions; his advice to every consumptive: "Go West, young man. Go West!"[11]

Chávez's humorous self-presentation emphasizes his difference as an Hispano from the West, whom some might perceive to be a foreigner physically, linguistically, and culturally. He aligns himself with mainstream British and American poets, but even in doing so, takes care to emphasize his Spanish roots with the reference to Don Quixote and the key role of the West in contemporary American artistic production with the mention of the cure for tuberculosis. Apart from the

FIG. 2.2. Photograph of Chávez and seminarians, which he captioned "Cake-Eaters of 1928: Kaiser, Diehl, Fritch, Meyer, Pfeiffer, Chávez" in his photo album "Chávez: Canticle of the Sun," courtesy Palace of the Governors Photo Archives (NMHM/DCA), Neg. No. PA-MU-082.14.

brief references to St. Anthony and seminarian Albert (Virgil) Kaiser, who had often invited Manuel to his family's nearby home, Chávez's presentation of the self is decidedly more ethnic than religious.[12] He subtly references the Santa Fe Writers Group as part of his identity in the photograph he captioned "Cake eaters of 1928" in his personal album, alluding to Bynner's 1926 play *Cake* that satirized Mabel Dodge Luhan.

Fellow seminarians also emphasized Manuel's ethnicity, as evidenced in a 1927 Christmas wish list addressed to "My Dear, Dear Santa Claus." The letter from "a little boy in the fourth class" humorously suggests gifts. Under Chávez, the entry reads: "Thinks Santa Claus was born in Santa Fe. He's our choo choo trained singer, and sounds like one, too. Knittles says that he sings like a cat out in Kansas, so you might as well pick up a fat, fluffy kitty somewhere and give it to him for accompaniment. But wait! He's been getting so brown lately that Kaiser calls him the Black Bottom upside down. Bring him some complexion soap or cream."[13] While the list jokes about the ethnicities of other seminarians, this entry implies beneath the tone of humor that Chávez's ethnicity is negative and needs to be washed away.

Chávez cites the influence of Taos artists Ernest Blumenschein and Joseph Henry Sharpe, whose paintings he saw in the Santa Fe art museum, and other artists who had an impact on his early work as well. He remembers watching Gerald Cassidy, Will Shuster, and Willard Nash painting in Santa Fe.[14] Shortly before his accidental death, Cassidy made lithographs for a historical novel about the old Southwest that Fray Angélico published serially in *St. Anthony Messenger* in 1931–32. Early on in the seminary Chávez painted and drew in several genres, often emphasizing aspects of his ethnicity and Southwestern themes. Like Carlos Vierra, he sketched the old missions of New Mexico and in a 1934 article, included ten of his own drawings of the churches. He did a pen-and-ink drawing of the old mission at Zuni for a 1931 calendar given out by Rev. Arnold Heinzmann, O.F.M., at Zuni.[15]

Chávez, of course, painted other kinds of art in this period such as a mural of St. Francis feeding the birds on a white wall in the newly built seminary. Unable to make the long trip home for holidays, he was frequently invited to the family home of the rector of the seminary, Fr. Floribert Blank, in Batesville, Indiana. For the eightieth birthday of Fr. Floribert's father, Chávez painted a gift for him—an image of Mr. Blank's cabin in the woods when he was an early settler in the

FIG. 2.3. Fray Angélico Chávez, pen-and-ink drawing of Zuni Mission, 1930, courtesy the Archives of the Franciscan Province of St. John the Baptist of Cincinnati.

Batesville area with smoke coming from the chimney in the shape of the number 80. In the novitiate at Mt. Airy, Fray Angélico painted an oil portrait of Archbishop McNicholas of Cincinnati on the brick wall of the basement.[16]

Besides helping to reterritorialize him to the Southwest in his semi-exile in Cincinnati and Detroit, Chávez's art and literary creativity in this period were small spaces of reprieve from the rigorous discipline of the religious life. Seminarians would rise early, go to prayers, then Mass and breakfast, and classes began about nine thirty. After lunch there was study hall. They ate dinner together in the dining hall in silence while being read to. After the "Deo gratias" they could talk for a short time. They slept in two dormitories. Evening activities included the "Reading Circle" in which each young seminarian would prepare a speech that was then publicly critiqued. "You'd shake like the dickens," one noted. After the senior year of high school, they entered the novitiate at Mt. Airy, a year of rigorous discipline spent cut off from the world. Novices wore habits at all times and even did chores in them. They picked fruit from the large orchard on the property. The curriculum for the year was the Rule of St. Francis and the scripture with no academic subjects. Upon rising, novices sang the "Divine Office," went to Mass, and then had breakfast. Complete silence was required at all meals. The guardian opened all arriving

FIG. 2.4. Fray Angélico Chávez, illustration for "Notch Twenty-One," 1930, courtesy the Archives of the Franciscan Province of St. John the Baptist of Cincinnati.

packages and took out what was unacceptable. Novices had very simple individual rooms with a bed, desk, and chair. No radios or newspapers were allowed. They underwent tonsure, symbolizing the renunciation of vanity and the things of the world. Once a month the priests used clippers to closely cut the novices' hair. At the end of the year, the novices placed their hands in the hands of the provincial to profess simple vows—that they would live the Franciscan life for three years. The boys were then put on a train for Duns Scotus College in Detroit, where they studied philosophy, logic, and epistemology, with classes entirely in Latin, along with other subjects such as history. This was followed by four years of theological study at Oldenburg, Indiana, and finally ordination to those who survived the thirteen years of rigorous training.[17]

The Early Fiction

Alice Corbin argued that the soil of New Mexico was crucial in the blossoming of the region's literature in the early twentieth century. "It may be that the advent of eastern writers, during and after the World War, had something to do with awakening native-born New Mexicans to a tardy appreciation of their own soil, just as the soil itself had power of re-creating the imaginative vision of the newcomers."[18] In Chávez's case, his contact with the writers' and artists' groups of Santa Fe in the 1920s and 1930s played a strong role in his early literary and artistic creation, and the distant cities of Cincinnati, Detroit, and Oldenburg, Indiana, where he spent most of his time in those years, functioned to set his native land and culture in relief. Precisely as he underwent a temporary exile from the Southwest soil, his writing and art became strongly imbued with ethnic motifs of this culturally important geographical space. His early fiction manifested a cultural hybridity in which religion, ethnicity, history, the Southwest, word, and image combined without losing their individual traces.

Early on Chávez began to write about the Southwest in the seminary newspaper, the *Brown and White*. His January 1926 "The Wonderland of the Americas" nostalgically invokes the land he misses with Spanish and English incantations: "O tierra gloriosa! O tierra digna de amor! O glorious land! O land most worthy of love! The glory of the West! The Eden of the Americas! New Mexico and Arizona."[19] Noting that others have argued that one must see the West in order to understand it, Chávez invites readers to imagine themselves there sensorially: "Now lift up your eyes to the pure sky of azure above. Then let them sweep over the vast stretches of enchanting desert. Inhale that dry, clean invigorating air. Smell and taste that sweet incense wafted from the pine and cedar and sage."[20] Chávez argues that Washington Irving must have had the Southwest in mind when he noted that America had sublime natural scenery. Highlighting the presence of Franciscans in the Southwest, he urges fellow seminarians to "Go West, young man, go West!"[21] Besides aiding the Franciscan goal of future missionaries for the Southwest, he also presents himself as an ethnic subject with expert knowledge of his native territory. In another early piece in the *Brown and White*, sixteen-year-old Chávez recounts the details of a day hike with a friend in the Mora valley in the summer of 1926. He describes for seminary "outsiders" the majestic terrain they scaled in the pine forest on their way to El Peñasco de Águila (Eagle Cliff). Arriving there, they see "an endless stretch of rolling prairie . . . the white-crested sierras glistening in the sunlight, the yawning canyons gliding in and out of the verdant valley, the craggy cliffs standing out in barren relief—all this presented a picture of silent, awful grandeur."[22] Just as the writers' and artists' creative vision was enhanced by the New Mexico soil as Corbin noted, so did Chávez depict singular experiences of the New Mexico landscape in his early writing.

The Southwest Fiction Series in St. Anthony Messenger

In his fourth year in the seminary, Chávez published his first short story in the school monthly. "A Desert Idyll" (February 1928) appears with his poem "The Deserted Mission" that describes the decay of a colonial mission in New Mexico. In both he points to the continuing legacy of Franciscanism in the Southwest, while describing the unique geography and ethnic culture of the region. The idyll—a small picture of a pastoral scene and a beautifully simple event—begins and ends with an image of a striking sunset that "paints" the desert. The conflict centers on the distinct Native American and Christian religious beliefs and practices. As his father has taught him, a young Indian sheepherder prays to the Sun God as he witnesses the stunning sunset. His mother, however, has converted to Christianity and now lies ill in the hogan. He promises to pray the following day that the saint will bring Christ to his mother. Again he prays before the sunset, but now syncretically. Holding out his arms to the sun, "he sang the only song he knew, the song his father had taught him," chanting while he prayed to the maker of the sun to send San Antonio to his mother, "to bring Thee to her!"[23] After this prayer, a Franciscan missionary passing on the road below asks him for directions. Named Padre Jerome in homage to Chávez's mentor, Fr. Jerome Hesse, the friar tells the boy that he is carrying the Blessed Sacrament and will take it to his mother. Since the boy at first believes the padre to be San Antonio because his habit matches the picture his mother has given him, he thinks that his prayer to St. Anthony has been answered perfectly.

While on one level this story encourages the future seminarians about their role in converting Native Americans to Catholicism, on another important level it allows Chávez to present himself as an expert on Southwest culture, deeply connected to the landscape and the traditions of the area. When the story was republished in June 1929 in *St. Anthony Messenger*, Chávez did a pen-and-ink illustration to accompany it, which, instead of depicting the key image of St. Anthony, portrays the Indian boy on a cliff praying to the sunset. Following the new cultural trends of the Santa Fe writers and artists, Chávez portrayed Southwest culture verbally and visually, focusing on specific ethnic traditions and practices. This story was the first of a series of ten narratives about the Southwest that he wrote and illustrated for *St. Anthony Messenger* from June 1929 to September 1930, the year he spent at the novitiate at Mt. Airy. That is, precisely as he received the Franciscan habit, took on a new name, and was encouraged to withdraw from the world he had grown up in, Chávez reconstructed key cultural elements of that world in his short story series. Although he was required to substitute Franciscan robes for the first-prize gaucho costume, he continued to assert his Hispano ethnic identity in his writing. He linked religious themes to his Southwest ethnicity and markedly revealed the influence of the Santa Fe writers' and artists' groups of the period.

The protagonist of "The Tesuque Pony Express" (July 1929) is a ten-year-old Hispano who travels on horseback every week from Tesuque to Santa Fe on family errands. Feeling as important as Don Quixote riding Rocinante, he absorbs the beautiful landscape as he travels and cannot remember one of the errands. Upon seeing the Cross of the Franciscan Martyrs as he enters Santa Fe, he remembers that he is to light a candle to St. Anthony in the cathedral for his grandmother. The narrative disequilibrium in the story results from his having lost the dime for the candle and lost his faith in the effectiveness of this religious ritual. He is concerned that despite his grandmother's devotions, the family lost crops this year. The remedy comes in the form of a woman artist painting on the hillside near the cross in a "multi-hued smock."[24] She asks the boy to carry her materials back to her house on Acequia Madre and pays him a dollar. With this unexpected remedy, the boy lights two candles before the statue, both his money and faith restored.

Chávez subtly inserts himself and other Santa Fe artists in this story. Gerald Cassidy and his wife, Ina Sizer Cassidy, owned a home at Canyon Road and Acequia Madre (924 Canyon Road), which they loaned to fellow artists Sheldon Parsons and his daughter Sara for a time,[25] and Chávez's father had recently built the family home at 712 Acequia Madre. The young Manuel links Franciscan history (the Cross of the Martyrs), Hispano popular religiosity (the grandmother's *manda*), and the Santa Fe Artists Group to the boy's renewed religious experience. The female painter who gives him money is a composite of artists such as the Cassidys, the Parsonses, and Chávez himself whose accompanying pen-and-ink drawing depicts the boy on horseback passing the cross that commemorates the Franciscan missionaries. Throughout the story, Southwestern motifs overcode the religious message.

As a kind of travel-guide narrative, "The Dude of Anchor Ranch" (August 1929) invites readers to follow the young Irish American diagnosed with tuberculosis whose priest advises him to go west to recuperate on an Otowi Canyon ranch. Like an educated tour guide, Chávez explains the meaning of the word *dude* (a non-cowboy), comparing it to the Romans' use of the term *barbarian*, and describes in detail the Southwest landscape and culture that the recuperating visitor experiences. He develops motifs of vision, underscoring the invitation he offers readers to "see" the Southwest through the story and accompanying drawing: the young protagonist cannot see the tuberculosis in his lungs but must accept the doctor's diagnosis; he converses with the priest while gazing at his reflection in a mirror in the office; and he recounts having seen a "talkie" about the Southwest in which the cowboys all had bowlegs. After his months at Otowi, standing on a cliff gazing at the sunset one evening, he sees the shadow of a bowlegged figure—his own now that he has ridden horses so consistently during his cure. A symbol of Chávez himself, the priest who knows the Southwest well has been completely correct.

Chávez links local Hispano ethnicity to cultures outside U.S. borders in "Romance of *El Caminito*."[26] Setting the story on a narrow path and shortcut to the Santa Fe Plaza, Chávez resolves the narrative problem through a wider international cultural base. As a local insider, he explains to readers the name and tradition of the path and recounts a fictional romance that blossomed there because of a young woman's initiative and agency. The boy whom the girl passes each day seems uninterested in her, yet she succeeds in attracting his attention through her stamp collection. After a delay in their conversations because a Franciscan friar appears on the path (similar to a scene in

Chávez's next narrative series, *Guitars and Adobes*), the boy finally shows his affection by offering to give her a prized triangle stamp from Liberia. Chávez validates local Hispano culture, at the same time linking it to larger geographic sites.

While other writers and artists in Santa Fe and Taos were highly interested in and supportive of the culture of Mexico in this period, Chávez criticizes the Mexican Revolution in "The Blasphemer" (November 1929). A visitor from Mexico to the small town "Buena Vista" (the name of Witter Bynner's street) creates a disruption. Named Zapata, the visitor symbolizes the anti-Church reforms of the Mexican Revolution. One Sunday morning, as the missionary padre rings the church bells, the cantina at the opposite end of the street is filled with men who had passed out drinking the night before. The owner, Don Sabino, tells them there is no need for men to go to church or to support the padre monetarily. When Zapata blasphemes and takes Sabino's remarks further, arguing that the Church is only out to get people's money, "the richest part of [the men's] mothers' blood began to boil in their veins."[27] Sabino violently kicks Zapata out and urges the men to come with him to church and donate generously. Hispano and Mexican ethnicities battle here, and religious renewal results.

Several of the stories in the series emphasize Hispano ethnicity through the themes of disguise, performance, and storytelling. In "My Ancestor—Don Pedro" Chávez satirizes the Eastern literary and scholarly establishment searching for authentic Southwest culture. Despite his superior, condescending attitude, Dr. J. Payton Smiggs is enthralled with the "authentic" story that the old Hispano Don Juan de Herrera tells about the role of Herrera's ancestor in the 1598 battle at Acoma. In his patronizing search for authenticity, Smiggs succumbs to the native informant's performance—a compelling fiction disguised as truth. The twinkle in the storyteller's eye hints that he plans to trap the scholar in his own game. As Herrera recounts blow-by-blow his ancestor's bravery at Acoma, the exciting story nearly overcomes Smiggs. Nonetheless, as the performance ends, he recognizes an obvious contradiction of the narrative—the death of the ancestor in the battle at age twenty before meeting the woman he would marry and from whom the family line would descend. Ever in control, Herrera responds to the request for explanation by simply answering, "Ah, Professor, that is the sad thing. My ancestor had to die so young and so inexperienced before he could tell us that!"[28] The performance has snagged the eastern expert by disguising a fictional historical tale as authentic. He closes his notebook and leaves.

Ethnicities confront one another again through performance and disguise in "Spanish and Irish." Here Hispano and Anglo ethnicities work out their differences through representations of Native American ethnicity.[29] Two Santa Fe girls, Lupe and Rose, are competing for the lead in the school play. Sister Antonia tells them to settle it themselves, so they devise a contest. Each will disguise herself, and they will meet at the archbishop's garden. Whoever recognizes the other first will get the lead role. Lupe painstakingly dresses herself as an old Santa Clara Indian woman, but is shocked to find only a real Indian smoking and selling pottery when she arrives at the garden. Intimidated by the man, she hides, waiting for Rose to appear, and finally leaves. Later, when the girls accuse each other of failing to show up as agreed, Lupe learns that Rose was playing the Indian man. Even though she herself was disguised as an Indian, Lupe had mistaken another copy for the real. The battle between the Spanish and Irish girls became a battle of fake Indian identities. The gender "lie" was more effective, however. Rose's performance was more successful (and signified her greater acting ability) because it engaged in doubly encoded difference. Lupe conceded that Rose won the lead.

In "Old Magdalena's Friend," donning ethnic clothing symbolizes a transformation of spiritual identity.[30] Clara Boyton has arrived in Santa Fe discouraged and skeptical about her religion after lengthy travel in search of her lost love. When her landlady Magdalena puts on her "seven-league black shawl" and carries her three-foot rosary to attend vespers, Clara rejects the invitation to accompany her. But Magdalena later inspires her to pray to San Antonio for help in finding what she is looking for. Clara dons Magdalena's long shawl and prays before the statue of the saint at the cathedral. She promises San Antonio money and to wash the altar linens if her request is granted. She is answered almost immediately, for when she recounts her *promesa* to Magdalena, it reminds the woman of the washing she has taken in from a young artist now in town, who, it turns out, is Clara's lost love. Clara disguises herself by performing the Hispano ritual of wearing a long shawl to church. This transformation symbolizes her renewed religious identity, her faith in the Hispano tradition of the manda, and ultimately her recovery of her lost man through San

Antonio's intercession. The Anglo learns from the Hispana, and the local ethnic tradition saves the day.

The first-person narrator of "Sierra Moon" functions as a local expert on New Mexico and, along with Hispano cowboy Fernando, employs double-coded language as a disguise or costume for the truth. Through linguistic disguise, Fernando humorously leads the city slicker visitor and readers down a false interpretive path to achieve a surprise ending. Fernando draws the group's attention to a mysterious pile of bones in the canyon below and tells the story behind them. While rounding up horses the previous year, he saw two figures approaching, old Isidro and Ramona who was "straining under the load of wood on her bent back."[31] Something seemed not right with Ramona, but the woodcutter kept hitting her back with his cane to make her continue. The shocked city slicker suspects slavery, but the storyteller continues: "A few paces away from me, Ramona stopped, her eyes rolling in agony. She sank to her knees without uttering a sound and rolled over on her side, dead."[32] Tearfully, Isidro tells Fernando that he didn't know she was sick that morning and experiences deep grief at the loss of his only companion. The adept storyteller reveals the linguistic disguise he has engaged in with the final line: "Isidro gave one last sad look at her, at those little hoofs and massive ears that would wag no more . . . swearing that there never was in the whole Southwest a burro so faithful as his Ramona."[33] Chávez's doubly coded language serves as a disguise or costume for the truth. Just as a costume temporarily conceals identity, the doubly coded signifier "Ramona" hides the figure's identity long enough to lead readers down a false interpretive path, preparing them for the surprise ending.

In "Notch Twenty-One," the first story published under Fray Angélico's new religious name, disguise, performance, and storytelling are key to an outlaw's triumphing. Here Chávez shows his interest in New Mexico history, setting the story in the 1870s in San Miguel County where Sheriff Miguel Armijo misses an important opportunity to capture "Beely de Keed."[34] Chávez gives key clues to the outcome in the first paragraph; Armijo has set his pistols on his desk, waiting for the outlaw to arrive. Behind him next to the open safe sits "young Jim Slocum," his guns strapped to his sides, sent up by the Lincoln County sheriff because he can recognize the outlaw. Chávez recounts historical details of this period of heavy outlaw activity: William H. Bonney, called "The Kid," was twenty-one and claimed that he needed to kill one more man to match his age. Slocum passes the time waiting with the sheriff by telling a story about the outlaw killing his friend in a bar in Lincoln, which Chávez illustrates adeptly in his drawing for the story. Slocum's story is the double of the one we are reading and prefigures its outcome. Vision is again a central motif, complementing the images of disguise and performance. Chávez's illustration, with several ethnic motifs of the Southwest, centers on the mirror behind the bar in a cantina in which Slocum and his friend briefly see the image of the outlaw as he enters. In Slocum's story, Billy the Kid rapidly kills Slocum's friend while he is drawing his gun. After Slocum has finished his story, the scene is repeated as the door of Sheriff Armijo's office bursts open and an outlaw enters. Standing behind the sheriff, Slocum quickly kills the intruder, and when the sheriff turns around he discovers the safe has been emptied and Slocum is gone. Billy the Kid has disguised himself as Slocum and achieved his twenty-first killing, distracting the sheriff with fabrications and storytelling. The sheriff's vision was impeded with the literal and figurative disguises, and his mistaken reading of signs led to the outlaw's triumph. Like the sheriff, readers are also fooled, thinking that the new intruder is Billy the Kid, as Chávez again leads them down a false narrative path.

Chávez's artwork for this story series presents aspects of the Southwest pictorially, emphasizing ethnicity and key scenes from the plots. He establishes a visual/verbal hybridity through which readers move back and forth between words and images to experience Southwest culture. Text and image enhance one another in partnership. The Southwest is rendered in images of Indians (and their imitators) in native garb, bowlegged cowboys, Spanish conquistadores, Hispana women in long dresses and shawls, a brown-robed Franciscan, the Cross of the Martyrs, a rural church, cantinas, and nature scenes with pine-covered mountains, hollyhocks, and the "opaque amber eyebrow" of the moon.[35] Many of these sketches resemble the illustrations in the 1928 *Santa Fé Fiesta Program*, in which the young Chávez published a poem. The contemporary style of representing the Southwest in drawings and sketches in Santa Fe influenced his artistic imagination in this period.[36] The verbal/visual hybridity of these illustrated texts works together with religion, ethnicity, history, and the Southwest to create Chávez's complex narrative identity.

FIG. 2.5. Ordination class, 1937. Standing left to right: Frs. Thomas Blomstrom, Cletus Kistner, Otto Krische, Edward Overberg, Placid Doyle, Emmet Rothan, Aelred Knittles, Carol Meyer. Seated left to right: Frs. Hugh Simpson, Edwin Schick, Angélico Chávez, Virgil Kaiser, Ignatius Brady, courtesy the Archives of the Franciscan Province of St. John the Baptist of Cincinnati.

The First Novel

Chávez formally received his religious name when entering the novitiate on August 15, 1929, and from January 1930 on, his many poems published in *St. Anthony Messenger* appeared with his new religious name, although the fiction series remained under his given name for several more months. Chávez chose a pseudonym for his next fiction series in *St. Anthony Messenger*, his first novel *Guitars and Adobes*, even as (and perhaps because) his poems and a translation appeared on the same pages of the magazine under his new religious name. The nom de plume, "F. Chalmers Ayers," creatively retains and mixes the order of the initials of Chávez's new religious name, subtly hinting at the real author's identity for astute readers who may have been following Chávez's writing on the Southwest in the magazine. It even retains the "ch," which is a single letter in the Spanish alphabet. Its refusal to mark gender and its implicit Anglo ethnicity point playfully ahead to Chávez's use of female Anglo pseudonyms on other fiction shortly thereafter and hint at his connection to the many eastern Anglo writers in the Santa Fe Writers Group. Semiotician Thomas Sebeok has noted that one's name becomes a quasi-iconic index that denotes the self. Precisely at the time that Chávez is given the new name Fray Angélico, he publishes stories under several pseudonyms, in a sense asserting his own creative control over this iconic index of the self.[37]

At the time Chávez wrote *Guitars and Adobes*, other novels and short fiction about the Southwest found ready audiences, such as Mary Austin's *Starry Adventure* (1931), Ruth Laughlin Barker's *Caballeros: The Romance of Santa Fe and the Southwest* (1931), and Frank Applegate's *Native Tales of New Mexico* (1932). In 1929 Oliver La Farge's *Laughing Boy* won the Pulitzer Prize. Plays about Southwest history such as *Pageant of Old Santa Fe* were produced at the annual fiesta, and the Santa Fe Players performed other dramas. The most well-known novel of the period, Willa Cather's *Death Comes for the Archbishop* (1927), is the first explicit intertext in Chávez's serialized novel, when he suggests on the first page that he wishes to present in his novel an alternate to Cather's picture of the Southwest in this historical period.

Published in eight installments in *St. Anthony Messenger* from November 1931 to June 1932, *Guitars and Adobes* continues the focus on Hispano ethnicity of his previous fiction. The novel reveals that Fray Angélico was already studying important figures in New Mexico history about which he would later write longer historical accounts. Digressive narratives within the larger novel treat Don Diego de Vargas, Archbishop Lamy, Doña Tules Barceló, and La Conquistadora as Chávez emphasizes their legacy in the characters' lives. He displays firsthand knowledge of New Mexico places such as Mora, Las Vegas, Taos, and Santa Fe. Especially noteworthy are the lithographs that Gerald Cassidy made for the novel and the brown ink in which the story and images are printed to chromatically signify the Southwest. In the last chapter, Chávez resignifies the novel's central motif of the house, subtly suggesting that it is Cassidy's house on Canyon Road and Acequia Madre, and he mentions other members of the Writers Group who lived on Camino Monte Sol in 1929 when the story ends. By obtaining Cassidy's artistic contribution and by alluding to the Writers Group, Chávez noticeably places this creative work within the burgeoning artistic and literary movements in Santa Fe at the time.

The novel is framed at the beginning and end by two deaths—that of Archbishop Lamy in 1888 and of an ordinary Hispana, Consuelo Ortega Rael, in 1929. Chávez's explicit denial at the outset that the novel is a sequel to Cather's in effect signals the opposite: that he strives to offer a vision of New Mexico in these years that much more accurately portrays Hispano culture. He presents an alternate ethnicity to the emphasis on French figures in Cather's novel.[38] As the story opens at the time of Lamy's death, Consuelo's mother, the widow Doña Genoveva, proudly traces her lineage to a captain under de Vargas in the reconquest. She hides her fortune under a slab in the fireplace and watches over an ancient guitar from Spain that her husband recovered years earlier from the famous saloon of Doña Tules and that, according to legend, will bring death to anyone who plays it. Throughout, the novel both affirms and denies the superstition about the guitar, subtly hinting at the end that Consuelo plays it shortly before her death. Five months earlier, Archbishop Lamy had come to Genoveva's house when she was ill and had played the guitar before she could stop him. She is convinced this is why he died on February 14, 1888. Meanwhile, her daughter begins to fall in love with Rosendo Rael, an industrious adobe maker who is falsely blamed for a burglary in their home. Doña Genoveva wishes her daughter to marry another man from a wealthy family who in fact is a gambler and troublemaker, and the real burglar.

When Rosendo loses his adobe-construction jobs because of the false accusation and because the Americans who have come are building their houses differently, he uses the adobes he has made to construct a house near the Atalaya hills and buys a beautiful piano for it. After Mass on Sundays he continues to tell Consuelo he loves her and is finally able to spend time with her at a dance on Agua Fria Street. At the novel's climax, Consuelo elopes with Rosendo, after seeing the beautiful adobe house with the piano. Padre Roque at the Santuario de Chimayó marries them in a double ceremony with a Native American couple. Pursued by the rival suitor, Consuelo and Rosendo escape to the mountains to begin their new life. They eventually settle in Mora, where Fray Angélico grew up, and have a daughter whom they name after Doña Genoveva. Three years later, through the intercession of Padre Roque, Consuelo receives a long letter from her mother. Eventually the evil rival dies during revelries at the Taos fiesta, and Doña Genoveva learns that it was he, not her son-in-law, who burglarized her house. She finally invites her daughter to come home to Santa Fe.

At this time an epidemic of *la viruela* (smallpox) breaks out in Mora, and the entire family is infected after Rosendo helps some of the ill. In poignant scenes, Rosendo and the child die, and Consuelo loses her mind and disappears one night with no one able to find her. The narrative moves ahead about thirty-five years to 1929 and the Santa Fe of the writers' and artists' groups. An artist has bought Doña Genoveva's house on Acequia Madre. Up the road on Camino Monte Sol, three writers at a gathering hear the music of an out-of-tune piano and guitar coming from near the Atalaya. The old woman with the scarred face who lives in the house calls herself Margarita and one night is killed during a violent storm as the house caves in while she is playing the piano. When the writers go to the house the next day, there are no musical instruments there, despite their having heard music for many nights. Chávez ends the novel on this note of mystery: "a mystery as intangible and uninterpretable as the one that holds the Old Santa Fe with the New in spite of the years, a tie of race, faith, and traditions, of love and romance, of guitars and adobes."[39] Chávez's historical novel eschews a happy ending in favor of a realism tinged with the uncertain. We cannot know everything about the past, but perhaps Spanish traditions and narratives carried down through generations provide a more accurate account of the past than Cather's novel.

One key means by which Chávez Hispanicizes Cather's version of events is by linking the motif of death to the ancient Spanish guitar. The Spanish name for the instrument preserved from Doña Tules' saloon is *la vihuela*, which Chávez creatively connects to its near homonym, *la viruela*, the word for smallpox. Inscribed on the guitar is a sentence in code that Archbishop Lamy deciphers because he knows Hebrew. The inscription contains words in Spanish spelled with the Hebrew alphabet, a hybrid text that gives historical testimony to the period of the reconquest in Spain in which Jews were told to convert to Christianity or leave the country. A subnarrative fictively recounted in one of Doña Genoveva's letters reveals the legend of the guitar. Here Chávez falls into a glaring anti-Semitism that he most likely imbibed in the milieu of the Cincinnati seminary. He writes,

"Most of [the Jews] had been driven out of the kingdom by the government in order to free the country of a peril more insidious than the open warfare of the formerly victorious Moors: for they had been assuming control of the financial, the political, and even some of the religious affairs, when the Spanish hierarchy sounded the alarm."[40] Seemingly defending the Spanish Inquisition, Chávez creates the character Salomon García, terming him "a notorious leader of the Jews," a "shifty Jew," and a "fanatical rabbi."[41] The Inquisition accused the converso García of plotting to overthrow the government and burned him at the stake. During the execution, an onlooker accompanied by a guitar improvised a ballad criticizing García. The converso's youngest son Benjamin then killed the balladeer and inscribed an encoded curse on the guitar: "La muerte canto—tócame y mueres" (I sing death—play me and you die!).[42] Eventually the guitar came to the New World and ultimately to New Mexico with Doña Tules' family.

The overt anti-Semitism Chávez expresses in this first novel written when he was just twenty, before the Holocaust would wreak its devastation, should be read in conjunction with information about the important contributions Jews made to Spanish and Latin American letters that Ilan Stavans documents in *The Scroll and the Cross: 1,000 Years of Jewish-Hispanic Literature*.[43] Stavans traces the relations between Jews and Hispanics through the centuries in the Spanish-speaking world. He presents key texts of the literary and intellectual contributions of Jewish Hispanic culture.

The Scroll and the Cross also provides information about how non-Jews have reacted to the Jewish presence, including such documents as the Edict of 1492, which forced the Jews out of Spain, and an analysis of anti-Semitism in the work of thirteenth-century poet Gonzalo de Berceo. Representing popular views of the time, Berceo portrays, for example, a statue of the Blessed Virgin that miraculously claims that "the Jews were doing Her injuries severe."[44] Thirteenth-century king Alfonso X (El Sabio) proclaimed a code of law with restrictions for Jews, arguing that they should live forever in captivity as a reminder of their role in crucifying Christ, that they wear a distinguishing mark on their heads to allow recognition, and that Jews who had sexual relations with Christian women deserved death. The poem "To a Nose" by seventeenth-century poet Francisco de Quevedo "might be one of the most anti-Semitic sonnets ever written in Spain, a peninsula known for its anti-Jewish literature," Stavans notes.[45] In contrast, a 1930 poem by Federico García Lorca highlights Judaism as a reservoir of ancient memory. By also including key writing by Hispano Jews in this volume, Stavans documents and gives voice to a vibrant intellectual culture, often developed under conditions of extreme adversity and often demeaned or overlooked by cultural arbiters. His work partially explains the long tradition of Hispano anti-Semitism that Fray Angélico Chávez inherited along with similar attitudes fomented in the Germanic milieu of the Catholic seminaries he attended. Stavans' book is a necessary companion to any reading of *Guitars and Adobes*.[46]

The guitar is a metaphor for the novel itself. Linking the themes of the curse, revenge, and foretelling, its enigma impels the narrative forward. Characters often debate whether playing the cursed guitar does or does not cause death, and although several voices of authority in the novel insist that such deaths are only temporally coincidental, Chávez playfully leaves doubt about the guitar's role at the end. Additionally, Benjamin's encoded curse is like Chávez's novel, since both involve writing by a minority group that carries a message about the past forward to future generations to prevent the forgetting of history. In form, Benjamin's dual-language message is similar to Chávez's bilingual narrative: both encode ethnicity through hybridity.

If the title of Cather's novel focuses on the death of Archbishop Lamy, Chávez's novel broadens our understanding of death in the period. Lamy's natural death is set in contrast to the tragic deaths of ordinary people from smallpox, especially the untimely deaths of little Genoveva and the good Rosendo. The villain suitor dies like a besieged cock in the *corrida de gallos* during the Taos fiesta. Consuelo dies after a tragic life when her house collapses during a violent storm. Some of her siblings had died in infancy, and her father was killed in a battle with the Navajos in 1873. The cursed Spanish guitar symbolizes the anxiety of Hispanos in New Mexico in this period about the pervasiveness of death. Chávez reconfigures the idea of death in the years preceding and following Lamy's demise, giving it an alternative ethnic nuance.

Another signifier of ethnicity in the title and plot is the adobe. In contrast to the death the guitar symbolizes, adobes signify life when they are used to construct homes to shelter people. Rosendo makes thousands of adobes for people's homes, and after clients reject him because of the false accusation, he builds a beautiful home to shelter his future family. In contrast to the guitar's embodiment of Thanatos, Rosendo's adobes symbolize Eros and life. The piano he brings links the home to the aesthetic. Inexorable death triumphs, as nature overpowers culture and the unrepaired adobes during the storm in 1929. The image of adobes also links Chávez to the preservation movement at the time led by cultural figures in Santa Fe, work that he himself would engage in after his ordination.

Hispano ethnicity imbues *Guitars and Adobes* and is particularly evident in the internal stories that Chávez inserts as digressions about Hispano historical figures. Citing details by a chronicler of the period, he tells the story of Tules Barceló who established a saloon and gambling house at the corner of the Calle del Palacio and what is now Burro Alley. Later, in 1950, Chávez would publish his own revisionist historical account of Doña Tules in *El Palacio*, including her death in 1852 when Lamy was bishop. In *Guitars and Adobes*, he augments and re-ethnicizes Cather's version of events by inserting the narrative of Tules Barcelona, as her name was believed to be at the time. In another narrative digression, Chávez tells the story of La Conquistadora, called at the time La Señora del Rosario or de la Victoria. As Rosendo prays before the statue to ask for help in winning Consuelo's love, he has a vision of the events of de Vargas' reconquest. In narrating Rosendo's vision, Chávez familiarizes readers with the associated Hispano traditions in Santa Fe relating to the 1680 Pueblo Revolt and de Vargas' 1693 reconquest using the same statue of the Virgin that Rosendo prays before. Chávez suggests that if Rosendo had read the original document that de Vargas drew up on the reconquest, he would have seen the signature of his forebear, Antonio Rael de Aguilar, and Consuelo's, Francisco Xavier de Ortega. Chávez named the protagonists in *Guitars and Adobes* to emphasize the authentic connection of Santa Fe Hispanos to centuries of the Spanish presence in New Mexico. That story did not begin with Archbishop Lamy, he insists.

Once again, as he undergoes the increasing discipline of the novitiate in Mt. Airy and Duns Scotus College in Detroit, Chávez directs an important part of his creative energy to a compelling narrative that reasserts Hispano ethnicity in the master historical text. His nostalgia for home was shaped by the intellectual and cultural preoccupations of the Santa Fe writers and artists. In *Guitars and Adobes* he joins forces with them by obtaining Cassidy's artwork and asserts his own authentic and historically accurate Hispano version of events. Instead of seeking a publication outlet in the Southwest or another national venue, he publishes the novel serially in the Franciscan national magazine, perhaps because of his youthful inexperience, his confinement in the seminary, and pressure from the editor for more of his compelling fiction.

Female Pseudonyms and the Stories in the Sodalist

At the height of the Depression, as he was finishing work in the major seminary St. Leonard's in Oldenburg, Indiana, Fray Angélico wrote a series of stories for the young female readers of the Catholic magazine the *Sodalist*. In this period, sodalities of the Blessed Virgin were clubs designed to encourage young women's devotion to Mary and enhance their moral development.[47] Chávez's stories impart advice and morals, with humor, erudition, and witty wordplay to entertain readers. Female protagonists predominate, often wiser and cleverer than the men. Young female characters must often choose between two suitors, and the narrative resolutions give advice on the most efficacious choices and the qualities of a good husband.

Fray Angélico published four of these stories under female pseudonyms, perhaps because the readers might be more receptive to instructional messages from a woman. However, his choice of the name "Ann Jellicoe" for three of the stories subtly challenges readers to connect them to previous stories by "Angélico Chávez." By leaving out the religious signifier "Fray," the byline suggests that the author is a layperson, not a religious; the omission of "Fray" also invites readers to make an easier connection to the pseudonym "Ann Jellicoe" without an intrusive, nonhomonymic extra word. The new pseudonym "Ann Jellicoe" echoes his real name phonetically, and the stories have similar structures, lessons, humor, and wordplay that careful readers might associate with Angélico Chávez's previous stories. Perhaps to mark his departure from seminary studies, he used the one-time pen name "Monica Lloyd" on the last story in 1938.[48]

Fray Angélico may have adopted a pseudonym the first time for a more practical reason—to avoid the appearance of two contributions by one author. In September 1936 both his article "How to Make Your Own Bookplate" and one of his stories appeared, and the editor or he himself might have suggested that he invent a pseudonym. In the

November issue that year, his poem had the byline "Angélico Chávez," while his story carried a pseudonym.[49] Perhaps Chávez enjoyed experimenting with the female authorial identities precisely at the time that his real-life identity was about to undergo transformation through ordination to the Franciscan priesthood. The gender hybridity of the pseudonym also employed another fictional ethnicity, that of an Anglo. Nonetheless, the gender and ethnic hybridity of a name such as "Ann Jellicoe" allowed observant readers to see the distinct elements of the new mixture clearly: just as a pun moves back and forth between the two or more meanings of the signifier, so do the names "Angelico" and "Ann Jellicoe" allow readers to enjoyably waver between male and female, Hispano and Anglo significations. Chávez also engaged in such rhetorical and thematic strategies in the story "Carrie's Notion" (1937) by giving the character Elmer Vogelmeister, whose surname means "Master of the Birds," the pseudonym "E. Byrd Masters."

The article on bookplates reveals Fray Angélico's analysis of the semiotics of names and identity precisely at the time he is inventing pseudonyms for himself. Additionally, he conjoins verbal and visual representational play and argues that making and using bookplates, while a signature would suffice to signify ownership, gives aesthetic pleasure. The issue of identity in this article combines concepts of ethnic and religious heritage, the aesthetic, visual and verbal signification, naming, and self-representation. He argues that "individual bookplates . . . bear some special design which reflects in an artistic way the identity, occupation, or even some personal traits of the owner. These lend individuality to one's private library, be it ever so small."[50] A bookplate imparts one's personality to a book. He shows readers how to visually represent their first and last names and engage in verbal-visual puns: "Angela Stone, for instance, can have an angel in the act of carving *Ex Libris* and her name on a stone. Frances La Fontaine would have a beauty in a picture of St. Francis standing by a playing fountain. . . . The one for Felix Katz would be a howler—two cats doing a jig."[51]

Chávez conjoins the verbal and the visual in one of his own designs for a bookplate. The illustration "Personal bookplate, drawn and designed by the author" includes a pen-and-ink profile of Fra Angelico da Fiesole; a Latin motto from the New Testament, "Impendam et superimpendar" (I will expend myself and I will be exceedingly spent); and a coat of arms that visually represents his name next to the verbal text of the name, "fr. Angélico Chávez." His inclusion of the accent marks on his name here adds another level of Hispanic ethnicity. He had the bookplate printed in brown ink on white paper to signify Franciscan identity through color. The small coat of arms, in apposition to the verbal rendering of his name, depicts two angel's wings suspended on two keys (the word *llaves* or "keys," from which his surname derived). The hybridity of aesthetic, religious, ethnic, and gender identity in this article parallels that of his other writing and creative production in this period.

As Chávez's stories in the *Sodalist* attempt to socialize Catholic girls, they also address issues of the day, portray Hispano and other ethnic cultures, and engage in humorous wordplay and cultural allusions. In "Time and Tide" (1935), for example, New Mexico Hispano culture is only a backdrop in contrast to other stories in which it plays a more central role. Twin sisters, humorously named Fructosa and Sinforosa Cana, are unmarried businesswomen who operate a hotel in Mora, where Fray Angélico grew up. Chávez anglicizes their names to "Time" and "Tide," diegetically because the townspeople found their names too much work to say, and formally to allow him to play on the aphorism "Time and tide wait for no man." Chávez also references "Bill" Shakespeare's relevant lines: "There is a tide in the affairs of men which, taken at the flood, leads on to fortune." In terms of romance, the Cana sisters had only experienced a desert to this point, but Chávez warns they were about to experience a flood and disprove "Bill's weather forecast."[52] With extensive wordplay and clever cultural allusions, Chávez adorns the rather simple plot with references to President Roosevelt and flood relief, Noah's ark, and the wedding at Cana. The transformation of a tide into the flood of fortune to which Shakespeare alludes involves a plot by two highway workers to pretend to be in love with the sister Time who carries large sums of money in her stocking. As one man drives her on a deserted road allegedly to elope with her, the other will stop the car and steal Time's money. But Time and Tide wait for no man, and the fortune seekers discover they have brought the wrong identical twin on the car trip. What Chávez terms "the attempted Cananite abduction" fails, and the women triumph over the scoundrels.[53]

Hispano culture functions more strongly in "Viola Comes of Age" with the byline "Ann Jellicoe." Set in Argentina, it develops identity through ethnicity, religiosity, and family heritage. The protagonist

Viola Molinar is a hybrid figure in appearance, personality, and name. Chávez notes that she is a blue-eyed blonde—physical traits inherited from the Celts who originally inhabited Spain—and has pensive moods in which her eyes grow dark, attributed to her strain of "Moorish fiery blood."[54] Her name is a linguistic hybrid of those of her two grandmothers, Victoria and Olivia. The story's narrative disequilibrium relates to religion and family heritage: Viola prays at the shrine of the fictional "Our Lady of Roybal." Here Chávez inserts his family identity into the narrative—his mother's name Roybal—perhaps to compensate for the absence of his paternal family name in the byline. He playfully implants a subtle signifier of identity that perhaps only family members and future scholars would decode.

Viola's mother fears that the visits to the shrine will lead to her becoming a nun instead of marrying and passing on the family's fortune. Ethnicity is invoked when her mother complains that the time at the shrine prevents her from practicing her Andalusian dance for the upcoming fiesta.[55] Viola prays to the Virgin that the handsome American miner she likes will turn out to be single and a Catholic. When he sees her at the shrine, he tells her that he is both, and also an Irishman—"the dark variety of Erin that inherited its brunette strain from shipwrecked survivors of the Spanish Armada."[56] As with Viola, Chávez integrates an inherited strain of Hispano ethnicity into the potential suitor and casts him as single and Catholic to urge readers to seek the same qualities in potential mates. Her mother is pleased that he attends vespers the night before the fiesta. The story ends with a tableau of Hispanic ethnicity, depicting Viola's gypsy dance: "Never was her hair more golden, or her lips more enticingly poutful, or her eyes more Moorishly big and enchanting. All the youthful *caballeros* applauded and whooped."[57] The narrative disequilibrium is resolved through a felicitous match that conjoins Spanish heritage, devout Catholicism, and maternal approval.

Chávez again linked Hispanic ethnicity to religion and ideals for young women in an adamantly anti-Communist story about the Spanish Civil War. "Spanish Joan," published under his own name, presents the figure of María Jaén, a brave Catholic girl in Spain who in an instant becomes a militant and is killed trying to save a convent of Franciscans from a mob of rabid Communists. Here, as in his 1939 essay "Ni los sepulcros respetan" (They Don't Even Respect Graves), Chávez presents a one-sided, inaccurate picture of the Spanish Civil

War in which those fighting for the Republican democracy were termed "Communists" by the Catholic Church and other supporters of the Fascist general Francisco Franco.

Describing "the night of Red Terror" in Málaga, Chávez portrays the Republicans as subhuman: "The Communist mobs surged about like incarnate demons, shrieking blasphemies and applying the knife and torch to everything that was God's."[58] After María's father and brother Manuel are arrested and burned alive by the "Soviet fiends," María wishes she had been born a man so that she could fight "these foes of her home, her country, and her Faith."[59] Remembering Joan of Arc, the girl takes up her brother's hunting rifle, refuses an escape route offered her, and forces the friars to escape safely while she holds off the "blood-thirsty throng."[60] After she is killed, and the "human devils" tramp over her body, the spirit of Joan of Arc comes down from the heavens to rescue the soul of the "Maid of Málaga." Chávez invites female readers to identify with María's militant defense of Catholicism, with a strong dose of Catholic anti-Communist indoctrination cloaked in details of Spanish ethnicity, such as the rose María wears near her temple as she holds off the enemy. Again he inserts himself subtly into the story by using his given name, Manuel, for the brother who is killed.

Hispano culture in New Mexico is a key element of identity in "Eve of San Isidro" (1937), published under the pseudonym "Ann Jellicoe." Although this story also focuses on a young girl's suitors, here the choice is a religious vocation over marriage. Now an elderly nun in Delaware, the protagonist is originally from New Mexico and tells for the first time the story of her youth. Much of her narrative, identity, and preoccupations coincides with Fray Angélico's own trajectory. It might be argued that "Ann Jellicoe" has superimposed his/her identity upon that of the character. Like the nun Sister Consolata, nicknamed "Sister Disappointed," Chávez was transplanted from New Mexico to the east and often needed to explain Hispano culture and correct misperceptions. On the eve of the feast of St. Isidore, the patron of the school, Sister Consolata informs the young graduate Ellen McIntyre that the saint was Spanish, not Irish. "In fact, there are two Saints by that name, the Archbishop of Seville and the Laborer of Madrid"; both the school and the church in the nun's village in New Mexico are dedicated to the laborer, she explains.[61] We can detect Fray Angélico's own nostalgia in the vivid image the nun offers the student: "I can still see the little town perched on the mountainside, with the New Mexico sierras looming behind, and the yellow plains spreading below for hundreds of miles. . . . I can see the Padre teaching the children their prayers under that old acacia tree by the chapel door."[62] Fray Angélico combines memory of place with a projected future image of himself as a village padre, beneath the guises of a female pseudonym and a female character's voice.

When she was eighteen, a young man Antonio asks for the narrator's hand. Explaining the Hispano custom of parents choosing mates for their children, the nun explains to Ellen that she left the decision to her father. Ultimately she rejects Antonio and discusses with the town priest an amorphous longing that she constantly feels. She asks, as María did in "Spanish Joan," why God had not made her a man so that she could become a priest. The padre then arranges for her to travel east to become a nun.

Fray Angélico overlays elements of his own story on Sister Consolata's, even having her express concern about the deteriorating condition of the Southwest missions and the work of the French missionary in her village to restore the church. Fray Angélico would engage in such restoration himself as soon as he was ordained, and here he uses the voice of the fictive nun to outline the religious and community work he will do on his first assignment. When Sister Consolata looks at the crucifix at the end of her narrative and tells Ellen, "I was never disappointed in love," we can imagine that Fray Angélico shared these sentiments about his own vocation.[63]

Several of Chávez's stories in the *Sodalist* center on an aphorism or common saying reconfigured both to teach a moral and for humorous wordplay. "A Stitch in Time" plays with the motif of sewing to illustrate a young dressmaker's integrity and ingenuity. Gertrude Miller's "stitch in time" saves a close championship baseball game. The story's conflict involves the pitcher's and catcher's rivalry for her affection. Having recently left the disrespectful pitcher for the catcher, Gertrude saves the day by an ingenious bit of playacting that she designs and executes.

L. A. Levy, banker and financial supporter of the team, demands that she pretend to renew her amorous relationships with both the pitcher and catcher so that they will play well together. She refuses on ethical grounds and stands her own against Levy's misogynist attacks accusing her of having disempowered the men, like Delilah.

He employs the motif of sewing as if this is all she will understand: "Yeah, a little snipper with scissors! Oi, you moderns womens. You ain't got no brains, no refinements, no moralities, no—."[64] Gertrude strongly defends herself and takes the upper hand by promising mysteriously to secure the team's win. In the last inning, just as there seems to be no hope for overcoming the dissension between pitcher and catcher, Gertrude openly flirts in the stands with the owner of the other team so that both players no longer want anything to do with her and finally work together to win the game. She reveals at the end that the other team's owner previously wreaked financial ruin on her family, and she was happy to devise this way for his team to lose. Levy tells her, "You sewed up the breeches—I mean, the breach in the team at the right time," and she responds that it was not merely a stitch in time that saved nine, but a double stitch because she also avenged the wrong done to her family. Chávez shows the predominantly female readers of the magazine that they can be strong and ingenious despite adversity and men's attempt to stereotype them. Of course, they also must not flirt with other men when not strategically playacting, or risk losing the affection of potential boyfriends.

Chávez depicts another ethnic culture in his love story about an Italian street vendor who competes with a doctor for a nurse's affection. In "Daily Apple" by Ann Jellicoe, fruit vendor Tony Valentino gives the nurse a bright red apple every day as she passes on her way to the hospital, hoping the gesture will keep the doctor away from her. He promises her an original song one day, and she hears him from below in the street singing Italian lines that Chávez translates for readers: "O wingless angel, pure and white / You make this hospital a Heaven bright."[65] Almost immediately, the song takes on a more literal signification when the nurse and doctor are called to an emergency: the street vendor has been hit by a van. As he lies near death in the hospital, he tells the nurse, "Miss Ellis, you make dis place a heaven for all. Tony, he go up to da big heaven. He pray for you two. . . . Maybe better dis way. What do American people say—an apple a day keeps da doc away?"[66]

"Rolling Stones" and "It's an Ill Wind" play on their respective aphorisms to overcome characters' dilemmas. The protagonist of the first story, Flora Leech, must decide between two suitors and between progress and tradition in the face of encroaching Yankee development in her small Tennessee town. The city-bred Algey Ludlow discovers a new species of moss on the idle millstones owned by Flora's father and names the strain *Floralacea*, hoping to entice her to marry him. The hometown suitor, Jim Huskin, proposes a clever scheme to revitalize the old mill and sell feed to the government at a lower price than the Yankee company. Flora makes her decision between the two after she slips into the water close to the turning waterwheel and Jim succeeds in saving her while Algey is primarily concerned about his scientific notes that have fallen into the water. The adapted aphorism conveys the moral as Jim and Flora converse at the end: "'I ask you for the hundredth time,' pleaded Jim, 'if you prefer me and the millstones to that cracked moss gatherer.' 'And I answer for the hundredth time,' said she, smiling, 'that a rolling stone gathers no moss.'"[67]

The saying "It's an ill wind that blows no one good" highlights the thematic and moral elements of the second story.[68] This time, the protagonist is a young man who goes wrong, dreaming of marrying his girlfriend but lacking sufficient money. Like Chávez himself, he is small in stature and plays a wind instrument—the bass tuba. (Chávez played the saxophone.) After an ill wind blows into town in the person of two career criminals who entice him into a burglary and then betray him, he staves off one thief's attempt on his life through his own "wind power." Trapped in a garage with the car engine running, the small man outlasts the hefty criminal in the struggle because he can hold his breath longer. In effect, a good wind triumphs over the ill wind. The victim of the burglary forgives him and pays him a five-thousand-dollar reward for helping to catch the thief, enabling him to marry.

"Winnie the Breadwinner and Saint Anthony," Chávez's last story in the *Sodalist*, appeared a year after he was ordained under the pseudonym "Monica Lloyd."[69] It recounts a young widow's struggle during the Depression to support her child and sister. An allusion to Detroit and the *Free Press* newspaper suggests that it perhaps was written earlier in the 1930s when Chávez was a student at Duns Scotus College outside Detroit. It contains none of the humorous wordplay, reinterpreted aphorisms, or the lightness of the other stories. Winnie and her sister are immigrants from Wales who now wish to return, given their suffering in the Depression. Thanks to the prayers of the sister and child before the statue of St. Anthony in the home, Winnie finds a part-time job that pays one dollar a day, which will go to back rent. Although they continue their traditional Tuesday night novena to St. Anthony at church, Winnie loses the job. The melodramatic ups-and-downs are resolved when a wealthy woman encounters the family outside the church, her own novena to St. Anthony having been answered. In thanksgiving she writes a check for the family's return trip to Wales before leaving quickly in her limousine. The predominant religious message is that a strong devotion to St. Anthony can ameliorate the most desperate circumstances suffered in the Depression. The story also subtly alludes to Fray Angélico's parents' loss of their house in the Depression and his mother's devotion to the statue of St. Anthony in the living room. After her death, family members found notes of petition that Mrs. Chávez had placed beneath the statue. (See figure 1.15.)

Chávez's stories in the *Sodalist* teach morals to young women through enjoyable plots, easy identification with characters, wordplay, and linguistic twists. Chávez inserts himself into many of these stories in unique hybrid constructs that cross ethnicities, genders, and professions, along with history, religion, politics, and linguistic play. He subtly overlays himself on both male and female characters, including a musician who betrays his family and friends by committing a burglary, a Spanish Civil War victim, a nun, and even the Blessed Virgin honored at a shrine in Argentina, as well as presenting himself through his given and religious names and female pseudonyms. Strikingly, several stories put Hispano culture center stage, pointing to the author as an ethnic subject whose personal expertise can correct misperceptions about an important regional culture in the United States and place that culture in the forefront.

Hybrid Poetic Expression

Chávez's early years of formation were also a period of intense poetic production. From 1925 until his ordination in 1937, he published a large body of poems in the *Brown and White, St. Anthony Messenger,* the *Provincial Chronicle,* the *Sodalist, America,* and the *Santa Fe New Mexican.*[70] We know that he wrote many of these poems between 1925 and 1932 because of a unique gift he made for his parents to commemorate his profession of solemn vows on August 16, 1933. He typed and collected his poems in a single bound book that he entitled *Cantares: Canticles and Poems of Youth, 1925–1932*. Years later, his sister-in-law Bernice Chávez found the volume in the basement of the family home on Acequia Madre and asked Fray Angélico if she could have it. He agreed and humorously signed the book for her: "To my dear Bernice, my terrible sister-in-law, to keep in the cellar, with all my love. Fr. Angélico Chávez O.F.M., Nov. 27, 1962."[71] In contrast, the dedication he typed to his parents at the beginning of the volume reads, "A ustedes mis queridos Padres, doy y dedico esta única colección de mis versos, no para que se la enseñen a todo el mundo, pero para que la guarden como señal de mi amor y devoción. Manuel, 16 de agosto de 1933 (Día de mi Profesión Solemne)."[72] Of the 166 poems in the private volume, 103 of them were published in periodicals, newspapers, and other volumes of poetry, sometimes under different titles. Chávez's tremendous spurt of poetic creativity from age fifteen to twenty-two as he was learning about canonical literature of the English and American traditions produced a large body of work from which he drew in subsequent years when asked for poems for publications. He later recounted that his English teacher Fr. Reginald encouraged him to write poetry at the time to help with his homesickness, and the large body of this work suggests that he was quite homesick as a young boy in the strange environment far from home.[73] Although he wrote important poetry in later years, especially *Eleven Lady-Lyrics and Other Poems* (1945), *The Single Rose* (1948), and *The Virgin of Port Lligat* (1959), he never wrote as much poetry as he did in this intense period of production and enthusiasm from age fifteen to twenty-two.

Religion imbues many of the poems, as do themes of Hispanic ethnicity and the Southwest. Once again Chávez establishes a hybrid identity in his literary creation that combines religion, ethnicity, history, the Southwest, words, and images. In his semi-exilic state between 1925 and 1937 where he experienced New Mexico in some summers but most years remained in Ohio, Michigan, or Indiana, a number of his poems focus on Southwest and Hispanic themes. The poetry of Bynner and other members of the Writers Group, and key publications such as Alice Corbin's *Red Earth* (1920) and her 1928 anthology *The Turquoise Trail*, influenced Chávez's presentation of Hispano ethnicity and the Southwest. His poem in Spanish "A La Conquistadora" won first prize in a contest sponsored by the Fiesta Committee in 1928.[74] As he recounts the key role of the Virgin in de Vargas' reconquest of Santa Fe three centuries earlier, he salutes the Virgin with the poem, as do the people of Santa Fe in thanksgiving for her protection. He writes the poem in Spanish, La Conquistadora's language, but also to assert his own brand of Hispano ethnicity during the Anglo artists' revival of the fiesta. The poem conjoins religious faith, historical traditions, and Hispano culture and language as Manuel Chávez makes his aesthetic contribution to the tradition in the public space of the 1928 fiesta leaflet.

Also that August, the *Santa Fe New Mexican* published Chávez's poem "'Foreign' New Mexico." Here he reminds readers that the Kingdom of New Spain predated the explorers and Pilgrims. He notes that the legacy of the conquistadores and the Franciscan martyrs is the Hispano people who "clung to every priestless mission wall, / Through centuries forgotten and unsung."[75] This "Atlantis" preserved Spanish culture and survived in isolation until the "tree" of U.S. expansion

> *spread its tender branches west,*
> *Encircling all this treasure, land, and race*
> *And making all its own.*[76]

Although New Mexico is the youngest state of the union, Chávez notes, it is in fact the eldest and the "least foreign to our glorious country now."[77]

That year Chávez also wrote of Santa Fe's Arabic-Spanish heritage in "On the Alameda," in which he compares the grove beside the river on Alameda Street to a mosque, the weeping willow to a jade dome, and the poplars to minarets. While imagining that he is in Arabia, he hears the Angelus bells from the cathedral and remembers that he is walking home with God or a companion. In a similar vein, in "The Archbishop's Garden," Chávez describes Archbishop Lamy's garden on the cathedral grounds, hidden by a high adobe wall. He and his companion can only see pink hollyhocks, the tops of junipers, and the spray of a fountain above the wall, but the passing farmer Isidro with his covered wagon filled with fruit, santos, and carved furniture kneels on the wagon seat to enjoy the view over the wall. Chávez most likely composed these poems on a visit home in summer 1928 or shortly after his return.[78]

The city of Santa Fe and its fiesta become the protagonist in "Tango," published in the *Santa Fe New Mexican* in 1929. Having dressed himself as a gaucho for the 1926 and 1928 fiestas, he reads the city's celebrations through another Argentine/Hispano motif—the tango. His sumptuous description of the city during fiesta in effect dresses it for display just as he dressed himself in ethnic attire for the occasion. Nature and culture interact, as the special landscape and geography of the Southwest are the optic through which Chávez reads the annual celebration. The wind drumming on the poet's windowpane with the rhythm of a fandango calls him out to the streets to see the parties, "singing of the charming tango."[79] In the fourth stanza, the poetic "I" changes to a personification of the wind, traveling at will throughout the city and proclaiming its superiority to the river that must pass by and never see the events again. The wind and river themselves "dance a wild fandango / Where the forest colors glisten."[80] Chávez compares the rich music and dancing of the fiesta parties in "The Great Salon of Night in the Canyon" to other famous dance rituals in Southwest pueblos and to the music the Franciscans brought to the area; despite the grandeur of these rituals, they cannot match the tango.[81] The poem's rich visual and auditory motifs and dancelike rhythm capture a modicum of the celebration's excitement. The strong elements of Hispano ethnicity in the poem become the native New Mexican poet's contribution to the "Great Salon of Night in the Canyon" where lately arrived writers, artists, and their friends revel.

Other key elements of Hispano culture in his poems in this period focus on history, place, the landscape, the old churches and missions, and the friar missionaries. One of his earliest poems, "The Deserted Mission," published in February 1928 on the same page with his story "A Desert Idyll," describes the ruins of a chapel where people worshipped three hundred years ago.[82] The Franciscan "cross and arms" still hang above the door, a symbol of the martyred priests who hoped help would arrive from beyond the canyon. Readers of the *Brown and White* should not regard this ruin as a loss, Chávez argues, because both the chancel and the cross have survived unbroken. In effect, the tradition and history of the ruins are more important than their demise; the deserted mission is the historical root of his colleagues' current missionary endeavors. A similar poem, "Pecos Ruins," was published with a drawing by Chávez in 1933.[83] The poetic voice assumes the persona of the ancient Native American people who founded Pecos Pueblo about AD 1300. Despite believing that its children's children would dwell there forever,

> *we fell*
> *By slow degrees to earth, as all men must,*
> *The red man back into the red, red, dust.*[84]

Like surviving kinsmen, the walls "remain to pray and shed / A tear" and function as a tomb and marker along with the wooden cross.[85]

One of a series of poems about the mission at Acoma, "Cibola's Cathedral," in *Cantares* (later published in *St. Anthony Messenger* under the title "The Church of Acoma" with Chávez's own pen-and-ink drawing), compares the church on the high cliff to other famous cathedrals that imitate nature with their grand stature. Unlike European cathedrals that mimic the clouds with their domes and the sunset with their red arches, Acoma can be viewed as "a mesa made by man."[86] Chávez compares the church to one Moses might have built on Mount Sinai, terming it the "Cathedral of the White-Rock-People" in "Church of Acoma II" (*St. Anthony Messenger*, September 1934) and titled simply "Acoma" in *Cantares*. Another poem in *Cantares*, "The Mission Guadalupe," perhaps written while Chávez's family still lived across from the Santuario de Guadalupe, is a canticle of praise. Chávez compares the church to a pueblo kiva in the morning, on the roof of which "the pink-painted dawn-priest" lights the ruby lamp on the rising sun.[87] During Mass, the poetic "I" sees the Beloved by the light of the lamp; at night, the darkened church is like the poet's heart, with the small ruby lamp continually burning inside, although unseen from the outside. We can imagine the young Manuel viewing the Santuario across the street at different moments from early morning until night, attending early morning Mass, and writing this canticle to record his meditation on the beautiful church.

Several of Chávez's poems in this period focus on the friar missionaries whose footsteps he wishes to follow. He pays tribute to the Franciscan role model he learned of as a child in San Diego, Fray Junípero Serra, in "The Song of the Padre," published in November 1933 in *St. Anthony Messenger* with his own illustration depicting the Franciscan gazing at the desolate Southwest landscape. Beginning with an epigraph from one of Serra's letters, Chávez assumes the imagined voice and perspective of Serra, or of any Franciscan missionary who has experienced homesickness. Having overcome his initial sadness and loneliness, Serra now enjoys the sunsets looking over the desert landscape and imagining that the mission bells are ringing "to those red and purple shapes," that is, to the wild grapevines and roses that are like the roses of Castile.[88] Chávez's accompanying drawing emphasizes the bleak reality that contrasts with the friar's memories of his homeland. Also in *Cantares*, the poem "Fray Serra" recounts Serra's journeys up and down California, sowing poppy seeds along the way "that marked his footprints for to-day."[89] If Serra read the desolate New World landscape in terms of his memories of Spanish grapes and roses, he left another flower across California by which he would be remembered in the future.

Chávez published "Cinquains to the Padre" in *St. Anthony Messenger* in July 1929 (his first poem in the national Catholic magazine) with a striking pen-and-ink drawing he did of a Franciscan walking with a tall staff beside a giant cactus, which Chávez captioned "El Padre." There are several differences between the version published in the magazine and that in the bound volume *Cantares*. Chávez made changes in the poem for the book he prepared for his parents three years later. In *Cantares*, the poem is dedicated to "W.B," that is, Witter Bynner; the title of the second cinquain is changed from "Not-sa-lid" to "Stone Rainbow"; and in the 2000 edition, the two last lines of the first stanza are elided into one, destroying the five-line cinquain. The stanzas depict five visions of the Franciscan friar: he is transfigured on the mesa as he is silhouetted by the moon (the image depicted in the drawing), and he is the iris that grows in the desert, the pine tree atop the mountain, the seaman sent by the Master of the fishing boat, and finally the

> *Sunlight on the Pueblo and the Villa:*
> *Like the Mission, brown and old—*
> *Still there.*[90]

Chávez wrote numerous poems on Franciscans in this period, joining them under the section "Cantares Franciscanos" in the book for his parents. He included a touching tribute to Fr. Eligius Kunkel, who died tragically on Memorial Day 1927 trying to save a fifteen-year-old girl. Rector of the cathedral in Santa Fe since 1920, Fr. Kunkel had taken a group of students for an outing at Lake Catron. Ernestina Chávez, who had suffered infantile paralysis but knew how to swim, apparently became agitated during the canoe ride, and the boat tipped over. Sixty-year-old Fr. Kunkel, who was in poor health, immediately tried to save her, but both drowned in the icy water, only a few yards from shore.[91] In his poem "In Memoriam" written in Cincinnati and published in the *Santa Fe New Mexican* on June 14, 1927, Chávez recounts his feelings the day after the tragedy as he stands before the statue of St. Anthony on the seminary grounds. Nature parallels his somber mood—the morning is "leaden and ashen" with dew dropping from the trees like tears. Chávez imagines that the statue begins to speak, describing its sadness for the lost brother in Santa Fe, "a good and valiant helmsman" who has "gone to a harbor away from that sea"; although in his ministry he had saved many souls from the depths, he succumbed to the deep while trying to save a body "that harbored a more precious soul."[92] Immediately the sun comes out, the friar rises, and he imagines that the statue is smiling, saying, "Go sing of our brother the priest" who is another Franciscan martyr.[93] Chávez completes the poem on June 5 and sends it to the Santa Fe newspaper in tribute to his Santa Fe pastor and Franciscan brother.

While many of his early poems focus on religious themes, a good number emphasize Hispano ethnicity and the Southwest. In addition to the poems on the Southwest landscape, the Spanish heritage of the region (including translations of Spanish poets and homage to their work),[94] Hispano traditions, Native American culture and religious practices, and the Franciscan missions, an important group of poems focuses on poetic and artistic creativity and the Santa Fe Writers Group. "Cantares," the first poem in the volume of the same name, was later published under the title "Singing Cowboy" in *New Mexico* magazine (March 1938) and in *Clothed with the Sun* (1939). Already in the 1932 volume he gave to his parents, Chávez links the Southwest theme of the rodeo that the Writers Group employed in its Poetry Roundups (1930–39) to the classical images of the winged horse and the muse's lyre. Changing the original word *weave* to *braid* in the 1939 edition, Chávez compares his poetry to "a lariat of words" that whistles in the air as he tries to catch Pegasus. In contrast to the golden bridle that Athena gives Bellerophon to rope in the horse in Euripides and Pindar, Chávez's lariat cannot catch the horse with wings.[95] Suggesting that Franciscanism is his poetic muse, in the first version, the poet explains that there is "no Muse's lyre here—/ It is the rope that sings"; in the 1939 edition, the wording changes to "It's not whirring wings I hear—/ It is the rope that sings."[96] In both versions, Chávez asserts his Franciscan identity (the white rope tied at the waist in the Franciscan habit) over his artistic self. The poem reveals his hybrid notion of self by tying together Franciscanism, the Southwest, the Writers Group, classical mythology, and the aesthetic.

In "Pegasus," a poem most likely written before "Cantares"/"Singing Cowboy," Chávez invokes the winged horse more positively and links it to images of the Southwest.[97] At dawn the poet sees Pegasus in the sky near the moon that is "a crescent on an Indian's ear."[98] Now its wings are "of cedar wood" because Bellerophon is in fact driving a burro, laden with firewood;[99] the everyday culture of the Southwest inspires his poetry as much as the lofty images of mythology. Here Chávez's hybridity grounds the aesthetic in the local, his native culture of the Southwest.

Chávez pays homage to his friend Witter Bynner in several of his early poems. Both writers continued in the tradition of lyric poetry despite the trend toward more experimental work of contemporaries such as Pound, Eliot, and Stevens. Bynner's "One Day When I Rode Pegasus" describes his chasing the muse as he rides the mythical horse, begging for enlightenment. Chávez owned a copy of the 1926 edition of Bynner's *Grenstone Poems* in which this poem appeared, and Bynner signed the book: "To Fray Angelico Chavez, blest lyrist." Chávez was perhaps in dialogue with Bynner's poem in his own "Pegasus" discussed earlier. In "A Poet's House," Chávez notes that Bynner's pagan house looks outward to the Indian pueblos and within "feeds the mind / With treasures from Cathay." But the good and kind poet inside "pours forth a soothing lay" that is "neither East nor West" but simply "song—the human way."[100]

Chávez begins "The Rondeau" with an epigraph from Bynner, "There were flutes once merry with stops," and playfully suggests that the roundelay he is composing is like trying to play the flute; he is not successful but does not regret having experimented with it.[101] Signing his name "Manuel E. Chavez," he sent Bynner a typed copy of his poem "To Witter Bynner" from the Cincinnati seminary, and Bynner wrote Chávez's address at the bottom of the page.[102] In the poem Chávez captures Bynner's biting humor and the support he gave to the young Franciscan poet. Chávez refers to Bynner's 1919 *The Beloved Stranger* in the epigraph and through direct allusions in the poem. As the Beloved Stranger arriving on Pegasus bringing a star, Bynner encouraged Chávez to write poetry; the teenage seminarian is a young bird eager to sing about his memories; "One gentle note of courage served to bring / A pleasing, though imperfect melody."[103] Bynner's kind words, "I like your poetry," however, are accompanied by the joke, "But, really, I don't like you at all!"[104] This early poem gives an inkling of the humorous and fun-filled get-togethers Chávez enjoyed at Bynner's house when home from the seminary and the inspiration for his poetry he received. Bynner's influence is evident in Chávez's poems such as "A Dance at Cochiti" (later published in 1938 and 1939) and "A Litany of Pueblos" (later published in 1938). They are reminiscent of Bynner's "A Dance for Rain" in Alice Corbin Henderson's *The Turquoise Trail* (1928) and the rest of his series of poems about Pueblo dances in *Indian Earth* (1929).

In his early poems on the process of aesthetic creation, Chávez engages in visual/verbal hybridity to express his dual interests in painting and writing. Besides illustrating many of his poems, he relies on visual intertexts in several (such as "The Angelus" from 1930, which comments on Millet's painting), and frequently he creates visual images with words. In "The Desert Artist" with his own illustration, he reads the New Mexico landscape through the image of God as the prime artist who paints the landscape in turquoise, deep purples, yellows, and orange "[w]ith a sage-brush dipped in rain."[105] In "The Painting Poet," which appears only in *Cantares*, Chávez focuses on his dual approach to his aesthetic re-creation of the Southwest; one end of a feather he uses is "sharpened to a poet's quill," while the other is "a painter's brush."[106] Explaining the harmony between his writing and painting, he notes,

> *I paint the sage upon the shady ground*
> *With pigment-words of silver-jades,*
> *And then I turn my wonder-pen around*
> *And with it add the purple shades.*[107]

Besides the numerous illustrations he created in conjunction with his writing, this poem relates in particular to the connection of his early poetry to his painting *By East García* (see figure 1.7), in which he depicted the newly built Amelia White house when he was home one summer from the seminary; here he visually represents Santa Fe as he did in numerous other poems in this period such as "Santa Fe Skyline," "The Archbishop's Garden," "The Cross of the Friar-Martyrs," "The Mission Guadalupe," and "Tango and Fandango." Similarly, the painting *Burros* and the poems "Pegasus" and "A Burro on the Plaza," along with various other references to burros in his poems, concretize the two aesthetic ends of the feather he "pluck[s] . . . with a cactus drill" in "The Painting Poet."[108]

In his last year at Oldenburg, Indiana, he published a new poem in *America* reflecting on the current Spanish Civil War (1936–39). "Calle de Amargura" (The Street of Bitterness) connects the Spanish phrase for the "Way of the Cross" to all the roads in Spain during the war, "God's fairest daughter by a red bull gored / Lies on the road to Jericho in pain."[109] He urges God to be a Good Samaritan to save Spain who is undergoing a kind of Passion: "Must Spain, like You, come to the sepulcher? / Then grant her, too the joys of Easter Day."[110] The motifs of the red bull, the Passion, and blood interpret the Civil War biblically, at the same time subtly upholding the Church's position that Communism was the evil force in Spain's struggle to form a republic. As an American of Spanish descent, Fray Angélico asserts his ethnicity in "Calle de Amargura" in a much sadder vein than his earlier references to Don Quixote.

Anonymous Playwright and Actor

At the beginning of February 1931, his second term at Duns Scotus College in Detroit, Fr. Reginald summoned Fra Angélico, as he was called at the time, with two other clerics and instructed them to research the life of St. Anthony and write a play to be performed for the upcoming seven hundredth anniversary of the Franciscan saint's death. Chávez threw himself into the project and within a week had written the play and then incorporated a few revisions that the other clerics and Fr. Reginald suggested. By February 14, the text received the imprimatur and was sent to the printer. Fray Angélico's name would not appear as the author, rather that of "The Friars of Duns Scotus College."[111] Meanwhile, auditions were held February 18, and the first informal rehearsals began under Fr. Reginald's direction. The costumes arrived May 29, designed by Chávez and Fr. Reginald with bright colors that were "very attractive and attracting," according to an entry in the journal kept by the friars of Duns Scotus College. On June 8, the press took pictures of the actors, and wide publicity in the Detroit newspapers and radio drew large crowds to the outdoor performances that began June 14. Scenes from the play were filmed on newsreel and also broadcast on radio, and although sometimes attendance was down (some blamed the economic problems of the Depression), it was profitable and reprised once more August 4–6.[112]

Despite the lack of public authorial attribution, Fray Angélico inserts himself in many ways into his dramatic composition. The title, *The Beloved Crusader*, subtly references Witter Bynner's 1919 *The Beloved Stranger*. Cast as the star, St. Anthony of Padua, Chávez also humorously names a Portuguese sailor after himself as "Manoel do Sal" and inserts Hispano humor by naming another sailor who is always drunk "Pato."[113] The author frequently lets his namesake Manoel function as narrator, allowing Fray Angélico to have it both ways by being the star and the principal narrator of the play as well. Early on, for example, as Anthony begins to tell Brother Beppo about his time in Morocco as a missionary, Manoel interrupts, "Fr. Anthony, let me tell the story! You are telling the truth, all right, but you are leaving some things out," thereby establishing himself as the superior narrator.[114]

The play is structured around retelling the great deeds of St. Anthony and the spiritual lessons to be learned from them. According to tradition, when the sinful people of Rimini told him to preach to the fishes, Anthony preached to the river, drawing thousands of fish that would not disperse until he told them to. When a novice ran off with a manuscript of Anthony's sermons, the friar prayed for him all night, and the thief returned with the manuscript in the morning. Thus, Anthony became known as the Finder of Lost Articles. Another story places Anthony in various countries at the same time, miraculously raising a dead man from his tomb to testify that Anthony's father had not killed him. Another witness recounts the story of a hungry mule that Anthony used to prove the real presence of Christ in the Eucharist. After depriving the animal of food for three days, the skeptical owner allowed it to choose between food and St. Anthony holding the host; the animal knelt before the Eucharist.

Chávez portrays Anthony as a humble and revered thirteenth-century spiritual leader whose life serves as an example for twentieth-century Catholics. Fray Angélico wrote sermons that Anthony might have preached into the play as well as spiritual lessons he taught as a key early Franciscan leader. The compelling theatre piece moves along quickly and interjects humor and nuance into the well-known episodes of the saint's life, as Fray Angélico plays multiple creative roles in the work as author, costume and set designer, lead character, key narrator, and solo singer. His early transgressive experiment overlaying Hispano ethnicity on the painting of St. Anthony in the seminary has now blossomed into a more extensive, dynamic portrayal of the spirituality and life of the key Franciscan saint whom he recognized as linked with his own ancestors from Portugal and the Iberian Peninsula.

Chávez's fiction, poetry, drama, and art during his years of seminary training engage in a complex hybridity in which religion, ethnicity, history, the Southwest, words, and images combine. While much of his writing employs religious themes, I have focused in this chapter on his self-presentation as an ethnic subject in many of these hybrid texts. In this period of semi-deterritorialization and partial exile from his home, Chávez reterritorializes himself aesthetically in the sometimes contradictory milieus of the Santa Fe writers' and artists' groups and the strict houses of Franciscan formation in the Midwest. Although he had been warned before entering the seminary that the Franciscans did not take Mexicans, he asserted his Hispano ethnicity continuously during his years there.[115] To the Franciscan community, the national Catholic audiences who read his work, and the Santa Fe literary and artistic community of the period, he presented himself as a native ethnic subject with firsthand expertise on Hispano culture and the traditions of the Southwest. His superiors' validation of his creativity during the seminary years helped to pave the way for the tremendous burst of aesthetic production that he would embark on immediately after his ordination in 1937 in the early years of his full-time priestly duties in Peña Blanca.

CHAPTER THREE

The Young Mission Padre and the Kaleidoscope of Culture

What a good writer writes is all of a piece—the threads of one's imaginative weaving sometimes run black and white, and other times scarlet and purple.

—John Gould Fletcher[1]

AFTER THIRTEEN YEARS OF SEMI-EXILE from the Southwest, Fray Angélico Chávez came home to begin his work as a Franciscan priest in July 1937. Assigned to the village of Peña Blanca near Santa Fe, he enthusiastically immersed himself in his new full-time ministry, at the same time embarking on perhaps the most prolific phase of his artistic creation. The nostalgia of exile evident in his poetry, fiction, and art from 1924 to 1937 now became the joyful celebration of Southwest culture and history in his literary creation, painting, and church restoration. While mediating the dispute between Santo Domingo Pueblo and the Church, traveling to nearby pueblos to offer religious services and instruction, ministering at Our Lady of Guadalupe Church and School in Peña Blanca—teaching catechism, leading the Boy Scouts, and directing the choir—and journeying to give missions across the state, Fray Angélico undertook the extensive repair and restoration of two village churches; designed and executed two series of large murals; participated in the activities of the Santa Fe writers' and artists' colony; wrote dozens of stories, poems, and essays; published his first two books; and began to place his creative writing in broader national venues. The hybrid identity he negotiated in the seminary years flourished again during his first priestly assignment from 1937 to 1943. Refusing to define himself unidimensionally, he carved out a space of energetic work in which he combined dedicated religious ministry, personal spirituality, architectural renovation, painting, creative writing, countercultural socializing, and historical research.

The years of separation from the Southwest and the rigorous training for the priesthood were almost over when Fray Angélico returned to Santa Fe for his historic ordination on May 6, 1937, and his first Mass on May 9.[2] The first native Hispano Franciscan priest in New Mexico in the centuries of Hispanic presence in the area, Chávez painted a remembrance card for the special occasion in shades of brown to pay tribute to Franciscanism. The text he wrote for the back of the card, "Quid Retribuam Domino?" (What do we give back to God?), reveals his sense of personal duty and his role in history. He explains the painting's depiction of the First Mass in Santa Fe after de Vargas' reconquest of the territory in 1693. To the celebrant's right, Capitán Don Bernardino de Chávez holds the statue of La Conquistadora, after the successful battle against the Indians.[3] As the descendant of this soldier, and the first "spiritual descendant" of the Franciscan padres, Chávez superimposes the image of himself as celebrant at his first Mass on that of the padre who first said Mass after the reconquest. The text closes: "On these days, in the Kingdom and Royal City and Cathedral of St. Francis, he is raised to the holy Priesthood by Archbishop Gerken and sings his First Solemn Mass within sight of that famous image of Mary. Pray to her for him. *Impendam et Superimpendar!*"[4] The Spanish royal coat of arms appears in the foreground, while soldiers hold the Spanish flag and the banner of Our Lady of Remedies on the right and the left. In the background are the imposing northern New Mexico mountains. These images and the text emphasize the importance, even on a day celebrating one person's accomplishments, of that individual's place in history and his connection to the community he will serve as a priest.

After taking up his duties as assistant pastor at Peña Blanca in July, Chávez immersed himself in a dynamic six-year period of ministry and creativity. The picture of this period is somewhat distorted by separating the veritable kaleidoscope of his cultural production into its component parts. A chronological account would reveal his constant

FIG. 3.1. *Remembrance of My Ordination*, by Fray Angélico Chávez, 1937, courtesy the Archives of the Franciscan Province of St. John the Baptist of Cincinnati.

interweaving of art, literature, restoration, history, and spirituality, and the fertile interaction among his endeavors. While it is impossible to understand Chávez separately as a poet, fiction writer, muralist, church restorer, historian, and missionary priest in these years, by examining the bright colors of the kaleidoscope in succession, we can view his trajectory in each of these fields.

Southwestern and Religious Poetry

One of Fray Angélico's first requests to the provincial minister after beginning his residence at Peña Blanca was for permission to publish poetry in *New Mexico* magazine.[5] On October 15 Provincial Ripperger replied, "You need both my permission and the Archbishop's. I gladly grant mine. Also show your manuscript to Fr. Robert [Kalt] for approval. Do not write too much for 'New Mexico' but keep *St. Anthony Messenger* well supplied."[6] Just as Chávez managed to develop his creative expression despite the rigorous academic schedule and the strict disciplinary control of the seminary, after ordination he would learn to negotiate his artistic life through the constraints of his vow of obedience. His writing had to undergo "censorship" (approval before publication) from several superiors. Chávez's fear of problems with obtaining an imprimatur from the archbishop later in this period would cause him to postpone publication of an important manuscript of poetry just before he left for World War II.

Negotiating his desire to become part of the dynamic Southwest literary movement flourishing at the time and the strictures of his religious order, he published poetry on Southwest themes in secular venues and religious poetry in Catholic magazines. Although this dichotomy is somewhat misleading because religion and spirituality often appear in his writing on the Southwest, it serves as a general framework to group Chávez's poetry. His dual interests in Southwestern and religious themes were logical outcomes of his birthplace, family heritage, and his extensive religious training. Seven of his poems appeared in *New Mexico* magazine from 1937 to 1939, ten in the *New Mexico Sentinel*, and one each in the *New York Times*, the *New York Herald Tribune*, the *Santa Fean*, and *LULAC News*. He also published poems in this period in numerous Catholic venues such as *America*, *Commonweal*, and *St. Anthony Messenger*.[7]

From Oldenburg, Indiana, in the last months before ordination, Chávez had sent two poems to *New Mexico* magazine, "Pecos Ruins" and "Cross of the Martyrs," published in March and August 1937. The latter, first published in *St. Anthony Messenger* in 1929 and included in *Cantares* under the title "Cross of the Friar-Martyrs," recounts the poet's climb to the hilltop in Santa Fe to see the large cross commemorating the Franciscans killed in the Pueblo Revolt of 1680. At first he thinks he sees no cross there but soon realizes that another "cross" stands on the hilltop:

> *There stood against the night*
> *With outstretched arms over the city's sleep—*
> *A friar bathed in light.*[8]

In a type of visual homonym, the image of the friar who carries on the Franciscan tradition of centuries repeats the image of the cross with his arms outstretched. Chávez employs this visual trope again in his 1938 mural in the refectory at Peña Blanca, *The Stigmata of St. Francis*, in which the founder of the Franciscan Order resembles a cross with arms outstretched.

FIG. 3.2. *The Stigmata of St. Francis*, life of St. Francis mural cycle, by Fray Angélico Chávez, Peña Blanca refectory, 1938, courtesy the Archives of the Franciscan Province of St. John the Baptist of Cincinnati.

In July 1938 *New Mexico* magazine published "Litany of Pueblos," also from *Cantares*, in which each verse invokes the patron saint of a Pueblo mission, followed by the refrain "Pray for us," as in a litany. Mindful of the broad readership of the state tourist magazine, Chávez calls the eleven saints by their English names—St. Jerome for Taos, St. Dominic for Santo Domingo, and St. Phillip for San Felipe. Alluding to an element of each saint's life, the poet praises the majesty of the small Pueblo churches. St. Bonaventure, unlike the lowly St. Francis in the cathedral in Santa Fe, is "Lord Cardinal throned on adobe, / Hold[ing] silent council with the chiefs that passed away."[9] Again, Chávez engages with motifs of the Southwest through religious and historical optics. The following year he would publish two more poems on Southwestern themes in the magazine, "Sandoval Sunset" and "Sangre de Cristo Range."

In June 1938, Haniel Long included two of Fray Angélico's new poems on the New Mexico Writers page in the *New Mexico Sentinel*, "Adventures in Cíbola" and "Southwest Sunset," which approach the history and culture of the Southwest from two distinct moods. The first, in rhymed, light verses, describes three periods of New Mexico history. "Crested Coronado / Mounted with bravado" and his men in search of gold tether their horses near the walls of Cicuye (now Pecos). Centuries later, "Beaver-crowned Kit Carson / Serious as a parson" journeys along the Santa Fe Trail with "wavy canvas dragons" (covered wagons) and arrives at La Fonda at the end of the trail. Now, in the early twentieth century, "Hatless Mister Babbit / Knickered like a rabbit" parks his coughing automobile at an auto camp after a long journey with his family, an allusion to the protagonist of Sinclair Lewis' 1922 novel *Babbit*.[10] Chávez calls the car a "flivver," slang for a second-rate, poorly made product, pointing out humorously that long-distance transportation is still a problem after all these centuries. The adventures of outsiders in Cíbola since 1540 structurally repeat one another.

In the foreword to his 1969 *Selected Poems*, Fray Angélico describes his life-long love of lyric poetry and his search for "that rare poem which, without any seeming effort, fixes a few simple Anglo-Saxon words into a thing of beauty that brings on rapture." After imitating poets who had achieved this such as Poe, Blake, Donne, Stevenson, and more recently Witter Bynner, Chávez continued to strive "after the magic itself." Later, "some of the magic did come, . . . when at long or shorter intervals a strange seizure of mind conceived and bore a verse or more with little conscious striving after phrasing or rhyme, and in the wink of an eye that often proved to have been hours lost from a day or a night."[11] He believed these poems were validated when members of the Santa Fe Writers Group published them in his first volume of poetry in 1939.

Chávez's 1938 "Southwest Sunset" exudes the magic that Chávez describes. The poet compares the sunset sky to an old Spanish bell that is

Tinged dull with verdigris inside the crown,
Its bronze-brimmed bodice swollen round
With music shimmering down
Cascading skirts of flouncing gold
Whose fringes tingle red with sound.

The poet imagines himself as the tongue of the bell, standing below, but unable to "strike that pulsing dome." Feeling both the limitations of self-expression and his tiny geographic presence as part of the natural and historical beauty of the region, he savors the aesthetic experience:

And so my heart, content to beat as one
With waves eternal from this moment's thrall
Cups up a canticle sans paroles
To sip alone when night and silence come.[12]

The wordless canticle he preserves from the scene will nourish him when night and silence have replaced the sunset. The synesthetic motifs of the poem link the sight of the sunset to the "music shimmering down" from the Spanish bell, connecting nature, history, and the aesthetic.

Meanwhile, Fray Angélico was publishing religious poetry in national Catholic and Franciscan venues. "Christ at the Well" is slightly revised from its first version, "Jesus at the Well," in *Cantares*. The poetic voice is Christ's, asking for "desert wine" from the well, and reminding followers that they will not be thirsty again if they drink his water. He asserts his divine identity by extending the metaphor of drinking and water: "[I] plunged the Dipper in the sky / And splashed the night with stars."[13] "Mulier amicta sole" (retitled "Clothed with the Sun" in the 1939 Writers' Editions book) praises the Virgin's rich attire, the "sun-spun" gown and "robe of cloth-of-sun," her crown of stars, and feet "slippered with the crescent."[14] Her clothing testifies to her identity as an ideal woman, the "truest, best, immaculate." The poem "Brother Francis to Brother Dog" (*Extension*, June 1938) humorously praises the importance of the dog since the beginning of humankind, but drolly cautions that our affection for this animal never allow it to replace the child on the mother's lap. Other poems published in *Franciscan Herald* in 1938, "Stigmata" and "Juniper's Lyric" ("Juniper's Carol" in *Eleven Lady-Lyrics*), correlate with the murals depicting the life of St. Francis that Chávez was painting in the Peña Blanca sacristy and refectory at the time.

Fray Angélico was invited to appear as a guest poet at the ninth annual Poets' Roundup August 6, 1938, in Santa Fe. In late April 1938, Haniel Long wrote to Chávez after reading the new story "The Penitente Thief," which Witter Bynner sent him. Long invited Fray Angélico to submit shorter pieces to the "New Mexico Writers" section in the *New Mexico Sentinel*, which he edited. Chávez likely wrote the poems "Adventures in Cíbola" and "Southwest Sunset" in response to this invitation. On July 18, Long wrote to ask Chávez to appear in the Roundup that year, which would take place in Miss Elizabeth White's chapel at three thirty on Saturday, August 6. Each poet would have eight minutes to read.[15] An unsigned newspaper article, probably written by Long, announced the ten poets who had been chosen by ballot to appear in the Roundup that year. The article noted that Father Angélico Chávez would make his first appearance at the event "as a poet in his native southwest," although many may have already discovered him through a poem published on the Writers Page.[16] Literary critic T. M. Pearce provided details of the 1938 Roundup: "Thornton Wilder introduced the participants at the ninth Roundup . . . and offered dramatic praise of the poets' contribution to the contemporary world." Two hundred people attended the event at the chapel of the Amelia White estate on García Street, paying one dollar each as a benefit for Writers' Editions books. Most wore ranch, Indian, or Spanish attire.[17] Fray Angélico wore his Franciscan robes for the event and shortly thereafter began to correspond with Wilder.

The tenth Roundup was held on August 5, 1939, at four thirty, again at Amelia White's home. Bynner and Alice Corbin Henderson

FIG. 3.3. Members of the 1938 Poets' Roundup, Santa Fe, New Mexico. Back row, left to right: Fray Angélico Chávez, Peggy Pond Church, Grace Meredith, Alice Corbin Henderson, Janis de Kay, Dorothy Belle Flanagan, William Dillin. Front row, left to right: Josephine Pinckney, Will Shuster, Haniel Long, Thornton Wilder, Witter Bynner, courtesy Clark Kimball.

read for the tenth time and were joined by Will Shuster, Haniel Long, Margaret Lohlker, Fray Angélico Chávez, and William Pillin. Peggy Pond Church was ill and unable to attend. An unsigned article in the *Santa Fe New Mexican* notes that the event was a benefit for Writers' Editions and that the group would publish Fray Angélico's first volume of poetry in October: "The Poets' Roundup at Santa Fe is known to be unique. It is the only place where the poets are trotted out before the public and given the same chance that musicians or painters frequently have. When the program was planned at Mr. Bynner's Wednesday night, all the old-time participants agreed that it would be a good Roundup, with plenty of variety in the poems and among the poets reading."[18] The historic Roundups ended after the 1939 event.

Between these two important poetry readings, Fray Angélico published more poems in *New Mexico* magazine and the *New Mexico Sentinel* and, with the help of his friends from the Writers Group, prepared the publication of his first book of poetry. A week after the 1938 Roundup, Haniel Long wrote to Fray Angélico praising his performance: "You made it a most memorable occasion, and I hope you will always read with us. I've written to Witter about your poems and am prepared to give the page (or most of the page) to them as soon as the manuscripts and introduction come to me."[19] The October 2, 1938, Writers Page was devoted entirely to Chávez, with an introduction by Bynner. The seven poems engage with Southwestern, religious, and general themes, showing the range of Chávez's poetry. "A Dance in Cochiti" depicts the fiesta dance for rain at San Buenaventura Mission. As the Indians dance before the statue of the saint in the aspen shrine, they employ skins, rattles, and pine branches, "[a]ll heathen symbols of the sky's white wine." Medieval scholastic theologian St. Bonaventure, the "Brown-robed Padre of Red-Hat-with-Tassels," is the lord of Cochiti, the poem suggests. Chávez compares the tassels of the scholar's hat (also pictured on the program of the play *Plurality of Forms* that Chávez wrote in 1932 at Duns Scotus College for St. Bonaventure's feast day) to the tops of the ears of corn that need rain to grow:

> *Make every tassel of the corn to see*
> *The roof-tops of your brown adobe castles: Father, rain!*
> *Sweet rain! Rain let it be—*
> *The sign between a Chieftain and his vassals!*[20]

Chávez connects the medieval saint to the village of Cochiti through visual signifiers, linking the statue's tassels to the corn tops on the enormous plants that will have grown after rain has come in response to the imploring dance. St. Bonaventure is the lord of Cochiti, the Chieftain's men are his vassals, and the houses are adobe castles. In joining these distinct images, Fray Angélico captures some of the syncretism of the Indians' religious practice.

In another vein, "Birds" metaphorically reads the world as a tree whose birds represent various humans. Most are unsatisfied as they fly in various directions, unsuccessful in their quest for food to quench their love or hate. Unlike the falcon in search of beauty as its prey, the poet ("A bird I know") finds beauty without pursuing it. Instead, he places himself within a hermitage:

Within a doorless cage with bars
He chose to live more staid and sage
To reach for the stars.

The caged bird sings, freely satisfying its need for mystery by interacting aesthetically with nature. The Huntsman spares his life, and although someday Time will "thrust / His ruthless hand into the cage," the bird will rise like the phoenix, "like One, / Clothed with the sun."[21] Metaphorically, Chávez explains his voluntary commitment to the constraints of Franciscan priesthood, arguing that his chosen way of life enables him to achieve both aesthetic expression and immortality. This poem became the lead entry in the 1939 *Clothed with the Sun*. In the seminary as well, Chávez had grappled with the issue of his vocation's constraints on his freedom; in "Prisoner," from *Cantares*, published on the October 1938 Writers Page and the next year in *Clothed with the Sun*, he argues that his life is a jail, but even though he could cut through the chain, he would not: "My soul's window / Is barred with love."[22] Perhaps his interaction with the countercultural writers' colony spurred him to explain again the constraints he had voluntarily agreed to live under as a Franciscan.

Although specifically writing about the Virgin Mary's acceptance of her role as the mother of Christ in "Ecce ancilla" (Behold the Handmaiden) Chávez may also be speaking of his own acceptance of his vocation, in a vein similar to "Birds" and "Prisoner." As Mary stands in her Eden-like "dawn-gardened room," she blushes "[a]t what a strange wind told her / During a strange rain's rush."[23] While Chávez's vocation did not involve Mary's intuition about her premarital pregnancy, he may be attempting to explain to a larger public the mode in which he experienced his vocation.

Chávez addresses the transformative role of art in two poems on nature on the Writers Page. He continues the motif of birds in "This Winter Day," noting that the song of a bird on a snowy tree branch transforms the barren tree into "one big blossom-avalanche." On a winter day the poet hears "a little word, / Your own" on the bird's wing; "And everything was bloom and bird / And all the blessed day was spring."[24] The polysemous "Your" refers to God, the bird, and the poet himself; art and poetic expression are transformative. Similarly, in "Sunlight," the poet argues that the daily sunlight of the Southwest is a "[s]urfeit of brightness with a train / Of yearnings for soft summer rain." Only when the sun shines after a cloudy rainfall can the poet really see its light and perceive nature in a new way. As theorist Viktor Shklovsky argued, art estranges the ordinary, interrupting people's automatic responses to the familiar and everyday.[25] Chávez notes at the end of the poem that everyone needs variety: too much sun "can be / A pall"; he implies that like lovers who see each other often, the sun and he must part for a while. "On our return we'll find we can't / part long—the sun is what we want."[26]

Also on the October 1938 Writers Page, Fray Angélico published the anguished poem, "Whose Broken Heart Is Brave." The poetic voice poignantly describes the pain of a broken heart that must be endured silently because grief "like lightening strikes no two alike." The brave broken heart, however, can begin to heal in experiencing the beauty of nature.

> *Bright canyons are earth's wounds, the sunset's flash*
> *Must gore the clouds, the sky, to paint the west—*
> *And Easter left unclosed one Wounded Breast.*[27]

Nature not only offers an assuaging beauty, but teaches that wounds are part of life and key to its beauty. Such scenes of nature will "tear the heart from anguish loose," and those undergoing emotional pain must try to heal themselves this way. As I will discuss later, it is possible that the anguish of this poem connects to another describing the wake of the young Rebecca Ortiz who died in 1939 in Peña Blanca; Chávez placed "To Rebecca Dead" immediately after "Whose Broken Heart Is Brave" in *Eleven Lady-Lyrics* (1945).

The Writers Page featured "A Caballero Recalls Lamy" with an apparent printing error under the title listing the dates as 1888–1938. In *Eleven Lady-Lyrics*, the subtitle is corrected to read: "Archbishop of Santa Fe, 1850–1885."[28] The poetic persona is an old-time Hispano in Santa Fe who remembers being "no higher than a hitching rail" when Lamy came. The old timer tells of the archbishop's leadership and compassion and emphasizes that "His hands were rough with building [the cathedral], / Although he did not cut or lay a single stone"; the archbishop's presence imbues the cathedral, since he was deeply involved in its design and early construction. A generation later, the caballero's son "was taller than a hitching bar" when Lamy was brought from his country house to the cathedral after his death, with "all the great warmth gone" and "every adobe home a deathbed attendant."²⁹ Chávez emphasizes the devotion of ordinary Hispanos of Santa Fe to the archbishop, a theme he also developed in the 1932 novel *Guitars and Adobes*.

After meeting Thornton Wilder in the summer of 1938, Chávez corresponded with him and published a poem in his honor in the *New York Herald Tribune*, February 26, 1939. Writing from New Haven on September 26, 1938, a month after he visited Santo Domingo Pueblo and participated in the Santa Fe Poets' Roundup, Wilder apologized for not having sent a letter to accompany the book he sent Chávez. The playwright had been suddenly summoned to replace the actor playing the stage manager in his play and had to memorize the lines and perform on stage. He disliked this "all-too-public labor" and was glad it would be over the following Wednesday. He commented about his trip home and how much he loved the desert region, especially the great experience of the Santo Domingo dance: "prayer, soft deep inner concentration without hysteria, without that egotistic 'give me, give me' insistence; a view of the Childhood of the Race in the best sense. Before long in some way, I am going to try and put some of that quality into a work and submit it to you." Wilder hoped soon to find Chávez's poems in the magazine files at Yale University library and invited him to send a new poem in his next letter. Further complimenting Chávez, he closed: "In my cluttered-up over-gregarious life it is a pleasure of think of you—a Franciscan brother, writing poetry, and working in that glorious country with the Indians. . . . [Y]ou must have many hours of gratitude at the deep rewarding elements of beauty and usefulness in the work." Wilder expresses part of the attraction of many East Coast writers to the different life of the Southwest.

Wilder wrote again January 9, 1939, praising the new poetry Fray Angélico sent. "The poems are truly beautiful and expressive and skillfully fashioned. . . . The sonnet 'for me' is a joy and a pride. The verses on 'grey' and 'gray' move gently to an ending of subdued power, and the Psalm is a radiant thing." Besides praising these poems ("Peña Blanca," "Grey," and "Psalm of the Shepherd"), Wilder compliments the murals Fray Angélico is painting at Peña Blanca, having received the 1938 Christmas card Chávez sent showing him painting *The*

Stigmata of St. Francis in the sacristy. Wilder writes that he dreams of "returning to the Southwest and calling on you."³⁰

Dedicated to Wilder, "Peña Blanca" appeared in *Spirit* in January 1939, the *New York Herald Tribune* in February, and later in *Clothed with the Sun*. In intertextual dialogue with Wilder's play *Our Town*, which had just run in Boston and on Broadway, Chávez eloquently captures Peña Blanca's connection to the earth. Our town is like the one you depict, he tells Wilder, "But here all's naked earth." People are born seeing "[t]he walls and roofs of clay" and are "re-wombed in earth" when they die, "[t]o wait for what we dreamed, a greener birth."³¹ In effect, Chávez argues, our Spanish American town is both like and unlike typical American towns because of our strong connection to the earth. The perspective of outsiders such as Wilder and the Writers Group helped to shape Fray Angélico's insider presentation of his small New Mexico town.

Among several poems from this period that deal with death, "Grey" sorts out the nuances of two spellings of the color. The *e* spelling evokes birds and new-painted sills—what we dream. In contrast, the *a* spelling conjures images of battleships, "an age-toned beam," and, most poignantly, "the casket-cloth / That sad, sad day." In contrast, the face the poet saw in the casket and cannot forget "stays with me / Quiet and grey,"³² perhaps a reference to the 1939 death of Rebecca Ortiz. The intangible and enduring memory merits the choice of the *e* spelling. The poem connects to others about loss and death that Chávez wrote at the time such as "Whose Broken Heart Is Brave," "To Rebecca Dead," "Who Pass by the Way," and "Peña Blanca."

In December 1938 poet John Gould Fletcher and his wife Charlie May attended a Christmas play and Indian dances with Fray Angélico.³³ They visited him again in March 1939 and corresponded with him for many years from Arkansas. A friend of Alice Corbin Henderson and Haniel Long, Fletcher had earlier published a volume of his poetry with Writers' Editions and won the Pulitzer Prize for Poetry in 1938. Together, Fletcher, Long, Corbin, and Bynner selected the poems that would be included in Chávez's 1939 Writers' Editions book. Fray Angélico had collected some of his published poems for a prospective book in early 1939 and in March asked the provincial for permission to look for a publisher.³⁴ In July 1939 Fray Angélico wrote with excitement to the new provincial, "I did not find a publisher, but a publisher found me." Several leading American writers living in the

Southwest "have seen my poems here and there and like them; so they spontaneously inducted me as a member of the Writers' Editions in order that they might publish my poems." The organization would retain 4 percent of the profit after costs, and the other 96 percent would go to the writer. They requested the manuscript by August 1 in order to publish it in late fall for the Christmas trade.[35]

Clothed with the Sun appeared in November "bound in a warm brown fabric of natural finish." Within a year, all but forty copies had been sold. Chávez was disappointed that the Catholic press seemed to ignore the book. He wrote, "When an official correspondent for the Catholic News Services sent in a story about a group of pink pagans publishing a book for a poor Franciscan missionary, headquarters [*St. Anthony Messenger*] wrote back that they did not advertise gratis. It is bigger news that a parochial pupil in Oshkosh wins a spelling contest." Fray Angélico wished that each of the Franciscan houses in the province had bought a copy of his book instead of *Gone with the Wind*. "It's a queer state of affairs when a priest author has to be grateful for indispensable help to radical writers and the secular press, and non-Catholic purchasers."[36] In these early years, already he felt unappreciated by fellow Franciscans.

St. Anthony Messenger did publish a half-page ad for the book with adulatory quotations from Bynner, Fletcher, and Henderson. Bynner wrote, "These poems make old truths and old symbols vivid for me with a new voice: the perennial freshness of literature." John Gould Fletcher commented, "It is not only that he has talent of a delicate, individual sort, but that his talent points in the right direction—that of giving and sharing life." Alice Corbin Henderson was quoted extensively: "Fray Angélico Chávez has a natural gift of phrase and image akin to that of the seventeenth-century metaphysical poets. Perhaps this is not strange—remembering how much seventeenth-century mysticism exists in New Mexico, and the fact that he wears the brown robes of St. Francis—but the discovery of a new poet for whom life is 'clothed with the sun' awakens that sense of strangeness which, as Yeats said, always accompanies beauty."[37] *Clothed with the Sun* was reviewed in local newspapers and several Catholic magazines including *Commonweal* and *America*; John Gould Fletcher published a review in *Poetry* but complained in a letter to Fray Angélico that the editor shortened the piece.[38]

As in his self-compiled volume *Cantares*, Fray Angélico dedicated this book to his parents, "Don Fabian and Doña Nicolasa."[39] He had previously published thirty-three of the thirty-six poems in this volume, a few under different titles. The new poems include "Pius XI," expressing his sorrow at the death of the pontiff in February 1939; "Psalm of the Shepherd," which self-reflexively struggles to find words for a pastoral poem about Christ's journey through the cosmos to earth; and "Morning," a short piece written to connect the sections of the book, "Morning," "Noon," and "Night." Appearing at the end of the first section, "Morning" compares the first hours of the day to a book always carried close to the heart: "Noon but ushers its last part, / Night is the dark, rich cover."[40] The poems are, as the title implies, "clothed with the sun" and mark one day's rotation around it—a short but rich period in the young new priest's life. About three-fourths of the poems in the volume were recently written, published between late 1937 and 1939, representing his intense period of creativity after ordination and his association with the Writers Group.

Chávez commented to his superiors about the irony that the allegedly radical writers in Santa Fe had chosen many religious poems of his to include in the volume. "Strange to say, these notoriously non-religious judges chose those poems that were most religious."[41] He writes about angels, the Blessed Virgin, biblical narratives such as the death of the Holy Innocents and the story of the Good Thief, female saints, the Eucharist, the Stations of the Cross, and alms-giving. In "Carmen Deo nostro," the poet argues that his life as a desert missionary is a song to God that can only be achieved with the two working together. First published in the *Franciscan* in 1938, the poem speaks to his fellow Franciscans who might experience low moments in their work.

"Sonnet of the Stations" (published as "Sonnet of the Via Crucis" in 1933), "The Angelus," and a new poem "Cherubs" engage in ekphrasis, the attempt to verbally represent visual representation. Chávez tries to express in words the visual impressions produced by paintings. He arranges the short, prayerlike lines in an eight- and a six-line stanza to form a sonnet and represent the fourteen Stations of the Cross. The lines verbally re-create the paintings of the stations in churches. Station IV, for example, reads "While Mary's eyes meet His, and two hearts cry."[42] In the lines of the second stanza, the poet prays to Christ for help in undergoing life's trials. In *Clothed with the Sun*, the poem "The Angelus" appears without the subtitle "Millet" in the 1930 version and *Cantares*; readers of the Writers'

Editions volume are presumed to know the intertextual painting. Chávez verbally re-creates the visual and auditory images explicit and implicit in Millet's painting: the figures bowing in prayer, the motion of the progressively fading light, and the sounds of the bells in the ensuing silence. Carrying Millet's image forward to nightfall, the poet meditates:

> *Neither ground*
> *Nor man nor wife nor sky are found,*
> *But God and I*[43]

The poem "Cherubs" describes the ways in which German and Italian artists depicted angels, noting,

> *They had such faith, it would have caused*
> *Them no surprise, had God allowed,*
> *To find small angels on their floor*
> *Or see their children on a cloud.*[44]

The poet urges modern artists to continue this anthropomorphism by depicting cherubs as mothers now dress their babies, since no one has ever seen angels. Fray Angélico, the poet/artist, deconstructs the aesthetic and spiritual dimensions of canonical religious art in this down-to-earth poem.

Chávez combined five previously published poems under the heading "Stigmata of St. Francis" in the middle section of the book. He retitled the 1932 poem "Stigmata of St. Francis" as "My Cross I Took," and the 1938 "Stigmata" was given the new title "I Vowed." "My Cross I Took" and "All for Love" were written in the seminary, while the other three in the cluster were written in late 1937 and 1938, as he was painting the St. Francis mural cycle in the sacristy at Peña Blanca. The key visual intertext of the poem series is Fray Angélico's famous painting *The Stigmata of St. Francis* (see figure 3.2). As St. Francis receives the stigmata with his arms outstretched like the crucifix, he is raised off the ground. The seraph, or six-winged angel that Francis recounted in his vision, glows above as an idealized mirror image of the saint. Chávez's poem series includes lines to depict this such as "After the Seraph fathomed him with fire" and

> *Dear Christ! . . .*
> *Complete the picture You began*
> *And have me crucified!*[45]

The first poem, "Marionette," written as Chávez painted the mural cycle, imagines that St. Francis is a marionette whose strings are pulled from above:

> *When God peered from the mountain's crest*
> *And lifted you with golden wires*
> *That pierced your hands and feet and breast.*[46]

Chávez worked across media (painting and poetry) to represent this key event in the life of the founder of his religious order.

Clothed with the Sun, as Chávez's first published book, offers representative pieces from his large poetic oeuvre that reveal his strong religious commitment, his identity as an ethnic poet writing on Southwestern themes, and the variety of poetic styles in which he worked. Poems such as "Peña Blanca," "Who Pass by the Way," "Adventures in Cíbola," "A Dance in Cochiti," "Singing Cowboy," and "Southwestern Night" locate his writing in the soil of New Mexico, as do implicitly those focusing on Franciscanism. In the next three years before his enlistment in World War II, he continued to publish poetry and wrote the poems that would later be published as *The Single Rose*. His poetry during these early years of ministry is closely connected to his other aesthetic efforts across several genres and media and must be seen as part of a whole.

Three Transitional Stories and New Mexico Triptych: Aesthetic Hybridity, Popular Religion, and the Southwest

After his ordination, a few more of Fray Angélico's stories appeared in *St. Anthony Messenger*. Much in the same vein as his early fiction, "Carrie's Notion," "Beads" (under the pseudonym Arthur Chapman), "Mateo Makes Money," and "Honest Art" carry over from pre- to post-ordination some of the themes of Chávez's stories in *St. Anthony Messenger* and the *Sodalist*. Like "It's an Ill Wind," in "Carrie's Notion," a young man wants to marry his girlfriend but as an aspiring writer doesn't have income to support her.[47] With advice from the

Catholic priest and an idea about a pseudonym from Carrie, he wins two thousand dollars in a short story contest and receives a writing contract. Fragments of Chávez's life are interspersed in the story so that a subtle self-reflexivity overlays the text. His presence overcodes that of the priest giving advice, the aspiring writer whose stories are rejected, the designer of the pseudonym, and the winner of the writing contest. As in his other stories in the *Sodalist*, women are strong, play key roles, and often devise ingenious solutions to problems. Carrie suggests that her boyfriend replace his cumbersome German name, Elmer Vogelmeister, with a pen name. Since the German means "Master of the Birds," she suggests he use the more authorial-sounding "E. Byrd Masters," reminiscent of Chávez's own "F. Chalmers Ayers." Chávez also inserts himself subtly into the story as the protagonist who writes about his own world using slightly altered names and events. Playfully, he attaches elements of his own identity to the process and plot of "Carrie's Notion."

"Beads" might be seen as an extension of Chávez's earlier story "The Blasphemer," in which he criticizes the anti-Church activities of the Mexican Revolution.[48] Once again his pseudonym (Arthur Chapman) retains his own initials, "A" and "Ch" (the fourth letter of the Spanish alphabet), as did the nom de plume "F. Chalmers Ayers." Arthur Chapman was the name of a little-known Southwestern writer of cowboy poetry who died in 1935. The authorial persona, "Chappy," meets a journalist friend from Cincinnati, Joe Sterkes, who tells him two related stories that teach the adage "Don't judge a book by its cover." When assigned to Mexico to write an undercover story on the Calles government, Sterkes ends up on a military work crew, where one elderly worker passes out. While nursing him back to health, Sterkes learns that he is a Franciscan priest forced to leave his convent in Jalisco during the war hostilities. Sterkes' "beads" on which he faithfully prays the daily rosary are a sign that assures the priest he is in safe hands. The educated priest quotes Shakespeare, Cervantes, and Lope de Vega, proving that his bedraggled looks belie his true talent and intelligence. Chávez inserts himself into the story by having it set during a train trip through Denver, like one of his own journeys home from the seminary. After hearing Sterkes' story, Chappy humbly follows his friend into church to pray the rosary.

Chávez's next two transition stories, published in November 1937 and February 1938 after he began his ministry at Peña Blanca, are firmly rooted in his Southwest surroundings. In "Mateo Makes Money," as sixty-year-old Mateo walks thirty miles from Santo Domingo Pueblo to Santa Fe to sell his wares, he remembers the story of the Virgin of Guadalupe whose image hangs on his wall. Suddenly he feels he is rising to the sky, seeing stars, smelling a sweet fragrance, and hearing a mild voice, which he imagines to be the Virgin's. In fact, wealthy tourists on the way to Santa Fe by car have hit him. Chávez satirizes their ignorance: "Guadaloop must be the chief's name," one man says when Mateo utters the Virgin's name. Another says, "How about us chipping in for the benefit of Pocahontas' grandpa?"[49] After they leave him a tidy sum, he believes Guadalupe has performed another miracle. He decides not to tell the archbishop, who, as Juan Diego experienced, won't believe him, or the people at the pueblo who will think he stole the money. Having superimposed the modified Guadalupe narrative on his life, he decides it will remain a secret between him and the Virgin. Although as the tourists throw money at him and Mateo feels like one of the clay rain gods he sells, Chávez's story is not a stereotypic, tourist's view of the Pueblo Indians. Since 1935 Santo Domingo Pueblo had been under interdict by Archbishop Gerken, which forbade all Catholic religious functions except last rites. On Saturdays, Chávez offered religious instruction at the pueblo and talked with the people. He was instrumental in negotiating the lifting of the interdict in July 1940. In this context, the 1937 story "Mateo Makes Money" reveals Chávez's view that the people of Santo Domingo retained a deep Catholic faith despite the interdict.

"Honest Art" is Fray Angélico's segue to the stories in his first book of fiction, *New Mexico Triptych* (1940). It focuses on an accomplished *santero* (carver of wooden saints) in Santa Fe.[50] As he is at work carving a *bulto* of San José, Arturo Vásquez tells the narrator about working earlier under the Federal Art Project, wondering how he could raise money to attend art school. Invited to a gathering of the writers' and artists' colony, Vásquez hears a French artist complaining that there is too much dishonesty in modern art. When the rich theatre mogul he is speaking to drops his wallet, Vásquez picks it up, finds hundreds of dollars inside, and decides to keep it to pay for art school. Later in the evening, the theatre producer praises his carvings and hints that he will help him through school because he is an honest artist. Vásquez's misinterpretation of this comment saves him; mistaken semiosis gets him back on the right path. His guilt overwhelming him, Vásquez returns the wallet and learns that his future sponsor was referring to art that did not cheat by tracing over a photograph or putting plaster on an imperfection in a sculpture. By ultimately practicing personal and artistic honesty, "Art" Vásquez receives the sponsorship and eventually becomes a successful santero.

The culture of Fray Angélico's new surroundings after ordination imbued these stories, just as it did his poetry. The plight of the Santo Domingo Indians to whom he ministered, and the relations between the arts colony and native artists such as the fictional Vásquez, became central themes in these transitional stories. Through them he paved the way to his masterpiece, *New Mexico Triptych*. In April 1938, Chávez's classic story "The Penitente Thief" was published in *St. Anthony Messenger* with a full-page illustration by another artist of a Penitente procession and the sensationalist tagline: "By all odds, the most gripping and unusual story that has ever appeared on these pages ... as haunting as New Mexican hills."[51] In fact, Chávez's story is part of the more accurate writing on the Penitentes appearing at the time, one important example of which is Alice Corbin Henderson's 1937 *Brothers of Light*. While Chávez fictionally recounts extraordinary, supernatural events, he offers a nonromantic, human view of the brotherhood, showing that there can be bad Penitentes among the many good men in the groups. Chávez's story appeared amid an explosive controversy over *St. Anthony Messenger*'s publication of an inflammatory article on the Penitentes in March 1938. A number of readers, including Fray Angélico and two other priests from New Mexico, wrote to refute Phil Glanzer's "Religious Rites of Horror," and the magazine issued a formal apology for publishing it.[52]

Witter Bynner and Haniel Long highly praised "The Penitente Thief" and invited Fray Angélico to publish on the Writers Page and participate in the Poets' Roundups. Long wrote, "The feeling of the all embracing love of God, even in the face of our miseries and vices is extremely beautiful in your story." When Fray Angélico inquired about the possibility of Writers' Editions publishing a volume of his stories like "The Penitente Thief," Long told him that the publishing house was "not in shape to undertake anything at the moment." At the end of June 1938, Chávez sent Long his story "Mana Seda," which had just appeared in *Missionary Catechist*, but after the Writers Page featured Fray Angélico's work in October, Long returned the story noting that he needed to rotate authors.[53]

John Gould Fletcher also highly praised *New Mexico Triptych* shortly after it appeared in May 1940, with the dedication, "To 'Coronado's Children' My People," through which Chávez points to his Hispano legacy, with the approaching Coronado Cuarto Centennial celebration in mind. Fletcher wrote,

> Your three stories seem to me the only ones I have ever read . . . by someone who has lived *inside* the New Mexican environment, which truly give me the environment correctly. You have a rich and a valuable gift—of understanding these, your own people *from within*. And of seeing how to them, this world—the world without—is close to another world, the world of their religion. . . .
>
> The best of the three is the "Penitente Thief." That is a story only you could do—only a Spanish Franciscan could do. And you have done it beautifully.
>
> I admire very greatly how to you the natural always leads to the supernatural. In this world which I inhabit— unprotected by mountains, mesa, traditions, or decencies— the supernatural seems to have fled as effectively as your angel, in the first story. And I cannot find the church that holds it anymore.
>
> . . . Your book is one which has given me, among so much that is distasteful, an hour of great joy. Like a cup of clear water when one is famishing. Few authors could have done these three stories.[54]

Members of the Santa Fe Writers Group, Fletcher, and other critics appreciated the spirituality and accurate portrayal of Hispano culture in Fray Angélico's stories. Chávez enhanced the poetics and themes of the stories and joined them as a whole through a metaphor related to his own art.

As he pondered how he might publish the stories, an element from his current artistic work gave him an idea. After completing the murals narrating the life of St. Francis in the sacristy and refectory at Peña Blanca in 1938, in May, October, and November 1939, he painted the famous Stations of the Cross on the walls of the church.[55] Both the refectory painting *Brother Juniper, Francis and Masseo, Francis* and twelve of the Stations of the Cross were painted as triptychs, similar

FIG. 3.4. *Brother Juniper, Francis and Masseo, Francis*, life of St. Francis mural cycle, by Fray Angélico Chávez, Peña Blanca refectory, 1938, courtesy the Archives of the Franciscan Province of St. John the Baptist of Cincinnati.

FIG. 3.5. Fray Angélico Chávez, frontispiece, *New Mexico Triptych*, 11.5 × 7.25, pen and ink, ca. 1940, Fray Angélico Chávez History Library and Photographic Archives, Nora Chávez Collection, courtesy Palace of the Governors Photo Archives (NMHM/DCA).

to the Chapman and Vierra mural cycle in St. Francis Auditorium in the Museum of Fine Arts in Santa Fe. Chávez's artistic and literary endeavors cross-fertilized one another. While he finished the large mural triptychs at Peña Blanca in 1939, he envisioned a way to connect his stories to form a whole. The model of the triptych became the glue to unite the stories, and he designed artwork for the book that would harmoniously support this visual theme.

Chávez's first task was to write a third story. In January 1940, just after Christmas, he wrote to the provincial that one was "breaking out in [his] mind," which would focus on Hispano traditions of the Christmas season to complement the other two stories on Lenten and May devotions. As in "Honest Art" and "The Santo Talks Back," Chávez focuses on the Hispano tradition of carving wooden saints in "The Angel's New Wings," which although written last, was placed first in *New Mexico Triptych* to follow the chronology of the Catholic liturgical calendar. Addressing the breakdown of popular religious traditions in a small New Mexico village much like Peña Blanca, the story vividly portrays the spirituality and talent of the old-time santeros.

The protagonist, santero Nabor Roybal, shares Chávez's mother's surname, with his given name referencing a martyr persecuted under Diocletian in 303 as well as the homophone *neighbor* when pronounced in English; Nabor's wood-carving proficiency is like the carpentry skill that Chávez's father passed down to his son and that Fray Angélico employed in his woodcarvings and church renovations. Chávez also inserts himself as the young village priest with a "lean, dark face," Padre Arsenio, who asks Nabor to repair the broken wings of the angel for the *nacimiento*, or Christmas crèche. Chávez critiques some of the new ways that have come to the village, focusing on the profound, enduring spirituality of the santero's relationship to his art, despite the breakdown of the old traditions and values. Nabor had carved the figures of the manger scene in his youth and each year proudly arranged them for Christmas in the village church. This year, the weakness of old age keeps him home, and one of the young people who sets up the scene breaks the angel's wings. As he carves bigger, lighter wings for the statue, the angel flies out of his hands and disappears.

Nabor searches throughout town for the angel, but the locals tease him by pointing to a bird that could be the carved angel that flew away. Chávez implicitly criticizes the tavern revelers, a prowler, the storekeeper's wife cavorting in a barn with another man—townspeople who also attend midnight Mass. Nabor, in contrast, finally sees the lost angel hovering off the ground, enveloped in an "unearthly glow."[56] As he experiences this vision reminiscent of St. Francis' seraphic apparition, Nabor hears the biblical account of the angel's message to the shepherds about Christ's birth: "*And suddenly there was with the angel a multitude of the heavenly army*, beings of the same size as the angel but not of wood, *praising God*."[57] Chávez italicizes the biblical text, leaving the details of the contemporary narrative in regular typeface. Nabor follows the angel who flies to the church for midnight Mass.

Fray Angélico implicitly connects Nabor to St. Francis, who made the first Christmas crèche, through the santero's "seraphic vision" and his careful construction of the wooden figures for the nacimiento. Nabor is so deeply connected to his sacred art that the figures come alive for him during midnight Mass, despite the reality that the figures are not there; people wishing to sell them for profit have stolen them. Where the townspeople in the church see a sparrow in the vigas, Nabor sees the wooden angel that flies down to enter the manger scene. In counterpoint to the Latin Mass rituals the priest performs, the biblical account of the birth of Christ is reenacted as the imagined wooden figures come alive for Nabor. As Padre Arsenio sings the line of the "Credo," "*Et incarnatus est de Spiritu Sancto ex Maria Virgine . . .* Mary woke and raised herself in her kneeling posture on the straw."[58] Joseph stirs and snores. Dramatically, Chávez, the Hispano Catholic priest, suggests that Hispano popular religious traditions are sometimes more spiritually efficacious than the official Church liturgy. In this case, they are a vernacular version of the Latin Mass. The carved figures of the manger, even when not physically present, offer a more dynamic, almost cinematic reenactment of the birth of Christ for Hispanos like Nabor. The old santero creatively imagines at the end that the figures leave because the angel tells them to flee to Egypt to avoid Herod. Like other Santa Fe writers and artists such as Alice Corbin and William Penhallow Henderson, Chávez tries to revive and support Hispano popular religious traditions. The only remaining figure at the end of the story is Nabor's old angel with its new wings, symbolizing the preservation and renewal of santero art in New Mexico.

The Bible also comes alive through contemporary reenactment in the second story, "The Penitente Thief." Divided into three parts, as are the other tales in the book, epigraphs from the Passion narrative begin each section. The story takes place over three successive years of Holy Week rituals of a small group of Penitentes whose numbers are dwindling because the archbishop has sent letters against their practices. (The story predates the 1947 reconciliation between the Church and the Penitentes.) If members of the brotherhood traditionally perform penance for their sins, Chávez selects two entrenched sinners as protagonists—men who, although they are on the fringes of the group's rituals, will have their own extraordinary experiences of the Passion reenactment each year in Holy Week.[59] They become contemporary versions of the two thieves crucified with Christ. Career thief Lucero, who had stolen Governor Lew Wallace's watch in 1880, is the more enlightened figure in the end and asks Christ for forgiveness like the Good Thief. Maldonado, the shyster lawyer who murders, remains trapped in evil, actualizing the implications of his name. Like Nabor's experience in the first story, these Penitentes are part of an especially profound spiritual reenactment, precisely as the popular Hispano religious tradition is in danger of dying out. Although the numbers of santeros and Penitentes were decreasing when Chávez wrote *New Mexico Triptych*, the characters in both stories experience strong revivals of the endangered traditions.

Two temporal planes intersect as the narrative proceeds—the progression of the biblical story of the crucifixion told in three epigraphs and the larger diachronic passing of three years of Penitente Holy Week devotions. Each year as Lucero and Maldonado are apart from the others in the *morada*, they experience increasingly extraordinary events. The first year, arriving late on Holy Thursday somewhat drunk, they join a procession with two unknown men and a Christ figure dressed in white carrying the cross. When he falls, they whip him with scourges, following the custom; the trickles of blood on the snow remind Lucero of one of his sins—the Navajo blanket he stole from Doña Luisa. At the *descanso*, Lucero and Maldonado remove the cross from the Christ figure's shoulder and fall asleep on the rocks. The other Penitente brothers do not believe their story after finding them alone, nearly frozen in the snow. Lucero's and Maldonado's experience in Holy Week that year brings to life the epigraph for the first section of the story, "There were two evildoers led with him."[60]

The following year, the two Penitentes find the three figures in the exact place they left them; the Passion narrative continues, with Lucero and Maldonado ritually scourging the Christ figure, and the epigraph noting "one on the right . . . the other on the left."[61] This year, the glow of the lantern reminds Lucero of his current crime—having stolen the gold chalice from the village church. They tie the Christ figure to the cross, raise it, and secure it with stones. Again, their fellow Penitentes do not believe their account of the extraordinary events and only the cross is standing. The group speculates that Lucero and Maldonado are bewitched because there are no marks from the cross being dragged in the snow. The events disrupt the usual rituals of the brotherhood, as the group forgoes the traditional reenactment of the crucifixion on Good Friday.

The third year, the two temporal planes of the narrative continue, culminating with the crucifixion and the Good Thief's words, "Do Lord remember me," as the epigraph. Both Lucero and Maldonado are gravely ill and unable to go to the morada on Palm Sunday. Doña Luisa, the kind woman whom Lucero has wronged, nurses him and forgives him when he confesses to having stolen her blanket. The lawyer Maldonado has now committed his most grave crime, murdering the widow whose pension he was stealing. Doña Luisa tries to get both thieves to confess their sins to the padre before their imminent deaths. After hearing three knocks at the door, Lucero sees the three figures from the previous year enter his room with glowing, beautiful faces. Again he accompanies them on the walk to the *calvario* and despite the Christ figure's admonition, steals a horse to try to make Christ's journey more comfortable. A posse of villagers catches him and strings him to a tree; again he has a vision of the Christ figure on the church cross that no one else sees. He asks for forgiveness for both himself and Maldonado, but Christ does not pardon the lawyer because he has not repented. The son of the murdered widow shoots Maldonado, and Lucero dies from hanging, exactly as the sun marks three o'clock. Chávez affirms the reality principle at the end by describing the two dead figures before the bare church cross. Like the missing santos that Nabor imagined in the first story, the Good Thief Lucero has imagined the vision of Christ he experienced three years in succession. Chávez suggests that although the numbers of Penitentes are diminishing, the annual reenactment ritual has a profound spiritual effect and healing power on even the most sinful members of the group. The powerful biblical narrative remains alive in the alternative spiritual rituals of Hispano Penitentes.

Chávez changed the first sentence of his 1938 magazine story to accommodate the illuminated letter he created for the book—a crucifixion scene superimposed on the letter *T*. It repeats the image of the crucifixion reenactment in Chávez's drawing on the facing page in which Lucero leads the stolen horse in front of the figure of the crucified Christ, with the morada and the New Mexico mountains in the background. The two illustrations relate to each other: with the image of the crucified Christ prominent in the background and outside the frame on the facing page in the illuminated letter, the well-intentioned "good thief" Lucero leads the horse he has stolen for Christ in front of and toward the crucified Christ he has imagined. The third drawing at the end of the story gives closure and a sense of continuance by portraying the tree on which Lucero is hung and the empty cross in front of the village church.

The third story was originally published as "Mana Seda" in June 1938 and like the other two, centers on longstanding traditions of Hispano popular religiosity. Where "Honest Art" focused on the revival of santero art in the period of the writers' and artists' colony, "Hunchback Madonna" depicts an earlier santero who made bultos and altar screen images for northern New Mexico churches in Ranchos de Taos, Santa Cruz, and San Juan. Both stories emphasize the important role of honesty in art and the artist's ability to right wrongs. If "Honest Art" emerged from Fray Angélico's association with Santa Fe artists, "Hunchback Madonna" bears the marks of his first year of ministry at Our Lady of Guadalupe Church in Peña Blanca. The annual May processions to the Virgin are overlain with the northern transplantation from central Mexico of the Virgin of Guadalupe story honored in the Peña Blanca church.

The villagers tell pilgrims the story of Mana Seda (Sister Silk), an elderly hunchbacked woman who was excluded in childhood from participating in the May processions and faithfully gathered flowers each year for other girls to carry to the altar. Now many flowers bloom on her grave. Mana Seda's physical absence from the public May processions during her life parallels the absence of an image of the Virgin of Guadalupe above the altar that the townspeople have been waiting years for. Fray Angélico develops a protofeminist reconfiguration of predominant ideals of female beauty that have even seeped down to popular religious practices. Internalizing the judgmental public view that her identity was coterminous with her deformity, Mana Seda participated in the May church processions for seventy-four years only as a helper and was excluded from the public religious display of ideal femininity of the girls chosen for the ceremony.[62]

While gathering flowers one year far from the village, she is caught in a storm, sees a vision of the Virgin to whom she prays for help, and encounters a santero/Christ figure named Esquipula who gives her shelter. As the flowers she picked fall from her shawl, Esquipula thinks of the Guadalupe narrative in which roses fell from Juan Diego's *tilma* as a sign to the bishop. He offers to paint the image of the Virgin that the village needs directly on her shawl, implying that the elderly woman is as worthy of this sacred image as was Juan Diego. Just as Fray Angélico painted the figures of Fr. Jerome, Archbishop Daeger, and the village townspeople into his murals, Esquipula uses Mana Seda as the model for his Virgin, including her hunchback in the image. The next day he arranges with the priest to place her at the head of the procession carrying flowers to the Virgin. Thus, her imperfect beauty is permanently ensconced above the altar in the santero's painting and accorded a well-deserved position of honor in the procession. Just as Fray Angélico superimposes the Guadalupe narrative on the May tradition, he overlays an alternative model of female beauty on the popular religious practice.

Chávez's artwork for the story depicts Mana Seda hunched over, picking flowers, with the image of the Virgin in the sky. The adjacent illuminated letter resignifies the Virgin as Guadalupe, prefiguring the semiotic process through which the santero, named after the Black Christ of Esquipulas, makes the Mexican Virgin visually present through art. All three panels of Chávez's triptych (see figure 3.5) show the protagonist in the foreground and the supernatural vision larger than life in the background. Narratively and visually, the book moves to a close-up of each of the successive panels in the opening *retablo* by enlarging the relevant illustration, then incorporating a motif from the drawing or one related to it in the illuminated letter that opens the story, and finally by narratively expanding the visual image in the story. Each of the three tales has three illustrations and three sections, extending the theme of the triptych formally and thematically.

The illuminated letters are micro-emblems of the verbal/visual hybridity of the larger book. The harmonious relationship between the two forms of representation allows readers to move back and forth between two codes: (1) a pictogram that resembles an element of the real world and (2) a signifier in the alphabetic code that does not look like the referents of the larger verbal sequence of which it is a part. The illuminated letters point to the organic nature of Chávez's aesthetic experimentation in this 1940 work. They and the other illustrations were not simply added to enhance readers' pleasure but rather were woven into the texts as essential narrative elements. The triptych form and the subject of the artwork and stories stem organically from key elements of his first two years of ministry at Peña Blanca: his church renovation and mural painting; his ethnic subjectivity and sense of himself as a writer and artist, strongly influenced by the Santa Fe writers' and artists' colony; his deep respect for Hispano popular religious traditions; and his strong Catholic spirituality. The dedication, "To 'Coronado's Children' My People," emphasizes his Hispano legacy and his place in that history. He highlights his people's ethnicity with the approaching Cuarto Centennial in mind. Just as *New Mexico Triptych* stems organically from Chávez's intense creativity in the five years after his ordination, it extends layers of meaning to his visual art of the period, notably, the murals and the extensive renovation of two churches he undertook at the time.

Art of the People and Church Restoration

While Chávez portrays himself in the priest in "The Angel's New Wings," several aspects of his identity also shape the artist-figures Nabor and Esquipula. Chávez had learned carpentry skills from his father, which served him well in church renovation, and like Esquipula, he painted with whatever materials were at hand. In practicing for the larger murals at Peña Blanca, for example, he did a self-portrait on a readily available practice surface—the back of a desk drawer—just as Esquipula painted the image of Guadalupe on Mana Seda's shawl.[63] Like Nabor's carved figures in the nacimiento that made the biblical narrative come alive, Fray Angélico hoped to make the Passion narrative come alive for parishioners through his life-size murals. Chávez's writing, painting, and church restoration in his first five years of ministry were "all of a piece," in John Gould Fletcher's words.

Fray Angélico's sense of missionary priesthood had been inseparable from the aesthetic since his childhood, and this conflation provided

FIG. 3.6. Chapel of Santa Dorotea, Domingo Station, New Mexico, before renovation, built by Father Albert Daeger, O.F.M., courtesy the Archives of the Franciscan Province of St. John the Baptist of Cincinnati.

FIG. 3.7. Chapel of Santa Dorotea, Domingo Station, New Mexico, after renovation and mural painting by Fray Angélico Chávez, 1938, courtesy the Archives of the Franciscan Province of St. John the Baptist of Cincinnati.

northern New Mexico with exquisite religious art and restoration beginning after his ordination. In September 1937 he began to renovate the chapel of Santa Dorotea at Domingo Station, encouraging the fourteen families who lived there to help him to save their deteriorating church. In a letter to his provincial that month, Chávez reported, "Got the Domingo (Mexican) people worked up to repair their chapel, which is in bad shape."[64] The front pediment jutted out eight inches from the roof, the tower supports were wobbly, and there were holes in the ceiling. Chávez advised removing the pediment, tower supports, and other weakened parts. With eighty dollars collected from the townspeople, donated lumber and adobe, and the help of two elderly men on weekdays, Chávez repaired and redesigned the exterior of the church, the roof, and ceiling.[65] He added adobe buttresses to support the front wall, designing one as a mission-style bell tower and chimney, replaced the wooden steps, filled in the lunette above the door to create a niche, and replaced the front windows on the facade with two large color murals of St. Jerome and St. Albert the Great.

Continuing his earlier artistic practice of painting contemporary figures such as Dolores del Río into images of holy figures, Chávez painted the faces of two Franciscan priests—his well-loved mentor Fr. Jerome Hesse and the first Franciscan archbishop of Santa Fe, Albert Daeger—into the images of the renowned fathers of the Church on the front of the chapel. Archbishop Daeger had begun building the church when he was a missionary at Domingo, and Fr. Hesse had completed the project. Besides paying homage to their roles in building the chapel, the young missionary padre gave grateful personal tribute to Fr. Jerome, his mentor for entering the priesthood, and to Archbishop Daeger, who had accompanied him on his first train ride to the seminary. Fray Angélico merged the long view of Church history with a local, close-up view by combining the images of St. Jerome and St. Albert with two of their contemporary namesakes. The townspeople recognized the saints depicted in the murals by connecting them to the two friars named after them who had previously ministered at the church. Nonetheless, when Fr. Jerome came to inaugurate the new chapel on February 6, 1938, the feast of Santa Dorotea (Archbishop Daeger had died in a 1932 accident in Santa Fe and thus did not see Fray Angélico's tribute), he "gave the artist missionary in charge a chiding look on seeing the murals and modestly declined to bless the paintings." Fray Angélico notes in the Peña Blanca House Chronicle that he himself then blessed the murals in Fr. Jerome's presence. He reported that a big crowd attended the vespers and the Mass and that his family from Santa Fe provided the music and singing.⁶⁶

Fray Angélico also remodeled the interior of the chapel, spending only $7.55 to redo the altar with simple statues, candlesticks, and small vases with flowers. He handcrafted and painted a large replica of the San Damiano crucifix, which was installed on November 29, 1938, on the new cloth drape behind the altar. Ten years later, however, a photograph shows that the crucifix had been replaced with a new reredos.⁶⁷

Chávez's restoration work continued at Peña Blanca. In late summer through September 1938, he remodeled the sanctuary, leaving it raised one level for visibility and building a new tabernacle dome in reinforced concrete and gold leaf over the original steel safe. He explained the color scheme he employed: "The rear curtains are deep red with horizontal double bars in gold tape. Tapestry is painted on the wall around Fr. Giles Hukenbeck's 'Guadalupe' in Vello, a permanent wall calcimine: ten shades of green with little blazons of cerise and gold. Canopy hangings of velvet pieces, alternately, blue and rose, to match the robes of the Virgin, trimmed with gold fringe and tassels. Larger tassels on corners are from old-time cinctures painted gold to match."⁶⁸ Working with slim resources, Fray Angélico recycled discarded materials and gave careful attention to both the overall aesthetic appearance of the sanctuary along with the close-up detail. He noted in the Peña Blanca House Chronicle that he recycled some of the old altar trimmings that he found in the barn by nailing them on the sacristy door, which he painted blue. He pulled the lights up to the ceiling to get them out of the way and they "look much better, and (believe it or not) give mehr licht!"⁶⁹

After renovating the sanctuary, Fray Angélico experimented artistically in the less public spaces of Peña Blanca in fall 1938 by painting large murals visually narrating the life of St. Francis. This art extended the image of St. Francis feeding the birds that he had painted earlier in the seminary and served as the proving ground for the Stations of the Cross he would soon embark on. By December 10 he finished a triptych of St. Francis on the refectory walls that focused on the everyday elements of the saint's alternative lifestyle. The panels portray Brother Juniper on the left, about to slaughter a pig, Francis and Masseo in the center, and Francis alone on the right (see figure

3.4). Fray Angélico's humor shows in the description he wrote in the House Chronicle: "Paintings finished on Refectory walls—a triptych. Center shows scene of St. Francis and Bro. Masseo eating on a rock. On the left is Bro. Juniper slicing off piggy's leg, and on the right St. Francis eating a panhandled bowl of something."[70] The painting echoes the St. Francis murals in the auditorium of the Museum of Fine Arts in Santa Fe, as do the later triptychs of the Via Crucis that Fray Angelico painted in the Peña Blanca church.

On the walls of the sacristy he painted images of the key moments of the narrative of St. Francis; initially, Francis kneels before the crucifix at San Damiano in his prerenunciation clothing; the next image, painted across both angled walls of the corner, depicts Francis renouncing his privileged lifestyle, placing his clothing at his father's feet in the presence of the bishop, and donning simple peasant clothing. *Confirmation of the Rule* shows the official recognition of the order, with the supernatural vision of the Virgin and Child in a glowing image in the background. In *Greccio*, St. Francis, as deacon at midnight Mass, prays by the crèche in a cave above Greccio, while the image of the Christ child glows in a halo of light. In *The Stigmata of St. Francis* (see figure 3.2), the glowing depiction of the supernatural again occurs in the mirrorlike aura above St. Francis as he receives the stigmata. The birdlike levitating posture of Francis is echoed in its counterpart above, a fusion of the image of Christ during the Passion with that of the six-winged angel that Francis recounted in his vision. Other paintings in the narrative sequence depict the investiture of St. Clare, the mission to foreign lands, and the death scene, *Transitus*. Chávez was especially proud of his rendition of *The Stigmata of St. Francis* and chose it for his 1938 Christmas cards.

It might be argued that Fray Angélico extended this visual narrative of St. Francis beyond these murals into his restoration of neglected churches in the area. Just as Francis repaired the church at San Damiano after perceiving a voice from the crucifix telling him to do so, Fray Angélico employed his artistic talent, his historical and ecclesiastical knowledge, and months of hard physical labor to carry on the legacy of Franciscanism in northern New Mexico. No matter how small, these churches might figuratively be seen as "cathedrals of the desert," as important to the people of New Mexico as the elaborate churches that hold the bishop's throne, or cathedra, in other places. More importantly, they would serve for many years as public, visually striking "sermons in stone," as Chávez termed one of the churches he restored, adapting Shakespeare's phrase.[71]

The following year, Fray Angélico looked into restoring the San Buenaventura Church at nearby Cochiti. He assured the provincial: "Concerning the Cochiti church restoration, I always intended to ask the Archbishop's permission before trying to connect with possible donors; first I consulted with Fr. Robert [Kalt], then you, for I believe this is the right manner of procedure. Nor do I intend to go ahead with the work if I can't get financial aid from the Historical Society and the Government. I think however that they would be willing, now that the Coronado 4to centennial is close at hand."[72] Apparently, however, Chávez was unable to raise funds for this restoration.

After the murals in the Peña Blanca church and rectory and on the facade of Santa Dorotea Church, Chávez undertook his most massive public art project, the famous images of the Stations of the Cross inside of Our Lady of Guadalupe Church. Designed and painted in three months in 1939, the seven-and-a-half-by-thirteen-feet murals are arranged in four triptychs and two single panels at the beginning and end of the visual narrative cycle. The paintings depict the townspeople, his sisters, and himself as life-size figures of the Passion narrative. Chávez used inexpensive materials available at the rectory—aluminum-based roof paint to prepare the walls and a set of Devore paints he had been given. As he began to outline the figures in charcoal on the prepared walls, the townspeople of the parish stopped to watch. One woman brought him a photograph of her twenty-year-old daughter who had recently died and requested that he paint the image near the figure of Veronica in Station VI. Chávez then took photographs of other townspeople and integrated them into the murals. In a series of self-reflexive gestures, he inserted himself visually and verbally into the narrative—as Pontius Pilate in Station I (surrounded by pillars and arches modeled on those of St. Francis Cathedral where he had recently been ordained) and with Latin inscriptions in Stations I and VI, "Angelicus Pinxit."[73] Employing a multilayered visual/verbal pun, he self-reflexively inserted himself into the narrative as both author and character—the executioner of Christ and the painter of the visual narrative to follow. Using again a trope deployed in the novel *Guitars and Adobes*, he writes the Latin message with Greek and Hebrew lettering in later stations in this playful authorial gesture of self-incrimination and attribution.

FIG. 3.8. Fray Angélico Chávez before crucifixion triptych, Our Lady of Guadalupe Church, Peña Blanca, New Mexico, 1939, courtesy the Archives of the Franciscan Province of St. John the Baptist of Cincinnati.

In keeping with both aesthetic and liturgical ends, Stations I and XIV were painted across from each other on opposing walls, so that Station XII depicting the crucifixion would be at the center of a triptych. In his humorous commentary, Fray Angélico noted that this arrangement would allow people to slip into the church, pray the Via Crucis, and sneak out the door without being noticed or, alternately, in a liturgical ceremony, for the priest to make an impressive procession before and after praying the stations.[74] Solemnly blessed in a ceremony on February 4, 1940, at seven in the evening,[75] the magnificent stations show the influence of the Chapman and Vierra paintings in St. Francis Auditorium in the Museum of Fine Arts in Santa Fe; Chávez's own St. Francis mural cycle in the refectory and sacristy; and his insertion of real people such as Dolores del Río and the archbishop of Cincinnati in his early paintings. The large scale of these paintings and the windowlike shape of each offered a series of figurative windows to the past in which contemporary New Mexicans were representationally joined to the people of Christ's time. The rich color and large scope of the murals offered a striking contrast to the usually smaller and darker paintings of the Via Crucis in churches. Fray Angélico gradually darkened the sky in the paintings as the Passion progressed.

Chávez integrated New Mexico Hispano ethnicity into the murals by painting the local people into the stations. The images retained both religious and secular designata for the Peña Blanca community, sometimes with a deep poignancy. Benedicto C. de Baca, the centurion in the foreground of Station XI, a few years later was a prisoner on the Bataan Death March and died on a Japanese prison ship. The deaf Víctor Mares was cast as the man who nailed Christ to the cross and stripped him of his garments, appearing in Stations I, III, and XI. Townspeople remember that he was very upset about this portrayal, saying "I didn't nail him to the cross!" and was reluctant for some time to enter the church and see himself in this role.[76] Chávez painted his sisters Consuelo, Adela, and Nora Chávez as the first three women on the left in Station IX, with Mary Baca as the Blessed Mother and Rosa Ortiz next to them. Jaime Baca's grandfather Esquipula Baca is the elderly man standing at the right. On the right side of Station VIII are two elderly women who walked a mile together to church every Sunday; Doña Marianita Armijo always wore a *tápalo* (like the character Mana Seda), and Doña Carlota Baca (Jaime Baca's great aunt) was blind.[77] As in "Hunchback Madonna" where the santero painted Mana Seda's image on her traditional black shawl for display on the high altar, Chávez attempted to praise and immortalize these devoted, unassuming women by painting them into the eighth station.

The story of Rebecca Ortiz is especially poignant. Pregnant and unmarried in the small 1930s village, the frail girl died in 1939 from complications of the pregnancy. Her mother Clotilde approached Fray Angélico after he had completed nearly half of the stations with a picture of Rebecca and the request that he paint her face into Station VI. He did this, also portraying Clotilde and Rebecca's sister Leonor next to her.[78] This gave him the idea to include the townspeople in all of the stations, and after photographing people with his Brownie Box camera, he redid several earlier stations with their images. Chávez also immortalized Rebecca in his poem "To Rebecca Dead," set at her wake. Here she is the hero who remained calm even when suffering the scorn of some in the town. Like Jairus' daughter, she knew greater pain than death during her life; she kept her sorrow and regret inside while presenting a calm face to the townspeople, some of whom had shown her "vile disdain." Now, at the wake, she calmly accepts the flowers offered from the same hands that "were raised to cast a stone" when her "stout heart ached from [her] mistake."[79] It is also possible that one intended addressee of Fray Angélico's 1938 Writers Page poem, "Whose Broken Heart Is Brave," was Rebecca, who perhaps had to endure her pregnancy and a broken heart silently.

The religious and secular referents of the figures in Fray Angélico's *Stations of the Cross* connect the official religious prayer cycle directly to the life of the people in Peña Blanca and their descendants. Chávez portrayed the ethnicity of those he painted to make the religious narrative come alive for and belong to the Hispano townspeople. As a local Hispano artist, Chávez gave his people the gift of life-size images of themselves immersed in the Passion narrative. "This is our story," he suggests, not one only about an ancient people in the Holy Land. In this sense, the *Stations* at Peña Blanca prefigures his 1974 magnum opus *My Penitente Land* in which he argues that Hispanos in New Mexico are inextricably connected to the spirituality, culture, and geography of the Holy Land.

The success of the St. Francis mural cycle, the beautified sanctuary, and the spectacular new *Stations of the Cross* encouraged Fray Angélico to undertake further restoration of the church and grounds. In mid-August 1940, he began the external redesign of the church by restructuring the two garages that opened to the courtyard. One garage would become a second sacristy and the other a passageway to the back where new garages would eventually be built. These changes were intended to make more room for trees and flowers. In subsequent months, Fray Angélico worked diligently to beautify the church grounds by adding major plantings. In January 1941 he planted a blue spruce and an Arizona juniper by the recreation room window; on February 13, two big firs and two aspens were transplanted from the forest with the help of Valerio Ortiz and the permission of the ranger; later he ordered flowering plants from Ohio. "Will [the trees] grow?" he wrote on February 13. "Quien sabe! They form a sylvan-looking clump near the side entrance to the Church." The beautification of the church grounds through these plantings was a crucial part of Fray

Angélico's church renovation. As he noted with pride and practicality on April 15, "It promises to be not only a beauty spot, but especially a delightful place to rest weary missionary bones and brains."[80]

Hoping to preserve New Mexico's history visually and materially, at the same time he was beautifying the church grounds in 1940–41 Chávez redesigned and rebuilt the facade of the 1869 church in territorial style to remedy what he considered to be the hodgepodge repairs: "A gabled farm roof was surmounted with a dog-house belfry and this was capped later on with a mosque-like derby painted with aluminum. False Gothic buttresses were set on the side and at every corner."[81] In a March 1941 letter to the *Provincial Chronicle* he notes: "What I did last fall was to change the façade of the church into a definite style, raising the front wall into a massive niche campanile for the bells. Then winter caught me. But in the meantime I have carved (in wood) a fancy frame for the front choir window, which will be installed as soon as weather permits. Then the portico will be remodeled to match the top of the façade . . . and the end is not near as I am working alone and penniless."[82] On September 1, 1940, Fray Angélico had preached at the two Masses at Peña Blanca hoping to rouse the people to help to remodel the church. He showed them his drawing of a proposed forty-eight-foot tower to rise from the north-middle side of the church, and the men of the parish promised to make five thousand adobes. Instead, the adobes were used to build a ten-foot-high, four-foot-ten-inch-thick pediment that held the bells in two niches completed by the first week of December; two thousand bricks were donated by José Ortiz y Pino of Santa Fe for the cornice atop the facade. Inclement weather forced the remodeling to stop for the winter, but on the parish's feast day, December 12, rows of paper bags with candles inside were mounted on the brick cornice of the facade. Although the bad weather prevented the traditional procession after vespers for the Guadalupe feast day, Fray Angélico was proud of the luminarias that highlighted the church's new pediment for the first time.[83]

Fray Angélico continued with the renovations throughout 1941. He carved a wooden frame for the front choir window, installed it April 23, and shortly thereafter added a wooden Spanish-style grill that he had made from maple mop handles. On June 4 he reported that he had finished the front porch of the church, using beams salvaged from an old railroad bridge. On August 28 he wrote that the old door in the north transept of the church was about to fall down, "so we put in new carved door posts buttressed with concrete on the outside." In early October, Fray Angélico's father worked several days fitting a new frame and doors for the front of the church, which had been donated by Fray Angélico's uncle Agustín Sosaya in memory of his daughter. Throughout October Fray Angélico plastered the front and sides of the church, helped by Brother Angeles and George Rivera of Sile.[84]

FIG. 3.9. Fray Angélico Chávez at north transept door he remodeled, Our Lady Of Guadalupe Church, Peña Blanca, New Mexico, 1941, courtesy the Archives of the Franciscan Province of St. John the Baptist of Cincinnati.

FIG. 3.10. Front exterior of Our Lady of Guadalupe Church, Peña Blanca, New Mexico, after renovation by Fray Angélico Chávez and parishioners, 1941, courtesy the Archives of the Franciscan Province of St. John the Baptist of Cincinnati.

We get some sense of the difficult physical labor involved in the renovation in an October 1941 letter:

> I wonder if from internal evidence, you can deduce my present state! I cannot typewrite, and this pen is held by a rubber-gloved paw! My right hand is badly burned by cement and lime—result of my plastering the front of the church. I'm only half done as the rains, unusual for these parts, are holding me back. As it is, I'll only be able to put on the first coat this fall, which is enough to protect the walls from the weather. Got a new pair of doors for the church front—12 panels and handcarved all. They look nifty.[85]

Jaime Baca, who spent summers at his grandmother's house in Peña Blanca, remembers that Fray Angélico did much of the work almost single-handedly:

> I remember one time he was trying to move some heavy beams [from the roof] and he ran across the road and got me and my cousin [Arturo C. de Baca] to go up there and help.... Then one time at a Sunday Mass ... he began to say "I need help," and then he started telling the men: "I know you have all kinds of excuses: you're busy with harvest time and politics. This is an election time and you say we're very busy with our politics." And then he said, "yes, this is when one Hispanic goes and stabs another Hispanic in the back to help some gringo." He told that to the people from the altar. And everybody kind of bowed their heads and nodded, yes, that's right.

Baca notes that Chávez, all by himself, removed the high roof with all its beams, leveling it down to make it like a mission church. Bertille Baca, another young student in Peña Blanca at the time, remembers some of the high school boys in town helping Fray Angélico—Mauro Montoya, Benedicto C. de Baca, Benito Baca, and other juniors and seniors at the school.[86]

As part of the renovations, Chávez asked his uncle Agustín (Gus) Sosaya to make new wooden doors for the church in August 1941. The model most likely in Fray Angélico's mind was the famous photograph of the carved door panels at Santo Domingo admired by Adolph Bandelier in 1880.[87] Chávez then carved panels with verbal and visual engravings on the doors, dedicating them to Sosaya's daughter María Dolores, who had died one week before Easter that year of double pneumonia.[88] Alternating vertical and horizontal panels surround a central image of the Sacred Heart on the top half of each door. Two vertical panels facing each other at the center of the doors depict the emblem of the Franciscan Order: a cross rising from the intertwined arms of Christ and St. Francis.

The three other panels on the top half of each door hold inscriptions about the family tragedy and the appearance of the Virgin of Guadalupe in Mexico in 1531. Those on the left door read, "En memoria de María Sosaya," "Estas puertas las hizo su Papá" (Her father made these doors), "Agosto de 1941." The right door panels are inscribed, "Nuestra Señora de Guadalupe," "Es la patrona de este lugar" (Our Lady of Guadalupe is the patroness of this place), "Diciembre de 1531." Fray Angélico links the death of María to the patronal Virgin of Peña Blanca and the Virgin's role in the history of the Americas. Square panels below give the Spanish names of eleven of the apostles, outlined by the appropriate visual images: hearts around Juan, shells around Santiago, arrows around Tomás, fish around Pedro, and crosses around Felipe. In the lower right-hand corner, a panel is left blank, refusing to invoke the name of Judas but making the betraying apostle present precisely by his visual absence. Using the verbal and visual in tandem on these simple wooden church doors, Fray Angélico linked his family history to the long narrative of Christianity in the Old and New Worlds in what he hoped would be a long-lasting tribute to his uncle, his cousin María, Franciscanism, and faith.

Nearly fifty years later in 1986, the Peña Blanca church was razed and a new one constructed. Although Fray Angélico is said to have made light of the destruction of the murals he painted by saying they were only *monos*, or "cartoons," others close to him note that he was devastated.[89] The decision to repair or to raze the church was difficult. After the sanctuary wall collapsed from undetected water damage, the town and the archdiocese debated the cost-effectiveness of restoration compared to building an entirely new structure. Some parishioners felt strongly that the murals and church needed to be preserved as vital elements of family, town, and religious history. Others worried that the expensive repairs on the old adobe structure would still not keep parishioners safe inside in years to come. David Grieves, an engineer under contract to the archdiocese, recommended razing the building because of the high cost to repair it, arguing, "The building itself is not what you'd call historically significant, compared to others."[90] Fr. Antonio Valdez argued strongly that to the contrary, the murals must be saved. Townspeople such as Oliver Sandoval and Manuel Baca staunchly campaigned to save the historical images of their relatives depicted in the stations. Baca hoped to walk his daughters down the aisle of the church with their family images on the walls: "We should leave it for them, because our fathers left it for us and their fathers left it for them."[91]

The new pastor, Fr. Myron Uhl, O.F.M., supported a ballot parishioners had been given on the issue shortly before he arrived in which ninety-six voted for a new church and thirty-eight for preserving the old one.[92] Jaime Baca remembers one proposal to retain the old church as a chapel and build a new one on land behind it. Fray Angélico's nephew Thomas Chávez, director of the Palace of the Governors in Santa Fe, obtained a lower repair estimate for the church than Grieves', but the Franciscans and the archdiocese proceeded with the demolition in 1986 after one Church spokesman was quoted in the press as saying that Fray Angélico's murals had no artistic value.[93] New Mexico lost a crucial component of its Catholic and Hispano heritage when the church was destroyed, and generations of Hispanos to come in the town of Peña Blanca have lost the beautiful religious representations of their twentieth-century ancestors. It is poignantly ironic that this key work of a Franciscan so devoted to history would have its continued historical presence terminated in 1986. In hindsight, we can imagine a kind of foreshadowing of the 1986 event in Fray Angélico's disillusionment after his tremendously productive first five years of ministry as the first native Franciscan priest of New Mexico.

Spirituality and History

While difficult for us to envision, given his overextended schedule, Fray Angélico made additional intellectual and spiritual contributions during the extraordinarily productive first five years of his priesthood. Although exhausted from physical labor and parish ministry, he often read and wrote late into the night, only to rise early for six o'clock Mass. He took on extra work when asked by superiors, such as designing the emblem for the newly formed diocese of Las Cruces in August 1940 and researching the history of Santo Domingo Pueblo.[94] Between September 1937 and May 1939 he published twenty short sermons in *St. Anthony Messenger* that reveal the themes on which he preached during his ministry. Until August 1940 he continued a monthly magazine column begun in 1935, "Out of the Centuries." He submitted a book manuscript of daily spiritual meditations for publication and began to publish articles on history. He wrote a long poem sequence and published several of its cantos. In 1938 he sent a picture he painted of Jemez mission to the provincial in Cincinnati and designed a book seal for the friary at Peña Blanca.[95]

The monthly "sermonettes" in *St. Anthony Messenger* give moral lessons, often illustrating the modern relevance of biblical episodes. Chávez reveals his predilection for art and beauty, for example, in the first sermon of September 1937. To those who complain that displays of pomp and splendor in religious and public ceremonies waste money that could be spent on the poor, he cites Christ's reproving Judas who complained that Mary Magdalene's ointment to anoint Christ's feet could have been sold for the poor. Even if no opulent displays of beauty had been created throughout history, he argues, we would still have the poor and no great art treasures. The poor love beauty and have contributed their labor to magnificent buildings throughout the ages. "It was not the poor . . . who complained when Mary poured the priceless perfume. . . The grumbler was Judas."[96] While Chávez does not take into account here the structural causes of poverty during the Depression at the time and seems to give preference to inanimate display rather than ordinary suffering people, he encourages readers to look for greatness in ordinary people in another sermon: "All of our daily acquaintances are not mere dumb, driven cattle, but each a captain of his immortal soul, each a possible hero."[97] Fray Angélico himself was just such an ordinary person who was already exhibiting greatness. Again in February 1938, he praises "the unsung heroes and heroines in every walk of life who, forgetting themselves, have borne bliss to others," as did St. Paul.[98]

In contrast to his sermon valorizing beauty over solutions to human poverty, Chávez addresses poverty and racism in a 1938 sermon. Expanding on the story of Respha, who stayed with the rotting corpses of her crucified sons, he urges readers to minister to the "social lepers" in our age, "people ostracized for their poverty, folks crucified, not for crime, but for their caste and color."⁹⁹ Other sermons focus on jealousy, passivity in the face of a wrong, taking responsibility for wrongdoing, and feigning friendship in order to hurt another. The concise magazine columns often employ humor and wordplay and bring a biblical episode to bear on a contemporary situation.

Fray Angélico also sought to publish in this period *Seraphic Days*, a book of daily meditations on the lives of Franciscan saints and Catholic feasts that he had written at Duns Scotus College. In 1938 he sent the handwritten manuscript to Fr. Sebastian Erbacher at Duns Scotus, suggesting that his mentor publish it without his name because of personal information revealed in the meditations. In November, Fr. Erbacher replied humorously and with enthusiasm that the manuscript "made me feel like trying to become a good Franciscan before I die, if it is not too late." He suggested that Chávez draw illustrations for each month and add a meditation for the newly canonized Franciscan saint Salvador of Horta, one for the profession of St. Francis, and one for Good Friday. In September 1939 Fr. Erbacher wrote a foreword for the volume.¹⁰⁰

Fr. Erbacher's foreword to the anonymous volume notes that while studying philosophy at Duns Scotus, a young cleric composed a series of meditations in the style of St. Francis and St. Bonaventure that appealed more to the heart than the mind and paraphrased Scripture in a nonscholarly fashion. He wrote the meditations not for public consumption but to enhance and evaluate his own spiritual progress. Because of personal notes about his spiritual development in the meditations, the author requested anonymity.

Following the calendar year, the meditations begin with the Feast of the Circumcision January 1 and end with the Birth of Christ December 25. Each has an introduction and three subsections narrating the life of a Franciscan saint or recounting the origin and meaning of the Catholic feast day. Each subsection ends with a meditative prayer pointing to human shortcomings and spiritual goals for those wishing to emulate holy figures. While Chávez frequently weaves in scriptural passages without the distraction of attribution, Fr. Erbacher added the citations when he edited the volume.

Although *Seraphic Days* is a book of spiritual meditations, it also reveals Fray Angélico's early interest in history and his efforts to recover forgotten historical narratives in an accessible, public form. The stories of less known Franciscan saints such as Hyacintha

Mariscotti and Veronica Giuliani are told alongside those of more well-known figures such as St. Paschal Baylon, King Ferdinand, and St. Anthony of Padua. However, since he was not yet engaged in original historical research, sometimes he uncritically transmits the received views of his time and those shaped by his position as a student-cleric. In the entry on St. Benedict the Moor, for example, Chávez praises the black saint's inner beauty in contrast to his racial difference from the perceived standard of positive whiteness: "It is well and profitable for me to behold the whiteness of this black man's soul. According to our standards, Benedict was far from handsome. His features were repellant to over-nice people; his skin was black. But, oh, if bodily eyes could see the whiteness of a saintly soul that is filled with grace."[101] Similarly, he seems to accept without question the dominant Church position against the Republican democracy in Spain in the 1930s, as in others of his writings. In his 1939 "Ni los sepulcros respetan" he virulently condemns the atrocities allegedly committed by what he terms the Communist Republicans during the Spanish Civil War. He does not consider other voices within the Catholic Church at the time that supported the fledgling democracy in Spain, such as Jacques Maritain. In the entry about St. Salvador of Horta in *Seraphic Days*, Chávez describes the political conditions in Spain at the time of his canonization:

> St. Salvador of Horta was canonized by Pope Pius XI during a period of storm and stress for his native land. At other times in history, Spain had saved Christian civilization by conquering its invading enemies at her very door. This time, hordes of the godless had entrenched themselves like deadly germs in the heart and arteries of Spain with the purpose of extinguishing her Christian life; and the source of infection, at least the worst sore, was in the very provinces sanctified by the birth, labors and death of Bl. Salvador.[102]

Although Fray Angélico brings several little-known historical narratives to a wider audience in this book, he does not engage in the critical research and questioning of his later work. In a strongly worded letter to Senator Dennis Chávez, which was sent to local newspapers at the time, he argues against the repeal of the Spanish arms embargo: the impression that Franco is a Fascist and Nazi is a figment of the press and leftists in the United States who have never printed Franco's own statements. The Loyalists and the Barcelona government are "Soviet in principle and in domination." Appealing to a shared ethnicity, he adds, "Mr. Senator, I am for Franco as a Christian democrat and because of the blood that runs in my veins and yours . . . [Franco's] stance [is] for that which made Spain glorious in the past, for that which gave our state and our people such a grand history and heritage." Fray Angélico tells Senator Chávez that now is the time for his Spanish American name to stand out in congress: "I hope to see the name of CHÁVEZ at the fore fighting for the right, and not merely silent at a rear desk . . . or on the list of absentees."[103] Although world events would escalate and he would soon risk his life to fight Fascism, his strong anti-Communist beliefs dominated his thinking in this period.

An important structural element of each meditation is self-critique. Chávez employs the pronominal shifter *I* that refers on one level to himself and on another to people who will later read the book for spiritual guidance; these readers may internalize each meditation as an occasion for self-evaluation and prayer. We can glean certain biographical information about Fray Angélico's personal thoughts and feelings when he wrote the meditations as a cleric and revised them later for publication. How do these handwritten passages of self-criticism change when they enter the public sphere upon publication, albeit anonymously? As polysemous texts, they hover between a subjective presentation of the authorial self and moral directives for self-criticism addressed to readers through the subjective persona of his or her *I*.

While self-presentation can never be relied on completely for accuracy, we can trust the veracity of Fray Angélico's self-criticism in the meditations in *Seraphic Days* to some degree because he was reluctant to have them published under his name and claimed to have written them as a cleric to advance his personal spiritual development. They offer clues to his state of mind during his years of formation and his early ministry after ordination—the goals he strove for and the criticism he directed to himself. In the first meditation he begins the new year by asking, "How then do I still shamefully desire earthly things? O Lord, help me to forget the things I left behind. . . Behold these worthless things I see about me, these books and manuscripts, my habit and other garments—I will readily part with them, if it is asked of me."[104] Meditating on the feast of the Holy Family, he recounts his struggle with the Franciscan ideals of poverty and humility: "Being a domestic of God, I think myself worthy of honors and comforts commensurate with such a dignity. Having severed all worldly family ties for Christ's sake, I expect the easy life of the wealthy. Nazareth, however, was not so."[105] According to a number of his meditations, Fray Angélico often struggled between his desire for his accomplishments to be recognized and the Franciscan ideal of humility.

Perhaps referring to his enjoyment of parties with Santa Fe literati, he chastises himself for desiring fine clothes and food: "I, who am nothing at times would be like those who are clothed in fine and fashionable garments, using dainty food and drink. . . . Jesus, make me poor, make me Yours."[106] St. Margaret of Cortona's grueling penitential rituals show "how meager and ridiculous my poor and infrequent acts of mortification seem when compared with such heroic penances. How ready am I to excuse myself even from fasting."[107] Comparing his religious community to a family on the feast of the Holy Family he confesses, "Yet how often there are ruptures in the religious family, in what should be a Seraphic family—and how often I am the cause. I become dissatisfied, not only with my brothers, but with our mode of life itself."[108] Such issues would persist for Chávez until he retired from the order in 1971.

Like many of the meditations in *Seraphic Days* on Franciscan saints, Fray Angélico's monthly column "From Out of the Centuries" in *St. Anthony Messenger* from 1934 to 1940 presents the achievements of Franciscans throughout history. Modeled on Ripley's "Believe It or Not" cartoons, the column recounts little-known tidbits of Franciscan history accompanied by his drawings and hand-lettered captions.[109] With humor and a focus on the extraordinary, he attempts to draw in readers with such captions as "LENIN remembered St. Francis in his last hours," "A German Friar had to carry the Holy Eucharist in an ENVELOPE," "LISZT was a tertiary," "The Franciscan order boasts of a COLORED SAINT," and "The word 'DUNCE' comes from a famous friar's name!"[110] In the sixty-eight columns, each with four or five anecdotes, over three hundred facts appeared.

Chávez primarily includes information about European, Latin American, and U.S. Franciscan history. He describes the art museum in Santa Fe based on the model of Franciscan missions: "The church proper forms a Civic Hall, called 'St. Francis Auditorium;' the convent section serves as a gallery for the paintings of Southwest

Art colonies."[111] He notes that the Southwest missions are the first American churches, since they were modeled on Native American buildings, unlike churches in the east patterned on British examples. Prefiguring his own later work when he researched and painted the original colors of the Castrense altar screen, his May 1935 column notes,

> A stone carving in bas-relief stood in olden days in the Spanish military chapel at Santa Fe. After the American occupancy, it was removed from the already ruined chapel and was used as a drop for letters in the post office of the town. What remains of the carving is preserved in the Museum of New Mexico. The inscription reads: "This building was made in the year of our Lord, 1791, at a cost of 8,000 pesos." So we see that our S.A.G. [St. Anthony Guild] stamps were preceded by a "St Anthony Guide" letter drop.[112]

He depicts the bas-relief of St. Anthony and the Christ child in the column's illustration.

While the entries are often humorous, the columns aim to educate through entertainment, bringing information to a wide audience through a popular genre. The series reveals that already from 1934 to 1940, Fray Angélico had begun historical research and worked to produce a revisionist historical narrative about the many contributions of the Franciscans in world history. His sense of ethnic identity is less prominent in these columns than is his Franciscan identity. A study of the over three hundred entries reveals his patient mining of secondary historical sources for little-known facts that cumulatively would write Franciscans into the larger historical narrative. Creatively, he designed each column to entice readers through a pleasing configuration of visual and verbal messages. Fray Angélico the artist, historian, Franciscan, and humorist shines in these innovative columns.

In April 1941, although still at work on the renovations on the Peña Blanca church, Fray Angélico began research on the ecclesiastical history of the Santo Domingo Pueblo in response to the *Provincial Chronicle*'s request. Archbishop Gerken had lifted the interdict on the pueblo on the feast of St. Dominic the previous August 4, making it a propitious time to document the Church's long history in the pueblo. In this early historical article, Fray Angélico delved into Church documents that would become his key focus in years to come. Besides secondary sources, he examined the Baptismal and Matrimonial Records of Santo Domingo from 1771 to 1836 held by the archdiocese in Santa Fe, the Baptismal Records of Santo Domingo and Peña Blanca from 1835 to 1940 in the parochial archives at Peña Blanca, and the House Chronicle written at Peña Blanca beginning in 1911. He divides the history of the Church at the pueblo into four eras: the founding and "Golden Era," 1591–1700; the century of stalemate, 1700–1821; the century of decline, 1821–1900; and the first half of the twentieth century.

Seven years after Spanish explorers under Castaño de Sosa named the village Santo Domingo in 1591, Oñate established a mission there under the title Our Lady of the Assumption. After a flood washed away the village in 1605 and it was rebuilt farther from the river, the first church was built in 1607 by Fr. Juan de Escalona. Chávez qualifies his choice of the term *Golden Era* for the seventeenth-century mission: Spanish Inquisition reports reveal continuous fighting between the friars and the military governors of the period in which the Indians were "the football in the controversy."[113] After the Pueblo Revolt and the 1692 return of de Vargas, the Santo Domingos rallied the Jemez and Cochitis to join the Tanos and Tiguas to fight against the reconquest of Santa Fe in December 1693. Again in 1696 they rebelled, killing five priests.

About 1706 the church and convento were built, with escutcheons of the Franciscan and Dominican orders carved on the wooden doors. Although the article is not footnoted to show what information Fray Angélico obtained from secondary sources, he notes that the oldest parish records he was able to find at the time started in 1771. Chávez had not yet undertaken the organization and documentation of the archdiocesan archives that he would engage in later for the invaluable 1958 volume *Archives of the Archdiocese of Santa Fe, 1678–1900*. He discusses the 1778 inventory of the convent library, which included valuable books, many of which "are now piled helter-skelter in a cupboard of the Santo Domingo sacristy, and closely guarded by the Indians. A small number of them has been pilfered by the Padre from time to time with the hope of grabbing some valuable handwritten record."[114] The article includes a reproduction of a page from a sixteenth-century work that Fray Angélico "borrowed" from the cupboard in the sacristy at Santo Domingo.

During the Mexican period, Chávez mentions the visits to Santo Domingo from 1837 to 1845 by the Very Reverend Juan Felipe Ortiz, vicar in Santa Fe for the bishop of Durango, about whom he would later research and begin to write a book, until illness prevented him from completing the project.[115] Another priest who drew his interest as his double namesake, Don Manuel Chaves, was pastor from 1863 to 1867 and became the subject of a retraction that Fray Angélico published a decade later. In "Apology to a Long-Dead Priest" (1952), Chávez notes that he "made a flippant remark about a former secular pastor [of Santo Domingo] as having apostatized, relying on common legend and hearsay. Recently I discovered that his life's story was exactly the contrary."[116] Later research in *La revista Católica* revealed that the earlier priest had led an exemplary life. Fray Angélico ends the retraction with a moral: "Let hearsay about priests go in one ear and out the other."[117] This early article on Santo Domingo laid the groundwork for much of Fray Angélico's future work on the history of New Mexico.

The last section of the article (published serially in two issues) focuses on the twentieth century, especially on the background and the lifting of the 1935 interdict. The Peña Blanca House Chronicle by Fr. Jerome Hesse from 1911 to 1919 recounts that on Palm Sunday 1913 no Mass was celebrated at the pueblo because the governor forbade children going to the sacraments. In 1917 the governor and his council spent a night in jail in Albuquerque for forbidding the Indians to register for the WWI draft.

Although before starting the article, Fray Angélico noted that it would need to be written "with much care and circumspection in order that the truth be told without *lese majeste* and the like," various condescending remarks about Pueblo Indians appear.[118] While Fray Angélico loved those he ministered to at Santo Domingo, his intense thirteen-year seminary training seems to have imbued him with a sense of superiority, as one with a message of truth that needed to be instilled in the native population. The historical period of his formation and early ministry was decades before Vatican II and ecumenism. Thus he writes of the pueblo's "heathen festivities," "the sadistic sanctions of the tribal laws," and asserts, "The Indians really have the minds of children. . . . One must take, as one does from children, actions and remarks which one would not forgive in adults."[119] Speaking of himself as the nice "Mexican Padre" who began to visit the pueblo when he arrived at Peña Blanca, he disparages the Indians: "[The padre] squatted on their filthy floors to dip greasy lamb-stew from the common pot and ate with much relish; he drank their ersatz coffee from unwashed cups lively with flies. He always picked up their ubiquitous citizens on the road. (Ordinarily white folks do not give a Santo Domingo a lift a second time, especially in winter when the windows are closed.)"[120] Noting that they invited him to lead prayer and give instruction every Saturday, he comments, "Was I good!"[121] The superior tone of the first-world ethnographer reporting on the culture of the primitive Other pervades this section of the article.

Several times Chávez attacks the artists and writers who were working for Indian rights at the time. Pueblo culture may outwardly seem to be democratic, he notes, "for which qualities it is much admired by shallow minds in Government, literary, and artistic circles. **But it is tyranny of the worst kind.** The Ogpu and Gestapo are mere upstarts. All this 'culture' (this word is used also in the scientific cultivation of germs!) is admired, abetted and defended by the U.S. Department of Indian Affairs, which listens to the vociferousnous [*sic*] of crack-brained artists and writers and their followers."[122] Later he argues that those in charge of the federal Indian bureaus do not see the inner ugliness of Indian life because they are too fixated on its external artistic aspects: "While they lift up the standard of liberty for Indians as a whole to be primitive and pagan, they blatantly ignore the more essential right of the individual to be Christian and decent."[123] While Fray Angélico socialized with the writers' and artists' colonies and shared his literary work with them, his primary loyalty was to the Church, and he often completely subscribed to its official positions. For example, in explaining the incident that finally sparked the 1935 interdict, he notes that the Indians wanted to have Mass on the day they chose: "If their calendar of heathen festivities fell on the day appointed for their monthly Mass, the Father may not enter the Pueblo, nor any outsider for that matter. *Here was absolute control of the Church by the layman.*"[124] Although Chávez worked for several years to mediate the conflict between the archbishop and the pueblo, he seems firmly entrenched here in the Church's ideology of control of the laity.

One stylistic sign of his desire to be a part of clerical inner circles is the article's bilingualism. In several instances he switches to Latin to recount embarrassing occurrences in the history of Santo Domingo.

Among them was his mistaken belief that Fr. Manuel Chaves left the Church: "*Hic viduus erat ab episcopo Lamy ordinatus qui sicut canis, ut ait Petrus, reversus in vomitum suum duxit feminam in comitatu Valenciae, et mortus est.*"¹²⁵ (In the 1952 retraction he notes that Chaves worked at the Jemez mission until ten days before his death, only then going home to Valencia to die in the care of his family.) Describing the immoralities of the "heathenish aristocracy" of Santo Domingo, he writes bilingually, "Of these let it merely be said that the *sancti innocentes vere sunt coinquinati* [defiled] and there is no question of conducting a B.V.M. Sodality."¹²⁶ Chávez adds to the paternalistic ethnographic tone of some passages in the article by code switching to Latin sporadically to address the inner circle of clergy in the ancient linguistic code of Church power.

We might also understand the disparaging remarks about the Santo Domingo people in this article as a subtle battle of ethnicities in which Chávez asserted the superiority of his own ethnicity and the Hispano legacy in New Mexico. Despite having been told in his youth that the Franciscan seminary did not accept Mexicans, and feeling that some in the Franciscan Order undervalued his people, he continued to affirm his ethnicity as he had in the seminary, now as the first native-born Hispano friar to minister in New Mexico. The legacy of his Hispanic heritage and his religious ministry were inseparable, as he worked in the pueblo and framed and wrote the article. Vis-à-vis the Santo Domingo people, he firmly believed that his heritage and religion were superior.

As in *Seraphic Days* and *Out of the Centuries*, Fray Angélico linked religious history and deep spiritual beliefs in this 1941 article on Santo Domingo. He presents one person's firsthand account of the dissension between the Church and the pueblo, which, although one sided and offensive to many now, is a product of his position within the Church in that historical moment. He aptly explains details of the lifting of the interdict and the ability of the Santo Domingo people to believe in two "true" religions: "Putting their two index fingers close together, they say: 'Both are equally true and good—God and the powers-that-rule.'"¹²⁷ Even with its shortcomings, the article offers an important documentary account of the Church's history at Santo Domingo Pueblo.

Another important element of Fray Angélico's spiritual writing in this period is the poems that he would later publish as *The Single Rose*.

Like *Seraphic Days*, he ultimately published this volume of mystical poetry without full self-attribution. Playing with a barely disguising pseudonym, he suggested that the book was a translation of the mystical poetry of "Fray Manuel de Santa Clara," alluding to his own given name and birthplace. Having published the poems separately in 1941 and 1942, Chávez asked Provincial Rolfes for permission to release them together as a book: "The reason I wish to publish these poems is that poets of note insist that I should, that they are of the best (of which I am no judge). They tell me also, and the publishers, that poetry sells better during times of stress like these."[128] Chávez suggests that this series of mystical poems would console people as the country entered World War II.

One month later, after the provincial approved the manuscript, Fray Angélico abruptly withdrew it. In early August he asked if the Cincinnati archbishop could give the additional imprimatur needed from one's bishop. When told no, he answered, "The Archbishop of Santa Fe thinks very little of the manuscript and I doubt very much if he will grant an Imprimatur. It matters little, for I don't feel like going on with the publication at present; nor do I want to give you the reason for I realize that you are burdened already with many matters, including complaining friars." One week later Fray Angélico wrote to Rolfes: "My book will not be published. Archbishop Gerken declined to give his Imprimatur, as I had expected; he thinks the manuscript bad spirituality and poor literature. In this matter I am not down-hearted, as it is only a hobby and not the main thing in life."[129] Although Chávez claimed not to be disheartened at the archbishop's rejection, it no doubt contributed further to his deep discouragement about the first five years of his ministry. His foreboding about the negative decision stemmed from strong disagreements he had previously had with the archbishop.

Two years earlier in July 1940, Fray Angélico's brother Eugenio Chávez and Lupe Fuentes from Mora, who both attended the Lourdes archdiocesan seminary, asked the archbishop for permission to enter the Franciscan seminary in Cincinnati. In his report to Provincial Rolfes, Fr. Jerome Hesse noted, "They did not meet with any friendly reception, not by any means. They were told that as long as he lived, he would not give them permission to enter our seminary; he said he had received special orders from Rome to educate native secular clergy; needed 4 priests right now, etc., etc."[130] The next day Fray Angélico himself wrote an angry letter to Archbishop Gerken:

> I must get some feelings out of my system, for your Excellency has accused me of "working against the diocese," and I am not humble enough, like Fr. Jerome to take it quietly.... Remember that only 2 years ago, I myself presented Eugene to you, and I myself took him to Lourdes. I've never tried to dissuade him. I paid no attention when Fuentes tried to contact me about becoming a friar. It was only recently that I told them, since they themselves had their minds made up, to see your Excellency, and find their way, as I did mine despite opposition, for I also had my troubles.... If Eugene Chávez persists in not returning to Lourdes, I feel obliged in conscience, and as his brother, to help him in his choice. I do not want to answer to God if now he should lose his vocation.[131]

The same day, Fray Angélico also wrote to the Franciscan provincial to ask if Canon Law permitted the archbishop to prevent the boys entering the Franciscan seminary. He also noted, "A good prospect in one of my missions also wants to go. Should I send him without the Archbishop's knowledge? ... I'm feeling fine and ready for a fight."[132] The strong position Fray Angélico took against the archbishop in this matter perhaps made him reluctant to ask for an imprimatur for the manuscript of *The Single Rose* in 1942.

On August 12, 1942, the same day he informed the provincial he was withdrawing the manuscript, Fray Angélico wrote to Fr. Robert Kalt, the superior of his friary who was away, to tell him he was going crazy in Peña Blanca. Disputes among the friars about dividing the ministerial workload and his perception that his superiors judged his first five years of priesthood to "have been a failure" contributed to his depression about living in the friary. He had been assigned to give missions in other places and noted that he forgot his concerns when he was away, "but as soon as I return to Peña Blanca, the sight of everything makes me sad and mad at the same time.... I want to obey and work, but I am sincere in telling you that this house and its inhabitants give me a spirit of despair and futility."[133] Fr. Kalt had already noticed his depression; in July he wrote to Provincial Rolfes: "Fray Angélico has been down in the dumps, hardly saying a word, gloomy; and yesterday he came to me asking to go to Santa Fe till Saturday night saying: 'he wants to get away from here for it seems that he is going crazy.'" Kalt recommended that Chávez be transferred but was not sure where. If he were to go to the cathedral as he wished, he would have disagreements with the archbishop. "Is it wise to let him have his way in everything? I am afraid he is spoiled somewhat already."[134]

In the next few months Chávez began talking with the army and his provincial about enlisting in the military as a chaplain. In November *New Mexico Quarterly Review* published cantos VI, XII, and XV of his manuscript of *The Single Rose*. His poems "Cologne Epiphany: 1943" and "Lady of Lidice" appeared respectively in *Commonweal* and *America* in December and the following February. In April 1943, his short story "The Colonel and the Lady" about Bataan won the first prize of the Catholic Press Association. Archbishop Gerken died on March 2, 1943, and finally on April 17 Chávez received the official telegram from the army notifying him of his acceptance. On May 3 he reported to Harvard for chaplain school.

While overall Chávez's first six years of ministry were a stellar period of literary, artistic, architectural, spiritual, and ministerial work, he also became discouraged and was anxious to go overseas in 1943. In 1939 his new friends Thornton Wilder and John Gould Fletcher both sent him critical letters about his novel *Guitars and Adobes*, which he hoped to revise for republication. Despite their enthusiasm for much of his current writing, the negative evaluations of both of these accomplished writers must have been a difficult blow for Fray Angélico. While Fletcher responded positively to Fray Angélico's request that he review *New Mexico Triptych* in the *Saturday Review*, Wilder wrote that he hadn't reviewed books for years and only made rare exceptions. He counseled the young Franciscan: "The arts should be like higher mathematics, a purely disinterested realm. One trusts that intrinsic merit will find friends, advocates and the only kind of publicity that counts and has dignity— the mind of some reader sympathetically stirred to enthusiasm who *talks about the book*."[135] Although Fray Angélico would continue his abundant writing throughout his life, no other period matched the daunting and exhilarating pace of his first years in Peña Blanca. The kaleidoscope of poetry, fiction, religious, historical, and spiritual writing, mural painting, and church restoration, along with full-time religious ministry, established Chávez early in his career as one of the most prolific men of letters and religious figures of twentieth-century New Mexico.

CHAPTER FOUR

Padre in the Pacific

Art in the Face of Death in
World War II and Beyond

FRAY ANGÉLICO CHÁVEZ SERVED HIS country in World War II from 1943 to 1946 and again in the occupation of Germany from 1951 to 1953. His writing in this period offers literary, autobiographical, epistolary, reportorial, and testimonial voices with details of everyday life, broader themes, descriptions of battles and landings, and personal thoughts. These cultural traces of the cataclysmic war tell the story of an Hispano chaplain and the troops he served and suggest the key role that art, spirituality, contact with other cultures, and everyday routine play in periods of extreme social upheaval.

On one level, Fray Angélico's artistic production during World War II reveals the Freudian opposition between Eros and Thanatos, the efforts of the life instinct to prevail against the death instinct. In a period of extreme degradation, destruction, and death, even a modicum of the aesthetic partially wards off the expanding signs of man's drive to destruction. Santa Fe artist Eliseo Rodríguez, for example, painted portraits from photographs of the wives, girlfriends, and mothers of his fellow soldiers in army camps in Okinawa during

World War II.[1] For the artist/priest Fray Angélico Chávez, the aesthetic and spirituality were crucial modes of surviving the horrors of war. He wrote poems in encampments and chapters of a novel while waiting to be shipped home. Believing that he had only a few weeks' stateside leave in April 1945, he hurried to collect his poems for his second book. He rescued a beautiful statue from a smoldering church in the Philippines, put it in a bomb casing, and carried it home. But above all, he wrote prolifically at every turn of the war. Art and writing represented life in the face of death.

In other writing during his three-year tour of duty, Chávez the historian and chronicler documented both the extraordinary and the day-by-day details of training, troop movements, landings, battles, and daily life. Besides the monthly reports to the provincial with details about the material conditions and spiritual practices of the troops, Chávez wrote dozens of letters to the Cincinnati headquarters, often expressing deep feelings and poignant observations to his superiors, his surrogate "parents." He published several articles recounting his war experiences and short stories depicting war themes. In this wartime writing, Chávez's hybrid identity emerges, as he perceives himself as a religious, ethnic, and newly defined American subject. Later in the 1940s and on his second tour of duty, he published two books of poetry, translations, and booklets on the Santa Fe Archdiocese and the cathedral. He also began to conduct original historical research. Shortly after his discharge from World War II, he began researching the historical documents in the archdiocesan collection and the Museum of New Mexico and learned paleography with France V. Scholes. With his appetite whetted from his preliminary 1941 research about Santo Domingo Pueblo, he returned from the traumatic experiences of the Pacific war front with a deep desire to immerse himself in researching the history of New Mexico. After the war Fray Angélico embarked on a new part-time career as a historian, and most of his publications from then on were devoted to history.

Poetry, Chronicle, and Essay: The Formation of an American Identity in Wartime

Even before the United States entered the conflict, Fray Angélico's correspondence with Arkansas poet John Gould Fletcher after the Poetry Roundup in 1938 and throughout the 1940s turned to the subject of the new war. Fletcher remarked in a July 1940 letter from the MacDowell Colony in New Hampshire that he was busy "getting . . . adjusted to the world as Hitler would have it."² One week after Pearl Harbor, Fletcher wrote that he had moved into a new home, "in the teeth of this new war," and hoped that Chávez's hands were healing from the work on renovating the church at Peña Blanca and that he would be able to complete his new long poem (*The Single Rose*).³ In June and July of 1942 the two poets carried on an epistolary conversation about the ethics of writing poetry in the tragic times. Fletcher told Chávez:

> My own Muse (drained and disheveled because of the war, and for other causes . . .) has begun to show signs again of responding to a hard wooing which I have been bestowing on her for the last several months. I am now writing poetry again. As you say, in these tragic times it almost seems a selfish thing to do (Nero fiddling as Rome burns and the corpses of Christian martyrs line every highway) to write poetry at all. Yet, I believe that there are values somewhere in this vast and overwhelming cataclysm that good poetry and the other arts can only hint at, but which these arts *surely must preserve*—if only for some far-distant age and time.⁴

As Fray Angélico corresponded with Fletcher about the ethics of wartime writing, he sent his poetry manuscript of *The Single Rose* to the provincial for approval, noting that people had told him poetry would sell well in the stressful time of war. Although both writers questioned the appropriateness of writing poetry in such a time, they felt compelled to continue this literary work as one means of reasserting values in the tumultuous times. Art could help to preserve the ideals that war threatened.

As part of this cultural work, Fray Angélico participated in a conference on folk art and literature at the University of New Mexico in April 1942, along with Nina Otero Warren, Erna Fergusson, and others. One of the key themes was Pan-Americanism, which Fergusson emphasized, having just returned from lengthy study in Latin America. This may have influenced Fray Angélico's unfulfilled expectation that he as a Spanish speaker would be sent to Latin America during the war. Also that spring, he published a strong letter to the editor in the *Santa*

Fe New Mexican praising Calla Hay for her criticism of a book by O'Kane Foster, "an insult to my people and to American democracy." Foster flaunts his Aryan superiority, referring to Hispanos as "washed up" and "unwashed," according to Chávez.⁵ An insult to Hispanos is an insult to Americanism, Chávez implied, just as he was about to enlist in the service to help in the war effort as an Hispano and an American.

Shortly after the United States entered the war, Fray Angélico reconfigured his 1938 poem "Whose Broken Heart Is Brave." Republished with a drawing of the American flag and the new dedication "For those Our Boys have left behind," the new version of the poem attempts to comfort the loved ones of American servicemen by encouraging them to connect spiritually to the beauty and hope of nature around them:

> *Bright canyons are earth's wounds, the sunset flash*
> *Must gore the clouds, the sky, to paint the west—*
> *Why, Easter left unclosed one Wounded Breast.*⁶

Nature also undergoes a symbolic destruction like war and can remind us both of death and resurrection and healing.

After the German massacre and destruction of the Czech village Lidice in June 1942, Fray Angélico wrote the poem "Lady of Lidice," published in *America* in February 1943; the Virgin who is "the remembering lover / of every small town" looks down from "God's lofty City" with wistfulness.⁷ Chávez emphasizes only the expressive gaze of the Virgin rather than using factual phrases to memorialize those killed in the massacre. For his contemporary readers, the facts did not need reiterating: the execution of 192 men and boys throughout the day of June 10, 1942, in reprisal for the May 27 assassination of Reinhard Heydrich, chief of security police; the removal of the women and children to concentration camps; and the burning of the Czechoslovakian town. The simple poem, like the belief in the Virgin's eternal love for the villagers, stands in aesthetic testimony to the unspeakable details of the massacre. Spirituality, love, and the aesthetic are countervailing forces to the brutality of war.

Also before he enlisted, Fray Angélico published "Cologne Epiphany: 1943" in the Christmas 1942 issue of *Commonweal*. On May 30 and 31, 1942, Britain launched the first thousand-bomber raid on the city of Cologne in which 868 planes assaulted the city, causing massive destruction.⁸ Because the cathedral of Cologne contains the reputed remains of the Magi, Fray Angélico imagines an Epiphany for the destroyed city at the beginning of the new year in 1943. If the dead Magi could see the sky above Cologne, "A blinding skyful would they find, / The deadly Pleiades of war."⁹ In the current war, Herod still wishes to kill

> *the Infant Jew*
> *Who shakes the mighty with the plot*
> *Of brotherhood.*¹⁰

And Rachel, whose prayers God accepted, weeps for her banished children. The destruction of Cologne may give way to an Epiphany in the New Year that might point the way for the Jews to escape Herod/Hitler's persecution.

During his stay at Chaplain School at Harvard in May 1943, Chávez wrote "Washington Elm" in response to a granite marker on the campus that commemorates a tree under which George Washington reviewed his troops. Having performed drills in the same area, Chávez meditates on the struggle in which blood was shed to found the country that now requires more blood in order to preserve it. The no longer present elm Washington stood under reminds the poet of a tree on an ancient hill "where Another won our liberty / In blood, as Washington remembered still."¹¹ He advises the inheritors of these sacrifices not merely "[t]o leave remembrance of both trees to stone!"¹² Chávez situates his incipient wartime service within the American and Christian traditions of self-sacrifice for a greater good. As in "Lady of Lidice," poetry is memory.

Fray Angélico's prose about this period reveals that his training was rigorous and that he wished he were home at Peña Blanca. He lived in crowded quarters in Perkins Hall with three Protestant ministers, attended classes in the morning, marched in the rain, participated in setup exercises all afternoon, and had a study period at night. He loved eating at Harvard Square, especially at Jim Cronin's restaurant. He felt competitive with the Protestant chaplains and proud of his superior knowledge of religion.¹³

From June 1943 to February 1944, Fray Angélico was stationed at Camp Chaffee, Arkansas, working with tank regiments in a new division being built from the ground up. On his arrival June 8 it was "raining pups when I hit the muddy tar-paper shack camp of my outfit," and he was "drenched and sick for civilian life." He enjoyed the friendship of several other Catholic priests at the camp, which helped to keep spirits high, as did his visits to his friend John Gould Fletcher's home. Fray Angélico believed that many of the boys who would come to Camp Chaffee would be of Spanish or Mexican descent, an explanation of why he had been assigned there. He ordered copies of *New Mexico Triptych* to loan to his fellow Protestant chaplains.[14] Fray Angélico published the lighter poem "To a Bishop Unfrocked" in December 1943 in *America* in which he describes the sartorial modifications modern society has made to turn Bishop Nicholas into the figure of Santa Claus:

> *They've made a cap from your birette*
> *To pull about your eyes,*
> *A makinaw from your mozette*
> *Of unascetic size.*[15]

The bishop's red soutane became a trousered suit, and the name and saintliness of Nicholas were feminized grammatically by reducing his title "[t]o an unfinished clause."[16] Perhaps in the context of his rivalry with the Protestant chaplains, he writes, "The sects are loading him with chores / To make the nickels ring."[17] At the end, however, the poet humorously admits that he prefers the saint in the heretical attire.

Also that month, Fray Angélico published the essay "Noche Buena" in the *Indian Sentinel*, issued by the Bureau of Catholic Indian Missions in Washington, D.C.[18] Narratively and visually recreating Christmas Eve ceremonies at San Felipe Pueblo, he situates the beautiful traditions in the context of the war raging around the world. The Indians in this remote village on the Rio Grande feel the war because many of their young men have gone to fight, but they continue to observe both native and Catholic feasts in this stressful time. Perhaps because of seeing the monument to George Washington at Harvard, he reminds readers that the large adobe church at San Felipe was already old "when George Washington beat the Hessians one Christmas long ago."[19] As in Cincinnati, he proudly reasserts his ethnic and religious pride and Southwestern heritage when encountering Anglo American history. At San Felipe, the syncretic religious ceremonies bring Anglo visitors, natives, and Hispanos together in time of war, carrying on a long-living tradition in the face of war and death. Chávez emphasizes the hybridity of the ceremonies. He reads the gospel and delivers the homily in both Spanish and English, with a longer English version to benefit the many visitors who have come to watch the Indians dancing before the crib. "What! Dancing in church! Yes, indeed," Chávez notes, arguing that visitors find an authenticity here that is missing from the overwhelming Christmas commercialism elsewhere. "I think they came to San Felipe to find something that looked more like Bethlehem."[20] He describes the padre's walk through the "Biblical streets" of the pueblo and compares the scene of Indians wearing skins, bells, and shells to a painting of the Bethlehem stable with "half-clad shepherds gazing in awe upon the Holy Child in Mary's lap."[21] Even before he has seen battle, Fray Angélico asserts life over death in this narrative and visual tableau of a centuries-old syncretic religious tradition of the Southwest celebrating birth and life.

In February 1944 Fray Angélico was sent to California and then departed for Hawaii. While there he wrote "In Extremis," published in July 1944 in *Spirit*. With thoughts about the imminent deaths he would see in battle, and perhaps even his own, he writes stanzas for each of the areas of the body to be anointed at death in the sacrament of Extreme Unction. The anointing will burn away the evil that the eyes saw each day, the tears, the sirens the ears heard, and the rank perfumes from the nose; it will burn the lips with coals "to utter and taste Him / How sweet the Lord is," and evil will be branded out of his hands and feet.[22] About to depart for the Pacific, Fray Angélico, as other soldiers, imagines death's proximity and his role as chaplain. Similarly in "Lady of Peace," he describes leaving a lei for the Virgin in the Honolulu cathedral.

To say goodbye
Before we sailed away
To where men die.[23]

He hopes to replace it with fresh flowers on his return, but if he does not, he asks the Virgin to honor his vow by giving him

Sweet release,
And lay your leis where I lie,
And peace.[24]

He makes a manda to the Virgin promising flowers in thanksgiving for her protection. If he should die, the flowers on his grave would be from her, and she would grant him peace.

In early July 1944 Chávez's division left Honolulu for Eniwetok Atoll, and from July 21 to 23 the division made the landing at Agat in Guam. Fray Angélico recounts that after the brief stop at Eniwetok, there were "plenty of confessions from then on and communions at Mass every morning. Afternoons and evenings I'd slip my habit over my denims and stand by a rail studying the waves, and the fellows came, stood by and talked and got absolution."[25] Chávez was a first-line chaplain and went in with the first wave of the landing. Dr. Randolph Seligman, who became friends with Fray Angélico and was one of three men from New Mexico in the division, took part in the assault landing and went ashore thirty-five minutes after the attack started. Twenty to thirty enlisted men were already killed, their bodies stacked up, and many were wounded. The battle for Guam continued until August 10, and the 77th Division lost 248 men. Fleet Admiral Chester W. Nimitz visited the soldiers on August 12.[26]

Besides ministering to American servicemen, Chávez also cared for thousands of Chamorro natives on the island who were without civilian priests under the Japanese occupation. On August 7, he wrote a lengthy letter to *St. Anthony Messenger* that was published as an article in October 1944. He was greatly impressed by the native people of Guam, noting that he was "still the missionary at heart." As the famished people lined up for food from the Americans, there were no complaints or pushing. Because most were Catholic, Fray Angélico attributes their respectful behavior to "the fruits of missionary labors of many years." He administered many sacraments and was amazed one Sunday while saying Mass atop a knoll when the people on their own sang the same melodies of old Spanish hymns used in New Mexico. "Then I sang the Hail Mary and other Spanish cánticos, and to my delight and surprise, the old folks joined in! They had sung these songs in their youth when Guam belonged to Spain."[27] His ethnic identity surfaces in this distant island with the Spanish hymns. In his August report to the Military Ordinariate in New York, he noted that he said eleven Masses with 12,450 in attendance, and he performed sixty baptisms, forty-two funerals, twenty-one Extreme Unctions, and had not counted the numerous confessions and Communions. While in Guam, Fray Angélico also outlined a book project on the Catholic faith: "During a rainy spell on Guam when everybody stuck in his hole like a rat, I made a complete outline for a book on our Holy Faith—the result of instructing converts without reference books, which made one think more than ordinarily.... Well that MS got lost when my trunk disappeared."[28]

Fray Angélico felt that he was living like an ancient hermit in his three months on Guam, suffering from the fleas and mosquitoes and sleeping with lizards. Nonetheless, his literary talent and humor inflect his writing: "I can't tell you where I am, and it doesn't matter in this continent of water dotted with lakes of land. Am in excellent health, though I haven't slept on an Army cot, much less a bed for two months. The food, scientifically stuffed with all the vitamins, has afforded ample nutrition but no pleasure in the eating. (An excellent idea for the monastic cuisine!)" He wished for more mail from his superiors to help allay the "nerves on edge from exhaustion, unpalatable food, restless sleep on damp ground, itching skin from insect bites and rough chemical-treated denim." Despite the beautiful scenery he complained of "dengue fever which is like malaria plus terrible aches in all the bones...; this plus the 'runs' and you wish you were dead."[29]

Poetry helped Chávez transcend the difficult physical environment. "Of Toads and Such" (*Commonweal*, November 1944) humorously places the hard circumstances in perspective. Although in bright times he had loathed the sight of toads, as he crouches now in the dark mud of the tropics, avoiding bullets, the poet comes to appreciate them. As the "warty guests" devour deadlier insects, he wishes they could also alleviate the stings he has suffered, and now he understands how St. Francis sang their praises in time of war: "From Solomons to Burma Road, / Praise God for Brothers Newt and Toad."[30] While in letters and reports he chronicled his physical suffering during the battle for Guam and on the ship, writing poetry allowed him an aesthetic and humorous respite.

Although his unit shipped out to New Caledonia for rest on November 3, it turned course for Leyte on November 15 to aid MacArthur's troops. As they made their end run around the island before the landing at Ipil in Ormoc Bay, Fray Angélico suffered from dengue: "Have to stand on [the] bridge above the front gates to catch [the] sea breeze and keep from burning up; even black and green mottled camouflage on other ships gives me nausea." After two cans of cold beer, he felt better the next morning as they pushed ashore at Ormoc at 7:07 a.m. on December 7, the three-year anniversary of the Pearl Harbor attack. Fray Angélico's chronicle of the landing recounts,

> The great front gates open and out we scramble on the beach followed by tractors pulling trucks and cannon. There is only rifle fire, for the Japs were caught with pants down in a surprise attack behind their lines, the only one not preceded by bombardment from ships or planes. Defense stiffens, Zeroes and Betties strafe us all afternoon and we have fun ducking; but those that are hit make for the ships. One destroyer hit amidship, magazine explodes, sinks. Night falls, with rain in bucketfuls all night. I'm with about 200 men back of line which has advanced about two miles. Next morning we learn some 11,000 Japs had passed the night in a jungle across a rice paddy from us. The after-knowledge makes me feel queer.[31]

After capturing Ipil on December 8, the division fought a hard house-to-house battle for the city of Ormoc, the Japanese headquarters, on December 10. Chávez recounts that the old Spanish mission church was blown up because it had been used to store ammunition. He rescued a sixteenth-century statue of the Immaculate Conception from the baptistery and brought it home in a shell case. During most of the battle, he rode in jeeps with the wounded from the lines to the hospital stations. In addition to administering the sacraments to the wounded, he went from cot to cot washing out blood and slime from the mouths of those with chest or abdominal wounds who weren't allowed to drink water: "A messy job no one saw, but the look in the eyes of the fellows was reward enough."[32]

In "Christmas on Leyte," a letter written on Christmas Day 1944 and published as an article a few months later, Fray Angélico describes the quiet celebration, "although the big guns did their part in not making it a 'Silent Night.'"[33] The soldiers quietly sang Christmas carols while the artillery was booming. Chávez said three Masses at different gun positions during the day on Christmas Eve but no midnight Mass was permitted because even two candles would be dangerous in the blackout. Joining his unit for the Masses were men from other battalions who were about to leave on beach landings, and fortunately they returned without casualties. Because his vestments had not arrived, he wore a black chasuble with gold and violet banding and used the nonfestive attire to speak about the real Christmas in contrast to the tinsel and glitter. No mail or presents had arrived from home, and Christmas dinner consisted of canned corned beef and synthetic lemon juice, although the troops were promised that turkey would arrive the next day. The infantry suffered the most on the holiday, having to attack the enemy and repel assaults. Chávez warns that from his outfit's position the war seems far from over and most expect that there will still be fighting on Christmas 1945.

Even after the island was officially declared secure, battles continued. Humorously, yet with graphic detail, he recounts one nighttime sea attack as he was sleeping under a tank by the waterline: "Our men heard them coming and waited, then turned loose with anti-aircraft and tank guns, rifles and machine-guns; their burning barges lit up the night and their yells played an accompaniment to our thunder, I was told on viewing the wreckage and corpses next morning—for I

FIG. 4.1. Chaplain Angélico Chávez administering Extreme Unction in the Philippines in World War II, courtesy Palace of the Governors Photo Archives (NMHM/DCA), Neg. No. PA-MU-082.01.

had slept through it all! I never heard the end of that." Although he writes this under the subheading "The Sleep of the Just," his humor does not disguise the devastation, suffering, and death of the battle. In his December 1944 monthly report, Fray Angélico noted that he administered thirty-one Extreme Unctions.[34] After this second landing and the difficult battles to take Leyte, he reported feeling run-down and losing weight. He told the provincial that he had written to the Military Ordinariate but had not received a reply: "I don't know if you can withdraw faculties, else I'd ask you to put a scare into the Ordinariate. In spirit, however, am OK and ready for the next push if I am left here."[35]

Chávez helped himself in this difficult period when surrounded by death, suffering, and danger by writing poems. In February 1945 "Sea-Birds" and "Ave Maris Stella" appeared in *America*. The first poem lightly plays with the name and legend of the seabird, the storm petrel, named after St. Peter because of its apparent ability to walk on water. The name "Mother Carey's chickens" in English derives from Spanish and Portuguese sailors' term for the Blessed Virgin, "Mater Cara." Like the images of the Virgin on ships, the birds protect sailors by warning of an approaching storm.[36] Perhaps Chávez's memory of Kipling's reference to the birds in "Anchor Song" and the 1938 movie *Mother Carey's Chickens* combined with his shipboard experience during the war to inspire the poem. The first stanza humorously attributes the birds' name to old British seamen with its bilingual wordplay—"Chickens Matris Carae." These seamen also saluted the quarterdeck because it contained a shrine to Mary. Chávez asks the dear Mother with her blue apron to send the birds "back to Peter's ship and crew" and to the image of the Virgin, or a sailor in blue on the deck who would feed the birds.[37]

In "Ave Maris Stella," the poet recounts a night spent at sea in which the dark cloudy sky was like a coffin lid and the ship swayed like a hearse. One calls out for Mary Star of the Sea in such circumstances, and when a star flashes, the doom leaves:

> Once more the sky is sky afar,
> The sea is sea alight with foam,
> The ship a safe and cheery car
> On rolling hill-roads going home.[38]

When the night sea and sky remind him of the closeness of death, poetry enables him to invoke the Virgin's protection and imagine the ship is a car taking him home through the rolling hills of New Mexico.

In "Communion on a Troop Ship" (*St. Anthony Messenger*, March 1945), Chávez compares the Pacific to the Sea of Galilee, or Genesareth, where Christ preached from Peter's boat and then caught many fish after the men had been unsuccessful. In this war, Christ's disciples, now sensing death, "gather closely, dozens deep" to receive Communion on shipboard as they are being transported to battle. Although the well-named Pacific is calm, the men's hearts are stormy until they receive the sacrament: "But soon the winds and waves are tamed / As Thou awakenest in each breast."[39] The poem aesthetically amplifies Chávez's prose account of the increased Communions and confessions during the division's journey to the Philippines in July 1944, emphasizing the importance of spirituality for the soldiers and the biblical parallels to Christ's work with the fishermen on the Sea of Genesareth.

"Sistine Madonna" (*St. Anthony Messenger*, May 1945) may have been written before the war, developing a similar theme to his 1940 poem "Cherubs." Chávez also may have retained a strong mental image of the Raphael painting and composed the poem from this memory in the Philippines. What draws the attention of the poetic voice is not the Virgin, the Christ child, San Sisto, or Santa Barbara, but rather the two cherubs looking up from the bottom of the frame, "One chubby palm beneath a perky chin."[40] There are no angel faces beneath their olive skin, the poet argues. According to legend, Raphael replaced a cloud with the image of two urchins who peeked in his window at the new painting, and Chávez imagines them saying, "'It ain't two angels, sir—it's only us.'"[41] Just as Fray Angélico painted the people of Peña Blanca in his murals of the Stations of the Cross, he imagines that Raphael included common street ruffians in the painting devoted to important holy figures in Catholicism.

In "Pacific Island Cemetery" (*St. Anthony Messenger*, July 1945), Chaplain Chávez remembers the soldiers buried in the Philippines as he gazes at rows of giant cereus plants that look like "cross-shaped stars" and palm trees that resemble sentries: "A lovely sight to view, but oh! the roots, the roots . . ."[42] Like the roots of mandrakes that resemble humans, the bodies of the war dead with "twisted limbs and bloated bellies mottled dark" become erased by the earth that covers them. "Forgive us, fellows, for forgetting what we know. . . . But you we will remember blooming white, O souls / More glorious than the Pleiades or Southern Cross!"[43] Chávez's poem in one sense gives new life to the war dead by realistically writing about the violent destruction of the bodies we no longer see. Chávez's art and spirituality resignify the dead as stars glowing white and bright in the heavens. They are the roots of new life.

Fray Angélico also asserted life in the face of death in a prose piece styled as a short story, "God Provides for Home and Nation: Salute to a Six-Star Family." He proudly recounts his parents' contribution to the war by telling of their raising ten children, six of whom are on active duty in the war. By revealing his parents' struggle to raise the large family, he emphasizes life at the moment that he and many others are facing death. This abbreviated life story of his family is a temporary antidote to the death surrounding him in the Philippines as he wrote it.

His father, a carpenter like his own father, later became a politician and married the daughter of a formerly wealthy sheep rancher in northern New Mexico. During the next three decades they moved with their growing family to various towns and rental houses as work became available, always centering their life around the local church and school. "There was no piano, no job, and no home, when the eldest boy, then fourteen, decided to enter the Seminary 'way out East in Ohio.' They had to borrow money for his clothes and costly train-fare, but did it gladly, though here was the first potential breadwinner flying the coop."[44] Despite poverty, they patriotically bought war bonds, and their children volunteered for military service. Always, they deeply believed that God would provide. He asserts that God did provide "for them and for their country," listing the names of the six Chávez children currently serving their country in the armed forces. By writing his family's story into the larger historical narrative, he subtly begins the revisionist historical work he would undertake in the postwar years.

Chávez was allowed bed rest in a base hospital after the troops took Leyte and prepared to deploy to Okinawa. He gained ten pounds in two weeks but nonetheless was sent home on leave in March 1945. While he waited for departure the first two weeks of March, he wrote the first chapters of a novel, perhaps the unpublished manuscript "I,

John." He finished the novel the following January while stationed in El Paso awaiting discharge, and because the manuscript was "so minutely scribbled and abbreviated that it look[ed] like Roger Bacon's code," the stenographer had difficulty typing it. Chávez had to rewrite the entire novel more legibly before the typist could prepare copies. In February he sent it to Macmillan, but ultimately several publishers rejected it.[45]

After arriving in San Francisco on April 8, 1945, from the Philippines, and then going home to Santa Fe, Fray Angélico socialized with family and friends and began immediately to collect his poems to publish as a book. May Sarton wrote that one evening in April 1945 she was invited to supper at Haniel Long's house in honor of Fray Angélico who was home from the Pacific: "He brought a sheaf of poems to read to us," she remembered.[46] Immediately on April 14, the day he arrived in Santa Fe from overseas, he wrote to the provincial for permission to publish a book of his poems: "I have enough of old material, together with stuff I wrote abroad, to make up a book." He asked that the provincial reply by telegram since time was short. Having been told that he was only on a brief leave, Chávez hurried to arrange the publication of the poetry book, perhaps to counteract his experience of combat, death, and sickness in the Pacific.[47]

The provincial replied favorably, and Chávez wrote that he believed he would receive an imprimatur from the new archbishop who was "well-disposed towards the friars." With May imminent, he closed: "May our Lady in her beautiful month keep you and bless you!"[48] This timing gave him the idea for the title of the book, *Eleven Lady-Lyrics*, and its organization around a series of poems about the Virgin. On May 13 Archbishop Byrne gave his imprimatur, and in June St. Anthony Guild Press accepted the book. Dedicating the book to Archbishop Spellman, head of the Military "Diocese," and to his fellow chaplains living and dead, "whose superior zeal and accomplishments in our arduous mission draw my unbounded admiration,"[49] he notes, "There is no poetry, nor time and inclination for poetic musing, during actual battle conditions, of course; but afterward, in those doldrums when ceaseless rains keep one bogged in a miserable shelter, with nothing to read and no light to read by, or when those brief but noisome tropic fevers rack the body and rob it of rest, the literary avocation furnishes some surcease and comfort, since like prayer, it needs neither workbench nor tools, nor even light."[50]

This portable form of aesthetic therapy afforded Fray Angélico temporary psychological escape from the hardships of war. Poetry could be mentally composed and roughly scribbled when there was no light, and perhaps it attained greater intensity during the feverish insomnia of tropical illness. The poems created overseas in *Eleven Lady-Lyrics* are overcoded with the austere conditions in which they were written. Their meaning is nuanced by the death, suffering, and physical deprivation that shaped their creation.

Besides these poems published in magazines during the war, *Eleven Lady-Lyrics* has five other poems about war. "Gold-Star Son" describes the pain a soldier undergoes hearing of his mother's death as he fights in the Philippines. The central visual image shows him mourning silently and alone after the beachhead battle in which "[h]is fearless heart sang clear and sharp." Now his harp is broken, and "[h]e sits alone and lets his grief / Drench all of him like tropic rain." Chávez contrasts the boy's suffering to "Rachels mourning soldier-sons / With kin to comfort and allay." With no family to console him, the boy sits on the alien beachhead, facing the waters of his Babylon. Chávez ends with hope and the triumph of the persistence of life over death with an allusion to the sun shining again "[o]n sighing beach and dripping leaf."[51]

In "The Sea," Fray Angélico expands on a line from Mexican poet Enrique González Martínez (1871–1952), "Rose, have you ever seen the sea?" which he cites bilingually. Chávez invites readers to visually compare the ocean to the mountains he remembers from New Mexico. The blue waves in the far distance are like the sierras constantly seen from a train, while the closer green waves are like hills sloping toward the shore, and

> *down the stretch*
> *White horses race in foam-maned herds*
> *To sprawl exhausted on the beach.*[52]

Ultimately, the sea is an inadequate cemetery "[f]or heroes buried in the waves" because no rose wreaths or wooden crosses can mark the "endless merging graves." While the Mexican poet directs his thoughts from roses to the sea, Chávez prefers the memory of the New Mexico earth where roses bloom.

In "Arma virumque," which references the first line of Virgil's

Aeneid—"Arma virumque cano" ("I sing of warfare and a man at war")[53]—Chávez ponders what kind of poetry can be written about war. While many elegies treat the subject, they are too sad to utter. Lyrics and odes do not fit the bill, especially because odes seem to be written "in water / Ignorant of blood."[54] Perhaps epics like those of Homer and Virgil will be written about World War II:

> *Then might some bard of epic arts*
> *Sift glory from the grief of hearts*
> *When these are dust, and slaughter*
> *Ripe for Iliads.*[55]

Only long after the events, when the hearts that knew death have ceased to grieve, will it be possible for the slaughter of war to be aesthetically communicated through epic poetry.[56]

Although not an epic, another war poem first published in *Eleven Lady-Lyrics* tells of a heroic G.I. nicknamed "Pockets" Kirk. More adept at pool than work, Kirk enlisted, thinking that the uniform would attract women. Nonetheless, in the Pacific he risked his life many times and "pil[ed] deed upon deed, / In which he bested better-vantaged foes." When "at last he got it, rescuing his pal . . . / We wept, because his dream could not come true."[57] Having hoped he could return to the pool hall to outwit time again with his cue, Pockets lost his battle with time on the front. Kirk, the ostensible deadbeat who only wanted to play, became an unsung hero of the war, deserving a poem to remedy this oversight.

Chávez ends the opening section of war poems in *Eleven Lady-Lyrics* with the pacifist message of St. Francis. "Assisi's Fool" recounts the melancholy return from war of Francesco, the formerly jolly son of Bernadon. As "Assisi saw him walk with Peace," some stopped feuding, believing him to be "[t]ouched by a star."[58] Others continued to wage war, blaming Francis' changed nature on the lunacy of the moon. The continued war of brother against brother to the present, Chávez suggests, is part of what "people are." Despite this aggressive tendency in human nature, Chávez chooses to assert Francis' message of peace to end the section of poems about war. Believing he would soon be returning to the Pacific, he wished to assert life forces over man's death drive, as he urgently made publishing arrangements for the poetry book.

The eleven "lady-lyrics" referred to in the title appear two-by-two at the beginning of each of the five sections and at the end as an epilogue. Nine are about the Blessed Virgin, and two are about the female biblical figures Ruth and Esther. Written in the seminary when he was seventeen, "Esther" first appeared in *Cantares* under the title "My Lady Esther," and Chávez made slight revisions for the later versions in *Spirit* (March 1940), *Eleven Lady-Lyrics*, and *St. Anthony Messenger* (October 1947).[59] Although a poem entitled "Ruth" appears in *Cantares*, the one in *Eleven Lady-Lyrics* develops Ruth's story differently, but both focus on the image of her holding wheat sheaves in the fields as prefigurations of the manger's straw and the Eucharist. Chávez also includes cantos that would later be published in *The Single Rose* and poems previously published in magazines.[60] Collecting poems on diverse themes, Chávez follows those on war with seven on the sacraments, the six cantos that would form part of *The Single Rose*, and thirty-three poems on diverse and sometimes lighter themes. In a 1946 review in *Southwest Review*, Robert Hunt, companion of Witter Bynner, praised the volume on many levels but criticized the section arrangements that broke the mood. Indeed, readers must move from war themes to sublime, mystical experiences to humorous light verse along with serious pieces such as "Nun's Golden Wedding" and "To Rebecca Dead." But Chávez's ordering plan is evident as he separates and arranges the poems. The humorous verse provides relief from the serious emotional experiences of some poems. "St. Blaise," for example, lightly celebrates the implicit homonym of the saint's name that is invoked to cure "inflamed throats" with lighted candles that indeed might cause a blaze. Most significant in this rapidly arranged volume is that Chávez insisted on immediately asserting his identity as a poet after having faced suffering and death overseas.

Chávez's various forms of writing during World War II—letters, reports, essays, poetry, and a novel—offer multiple perspectives on his changing identity in which he continued to join spirituality, creativity, ethnicity, and a new understanding of American identity in a war that so strongly challenged G.I.s physically and psychologically. Believing that his ethnic identity would be tapped as a key asset as he volunteered for service, he focused on other aspects of identity when his Hispanic experiences were not used. During his training at Harvard, he highlighted his theological acumen in a perceived competition with other "PB" (Protestant Brethren) chaplains. At Camp Chaffee, after realizing that he would not be assigned to minister to Spanish or Mexican servicemen, he ordered copies of *New Mexico Triptych* to share with fellow chaplains, proudly asserting both his literary and ethnic identity. While stationed in Hawaii, his letters attest, he practiced solidarity with another minority group by defying segregation orders and insisting that a black soldier be given the honor of altar server at his Masses. Perhaps he remembered being erroneously told as a boy that the Franciscans did not accept Mexican seminarians. His letters subtly suggest that he was aware of racism in the service when he notes that he was assigned to minister to a battalion of black troops even though there were only a dozen Catholics in the group. By insisting that his black altar server stay with him when he returned to the white area, he shows his commitment to social justice, Christian love of others, and identification with another excluded minority group. Overwhelmingly at the Pacific front, he saw himself as a spiritual minister to the servicemen. But when his ministry involved recently liberated Filipinos whose religious songs were close to those of Hispano New Mexico, he proudly emphasized his Hispano heritage in letters to the provincial in Cincinnati.

Chávez also asserted himself as an American citizen, as he and the rest of the country redefined themselves during the wartime emergency as a unified, patriotic people who put their lives on the line to defeat Fascism. In his article about his "six-star family," he notes the contributions of his parents and siblings to the war effort, showing that the Chávezes, although poor, gave extraordinary assistance to the country in this time of crisis. Their particular story as Hispanos from northern New Mexico, he asserts, is a key part of the larger narrative of American history. Poems such as "Gold Star Son," "Communion on a Troop Ship," "Pacific Island Cemetery," and "'Pockets' Kirk" valorize and pay tribute to his fellow American G.I.s, as does the chronicle of his war experience, "With Fr. Angelico in the Service." In these pieces, he asserts that the soldiers about whom he writes should be part of the American literary landscape. His poem "Washington Elm" views the then current American war in the tradition of the American Revolution. During the war he wrote about American Christmas traditions and the modern Santa Claus. On his return to Santa Fe in April 1945, he quickly contacted his friends in the Santa Fe Writers Group, asserting his identity as an American poet by reading his sheaf of poems to them at a dinner party. His hybrid identity during the war was formed by his deep Catholicism, his ethnicity, and his sense of himself as an American. During his wartime experience he asserted his identity as a writer whose disciplined, consistent creation of written texts asserted life over death.

The Emerging Scholar and Historian

The life-changing experience of suffering, battles, and death in World War II gave Fray Angélico his most profound understanding to date of his role in world history. His readings of classical literary and historical descriptions of war during his rigorous education under the Franciscans were abstract in comparison to the firsthand experience of this cataclysmic historical event. Although he had published a few essays on historical themes in the seminary and undertaken some historical research for the essays on Santo Domingo Pueblo, after the war he began to immerse himself in research and writing history. He commented on the difficulty of getting poetry published in the postwar years when he explained to his superiors his desire to pursue historical research. Similarly, he was unsuccessful in finding a publisher for the novel begun overseas.

In September 1945 he told his friend Bishop Metzger in El Paso for the first time about a plan he had been thinking about during the war, "a wild scheme for the Indian Missions." Metzger encouraged him to write up the plan, which Chávez did while waiting to be discharged.[61] He corrected the proofs of *Eleven Lady-Lyrics* in August and November and waited impatiently for the book to finally be published in December.

Chávez spent much of his time in the first year after his return trying to obtain a discharge from the service. While ministering to many servicemen as the only priest at Fort Bliss in El Paso, he wrote numerous letters and unsuccessfully tried many avenues to speed up his return to New Mexico. He finally received word in late February 1946 that he would be discharged April 28 but would be given a promotion to major and sixty days' leave immediately. On the last day of his travels across the country during his terminal leave, he presented a sermon at a Mass celebrated in St. Patrick's Cathedral in New York City by Francis Cardinal Spellman entitled "Poetry and the True Nature of Man," during the Catholic Poetry Society meeting.[62] One welcome break in his struggle to obtain a discharge was in early October 1945, when he flew to Mexico City for nine days to attend the Inter-American Congress of Our Lady of Guadalupe. After his return he worked late at night on an article documenting the experience, "I Saw Her Picture." He notes that writing the essay was a manda or "promise" he made to the Virgin when he visited the shrine.[63] In the article and other letters written to fellow Franciscans, Chávez described the important historical event in which bishops, clergy, and dignitaries from all of the Americas attended the ceremony to mark the replacing of the fifty-year-old silver crown painted on the image of the Virgin with a new image of a gold crown. "At the close of the worst war in history, this coronation was a canticle of peace and a consecration of the entire Western Hemisphere to Our Lady."[64] He describes his inability to appreciate the beauty of Xochimilco after his war experience: "The 'islands' are covered with all sorts of flowers and flat-boats filled with them look like floating gardens. But the Philippine jungles were too fresh in my memory so that the black mud and smelly tropic water spoiled things for me."[65] The historical events commemorated in Mexico are part of the larger world history of the war he has just participated in.

Back in Santa Fe after traveling across the country during his sixty days' terminal leave, Chávez agreed to take on an important history-writing project on short notice. In three weeks in May 1946, he researched, wrote, and illustrated *The Old Faith and Old Glory*, a thirty-six-page booklet about the history of the Church in New Mexico in the one hundred years since the American occupation. Chávez hides his authorship in the anonymous publication of the Santa Fe Archdiocese, later noting that he was unsatisfied with the appearance of the booklet when it came back from the printer. In a caption under a photo of the new facade of the church at Peña Blanca, he writes, "Built and plastered by the Padre himself," omitting his name from the historical document.[66] Similarly he leaves himself unnamed when he notes that the archdiocese provided the war effort with three priests as chaplains. Only his signature on the front cover illustration names him specifically. Apologizing at the end for the book's brevity and omissions, he writes, "A sudden realization of the approaching centenary has forced us to collect data, pictures, maps, and write this account within the space of less than three weeks ... if any important facts were missed ... it is simply because the material was not at hand when the writer finally sat down to compile the account."[67] It is likely that during his cross-country trip in April, Chávez himself realized that August 1946 marked the centenary of the American occupation of New Mexico, and as soon as he arrived home, he approached the new archbishop for permission to quickly compile the history.

The Old Faith and Old Glory is strongly shaped by Chávez's recent war experience and the deep American patriotism in the country in the war years. Catholicism in New Mexico greatly benefited from the American conquest, Chávez argues, unlike what might have happened had the territory remained under Mexico, with the 1920s persecution of the Church under President Calles. General Kearny promised freedom of religion. Through the work of Archbishop Lamy and hundreds of priests and religious who came to New Mexico in the ensuing years, the Catholic Church recovered from its deterioration under Mexican rule after the secularization of the missions and the expulsion of the Franciscans. As the railroad expanded, Catholicism experienced a threat by encroaching Protestantism, Chávez argues. Between 1879 and 1891 these sects founded over sixty schools across the Territory and "blacken[ed] Catholicism in the eyes of simple folk . . . [with] canards about the evil secret lives of priests and nuns, the adoration of images, and other such lies."[68] Chávez argues that through the Spanish weekly, the *Revista Católica*, and the effective preaching of several of their priests, the Jesuits saved the day, greatly helping to correct the Protestant misinformation. Presenting a one-sided view of Protestantism in New Mexico before the ecumenism of post–Vatican II, Fray Angélico writes from within the dominant Catholic ideology of the time.

Chávez's proud Americanism overlain by memories of the recent war begins on the front cover with his drawing of the "makers of America in New Mexico," which was patterned on the famous photograph of the flag being raised at Iwo Jima in World War II. Now, in Chávez's depiction, the group raising the flag in the 1846 period consists of a trapper or scout, the soldiers of the Mexican War, native New Mexicans, and an Indian. Archbishop Lamy stands to the side to offer guidance, with the Cross of the Martyrs in the background to symbolize the faith the Spanish Franciscans brought. The intertext of the Iwo Jima photograph places the one hundred years of New Mexican Catholicism within the narrative of American history. Fray Angélico's optic perhaps unconsciously parallels Spain's ideology in the wars of conquest centuries earlier in which the interests of the Spanish Crown and the missionary goals of the Church were coterminous, harmonious parts of a whole. Chávez's overlay of the recent world war on his reading of the Church's history after the U.S. conquest powerfully reveals how the contemporary moment shapes historians' work.

Two of Chávez's pen-and-ink drawings frame the narrative on the front and back inside covers. The first, a map of the New Mexico settlements in 1846, has drawings of the period including the raising of the American flag, the Acoma mission, an Indian horseman, an Hispano driving an oxcart, and Bishop Lamy, who, the hand-lettered text notes, "found only ten priests in the whole territory." The inside back cover shows the map of the archdiocese one hundred years later in 1946 with many more churches and lists the current pastors. Complementing the Iwo Jima–like image on the cover, which represents 1846, Chávez uses a 1946 photograph of Archbishop Byrne and priests with the American flag on the back cover. These carefully designed visual brackets on the book enclose Chávez's narrative, the photographs he selected, and five other maps he drew to help readers visualize the progression of Catholic history in New Mexico.

From Church records and secondary sources such as Archbishop Salpointe's *Soldiers of the Cross*, along with his own experience of twentieth-century history, Chávez documents in detail the consistent growth of Catholic parishes and schools in New Mexico. He recounts the arrival and work of the many orders of nuns, the recruitment of priests and brothers, the training and ordination of native diocesan priests, and the construction of new churches. He proudly delineates the contributions of the Franciscans after their return in 1900, along with the hard work of other religious orders. He praises the reconciliation possible in America when after the French defeat of Germany in World War I, French-born Archbishop Pitaval consecrated his successor, Franciscan Albert Daeger, the son of German immigrants.

Chávez also overlays the history of the archdiocese with his pride as an American, a New Mexican, and an Hispano. He emphasizes New Mexicans' contributions to the Civil War, the Spanish-American War, and World War II—especially in the early years and the Bataan Death March. He proudly recounts the naming of Fr. José A. García as vicar general of the archdiocese after the war, "the first time a native priest has held any position of note since Fr. Juan Felipe Ortiz was Vicar for the Bishop of Durango before 1846."[69] While Chávez's pride as an American, a veteran, and a Catholic primarily structure this history, his hybrid identity also surfaces as he expresses regional and ethnic pride, and joins verbal and visual genres—written narrative, art, and photography—in his first book of history after the war.

After his assignment to the cathedral in July, he undertook two writing projects connected to his new living and work situation. His duties involved traveling to preach missions to the Spanish-speaking people, and Provincial Mollaun recommended that to help in that work Fray Angélico translate *The Way of the Cross* into Spanish. Fray Angélico suggested that he translate St. Leonard's Italian stations, which he had seen in the novitiate. He would include both English and Spanish translations, along with a brief history of the devotion and St. Leonard's work to promote the Way of the Cross.

By mid-August he sent the Spanish translation to Cincinnati. Fr. Honorius suggested cutting down the longer stations so that each would fit on one page, but Fray Angélico objected vehemently: "The translation . . . was to promote a Franciscan Saint (we are always talking about that) and that is why I made a complete and faithful rendering. . . . [I]f St. Leonard's meditations are to be mutilated I beg you to have my name deleted."⁷⁰ Fray Angélico reveals his commitment to historical accuracy and faithfulness to the original in the translation. In early October they still disagreed, and it was suggested that Fray Angélico instead translate another English version. In objecting, he asserted his ethnic expertise: "Each people has its *genius*, or mode of thinking and feeling. . . . Italian and Spanish are much alike, and that is why St. Leonard's meditations struck me as just the thing to translate."⁷¹ He proposed using smaller type and including a verse of "Stabat Mater" in Spanish under each of the illustrations. The following year the booklet was published under the title *El Vía Crucis de San Leonardo, adapted by P. Fr. Angélico Chávez, Franciscano*. Chávez joined his Hispano ethnicity and Franciscan identity in his translator's byline.

As he was preparing the booklet on the stations, he began to write a history of St. Francis Cathedral where he was assigned. An offshoot of his recently completed history of the archdiocese, the fifty-page booklet would be completed by spring for the tourist trade, Chávez hoped. In early December he reported that the manuscripts of the stations and the cathedral history were both ready for the printer. By early January he had given the archbishop the manuscript and a dummy layout of the cathedral booklet for approval. Besides writing the original 1947 edition, Chávez revised the booklet in 1968, 1978, and 1987, adding information on new historical discoveries and renovations made over the years. In 1995 the booklet was updated to include Archbishop Robert Sánchez's resignation and the installation of Archbishop Michael Sheehan.

The 1947 edition, titled *The Santa Fe Cathedral of the Royal City of the Holy Faith of Saint Francis*, is completely different from the subsequent revisions and is, in fact, another booklet altogether. The small figure of Fray Angélico in Franciscan robes standing by La Fonda, with the cathedral in the background, appears on the cover of the book in a photograph by Robert Martin. (See fig. 4.2.) Chávez's poem "Of Toads and Such" appears at the end, with a note that his book *Eleven Lady-Lyrics* is available for $1.25 in bookstores. Fray Angélico is listed as the copyright holder and as the author ("Text and Format by Fray Angélico Chávez, O.F.M."). In contrast to his anonymity in the book on the history of the archdiocese, Chávez prominently features his name along with visual and poetic signs of his identity at the beginning and end. Both his war experience and Franciscan identity overlay the booklet. Full of life after facing death in the war, he proudly highlights his name and identity in this new work making Church history available to the public.

Chávez begins the 1947 edition with a reproduction of an old painting of St. Francis in the cathedral, arguing that to understand the history of the cathedral one must return to the thirteenth century and St. Francis. The Franciscan discoverer of New Mexico erected a cross to establish the New Kingdom of St. Francis, and later the capital was founded as the Royal City of the Holy Faith of Our Father St. Francis.[72] Chávez chooses a visual motif to structure the pamphlet—the official herald or "arms" of the archdiocese, which emblematizes the history of the Southwest and the cathedral. To structure what he terms a "narrative in word and picture," Fray Angélico makes two main divisions in the booklet, "The Making of the Shield" and "The Restoring of the Shield," with subdivisions such as "The Cross and Arms" and "The Shield Blotted Out with Blood." Rather than writing a simple chronological account, Chávez creatively re-envisions the cathedral's history through this visual emblem whose shorthand he will decipher and expand in the larger verbal/visual narrative.

Chávez writes the booklet in literary style and includes small-typeface paragraphs at the bottoms of pages with miscellaneous

FIG. 4.2. Fray Angélico Chávez, 1946, School of American Research Image No. 7014, photograph by Robert H. Martin, courtesy New Mexico State Records Center and Archives.

historical information to augment the main narrative. Each chapter in the first half centers on a key historical date and the correlation of its events to the visual trope of the cathedral's coat of arms. Beginning with the first Spanish exploration, Chávez draws readers into the story of Fray Marcos de Niza: "One day in the year 1539, a weather-beaten man in a gray gown stood on a mound facing Hawikuh, one of the Zuni Pueblos. For the moment, he was the center of vast distances, whose horizons were rimmed with wavy blue ridges or broken by sharp terraces of tawny hues. Over all arched a depthless dome, like flawless turquoise." Ekphrasis allows readers to visually experience the key moment. Next, he argues that Coronado's 1540 expedition looking for the Seven Cities of Gold, and the deaths of Fr. Padilla and Fray Juan de la Cruz, gave the shield its colors of red and gold—symbolizing the colors of Castile but also the gold the explorers sought and the blood the Franciscans shed. Chávez continues the metaphor throughout the booklet, referring to Mexican independence and secularization as the fading of the shield, to later years as "The Restoring of the Shield," and the stories of the eight archbishops from Lamy on.

The readable historical narrative with its literary style and motifs interacts with many historical photographs and illustrations and brief historical vignettes explaining figures and events such as "Black Stephen" and "The Martyrs of St. Lawrence Day, 1680." Fray Angélico carefully explains in the latter that no one has established yet that all these men died for the faith, and the Church has begun investigations on them. These notes reveal the beginning stages of his historical research after the war. On November 20, 1946, as he was finishing the cathedral booklet, the Franciscan provincial asked him to begin research on sixty-seven friar-martyrs for possible beatification. Fray Angélico immediately agreed to take on the project and began checking manuscripts for data about their lives.[73] He also had barely begun research on La Conquistadora. In a small note on the statue in the booklet, he writes that a rare document about the confraternity already existing in 1685 was discovered in June 1947, without crediting himself. Sometimes the notes are polemical, as, for example, "Causes of Indian Massacres," in which Fray Angélico mentions various theories about the Church's repression of native religious traditions, corporal punishment, and the Spanish governors hanging medicine men. He notes that today some conservative Indians preserve ancient pagan customs and forbid Christian Indians to receive the sacraments.[74]

Later editions of the booklet are substantially different. *The Santa Fe Cathedral* (1987, updated 1995) omits the introduction about St. Francis and the motif of the shield and focuses more centrally on the cathedral itself. It begins with the "Oñate Conquest Period, 1610–1680," followed by succinct accounts of three successive eras. Now Chávez adds material from his extensive historical research. He corrects his earlier error about the first name of Santa Fe and notes that the title of the original church on the east side of the plaza was "Our Lady of the Assumption." He includes reproductions of Carlos Vierra's paintings of the Pueblo missions at Sandia, Acoma, and San Felipe to suggest what three of the successive Santa Fe churches must have looked like in 1610, 1631, and 1718. Fr. Alonso Benavides referred to the first church as a jacal or shanty when he came in 1626, bringing a statue of Our Lady of the Assumption, thereafter called "La Conquistadora." Benavides ordered a new church built, which lasted until the Pueblo Revolt of 1680.

In the mid-seventeenth century, the church's name became "Our Lady of the Conception" because Franciscans in Spain and its colonies were working to have the dogma of the Immaculate Conception established. The Franciscans dyed their gray habits blue in this period to promote their cause. After the reconquest, de Vargas erected a small temporary church behind the Palace of the Governors by the north town wall, dedicating it to St. Francis. This served as the parish church from mid-1694 until the new church was finished in 1718, which was placed forward on the site of the Benavides church and thereby decreased the size of the plaza. On the church's north side, the chapel of La Conquistadora was built. At this time, St. Francis became the patron of the church.

Fray Angélico emphasizes ethnic pride when he notes that probably the first native priest in what is now the United States was Don Santiago Roybal, born in Santa Fe in 1694. He served as the vicar of succeeding bishops of New Spain from 1730 until his death in 1774. Chávez digresses to explain why the people of New Mexico continue to identify as Spanish Americans and not Mexicans and have kept the language of Cervantes along with rural Castilian customs. Being only very briefly under Mexican rule from 1821 to 1846, they did not acquire Mexican national aspirations, language, and customs. While Chávez is correct that twenty-five years is a short period of history, he presents a somewhat unidimensional view of Hispano culture, rather than a more nuanced understanding that would take into account Hispano culture's hybridity and the elements of Mexican culture that also imbue it. In other writings at the time, for example, he proudly recounts visiting the shrine of the Virgin of Guadalupe in Mexico, a strong presence as well in New Mexico, as noted in his 1939 story "The Hunchback Madonna." Most likely, Chávez asserts Hispano ethnic pride so strongly throughout the booklet because he wishes to make central the role of Hispano Franciscanism in the church's history. He also more strongly emphasizes La Conquistadora in the 1986 edition and the importance of the appointment of Archbishop Sánchez.

Chávez describes the changes in the church during the tenure of various archbishops and unabashedly expresses his own criticism of some of the modifications. He explains that in the aftermath of Vatican II, Archbishop Davis was prompted to enhance liturgical worship by removing the "clutter of past centuries in favor of the more meaningful simplicity of former ages."[75] However, Chávez criticizes the "unfortunate destruction in 1966 of the hidden 1717 adobe apse (where the Cristo Rey reredos and the friars' stone casket had been), as well as the just as old sacristy next to it."[76] He comments, "But, sad to say, this entire renovation which was in undisguised modern steel-and-concrete construction, clashed entirely with the soft Romanesque look of Archbishop Lamy's original building. . . . It would take some twenty years for a remedy to be applied to the unfortunate situation."[77] He ends the booklet with pictures and description of the major renovation for the centenary in 1986 in which he played a major role. The revised booklet is overcoded and shaped by Chávez's own renovations of the cathedral and those he did in other northern New Mexico churches from 1937 on. He is both a historian and a participant/witness to some events he recounts.

In this flurry of research, writing, and publication as soon as he returned from the war, Fray Angélico also sought to publish his orphaned volume of spiritual poetry written just before he went to the war, *The Single Rose*. With the help of Dominican priest Fr. Vincent Kienberger, he received the archbishop's imprimatur and then sent the manuscript to Cincinnati on September 19, 1946, for censorship.[78] Having finally gotten these approvals, yet receiving rejections from several publishers, he asked permission in July 1947 to accept the generous offer of the Catholic printer who did the cathedral booklet to print one thousand copies of the poetry manuscript for the minimal fee of $300. Additionally, he arranged for Mrs. O'Bryan, who ran Los Santos Bookshop, to split the fee with him and publish the book under the bookstore's imprint.[79] After Fr. Cletus, head of the cathedral friary, offered to pay the $150 from house funds, Provincial Mollaun gave his permission for the arrangement on September 1. In the final days of December, the book was released, unfortunately too late for the Christmas trade as Fray Angélico had hoped.

Fray Angélico had written these poems as World War II began and believed that their spiritual message would comfort people in time of war. Rhetorically and thematically they bear similarities to the meditations in *Seraphic Days*, which he had recently prepared for publication. As he was remodeling the facade of the Peña Blanca church in fall 1941, his hands sore from the cement and lime, John Gould Fletcher wished him well on completing his new long poem in a letter written just after the Pearl Harbor attack. Although part of his tremendous period of creativity in Peña Blanca after his ordination, the volume is also overcoded with his early experience of the war, his difficulties with Archbishop Gerken, and the postwar period of January 1948 in which it was finally published. In March, May, and July 1941, he published one stanza of Canto 16 and Cantos 3 and 7; in March 1942 he published the prologue, and in November Cantos 6, 8, and 15. Chávez lists the piecemeal publication of much of the poetry in the volume in a note after the table of contents. Now in 1947–48, all of the poems could be published together along with the poet's own exegetical commentary.

Combining his characteristic impishness with the serious tone and subject of mystical poetry, Chávez pretends to be translating the Spanish mystical poetry of Fray Manuel de Santa Clara, subtly inviting readers to remember that his own given name was Manuel and that his hometown of Wagon Mound was originally named Santa Clara. Facing the title page is an ostensible fragment of the original document, with old Spanish orthography. In reality, Chávez wrote the long poem in English and translated part of the prologue to create a fake "original" in Spanish. He uses such spellings as "fermosa" and "fermosura" to imitate older Spanish spelling. He continues the pretense that he is translating the work of a Spanish mystic poet in the commentary, referring to "the religious" and "the would-be lover" whose poetry he is interpreting. In Canto 8 the mystic wishes he had a magic lamp like

Aladdin's to be able to call the Beloved at will. In the footnote subtle humor underlies the serious commentary: "The Arabian Nights, in which the magic word is **'sesame'** which the author confuses with the Hebrew word **'shibboleth,'** which was a password."[80] He himself is the "author" he refers to, and his carefully selected words in the poem did not involve confusion.

Fray Angélico also foregrounds his Spanish ethnicity by imitating the famous mystics San Juan de la Cruz and Santa Teresa de Ávila, "two illustrious stars of Carmel."[81] No one today is likely to attain the high level of these saints' mysticism, Chávez argues, and many who want to devote their lives completely to God fail because of their ties to the material world. These souls are unripe or "verdes," Chávez argues, writing bilingually both to assert his Spanish ethnicity and to preserve the pretense that he is translating a work in Spanish.[82] Similarly, several times he introduces Spanish expressions such as "ni pez ni res" (neither fish nor fowl).[83] Suggesting that Spanish expressions more aptly communicate his precise meaning, he writes, "Our Spanish tongue has a word for this rare combination of white and red, namely, **color de rosa**" and "but while the latter falls into the Beloved's arms, the former meets with a closed door, as we say in Spanish. (**Le dan con la puerta en las narices.**)"[84] Although Chávez uses Latin words as well, he connects himself personally to the Spanish phrases as if he were an insider ethnographer explaining his culture for outsiders. He proudly refers to "our Spanish tongue," "as we say in Spanish," "St. Lawrence, our first Spanish martyr,"[85] and "our yellow grapes of Malaga"[86] to assert his ethnic roots, as well as to playfully create the double meaning that the commentary has been written by the Spanish mystic Fray Manuel de Santa Clara.

Following the tradition of the great mystical poets, Chávez nearly doubles the size of the book by writing extensive commentary about each canto at the end of the long poem. The text and commentary function as tandem texts in which Fray Angélico engages in exegesis of his own literary creation, inviting readers to go back and forth between the two discourses. The commentary is both erudite and ordinary, with the teaching and moralizing of a sermon. Showing that he is both a reader and a writer, Chávez cites numerous biblical passages to support the mystical journey of the poet. Sometimes subtle humor teaches a lesson: "One would think that by this time this religious has learned, as most religious soon do, that the quest for perfection is a life of work and prayer and self-denial. . . . But no! he tires of the drab husbandry of meditation and self-sanctification and . . . laments his frustration with self-pity."[87] Through such commentary, Chávez bares the device of his own poetic composition, self-reflexively critiquing the spirituality of the first-person poetic voice he has created.

Like *Seraphic Days*, the poem and commentary emphasize the almost permanent state of imperfection of one who strives to be good. Now the self-admonition is displaced to the poetic persona of the religious striving for mystical union with Christ, and is especially articulated in the exegetic commentary following the poem. For example, "This need not mean that he fell into grave sin, or any sin at all; but for the pledged lover of the Beloved, any form of dissipation or mingling with the world, even in thought and affection, is in a way a breach of faith."[88] *The Single Rose* implies that the struggle against imperfection and toward union with the Beloved is perpetual. The long narrative journey that the poetic "I" recounts through the cantos focuses on the unfulfilled desire to see and possess the Beloved fully. Nonetheless, the poetic voice remains the desiring subject in the final line of the epilogue, "The love I love wants all or naught."[89]

In retrospect, we should also understand *The Single Rose* in the context of the upheaval of World War II, given its composition as the war was beginning, the publication of some of its cantos before and during the war, and Chávez's perseverance in publishing it as a whole shortly after he returned from overseas. The spiritually erotic level of the mystical desire in the poem constitutes an insistence on life in the face of death. The persistent striving for spiritual perfection in the poem and the longing for union with the Beloved are not to be defeated by man's drive toward death and destruction, patently evident during the long years in which the poem saw the light of day piece-by-piece and finally as a whole. Chávez ends the commentary with a challenge to readers to strive for perfection. Divine love, Chávez suggests, is perhaps the only effective remedy for the world's inhumanity.

In this period of immense writing productivity upon his return from the war, Fray Angélico continued his priestly duties, ministering to Hispanos in the cathedral parish and interrupting his work frequently for two-week missions around the state. Even though St. Anthony Guild rejected *A Single Rose* before the war, he persevered and published the volume later. Although the novel he wrote aboard ship was rejected, this was only a minor setback in the context of his immense productivity and success in the year after the war. His sense of his own role in history after military service, the historical research he did for the booklets on the archdiocese and the cathedral, and the provincial's request that he undertake the research on the friar-martyrs inspired him to move more completely into historical research as 1947 began.

CHAPTER FIVE

Re-envisioning History

Hispano-Franciscan Identity, Documentary Recovery, and the Creative Impulse

ELATED TO BE HOME AFTER the war, Fray Angélico Chávez worked energetically to publish attractive volumes of his poetry, commemorative booklets on the history of the archdiocese and the cathedral, and *El Vía Crucis de San Leonardo* for the Spanish-speaking. Fray Angélico's literary and artistic creativity underlies these texts: beyond the expected artistic vision of the poetry volumes, the three booklets that recover history also reveal the strong aesthetic vision and creative hybridity that he would not abandon as he committed his time more fully to the writing of history in subsequent decades. Whether including his own drawings and maps in the booklet on the archdiocese, Robert Martin's artistic photograph of Chávez on the cover of the cathedral booklet and his own poem on the back, or insisting on aesthetic integrity in the layout, illustrations, and length of the Stations of the Cross booklet, the emerging historian remained an artist. His abundant scholarly publications on history in the decades to follow would also include creative hybrid texts on history such as the 1954 autobiography of La Conquistadora, *The Lady from Toledo* (1960), and *My Penitente Land* (1974).

At the same time, Chávez's extensive work in history became an important new site of identity formation for him. Long before contemporary postmodernism's rejection of unidimensional and stable notions of self-definition, Fray Angélico insisted on his own developing and multiply conceived identity. In addition to the aesthetic and scholarly hybridity of several of his historical writings, from the outset of his career as a historian, he asserted his Hispano, Franciscan, and family identity. Although somewhat evident in his early essays on historical themes written in the seminary and the articles on Santo Domingo Pueblo done just before the war, Chávez's ethnic and religious identity strongly imbued his professional historical writing from 1947 on. From his position as an Hispano and a Franciscan, he sought to rewrite and correct history through careful study of primary documents that he had special access to as a Franciscan, and to correct previous documentary research as a bilingual, native Hispano.[1] Additionally, his early work in archival archdiocesan documents and secondary sources revealed the key role of his family ancestors in New Mexico's colonial history. In several cases, the information he discovered about his ancestors caused both pride and conflict. As a fair-minded historian, he negotiated the personal conflicts that certain discoveries caused between the role of his ancestors in history, his ethnic pride as an Hispano, and his Franciscanism. Fray Angélico's historical research soon led him to an expanded sense of ethnicity and family identity in which the entire Hispano community of New Mexico represented a single family ancestrally, culturally, historically, and spiritually.

Martyrs, Mysteries, and Family Ancestors

After the Franciscan provincial requested in late November 1946 that Fray Angélico investigate the documents in New Mexico about the friar-martyrs of the Southwest, he immediately agreed to do so. Finishing a two-week series of missions in early December, he wrote that he was glad he had taken January off so he could finish the projects and begin the work on the martyrs. Even this new historical project became overlain with his postwar relationship to military service because in early January he wrote to the provincial to ask permission to join the Army Reserve at the request of the state chaplain. Without Chávez realizing it, this apparently innocent request would soon lead to his being assigned to active duty and being taken away from the exciting research he began with such enthusiasm in the late 1940s.²

By January 7, 1947, he reported to the provincial that he was not finding much on the martyrs for 1538–1680, but what he was uncovering would help ascertain motives for the rebellion and how the friars treated the Indians in different periods. Because the written history to this point was by non-Catholics, Chávez hoped to approach the subject with what he termed "the right slant" that would include "a) the Catholic mind, b) the Spanish mind, c) the Franciscan mind." Within a month of taking on the project, he had decided also to write "the history of the old Spanish times in New Mexico from the friars' point of view, for they are the chief protagonists after all. This will throw light on the martyrdoms, and whether they can be called such in a canonical sense."³ Although he focused on this limited historical perspective, Chávez understood his work as revisionist history from the start. The written documents the Franciscans had left and his own perspective as a twentieth-century Catholic and Franciscan missionary would shape the history he would write. By late February he had decided to undertake "a full History of THE CUSTODY OF THE CONVERSION OF ST. PAUL in New Mexico from 1539–1925" (the Franciscans) and had begun to write data on all the old friars on large index cards as he uncovered information. The scope of his first large historical project was enormous: "First I'll tackle all published books and publications, and from there follow up original sources for correct translation and interpretation, then I'll go through unpublished manuscripts which are legion here in Santa Fe and the university of Albuquerque. . . . Then there are the old parish registers in the archiepiscopal archives, the province, and some parishes." Conceding that it was a monumental task, Chávez predicted he would complete it in ten to fifteen years.⁴

Marc Simmons describes Chávez at this point as "bitten by the documentary bug."⁵ Fray Angélico became quickly enthralled by the wealth of new material he had been asked to work with in this life-changing assignment and elatedly began to pursue multiple research directions that had little to do with the provincial's initial request. Although he justified the new projects as providing background for the study of the Franciscans, he ultimately did not pursue that project due to lack of primary source information. Finally at this time, Fray Angélico had found a scholarly field that fit him perfectly. It was as if his youthful fascination with Fray Junípero Serra and the Franciscan legacy in New Mexico had not only led him to becoming a Franciscan, but to charting a new course as a historian to document multiple facets of the narrative of his land. At age thirty-six and a veteran of a devastating war, Chávez was not engaging in youthful experimentation. He had found his intellectual calling and would not abandon this work until physical disabilities prevented him from writing in his eighties. His first enthusiastic historical discoveries appeared in "The Archibeque Story" and "The Mystery of Father Padilla" in *El Palacio* in August and November 1947. He also wrote "The Gallegos *Relación* Reconsidered" in early 1947, but it took many months to be vetted by *New Mexico Historical Review* and did not appear until January 1948. In fall 1947 Fray Angélico wrote about his discovery concerning the Doctrine of the Assumption in a 1609 painting in the mission church in Galisteo.[6] The article, "An Ancient Painting of the Assumption in the U.S.," published in May 1949, will be discussed later.

Chávez wrote "The Gallegos *Relación* Reconsidered" in early 1947 at the time of his initial research about the early missionaries. His excitement about his new discoveries as a historian and a revisionist decoder of texts pervades the piece. He writes in an authoritative voice, unabashedly articulating his sense of personal expertise on the subject as a Franciscan, despite his status as a neophyte historian. It is as if he is saying, "This is *my* history; the others have told it incorrectly." His pen name, Fray Angélico Chávez, linked him to the early *frailes* he was writing about, and he proudly refers to himself in the contributor's note as "New Mexican poet and acting church archivist at the Cathedral, Santa Fe, New Mexico." Even though his provincial did not agree to assign him as cathedral archivist, he gave himself the lower-case title in this article as a means of validating his work and publicly establishing his expertise on the subject. Although he concedes that the impetus for his new discoveries was the hunch that Gallegos had lied in his *Relación* "for his own ends," this intuition led him to a careful textual examination of the Gallegos document and other reports that confirmed his suspicion.[7] Masterfully, he contests the accepted notion that eyewitness testimonies are the most accurate historical documents and aims to re-center the leadership role of Fray Agustín Rodríguez that Gallegos underplays in his chronicle of the events.

Working with a copy of the original Spanish text of the *Relación*, Chávez argues that the common soldier and chronicler Hernán Gallegos had his own agenda and that his attempt at self-aggrandizement pervades the document. Gallegos suggested that the ailing Capitán Chamuscado was the leader of an expedition (when no military expedition as such had been approved) and that he merely brought the friars along for the trip. In fact, Chávez argues, Fray Agustín Rodríguez had proposed the journey for evangelization, and the viceroy approved it and allowed volunteer soldiers to accompany the friars only to protect them. Chávez also argues that Gallegos did not write the journal day-by-day as required and therefore made mistakes such as claiming that the group departed one location on September 28, traveled four days, yet arrived at the new place on the feast of San Miguel, which was celebrated September 29. In his deposition to the viceroy, Gallegos omits crucial information about Fray Santa María who allegedly defected. Although the extant version of Gallegos' *Relación* mentions this key event, Chávez finds disturbing its absence from other contemporary documents, suggesting that Gallegos perhaps added the information to a later copy of the *Relación*. Asserting his identity as a Franciscan, Chávez challenges Gallegos' contention that Santa María left without his superior's permission: "Had Santa María left without permission, I am certain as a Franciscan that Fr. López, his religious Superior, would have signed the protest also. If we only had the Chronicle which the friars undoubtedly kept faithfully (this I also know as a Franciscan). But it was lost, either when López and Rodríguez were later killed, or else when *Santa María was slain*."[8] Chávez inserts himself personally as a Franciscan and a chronicler into the article. Having written the Peña Blanca House Chronicle, Chávez seems almost personally to identify with Fray Santa María, whom he believes might have served as the Franciscan chronicler during the sixteenth-century religious expedition.

In addition to his personal knowledge of the long-standing practices of the Franciscan Order, Fray Angélico brings together several accounts of the events, mindful of how stories change over the years. After reconstructing a more reliable version of the deaths of the three Franciscan missionaries who worked in New Mexico in 1581–82, he strongly concludes with a harsh critique of the "more than two centuries of blood and tears and constant failure [of evangelization], because of unscrupulous little 'conquerors, colonizers, and discoverers,' and '*escribanos*.'"[9] He argues that soldiers such as Gallegos with personal ambitions and agendas hindered the work of the missionaries for over two centuries, leading to the "tragic deaths of so many Franciscans."[10] This product of Fray Angélico's early research on the Franciscan martyrs, as Marc Simmons points out, "won [him] admission to the select fraternity of Southwest historians"; noted University of California at Berkeley historian Herbert Eugene Bolton, whose former graduate students' work the article on Gallegos criticized, later told Chávez of his high regard for the article.[11]

Fray Angélico also published two shorter historical pieces in *El Palacio*. He commented to his superior that he wished to preserve his research in print, "which is more compact and permanent than typed or handwritten notes," and that he wrote the second article on Fr. Padilla to repay the museum staff "for all the courtesies and help given me in my work."[12] He wrote "The Archibeque Story" quickly in August 1947 after reading an article in *New Mexico* magazine that his new research in the Church archives disproved. Fray Angélico's attention was probably drawn to this mistake in historical accounts because it involved the names of several of his ancestors, which he had seen in the marriage records. His careful research and calculations revealed that the Frenchman Juan de Archibeque, whom historians believed had ambushed and shot the famous explorer La Salle and was later murdered in retaliation by the Frenchman Cavelier, was not the man killed in the latter's attempt at vengeance. The marriage records of the time proved that the Juan de Archibeque who came to Santa Fe with the de Vargas reconquest in 1693 and who was later killed by Cavelier was in fact the son of the man thought to have killed La Salle: "[A]nd so Cavelier avenged himself on an innocent man while his victim never knew exactly why he died."[13] Fray Angélico's research revealed that the elder Juan de Archibeque petitioned to marry Manuela de Roybal, one of Chávez's own maternal ancestors, and that his son Juan married Manuela's sister María de Roybal three years earlier. The younger Juan was a mere boy at the time of La Salle's murder.

Similarly, "The Mystery of Father Padilla" (November 1947) clarified a case of mistaken identity in popular legend.[14] The story claimed that the body of Fray Juan de Padilla, who accompanied Coronado in 1540, was buried in the sacristy at Isleta and mysteriously rose to the surface of the earth about every twenty years, miraculously preserved from complete decay. Chávez wondered why previous ecclesiastical investigators who disinterred the body when it rose and who wrote reports failed to examine the burial records at Isleta to see that the friar interred there was not part of the Coronado expedition, but rather the eighteenth-century Franciscan, Fray Juan José de Padilla, who died and was buried on the same day, February 5, 1756. Chávez uses baptismal, marriage, and burial records to chart the missionary activities of the eighteenth-century priest. He transcribes the first and second burial records, which "had escaped the notice of subsequent investigators."[15] The second entry (1775) alludes to the violent death of the prelate, "a puñalados" (by stabbing), and Chávez speculates that this would not have been at the hands of Indians or it would have been classified a martyrdom. The third document written in 1819 when the body is again disinterred alludes to a scar behind the ear. When the well-preserved corpse is again officially examined in 1895, Chávez wishes that the report had included information about any additional stab wounds. Having established the true identity of the buried friar, he poses two problems at the end of the article: "Who killed Padre Padilla and why, and what preserves the body and makes it rise?"[16] The fascinating preserved body becomes a text for Chávez to decode and explain, using contemporary documentary accounts of its material state at each stage.

Five years later he published a follow-up article, "A Sequel to the 'Mystery of Father Padilla'" in homage to another recently deceased Franciscan who served at Laguna, Fr. Agnellus Lammert. He reprints a letter that Fr. Agnellus wrote to him on March 11, 1948, reporting on a new exhumation of Fr. Padilla on March 9 prompted by Chávez's November 1947 article. He encloses a copy of the official report (which was supposed to be kept secret) along with his own copious observations as a witness to the disinterment and reburial. He tells Fray Angélico: "I examined the mummified torso as closely as I could but did not find any marks of a knife. (If he was stabbed it might have been in the neck—we did not turn over the body.)"[17] Fray Angélico must have been frustrated to learn that although his article prompted the new exhumation, and he was the primary Franciscan expert on the subject, he was not able to witness the disinterment. We do not know if he was invited or if any attempt was made to include him. He had heavy mission work during this period that required frequent travel, and on March 10 he wrote to the provincial from St. Vincent's Hospital where he was suffering from the flu and confined to bed rest for a week on the doctor's orders.[18] Perhaps his illness prevented him from attending the disinterment. He waited until after Fr. Agnellus' unexpected death in September 1952 to publish the new information as a tribute. Much later in his 1968 *Coronado's Friars*, Fray Angélico adds to the narrative of the eighteenth-century missionary: "Fr. Juan José de Padilla . . . arrived mysteriously wounded, and seeking the aid of Fr. Pascual Sospedra, at the mission of Isleta. He died after receiving the last sacraments and was buried in a hollowed-out log. The rough casket rose to the surface in June 1775. . . . A board floor over the heavy beams, installed in recent years, now conceals any further phenomena of this nature."[19] Fray Angélico would have to be content with other people's reports about the mysterious corpse buried so close to him in New Mexico.

While Fray Angélico identified traces of himself as a Franciscan and an Hispano in the historical documents he examined, his research also shaped his identity when he uncovered information on his family. In the early articles about his noteworthy ancestors in colonial New Mexico, he struggled to paint a fair picture of his forebears, including some who were involved in controversy. In the April 1948 article on Don Fernando Durán de Chaves, an important figure in the Pueblo Revolt, Fray Angélico begins with the figure's grandfather, Don Pedro Durán y Chaves, who poses a personal conflict for the Franciscan writer-priest who is also a Chávez: several complaints to the Inquisition accuse his forebear of actively undermining the friars' mission to the Indians in New Mexico by taking the side of the local military government against the Franciscans. Don Pedro led a punitive campaign against the Jemez Pueblos in 1624 and was accused of being a crony of the nefarious governor Don Juan de Eulate. Fray Angélico argues, however, that the charges did not suffice for a citation from the Holy Office. He grants that Don Pedro, caught up in the political struggles of the time, sided with the military government; he proudly notes, however, that Don Pedro's son Don Fernando Durán de Chaves was "unlike his father, [and] sided rather with the Franciscans."[20]

Don Pedro's grandson Don Fernando escaped with his family during the 1680 Pueblo Revolt. In 1693 de Vargas gave him the honor of carrying the standard of Nuestra Señora de los Remedios in the re-entry into Santa Fe. Chávez infers that in 1704 de Vargas died in the Chávez home because Don Fernando and his son signed as witnesses of de Vargas' will. Don Fernando suffered when his eldest son, Bernardo, died in an accident in 1705 and again when he learned in 1709 that he had fathered a daughter before his marriage. As his family began to lose power in the region, he and his sons were arrested for savagely attacking the new alcalde of Alburquerque, calling him a "mulatto-dog" and "un perro Indio Griego."[21] Chávez characterizes Don Fernando as "a man who was brave to the point of recklessness and pious to the core."[22] This early research on family names led eventually to his 1954 *Origins of New Mexico Families* and his 1989 *Chávez: A Distinctive American Clan of New Mexico*.

Complementing the article on the Chávezes is the August 1948 piece on his maternal uncle seven generations removed, El Vicario Don Santiago Roybal, and several other maternal ancestors. Roybal was the highest-ranking clergyman in New Mexico for over four decades as the vicar and ecclesiastical judge representing the bishop of Durango from 1730 to 1774. A native New Mexican, Roybal managed to become educated at a time when there were no schools. His father, who had fought with de Vargas' troops in the reconquest, sent his son to study in Mexico where he was ordained. Roybal's maternal great-grandfather, Francisco Gómez, had held the banner of the Inquisition at the solemn Mass Fray Alonso de Benavides celebrated in Santa Fe in 1626. Gómez was a violent critic of some friars and unpopular with political leaders. He was accused of secretly practicing Judaism, and after his death, his son was tried before the Inquisition for heresy and being a crypto-Jew. The son, Francisco Gómez Robledo, exonerated himself, his father, and his brothers, and Fray Angélico argues that though he might well have been of Jewish extraction, he was a staunch Christian centrally involved in the Confraternity of La Conquistadora. Chávez provides details on the difficult relations between the secular clergy and the Franciscans in which his ancestral uncle Fr. Roybal was strongly involved. But he praises the cleric's integrity and morals, despite "his youthful show of aggressiveness in the use of his high office"; Chávez notes, "He was certainly one of the great men of New Mexico—perhaps her greatest native son. As regards our entire country, he is, unless the contrary can be proved, *the first man born within the present boundaries of the United States to become a priest.*"[23] Chávez manages to negotiate various tensions between family, ethnic, and religious pride to accurately present the information he has uncovered, giving testimony to the complexities of history.

La Conquistadora as a Paisana

During his first two years conducting historical research while assigned to the Mission Band at the Santa Fe cathedral, Fray Angélico threw himself into his newfound scholarly work. He told the provincial that he put more time into this research than a pastor or assistant did on pastoral work. He lived as a hermit, foregoing visits to confrères at other missions and his much-loved fishing trips in the summer. He also worked long into the night; instead of examining documents in the chancery, "with the good Chancellor's knowledge, [I] sneak the documents back to my room a few at a time."[24] This enthusiasm and dedication to work produced a wide array of copiously researched articles. At the same time that he was writing on Archibeque, the Gallegos *Relación*, Fr. Padilla, the Chávezes, and the Roybals, he wrote three articles on La Conquistadora, two others on ancient paintings of the Blessed Virgin, and several more popular-style articles to disseminate his historical findings to a wider audience.

In late November 1947, Fray Angélico told the provincial that he was working on a book-length article on Our Lady of the Rosary (La Conquistadora) that spanned the entire period of Franciscan history in New Mexico using previously unknown material. Besides preaching three full missions and two retreats that fall, he had managed to conduct this research. He especially enjoyed the mission and retreat work in Albuquerque because it allowed him to look up manuscripts in his spare time at the university library, while in contrast, the stay in mountain villages "was a torture" with the icy sierra winds. He took notes to work on while on assignment there to help him forget the cold.[25] On December 9 he wrote that although he thought he had all the material for the long article on La Conquistadora, "she smiled on me recently by leading me to most important fragments that will upset historical theories." Additionally, he had sent Fr. Herculan Kolinski in Cincinnati a projecting wood sliver from behind the statue's ear for identification; Fr. Herculan and a university scientist were able to classify it as willow wood but could not identify the country it came from. On December 26 he wrote that he was following up on leads that pointed farther back into the sixteenth century for the devotion to the statue.[26] Although Fray Angélico was experiencing bouts of depression in these months, his new historical discoveries and research helped him to come through the difficult time. His research not only helped his postwar adjustment, but resulted in a landmark two-part article on La Conquistadora in spring 1948 and Dr. Sylvanus Morley's invitation to republish the articles as Chávez's first book of history.

In April and July 1948 his groundbreaking study of the ancient wooden statue's history was published, correcting errors in previous accounts and dating the devotion in New Mexico much further back than previously believed.[27] Concerned that historians viewed as legend the popular stories about Hispanos' devotion to the statue, he documented the earliest references to La Conquistadora in the surviving records. Chávez proposed that the three-foot-tall wooden statue of the Blessed Virgin was the one that Franciscan father Alonso de Benavides brought to New Mexico in 1625 under the title of Our Lady of the Assumption. Although many believed that the statue had first come with the reconquest, Chávez documented the existence of the Conquistadora confraternity earlier in the seventeenth century.[28] Hispano settlers who fled to El Paso after the 1680 Pueblo Revolt carried the statue, and it accompanied de Vargas on his second campaign of reconquest in 1693. Chávez demonstrated that the de Vargas party brought only a banner with an image of the Blessed Virgin on the first trip to Santa Fe in 1692, not the revered statue. In 1693, during the battle to retake the territory, the statue was placed on a makeshift altar outside the town. Fray Angélico disputes the longstanding legend that de Vargas made a vow to repay the Virgin, should he be victorious over the Indians, by building a chapel on the site and holding yearly processions in thanksgiving. There is no mention of such a promise in de Vargas' journal, and Rosario Chapel was not built until 1807. Rather, de Vargas resolved to build what is now the north chapel of St. Francis Cathedral, although he died before it was constructed in 1717.

Chávez's creative deduction that the statue came to New Mexico in 1625 caused him great joy, as Pedro Ribera Ortega, a former altar server for Fray Angélico, remembers. Ortega told historian Marc Simmons that Chávez was elated one morning before Mass because he had found a document recording the dimensions of the packing case enclosing the statue Fr. Benavides brought with him—dimensions that corresponded to those of La Conquistadora.[29] He therefore proposed in the 1948 articles that the original statue depicted the Assumption of the Blessed Virgin and was displayed in the *parroquia* dedicated to the Assumption, which Benavides saw when he arrived in 1625, and later in the new church. Sometime in the next thirty years, a confraternity dedicated to Our Lady of the Rosary was founded and adopted the statue as its patron. In the decades before 1680, the statue was "mutilated," as Chávez terms it, when "puppet arms" were attached to it so that it could be dressed as Our Lady of the Rosary. Chávez theorizes that although people referred to the statue then as "Nuestra Señora del Rosario," they also remembered that it had arrived in the days of their forebears and therefore also called it "La Conquistadora."

Fray Angélico reveals that the earliest record of a *mayordomo* of La Conquistadora's confraternity was one of his own ancestors, the son of Major Francisco Gómez who had accompanied the statue to New Mexico. Although Gómez's son, Francisco Gómez Robledo, was imprisoned, tried, and acquitted by the Inquisition from 1661 to 1664 after he was accused of being a crypto-Jew, he remained president of the confraternity throughout his ordeal and until his death in 1684.[30] Fray Angélico brings his expertise on Church history and religious traditions to his reconstruction of the statue's history, and likens his work on the early documents to a jigsaw puzzle whose complicated pieces he attempts to put together but that has pieces still missing, to be filled in later.

Chávez's initial historical writing on La Conquistadora drew him into the aesthetic aspects of the statue, as he documented its garments and physical appearance in various periods and the reconstruction undertaken by Gustave Baumann in 1930. Besides the damage done during two centuries of frequent changing of the statue's clothes, its base had been sawed off to fit it into a niche, which Chávez terms an act of vandalism. He describes the wear and tear on the statue in detail: "The face . . . was brittle and ready to fall off . . . ; some of the fingers were broken off; the tip of the bent right knee had also been sliced off."[31] Chávez criticizes the "unskilled and reckless hacking" of the statue's head when someone decided that a human hair wig would look better than the beautiful "original carved locks framing her face . . . parted in the middle and flow[ing] down to the shoulders, revealing only the lobes of her ears."[32] Chávez was pleased that Baumann, "a real artist," repaired this damage in his 1930 restoration.[33] Fray Angélico also intervened into the aesthetics of the statue by encouraging local women to make new dresses following the description of the original style of dresses in the documents he found. He was concerned that the elegant dresses of past centuries had been replaced by "the flat-chested, rear-bustle Victorian look," even now in the 1940s.

Aesthetics also played a key role when the articles were republished as a beautiful book in August 1948. Chávez told the provincial in March 1948 that the editors of *New Mexico Historical Review* "were so crazy about [the article] that the famous Dr. Morley wants to publish it in book form also!"[34] Archeologist Sylvanus Morley put the articles together and arranged for artist Jean Charlot to paint the image for the cover. Fray Angélico was thrilled with the five-color cover and the beauty of the volume.[35] The renowned French artist Charlot had worked with Diego Rivera in the early 1920s painting murals and as the archeological artist at the ruins of Chichén Itzá in Yucatán. When visiting Dr. Morley in Santa Fe, he agreed to do the cover illustration and title page vignette for the book on La Conquistadora. With an edition of two thousand copies, the books sold for only two dollars to cover expenses. The beautiful silkscreen cover in light pastels over an ivory background depicts the Santa Fe Virgin in large scale over two much smaller buildings representing the church and town. As in Fray Angélico's own drawings for *New Mexico Triptych*, the larger-than-life supernatural figure hovers over the tiny images of mortals below. In contrast to the statue's much smaller actual size, the enormous image in Charlot's illustration suggests that La Conquistadora is a benevolent supernatural figure perpetually guarding the small mortal villa of Santa Fe. The blue and gold visual pattern silk-screened on the back cover suggests the design of a beautiful brocade garment for the statue. Holding rosary beads and the Christ child, La Conquistadora wears a wig and a tall gold crown along with the regal garment, reminding viewers of the statue's earlier role as Our Lady of the Rosary and the royal attire originally used to dress her.

The aesthetics of Fray Angélico's first book of history was augmented by the images of his friend Robert Martin who photographed the statue without the dresses to show the fine workmanship of the original carver and of Gustave Baumann in his 1930 restoration. Fray Angélico had encouraged the women of St. Francis Parish to sew new dresses for the statue, one of which was made from Archbishop Lamy's cope. Martin's photograph of the statue in this attire during its week in Rosario Chapel in June 1948 is the book's frontispiece. Another photograph (following page 54) of the procession returning from Rosario that year shows Connie Hernández (whose mother sewed new dresses for the statue on the family's kitchen table) carrying the statue with Dolores López and Deanie Ortiz, with Fray Angélico in Franciscan robes and sunglasses following behind.[36] Chávez's sense of the aesthetic deeply imbued his historical research and led to his encouragement of the local women to refashion aesthetically and historically accurate garments for the statue. Martin's photographs add

FIG. 5.1. La Conquistadora procession, downtown Santa Fe, New Mexico, ca. 1948. Left to right: Fray Angélico Chávez, other priest and altar boy, Connie Hernández, Dolores López, and Deanie Ortiz. Robert H. Martin image, No. 10220; photograph by Robert H. Martin, courtesy New Mexico State Records Center and Archives.

a further aesthetic layer to the statue's historical narrative in the book. Chávez did not abandon art when he moved into historical research and writing; on the contrary, his sense of the aesthetic could not be separated from this new work.[37]

Dr. Morley died one month after the book was published, and Fray Angélico played a key role in his deathbed conversion to Catholicism as we have seen. Twenty-five years later Fray Angélico revealed that Morley had also played a key role in bringing his research on La Conquistadora beyond intuition and hunches. When he showed Morley the first version of his article, the director of the museum told him that he had no documentary proof for his points. Chávez then found evidence for his contentions in the old fragments he was organizing in the archdiocesan archives. "Dr. Morley then told me that I was the first historian to write his story first and find the documentation afterwards."[38] Chávez recounts that the dress from Guatemala that Morley donated and the brass crown given by Chávez's mother and aunts made everything match the descriptions he had discovered in the ancient inventories. Mrs. O'Bryan, who ran the Los Santos Shop, made three dresses from old vestment brocades in the cathedral museum, and Miguelita Hernández made a long processional mantle with filigree jewelry that Mr. Adolfo Ortiz made available at a low cost. Fray Angélico turned his groundbreaking research into a practical application in which the community participated in rebeautifying the statue to make the historical legacy come alive again.

His desire to share his new historical discoveries with a larger audience is also evident in the more popular article, "Queen of the Southwest," published in *St. Anthony Messenger*, which had a national Catholic readership.[39] As he had done in the 1946 *The Old Faith and Old Glory* and would do in the 1951 *Lamy Memorial*, Chávez situates New Mexico history in the larger context of American history. He asks readers to imagine that the Pilgrims had been Catholics and brought a statue of Our Lady with them, enthroned it in their first church, and stood it on the main table at the first Thanksgiving Day. Years later, what if their descendants had carried it in procession during the Battle of Bunker Hill and later when the Declaration of Independence was drafted? What if George Washington had carried it across the Delaware and asked Mary for intercession for his victory at Yorktown, and what if Abraham Lincoln had proclaimed days of prayer to the Virgin during the Civil War? That statue, Chávez argues, would be a national treasure, linked to important historical moments. While there is no such statue in New England, one was brought to the American Southwest much earlier than the Atlantic seaboard settlements.

The article presents a detailed chronology of the first centuries of New Mexico from 1600 to 1770 when the settlers named La Conquistadora patroness of the kingdom, six years before the Declaration of Independence. Fray Angélico's technique of recounting his newly discovered story of the origins of La Conquistadora by rhetorically transposing it to the eastern colonial context shows that as an Hispano writing about New Mexico he believed that there are at least two American histories—that of the dominant Anglo mainstream and that of the ethnic group that lost the Mexican-American War. While the latter may be less well known, Chávez suggests, this history contains milestones and record-setting events that must be included in the narrative of American history. Years later when the statue was stolen in 1973, Chávez continued this comparison: "If somebody stole the Statue of Liberty, it would be to the nation like the loss of La Conquistadora is to New Mexico. . . . We might compare it with something that's much newer—the Liberty Bell."[40] In terms that the larger American public can relate to, he emphasizes the historical and emotional value of the statue along with its pre–American Independence arrival in the Southwest. Despite his multiple publications on the statue in different venues, this history still remains part of the regional and ethnic context, rather than a well-known part of mainstream U.S. history.

By the time his first groundbreaking book on La Conquistadora was published in late 1948, Fray Angélico was stationed in Peña Blanca, having been released from his grueling schedule of giving missions. Throughout the winter of 1948–49 he worked painstakingly to complete the translation and annotation of the Domínguez volume, *Missions of New Mexico, 1776*, which France Scholes asked him to do after Dr. Morley's funeral. He completed several articles on material he discovered in the archdiocesan archives and continued his investigation of the La Conquistadora documents. On June 18, 1950, for the annual Conquistadora procession, he published a popular article in the local newspaper about the statue and prepared a version with footnotes and references for *El Palacio* that October, "La Conquistadora Is a Paisana." Here Fray Angélico unabashedly

FIG. 5.2. Fray Angélico Chávez in the History Library, Museum of New Mexico, 1949. Photo by Charles Herbert, courtesy Palace of the Governors Photo Archives (NMHM/DCA), Neg. No, 15369.

reveals his own emotional connection to the statue and prefigures the lengthier creative autobiography that would appear in 1954.

Chávez notes with emotion that for 325 years, direct descendants of those devoted to the statue in early New Mexico have played prominent roles in the continuation of the religious observance. He reveals his ethnic pride about this: "Religious piety mingled with ancestral pride raises my emotions to the point of tears. After reading this, every New Mexican of Hispanic ancestry will, I am sure, feel the same way."[41] Addressing his fellow Hispanos, Fray Angélico argues that La Conquistadora is a "paisana," almost a living person to whom they and their ancestors have strong familial ties. In effect, they must continue the longstanding devotion to the Virgin to be true to their forebears and their ethnic identity. The introductory paragraph reveals the seeds of Fray Angélico's 1954 autobiography of the statue. Overlaying his own characteristics on the statue, forty-year-old Chávez attributes his current age to her: "It is as though a prominent New Mexico lady of the Seventeenth Century had, by some divine or scientific miracle, remained alive and handsomely fortyish down to our day."[42] In the follow-up book, Chávez would overlay his authorial identity on the statue, speaking throughout in her imagined voice as she supposedly tells her own story. His early ethnic and spiritual self-identification with the statue leads him to the creative merging of his voice with her imagined one to form a hybrid narrative "I" in the 1954 book.

In "La Conquistadora Is a Paisana" Chávez definitively states that Fray Alonso de Benavides brought a three-foot statue of the Assumption to Santa Fe in 1625, which he enthroned in a special chapel of the Santa Fe parish church that he had built four years later. Chávez notes that while he could only tentatively deduce this in the 1948 book, the evidence he has discovered about the Gómez Robledo family now supports that deduction. Francisco Gómez, a Portuguese man of Jewish extraction who commanded the soldiers accompanying Benavides and later was appointed interim governor, married Ana Robledo, who was born in San Gabriel del Yunque, the first Spanish settlement in New Mexico. As late as 1664, Ana was in charge of the statue's wardrobe and accused Governor Peñalosa of taking a new silk mantle she had donated to the statue. Although their eldest son, Francisco Gómez Robledo, was a philanderer with two children born out of wedlock, he was "most tenderly" devoted to the Virgin, serving as mayordomo prior to 1659 and also in 1684 when the Spaniards had retreated to the mission Guadalupe del Paso after the Pueblo Revolt.[43] Although Fray Angélico had intuitively concluded in the 1948 book that someone had carried the statue when the Spaniards fled Santa Fe in 1680, he now names this person as Josefa Sambrano de Grijalba, the wife of the grandson of Francisco Gómez, who carried the statue in her arms on the journey.

In a simple, clearly written narrative, Fray Angélico presents the names of the Hispano forebears devoted to La Conquistadora such as the Roybals, the Senas, the Ortizes, and the Bustamantes, including his own family ancestors. As he discovered this information during three years of research, he encouraged his family members to participate in the tradition. His mother and her two sisters, Aurelia and Victoria (Mrs. George King Sr. and Mrs. A. A. Sosaya), donated a "more queenly" crown to replace the statue's "little insignificant" one.[44] His father, who had worked as a carpenter in Los Alamos since the inception of the Manhattan Project, made a new octagonal pedestal for the statue to replace the one previously sawed off. Fray Angélico then covered the pedestal with pieces of Spanish rococo molding from the cathedral museum, which he painted in bronze. His literary and artistic identity joins his sense of ethnic pride and spirituality as he situates his family's contribution in the context of current events: "This manner of acquiring the pedestal was designedly a poetic prayer that La Conquistadora may keep the Satanic horrors of atomic destruction, which originated not far from her throne, firmly suppressed beneath her feet."[45] Chávez notes that in directing this work for La Conquistadora, he was fulfilling an old ancestral tradition. He invites all Hispanos in New Mexico to continue this family heritage by paying homage through their continued devotion to La Conquistadora, who is their paisana. In this important 1950 article he sows the seeds of his 1954 books on the origins of New Mexico families and the autobiography of La Conquistadora.

Ordinary and Extraordinary People and the Hispano Linguistic Heritage

While Fray Angélico was writing about La Conquistadora and revitalizing the devotion to her, he produced a series of historical articles based on his research findings. Having compiled many notes as he poured over the old Church documents, he discovered and brought together various subthemes as tributaries of the original project on the first Franciscan friars. After writing the history of his early ancestors, he published five articles on New Mexico place-names and five on interesting, little-known stories about people or unique objects in New Mexico history. Two, for example, dealt with special paintings of the Blessed Virgin he encountered while stationed at Santa Fe.

In November 1947 Fr. Cletus wrote to the provincial that Fray Angélico had made an interesting discovery about the doctrine of the Assumption in a painting from 1609 found nearby and was writing an article about it.[46] Published in May 1949 (although Fray Angélico told his provincial he had finished it on December 9, 1947),[47] "An Ancient Painting of the Assumption in the United States" analyzes a hide painting believed to be the oldest image referring to the Assumption of the Blessed Virgin in the United States, which was hanging on the sanctuary wall in Galisteo. Chávez expresses concern that even in the late 1940s, the Assumption had not yet been officially declared dogma even though there was great enthusiasm for this ancient belief. Because of Mary's divine Motherhood and Immaculate Conception, people were reluctant to think of her "rotting in the grave,"[48] and this early painting proclaims "ASSUMPTA EST MARIA IN COELUM" (MARY IS ASSUMED INTO HEAVEN). Chávez argues that Franciscans continue to be in the forefront of advocating that the Assumption be proclaimed dogma, and he reads this painting as another piece of evidence of Franciscan support for the doctrine.[49]

Besides invoking the Assumption, the image also represents Our Lady of Begoña, the special patroness of Basques and the ancient Kingdom of Navarre. Chávez speculates that a Franciscan friar from this region of Spain painted the image in New Mexico centuries ago, even before the Atlantic coast of the United States was settled. The 1608 date on the painting is perhaps the one on the image that the friar copied because it would be too early for Spanish settlements in the area. Chávez's research showed that almost half of the old Franciscan missions in New Mexico were named for titles of Mary, especially the Immaculate Conception, more than two centuries before that dogma was declared. He includes a photograph of the hide painting and explains its symbolism, expressing pride that a Franciscan in western North America may have painted this crude but masterful work on the primitive material available at the time.

After another old painting of the Blessed Virgin was donated to the cathedral in fall 1948, Chávez wrote an article on the history of the image and the family that owned it, which was descended from one of the original conquistadores who accompanied Oñate in 1598. "Journey's End for a Pilgrim Lady and a Family" characterizes the donated painting *La Divina Peregrina, Nuestra Señora del Refugio* as a copy made in 1771, probably brought to Santa Fe by Fray Buenaventura Merino.[50] Fray Angélico recounts the provenance of the painting in reverse chronology, beginning with Alberto Trujillo, an elderly organist at the cathedral whose beautiful music Chávez remembered hearing in his youth in the 1920s. Trujillo's grandmother had received the painting as a gift, probably from Fr. Merino toward the end of the eighteenth century. Trujillo's widow finally moved from their home on East Palace Street in fall 1948 and gave the painting back to the cathedral, which started Fray Angélico on the path of researching the family's history and that of the painting. He connects the end of the family, and the pilgrim Virgin's journey, to the end of the first Franciscan presence in New Mexico, as Fr. Merino was the last friar appointed pastor ad interim after the secularization. Linking art to the narrative of history, Chávez suggests that the painting is a beautiful epitaph to both the family and the early Franciscans.

While Chávez learned from interviewing Trujillo's widow important information to complement his documentary research, his next piece in *El Palacio* involved speculation and imagination about a black drummer in de Vargas' era to augment the written documents. Chávez stresses the importance of also studying "the little people in regional history" who are often forgotten because of historians' preoccupation with the powerful figures of the past.[51] In various Church documents, Sebastián Rodríguez Brito stated he was from Angola, San Pablo de Luanda in Guinea, and Río Llanero. He claimed he was born in 1642 and that his parents were both "negros bosales" from San Pablo de Luanda. Chávez speculates that "Río Llanero" sounds like "Rio de Janeiro," so perhaps Rodríguez traveled from Guinea to Brazil and then to New Spain. Some of Chávez's statements in this 1949 article are offensive to today's sensibilities. "Sebastián is a true black, since both his parents were 'jungle' Negroes" is Chávez's explanation of the term *negros bosales*.[52] His visual and literary imagination entices him to invent an image of Rodríguez beating the drum for de Vargas' military entourage: "One can see his ivory-toothed grin as he frantically beat his drum" and "the coal-black face and toothy grin of Sebastián Rodríguez, strutting high, manipulating his drumsticks as only a Negro can."[53] Although Chávez believes he is revising history to include the important role of little known figures, his manner of placing this person at center stage falls into stereotypes and racialism. Nonetheless, he emphasizes the key role Rodríguez played as both drummer and herald for de Vargas' important announcements. Later in Santa Fe, Rodríguez was wealthy enough to purchase property.

Chávez's research in this period also led him to the discovery of "The Mad Poet of Santa Cruz." Addressing the folklore society, he argues that folklore is not created by a kind of spontaneous combustion, but rather is the purposeful creation of a talented person whose creations people enjoy and pass down. Because of the lack of printing in New Mexico throughout the colonial period, the names of such creators have not been preserved. The exception of Villagrá's account of the Oñate conquest is extant only because it was published after he returned to Spain. Another anomalous case is that of an eighteenth-century poet, Miguel de la Quintana, whose poetry and name have been preserved because the Inquisition investigated him. "Had not some injudicious Padres suspected him and his verses of heresy, we would not have this information and even autographs of his poems, so important for being the first and only signs so far discovered of New Mexican literature since the time of Villagrá."[54]

Educated in Mexico City, Quintana came to New Mexico during the 1693 de Vargas resettlement and worked as a secretary, composing lengthy well-written reports of land disputes and criminal court proceedings in a clear, legible script. He was also a poet and upon request wrote occasional verses, *coloquios* at Christmas and feast days, and maybe short dramas. When he was sixty-two, he experienced a marked change, and two young priests from Santa Cruz denounced him to the Inquisition. He became reluctant to attend Mass and confession, and his poetry and prose took strange turns. He felt compelled to give this writing to the priests, who then used it as proof against him to the Inquisition. Chávez recounts the puzzling details of Quintana's writings and the proceedings. As a twentieth-century priest, Chávez then diagnoses Quintana with the disorder of abnormal scrupulosity. He reads the textual records of Quintana's troubled time through the lens of modern psychology and his experiences as a priest, explaining to readers in detail the symptoms and behavior of people with this disorder. He excuses the two priests who denounced Quintana because of the witch-hunting era in which they lived and praises the Inquisition in Mexico City for its surprising wisdom in recognizing that Quintana was not a heretic. We are indebted even to the denouncers, Chávez adds, because their impetuous actions resulted in our knowing about this talented poet who was not insane and may be the author of much that has survived as folklore in New Mexico.

In his fifth article on unique people in New Mexico history, Chávez debunked the unsubstantiated stories of writers over the years about the nineteenth-century Santa Fe figure Doña Tules Barceló. Chávez's sense of ethnic identity comes to the fore in this article as he attempts to correct the scandal surrounding her in previous accounts by W. W. H. Davis, Josiah Gregg, Ralph Emerson Twitchell, and Susan Shelby Magoffin: "The accepted indictment of her in the past has also been the indictment of a whole people."⁵⁵ That is, Chávez suggests, we Hispanos are affected by these Anglo writers' misrepresentations of our culture. He documents from Church records that the only baptismal and marriage records for the Barceló name in all of New Mexico are in Tomé, not Taos where writers had claimed she was from. Gertrudis Barceló married Manuel Sisneros in Tomé in 1823; the records refer to her and her family as *Doña* and *Don*, terms bestowed only on people of the highest social standing. "That Tules started out as a low harlot in Taos and gained the title of *Doña* in Santa Fe by her sinful affluence is a figment of Gregg's imagination," Chávez argues. He asserts that Gregg and Magoffin condemned Barceló through a Puritan Anglo American outlook as opposed to the Latin mind that saw nothing in nature or Scripture that forbade tobacco, liquor, or gambling as sins in themselves. Chávez explains that he uses the terms *Puritan* and *Latin* instead of *Protestant* and *Catholic* because at issue are the customs of social and racial groups rather than of religion and morals. After extensively discussing these ethnic differences he concludes that the only information "the impartial eye of sober historical research" tells us is that Barceló ran "a house where open gambling, drinking, and smoking were enjoyed by all and sundry with no thought of being socially degraded"; just as today, some enjoy these pleasures in moderation while others engage in excess.⁵⁶

To refute Davis' additional contention that Doña Tules' funeral and burial were excessively costly and scandalous, Chávez examines the records and explains the Hispano and Church customs of the time. There was no Sunday collection to support the Church in New Mexico; rather people paid stipends for baptisms, marriages, and funerals. Instead of offering the prescribed annual *primicias* (first fruits or tithes), even well-off Hispanos often asked for reductions or credit. Consequently, after the secularization of the missions in the nineteenth century, priests tried to obtain as much as they could from the well-off for the extra services these parishioners wanted. The rich competed with each other to have the most candles lit and the most *pasos* or "stops" in their funeral processions where priests offered prayers and collected more fees. While there is no burial fee in Doña Tules' name in the Church records, she or her family likely requested an opulent funeral. However, Davis' contention that she paid the outrageous sum of one thousand dollars for her burial is misleading; Chávez points out that Church fees were in native pesos, not American dollars, in this early transition period in 1851, and they were worth only about ten to twenty-five cents. He insists that Doña Tules' legacy must be understood as bringing the raucous glamour of a gambling house to the quiet Mexican frontier town; she was at the same time a respectable, faithful wife. He insists on correcting the legends about her both as a historian and as an Hispano who believed that the Anglo visitors who had written about her did not understand the area's ethnic culture and customs.

Just as La Conquistadora and Doña Tules are paisanas for whom inaccurate legends must be put to rest, ethnic pride and the desire to set the record straight underlie Fray Angélico's five articles on New Mexico place-names.[57] For the first article, the editors of *El Palacio* featured Fray Angélico's picture on the cover of the November 1949 issue and a short article on his life and work. This format gives testimony to Chávez's new prestige as a historian, although he had not been formally trained in this field. His article "Saints' Names in New Mexico Geography" brings together his recent research, linguistic skills, and knowledge of Church history and hagiography.

Besides delineating the stories of the saints for whom various towns are named and fifteen titles of the Blessed Virgin in place-names such as Pilar and Belén, Fray Angélico corrects many misconceptions about the origins of religious names in New Mexico. The name of Acacia, in Socorro County, is a corruption of San Acacio's name, probably confused with the acacia tree. San Diego is the name of the fifteenth-century Franciscan lay brother, St. Didacus of Alcalá, whose name should not be confused with Santiago's, as many American writers have done. *Santiago* is a contraction of *Santo Iago*, ancient Spanish for "St. James the Greater," one of the twelve apostles who brought Christianity to Spain. "Santiago" is the battle cry of Spaniards because the saint is said to have appeared on horseback to help the Spanish armies; many carved wooden santos of the saint were made in New Mexico, and the feast was formerly celebrated in every village as almost a national holiday. The seventeenth-century pueblo Socorro was not named after La Virgen del Socorro as recent writers have claimed, but rather because the starving colonists got *socorro* or "help" from the Piro Indians; the Franciscans gave that church the title of "Assumption," not "La Virgen del Socorro." San Juan in Rio Arriba County was named for St. John the Baptist by the Oñate colonists, who added the phrase "de los Caballeros," not in honor of the local Indians who offered them hospitality, as many have written, but because they would become hidalgos for having been first settlers of the new land.

Chávez explains that although Governor Tomás Vélez Cachupín tried to name the pueblo at Abiquiu after his patron Santo Tomás, the people insisted on Santa Rosa, for St. Rose of Lima, the first canonized saint of the New World who was especially popular in all the Spanish colonies. He explains that the word *Santo*, not *San*, is used before the names beginning with *Do* or *To* to preserve euphony, as in *Santo Domingo* and *Santo Tomás*, and that the word *Guadalupe* is of Moorish origin. Besides the correction of longstanding misinformation on saints' names for locales in New Mexico, Chávez presents a systematic catalogue of these religious names as a means of preserving this history and making the information available to the public.

His documentary research also revealed information on place-names derived from Spanish proper names, the subject of his next article. The name of Albuquerque, which was a Spanish town originally in Portugal, might have derived from the Latin *albus quercus* meaning "white oak." While the word may also be of Moorish origin because it begins with the prefix *al*, it is definitely not, as some have argued, from *albaricoque* (apricot), Chávez insists. His research shows that before the Pueblo Revolt it was called El Bosque Grande de Doña Luisa and also La Estancia de Doña Luisa de Trujillo. In 1706 it was called San Francisco Xavier del Bosque Grande. Later that year, Governor Francisco Cuervo y Valdés named it the Villa de Alburquerque after the viceroy, the Duque de Alburquerque. However, just as the people insisted on Santa Rosa rather than Santo Tomás as the patron of Abiquiu, so did the people in Alburquerque continue using the name San Francisco Xavier de Alburquerque, despite the viceroy's order to change the patron to San Felipe in honor of the king. Only in 1777 did people use "San Felipe Neri" as the title. Chávez argues that Hispanos often dropped the second *r* of the name, while Americans dropped the first one, and the city's name ultimately dropped the first *r*.

Chávez locates the origin of the present county name De Baca in thirteenth-century Spain during the Moorish Wars. The king rewarded a man who had marked a strategic river ford with a cow's skull by giving him the title "Cabeza de Vaca" (cow's head). Captain Cristóbal Baca came to New Mexico from Mexico City in 1600, and he and his descendants were called simply Baca. Not until 1800 was the full name used in New Mexico. Even though people widely believed that the Bacas were a distinct family from the Cabeza de Bacas, Chávez argues that both civil and Church records show them to be the same family. Chávez explains simple origins of proper names such as Valencia, which refers not to the city and province in Spain but to Juan de Valencia whose ranch was located on this site in the seventeenth century. A more complex origin lies behind the confusion between Don Fernando de Taos and Don Carlos Fernández de Taos, an eighteenth-century landowner in the area. Chávez explains names he has a personal connection to, such as Chávez, which derives from the Portuguese word for keys, and Peña Blanca, referring either to the white rock in the area or to the early figure José de la Peña. This early documentary work on proper names in New Mexico was the beginning of his extensive studies to come—*Origins of New Mexico Families* (1954, 1973, 1975, 1992) and "Addenda to New Mexico Families" (*El Palacio*, 1955–57).

In the last three articles in the series, Fray Angélico explains religious place-names that do not refer to saints, New Mexicanisms in place-names, and Aztec or Nahuatl words in the area's names. He clarifies that names such as Nacimiento and Sacramento have special meanings, the former referring to the birth of the Blessed Virgin and the latter, short for "El Santísimo Sacramento" (the Most Blessed Sacrament), referring to the Eucharist, not to sacraments in general. At the beginning of the nineteenth century, the name Sangre de Cristo (Blood of Christ) replaced the name Sierra Madre for the southern portion of the Rockies, because of the Penitentes' special devotion to the Passion and death of Christ. The villa of Santa Fe was originally named by Peralta not primarily for its meaning "Holy Faith" but to follow the tradition of naming towns in the New World after Santa Fe near Granada, which Ferdinand and Isabella had founded during their conquest of the Moors in 1492.

In a lengthy list of New Mexican adaptations of Spanish in various place-names, he explains that sixteenth- and seventeenth-century Castilian was spoken in New Mexico, along with a few provincial expressions from Galicia and Extremadura. Over the years, New Mexicans gave new shades of meaning to these old words. *Abuelo*, for example, appeared in the earliest documents according to its provincial pronunciation "ahuelo" or "aguelo." The name El Rito does not refer to the Native American rituals, but to the old Spanish term for "little river," *rito*, spelled "riito" in the eighteenth century. Ojo Caliente (Hot Spring) uses the old Spanish word for very small springs; in New Mexico *ojo* became the generic word for spring instead of *fuente* because most of its springs are small.

In the last article, Chávez explains several words of Nahuatl origin brought to New Mexico when the colonists came north. Atrisco was named after Atlixco, a beautiful valley and city southwest of Puebla. Los Cuates in Union County derives from the Nahuatl *cuahtl* meaning "twins." In use since the first colonists came north, the term *cuate* replaced the proper Spanish terms *gemelo* and *mellizo* in New Mexico. Even the name of the state derives from the Nahuatl words *Mexitli* and *Mexica*. At the end of this last article, Chávez also corrects a few previous entries such as the one for Peña Blanca; he now notes that the settlement was first known as El Rancho de José Miguel de la Peña, then El Rancho de Peña, and then El Rancho de la Peña Blanca. This series of five articles in *El Palacio* reveals that Chávez's research in documents of the colonial period sparked a corollary interest in linguistics and philology and the variations in Spanish preserved in New Mexico's place-names. Often thereafter he would bring this linguistic expertise to the public in his articles, books, and commentary.

As these articles were published, Fray Angélico traveled to California for three weeks of research at the Huntington and Bancroft libraries where he took copious notes on the documents relating to New Mexico in the collections. Chávez provided information on the documents to the Museum of New Mexico, which had funded his trip, and the museum ordered microfilm copies. He also published an article on the documents in *New Mexico Historical Review* in July. In these ways he helped to return copies of these New Mexico documents to their place of origin, making the material accessible for his own work and for that of other scholars and researchers for generations to come. This full-time research for three weeks invigorated him. He returned to Peña Blanca in high spirits, noting that he felt better than ever. Nonetheless, he quickly became frustrated again because the archbishop asked him to write a book for the centenary of the Archdiocese of Santa Fe and Bishop Lamy's assignment to New Mexico. Chávez was reluctant to stop his other historical projects and felt like "a flunky who is patted on the head just like a nice dog that knows how to do a few tricks."⁵⁸ He wrote the book, *Lamy Memorial*, from February to July 1950, and it was published in October.

Like *The Old Faith and Old Glory*, which Chávez had undertaken with enthusiasm immediately on his return from the war, perhaps because it was his own idea, *Lamy Memorial* documents the history of the Archdiocese of Santa Fe from its beginnings as a vicariate apostolic in 1850 to its elevation to diocese in 1853 and then to archdiocese itself in 1875. Where *The Old Faith and Old Glory* celebrates the growth of the Church in New Mexico under American rule, the book on Lamy commemorates the French prelate's foundational role in reviving institutional Catholicism in the territory from 1850 on. In honor of the centenary, the book recounts the history of the two and a half centuries before Lamy's arrival, the French bishop's story, and those of succeeding archbishops, with small historical sketches of the principal parishes, seminaries, and religious orders in the archdiocese in 1950. Chávez was able to write this book in a relatively short period because individual parishes completed questionnaires and because of his extensive research in ecclesiastical documents.

A great deal of this research overlays his conceptualization and structure of the volume. He constructs a diagram of the "family tree" of the diocese, illustrating which diocese "begat" subsequent ones, and tracing the Santa Fe Archdiocese back to its time under the Franciscan Province of the Holy Gospel. Just as he reconstructed New Mexico history through family trees of its colonists and their descendants, he would use this model as one means of conceptualizing the growth of the diocese. His handwritten signature "Fr. A. C." is at the bottom of the diagram, although he chose not to have authorial attribution anywhere else in the book. Chávez devotes an entire section to the history of La Conquistadora in keeping with his recent discoveries. Asserting Hispano ethnicity, he integrates the statue into the book as a parallel figure to Lamy. With almost equally long texts for the two figures, preceded by full-page photographs of both, he includes color photographs of the statues of Lamy and La Conquistadora as central images on the front cover.

In May 1950 the *Santa Fe New Mexican* published a watercolor sketch by Fray Angélico that, according to the caption, "will be on the cover" of the Lamy centennial book. The painting depicts the cathedral in the background with the large statue of Lamy on the side, the Conquistadora in the center, and Archbishop Byrne in the foreground.⁵⁹

As he had done for the 1946 book on the archdiocese, Fray Angélico did a painting for the cover. In the intervening months before publication, Fray Angélico's work must have been rejected, and instead a similar photograph appeared with an inset of the statue of Lamy. Fray Angélico's original sketch depicts Hispanic women and Franciscans in their brown robes more prominently, directly behind the archbishop, than does the photograph finally used. In a short section interpreting the final cover, Fray Angélico notes that the statue of Lamy dedicated in 1915 dominates the cover layout, although it is to the left of the larger, central image of the cathedral and La Conquistadora. He explains the allegorical level of the larger image: "The focal point is occupied by the Queen of New Mexico and Santa Fe, Our Lady of the Conquest.... She is surrounded by Catholics of every national derivation representing the faithful of our American Archdiocese today, all united in the same ancient Faith."[60] Chávez interprets for readers the visual symbols on the cover in Robert Martin's photographs, attempting to anchor the meaning of the images according to his conceptual plan for the book based on his recent work on revising New Mexico history.

Of New Mexico's 250 years before Lamy's arrival, Chávez poetically writes, "These foundations were lowly and crumbling, it is true, like the old adobe walls of which the churches were built, but they were cemented with blood, with the blood and tears of countless pioneers."[61] Lamy realized this, which led to his successes, but his failures can be attributed to his not understanding the huge territory and its long history. After Peralta became governor in 1609, seventy years of quarreling followed between the friars and government figures, most of whom, Chávez argues, tried to exploit the Indians while the missionaries tried to protect them. He admits that some of the friars were also at fault in the disagreements and suggests that the Pueblo Revolt occurred not from the native people's desire for independence but from confusion and hate created by the abuses of the authorities.

Already in 1630, Fray Alonso de Benavides proposed the creation of a diocese in New Mexico, but the civil leaders pushed for a bishop in Mexico or Guadalajara so that distance would allow them to continue in their ways. By 1800 widely separated pueblos and villages functioned under only one priest. Chávez argues that the faithful in New Mexico were "spiritually abandoned" at this time.[62] Only two known cases exist of native priests being ordained in New Mexico between 1600 and 1800. Quarrels between the religious orders and the secular clergy contributed to the Franciscan decline in New Mexico. From 1797 to 1850—the Secular period—New Mexico was no longer a Franciscan mission under the Spanish Crown. One positive aspect of the fifty-year Secular period, however, was that thirty New Mexican men went to Durango for studies and were ordained. After the United States took over, however, many of them returned to Mexico in protest. Two of them, Padres Martínez and Gallegos, "left a bad name."[63] Chávez argues, however, that they were the victims of circumstances rather than villains as legend and writers have characterized them. This allusion prefigures the lengthier revalorization of these two key priests that Chávez would publish in 1981 and 1985.

Chávez notes that Lamy brought the area into modernity ecclesiastically. Placing Lamy within American history, he interprets the archbishop's large photograph on the facing page as almost "a composite photograph of Stuart's head of George Washington and any of several portraits of Abraham Lincoln."[64] Chávez implies that Lamy is as important in his context as the two famous U.S. presidents in theirs. After briefly summarizing Lamy's work in New Mexico and pointing out the difficulties he faced because he was perceived as an American as well as a Frenchman, Chávez notes that "his troubles with some of the native priests were unfortunate and not of his own making," a thesis he would later revise.[65] He ends the brief narrative on Lamy by again asserting the archbishop's comparison to the American presidents in large type: "TODAY ACROSS A CENTURY THAT HAS WITNESSED THE CONTINUATION OF HIS LABORS, HIS PORTRAIT AND HIS LIFE SHOW HIM AS THE GREAT FATHER THAT HE WAS . . . LIKE WASHINGTON, FIRST IN THE HEARTS OF HIS COUNTRYMEN: LIKE LINCOLN, A MAN OF THE PEOPLE."[66]

After writing about the archbishops who succeeded Lamy, Chávez presents information on each of the parishes now in the diocese. He argues that the book is neither a comprehensive history nor a literary work but a pictorial album and memorial to Lamy on the centenary of his appointment. In the section on seminaries, he repeats an earlier point in the book: "The source of inner life and vitality of a Catholic area, or a diocese, is a Seminary that steadily produces native vocations to the Holy Priesthood."[67] He praises Archbishop Gerken's establishment of a minor seminary at Lourdes School near Albuquerque and the new Immaculate Heart of Mary location near Santa Fe. Anonymously remembering his own distant journey to become a priest, he notes that a few native priests were ordained in the two preceding decades through their own initiative and going far away for their training.

In this period of renewed creativity after World War II, Chávez plunged wholeheartedly into his new part-time work as a historian, renewed and invigorated by the gold mine of untapped resources in the unorganized archdiocesan archives. While carrying on his missionary work from the cathedral headquarters and then as assistant pastor at Peña Blanca, he continued, as he had in the vibrant first years after he was ordained, to work from dawn to late night on these multiple tasks, while continuing to socialize with old and new friends. He began to study paleography with France Scholes in Albuquerque, gave guest lectures and sermons, traveled to archival collections to do research, led the revitalization of the Conquistadora devotions in Santa Fe, and wrote books on the cathedral, Lamy, and the history of the Church in New Mexico since the American occupation. He also published numerous articles after careful study of the documents he uncovered and began to organize in the archdiocesan archives. He published his first book based on this historical research and began work on several other books that would appear in the 1950s. Besides accepting writing assignments from his Franciscan superiors, such as the translation of St. Leonard's *Stations of the Cross*, he put aside the other work he loved to complete tasks for the chancery—including the three books on the archdiocese and writing other material for Archbishop Byrne, such as Byrne's introduction to *Eleven Lady-Lyrics*, his pastoral letter accompanying his photograph at the beginning of *Lamy Memorial*, and the official declarations on the Penitentes and a racial question, both of which were quoted in *Time* magazine.[68] Fray Angélico's artistic creativity could not be suppressed, despite the breakneck pace of his newfound passion for history; while he did not produce new poetry in this period, he wrote several short stories, helped to design historically authentic dresses for La Conquistadora, collaborated with photographers Robert Martin and Laura Gilpin by translating part of Villagrá's poem for Gilpin's 1949 book *The Rio Grande, River of Destiny*, and added artistic layers to tasks such as the booklet on the cathedral by printing his poem "Of Toads and Such" on the back cover. He even made a small contribution to church building by designing the facade for a new church in Clovis completed in 1948.[69] The multiple aspects of his busy life in this period did not exist in separate boxes or layers, but rather functioned as overlapping pieces of a whole, constantly interacting and cross-fertilizing one another. All this would have to be put on hold once again when the newspaper headline on July 24, 1950, announced that two battalions of the New Mexico National Guard had been activated.

CHAPTER SIX

Hispano Genealogy, La Conquistadora, and the Penitentes

Revisionist History

Chronicle of the Second Tour of Duty

Chávez, the writer and historian, was careful to chronicle his second period of military service for posterity. Deprived of time and hospitable circumstances for writing for two years, he happily plunged into literary self-expression when he arrived at Jemez on August 13, 1952. Although he was not able to do serious work right away, while adjusting to his new assignment and learning the routine of the post office during the first month, several articles began to appear very quickly.[1] His first was a sequel to his 1946 narrative about his World War II experiences where he attained the rank of major. Playing on the opposing titles accorded by the military and the Franciscans, the Friars Minor, Chávez humorously entitles the piece "From Major to Minor, or: High on the Muster-Role to Low on the Totem Pole" to describe his journey from high-ranked army officer to lowly newcomer friar at Jemez Pueblo. Immediately on returning, Chávez writes about his tour of duty both from a desire to tell fellow Franciscans the story of his latest adventures as well as to document it for the historical record. Unlike the long-dead missionary friars, such as Fr. Padilla whose stories he had to piece together from decrepit documents that left many unanswered questions, Chávez insists on telling his own story exactly as he wishes it to be remembered in generations to come. His narrative is quite partial a text compared to the detailed letters he wrote to the provincial during his tour of duty; it glosses over severe problems that he revealed in the letters. He modifies the story now in retrospect after being released from the unwanted tour of duty, with the calmness and wisdom of someone no longer in the thick of things. He adds information not in the letters home, analyzing in hindsight some of his motivations. Even before postmodernist theory emphasized the partiality of all historical discourse and the always inadequate nature of self-representation, Chávez unselfconsciously demonstrates these tenets.

Fray Angélico describes his first year at Fort Bliss as "blissful" because of a wonderful group of friends, including chaplains he knew in World War II whom he humorously terms "retreads." He only briefly alludes to "the headaches that only military headquarters can cook up."[2] In fact, he had major troubles with one of his superiors, got into a fistfight, and finally was able to get the superior officer transferred.[3] After three months of walking to his duties across the huge base, he finally was given a car to use from the friary at Santa Fe. He arranged to move off the base to Roger Bacon seminary and made a good friend there, but this priest was abruptly sent back to Mexico, and Fray Angélico left after no longer feeling comfortable there.

Having initially felt tricked when he agreed to join the reserves that were shortly thereafter activated, Fray Angélico describes some of the machinations he and his friends employed to prevent him from being sent a year later to Korea. The University of New Mexico formally requested that the Pentagon release him for three months to finish preparing an important historical document for publication, probably Domínguez's *Missions of New Mexico, 1776*. When that was denied, others in Santa Fe tried to pull strings with Washington politicians. Fray Angélico does not mention—perhaps he did not know—that his brother Fabián Chávez worked to have him reassigned to Europe rather than Korea.[4] When Fray Angélico saw a reply from the chief of chaplains criticizing him for not accepting orders like a soldier, he wrote a long angry reply, partially quoted in the article. Now in 1952 with hindsight, he claims he was disappointed in the changed assignment to Europe, as if "God's will had been tampered with."[5] Although these thoughts may have crossed his mind, he may be placing them center stage in this essay written for other Franciscans, to emphasize his priestly obedience and humility. Other evidence shows that he desperately did not want to go to Korea. Now that the ordeal of the second tour was over, the telling of that history could be modified in retrospect.

He recounts his arrival in Bremerhaven and then Heidelberg on September 12, 1951, and his enchantment with the medieval city along with his visit to Theresa Neumann. When sent to Nuremberg two weeks later, he almost froze during night maneuvers in the woods. While awaiting his assignment, he traveled to Rome and for eight days delighted in seeing the famous churches and masterpieces he had only known from books and pictures. He celebrated daily Mass at St. Peter's, including once over the exposed body of Pope Pius X. Chávez humorously recounts the story of a large audience with Pope Pius XII in which his was the only voice shouting "Viva il Papa" when the Pope greeted the Americans: "I felt like a you-know-what. Curiously rising on tip-toe, I beheld his Holiness . . . throw out his arms in mirth as he chuckled out loud . . . the Holy Father heard my pipsqueak voice and . . . I caused the most heavily burdened man in history to laugh."[6] Small-statured Fray Angélico humorously yet proudly recounts his episode with the Pope in which his attempted leadership of the American group resulted in an instant of personal contact with the head of the Church.

Chávez's humor pervades the story of his adventures on the second tour. He describes allowing his leave time to accumulate "with canny malice aforethought" so that he could travel in Spain shortly before coming home.[7] His humorous hand is also visible in the captions on a photo of him and two other chaplains at Fort Bliss with the tall prize-fighters Max Baer and Primo Carnera: "Five Giants—One of them not so big but well protected. . . . Primo wanted to send this picture home to show the company he kept."[8] In this first article after his arrival home, Fray Angélico inserts himself into the written record of history, modifying events slightly with hindsight; he chronicles the episodes of his time away while presenting himself both seriously and with characteristic humor.

That spring Chávez had sent information about his activities to the *Chronicle* with a picture of himself in vestments he designed modeled

FIG. 6.1. Left to right: Father O'Connor, Max Baer, Father Angélico Chávez, Primo Carnera, and Father Brennan at Fort Bliss, Texas, 1952, courtesy the Archives of the Franciscan Province of St. John the Baptist of Cincinnati.

on an original Roman chasuble.[9] With this image he inserts himself pictorially into the historical record, precisely at a moment in which he attempted to reconstruct Catholic history by reproducing and wearing ancient vestments. In another narrative he wrote in the issue, he describes the importance of the new dress he had commissioned for La Conquistadora out of prewar German gold cloth. Offering it to the Virgin in the name of all New Mexicans in the service, especially those in Korea, he designed it with gold cords and a tassel to form a monogram of the letter *M* on the back of the mantle. Catholic history and Hispano traditions of popular religious devotions came together with vestimentary visual display in Fray Angélico's Speyer creations. He continued his family's and New Mexicans' devotional tradition from the 1600s.

Following up on the vestimentary designs, Fray Angélico the painter elaborates on the chromatic visual effects of Mass vestments in another article published shortly after his return. "Yellow Is Yellow Is Yellow" in *Homiletic and Pastoral Review* is a sermon directed to other priests rather than to a congregation. He warns fellow priests that the Church does not authorize the yellow vestments now appearing more and more often. "Vestments of yellow or heavenly-blue color are forbidden," he translates from the Latin.[10] Priests are confusing yellow with the permissible gold.

Chávez analyzes the incorrect vestments in detail as if they were paintings. As an artist, he brings his firsthand knowledge of colors, materials, and visual effects to his sermon. While manufacturers may be passing off the new vestments as gold, he notes, the material is merely a yellow with sheen. Gold is not a color proper but rather a metallic. The cloth-of-gold vestments that the Church prescribes must be closely woven with gold metallic thread, not a sparse overlay of gold thread on a yellow vestment: "Close by they are gold-looking and good looking; three yards away they look like mustard."[11] This is no doubt why Chávez chose the expensive cloth-of-gold for the dress and mantle he had made for La Conquistadora in Speyer.

Chávez suggests that the Church become open to new liturgical colors, pointing out that except for white, the other accepted colors are relatively new. He would especially like to see rose used more frequently, along with blue, the Blessed Virgin's color. Despite strongly criticizing the new yellow vestments and authoritatively employing his expertise as an artist, Fray Angélico humorously humbles himself at the end of this sermon to fellow priests: "Yellow is yellow and it is forbidden—but do not throw away your new and costly yellow set, for I could be wrong, y'know."[12]

On November 6, 1952, he sent the *Provincial Chronicle* his article "Old Guadalupe in Spain." He wrote that the photos he took on the road demonstrated how much like the New Mexico countryside Spain is. Fr. Casey replied that if Chávez hadn't told him, he would not have known that the mountainsides were from Old rather than New Spain.[13] The seeds of Chávez's 1974 book *My Penitente Land* had been planted.

History after the European Tour: From Colonial Churches to Hispano Genealogy

In April 1949, Chávez's article "Santa Fe Church and Convent Sites in the Seventeenth and Eighteenth Centuries" was the lead piece in *New Mexico Historical Review*, and it functions as a companion article to "How Old Is San Miguel," published in 1953 in *El Palacio* after his return from Europe. In both, Chávez conducts detective work on the early church sites of Santa Fe. In the first study he uses documentary sources to show the relative positions of the three church-convento layouts in 1629, 1697–1717, and 1804 on the site of the present St. Francis Cathedral. His detective work allows him to correct errors about the location of the first church in Santa Fe: it was almost directly behind the present cathedral, with its front entrance along the north-south line to the rear of the cathedral where the two-story St. Vincent's hospital was when Chávez wrote the article, not in the front facing the post office as was commonly believed.

Chávez explains that unlike monks who lived in secluded monasteries, Franciscans lived in conventos, or gathering places that were halfway between monastic and secular life, and in New Mexico were joined to the church building of the parish or mission. The first permanent parish church in Santa Fe was built in the term of custos Fray Alonso Benavides, 1626–29. The convento may have been built first because in 1631 the work on the church was apparently not completed according to records. The Lady Chapel of the parroquia was completed during Benavides' term, and the church was attached to the north of the convento to shelter the friary from wind and weather.

Fray Angélico neatly drew a scheme of the three successive convento-churches from 1629 to 1804. Since there is no record of the exact location of the 1629 structure, he labeled the sketch "descriptive"—part of his attempt to illustrate how the buildings occupied different areas of the site in the three periods. In boldface outline, he shows which sections of the 1717 church are still in use. After the original buildings were razed during the Pueblo Revolt, de Vargas vowed to rebuild the church, but he was too busy fending off Indian attacks. When Cubero bought the governorship from the king in 1697, he wished to undermine de Vargas' popularity, Chávez speculates, and therefore moved immediately to build a convento for the Franciscans, which was completed within fifty days of his arrival. The permanent church was not built until 1714–17 with the assistance of the Confraternity of La Conquistadora. Busily at work translating Domínguez's 1776 report on the churches, Fray Angélico uses Domínguez's description of the length of the 1717 church to show that its front entrance was at about the middle of the present cathedral, with the plaza originally extending all the way up to that point. Burial records show that a cemetery in front of the church was in use by 1732 and that houses were built between it and the now-smaller plaza in this period. On the basis of his new detective work with Church documents, Chávez corrected several misconceptions in historical accounts and invited future scholars to ascertain the exact positions of these buildings through professional survey work.[14]

Similarly, he corrects errors about San Miguel Chapel in the 1953 article "How Old Is San Miguel?" By carefully reading Church documents and critically examining secondary sources, he recounts the chapel's history and shows that its walls stood after the 1680 Pueblo Revolt, giving it a claim to being the oldest church in the country. "If someone will establish honestly that the old church of Saint Augustine, Florida, has nothing left but its original site, or its foundations at the most, then San Miguel can rightfully boast of its title as the oldest church in the United States of America."[15]

Chávez deduces that San Miguel Chapel was built around 1610 because documents show that it was taken for granted by 1628. It was built sturdily with very thick walls as part of the padres' emphasis on converting and serving the Indians. Chávez corrects several errors of previous historians. First, he disputes the belief that Tlaxcaltec Indians lived there, perhaps brought by Oñate; Fray Vélez Escalante referred to this group living near San Miguel in Analco, but he wrote 175 years after Oñate, and Bancroft found no earlier reference to the Tlaxcalans in the area. Chávez argues that the Indians in this neighborhood came from the Valley of Mexico (the only "Mexicans" of that period), from other tribes of New Spain and later Apache captives, and Pueblo Indians brought in to do construction. Second, historians such as Hodge, Hammond, and Scholes had confused the hermitage of San Miguel with the parroquia built by Benavides. He explains that a hermitage was a small dwelling place for friars that was not a full-fledged convento, sometimes with a small chapel. By 1640 when the brutal governor Rosas burned down the hermitage and had the bells removed, it had been converted into a clinic and hospital. Historians who did not distinguish carefully between these terms mistakenly argued that Rosas burned the church down. Fray Angélico cites the testimony of friar witnesses and a captain who refer to the destruction of "el hospital" and "la enfermería" of the villa of Santa Fe at San Miguel. The church remained intact until the roof was destroyed in the 1680 Pueblo Revolt.

A third misconception Chávez points out is crediting the 1710 restoration to the mayordomo of the Confraternity of St. Michael and the governor whose names are carved on a beam inside the chapel. Rather, he argues, citing the transcripts of the confraternity's *testimonio* published by George Kubler, the members of the confraternity gathered funds for the restoration all over the kingdom and finished the project when de Vargas was unable to do so. The confraternity used the chapel for celebrations of St. Michael's feasts and when members died. The chapel is not mentioned for decades in Church records, Chávez notes, except for a few burials such as that of one of the confraternity's charter members, Don Bernardino de Sena, in 1765.

As he had in the article on the Santa Fe parroquia, Chávez employs information from Domínguez's manuscript on the missions of New Mexico in 1776, which he had translated. Since Domínguez missed practically nothing in his descriptions, we can be sure, Chávez argues, that there were no towers on the San Miguel Chapel in 1776 and the rear wall behind the altar was rectangular. At the beginning of the eighteenth century, after the rear wall had fallen down, Don Antonio José Ortiz built on a sanctuary in a triagonal shape at the back, a section not present during Domínguez's visit. In the nineteenth century a wide tower was built in front, and the remodeled front with the gabled roof and the inclined stone buttresses are from the twentieth century. Both in this article and the study of the Santa Fe parroquia, Chávez joined his material experience of church renovation with his new skills as a historian to correct errors about the first two churches of Santa Fe. He asserts his identity as a Franciscan and a priest several times, such as in explaining the difference between a convento and a hermitage. His priestly experience is evidenced in a single extra punctuation mark inserted when he recounts Fray Domínguez's description: "On the Gospel (north!) side was the sacristy."[16] The exclamation point reveals his impish yet insistent personality and his determination to correct the historical record. He especially wishes to correct his own mistakes; he apologizes in a footnote for an error in his 1947 booklet on the cathedral where he asserted that St. Francis was the titular patron of the parroquia from the beginning.[17]

Also in the April 1953 issue of *El Palacio*, Fray Angélico published an article on the family who built the nineteenth-century chapel of San José de Chama, six miles north of Española. Mariano Chávez of Chama brought Fray Angélico some old family documents that included the bishop of Durango's permission to build the chapel in 1844. On the reverse is a notation that the bishop himself blessed the chapel when it was completed in 1850 on his visit to New Mexico. This document, Chávez argues, makes the chapel twenty years older than Kubler surmised in his important 1940 book on the missions.

Translating the document, Fray Angélico reveals that Don Miguel Mariano Chávez asked permission to build the public chapel in 1844 in fulfillment of a promise he made to "the Most Chaste Patriarch, the Lord Saint Joseph."[18] The document inspired Fray Angélico to do further research in Church archives to write the story of the nineteenth-century Chávez and his ancestors. His literary imagination active, Fray Angélico notes, "The other documents in this family file are unimportant in themselves, but most helpful and revealing, once we become interested in the personality of the man who undertook to build the chapel at Chama."[19] He interprets them together with Church documents such as Don Miguel's baptismal record, showing he was born in 1783 and baptized at the mission of Santo Tomás de Abiquiú. Fray Angélico traces the family history to the youngest son of Don Pedro Durán y Chaves, Eusebio.

The article on the builder of the chapel at Chama is a sample of the monumental work Fray Angélico was preparing at the time, *Origins of New Mexico Families*. By late August 1953, he had mailed the huge manuscript, handwritten on small tablets, to his provincial in Cincinnati for approval. Both he and Mariano Chávez, who had given him the original document, could trace their ancestry to the famous Don Fernando Durán y Chaves who fought in the Pueblo Revolt and the de Vargas reconquest. Fray Angélico brought together his literary imagination, historical research skills, and his ethnic pride in his own ancestry and that of other New Mexico Hispanos. In this article, a single noteworthy historical document opened the way to his construction of a larger narrative of other fragments that became meaningful when studied and interpreted together.

Fray Angélico engages in similar narrative strategies in his next article, "The First Santa Fe Fiesta Council, 1712." Here again he presents an important historical document and then branches out to genealogical research on the names it contains. His literary imagination shapes the opening of the article as he places readers in the concrete milieu of the day the document was composed: "It was a wet and stormy day in September, 1712, when several citizens of Santa Fe joined the City Council in a special meeting to formulate plans for a perennial fiesta in commemoration of General De Vargas' first Reconquest of the ancient Capital. But let the original minutes and ordinances speak for themselves in the quaint rambling phraseology of those times."[20] Breaking the page-long sentences into short paragraphs for smoother comprehension, Chávez gives readers the opportunity to read a primary source for themselves, sharing his joy in historical discovery firsthand. The town leaders had gathered in Lieutenant Governor General Juan Páez Hurtado's house because severe storms had made the official meeting house unfit. Although they had reconquered the territory on September 14, 1692, in twenty years no fiesta had been celebrated to commemorate the victory. The leaders voted to fund an annual fiesta that would include vespers, Mass, a sermon, and a procession on September 14 in perpetuity. Chávez points out that the group chose to celebrate de Vargas' first *entrada* in 1692 rather than the second more difficult one the following year. And rather than commemorating the general pacification of the Pueblos of New Mexico, they focused on the entrada into Santa Fe and the ceremonies de Vargas described in his journal. The leaders saw the fiesta as a particularly local celebration, rather than one commemorating the larger role of the events in the history of New Spain. Perhaps they realized that weather would prevent a commemoration in December to celebrate the more significant 1693 event, Chávez speculates, or perhaps they automatically included the second with the first. He does not mention the human tendency to remember and celebrate more pleasant memories or the possibility that these early eighteenth-century colonists viewed the first entrada as especially important because it marked Spain's return to the area after the involuntary twelve-year absence.

Again in consort with his nearly completed manuscript of *Origins of New Mexico Families*, Fray Angélico presents the genealogy of the members of the first Fiesta Council of 1712, including the information he had gathered in New Mexico Church records and in California archives. He points out that the lieutenant governor Juan Páez Hurtado was probably the originator and prime mover of the idea of a fiesta because de Vargas had been his hero, close friend, and benefactor. Again correcting historical accounts, Fray Angélico points out that credit for originating Fiesta has mistakenly been given to the Marqués de la Peñuela, governor in 1712, whom this document shows was absent from the meeting. Spanish governors in New Mexico did not want to celebrate the accomplishments of their predecessors, Chávez tactfully notes.

Chávez speculates that Fiesta was celebrated at least as long as Páez Hurtado was alive for there are no records to document it. Although the 1953 fiesta advertised itself as the 241st, Chávez notes that the celebration in fact dates from the period around World War I when "Anglos" who valued the Spanish historical background saw the possibilities of the decree of 1712 and got Hispanos excited about joining them in "one big spontaneous folk festival."[21] The newly returned Franciscans resumed the custom of vespers, Mass, sermon, and procession. Writing from his own firsthand memories of Fiesta in these early years, Chávez notes that in these times, the celebration was a genuinely Spanish American folk festival with some Indian participation, as it should be. But for the past decade, Hollywood western cowboy costumes and hillbilly music had taken over, along with Mexican music and costumes. Fray Angélico seems to have forgotten that he himself wore an Argentine gaucho costume in two fiestas when home from the seminary! He argues that these changes, although representing Southwest culture, should be dropped in favor of "a genuine Spanish-American folk festival and nothing else . . . [with] some Pueblo Indian participation which the Fiesta's original event calls for."[22]

Bringing his research to a larger audience as a public intellectual, Chávez published a two-part article "The Kingdom of New Mexico" in *New Mexico* magazine in 1953 focusing on New Mexico's status as a kingdom in its first 161 years. The area's name did not come from the Republic of Mexico but from the City and Valley of Mexico that the Aztecs called "Mexitli." Soon after Cortés' arrival, the Spaniards heard rumors about the wealth in the far north and called the area "La Nueva México." Fray Marcos de Niza termed it "the New Kingdom of St. Francis" in 1539, and because it was so hard to get to, the fantasy of wealth persisted. Chávez speculates that this explains its designation as a kingdom. Numerous official documents bear the title "kingdom" up until 1771 when Spain annexed it to the northern provinces of New Spain. In his references to the numerous documents that use the term *kingdom*, Chávez proudly and humorously states, "One grandpappy of mine in 1718 called it 'this miserable kingdom,'" in reference to Don Fernando Durán y Chaves II.[23]

In the second installment, Chávez attempts to correct errors, sometimes unconvincingly. He takes issue with a reporter who twisted the word *peasant*, which he used in a lecture. The original settlers were not peons, but idealistic people who wanted to obtain the title "hidalgo" by staying a certain number of years: "The Spanish colonists of New Mexico risked life and limb to be called 'a somebody' eventually" and were not fugitives and deserters.[24] He also critiques property lawyers in New Mexico who promoted the error that New Mexico once belonged to the Republic of Texas. Instead, Chávez argues, after Mexico and Texas agreed to the Rio Grande as their boundary, officials in Washington mistakenly extended the boundary all the way up the river to its source, giving Texas New Mexico's settlements east of the river and a large part of Colorado. Fray Angélico's version of this history presents Texas' and the United States' political maneuvering over boundaries at this time as simply a mistake, when in fact both strongly desired to lay claim to the territory east of the Rio Grande all the way up to the source and intentionally did so. There was no "innocent" or "mistaken" drawing of maps in this period. Although Chávez is proud of being an American, he narrates history here from the perspective of the Spanish settlers in New Mexico, where the Americans were the squatters and "walked in and took New Mexico."[25] He urges preservation of the Spanish character of New Mexico and this Spanish history. Although poverty and suffering existed in the area, it was also a kingdom, and there were glorious aspects to its history. Just as Massachusetts retains the name of Commonwealth, New Mexico should have retained the name Kingdom when it entered the Union.

For the series, Chávez designed and drew a coat of arms for the state, urging his fellow New Mexicans to adopt it. He disliked both the design and historical inaccuracy of the current state seal, which shows a big U.S. eagle protecting a small Mexican one. It was fashioned when U.S. leaders thought that New Mexico derived from Old Mexico, not understanding that "La Nueva Mexico" existed long before the republic that gained its independence in 1821. "It does not tell the true story of New Mexico as a kingdom and a name over two centuries old when the Republic of Mexico was born."[26] His drawing depicts a crown of crosses at the top to show that it was a kingdom, with a flat, square shield characteristic of Spain. The place of honor depicts the flag of the thirteen original American colonies, then the Mexican national flag with the eagle (the mythical symbol of the Aztec capital Mexitli), then the castle and lion of Castile and León, where many of New Mexico's families came from. A tiny Zia sun symbol at the bottom represents the Indians. Fray Angélico justifies this miniscule representation of the Native American presence by arguing that the symbol already is the center of the state flag. Despite his attempted justification, he clearly wishes to reassert the important role of Spanish culture in New Mexico history and pictorially subjugates the tiny Zia symbol at the bottom to the crown of crosses at the top and the large symbols of the three nations that have ruled over the native peoples since the conquest.

Groundbreaking Companion Books

In the first half of 1953 while these articles were in press, Fray Angélico completed two groundbreaking books that proved so popular they are still in print. In early August when Provincial Vincent Kroger was visiting New Mexico, Chávez gave him the completed manuscript of *La Conquistadora: Autobiography of an Ancient Statue*, which Kroger read on his trip home to Cincinnati. He wrote to Chávez immediately, highly praising the manuscript.[27] Meanwhile, on August 23, Fray Angélico sent Kroger "what appears to be an adobe wrapped in brown paper," a group of notebooks, or small tablets, that comprised "the actual manuscript" of *Origins of New Mexico Families*.[28] Chávez advised the provincial that the book was purely a scientific dictionary with reference notes on the families of New Mexico and therefore dry reading. The two books, born at the same time soon after Fray Angélico's return from Europe, complement each other and are intertwined: one, a hybrid re-rendering of history creatively telling the story through the eyes of one figure—an ancient statue that is almost a person—and the other a kind of collective biography of a people, painstakingly documenting information about hundreds of families who came to New Mexico in the seventeenth and eighteenth centuries, from whom many contemporary New Mexicans are descended. The dynamic imagination of one book contrasts the important documentary catalogue and reference nature of the other, yet both represent Fray Angélico's continuing commitment as a public intellectual to disseminating his research in accessible form to a wide audience.

On March 10, 1953, he wrote to his dear friend José Cisneros in El Paso about an idea that had hit him the night before. Having worked all winter to complete the three-hundred-page manuscript of *Origins of New Mexico Families*, he thought of asking his talented artist friend to do some drawings to make the book more appealing. While at Fort Bliss, he had talked with Cisneros about collaborating on a literary work, "aquella historia interna de mi pueblo, en que quería unir su nombre y talento con los mios" (that inside story of my people in which I wanted to join your name and talent with mine), but now Chávez suggested that they collaborate instead on this project. He asked Cisneros to draw a frontispiece of Oñate, art and lettering for the title page, and a frontispiece of de Vargas to open the second section of the book. He included detailed small drawings to show his friend what he wanted. Oñate was to be on horseback, next to a friar without a beard, and a soldier with his wife. The Chávez coat of arms was to be at the center of the title page. The second frontispiece was to show de Vargas and a friar looking up the image of the Virgen de los Remedios on the standard carried by El Capitán Don Fernando de Chávez next to his wife. Don Fernando was to be drawn with his shield over his chest. After Cisneros' positive reply, Chávez wrote that his friend could adapt the drawings freely and that what he had in mind was the cover and frontispiece of Hallenbeck's book on Niza.[29]

After Cisneros sent the first sketch in early April, Fray Angélico was very pleased with the drawing of de Vargas and praised the artist for having guessed so well in making Don Fernando de Chávez look like Fray Angélico's father. Within twenty-four hours, Chávez had another idea. He hurriedly wrote again to Cisneros, enclosing photos of himself, his father, and his mother for the artist to copy into the images of the Franciscan friar, Don Fernando, and his wife.[30] Just as he had inserted the townspeople of Peña Blanca into the larger narrative of the *Stations of the Cross* he painted in 1940, here he visually placed his parents and himself as a Franciscan into the history of New Mexico's first families of colonists. The Chávez faces would visually connect with the Chávez coat of arms drawn on El Capitán's uniform and on the initial title page of the book and with the author's name and lengthy self-description on the first and second title pages.

Fray Angélico was extremely pleased with the pen-and-ink drawings that arrived the morning of July 4. He described himself like a child awaiting Christmas when he knew they were on the way. As a fellow artist he could find nothing lacking in the work, whose "valor intrínsico me deja atónito con este tesoro en mis manos" (intrinsic value leaves me astonished with this treasure in my hands). Contributing his own artistic vision to the project, he told Cisneros that he would use the second drawing of de Vargas, which went better with the dark clothing in the drawing of Oñate.[31] Chávez's correspondence with Cisneros in these months reveals that the two were partners in artistic collaboration on the book. Fray Angélico had an artistic vision for the work, and Cisneros' visual talents joined together with those of his friend. Their friendship even survived Fray Angélico's changing one of Cisneros' drawings. Wanting to draw something for the book on La Conquistadora that was being prepared at the same time, Cisneros sent a drawing of the statue. The publisher rejected it because the face didn't look like the statue's, so Fray Angélico took it upon himself to erase the face and try to make a new one himself:

> Ahora que me la devolvió, tuve la osadía de borrarle la cara e imponer una de mi puño—a ver si así la acceptaba. Salió muy parecida la que dibujé yo, pero (válgame Dios!) mis pobres lineas choquéan horriblemente con las profesionales de Ud., de manera que he echado a perder aquella obra tan linda que me había ortorgado. Confio que Ud. me ha de perdonar mi tontera.
> No tema ahora que yo vaya hacer semejante cochinada con los dibujos de Oñate y De Vargas![32]

On the title page, Chávez credits Cisneros with four illustrations for the book on New Mexico families, which, because of funding difficulties, came out after the book on La Conquistadora. The small drawing of the Virgin on the second title page of the *Families* volume is probably Cisneros' drawing, either with Fray Angélico's version of the face, or as Cisneros repaired it. Chávez suggested in a September 25 letter that Cisneros could fix the defacement if necessary.

Fray Angélico again reveals himself as artist, poet, and historian in the four-line poem he wrote to fill in the empty space above the titles on the two title pages. He serializes the poem by using an ellipsis at the end of line two and at the beginning of line three, which is continued on the title page for the second half of the book. He told Cisneros that the lines were neither in Portuguese nor Gallego; rather, he spelled *Senhor* with an *h* because there was no *ñ* available. He intended the verses to unite the two title pages through the coat of arms and the drawing of the Virgin:

> Las Cinco Chagas de mi Senhor
> Cual Cinco Chaves de azul en or
> En manos tuyas, Conquistadora,
> Abrirme han puertas de fino amor.

Using the old spellings of *llagas* (wounds) and *llaves* (keys), Chávez compares the five wounds of Christ to the five keys on the Chávez coat of arms with which La Conquistadora opens doors of fine love for him. His harmonious use of words and images here creates what W. J. T. Mitchell terms the imagetext; the artist in him wished the space on the title pages to be balanced, and the poet in him invented a beautiful remedy for the problem. There are many other examples of this in Fray Angelico's oeuvre, for instance when he "signed" the anonymous book on St. Francis Cathedral with Robert Martin's picture of him with the cathedral in the background and his poem "Of Toads and Such" reprinted on the back cover.[33]

Although Chávez feared that the book on New Mexico families would be dry reading, he insisted on making it a beautiful work of art. As he was preparing it for publication, he wrote short reviews of Francis L. Fugate's 1952 *The Spanish Heritage of the Southwest*, which was illustrated by Cisneros and printed by the talented bookmaker Carl Hertzog. Exuberantly praising Cisneros as "a rare historian with a pen and pencil," he credits Hertzog with imparting magic to the text and drawings. The three-toned drawing on the "adobe-hued" cover of the paperback edition makes it wonderful, but how much more so must be the special limited hardbound edition, with hand-colored drawings by Cisneros, Fray Angélico wonders. He pays little attention to the book's content, but rather attends to its presentation and similarly praises the artwork in superlative terms in other reviews, calling the book a "jewel" or a "painting."[34] The artful presentation of this book strongly influenced Chávez's desire to make his own volume on the families a work of art.

The introduction to *Origins of New Mexico Families* makes some of the same points Fray Angélico argued in the articles on the Kingdom of New Mexico. He also emphasizes that the material included was a by-product of his research on the Franciscan missionaries, especially his work to chart the history of La Conquistadora. The two books he wrote in 1953 are like siblings branching out in two directions, stemming from a common research root and paternity in the early pioneers in New Mexico. The story of La Conquistadora and the story of the origins of New Mexico families are coterminous. Organizing and researching the loose archdiocesan documents, Fray Angélico began to cross-file and compare names, turning up stories about the early Spanish families and their descendants through recorded events. This material provided a unique knowledge of the period, unattainable any other way. By publishing this material in the 1954 book, he aimed to make it available to thousands of the descendants of these families in New Mexico, rather than only a small group of scholars. It belongs to New Mexicans as their patrimony.

The immensity of his work on this project is staggering. Without a computer, he compiled and cross-referenced numerous allusions to the colonists and their descendants. While there were many names and events in the documents, many references were also inadequate and partial, requiring skillful detective work to determine, for example, that a given male might be the son of another man named in a record. Although he argues that the book was feasible only because the population was small and homogeneous in the first two centuries, his extensive work is evident in the numerous names, references, and sample family trees in the book. He notes that an adult in New Mexico in 1953 would have to find over five hundred grandparents in de Vargas' time, while the sample family trees in this book could show only some of these lines.

Chávez summarizes the early history of the region, noting that Oñate arrived in 1598 with about 130 Spanish soldiers and their families, and about 80 additional solders arrived in 1600. Because of mutinies, battles, and desertions, fewer than forty of these names became linked to permanent families of New Mexico. Soldiers who came in the next eighty years married the daughters and granddaughters of the first colonists. In exile after the Pueblo Revolt, some of the refugees left to settle south in New Spain, and when de Vargas came to undertake the second colonization in 1692, there were too few families to attempt resettlement. He recruited newcomers so that the reconquest colony included distinct groups: native New Mexicans, soldiers from Spain, "Españoles Mexicanos" (sixty-seven Spanish families living in the Valley of Mexico who came in June 1694), families from Zacatecas who came in May 1695, and New Mexicans from Guadalupe del Paso. Now, besides Santa Fe there were two new villas, Santa Cruz de la Cañada and Alburquerque. When New Spain became the Republic of Mexico in 1821, there was a mixture of closely related people living in this small stretch of the Río del Norte valley, and this same group existed when the American army of occupation came in 1846.

While some of the conquistadores may have had distant noble ancestors, all now were ordinary people, undertaking the treacherous journey and colonization because of the promise of the title "hidalgo." Although some stories of misdeeds have come down, the majority of the people were virtuous, displaying courage, fortitude, and idealism. There is no written record of this, however, since "court records do not concern themselves with men's virtues."[35] They enjoyed adding ancestral names to their own and sometimes whatever titles they had, such as "Capitan, Alcalde Mayor, Regidor que fué, Hermano de la Tercera Orden..."[36] Fray Angélico humorously imitates this practice in an eight-line entry on the second title page of the first edition of the book: "FRAY ANGÉLICO MANUEL GÓMEZ DURÁN Y CHÁVEZ ROYBAL Y TORRADO, Priest and Preacher of the Order of Friars Minor; Son of the Province of St. John the Baptist; Chronicler, Porter, and Third Assistant at the Mission of San Diego de Jémez, Postmaster of the Pueblo; Regent of the Museum of New Mexico..."

Fray Angélico emphasizes that during the first two centuries, New Mexico was essentially one large family. He attempts to show this by a series of extensive family trees relating to his own family's ancestry, such as Chávez, Robledo-Romero, and Baca from the seventeenth century. In charts for the eighteenth century, he lists his ancestors who were "Españoles-Mexicanos" (those from the City and Valley of Mexico) and the French, north Spanish, and Andalusian component of his ancestry. He argues that by charting a single ordinary family, he can show the extensive interconnections that make New Mexico Hispanos almost a single family. The family-tree diagrams reveal an additional aspect of his tireless work for this volume. He painstakingly assembled them by hand, after having proof sheets made of the names. In a letter to José Cisneros, he wrote, "Luego corto cada nombre y lo pego en su lugar, y despues hago las lineas con tinta-negra. Es un metodo que lleva mucho trabajo y require paciencia."[37] He also worked extensively on calling on his New Mexico and Franciscan families to help underwrite the book by purchasing copies before publication. While his superior wondered how he would ever raise the money after the state funding was unavailable, Chávez's perseverance and commitment to the project succeeded in raising the funds to make this important research on historic family origins available to the larger New Mexican family.

Fray Angélico's nephew Thomas Chávez worked with him to produce a revised version of the book, which was published by the Museum of New Mexico in 1992. Immediately after the first edition appeared, Fray Angélico's further research uncovered new information that he published in a series of articles in subsequent years. The new edition includes these articles at the end, making all Fray Angélico's work on the subject accessible in one volume. The title was modified, as were the two title pages. Fray Angélico also changed the phrasing of his dedication to St. Francis to emphasize the poverty he shared with the founder of his order. Where initially the dedication was to St. Francis "whose barefoot sons shared in the adventures and the hardships of the people treated here," in 1992 he calls St. Francis his true father, noting: "Failing to find a Maecenas or a Lord Chesterfield to finance this venture, even among those who ought to care, I dedicate it to thee, so lacking in funds, like myself." While he overtly expresses his discouragement about finding funding for the book in the 1992 dedication, he expressed his feelings much more subtly in 1954. Explaining the first dedication to his friend José Cisneros, he wrote, "La dedicación fue una inspiración de ultimo momento; Asi le dije la verdad poeticamente a mi P. San Francisco, y a la vez una poca de ironia hacia mis paisanos. Con lo poetico se quita u esconde la amargura."[38] Chávez wants to remind fellow New Mexicans that their success and survival in the area were achieved not on their own but with the crucial help of the Franciscans. Previously, he discussed the tensions between some Spanish officials and the Franciscans, whereas here he employs poetic irony to make his point subtly.

While *Origins of New Mexico Families* represented years of copious, detailed work, *La Conquistadora: The Autobiography of an Ancient Statue* was written, surprisingly, in a few short weeks in the summer of 1953. Time pressures joined with Fray Angélico's creative genius to produce a masterful literary text that flowed almost naturally from the exciting knowledge of his recent historical discoveries and his personal identification with the statue. The Franciscan Commission planning the order's 1954 Marian Year celebrations suggested taking La Conquistadora on a national tour by air so that people across the country could become familiar with the important statue. They commissioned Fray Angélico to write several articles and a book-length popular history of the statue for the tour. As he told his friend José Cisneros in a July 4 letter, "No se cómo me irá—escribir un libro de cien o más páginas durante dos meses de tanto calor" (I don't know how it will go—to write a hundred-or-more-page book in two months with so much heat). But by August 3 Fray Angélico had finished the manuscript, "gracias a Dios, después de muchísimo trabajo, y ya me comían los redactores porque no les mandaba el manuscrito mas antes" (thanks to God, after a lot of work, and with the editors on my back because I hadn't sent them the manuscript earlier). Now he only needed to type it from his handwritten version. When Cisneros' friend Carl Hertzog heard about the project, he offered to publish it in a deluxe edition, but Fray Angélico declined the generous offer because he had already promised it to St. Anthony Guild Press, and it was intended for wide dissemination rather than as an expensive edition.[39]

After his previous intensive research, Fray Angélico knew La Conquistadora's story inside out. When asked to quickly write a popular book in the heat of the Jemez summer, his well-honed literary imagination offered him a solution as well as a creative outlet. Since 1947 he had written a few short stories from time to time, and now he would merge fiction and history in an innovative narrative in which he assumed the identity of the statue under the pretext of allowing her to tell her own story. Having repeated his new historical findings about the statue in multiple venues in recent years, perhaps boredom inspired this creative man to find an alternative mode of narration. Becoming La Conquistadora fictively was also a logical outcome of his intense involvement in the statue's historical and ongoing narrative since 1947—learning of his ancestors' longstanding involvement with the statue, writing its history, working with Bauman to reconstruct a replica, redesigning the wardrobe, reviving the confraternity, and the intense pilgrimage he was about to undertake in the Marian Year with the statue. By the summer of 1953, much of his identity was tied up with the precious statue, and now this identity would be concretized in the innovative literary text. Having become the "semi-pregonero" (town crier) of the statue's history, as he called himself in his July 4 letter to Cisneros, he related to the small figure as a protective, caring parent who was at the same time a figurative child of the Virgin, as do many of the statue's devotees. In addition, his deep love of the Virgin, nurtured since childhood and expressed poignantly in poetry, also informed his work and writing on La Conquistadora. Now he would take these multiple relations a step further by assuming the statue's identity and telling 325 years of history apparently through her ancient eyes, although in fact articulating his own views.

While ostensibly the book is about La Conquistadora, in fact its primary subject is the New Mexico history, in which the central characters are Fray Angélico's ancestors. Through the personification of a revered inanimate object, Chávez can express strong opinions and teach lessons under the cover of the impeccable Mother of God, who is implicitly trusted. The ambiguous "I" allows Fray Angélico to have it both ways—to tell his story through the rhetorical device of telling that of the statue. As he argued in "La Conquistadora Is a Paisana," the statue's story is really that of the New Mexico people. Through the old wooden statue, Fray Angélico establishes a pseudo-focalization or textual point of view whereby a surrogate acts as an agent who sees and recounts events. The implicit textual presence of Fray Angélico as author is the real focalizer. Readers suspend disbelief and play along with the literary device, enjoying the creative fun.

Although Fray Angélico makes several attempts to justify embedded narratives and digressions as the statue tells the story, he ignores other logical inconsistencies and allows the enthusiastic narrative voice to flow on, brimming with information. His goal is to disseminate facts in an easily readable text rather than to craft an impeccable literary work. Before and after an eight-page digression to tell the story of the Virgin of Guadalupe, La Conquistadora assures readers that her own story relates to it and that she enjoys retelling this tremendous event. Or, when providing details about the birth, Baptism, and Confirmation of Francisco Gómez Robledo, the statue remarks that she includes this information "because this boy grew up to be my knight and champion."[40] Among the inconsistent narrative turns is the statue imagining, when entering El Paso del Río del Norte, that "one of those great bluffs . . . would make a grand pedestal for a gigantic statue of the Savior, Christ the King of all creation" without regard to chronological consistency or in a subtle attribution of clairvoyance to the statue.[41] Similarly, the statue imagines that a single white cloud is like another cloud that would appear 325 years later "shaped like a giant mushroom and casting invisible death for leagues around the flats of Alamogordo."[42] Chávez, as the external focalizer of this first-person narrative, describes historical events that the wooden statue could not have known about at the time, just as an adult narrator would shape a first-person account of his or her childhood.

Chávez uses the fictional autobiography to correct and explain several historical events. He blames the Spaniards' abuse and even the misdeeds of certain friars for the Pueblo Revolt, including governors and local leaders who exploited the Indians. He offers an explanation of why the 1692 bloodless reentry into Santa Fe was celebrated rather than the military victory of 1693. Don Juan Páez Hurtado, a personal aide of de Vargas, participated in the first peaceful entry but was away recruiting new colonists when the 1693 battle took place. When he inaugurated the fiesta in 1712 to commemorate his friend de Vargas, he chose the expedition he had participated in and remembered well. He also carried on de Vargas' devotion to La Conquistadora and became head of the confraternity. Chávez sometimes uses utterances that a revered statue of the Virgin would not likely employ. In telling the story of Ana Robledo's anger in 1664 when Governor Peñalosa took one of La Conquistadora's mantles that she had made, the Virgin uses strong language against the governor, calling him "the liar!"[43] Chávez makes history come alive for readers by merging his own voice with that of the statue. He freely overlays his theories and opinions on hers. Speaking about the devotion to Our Lady of Light, which displaced rituals devoted to La Conquistadora in the mid-1700s, the statue says, "But sometimes I wonder if the devotion to Our Lady of Light had depended too much, perhaps, on loud fanfare and pomp, on the power and affluence of the great."[44]

Along with chapters focusing on various important ancestors in early New Mexico history and the devotion to La Conquistadora, Chávez also explains the statue's connection to other representations of the Virgin in Spain and the colonies, including others called "Conquistadora." The first Conquistadora was a small statue of Our Lady of the Angels that Cortés brought with him, which was eventually taken to Puebla. When Francisco Gómez Robledo came before the

Inquisition in 1661, the popularity of this Virgin was at its height, and a book was published to prove the statue was a true Conquistadora. Chávez suggests that perhaps Gómez Robledo brought back the idea of calling the Santa Fe statue a Conquistadora. The small dark statue of Guadalupe in Extremadura whose shrine Fray Angélico visited in 1952 was the first Virgin to be dressed in regal garments in Spain. Fleeing the invading Saracens after 700, Spaniards hid their holy images, and some of these were found six hundred years later. One such image is the small statue of a black Virgin that a peasant found buried in a mountain range that the Moors had named Guadalupe, meaning "hidden river." According to legend, a church was built at the site following the instructions of the Virgin who appeared to the peasant. In 1340 King Alfonso XI won a great battle over Abu al-Hasan 'Ali, ruler of Morocco, after praying for help to Our Lady of Guadalupe. When riches from the colonies were shipped back after 1492, luxurious crowns and dresses were made for the statue; therefore, Chávez's La Conquistadora argues, the tradition of dressing the Spanish Guadalupe was the precedent for her own collection of dresses and jewelry. Fray Angélico points out that so important was the Extremadura Virgin of Guadalupe to the Spaniards who came to New Spain, when the Indians said "Tecuatalope" or "Santa Maria de Coatlalopeuh" (Holy Mary Who Chased Away the Serpent), the Spaniards heard "Guadalupe."

The story of Our Lady of Remedies, also a key part of New Mexico's history, bears similarities to the Guadalupe stories both in Spain and New Spain. In 1540, nine years after Juan Diego's experience, another Indian in the Valley of Mexico found a very small statue of the Virgin that Cortés' army had hidden beneath a maguey tree during La Noche Triste massacre of 1520. After visiting the Virgin of Guadalupe's shrine, he was cured of his ailments, and Guadalupe told him to build a chapel on the spot where he found the statue of Remedios. Chávez recounts that a rivalry based on racism developed between the two representations of the Virgin, in which Spaniards looked down on Guadalupe and her Indian devotees and adopted the Lady of Remedies as their patron since the statue had come from Spain with a conquistador. The latter became known as La Gachupina, "the European-Spaniard," and Guadalupe was called La Criolla, "the Creole." This explains why there was no mission named for Guadalupe in the kingdom of New Mexico until the one in El Paso del Norte, many years later. Chávez argues that de Vargas and La Conquistadora effected a reconciliation of the competition and rivalry between the two Virgins in New Mexico.

The chatty tone throughout the book establishes a sense of friendship and near intimacy between narrator and reader. La Conquistadora expresses the feelings Chávez attributes to her, speaking of the mutilation her body suffered and the many dresses made for her throughout the centuries. The double "I" narrator describes the changes made to the statue so it could be dressed as almost a tortuous martyrdom: "Someone began slicing off my shoulders, until my arms down to the elbows were completely gone. . . . Next they drove crude iron hooks into my armless shoulders, and from them hung shapeless arms that moved also at the elbows, like those of a puppet. . . . Little pierced iron wedges were hammered into my ear lobes, to hold earrings. And they drove a hole into the top of my head; this was to receive a small spike that held my crown in place."[45] The statue has been changed from an actress to a puppet. She is relieved, however, when given regal dresses, mantles, and jewelry and "began to feel glad that they had spoiled my original beauty."[46] What woman, the narrator asks, wouldn't prefer many gowns to a single dress of gold leaf? Chávez tries to attenuate his anger that the historical treasure was violently altered by focusing on the new aesthetics that replaced the old. He falls into contradictions as he creates a martyr narrative to evoke sympathy in readers for a statue that somehow both can and cannot feel, and into stereotypes about women to assuage the damage. Later, as he and the statue describe in detail the many dresses given to her over the centuries, they again stereotypically assert that female readers will be especially interested in these vestimentary descriptions. Fray Angélico's own strong interest in the dresses belies this assumption.

His nonnuanced opinions about the "savages" whom the conquistadores waged war against, and his strong aesthetic dislike of the santos that the Conquistadora vehemently distinguishes herself from, are at odds with today's sensibilities. Nonetheless, the book as a whole is a masterwork of creative hybridity that attractively presents history, religious faith, and ethnic heritage to a wide audience both in New Mexico and nationally. Chávez uses photographs to make the statue come alive visually for readers, beginning with the front cover and frontispiece photographs by Laura Gilpin depicting him lovingly touching the hem of the statue's dress, seeming smaller than the central image of the Virgin. Another photo by Robert Martin opening chapter 1 shows Fray Angélico's collaboration with artist Gustave Bauman to design a replica of what the statue might have first looked like using information from historical records. Successive images include Robert Martin's images of the statue in the gold dress Fray Angélico had made in Germany, in the mantle made from Archbishop Lamy's cope, and a close-up shot of the statue's face intended to illustrate the sad expression Fray Angélico attributes to her. The composite narrator reminds readers at the end that they can see La Conquistadora in her chapel in St. Francis Cathedral if they come to Santa Fe.

The autobiography of La Conquistadora was part of a larger project to increase knowledge of and devotion to the statue during the 1954 Marian Year. Beginning in May, Fray Angélico drove the statue to every parish in New Mexico on a pilgrimage. Where he had described the statue's previous historic trips in the autobiography—the 1625 journey from Mexico City to Santa Fe with Fr. Benavides, the treacherous departure from Santa Fe to Guadalupe del Paso during the Pueblo Revolt of 1680, and the triumphant return with de Vargas in 1693—now he would participate in that history himself by taking the statue on her first trip outside of Santa Fe since 1693, traversing some of the same land she had crossed centuries earlier. The arduous work of being "on the road" for three months and returning to Jemez on weekends to say three Sunday Masses was mild in comparison to the daunting journeys of his forebears in earlier centuries with the statue. And where some might take a deserved break from scholarly work during such a trip, Fray Angélico continued to work steadily while he traveled on his translation and editing of Domínguez's *Missions of New Mexico, 1776* and the book on New Mexico families. By early September, he sent the provincial four large notebooks with the typed Domínguez manuscript for censorship.[47]

Archbishop Byrne launched the tour on May 2 in Zimmerman Stadium in Albuquerque where fifteen thousand people attended a Solemn Pontifical Mass, with a sermon by Bishop Metzger of El Paso. Marian hymns, a living rosary, and a procession preceded the Mass, with members of the National Guard carrying La Conquistadora. The Mass was followed by public recitation of a prayer to the Virgin, which Fray Angélico had written, and Benediction. A special message from Fray Angélico summarized the history of the statue and announced the start of the pilgrimage in which the statue would "reclaim her

FIG 6.2. Soldiers bearing La Conquistadora with Fray Angélico Chávez at left, Zimmerman Stadium, Albuquerque, New Mexico, May 2, 1954, courtesy the Archives of the Franciscan Province of St. John the Baptist of Cincinnati.

'kingdom' by visiting every parish in the Archdiocese," followed by a crowning ceremony with the archbishop in Santa Fe at the fiesta.[48]

After seventeen days of visiting parishes in Albuquerque, Fray Angélico and the statue moved on. On June 7 he brought it to Our Lady of Guadalupe Parish in Clovis where it was displayed on the front porch of a home with two National Guard men as honor guards as people came for veneration. At 7:00 p.m. people processed six blocks to the church while the children sang the Rosary. During Mass,

Fray Angélico gave a sermon in Spanish and the next day took the statue to Sacred Heart Church in Clovis.[49]

Fray Angélico describes the pilgrimage in detail in articles and letters. He tallied seventy-nine parishes and sixteen other churches visited, with eighty-five sermons and eighty-two processions between May 2 and August 31. The first week of September he arranged the details for Cardinal Spellman's coronation of the Virgin.[50] Years later after he had left the order, he recounted some of the more difficult aspects of his role in the Marian Year celebrations and subsequent special events relating to La Conquistadora. In a newspaper article he notes that after writing the autobiography, he was "ordered" to make the trip to each parish and that it was "a grueling if most happy task" to travel to ninety-seven parishes, preach a sermon at each, plus say his three Masses each Sunday back at Jemez. He was pleased because as a result of reading his book, Cardinal Spellman agreed to come to Santa Fe to crown the statue on September 5. However, after the ceremony, the cleric in charge announced that all the monsignors and pastors were invited to a banquet with the cardinal. When Fray Angélico asked about himself, he was told, "You heard what I said." Too tired to drive back to Jemez, he had drinks at La Fonda with Maurice Loriaux, the artist who ran a workshop for ecclesiastical art and furnishings. Chávez recounts, "I began wondering aloud why I had not been invited to the banquet. Or why I was never asked to participate in any ceremonies for La Conquistadora in the cathedral or during the annual Conquistadora Processions. . . . Sometime later the Archbishop scolded me because, as he said, I had been seen drinking at a bar. I merely grinned, for it was a good joke."[51] These and other revelations in the newspaper article by Fray Angélico show that despite all his work for the Church, he had a growing sense of being unappreciated.

In 1956, with the archbishop's permission, Chávez began to revive the cofradía of La Conquistadora, inactive since the early 1800s. The group took on the project of renovating the Conquistadora Chapel where the statue had stood on a simple pedestal off to the side for years. Fray Angélico raised four thousand dollars for the project by writing to Cardinal Spellman and other bishops for contributions. Imaginatively, he had two old side altarpieces with paintings fitted one on top of the other and installed in the chapel to create a reredos and throne for the Virgin. E. Boyd of the museum removed the white enamel that covered the altarpieces to reach the original colors and gold leaf. Chávez disappointedly reported, "Unfortunately, others soon had it painted with garish colors before we knew it." Chávez attended the Papal Coronation of La Conquistadora performed by the apostolic delegate, although he was not invited to participate in the ceremony. Later, Mrs. Elizabeth Hegeman of Albuquerque, who had donated the diamond cross placed on the statue in the ceremony, asked Fray Angélico why her wishes had not been followed that he put the cross on the statue during the coronation. Chávez told her, "Ma'm, you couldn't have done worse."[52] While Fray Angélico waited until after he had left the order to reveal these difficulties, they hurt him deeply, and as a historian, he wished ultimately to leave a public record of them in a 1973 newspaper article.

The Historical Origins of the Penitentes

After the illustrations for *Origins of New Mexico Families* had been arranged with José Cisneros and he had finished reading the proofs for the La Conquistadora book in late September 1953, Fray Angélico turned his attention that fall to writing a groundbreaking article on the Penitentes. In March 1938 he had written a letter to *St. Anthony Messenger* criticizing the inflammatory article on the Penitentes published that month by Phil Glanzer, "Religious Rites of Horror," and the editor had apologized for the article when publishing Fray Angélico's critique in July 1938. In April 1938, *St. Anthony Messenger* published his soon-to-be-famous story "The Penitente Thief," discussed in chapter 3, which presented a realistic, nonsensational portrayal of the brotherhood. Now, after immersing himself in historical research and writing for several years, he attempted to counter "the mass of confusing misinformation which has held sway for more than a century" about the Penitentes.[53] Chávez blamed both American clergy and secular writers who, for different reasons, propagated erroneous views that were then passed down to other writers, often resulting in sensationalism. The Catholic hierarchy wished to suppress or at least control the society's activities, and American newcomers who did not understand Christian penance and the penitential tradition of Spanish culture wrote distorted accounts of what they viewed as strange customs. From a historical perspective, writers had mistakenly dated the Penitentes' presence in New Mexico to 1598 and claimed that the brotherhood had degenerated from the Third Order of St. Francis. Chávez corrects both of these errors and explains the Spanish penitential traditions that underlie the popular religiosity of the Penitentes.

After explaining the errors of writers such as Darley, Harwood, Archbishops Lamy and Salpointe, Gregg, Lummis, Davis, and others, Chávez discusses the founding of the Penitentes in New Mexico. Given that there is no reliable extant information on founders and dates, he employs the methodology of establishing a terminus a quo and a terminus ad quem from other historical evidence to situate the origins of the group. To find the latest period in which they did not exist and then the earliest period in which they did exist, he brings together two documentary sources: Fray Francisco Atanasio Domínguez's 1777 report on his findings the year before, which Chávez had recently translated, and the decree of Bishop Zubiría written in Santa Cruz in 1833. Fray Domínguez's punctilious report on all the New Mexico missions names every religious society including their mayordomos, funds, and properties, but nowhere mentions the Penitentes. "From the way Father Domínguez condemned, reproved, and even ridiculed certain abuses down to the smallest detail, it is obvious that the Penitentes, had he found them in existence, would have provided plenty of rich grist for his mill."[54] At the other terminus is Zubiría's 1833 decree in which he condemned the brotherhood of Penitentes at Santa Cruz. Criticizing their excesses of corporal punishment practiced outside the control of the Church, he forbade their meetings, membership in the groups, and forever abolished the brotherhood. Since Zubiría writes that the Penitentes have been at Santa Cruz "for a goodly number of years" and doesn't mention their existence in other areas, Chávez theorizes that the Penitentes most likely had their beginnings at the turn of the century between 1790 and 1810. Therefore their origins definitely do not date to the first two centuries of New Mexico's colonial period.

Fray Angélico uses his knowledge of Spanish culture to explain three historical references to flagellation in New Mexico before 1790, which historians had misinterpreted as evidence of Penitente practices: the account of Oñate scourging himself in 1598, Fr. Benavides' allusion to public flagellation in Santa Fe before 1630, and Fray Domínguez's report about the Asturian priest Fr. Fernández in Abiquiu, who held the Way of the Cross every Friday in Lent, followed by extinguishing the lights and flagellation. Chávez argues that these instances can be explained by the concept of primitive Christian penance that remained part of the Spanish soul for centuries after it became weaker in other Christian countries. Already formulating some of the central ideas of his 1974 *My Penitente Land*, Chávez notes that Spain did not experience the changed attitudes toward the body and discipline of the hedonistic Renaissance, nor was it affected by the Protestant Reformation's emphasis on faith alone and predestination. "The Spanish-Catholic mind and heart still thought and felt about religious matters, and penance in particular, as did the Catholics of the Middle Ages and beyond. The inherent traits of the Spanish character helped, perhaps, and the harsh central plateaus and landscapes of their land contributed to some extent."[55] Fray Angélico's recent travel in Spain in June 1952 helped to shape these views on "the Spanish soul." He explains that Oñate's privately scourging himself during Holy Week would have seemed normal to his fellow Spaniards because it was commonly practiced throughout Spain and its colonies, and the padre of Abiquiu was a continuation of this tradition. New Mexico still had a medieval character at the beginning of the nineteenth century because of lack of contact with modernizing Spain, its colonies, and other cultures.

Surprisingly, Fray Angélico buries one of his central arguments on the origins of the Penitentes in New Mexico in a footnote. He notes that in Mexico, the masses of people ignored both Church and royal decrees against public flagellation. Fray Agustín de Vetancourt mentions "Procesiones de Sangre" between Mexico City and Veracruz in 1616 and 1641, which were acts of rogation during drought and pestilence. Alice Corbin Henderson quoted vivid descriptions of public flagellation in Mexico as late as 1843, and Chávez concludes using italics for emphasis: *"This late resurgence in Mexico is evidently the source of the movement in New Mexico brought up by some migrant at the turn of the century."*[56] He also suggests the possibility that the practice came to New Mexico by way of a book brought to the area. Most emphatically, he insists that the Penitentes did not originate in the Third Order of St. Francis as had been argued for almost a century. In this article he attributes the mistake to Archbishop Lamy who felt that the brotherhoods had degenerated from the Third Order of St. Francis after the Franciscans no longer ministered in the area. Believing that a connection to the Third Order would regularize the group's religious practices, Lamy issued a set of rules for the Penitentes under the Third Order. "What Lamy accomplished was to leave the idea of their Third Order origin implanted in the public mind, including the Penitentes themselves."⁵⁷ He notes that despite the name of the Third Order appearing on documents the *hermanos* have shown him, the regulations are in no way like those of the Third Order. He also found no evidence that the archbishop had authority or knew how to establish the Third Order, nor that the Penitentes ever wore the required scapular and cord of St. Francis. Later in his 1981 *But Time and Chance*, Chávez modified his position that Lamy began the misunderstanding by noting that Padre José Antonio Martínez of Taos confused the Third Order with the Penitentes, perhaps because of the former's name, "the Order of Penance." Martínez formally requested in 1831 that sixty brothers of the "Third Order" from Santa Cruz be allowed to hold their rituals in Taos as long as no abuses occurred. Lamy was similarly to confuse the two groups after his arrival.

Especially significant, Chavez argues, is that the brotherhood appeared full-blown with a recognizable terminology for itself at this time in New Mexico documents. He argues that these are the same terms in use among the penitential societies of Sevilla, such as Hermanos de Luz (Brothers of Light), who carry candles, and Hermanos de Sangre (Brothers of Blood), who scourge themselves. The term *Nazareno* in the title of the brotherhood does not refer to Jesus being from Nazareth but rather to the Nazarenos in Sevilla who dressed in long red or purple gowns and long black wigs, carrying heavy crosses. Etymologically the term comes not from Nazareth but from the Hebrew *Nazarite*, meaning "one consecrated to God" and recognized for not cutting his hair, such as Samson and Samuel. Chávez also compares the New Mexican Penitente hymns to those of Sevilla. He argues that perhaps because Andalusians did not settle New Mexico as a body, the penitential traditions they brought to other areas of Latin America did not migrate to the far north until the Secular period after 1790.

Fray Angélico's arguments about the origins and roots of the Penitentes countered the numerous misconceptions in publications and documents. Even Aurelio M. Espinosa, who wrote quite accurately about the brotherhood in 1910, twenty years later mistakenly linked the Penitentes of Oñate's conquistadores to the Third Order of St. Francis, Chávez notes. While Fray Angélico defends the importance of the Penitentes, who helped preserve during a critical period "many old Christian and old Spanish nuggets of virtue, courtesy, and folklore which we have since squandered away," with seeming contradiction he argues that they should be a thing of the past.[58] Perhaps his position as a priest in the 1950s outweighs his obvious appreciation of the Penitentes as he suggests that more modern organizations such as the Knights of Columbus or the Holy Name Society might be better means of finding male camaraderie. This remark, along with two negative allusions to the primitive santos, which also arose during the Secular period, should be placed in the context of his extremely positive portrayals of santeros in earlier short stories: "Honest Art," "The Saint Talks Back," "Mana Seda" ("The Hunchback Madonna"), and "The Angel's New Wings."

When Fray Angélico returned to Santa Fe from World War II, he immediately began to assist in the reconciliation efforts between the Church and the Penitentes. In August 1946 he asked the provincial for permission to establish confraternities of the Third Order, arguing: "One big aim is to get all the Penitentes cleaned up and established as Fraternities of the III Order. This will take a long time. Maybe it will work, for the outlook is good."[59] He was referring to the strongly progressing efforts at reconciliation under way and led by Miguel Archibeque. In residence at the cathedral at the time, Fray Angélico probably assisted in the negotiations in the summer of 1946. In another letter he told the provincial that he had written Archbishop Byrne's official declarations on the Penitentes, released in January 1947, which were written about in *Time* magazine.[60] Roque García, son of a Penitente and altar boy of Fray Angélico, remembers traveling to Roy, New Mexico, with Fray Angélico to serve a special Mass for the Penitentes officiated by Archbishop Byrne.[61] While he fulfilled his role as a priest working in the Santa Fe Archdiocese during the last years of the longstanding tensions between the Penitentes and the Church hierarchy, he also brought understanding of the important role the Penitentes played in New Mexico religious and cultural history to the discussions. Overall, in his writing and ministry, he strongly supported the Penitentes.

After turning his unwanted second tour of duty into an opportunity for some degree of creative expression and a journey to see firsthand the land of his Iberian forebears, Fray Angélico returned invigorated with a strong desire to continue with his historical documentary research.

Having accumulated several years of discoveries as the first person to organize and work with the original Church documents in the archdiocese, he was now ready to publish one of the key works of his career, *Origins of New Mexico Families*, which has served the people of New Mexico for decades. His dedicated work with the popular devotion to La Conquistadora inspired him to make this history available in the enticing format of an autobiography in the statue's imagined voice. Similarly, both his historical research and his work with the Penitentes as a mission padre led to his important work of situating the historical origins of the group. Despite his strong commitment to writing history in the 1950s, art and literature would drive his work again as the decade progressed.

CHAPTER SEVEN

The Historian's Return to Art and Literature

WHILE LITERARY AND ARTISTIC CREATION predominated in the first decades of Fray Angélico's life, it moved somewhat to the background during his immersion in historical studies in the late 1940s and 1950s. We have seen that a number of his historical publications and projects were overlain with aesthetic concerns, but his primary project in this period was to find documents, write the new history he had uncovered, correct misconceptions, and reveal the ethnic and religious roots of his people. The early families and the committed Franciscan missionaries of the colonial period were his spiritual and ethnic forebears, so that both religious and ethnic pride shaped his historical studies as he researched their history in the colonial period.

Art inflected his historical work overtly in this period. His books on the archdiocese and the cathedral included his drawings and his careful aesthetic design; the first book of history on La Conquistadora was encased in visual art, and the narrative was overlain with Chávez's aesthetic sensibility; and the creative 1954 autobiography of La Conquistadora hovers between literature and history as a genre.

The new dresses he designed for the statue and the renovation of the Lady Chapel were both historically and aesthetically imbricated. He painted the frontispiece and sketched designs for the drawings for Domínguez's volume on New Mexico missions and worked closely with José Cisneros to produce illustrations for *New Mexico Families* that made the reference book more reader-friendly.

In the mid-1950s, however, he turned his attention more directly to art and literature once again. He composed music and translations for a St. Francis prayer, "Salve Sancte Pater," and did new Spanish and English translations of the hymn "The Responsory of St. Anthony." His visual artistry contributed to these musical projects as he wrote the score and hand-lettered the words for reproduction. He completed a volume of short stories based on an artistic motif, published in 1957 with illustrations by Peter Hurd. In May 1956 in *Spirit* magazine, he published "The Virgin of Port Lligat," a groundbreaking poem that received the accolades of T. S. Elliot and others. Subsequently, he wrote interpretive notes for the poem and published it in a beautiful volume with a reproduction of the painting by Salvador Dalí on which it was based. In 1957 he completed the manuscript of a novel about colonial New Mexico, *The Lady from Toledo*, which was published three years later with his own illustrations. In 1958 he contributed a pen-and-ink drawing to accompany the reprint of his poem "To a Fly (On an Old Friar's Head)" in *Catholic Life Annual*. And shortly after he was assigned as pastor of Cerrillos in July 1959, he began his artistic renovation of two churches in the area. As he had twenty years earlier in his first assignment at Peña Blanca, Fray Angélico worked in several artistic venues simultaneously by writing fiction and poetry, illustrating his books, and beautifully remodeling churches.

In 1955 while searching for a simple hymn about St. Francis to teach his Spanish-speaking Third Order Franciscans at San Ysidro, Fray Angélico got the idea to translate the night prayer "Salve sancte Pater," recited for centuries by Franciscans as their concluding evening devotion.[1] Although not trained in writing music, he composed a melody for the Latin words, which made his translations of the prayer into both Spanish and English easier to create. Although the sounds in the original Latin rhymed, Fray Angélico explains, it is because of the language's inherent assonance, and he did not attempt to create perfect rhyme in the translations. The tertiaries at San Ysidro learned the music easily and were quickly singing the hymn in all three languages.

FIG. 7.1. Hymn "Salve Sancte Pater" translated and hand-lettered by Fray Angélico Chávez, 1955, courtesy the Archives of the Franciscan Province of St. John the Baptist of Cincinnati.

FIG. 7.2. Pen-and-ink illustration for poem "To a Fly (On an Old Friar's Head)" by Fray Angélico Chávez, 1958, courtesy the Archives of the Franciscan Province of St. John the Baptist of Cincinnati.

Fray Angélico hoped that other Franciscans would enjoy using it for their Third Order groups.

Subsequently, he re-translated another hymn, "The Responsory of St. Anthony," which he believed had lost the richness of the original Latin and melody as it was now recited in English at novenas to the saint. "The melody, like the words themselves, is another outstanding example of Franciscan warmth and joy, enlivening the usual somberness of Gregorian Chant."[2] He developed a vernacular rather than exact translation of the Latin to give it more popular appeal. He explains the difficult task of matching the new translations to the music and how he had to adapt a slightly different rhyme scheme for each language, keeping in mind the inherent ideas and wordplay of the Latin original. "The final results look simple, but are really the fruit of many months of humming, mulling, emendation, and compromise."[3] He shows tremendous creativity in the translations, changing word order, finding equivalent expressions, and merging syllables to fit the music. For both this hymn and the "Salve Sancte Pater," Fray Angélico also drew the musical notes by hand and neatly typed and hand-lettered the verses in the three languages beneath the notes.

As vice-president of the Catholic Poetry Society of America, Fray Angélico was invited to preach the sermon at St. Patrick's Cathedral during the Congress of Poetry celebrating the society's twenty-fifth anniversary. His talk, "Poetry and the Ten Commandments," was postponed until the next day's plenary session in the Waldorf Astoria before an audience of two hundred and was published one month later in *Spirit* magazine. In the sermon Chávez argues that the Decalogue affects both art and the artist. He criticizes "art for art's sake" and poets who openly flout moral law, such as the bohemian artists of the Paris Left Bank and "those godless eggheads who controlled the

FIG. 7.3. Fray Angélico Chávez addressing the Catholic Poetry Society of America with Cardinal Spellman (center); Waldorf Astoria, New York City, October 21, 1956, courtesy the Archives of the Franciscan Province of St. John the Baptist of Cincinnati.

poetry pages during the late pink-dominated decades of our era." A product of his upbringing and his conservative anti-Communist religious training, Chávez makes no allowance for well-intentioned socialist and radical writers of the 1930s who believed strongly in the moral value of more equal distribution of wealth. In arguing that "no human being, no matter how gifted, is exempt from the moral law," Chávez posits only one true morality, that of the Decalogue, and argues that the poem must come under God's law. It does not have to be pietistic—that should be left for prose—but it must be "of the spirit, and spirit must include God and His laws."[4] Nonetheless, an atheist may compose good poetry, Chávez concedes, because even without desiring it, the flowering intellect gives glory to God. Cardinal Spellman praised his speech, and a good number, though perhaps not all, of the other Catholic poets in the audience were likely sympathetic to his views on art and religion.

While in Washington, D.C., in January 1957 going over the complicated proofs for *Archives of the Archdiocese of Santa Fe, 1678–1900*, Chávez arranged with José Cisneros to draw endpaper illustrations for the front and back with a map showing the settlements and churches from 1694 to 1850. In blue and white to pay homage to the color of the Franciscan robes and the friars' devotion to the Blessed Virgin, and encircled with the white cord of the Franciscan habit, the illustrations depict a friar instructing Indians before a large wooden cross and a Pueblo church and a procession of colonists with La Conquistadora, led by a friar and two Indian acolytes. Fray Angélico wanted historically complementary artistic images to be the gateway to this valuable historical reference text.

Later that year, when he was again in Washington to translate two film scripts into Spanish for the National Council of Catholic Men, he gave a talk to prospective Catholic writers. He urged them to write at every available opportunity and be willing to sacrifice social pleasures for the somewhat lonely life of a committed writer: "Yet you are not alone when you are writing: you are with your ideas.... You are actually making something." He urged writers to avoid materialism and naturalism and to present the Christian view of life. The naturalistic or "photographic" style usually depicts sordid scenes or themes, such as the indecent descriptions in stories of the South. Good literature, in contrast, describes sordid themes with decency. He also urged writers to carve out a fixed time each day for writing, even if only an hour, to imitate good writers at first, and to aim for writing that is worthwhile, rather than only to make money. This advice reveals Fray Angélico's own goals and habits of writing.[5]

Verbal-Visual Hybridity in Fiction and Poetry

From time to time after he returned from World War II, Fray Angélico wrote short stories. *Southwest Review* published "The Fiddler and the Angelito" in 1947, and "The Black Ewe" appeared in *New Mexico Quarterly* in 1950, as did "A Romeo and Juliet Story in Early New Mexico," although it was a nonfictional account of historical events told in story form. In *St. Anthony Messenger* he published "The Bell That Sang Again" in 1953 and "Daydream in the Chapel" in 1954, which earned him one hundred dollars that he intended to put toward the fund to publish *Origins of New Mexico Families*. Although the *Messenger* usually paid forty dollars per story, Fray Angélico asked for the higher fee "as a charitable donation to my printing project."[6] He published "Wake for Don Corsinio" and "Poor Little Man" in *St. Anthony Messenger* in 1955 and 1956, respectively.

About the time Fray Angélico sent in the 1954 story, he began to think about collecting the recent fiction into a volume. An influence may have been his friend Paul Horgan who wrote on July 1 that a book of his own stories would be published shortly in England. Noting that he'd been unable to drive to Vaughn to see Fray Angélico and "My Lady" because he was reading proofs for *The Great River* and the volume of stories, Horgan wrote in a quickly typed letter: "Macmillan of London are doing, in August, the little volume of novelettes called Humble Powers, containing One Red Rose, the Devil in the Desert and To the Castle. The last one is 'your' story, under its rightful and original title."[7] When he was visiting Rome during his second tour in the army, Fray Angélico had first read Horgan's story in which he was cast as a World War II chaplain. Horgan and Chávez had much in common as Catholics in New Mexico, writing history, fiction, and art. Their friendship occasioned intellectual interchange and cross-fertilization. Fray Angélico's stories clearly influenced Horgan's 1955 *The Saintmaker's Christmas Eve*, published with his own illustrations. Like Chávez's Christmas Eve story in *New Mexico Triptych*, a santo comes alive for the santero who crafted it. Unlike Chávez, Horgan does not use Spanish expressions so that the story lacks the ethnic tone of its antecedent, and he is more critical of the priest who visits the pueblo, whereas Chávez portrayed the priest positively. A novella, Horgan's story is lengthier and develops characters more fully, but Fray Angélico's influence is evident.

Horgan recommended Chávez's coming book of stories to Robert Giroux, editor in chief of Harcourt, Brace and Company, who was interested in reading the manuscript: "I told him that your book was sure to have a goodish annual sale for years in Santa Fe and environs, where travelers look for interpretive works of the region. I am sure you'll have an intelligent and sympathetic reception. He is a Catholic." He also recommended his literary agent, Virginia Rice.[8] Horgan had previously used his connections to obtain Laura Gilpin's photograph for the cover of his friend's book on La Conquistadora.

Chávez and Horgan's friendship involved mutual assistance, wit, and fun. The two wrote well-wrought reviews of each other's work and helped one another out whenever possible. Despite his heavy schedule, Chávez made time to carefully read the manuscripts of Horgan's two-volume *The Great River* and *Centuries of Santa Fe*. In October 1955, Horgan wrote to Fray Angélico from India, asking for quick help on a bibliographic reference and information for *Centuries of Santa Fe*, which he had just completed after a summer of hard work. He needed the citation for the recent edition of the Oñate papers and also requested Fray Angélico to make a chart with the names and positions of all the saints in the reredos now in Cristo Rey Church. He also asked for suggestions on how he might obtain access to documents in Rome on Archbishop Lamy for the biography he intended to write. Fray Angélico quickly sent the information and a sketch of the Castrense altar screen. Horgan was grateful for the "instant reply to my yelp for help" and for saving him from "some horrible howlers." He congratulated Fray Angélico on having submitted the stories to Knopf and noted once again that he was still willing to propose the book to his new publisher Farrar, Straus, and Cudahy.[9]

Horgan did not gain access to the documents on Lamy in Rome until 1959, after his tenacious perseverance in pushing his own case at the Vatican to be exempt from the hundred-year rule. He recounted the experience in a compelling article in *America* in 1991, which ends with an example of Fray Angélico's intelligent analysis of Horgan's feat. Having journeyed to Rome and despite many negative rulings on his request, Horgan made a bit of headway in telling the story of why he wanted to write Lamy's biography to the procurator general of Maryknoll in Rome who could open doors. So compelling was Horgan's narrative that the procurator called the next morning to tell him to write it up quickly because he had arranged an audience for Horgan with the cardinal in charge of the archives—the head of Propaganda Fide—after the cardinal's return from a meeting with the Pope. The cardinal read Horgan's short narrative and then asked specifically about his having been named a Knight of St. Gregory by Pope Pius XII for services to literature. To his amazement, the cardinal immediately exempted him from the hundred-year rule and allowed him access to all the Lamy material. Later, he told the story to Fray Angélico, along with his idea that the cardinal had ruled favorably because his own middle name was Gregory. Chávez debunked this as superstitious and pointed out that the cardinal had met with Pope John XXIII moments before. "Who had already proclaimed an era of new openness in the Church? Who else could give permission with one word to break the hundred-year rule, given cause?" Chávez asked his friend. "Pope John," Horgan answered. "There you are," was Chávez's reply.[10]

Horgan apparently tried unsuccessfully to help Fray Angélico place a story in late 1952. He wrote, "Ooops! *The Atlantic* slipped. Now it has gone to *Harper's*. If they don't schedule it, I would like, with your permission, to send it to my agent, Virginia Rice, to try on the rest of the market."[11] Perhaps the story in question was "The Bell That Sang Again," which Fray Angélico eventually published in *St. Anthony Messenger* in October 1953.

After Horgan encouraged him about the volume of stories in 1954, Chávez wrote several more and on Witter Bynner's advice, sent the collection to Knopf.[12] Horgan's publisher eventually accepted the book, however—the most important national venue in which Fray Angélico's fiction appeared. Peter Hurd agreed to do the illustrations, and Fray Angélico sent him the completed manuscript in September 1956. They met in November to discuss the illustrations, and Hurd completed them in early March. Writing from New York City on October 4, 1957, Horgan told Chávez that he had just been given a copy of the beautiful collaborative work between his two friends.[13]

In his first volume of fiction, *New Mexico Triptych* (1940), Fray Angélico had joined the visual genre he was working on at the time—triptychs of the *Stations of the Cross* in the church at Peña Blanca—to the verbal genre of storytelling. As a hybrid text, the book linked the visual and verbal in both theme and form. His 1957 volume of stories, *From an Altar Screen*, attempted a similar hybridity. At this time, Fray Angélico was working artistically on two altar screens—his color study of the Castrense reredos for the *Missions of New Mexico* book and the construction of a new reredos from old materials for the Conquistadora Chapel in St. Francis Cathedral. In the author's note, Fray Angélico poetically links the visual motif of the retablo to the stories in the book. Each of the seven narratives is a retablo panel drawn from the "New Mexican sky, scape, and village; . . . from the shadows cast by firs and piñons at certain hours, from the still air of adobe homes and chapels at dusk. The outlines of each figure are from folks known through the years. . . . The whole thing is more of a tableau . . . picturing the soul of a simple people at various periods across a couple of centuries. The more or less exact date of each tale appears hidden somewhere in the background of each panel."[14] If Fray Angélico commented critically on the primitive santos in his autobiography of La Conquistadora, here he portrays santero art positively, as representing the soul of the New Mexico people.[15] "Any resemblance to actual catalogued *retablos* is meant to be that way," he says of his stories, emphasizing his people's close connection to the santos.[16]

Set in seven distinct historical periods, the stories teach moral lessons beneath the pleasurable trappings of Hispano ethnic traditions, history, and religiosity; the suspenseful resolution of an enigma or a character's temptation; and correlations between biblical and saintly prefigurations of the characters. In every story, one of the figures represented on Chávez's metaphorical altar screen seems to step out from the *nicho* or painting to come alive for the characters. Santa Ysabel appears in order to dissuade the young widow named after her from taking her own life. A child, perhaps the one depicted in the Virgin's arms or one of the painted cherubs, comes alive to force the town fiddler to do his duty. Santa Bárbara appears to a man who has fallen into alcoholism and poverty after the death of his wife, Bárbara. San Acacio's early Roman martyrdom is reenacted in the death of a World War II soldier named after the saint. Chávez crafts the plots to correlate with the traditional narratives carried down through the ages about the holy figures. As Fr. Thomas Steele has argued, Fray Angélico assimilates these figures into the patterns of life and culture in New Mexico over the centuries.[17]

When the book was republished in 1977, Fray Angélico corrected the title that the first publisher had changed, as well as two incorrectly placed Hurd drawings. He tweaks the motif of the altar screen and places the author's note at the beginning instead of the end to shape readers' interpretation of the stories to follow. With the intended title, *When the Santos Talked*, he emphasizes the notion of the images coming alive to help people resolve problems, which has been essential to Hispano religiosity in New Mexico.

Fray Angélico makes the images of the saints come alive in these stories to teach both moral lessons and history. He entices readers to this history by bringing New Mexico forebears to life through imagined accounts of their human foibles. In introducing the story of Doña Casilda's near seduction in the late eighteenth century, he notes that he must also detail the important historical landmarks, objects, and people connected to her: "They have to clutter up the tale, like so many stakes holding a great tent taut and fast."[18] He describes the architecture and layout of the buildings on the plaza in detail to place readers there almost physically. Descriptions of husbands' deaths in campaigns against Indians, the presence of French merchants, and Spanish religious and civil ceremonial pageantry establish the historical setting of the tale. Writing this story at the time he was finishing work on *Missions of New Mexico*, he uses details from Domínguez's description to visually re-create image-by-image what the protagonist sees in the interior of the military chapel on the Santa Fe plaza dedicated to Our Lady of Light. The bishop of Durango's visit to Santa Fe to dedicate the military chapel in 1761 is a key background element, as Chávez imagines that the bishop gave the protagonist a small painting on copper of Our Lady of Light to protect her, just as the painting depicts the Virgin protecting the child from a dragon. Chávez captures the immense importance of visual imagery in Catholic spirituality in this period. As Casilda views the large original painting in the huge stone reredos during the ceremonial Mass, she tunes out the priest's Latin droning, focusing on the image of the Virgin. Fray Angélico, who precisely at this time was painting a color image of the old reredos as it would have looked with paint in 1776, describes the vivid color image that Casilda would have seen: "the figures and colors were richly distracting. They were exactly like those in the miniature above her bed, as though the picture had been stretched out by magic to become this one on the altar, or the other way around. In fact,

Casilda could do the trick at will by squinting hard."[19] Fray Angélico has Casilda engage in precisely the same visual exercises that he himself used to reproduce the large painting for the miniature image frontispiece of *Missions of New Mexico*.

Art and history are connected to spirituality for the Franciscan writer, and the painting's key role within the narrative is not aesthetic or historical but to protect Casilda from falling into sin. Comandante del Fuego literally burns up and explodes after seeing the Virgin's image in Casilda's bedroom, revealing his true identity as the Devil—the dangerous dragon in the painting. The medieval worldview portrayed here leaves no room for women and men to negotiate and come to terms with sexual desire. The woman cannot be expected to make a proper decision on her own about whether or not she will enter into a relationship, but needs supernatural intervention to protect her from evil. Writing in the Marian Year 1954, Fray Angélico casts the Blessed Virgin as the model of female chastity, with good and evil as absolutes. Nonetheless, when he revised the story for the 1957 collection, he added sentences and paragraphs that emphasized Casilda's loneliness, showing her human vulnerability and hinting that Hispano superstitions and customs of the time prevented her from marrying again after three husbands died.[20]

The moral lesson of another story in the collection involves the righting of a wrong by punishing the woman instead of the more powerful man when both are involved in sexual transgression. In lines he added to the revision of the 1950 story "The Black Ewe," Chávez raises suspicions and invites readers to solve an enigma. The shepherd Agapito worries about the ambiguous meaning of the pronoun *her* when the *patrón* tells him to leave the special black ewe in the corral so that he can enjoy the sight of her: "*When the master used the female pronoun, however, Agapito could not help thinking of something else.*"[21] Another of the revisions he made to the story for the 1957 volume adds to suspicions: "the master often came to San Blas and stayed a few days each time to oversee the work, so he said; *for he seldom went out to the pastures where the sheep were grazing.*"[22] Even in the revision, Chávez gives only meager clues, however, wanting to surprise readers with the ending. The ambiguous pronoun now represents the single identity that the ewe and the woman share in this cautionary parable. The tall, strong figure of a *genízaro*, probably the husband of the woman the master is sleeping with on his visits to San

Blas, corporally punishes her by enacting violence on the black ewe. When the genízaro commands Agapito to shear the sheep, the two subservient figures finally stand up to the master, and Agapito thereafter can raise his eyes to look at the master directly. The unfaithful woman, however, suffers severe physical punishment and lies in bed debilitated and shorn of her hair. Agapito's punishment also in effect repays the kindness of the patrón's wife, Doña Eduviges (whose name Chávez changed from Isabel so that he could use this saint's name in "The Bell That Rang Again"), who had nursed him after a snakebite, paralleling the kind acts of her namesake, St. Hedwigis.

In several stories the wooden santos or retablos come to life to help people cope with death. Just as the colonel in "The Colonel and the Santo" feels he is entering a painting when the chaplain takes him to the New Mexico home of the dead soldier he called Cash, so will Cash become the figure of San Acacio in the painted santo in his mother's home. When the mother affixes her son's medal to the image of the crucified soldier, the saint takes on a figurative life and assumes a kind of humanity. Rather than succumb to the gruesome details of her son's death, the mother associates them with the crucifixions of Cash's early Roman namesake and that of Christ.

When the fiddler and *leñero* in "The Fiddler and the Angelito" tries to escape playing for the wake and burial of a village boy by looking for more wood to sell on his burro, the child comes back to life as an angel to insist he play the violin. Changing words from the original 1947 story, Fray Angélico contrasts the "barren dead wood and the dried entrails of sheep" of the violin to the "paunchy female burro" with a "somewhat swollen belly,"[23] who would be able to wander off to "possibly assure herself of a successor" while the fiddler played for the dead child's wake. In imagery and plot, the story encourages the idea of life's triumph over death.

Similarly, in "Wake for Don Corsinio" (originally titled "Poor Little Man" in 1956), Santa Bárbara comes to life from a retablo dearly loved by Corsinio's wife, Bárbara. Like his other possessions, he had sold it for money to sustain his alcoholism after her death. Santa Bárbara, the protector against lightening, saves him from death during a storm, although he seems to be dead and his neighbors prepare a wake for him. His dead wife appears to him as Santa Bárbara to assure him he did not cause her death and help him recover from it. The saint's coming to life within the story re-establishes the narrative equilibrium that has been disrupted both by his apparent death and the previous real deaths of his wife and son.

When the carved wooden statue of San José comes alive for José Vera in "The Lean Years," it is part of a parable about coping with tribulations that come even to good people, resisting temptation, and fecundity ultimately triumphing over barrenness. The furniture maker José carries on his father's name and carpentry skills, and spiritually he carries on the biblical tradition of his namesakes Joseph of Egypt and Joseph of Nazareth. Where Joseph of Egypt saved his people from starvation in seven years of drought, and Joseph of Nazareth cared for his wife and her child, so will José Vera care for his paralyzed wife with whom he cannot have children. The biblical narratives of the drought and virgin birth become parables to guide José in his contemporary troubles.

The village of La Cunita, a figurative cradle protected from the evils of the nearby city Las Vegas, shelters its twenty families and José Vera as he is about to marry Soledad. During the wedding reception a roof collapses, paralyzing the new bride. After José's friend Urbán, whose name symbolizes the evils of the city, gets him drunk, the little wooden statue of San José at the town chapel comes alive and waddles into José's home, advising him to care for Soledad as if she were both his wife and child. Despite following this advice, José is unhappy and travels to Las Vegas to sell the toys and furniture he made, where he faces the urban temptations of alcohol and adultery. Instead of succumbing, José brings home the seeds of hollyhocks or "varas de San José." The Spanish name for these American flowers plays on José Vera's name, reminding him to remain strong like St. Joseph and be content with symbolic fecundity—here the beautiful flowers he will plant to console his wife in her last days. These real flowers will replace the paper flowers the townspeople attach to San José's staff during the saint's fiesta. And after the "seven lean years" and his wife's death, José will re-marry, have children, and cultivate more beautiful hollyhocks in Soledad's memory.

Although a publisher's error transposed Peter Hurd's drawings for this story and the following one, "The Colonel and the Santo," readers can perhaps make the adjustment mentally. His image of Cash's rural adobe house with crosses in the windows recaptures Chávez's verbal description of "the painting" that the colonel felt he was entering: "some clumps of bluish-green sagebrush . . . a small adobe house dozing cool and quiet under the glossy umbrella of a giant cottonwood."[24] In the drawing intended for "The Lean Years," Hurd depicts the stern-faced San José santo with his staff and the Christ child, with rays of light emanating from him to symbolize his extraordinary "coming alive" for José Vera, who lies drunk in bed. In "Wake for Don Corsinio," Hurd selects key elements—a wooden retablo of Santa Bárbara holding a sword with rain in the sky behind her and two candles lit for Corsinio's wake. Although Fray Angélico chose not to create his own drawings for this collection, the collaboration with Hurd produces a rich visual-verbal montage similar to that of *New Mexico Triptych*.

Fray Angélico's tandem preoccupations with the verbal and the visual come into play in many of his works, in particular his poem "The Virgin of Port Lligat," published without illustration in a poetry magazine in 1956 and subsequently in book form in 1959 on the recommendation of T. S. Elliot, along with a photograph of the painting that inspired it and lengthy explanatory notes. Motivated by Fray Angélico's fascination with Salvador Dalí's 1950 painting *The Madonna of Port Lligat*, the 113-line poem celebrates the link between nuclear physics and religious mysticism. Selecting from Dalí's immensely transgressive oeuvre a painting that Pope Pius XII had approved of, Chávez writes a highly creative yet orthodox religious poem that was awarded an imprimatur by his religious superiors in 1958.[25] The publisher who wished to release the poem in book form asked Fray Angélico to write a commentary to lengthen the text. A deluxe edition of five hundred copies was ready May 1, 1959, and the trade edition May 18. "The deluxe is intended not only to honor the Mother of God, reach the pagan book collector, but also help launch the cheaper trade edition," Chávez wrote. He was disappointed that only two subscribers from the province had made advance purchases. "Cui bono?" he commented to Provincial Kroger, echoing the title of his friend Gerald Cassidy's noted 1911 painting of a Taos Pueblo Indian, implicitly asking onlookers, "Who benefits from this?" With this intertextual allusion, Fray Angélico again suggests that he is a friar treated as an Other within the order, perhaps because of his ethnicity. By late May 1959 he was happy to report that both Archbishop Ritter and Cardinal Spellman had written with high praise for the book.[26]

In his commentary, Fray Angélico engages in several strategies of containment to attain interpretive closure over Dalí's painting and his own poetic text. While Chávez deploys a variety of visual and verbal aesthetic modes in the book, he ultimately privileges the verbal as he attempts to limit the polysemy of the painting and his poem. Nonetheless, the image was a site of fertile fascination for Fray Angélico and inspired him to produce a vibrant interartistic work. Chávez recognized the dialogic relation established between his poem and the reproduction of Dalí's painting in the 1959 book, and in a typescript emended for a future edition, he employs a different title that emphasizes his own equality with the painter in the joint aesthetic work: "'A Dalí-Chávez Duet': *The Madonna of Port Lligat*—A painting by Salvador Dalí, *The Virgin of Port Lligat*—Ode by Fray Angélico Chávez."[27] In this later typescript, Chávez adds a "Poet's Foreword," highlighting the key role the painting played in his poetic creation after he happened to see Dalí's work reproduced in *Life* magazine. Realizing the inadequacy of publishing the poem without its visual intertext as he had done in 1956, Chávez included a black-and-white reproduction on the cover and as the frontispiece of the 1959 book edition, and he added an ekphrastic description of the painting in an introductory section entitled "The Setting."[28] The reproduction is an inferior copy of the original, and the primary visual image in the book begins the duet with a handicap. Despite the centrality of the image and the open possibilities of interpretation it offers viewers, Fray Angélico's words have the upper hand in this so-called duet.

In both his 1949 and 1950 versions of *The Madonna of Port Lligat*, Dalí combined his awe of the 1945 atomic explosion at Hiroshima with his renewed religious mysticism. Believing that he could understand and master the forces and hidden laws of nature through mysticism, Dalí advanced the concept of "dematerialization," the equivalent in the age of atomic physics of "divine gravitation."[29] In the "Anti-matter Manifesto" of 1958, he argued that that because physicists were producing antimatter, painters who were "already specialists in angels" should paint it; the latest microphysical structures were to function as the new brushstrokes of the postatomic age.

In the *Port Lligat* pieces and other paintings of the period, architectural, natural, and human representations are partially broken up and floating in defiance of gravity. Dalí engages in a kind of atomic iconoclasm of the Renaissance intertext for the Port Lligat Madonnas—Piero della Francesca's fifteenth-century Brera altarpiece, *Madonna and Child with Angels and Six Saints*. Where the hands of

Piero's Virgin are joined together in the traditional upward gesture of prayer, Dalí parts the Madonna's hands to create a triangular space above the child's head; besides the obvious reference to the Trinity, the repositioned hands also signify the incipient kinetic gesture of the laying on of hands, expanding the healing powers of the gesture that is biblically reserved for men to the female figure in the painting.

Dalí visually resignifies both the Madonna and the angels of Piero's painting by adding the overarching signifier of the face of his partner, Gala. Intertextually linking the *Madonna of Port Lligat* paintings to his various other works in which Gala appears, this resignification was a political gesture as well. Dalí showed the earlier version of the painting to Pope Pius XII on November 23, 1949, and, a biographer notes, organized another audience with the Pope in 1955, ostensibly to show him the 1950 larger version; in reality, Dalí sought the second audience to obtain an authorization to marry Gala in the Church, now that her husband Paul Éluard had died.[30] By giving Gala an even greater visual role in the second painting, now on the face of the angels as well as on the Madonna's, Dalí engaged in politically charged visual semiosis, hoping that the sacred part of the figures' double referents would impart sanctity and approbation to the worldly element.[31] And since semiosis is a transitive activity in which various viewers perform different kinds of work in the process of decoding, the Pope's sacred reading of the text would not preclude other publics from extracting more transgressive signifieds.

In the 1949 *Madonna of Port Lligat*, the Madonna's head and chest are split, blood appears on the Christ child's head, and his body is jarred to the right as if by the force of an explosion, in contrast to his more peaceful position in the 1950 version. While the Virgin's garment is torn in the 1949 painting, it is instead lifted and open in the 1950 version, exposing a foot unsupported by the pedestal and evoking a greater sense of floating. The Virgin's head is slanted to the left in the final version, reversing the direction of the first painting, perhaps so that the head may now complete the curve of the rhinoceros horn below, an image added to the second version. In both paintings, although Piero's architecture and human imagery are somewhat fragmented, the image is a much minimized simulacrum of the real force of an atomic explosion. And the egg remains unshattered above, a symbol of the female and procreation, here with divine progeny.

In his attempt to secure interpretive closure over Dalí's work, Fray

Angélico purposely ignores the painter's more transgressive side, terming the rhinoceros in the pedestal with its phallic horn, for example, one of "the artist's strictly private symbols."[32] Similarly, Chávez does not develop any of the imagery in Dalí's 1949 *Leda atómica*, an obvious intertext of *The Madonna of Port Lligat* with Gala again as the Virgin in a more transgressive representation.[33]

Fascinated by the imagery in the 1950 *Madonna of Port Lligat*,[34] and despite his nonengagement with the transgressive elements of Dalí's work, Fray Angélico offers both a critical exegesis and an exquisite poetic reelaboration of the work. In "The Setting," the verbal introduction to his book, he employs the visual metaphor of three images that will structure the poem to follow: the first, his interpretation of certain images in Dalí's painting; the second, an intellectual metaphor redeveloping the figure of the Sphinx; and the third—which he terms both visual and intellectual—the image in astronomy and nuclear physics of the orderly floating of the constellations and the parallel floating of particles inside the atom. With an imaginary visual intertext, Chávez envisions that the three images are painted on transparent glass or film—the Dalí Madonna, the reconfigured Sphinx, and the cosmic and nuclear galaxies, "to reconcile different planes of knowledge and experience in art, science, and theology."[35] As Krieger has argued, poets often prefer that the visual intertexts they verbally imitate be fictive, to enable the poetry both to exceed the visual image with language and to have a freer rein with the verbal description.[36] In effect, Chávez displaces and transcends Dalí's painting with his imaginary tripartite image on transparent glass. Despite the extensive imbrication with the visual that characterizes Chavez's verbal utterances here, and the fascination and inspiration he draws from the painting, the book also ultimately privileges the verbal because of its interpretive gestures and literary and religious ends.

Chávez's reading of Dalí's painting is selective, as are all interpretations, and focuses on the visual signifiers that will nurture his poem. The floating images in the painting invoke the divinely ordered suspension of galactic bodies and subatomic particles for Chávez, as he narrates the progression of human knowledge through Newton and Copernicus to the nuclear age. The "geometric openings in the Mother and Child" are a bold stroke of surrealism;[37] how can they shock people, he wonders, who gaze with complete calm at images of the Sacred Heart hanging out in "gory detail" from Christ's chest.

Notably, Chávez changes Dalí's title of Mary from "Madonna" to "Virgin," insisting on her purity even as he relates her to Eve. Dalí's Madonna "Is all Eve's daughter to her feet," yet because she is suspended "Untouched, and touching nothing, free," she embodies a "personal stainlessness . . . retaining her physical integrity before, during, and after the Virgin Birth of her Son."[38] Chávez reintegrates the transgressive subtexts of Dalí's imagery into orthodox religious doctrine. The poet has it both ways: open enough to enjoy Dalí's liberal reworking of religion, he at the same time re-secures the images to official dogma.

In addition to developing the symbols of the tabernacle, bread, and nurturance in the absent chests of the Madonna and child, Chávez reads the image of "The Word" into these spaces. On one level he reasserts the word by superimposing a biblical quotation in the geometric opening of Dalí's Madonna:

Her open breast the Prophet's aleph-shapen cry
Of sweet unsphinctered mystery:
"Behold, a Virgin shall conceive and bear a Son!"[39]

Recasting the Virgin as "The Sphinx of this our era," Chávez interprets the opening in her chest as an "unsphinctered" version of the "constrictor muscle of the cervix" from which will "bloom" the quotation from Isaiah about the Virgin birth.[40] The Word in Chávez's poem additionally fills in Dalí's visual opening in the sense that the Christ figure is now the answer to the Sphinx's riddle, walking on four legs in Bethlehem, two in Jerusalem, and three as he drags his cross to Calvary. In the Virgin's bosom is framed the "pending word in mouth . . . her riddle and reply."[41] Chávez develops a sacred rearticulation of the image of the Sphinx, in contrast to Dalí.

While we might read Chavez's central motif of the Word as a further assertion of the verbal over the visual, perhaps it is more useful to view the issue conversely, instead focusing on his strong fascination with the visual that often manifests itself as what Mitchell terms "ekphrastic hope." Even though Chávez attempts to anchor the semiosis of Dalí's painting with verbal exegesis and poetic re-elaboration, he performs a similar process on his own poem by including thirty-five pages of line-by-line notes in the book. Rather than trying to displace the visual object, Chávez exhibits his excited fascination with it. Without Dalí's painting and the new vision it presented, Chávez would never have written this poem—in effect a partnership and kind of duet. Although the verbal might be said to predominate in many ways, the book remains a prime example of what Mitchell terms the "imagetext," a composite, synthetic work that combines image and text.[42] In such cases, it is more useful to focus on its rich semiotic hybridity instead of the rising and falling scales of balance between the visual and verbal.

Historical Findings in Search of a Creative Venue

In 1957 Chávez completed the manuscript of another literary work relating to the Blessed Virgin, *The Lady from Toledo*. Like the autobiography of La Conquistadora and *The Virgin of Port Lligat*, it grew from the Catholic Church's emphasis on the Blessed Virgin in the 1954 Marian Year. As had occurred both in his writing on La Conquistadora and his poetic homage to Dalí's Virgin, he worked for several years to re-elaborate his first publications on the subject, adding new historical findings and additional ideas in subsequent texts. He had difficulty finding a publisher for *The Lady from Toledo*, and it was not published until 1960. Meanwhile, he wrote a scholarly article on the subject, "Nuestra Señora de la Macana," published in 1959. Almost a decade later, after further research, he published an even more detailed treatment of the subject in his controversial article "Pohé-Yemo's Representative and the Pueblo Revolt of 1680." Many of Chávez's projects were intertwined works that developed and grew over long periods, rather than isolated, completed works after which he moved on to new topics.

Although *The Lady from Toledo* announces itself as an aesthetic work about a small statue of the Blessed Virgin, in fact it is a largely historical work about the Pueblo Revolt and colonial figures who were Fray Angélico's ancestors. In my view it fails as a novel because it is overwhelmed by Chávez's desire to recount historical minutiae he had discovered in years of research on the period. Two sections of the book are compelling novelistically, but multiple digressions impede narrative flow throughout most of the book. His first novel, *Guitars and Adobes*, worked much more effectively as a novel because Chávez had not yet become overwhelmed by the innumerable historical findings he uncovered in the late 1940s and 1950s. He succeeded in adapting some of this material to fiction in shorter venues such as the stories in *From an Altar Screen*, but he allowed the historical information to weigh down the aesthetic intention in the 1960 novel.[43]

As with his work on La Conquistadora, he brought his historical findings to both scholarly and creative venues. He tells the stories of both ancient wooden statues that played important roles in early New Mexico history in academic texts as well as in imaginative, personalized accounts. In the 1960 novel, however, the story of Nuestra Señora de la Macana (Our Lady of the Aztec War Club), formerly known as Our Lady of Sagrario in Toledo, Spain, is only a narrative frame established on the front cover, the opening and closing illustrations drawn by Fray Angélico, and the first and last chapters, while the bulk of the novel deals with the Pueblo Revolt of 1680. The story of the statue's time in New Mexico is the occasion for Fray Angélico, through the persona of his ancestor Ana Robledo, to narrate the stories of his family ancestors from 1600 to 1680 in New Mexico. Thus, the book is an extension of *Origins of New Mexico Families* and his other publications on his colonial forebears.

A paralyzed girl, María Romero, whom the Virgin miraculously cures and who foretells the destruction of the Spanish colony in northern New Spain, appears at the beginning of the novel as the diegetic audience of her great aunt Ana Robledo's stories about the origin of the statue, key historical events, and religious disagreements between the Pueblo Indians and the Church. At the end of this section, the small statue of the Virgin of Toledo that María's family has brought from the Valley of Mexico, and which she keeps in a niche in her room, cures her as she is near death. Growing larger and coming closer to her, the Virgin tells her to get up and tell everyone that the kingdom and custody will be destroyed soon because the Spanish colonists have not respected the priests and therefore hurt the conversion of the native Indians. María's cure from paralysis will be the divine sign that people must repent and change their ways if they hope to be saved from the coming disaster, the Virgin tells her. The colonial religious narrative was intended to dissuade and strike fear in those civil authorities who allowed the natives to retain practices that the Church condemned as idolatrous.

The rest of the novel describes in detail the disaster that befell the Spaniards and allows Fray Angélico to introduce his theory about the role in the Pueblo Revolt of Diego Naranjo, a mulatto from Mexico, whom the Spaniards characterized as the Devil and the Indians believed was the human representation of the god Pohé-Yemo. Chávez argues here and in the related article that although popular legend must be corrected and verified, it also sheds new light on the "black-and-white sketches left by governors and captains."[44] The legend recounts that the statue of the Virgin of Toledo predicted the destruction of the missions six years before it happened and that the Indians then rebelled under the leadership of the Devil who appeared as a giant. When the rebels attacked Santa Fe, an Indian chief broke the small statue of the Virgin with his *macana* or "war club," and then the Devil hung him. The statue was taken to the Valley of Mexico and was restored, but the wound continued to open and be repaired over the years.

Chávez remembered related evidence uncovered in his historical research and brought it together to tell the fuller story behind the popular legend. He argues that the Devil of the legend was Diego Naranjo, a mulatto with bright yellow eyes, who, after coming to northern New Spain as a fugitive slave shortly before 1621, encouraged native rebellions against the Spaniards from his mysterious position as the representative of the god Pohé-Yemo. He had attained this prestigious position through his large size and frightening appearance along with his ability to perform magic and speak Spanish and several native languages, thereby uniting the divergent Pueblo peoples to rebel against the Spaniards. A year after the 1680 revolt, when Otermín questioned him about the events, he misled the Spaniards again by blaming three spirits for the revolt, which subsequent historians wrote into the narrative and Fray Angélico rejects as the eighty-year-old Naranjo's deliberate invention.

Chávez imagines in this fictional rendition of some of the historical figures a key final moment in which Diego Naranjo confronts Juan el Tano, an Indian first loyal to the Spanish but who later fights against them. After Juan el Tano sacks María Romero's Santa Fe house, hitting the small statue of La Virgen with his macana, he repents, wraps the statue in a scarf, and throws the bundle up to a Spanish soldier on the roof of the Palace of the Governors. Indians who see him do this bring him before Naranjo. Then the group kills him and Naranjo dons a kachina mask to hang the body from a tree. "The Spaniards standing guard atop the Palace roof saw what appeared to them . . . like a fearsome dark giant with the face of the Devil himself. Big sharp horns stuck out of his big black drum-shaped head. . . . The monster was hanging from the river tree the limp body of . . . Juan el Tano."⁴⁵ Employing a verbal/visual metaphor, Fray Angélico argues that fictional renditions such as the encounter he imagines between Naranjo and Juan el Tano function as the "third color plate" needed to fill out the picture, and only fiction can produce this added level of color for the strictly historical narrative.⁴⁶

The strength of *The Lady from Toledo* lies in dramatic scenes such as this that imaginatively explain the seemingly absurd, medieval-like legend about the Devil and the Pueblo Revolt, placing readers narratively in the historical moment. Chávez argues that often, "legend and folklore are but the foam, the flowering of history. Under the airy froth flow the tides of human life; beneath these currents, tracing these roots, one can come upon the intimate aspirations and sorrows of real people."⁴⁷ But he undercuts his admirable goal in this novel by overwhelming the drama and the solving of the puzzle with lengthy digressions that instead of providing a flavor of the times, tediously lead us away from the main story. He spends more than twenty pages describing Padre José de Trujillo's journey from Cádiz to New Spain, the Philippines, and eventually to the cliff pueblos of Moqui where he wrote about the Virgin's cure of Ana and the prediction of the rebellion. His role in the story of the statue and the revolt could have been told without so much time spent on his journey to the missionary priesthood, the people who influenced him, and countless other details. Fray Angélico is proud, nonetheless, that he is for the first time bringing the story of Our Lady of Toledo to present-day New Mexico, whose people "salute her across an international border."⁴⁸ While his account centralizes the perspectives of the Spanish and the Church in the events, he argues that Native Americans and even those descended from Naranjo join in his salute to the Virgin.

A product of his time and imbued with the ideology of his strict religious training as a Catholic missionary, Fray Angélico expressed complex attitudes about race, some of which are offensive to today's sensibilities. This is the priest who deliberately disobeyed orders and invited a black soldier to be his acolyte in the segregated U.S. Army during World War II, yet wrote home to the provincial that "a darkie" had stolen his wallet from his pants pocket while he slept. He supported the black Civil Rights Movement in the 1950s and 1960s and several times asked his superiors for permission to move out of the friary to take up residence with the Pueblo Indians. He lovingly ministered to them, spent Saturdays teaching catechism during the period of the interdict, and worked hard to negotiate an end to this official Church punishment of the Santo Domingo people. The generosity and self-sacrifice of his lifelong goal to be a missionary to the native people of New Mexico was nonetheless linked to an underlying sense of superiority inherent in the Catholic and Franciscan enterprise of saving pagan souls for the perceived true religion. All of Fray Angélico's missionary training and his first decades of ministry took place in the pre-ecumenical period before Vatican II, prior to the Church fostering greater acceptance of other religious traditions. Nonetheless, Fray Angélico's movement from protoracist attitudes toward Native Americans in his early work on the Pueblo Revolt and the Virgin of Toledo to offensive racial statements in the 1967 article on Diego Naranjo in the *New Mexico Historical Review* is surprising given the sociopolitical milieu of the late 1960s in which the article is published.

He argues, for example, that historians have failed to consider that "some of the principal and most intelligent ones among the leaders were not pure-bred Pueblo Indians . . . [because] during the first eighty years certain mestizos gravitated into pueblo life [and] . . . their native and acquired capabilities were superior to those of the inbred pueblos. . . . Otherwise, the ordinary run of Pueblo Indians had been happy with the many material benefits brought them by the padres."[49] Fray Angélico is wearing historical blinders when he assumes that there was no discontent among the conquered native peoples of northern New Spain and that an outside leader claiming to be a god's lieutenant could rally perfectly happy, geographically and linguistically separated peoples to unite to risk their lives in armed rebellion. If the Pueblo Indians were as passive and content as Fray Angélico argues, why did the friars need to engage in continuing arguments with them to eliminate kachina rituals and ceremonies in the *estufas* or kivas? More offensive is his contention that Native Americans were genetically inferior to the mixed-race people who took up residence among the Pueblos, such as Diego Naranjo. Later he argues, "It is not the first time that an African spoiled the best-laid plans of the Spaniard in American colonial times, but it was the most dramatic. More active and restless by nature than the more passive and stolid Indian, he was more apt to muddle up some serious Hispanic enterprise."[50] The additional historical research Fray Angélico conducted to uphold and correct his hunches about the revolt in the 1960 book on the Virgin would have been better served had he not resorted to racialized arguments in the 1967 article. Marc Simmons notes that Chávez based his theory on extremely tenuous evidence but always insisted that he had proven the case. Nonetheless, Fray Angélico's article on Pohé-Yemo won the annual award for the best article by a nonprofessional historian in the *New Mexico Historical Review* in 1967.[51]

Church Restoration in the Early 1960s

On July 6, 1959, Fray Angélico was assigned as pastor of St. Joseph Church in the isolated town of Cerrillos, and as in his first years at Peña Blanca, he immediately began local church remodeling and restoration. He first directed his efforts to restore the chapel of San Francisco that was under his jurisdiction in nearby Golden. Originally called El Real de San Francisco by the Spaniards in the colonial period because of the gold in the surrounding hills, the town was renamed Golden by the Americans, and although once a booming mining town, its population had dwindled to only four families by the time Fray Angélico became responsible for the church. Two major events inspired Chávez

FIG. 7.4. Chapel of San Francisco, Golden, New Mexico, 1941, courtesy the Archives of the Franciscan Province of St. John the Baptist of Cincinnati.

to renovate the church: on March 31, 1960, a whirlwind tore off the roof, and in the spring and summer of that year, State Highway 10 was widened and paved, cutting through the hill where the Golden church stood, leaving the chapel prominently visible. "This act of God, plus the acts of the highway department, and the intrinsic historical character of the building, gave me the idea to restore the building in the old mission style," Fray Angélico noted with his characteristic humor.[52]

In 1918 his mentor Fr. Jerome Hesse had modernized the chapel by adding a pitched roof of lumber and corrugated iron, which, in Fray Angélico's view, "made it look like the drab inconspicuous chapels in scores of other New Mexico villages." This roof was torn off by a storm in March of 1959, and the replacement was even worse, Chávez noted, because it was completely flat with very wide eaves and a flat-roofed belfry. "Exactly a year later [another] high windstorm . . . picked up the kite-like roof, with bell and belfry, and deposited the whole thing upside-down several yards away to the east."[53] Fray Angélico commissioned Joe Schmidt of Cerrillos, the son of the builder of the 1918 roof, to construct the new roof according to Chávez's specifications. Fray Angélico solicited and received building material for the Golden church from the Big Boy lumberyard in Santa Fe at the site where the Eldorado Hotel now stands.[54]

While the roofers worked, Fray Angélico built the front pediment himself, fashioning a new niche for a statue of St. Francis. Over the summer he constructed a new bell tower from stone and cement in the old mission style with the help of a man from Cerrillos to mix the cement and hoist up the material. He placed the tower on the west side of the church so that it would be visible from the highway. The beautiful bell that he had ordered from Holland with the insurance money proved to be too thick and heavy for the new tower, so Fray Angélico installed it in St. Joseph Church in Cerrillos.[55] He turned to his younger brother, Fabián Chávez, who was then Senate majority whip in the New Mexico State Legislature. Contacting his friends connected to the railroad, Fabián Chávez was initially unable to procure an old railroad brass bell for the church. Eventually, through Bryan Johnson's efforts, the home office of the Santa Fe Railway in Chicago donated a bell for the church. Fray Angélico humorously remarked that this "golden bell" that he hung in the church steeple looked especially good in the sunlight. "However, it sounds lousy—it sounds like a train bell."[56]

For the interior renovation, Golden resident Mrs. Ernest DeGeer obtained the wooden pews from the church at neighboring Madrid and had a local carpenter shorten the benches to fit the St. Francis Church. When rain leaked through the new roof, warping the wooden floorboards, Mrs. DeGeer and other residents wanted to replace the floor. Fray Angélico insisted that it be left as it was, appreciating its new irregularities just as he had insisted that the outside walls have wavy rather than straight lines. "The floor looks old now," he argued.[57] Chávez was also instrumental in the return of an old wooden statue of St. Francis of Assisi that had been stolen from the church at Golden in the 1950s, apparently because of the belief that the statue contained a treasure.[58] According to Chávez's research, the statue had been part of the original parroquia church of San Francisco in Santa Fe since 1717 and was sent to Peña Blanca and Golden after the new cathedral was built. Carved in Mexico City at the beginning of the eighteenth century, the statue was not considered modern enough for the new cathedral. At Golden, it was repainted with house paint, as Chávez was dismayed to discover. E. Boyd of the Museum of New Mexico restored the five-foot-high statue, revealing the original blue-hued Franciscan garb of the saint. Later, during the renovation of St. Francis Cathedral in 1986, Fray Angélico arranged for it to be returned to the cathedral where it is now prominently displayed in the center nicho of the new altar screen. Archbishop Robert Sánchez thanked him formally in a letter for the suggestion to use the statue in the new reredos: "It seems as though your recommendation to use the old statue of St. Francis which is at Golden for the reredos is an inspiration from the Lord. . . . I would like us to proceed . . . and have the proper nicho prepared for it in the reredos."[59]

With the Golden renovations Fray Angélico created a stunning new visual presence for the church that, according to his research, had been dedicated to San Francisco de Paula, in honor of one of the original settlers. To those who asked why he bothered to restore a church in a ghost town, Chávez explained that he was creating "a sermon in stone" for all passersby on the new highway, which would give testimony to the history of Catholicism in New Mexico visually and aesthetically.[60] A striking photograph of the church appeared on the cover of Ralph Looney's popular book *Haunted Highways: The Ghost Towns of New Mexico* (1968), drawing many others besides passersby to see Fray Angélico's historical "sermon in stone."

FIG. 7.5. Chapel of San Francisco, Golden, New Mexico, after renovation by Fray Angélico Chávez, 1961, courtesy the Archives of the Franciscan Province of St. John the Baptist of Cincinnati.

In spring 1961, while the work at the Golden church was under way, Fray Angélico began to renovate the sanctuary of St. Joseph Church in Cerrillos.[61] In these final years before the sweeping liturgical changes of Vatican II would be put into effect, Fray Angélico designed one of the last traditional high altars holding the tabernacle and facing away from the congregation toward the crucifix. The centerpiece of the remodeling was a large colorful window in the wall behind the altar designed to provide beautiful light in the sanctuary and mimic the effect of a stained glass window without the expense. Fray Angélico opened the rear adobe wall to accommodate a nine-by-seven-foot window and filled the inside with ornamental blocks in a cross-and-circle design. On the outside, he constructed a strong frame with four large sashes containing small panes of glass. Then, from the inside, he overlaid each pane with stained-glass panes of blues, violets, and reds. The beautiful window served as a backdrop for a life-size crucifix that Fray Angélico moved to the sanctuary from the rear of the church; the dimensions of the crucifix had determined the size of the window.[62]

In July he designed a baldachin or canopy for above the altar and had it crafted by the Santa Fe Studios of Church Art. It had gold tassels and was made of pine tinted slightly white to achieve the effect of "ivory watered-silk."[63] Next, he painted the rear and side walls of the sanctuary a greenish-blue with gold-leaf fleurs-de-lis spaced evenly on the surface. In October he ordered a new altar from the same Santa Fe studio, which, according to Chávez's account, did not adequately follow his design. He added a third step, making the new altar more easily visible; the finely crafted, gold-plated tabernacle had a revolving door and was covered by a gauze curtain with gold thread. In the wall behind the altar he installed an old tabernacle safe from Peña Blanca to serve as a closet.

Although Fray Angélico economized by doing the work himself with help from a few parishioners, the church had to be rewired by professional electricians. To pay this debt, Chávez invited "padrinos from the highways and byways" for a celebration on November 11, 1961. Fray Angélico's parents were present, and his brothers and sisters sang in the choir. Enough money was donated to pay the debts and to paint the interior of the church. Two large statues from Spain were also donated: the Sacred Heart of Jesus and the Immaculate Heart of Mary. Fray Angélico was pleased that they fit the baroque character of the Cerrillos church with their rich coloring and gold decoration.

Like the finely drawn music verses and notes, the sermon on poetry and faith, the volume of short stories, the poem and explanatory notes, and the historical novel with his drawings, Fray Angélico's meticulous church renovation in this period gave testimony to his continued commitment to the aesthetic. Verbal and visual art coexisted harmoniously on a continuum for him, and while practical necessities sometimes inspired the aesthetic creation, he never followed a purely utilitarian path in these projects. In keeping with the religious traditions of his early ancestors in northern New Spain, he created beautiful religious art with few economic resources. He was always faithful to the rich historical traditions he and others had documented in research. He would never tear down a battered church or chapel, throw away a short story or poem previously written, or allow a precious historical document to decay from lack of preservation or organization. Instead, in keeping with the Franciscan ideal of chosen poverty and respect for tradition, he recycled and renovated—whether it be a poem, a short story, archival discoveries, or a chapel. He was devastated when the local leaders of the Catholic Church and parishioners made the decision to tear down the beautiful church he renovated at Peña Blanca, not simply because his large paintings and handiwork were destroyed, but because a key element of the historical tradition he had worked to preserve throughout his life was deliberately razed to rubble in deference to modernity and the new.

History and Franciscan Biography: Images of the Self in History

If Fray Angélico's attempts to bring history to creative venues were often but not always successful, his continued historical research fomented his scholarly reputation and garnered him numerous invitations to write articles and give talks. As he continued to collect and catalogue historical documents and to retell and revise the accounts of Franciscan missionary work in early New Mexico, he also expanded his identity formation in the process as he engaged more deeply in modern versions of the patient and committed work of the early Franciscans. To piece together and recount their stories was in a sense to tell his own story as one who carried on their tradition. One of his most valued and useful contributions was his two-year work in 1955–57 to produce a richly annotated catalogue of the Archives of the Archdiocese of Santa Fe.[64] Although he undertook the time-consuming, closely detailed work to aid his own historical research and make the information available to others, the book had larger implications as part of American history. As Mario T. García has argued, in *Archives of the Archdiocese of Santa Fe, 1678–1900* Chávez showed that New Mexico and its Hispano population "possessed a history because they could document it. Here the role of the Church as the guardian of historical identity was crucial."[65] Not only did this book help to write Hispano New Mexicans into U.S. history, but it revealed the key role of the Catholic Church in preserving that history for future generations.

The editors of the Franciscan history series allowed Chávez to include the relatively small amount of diocesan material along with the Franciscan material, so that the book became a catalogue of the Archdiocese of Santa Fe. The documents of the mission period are important in their totality, he argues, for taken together they supplement other sources with unexpected and unknown data. Instead of merely listing the documents, he specifies the significant historical findings that they offer. As a part-time researcher and full-time missionary, Fray Angélico took several years to complete the project. He notes that he was able to richly annotate Fray Francisco Atanasio Domínguez's record of the New Mexico missions with material he found at the time in the archives, and there would have been even more such documentation had he completed cataloguing the archives then. Similarly, in cataloguing the loose *diligencias matrimoniales* (prenuptial investigations) for the *Archives* volume, he discovered more New Mexico families after his 1954 volume on the subject appeared and published this material in the subsequent articles in *El Palacio*.

He divided the documents into the three categories of diligencias matrimoniales, mission documents to 1850, and diocesan papers from 1850 to 1900. He filed and numbered the documents according to years so that he could add additional documents as they were discovered and carefully retained in parenthesis previous, sporadic numberings in deference to already published scholarly work that had used this numbering. He used colored tape to allow researchers to easily distinguish the five categories of bound documents: Books of Patentes (copied letters from Franciscan superiors, the bishop of Durango, or civil authorities), Books of Accounts, and Books of Baptisms, Marriages, and Burials. In each category he found important overlooked information that broadened the picture of New Mexico history. For example, Don Antonio José Martínez, as Padre Martínez of Taos was called in the nineteenth century, printed the first forms for the diligencias matrimoniales on his press—the first printed documents in the West. A 1731 *patente* from Visitor Menchero forbade friars to go to Santa Fe without the written permission of the vice custos, or face the penalty of six months at Zuni. Another patente earlier that year emphasized the need for catechisms and schools in Spanish for the Indians to alleviate the problem of having to use interpreters for confession. One friar complained about the scarcity of paper in 1818. Sometimes priests added a single name to all the Indians baptized: Fr. Lago added "Dolores" to the name of every male and female he baptized in 1793–94. In an 1819 note in a box of Cochiti documents a friar recounted that after he found Indians adoring idols, he confiscated and broke them and then burned them in the plaza.

Throughout the book, Fray Angélico is an interpreter-detective who decodes the recorded information and reshapes the contemporary narrative about the past. He deduces, for example, from the books of baptisms that because eighteenth-century christenings at Acoma were multiple, the friars did not live continuously at this pueblo but most likely at Laguna. He includes censored entries that were crossed out, choosing historical accuracy over the desires of certain predecessors to expurgate the records. One crossed-out 1734 complaint at Zuni concerned two hundred Indians dying in a smallpox epidemic and burying their dead secretly. Because the governors were no longer providing soldier escorts, the friar could do nothing about recording the deaths. The complaints also concerned accusations of widespread idolatry and Indian barbarity and the isolation the friars felt. Several other censored accounts complain about trouble the Indians caused, such as disrupting Mass with the false alarm of an Apache attack to keep people from hearing Mass, preventing women from praying in church, not marrying properly, and in one instance, blaming the priest after an Apache attack, surrounding him, and asking him to leave the pueblo. Later, the secretary of the custos ordered that these complaints be deleted and that no others be recorded in the entries.

This 1957 book is also a record of the sources that inspired Fray Angélico's groundbreaking historical articles after World War II. He records information on place-names used in various documents at different times, floor plans of various churches, the cofradías, the Penitentes, and details of everyday life. Devotional societies were allowed to raise funds once a year by taking out La Conquistadora and Our Lady of Light in portable niches and leaving the statues in various homes overnight. This information may have inspired his 1956 revival of the cofradía of La Conquistadora to raise funds for the renovation of the Lady Chapel. What Fray Angélico learned about the historical work of the missionaries through these documents affected his own sense of his contemporary missionary work as well as his efforts to preserve old churches, safeguard documents, and write history from them. His youthful fascination with the Franciscans, which led to his vocation, was now imbued with detailed historical information decoded, ordered, and interpreted from the handwriting of three centuries of his predecessors in New Mexico.

In May 1961, as he was knocking out the rear wall of the sanctuary at Cerrillos and the townspeople of Golden were plastering their chapel, Fray Angélico published "'Black Legend': Bigotry in Disguise" in the *New Mexico Register* to counter a travel brochure that attributed the Pueblo Revolt to the cruelty of the conquistadores and Franciscans in New Spain. He argues that the truth lies in between the opposing beliefs that the Spaniards were completely benevolent and the Black Legend developed by the British and Americans that colonization and evangelization constituted the blackest oppression of the Indians. While some settlers and missionaries did oppress the Indians, notable historians such as Bancroft, Bolton, and Scholes have disproved the Black Legend, Chávez argues. In New Mexico, the Spaniards preserved and protected the Indians in their communities, and if abuses occurred, they were brought to court. Writing in italics for emphasis, Chávez argues, "*If it were not for the Spanish colonial policy regarding the Pueblos, and the good the missionaries did them in furnishing them with tools and livestock along with Christian teaching, there would be no Pueblos left at all for the tourist bureau to advertise.*"[66] The cause of the Pueblo Revolt, he insists, was not Spanish oppression, but the uneven enforcement of bans on the "grossly immoral" kivas and kachina dances. When Governor Otermín began to enforce this ban, the medicine men staged the rebellion. While Fray Angélico is attempting to create a more nuanced understanding of colonial times, his perspective as a Franciscan priest strongly shapes his understanding of this history. His identity is tied up with what he writes. Additionally, as García has argued, he is promoting an ethnic view of American history from his position as an Hispano to counter the standard Anglo narrative of U.S. history.

Chávez developed these ideas further in an address to the Catholic Art Association in August 1963, which later that year was published as "The Survival of American Indian Culture amid Missionary Activities."[67] He inflects his historical findings of the previous decades with contemporary phenomena such as Vatican II, the Civil Rights Movement, and television. He tries to present a positive view of Indian spiritual beliefs and practices, shaped by his own sense of Hispano ethnicity and, most profoundly, by his identity as a Franciscan priest. His remarks address the concerns of some of his fellow friars who object to certain Native American spiritual customs, as well as people who espouse the Black Legend, which Chávez considers anti-Spanish and inaccurate. While he aligns himself entirely with the Franciscans in the article, he also offers a special understanding of Indian culture based on his continuous experiences with Native Americans since 1937 and his extensive reading about their culture.

Groundbreaking historical events of 1963 mark this essay. Chávez discusses the adaptation of Southern black slaves to their masters' Fundamentalist Christianity, their identification with the Israelites under the Pharaohs, and the development of a moving music that has enriched American culture and now "plays no small part in the current efforts of the Negro to reach the Promised Land of national American equality."[68] The ecumenism of Vatican II has caused there to be a wider interest in black and Native American spiritual cultures, which are historically very different. The Indians believe in a natural Power, not a person or a god, and tap the reservoir of Power for their material welfare and then replenish it. As in *The Virgin of Port Lligat*, Chávez argues that the universal power that the Indians commune with is what scientists discovered as the nuclear interchange of matter and energy: "Had those scientists at Alamogordo been Pueblo Indians they would have prayerfully offered a piece of crude uranium, topped with a thunderbird feather, in deep apology to a violated Nature."[69]

Once again, Chávez counters the Black Legend. How was it that the lone Franciscans who had no soldiers to support them in the early years converted the Indians to Catholicism? Chávez attributes this to the material benefits the Franciscans introduced and their acceptance of the retention of Indian customs during the Christianization. They brought metal tools that allowed the Indians to build more comfortable dwellings and introduced their own Moorish legacy of the adobe, which allowed Native Americans to build more secure dwellings. New grains, fruits, and vegetables, along with better farm tools, irrigation systems, and farm animals, greatly increased the quality of Native American life. Chávez argues that the missionaries engaged in "Christianization without Europeanization," much like the current Church practices promoted in Vatican II policies of ecumenism.[70] The only practices the Franciscans morally objected to were witchcraft and indecent dances, but today the Native American dances that sometimes turn into debauchery are not as bad as the rampant sexuality in the "white man's movies, magazines, and other spectacles."[71] He expresses a solidarity with Native Americans who are an oppressed minority in the United States, like Hispanos: "After two thousand years of Christianity the blond Nordic somehow has a lurking feeling that he is somewhat superior to the darker complexioned Caucasian of the South—this feeling running progressively down through the brown and yellow races to the poor Negro at the bottom of the totem pole."[72] He urges Native Americans to preserve their customs, "except anything that would violate the first and sixth Commandments."[73] Ultimately he defends Native American spirituality and culture from his years of working in the pueblos, an ethnic solidarity with them in the face of the mainstream's sense of superiority toward minorities, the Civil Rights Movement, and Vatican II.

As the 1960s progressed, Fray Angélico wrote the stories of key early colonial Franciscan missionaries for both scholars and the public. He sought to correct errors in published material and to bring to light little-known friars who deserved being written into the larger narratives of the history of the Americas. Four articles on the history of three seventeenth-century friars preceded the 1968 *Coronado's Friars*. Chávez brings his own Franciscan missionary experience to bear on these stories, and his identity is strongly connected to these friars. Shortly after his abrupt return to Peña Blanca from Atrisco on December 10, 1964, he wrote in his Christmas letter to the provincial how happy he was and that he had completed and typed his article on two colonial friars and started another "to clear up the historical hodge-podge on Fr. Padilla."[74] This last was probably the beginning of the book that would become *Coronado's Friars*. In the first seven months of 1965 he wrote a résumé of the Franciscan missions in New Mexico, Texas, and Arizona (1539–1965) for the Seraphic Curia in Rome. He also began translating and annotating the lengthy sixteenth-century Oroz manuscript housed at Tulane University. In it he found key information for the work on the early Franciscan friars he was starting.[75]

The first pair of articles appeared in April and July 1965, recounting the finding of the tombs of Frs. Zárate and de la Llana and retelling their stories. In the scholarly piece, Fray Angélico reveals details of his removal of the friars' casket from a wall of the former sanctuary of the cathedral when he was directing the restoration of La

Conquistadora Chapel in 1957. "Solicitous as well as curious about my ancient Franciscan brethren left so abandoned, I took a hammer and chisel and chipped away the upper beam of the 'grave' to discover a well-proportioned stone casket and, under its two removable lids, further inked inscriptions which no light had faded. Immediately I got the contractor to open a fitting niche in the left-hand side wall of the Conquistadora chapel, and thither we reverently carried this 'treasure' on March 15, 1957."[76] In 1759 to honor the centenary of Fr. de la Llana's death, Governor Marín del Valle commissioned the sculptor who carved the Our Lady of Light Reredos to make a stone casket for the remains of the two friars in the cathedral. Chávez gives brief accounts of the lives of the two friars in the scholarly article, using primarily secondary sources and offering supplemental information in the footnotes.

In the companion article for *St. Anthony Messenger*, Chávez shows his literary talent by presenting the same information in a livelier format.[77] Why, he asks, are some saintly people who are highly regarded in their own time forgotten subsequently? Perhaps because they have finished their work in God's plan, and it is time for others to take over, he suggests. The two friars whose relics lie in the cathedral are examples of this. Conscious of the magazine's larger U.S. audience, he reminds readers that Fr. Zárate came to New Mexico before 1622, about the time the Pilgrims landed on Plymouth Rock. After evangelizing among the Humana Indians, Fr. Zárate was assigned to the isolated pueblo of Picuris where he was at first treated badly but later came to be loved. Twenty-five years after his death in 1632, his fame had grown extensively; his body was exhumed and found to be still intact and pliable and then reburied again in the Picuris church. Fr. de la Llana was born in Mexico City in 1607 of Basque parents and learned the Aztec language for his missionary work. He came to New Mexico sometime before 1634 and lived alone with the Indians in the isolated pueblo of Quarac where he died in 1659. There is much written about them in the chronicles in Mexico, which report that Fr. Zárate became invisible to the wild Comanches who had come after him in his church and that on the feast of St. Bonaventure in 1659, Fr. de la Llana foretold the time of his death five days later. Both men were very prayerful and did much penance.

The people of New Mexico kept the memory of these friars alive for more than a century through oral tradition. A full fifteen years before the American Revolution, they honored the centenary of Fr. de la Llana's death by exhuming both bodies and reburying them in the cathedral in Santa Fe with great pageantry. Fray Angélico tells the details of his discovering the stone coffin and the blue Franciscan habits in which the bones were wrapped, speaking freely of his surprise and emotions. He emphasizes that he had the coffin moved to La Conquistadora Chapel so that it would be in full view of both the faithful and visitors. In the Wild West the friars were eventually forgotten as history changed rapidly. He hoped to reverse this forgetfulness by having moved the coffin to a more visible location and writing both academic and popular articles about them.

Another forgotten missionary was Fray Bernardo de Marta. There was no trace of his grave at Zia in 1759 when the remains of the other two friars were reburied in the cathedral, or Governor Marín del Valle would also have included him in the coffin. Born in Catalonia, Fray Bernardo and his brother requested assignment in the Indies after their ordination, hoping to become martyrs. In 1606 they were separated—the elder sent to the Philippines and Fray Bernardo ordered to stay in the Americas. In Puebla his piety and musical talents earned him the name "the organist of heaven." He probably arrived in New Mexico in 1609–10 and was in charge of Santo Domingo, then Galisteo, and finally Zia until his death. He advised his fellow Franciscans to avoid confrontations with the authorities although they did not always heed his advice. Chávez wonders if Fray Bernardo had even a rudimentary organ in New Mexico, but the early friar was probably the first professional organist in New Mexico. The date of his death is uncertain.[78]

The popular article has a bright red inset image of an organ, and Fray Angélico claims with more certainty that Fray Bernardo died ten years after he arrived in New Mexico in 1610 and made a great sacrifice to live there because there were no organs in the area at the time. The organist of heaven could no longer play sacred music, Chávez tells his readers sympathetically. When young, he and his brother had been trained in music and chant at the cathedral in Zaragoza, far from their village in Catalonia, suggesting that they were either orphans or given to the Church by their parents. In this popular version of the story, Fray Angélico adds color to the episode of their separation in 1606 in Mexico City: "We would call this a rough deal. It makes me want to think that the Superior General was a heartless sort of fellow, to separate these two fine brothers who since childhood had been inseparable."[79] Although he expected martyrdom when assigned to New Mexico, Fray Bernardo experienced "only loneliness in a vast silent world of high mountains and endless desert mesas, and no great organ with which to fill that great void with the music that welled in his heart."[80] Friar Bernard has been forgotten like the early Franciscans buried in the cathedral. Almost as if resurrecting a part of himself, Chávez infuses his own experience into the telling this story.

Fr. Antoine Tibesar, who headed the American Academy of Franciscan History, had urged Chávez to write a book on the life of Fray Juan de Padilla. By Christmas 1958, Fray Angélico told the provincial, he had decided to do the project but would broaden it to include all forty of the Southwestern martyrs. He proposed that he be allowed to leave Jemez and be assigned to a temporary affiliation with the academy, which would allow him to travel to various collections to complete the research for the book. "I have always wanted to cap off my mission research with a work on these martyrs, something definitive that might also serve as a *corpus actuum* if the question of their beatification should come up." Provincial Kroger responded positively, although he expressed concern about manpower in New Mexico, and promised to take the proposal to the Definitorial Congressus in June.[81] Six months later, however, Fray Angélico was assigned to Cerrillos as pastor. The book would not be published until a decade after Fray Angélico took on the project, and it would be a scaled-down version, investigating the stories of only the first few friars who came to New Mexico. While a good deal of *Coronado's Friars* focuses on the life of Fray Juan de Padilla, it also tells the stories of the five other Franciscans on the 1540 expedition. Ever the meticulous, patient detective, Fray Angélico untangles numerous contradictory, fragmentary, and erroneous written accounts about these friars and presents their revised stories according to what the extant information would allow.

Coronado's Friars corrected written accounts from as early as 1583 about the exact number and names of the friars on the Coronado expedition. "Fray Juan de la Cruz" was a mistaken name attributed to the lay brother who accompanied Fr. Padilla—Fray Luis de Úbeda. There were five distinct friars officially on the expedition: the three ordained priests Fray Juan de Padilla, Fray Antonio de Castilblanco, and Fray Juan de la Cruz and two lay brothers Fray Luis de Úbeda and Fray Daniel el Italiano. To sort out the mistaken accounts, Fray

Angélico had to "[interpret] the material available through a minute textual criticism of the original information sent to [the minister general in Rome] by different writers, and this in relation to the early historians who copied from them."[82] Fray Angélico includes lengthy footnotes and documents in an appendix to prove his case. His most important discovery is a deduction he made that was influenced by the techniques of textual criticism used by modern biblical scholars. Realizing that the late sixteenth- and early seventeenth-century writers often employed almost identical phrases and paragraphs although working separately, Fray Angélico concludes that they had to be using a common source previously unidentified by historians. After much comparison, he identifies that source as "RB," Fray Rodrigo de Bienvenida, who recorded many notes on his fellow Franciscans in New Spain. Chávez illustrates the genealogy of the early historians' material by drawing a family-tree chart of the early texts, starting with RB who wrote from 1552 to 1575, through Mendieta, Muñoz, Oroz, Torquemada, Gonzalo, and finally Tello in 1652.

Chávez argues that although Fray Marcos de Niza accompanied the expedition, he was not an official part of it since he had recently been elected provincial of the Holy Gospel Province in Mexico and could not be away as a missionary at the same time. Fray Marcos went partway with the expedition but turned back, probably in shame, when the city of Cíbola he had claimed to have seen from afar in 1539 turned out to be the Zuni pueblo Hawikuh. On the 1539 expedition, an advance scout sent word that led Fray Marcos to believe he had seen one of the fabled seven cities. When the scout was killed, Fray Marcos only dared to look at the pueblo from a great distance and reported that it was one of the great cities called Cíbola by the Indians. A Frenchman from Aquitaine, Fray Marcos' command of Spanish was not perfect. In Mexico, his oral account was written up in fluent Spanish and in more glowing terms, and Fray Marcos signed it.

After treating Fray Marcos only briefly, Fray Angélico focuses on the five Franciscans who comprised the official missionary band of Coronado's expedition. He devotes substantial space to the most well-known friar, Fray Juan de Padilla. When he heard about the Coronado expedition he immediately asked to participate. Employing his literary skills, Fray Angélico makes the historical figure come alive: "We can almost hear Fray Juan de Padilla scolding some soldiers for their desperate curses, . . . envisioning himself already converting the

Portuguese-speaking King of the Seven Cities."[83] When a group of Indian leaders from the east visited Coronado's party in Hawikuh, they recounted tales of giant humped cattle, a rich land called Quivira, and their pueblo called Cicúye. The members of the expedition were the first Europeans to visit the pueblos up and down the Rio Grande, and in Cicúye they were given a captive from Quivira whom they nicknamed "the Turk" and who told Fr. Padilla about the source of a golden bracelet and jewels. After conquering the Indians at Tiguex, the expedition journeyed to the settlements of the Wichita Indians, or Quivira, but disappointed not to find the seven cities, they returned to Tiguex. When Coronado ordered everyone's return to Mexico, the stubborn Fr. Padilla refused to go, staying behind with Brother Luis de Úbeda. Padilla met his death very soon, as he set out again for Quivira. Brother Úbeda stayed with the people of Cicúye at their invitation, and historians do not know what became of him.

The other Franciscans Fray Angélico identifies as members of the expedition include the burly Brother Daniel the Italian, a master embroider and vestment maker who taught the Indians embroidery and engaged in extraordinary penances. He died peacefully in Guadalajara, probably in 1567. The young Fray Antonio de Castilblanco preferred to work at provincial headquarters and with the Spaniards and became the confessor and friend of Coronado. Fray Juan de la Cruz was a French priest from Aquitaine as was Fray Marcos de Niza. Chávez resolves the contradictory accounts of the identity of Fray Juan de la Cruz, whom several sources had claimed was the lay brother. By comparing the manuscript of the *Oroz Relación* (1584–86), which he was working on at the time, with the other accounts, he showed that Fray Juan de la Cruz was in fact a priest in the expedition. Fray Juan probably arrived in Mexico in the 1520s and was so loved that over one hundred Indians protested his being transferred and then were massacred by the provisor of Michoacán, Juan García Zurnero. Perhaps because the Indians respected him, Chávez speculates, Coronado invited Fray Juan to be part of the expedition.

Returning to one of his early motivations for studying the first Franciscan missionaries in La Nueva Mexico—to investigate whether they were in fact martyrs—Fray Angélico notes that because the other friars returned safely to Mexico with Coronado, only Fr. Padilla and Brother Úbeda might possibly be considered martyrs. Later Fray Alonso Benavides, custos of New Mexico from 1625 to 1629, proposed the canonization of Fray Marcos, Juan de Padilla, and Juan de la Cruz, along with three other friars killed in 1582. Chávez argues that none of them deserves the status of martyr. Fray Marcos had died later in bed in Mexico, and "Fray Juan de la Cruz" (actually Fray Luis de Úbeda) probably had died a natural death. Neither were Fr. Padilla and the others who died in 1592 martyrs: "Although they had been slain by the natives, [they] had not died because of any hatred for a faith about which these poor aborigines knew nothing at all. If at all martyrs, they were only such out of their zealous desires."[84] Having finally established the identities and exact number of the Franciscans in the Coronado expedition in this intricate study of contradictory historical accounts, Fray Angélico concludes that the 1540–42 expedition represents one of the greatest feats of "derring-do" in the history of North America, despite its failure to find gold or save souls.

In the first eight months of 1965 when Fray Angélico was peacefully resettled at Peña Blanca and devoting much of his time to research and writing, he began the translation and detailed annotation of the *Oroz Relación* housed at Tulane. Three years later in July 1968 he reported to Provincial Huser that he had finally finished the manuscript for Tulane—753 typewritten pages—and that they wished to publish it.[85] Although Tulane backed out of the project and it was finally published in 1972 by the American Academy of Franciscan History, it is most closely connected to this period of Fray Angélico's life (the early and mid-1960s) when he worked painstakingly to uncover the details of the early Franciscans. Nonetheless, there is an important mark of 1972 in the dedication to his parents, who died in 1966 and 1969, respectively, in which he recounts their ancestral roots in sixteenth-century Spain, similar to those of the friars who appear in the book, and hints at the hardships his parents endured in the modern twentieth century: "Both heirs of ten generations of cultural and economic disadvantage in their native New Mexico (often referred to by their forebears as 'this miserable kingdom'), but who prepared all their many children to compete successfully within an alien modern culture in our century."[86] Having just left active ministry as a Franciscan when the book finally went to press, Fray Angélico emphasizes through this tribute to his parents the difficulties that generations of Hispanos have undergone in New Mexico from the colonial period to the present, including cultural and economic disadvantages and a sense of alienation. Here he associates his personal sense of never being fully accepted in the order with the hardships his parents and Hispano ancestors experienced, including the early Franciscan missionaries.

Apart from this strong statement in the dedication, the book itself is a product of the mid-1960s when Fray Angélico compared manuscripts and historical accounts in detail to write corrected versions of the lives of the first Franciscans in New Mexico. Other historians had used much of the information in Fray Pedro Oroz's manuscript, but Fray Angélico argued the importance of publishing an annotated version in English. Oroz's correct identification of Fray Luis de Úbeda as the lay brother who stayed with Fray Juan de Padilla in New Mexico led Fray Angélico to uncover the common source of the other sixteenth-century accounts—Fray Rodrigo de Bienvenida. Additionally, Chávez's annotations of the manuscript demonstrate that it is not merely a copy of other well-known writings, but a key to the not previously recognized sources of those accounts. While Oroz was primarily a copyist, he was also an original contributor, and without his patient, persistent writing, a large body of colonial documents would have been lost. Chávez's notes also corrected many errors in Oroz and Mendieta that had been "slavishly copied by every historian."[87] He linked his own identity to the sixteenth-century writer, copying and editing the material in the codex just as Oroz himself had done centuries before. Fray Angélico was a modern incarnation of the colonial missionary, writer, and copyist.

Chávez used the occasion of his work on the manuscript to add an additional biography to his series on the early friars as a lengthy introduction to the book. Bringing together many sources to expand on the very brief résumé of Fr. Oroz's life by Fray Juan de Torquemada, Fray Angélico writes the most extensive, detailed biography in his mid-1960s series on the early Franciscans. Narrating with specifics the ugly power struggles between the Franciscans from Spain and those born or educated in New Spain in Oroz's time, he chronicles how the generally well-loved priest reluctantly accepted ecclesiastical leadership positions when he would rather have been teaching, ministering to Indians, and writing books. Fray Angélico suggests that controversies of the period may have motivated Oroz's work of gathering and copying legal documents about the rights and privileges of his order in the New World. He resigned as provincial before the end of his term, returning to his manuscript documents, but in 1582 he was appointed commissary general of New Spain. Later, during what Fray Angélico terms "perhaps the most shameful episode in the entire Franciscan history of New Spain," Fr. Oroz joined fellow New World Franciscans in signing declarations refusing to obey his controversial successor commissary, Fray Alonso Ponce.[88]

Besides recounting the details of these contentious years of the colonial period, Fray Angélico's biography of Oroz also reveals his personal identification with the colonial friar as a writer and meticulous copier of texts. Responding to a request from the minister general in Rome for information on the missions of New Spain, Fr. Oroz began to prepare his *Relación* in late April 1584, based on the historical writings of his fellow friar, Fr. Mendieta. Fray Angélico concludes that he had only six months to plan the book, arrange the material, and copy it in neat lettering. Then, Chávez calculates, Oroz used the next months to produce the hand-lettered official report from the first document to be sent to Rome: "Father Oroz must have gone at his labor of love with a will, devoting most of his daylight hours to it, each blocked hand-lettered page coming out like those of a printed book."[89] Despite his meticulous work, someone in authority whom Fray Angélico cannot identify with certainty (although he notes that this occurred about the time Fr. Oroz's successor Fr. Ponce arrived) ordered the manuscript to be shortened, recopied by someone else, and signed by three friars as coauthors before being sent to Rome. With his own experiences in mind, Chávez writes, "Father Oroz was left with his rejected masterpiece in his hands. He must have felt terribly hurt and disappointed."[90] Later he painstakingly recopied the entire manuscript and dedicated it to the viceroy's wife, hoping she would help to publish it.

Chávez's decision to spend three years translating and copiously annotating the lengthy *Oroz Codex* reveals his understanding of the historical importance of the material and his personal identification with this colonial Franciscan missionary, writer, and historian who with great artistry patiently edited and copied important historical documents centuries before carbon paper and the photocopier. Fr. Oroz's ability in the daunting physical circumstances of sixteenth-century Mexico to combine evangelization, teaching, and the difficult politics of religious administration with the lengthy historical writing he left for future generations must have been a source of identification for Fray Angélico himself, despite the privileges he enjoyed merely by living four centuries later.

While he returned to literature and art in this period from the mid-1950s to his departure from the order in 1971, Fray Angélico continued his work as a historian, finding further connections of his twentieth-century identity to the early Franciscans in New Spain. Nonetheless, he returned once more to literature at the end of the 1960s by publishing a final volume of poetry. In February 1969, he sent to Provincial Huser what he would later term his "swan song of poetry," the manuscript of *Selected Poems: With an Apologia*. His mother had died the month before, and now almost sixty, Fray Angélico was no doubt looking back on his decades as a Franciscan priest, a war veteran, an artist, a poet, and a historian. The turbulent 1960s and the death of his parents helped to shape this reevaluation and the life-changing decision he would soon make. Poetry had been a key part of his identity through the late 1940s when he had turned his intellectual efforts to history. He used the occasion of this volume to evaluate his identity as a poet and mark the rite of passage he was about to undergo at the beginning of the new decade. The provincial sent the manuscript of carefully chosen poems to Fray Angélico's early mentor, Fr. Hyacinth Blocker, for censorship, and Becker returned it with high praise: "Angélico . . . has written Poetry (with a capital P) and not the curious hieroglyphics that pass for poetry in erudite circles today. [He] . . . is the one genuine poet our province has produced. I have always regretted his decision to give up 'creative' writing, both poetry and prose, for historical research, although in the latter field he has . . . accomplished more for New Mexico than many other historians." Uplifted by this praise, Fray Angélico regretted that Fr. Blocker did not live to see the 1970 published volume.[91]

In the foreword, Fray Angélico explains his relationship to poetry and his decision to discontinue writing it. Lyric poetry for him always involved a rare quality of pleasant "strangeness," from his early days of reading Robert Louis Stevenson, Burns, and Tennyson to his later discovery of Stevenson's "Requiem." He strove to attain the impact of this poem in his own poetry and always looked for the rare poem that, like Stevenson's, "without any seeming effort, fixes a few simple Anglo-Saxon words into a thing of beauty that brings on rapture." Describing his own writing process, he notes, "In time some of the magic did come . . . when at long or shorter intervals a strange seizure of mind conceived and bore a verse or more with little conscious striving after phrasing or rhyme, and in the wink of an eye that often proved to have been hours lost from a day or night." After 1959 this excitement slowed down, and his style of poetry became outmoded. The volume's poems are a "farewell to an era" and those that others have valorized. He was especially proud of "Lady of Peace," having written it as his warship departed Honolulu for the Philippines and realizing that it was Stevenson's "Requiem" restated from his own situation while sharing the tropic isle and sea: "Then I knew that my journey after beauty in the simple lyric had made the full round, and I was content."[92]

Fray Angélico selects poems on the Southwest, World War II, St. Francis, and other religious themes, especially the Blessed Virgin. To "Peña Blanca," published in the *New York Herald Tribune* in 1939, he adds the new 1965 poem "Southwest Landscapes and St. John 6" in which he envisions the events recounted in chapter 6 of John's Gospel reenacted in the contemporary Southwest near Peña Blanca. The patch of green grass near the desert pass that the poetic voice sees on his way to say Mass, for example, reminds him of the springtime green grass where Christ fed the multitude loaves and fishes as described in John's chapter. The Mass he is about to offer "shows how the sign made on the grass / has come to pass, has come to pass." The poetic voice imagines several landscapes in the area as correlatives of events in John's Gospel.

Another more recent poem carries on the theme of the power of atomic energy from "The Virgin of Port Lligat." "Inedible" (1957) urges readers to beware of the mushroom of Alamogordo, which "spreads its ghostly parasol" and "Sows spores of terror far around its girth." The "botanists" who created this mushroom cannot stop its further growth, and despite projected future benefits, "The fact remains that somewhere some gourmet / Can cook the poison species nonetheless." Although fascinated with the philosophical and theological implications of the atomic bomb, Fray Angélico wisely warns of the dangers of nuclear proliferation. He ends this last volume of his poetry with "L'Envoi," written in 1947 after his return from the war front and his brush with mortality. In it the poet asks forgiveness as he imagines seeing God face-to-face:

> *The very stars like bees will swarm on our delight,*
> *Like hummingbirds in orgy when space becomes a garden*
> *In sunshine of Thy Face the day on which I see Thee.*

Fittingly, Fr. Jack Clark Robinson, O.F.M., read this poem at Fray Angélico's wake and vespers service in St. Francis Cathedral, March 21, 1996, sending him off with the last poem he included in his final volume of poetry.

CHAPTER EIGHT

The Renaissance Man as Public Intellectual

Declaration of Independence

When Fray Angélico Chávez posted his undated letter announcing his separation from active ministry on June 30, 1971, at the Peña Blanca friary, the act was not as historical as the famous declarations of Martin Luther and Thomas Jefferson but involved great personal courage. His decision had not been made quickly or spontaneously as his articles at the time and the letter itself evidence. It was to have profound effects on his writing and the quality of his life in his last decades. At age sixty-one, after owing obedience to Franciscan superiors since he was fourteen, Fray Angélico no doubt felt a tremendous sense of freedom as he walked out the door and moved home to Santa Fe.

A decade earlier on June 13, 1962, he presented "A Canticle of Gratitude" at the Mass in St. Francis Cathedral celebrating the twenty-fifth anniversary of his ordination. In this prayer composed in English and summarized in Spanish, he expresses happiness and gratefulness for his Franciscan vocation, in striking contrast to his letter of a decade later announcing his departure. Without doubt the prayer was heartfelt and sincere on his silver jubilee, as people often relegate frustrations to the background on celebratory occasions. He gives thanks for his Catholic faith, his call to the priesthood, his Franciscan vocation, his missionary assignments among his people, and unexpected blessings such as his success as a writer, serving as chaplain, seeing the numbers of native clergy grow, and the presence of his parents and family at the celebration. He praises the permanency of the priesthood that allows "a poor imperfect man to stand in the very shoes of God as an advocate of his fellowman." While other leaders depart, "God's Priesthood is for ever." This strong sense of his permanent identity as a priest continued after he left ministry in 1971 and explains his refusal to request official laicization as his provincial wanted. In expressing gratitude for his vocation, he notes that he has never doubted his choice, and

FIG. 8.1. Fray Angélico Chávez's Silver Jubilee, St. Francis Cathedral, June 13, 1962. Left to right: Frs. Salvador Aragón, Aelred Knittles, Angélico Chávez, Emeric Nordmeyer, and Michael Baca, courtesy the Archives of the Franciscan Province of St. John the Baptist of Cincinnati.

he remarks that in fulfilling his boyhood dreams to minister to his people as the Franciscan martyrs did, "there has been no room for frustration." In the Spanish version, he mentions his religious father, St. Francis, along with San Antonio de Padua, Santa Clara, and Fray Junípero Serra, the key missionary of his boyhood dreams.[1]

Although his frustrations had not yet reached the boiling point, neither would it have been appropriate to mention them on this occasion. In contrast, his letter of departure, written after the tumultuous social change of the 1960s, spells out these frustrations clearly in the context of the times. He notes that his principal reason for leaving is a "dogmatic Scriptural problem." He believes that "the closest approach to the only Scriptural evidence of faith was the Dutch Catechism, and this Rome condemned."[2] In March 1966, Dutch cardinal Bernard Alfrink gave the imprimatur to the innovative adult catechism and four hundred thousand copies were published. Many in the Dutch Church at the time were in the vanguard of radically rethinking Church doctrine and its role in society. In 1965, for example, the Vatican had asked Cardinal Alfrink to cease allowing the distribution of Communion in the hand in his country, a liturgical practice that later became widespread. Descriptions of the Dutch Catechism vary, with some praising its emphasis on the witness of faith, self-liberation, and social justice, while others argued it posed a serious challenge to official Church dogma. In his study of Dutch Catholicism, Fr. John Coleman, S.J., argues that the book is a new kind of catechism for adults, "one that avoids technical, theological language to express the faith in a modern, lively, almost poetic idiom." He praises the book's ecumenism and notes that it left certain issues such as the biological virginity of Mary "open for further doctrinal development."[3]

In June 1967 a commission of six Vatican-appointed cardinals ruled on a series of doctrinal errors in the catechism and told the Dutch bishops to correct them. The changes made did not satisfy the cardinals, and in February 1968, the Dutch hierarchy issued a defense of the catechism, openly challenging the Vatican. In October, the cardinals condemned the Dutch Catechism, citing doctrinal errors such as the nonliteral interpretation of the virgin birth, the fall of humanity through Adam, and the transubstantiation in the Eucharist, in addition to the denial of the infallibility of the Church and the hierarchy's power.[4] Fr. Coleman points to the Dutch Church's reforms in the pre–Vatican II period, which enhanced its leadership in changes after the council, especially its inclusion of the laity in decision making and the nominations of bishops by the clergy. Although Cardinal Alfrink publicly noted that the Dutch Catechism was to be a new kind of catechism for adults, which would help Catholics pursue the ideas of Vatican II rather than present infallible teachings, Rome objected to its being termed a catechism and to some of its content. We do not know if Fray Angélico agreed with all of the positions in the catechism, but his letter of departure cites his agreement with the text's scriptural interpretation. He criticizes the bishops' reversion to "the old non-scriptural mentality. Since May 16, 1969 when I woke up with this conviction, I have suffered great mental and spiritual anguish, but have hung on for two years, praying for the Holy Father and the bishops to touch on the crucial Scriptural problems. Instead, they and the press keep wrangling on about peripheral matters like celibacy, etc."[5]

Fray Angélico's strong dissatisfaction with the curbing of the reforms of Vatican II under Pope Paul VI must be placed in the context of the conservative Catholic milieu in which he lived and worked throughout most of the twentieth century. In 1910, the year of his birth, Pope Pius X published the *Oath against Modernism*, which all hierarchy, professors of philosophy and theology in Catholic institutions, clergy, and seminarians were required to affirm until it was abolished in 1967 after Vatican II. The oath asserted that Church dogma would never be modernized or adapted according to the times, that human reason affirms God's existence, and that prophecies and miracles recounted in the Bible are literally true, among other tenets. Having lived through this strict milieu of hierarchical resistance to change and modernization for six decades, Fray Angélico was moved to leave religious life when this resistance again surfaced after Vatican II. His first writings after his departure reflected his new freedom outside the Franciscan Order to explore various official tenets.

The English translation of the Dutch Catechism in 1967 had a profound influence on Chávez's life and writing. Moving beyond the rote catechism questions memorized by children who are learning about the faith, it updated and vastly expanded adult Catholics' knowledge of the history of their religion and its place among the other world religions. It aimed to share the vast religious knowledge of priests and hierarchy with ordinary Catholics, educating people about the Bible and religious history much beyond the small excerpts of Scripture read in Sunday liturgies. The Dutch bishops argued that the Church must think out new forms of truth in each age, just as the evangelists adapted previous versions of the Gospel according to their own milieus. The catechism notes that John's Gospel, for example, is "a new account from an eyewitness, penetrated by more than sixty years' experience of Jesus through the Holy Sprit. . . . Each of the gospels shows in its own way what a given community of believers found most important."[6]

Fray Angélico's concern with the Vatican's repression of various postconciliar reforms joined his frustration with the "ecclesiastical colonialism" he experienced as an Hispano priest. He objects to the Church having treated his ethnic minority as an inferior people. He had addressed the organization of Chicano priests, PADRES (Priests Associated for Religious, Educational, and Social Rights), in February 1971 at Immaculate Conception Seminary in Santa Fe, and Monsignor Tito Meléndez had nominated him for the position of pastoral vicar of the archdiocese in March 1971, mentioning that Fray Angélico was a Chicano who had the backing of PADRES. With the growing consciousness of Chicanos and other U.S. Latinos in this period of ethnic pride, political strength, and rejection of historical oppression, Fray Angélico felt emboldened to articulate his experience of "ecclesiastical colonialism" as a friar-priest in the Archdiocese of Santa Fe. Where Chicanos employed the concept of internal colonialism to describe their second-class status as U.S. citizens after the American takeover of the Southwest in 1848, Fray Angélico saw a similar pattern in the ways in which the Church treated Hispanos throughout the centuries and in his own experience in the Franciscan Order and under the archdiocesan authority.[7]

These concepts were also central to the early formulations and political activism of PADRES at the time. The new organization of Chicano priests formally protested the systematic discrimination they and their people experienced in the Church, their exclusion from positions of power within the Church, and their status as second-class Catholics. The group organized a campaign to nominate Chicano priests for episcopal positions, and this included Msgr. Meléndez's letter nominating Chávez. In April 1971, for example, his fellow Hispano priest from Santa Fe, Fr. Rafael Aragón, complained in an article in the *National Catholic Reporter* that the Church treated his people as children. He used the term *racism* to describe Fr. Patricio López having to say Mass for two hundred Mexicans in a community center in Albuquerque because they were not welcome in the parish church.[8] Fray Angelico's letter of resignation uses some of the same language and ideas espoused by the members of PADRES. The activism and concerns of PADRES influenced his decision to leave active priestly ministry in June 1971.

In November 1970, six months before his departure, Chávez addressed eleven hundred people at New Mexico State University at the inauguration of President Gerald W. Thomas.[9] He attempts to define New Mexican Hispano identity with subtle reference to current issues raised by Mexican Americans in the Chicano Movement. Employing his extensive study of baptismal and marriage records and premarital investigations, he argues that Hispano New Mexicans are quite different from Mexican Americans in history, culture, racial background, and political concerns. Although the saying claims that blood is thicker than water, Chávez argues instead that "one's cultural background in one's very own homeland of centuries is thicker than blood."[10] That is, although the contemporary Mexican American struggle is a rightful one and might be worth joining, Hispano New Mexicans have not suffered as much as the most recent immigrants from Mexico who "have not fared so well at the hands of waspish Anglos, the ones who wave the flag but deny other peoples their civil rights."[11]

Chávez explains the historical differences between the Spaniards, Hispanos, Mexicans, and Indians without valorizing one group over another. These ideas would be developed further in his *My Penitente Land* (1974). He characterizes the early Spanish settlers as pastoral rather than agricultural people who found geography similar to their homeland in the colony of New Mexico. The language that Cervantes recorded was passed down orally in New Mexico because there was little written material in the isolated northern reaches of the colony. Documents reveal that in the years after the 1693 reconquest, settlers still believed they were full-blooded Españoles with noble ancestors, forgetting that some early settlers had married Tlaxcaltec women and other mestizos who came north. As their land holdings grew, the pastoral Hispanos needed menial labor to assist them and so began in the eighteenth century to "adopt" the wild Indians of the Plains, raising them as Catholics with Spanish names and giving them their freedom when they married. Chávez terms this "External Hispanization," which caused the genízaros to lose their tribal identities. Many of their descendants today consider themselves Hispano or Spanish American, he argues.

As Fray Angélico outlines the quite different development of the colony in central Mexico, he previews his controversial view of the Virgin of Guadalupe story that he would develop more fully in *My Penitente Land*. Terming it "a legend to the effect that the Virgin Mary had appeared to a simple Aztec Indian and imprinted her image on his humble cloak," he notes that the printing of the legend by two criollo clergymen in the seventeenth century helped to unite the criollos, Indians, and mestizos.[12] As the legend grew during the following century, it helped to inspire the 1810 rebellion against Spanish rule, and a flag with the Virgin's image was carried into battle. Already in late 1970, then, before Fray Angélico left active ministry, he spoke and wrote about the Virgin of Guadalupe as a legend rather than a miracle.[13]

Chávez argues that having been part of Mexico for so brief a period (1821–48), many Hispanos in New Mexico identify as U.S. citizens first, and then Spanish Americans. Since their education has been in the U.S. system, they know little of Mexican history and its people. Although many are Catholics, they see the Virgin of Guadalupe as an important representation of Christ's mother, but without the fervor of Mexicans who link the Virgin to national freedom. He argues that many New Mexicans did not join Mexican American Reies López Tijerina's movement because they did not hate the Colossus of the North as Tijerina did, based on his Mexican heritage. New Mexicans know, Chávez argues, that not only Anglo Americans but Hispanos as well took away their land by legal trickery.

This important 1970 article reveals Fray Angélico's nuanced interaction with ideas of the Chicano Movement in full flower at this time. While he applied the model of internal colonialism to the Catholic Church's attitude toward minorities, he was careful to distinguish three different "thrusts" of the Spanish cultural influence in the Southwest, rather than a single, homogenous Hispano presence. The historical legacies of these three varieties of Spanish culture in Mexico and the Southwest mean that a single political movement, no matter how correct and justified, might not be appropriate for all Hispanos in the Southwest. Fray Angélico's personal and generational experience and his documentary research led him to respond to the radicalism of the Chicano Movement with both support and a call for more nuanced understanding of history and culture.

At this time also, six months before he would leave ministry, *New Mexico* magazine announced in its November/December 1970 issue that Fray Angélico had been hired as the magazine's new book reviewer. After his mother's death in 1969 and his disillusion with the Vatican's repression of the Dutch Catechism, Fray Angélico gradually moved to put into place the material conditions that would allow him to leave full-time ministry in order to write. The work he arranged with *New Mexico* magazine (he had not published there since 1956) would be one step in financially supporting himself in this endeavor. While he would continue to produce several important volumes of scholarship after leaving, his writing for the magazine allowed him to function as a public intellectual, bringing his extensive knowledge to a wider audience.

Fray Angélico told a newspaper reporter in 1981: "I was treated better by the Army than by the Church," noting that in his three years of service he was promoted from first lieutenant to major.[14] Judge Antonio Chávez also recounts that his brother's disillusionment with the Church involved both questions of faith and his poor treatment by other priests and the hierarchy. Throughout the decades of his ministry to the Indians, he learned their languages, wore simple clothes, and engaged in the difficult manual labor of rebuilding and restoring churches. Over the years he also produced a large number of publications but continued his simple life of ministry and service:

> And then the crash came, some of the things that were said about him, some of the things that were done to him by his own brethren within the Church—and the non-acceptance of some of the things that he wrote, especially about Guadalupe and Chimayó and things like this. . . . But he'd already preached it—he'd already had it in articles and things like this. And at Chimayó he'd already told them what the history of it was, how the family apparently started it and, you know, their family being from Mexico, they were copying from Guatemala. Things like that.[15]

Fray Angélico's disillusion and decision to leave ministry was long in the making and the result of a variety of factors including doctrinal disagreements, feeling unappreciated and unaccepted by other clergy, the influence of PADRES, the radical milieu of social change in the

1960s, and the profound changes of Vatican II, but above all, the avid desire of a scholar and writer to devote himself full time to this work. The posting of the letter at Peña Blanca on June 30, 1971, and the beginning of this new life would have profound effects on his writing thereafter.

Magnum Opus: My Penitente Land

Fray Angélico's new freedom, the radical spirit of the times as the 1960s spilled into the early 1970s, and his disillusion with the Church's treatment of his people combined with his decades of thorough research on the primary documents of the history of Hispanos in New Mexico to produce a radical new book, *My Penitente Land*. Denied a Guggenheim fellowship for this groundbreaking study, Fray Angélico nonetheless plunged into the project as soon as he left ministry. His sister Nora recounts that he wrote in a small script, tablet after tablet in his parents' home, and insisted that he not be bothered while working. When he returned from a visit to his brother in Los Angeles on August 15, 1973, he wrote to friends that he was typing the last one hundred pages of the "big" book. In February 1974, editor Jack Rittenhouse of the University of New Mexico Press wrote an enthusiastic response after having read the manuscript. He apologized for the press's treatment of previous works Chávez had submitted and asked for a one-month option to accept the book. Rittenhouse noted that people's knowledge of New Mexico history would remain two-dimensional unless they read this new book: "[Y]ou add dimension, depth and understanding. . . . [Y]ou literally poured yourself into this work, letting it flow like a stream from a spring . . . at times revealing more about the author than the subject. . . . Whether or not we get a chance to do this book, I consider it not only an honor but a major experience in being allowed to read it. I will never be quite the same person again." In July 1974, as he was reviewing the final copyedited manuscript that UNM Press would publish in October, Chávez took a further step to independence by moving out of his parents' home to 214 McKenzie, Apt. C. He wrote to a friend, "On the Fourth of July I declared my Independence and found me a little pad on a back street near the Santa Fe Plaza."[16] *My Penitente Land* is profoundly shaped by the growing physical and intellectual freedom Fray Angélico experienced as he wrote it.

Still a poet at heart, he combines his vast historical knowledge with his artistic proclivities to write what Fr. Thomas Steele terms "a prose poem . . . composed by a poet who knows history."[17] The innovative text transcends traditional generic categories; a profound study of history, it combines intuition and intellect to take interpretive risks. It situates contemporary Hispano identity in New Mexico as an outgrowth of centuries of monotheistic religious tradition going back to Abraham and oral tradition one thousand years before the Torah was compiled. The *ánima hispánica* persists in the New Mexico landscape and its people's traditions, the book argues. Expanding on Miguel de Unamuno's study of *lo castizo*, that is, the purely Spanish that persists in Spain despite the periods of foreign conquest, Fray Angélico attempts to go beyond Unamuno's "pictorial intuition" to present a "more ambitious mosaic or tapestry of Palestinian–Castilian–New Mexican landscapes and peoples" from both an artistic and historical perspective.[18] He centers his argument on "a landscape's essence simmering in living blood" and argues that although science might argue with his contentions, art should not resist them; Fray Angélico insists that the aesthetic perspective is necessary to understand the history of Hispanos in New Mexico.[19]

At this time of major change in his life, he remembers a key episode of his childhood as the seed from which this book grew; after he and a young friend taunted the local cobbler/barber with a denigrating verse about the Penitentes, Fray Angélico's mother reprimanded him and explained that the Penitentes, although not perfect, were sincere Christian men who scourged themselves during Lent because they loved the suffering Christ. He began to connect questions about the origins of the Penitentes to his people's ancestry including their current similarities and differences from Spain. After later researching documents of Spanish colonial history, he established that the Penitentes had not come to New Mexico with the colonists but rather at the beginning of the nineteenth century and were not a development of the lay Third Order of St. Francis. The documents also showed him that the Hispanos of New Mexico had become linguistically and culturally different from both Spain and Latin America over three centuries. Expanding on Longfellow's image remembering his youthful will as "the wind's will," Chávez connects his willful treatment of the hermano in Mora to both the future and the past: "[T]he hidden mustard seed of long ago developed into a full-grown tree at last, ready for me to paint in broad strokes as best I can."[20] *My Penitente Land* is this full-grown tree with deep historical roots, "painted" uniquely by the artist, poet, and historian Fray Angélico. The book is "the intimate story of my people of New Mexico upon their very own landscape" and cannot be told apart from the story of the Penitentes.[21] "[We] Hispanic New Mexicans are all Penitentes in some way," Fray Angélico observes.[22]

Two other events in his life were also foundational for *My Penitente Land*. Shortly after Chávez was ordained, a visiting priest from Spain pointed out the similarity of the northern New Mexico landscape to Spain, noting that the local Hispanos were "tipos castizos" like those from his homeland. The two discussed the presence of Penitentes in this area of New Mexico as in Spain, and Fray Angélico began to associate vague ideas of landscape and people with penitence, which would eventually grow into the "mustard tree" of this book. Later, on leave from his military assignment in Germany, he finally saw the Spanish landscape and the historical venues of his forebears. *My Penitente Land* would not have been possible without his life-changing 1952 trip to Spain, and he cites several episodes to exemplify this.

Chávez quotes extensively from Unamuno's 1895 essay "La casta histórica castilla," which argues that the Spanish landscape played a strong role in forming the ánima hispánica.[23] He admires Unamuno's "word picture of a landscape" and adopts the Spanish writer's thesis that landscape gives rise to a particular religious belief.[24] Despite its immense beauty, his country's landscape is uniform and monotonous, lacking intermediary shades; nor is it a sensuous terrain that encourages comfort or nesting instincts. It leads people to monotheism rather than pantheism because instead of communing with nature, "se achica el hombre" (man is diminished), and his soul feels parched like the landscape.[25] Fray Angélico applies this idea to biblical times. The barren landscape of the Palestinians gave rise to a pastoral economy and monotheism, unlike the agricultural economies of the Nile Egyptians and eastern Mesopotamians who were polytheistic. New Mexicans are linked to the monotheistic traditions of Spain and Palestine through their landscape.

While Palestine and Castile "were landscapes ancient with people" Fray Angélico poetically observes, when the Spaniards colonized the Americas, Native Americans also had a long history of harmony with the landscape, having "honeycombed tall sandstone cliffs for dwellings."[26] He echoes D. H. Lawrence's 1928 analysis of the temporal depth that the British writer encountered in New Mexico where Native Americans preserved culture and traditions going back centuries, unlike the geographic breadth Lawrence had accumulated traveling the world.[27] Like the people of the Nile and Euphrates, Native Americans had an agricultural economy and a related religious outlook.

The Spaniards, who introduced a pastoral economy and monotheism in La Nueva Mexico, were primarily *extremeños* and *manchegos*—Semitic Iberians bringing the castizo traditions of the high plateau. A plain, illiterate people, these colonizers primarily sought *hidalguía*; the quest for gold was a means to becoming hidalgos and owning their own land. Villagrá's 1610 account of Oñate's proclamation of formal possession of New Mexico in 1598 overlays the events with biblical comparisons of New Mexico's landscape to Palestine. Fray Angélico compares the epic poem to Genesis and Exodus.

The visual artist in Fray Angélico combines with the poet and historian in his analysis of the connection of New Mexico's landscape to Hispano religion, culture, and history. Complementing Unamuno's word picture, Chávez remembers trips he made as a young historian through New Mexico to El Paso in which he retraced in reverse the journeys of the early Spanish colonists. He imagines "visionary tableaux," "action scenes," and "successive motion picture frames" as he travels from Albuquerque to Socorro, the Jornada del Muerto (the Dead Man's Route), and Robledo and Doña Ana, named after his forebears.[28] He now recounts the history of these places in the direct order in which the early Spanish colonists traveled. He compares the historical events they experienced to episodes from the Bible. His ancestor, Luisa Robledo, who led the Spaniards in pelting Indian attackers with stones, is a reincarnation of Deborah from Judges. The Franciscans are "God's Spanish Levites," and New Mexico represents the "extreme western Canaan of the New World."[29]

Chávez compares the Indians to the "poor native Canaanites" whose land the Hebrews appropriated.[30] He attributes a similar "manifest destiny" to the Spaniards and critiques the misdeeds of the early "maverick plunderers" such as Cortés, Pizarro, and Nuño de Guzmán, along with the cruelty of Coronado's men in 1541. He strongly criticizes Oñate's vengeful siege of Acoma, recounting elements of Villagrá's literary account, but faulting the writer for "giv[ing] no hint of this master's terrible and inhuman vengeance upon Ácoma" when he ordered a foot cut off of males twenty-five and older, as reported in the records of Oñate's trial in Mexico City.[31] Chávez compares the natives of Acoma to the besieged Jews on the heights of Masada in AD 73. Had the Acoma leader known about Spanish manifest destiny and Oñate's cruel vengeance, he might have put his people to death, as did the Jews at Masada.

Chávez deconstructs Villagrá's 1610 epic poem written to restore Oñate's honor by attributing to him what was then the epitome of Hispanic piety—penitence and self-flagellation. "The blood of Ácoma had to be covered up by Oñate's own, as it were," Chávez argues.[32] Although the chronicler who documented the Holy Week ceremonies of March 1598 did not mention flagellation and most likely would have had it occurred, Villagrá's poem portrays many of the colonists engaged in the penitential practice at official religious ceremonies and Oñate and his nephews "spill[ing] a sea of gory crimson ... cut[ting] themselves to pieces" with whips.[33] Fray Angélico argues that the centrality of the cross to Oñate's act of possession at La Toma along with Villagrá's exaggerated depiction of the blood shed in the first Holy Week ceremonies represent the idea of intense personal suffering so predominant in Hispano New Mexico through the centuries.

Diego de Vargas' 1692–93 reconquest symbolized the return from Babylonian captivity for the Spaniards who had fled to El Paso in 1680. De Vargas imitated King Ferdinand's campaign against the Moors in Sevilla in which the latter entrusted himself to the Virgin, reportedly with the words, "Valme, Señora." De Vargas offered a similar prayer to La Conquistadora, later establishing a shrine at the site of victory, as did Ferdinand for Nuestra Señora del Valme. Fray Angélico argues that this parallel to the Catholic king who liberated Spain explains why de Vargas and the *reconquista* have been remembered and commemorated more than other important events in New Mexico history. Hispanos have turned the reconquest into a myth, telescoping the 1692 peaceful re-entry and the 1693 military victory "paid for with considerable Indian blood."[34] The annual fiesta in Santa Fe mythifies the reconquest, avoiding its violent aspects.

In the 1714 La Conquistadora Chapel of St. Francis Cathedral are two visual images that epitomize Hispano New Mexico's connection to Palestine and the pre-Tridentine Catholicism that Spain brought to the Americas. The statue of La Conquistadora in the central reredos and the stark crucifix with the bloody figure of Christ on the side wall contrast what Chávez terms the "romantic, Aryan view" of the marble statuary in European churches.[35] The real hair, clothing, and bloody red paint on the images in La Conquistadora Chapel, like the native santos that would later be crafted, are more faithful to Spain's realistic "Nazareno" tradition, the bloody descriptions in Isaiah of the Suffering Servant, and the finely dressed Esther before her king. This visual culture would persist in New Mexico with the lack of Bibles during the colonial period.

Chávez offers revisionist accounts of three key religious motifs in New Mexico: the shrine of Chimayó, the Penitentes, and the Virgin of Guadalupe. Since ancient times, the Tewa believed in the curative powers of the earth at the sacred site Tsimayo, by the turn of the nineteenth century part of the rancho of Bernardo Abeyta. About 1813, one of the secular pastors from Durango, or a member of his party, told Abeyta about a similar sacred site in Guatemala dedicated to the Black Christ of Esquipulas where the earth also had curative powers. Abeyta built a shrine over the pit of sacred dirt and in 1816 erected the Santuario de Chimayó to which numerous pilgrims came. Chávez compares Chimayó to patronal shrines built in medieval Spain and elsewhere. For Hispanos in New Mexico, Chimayó represented the first incident of sacred waters that dried up into a *posito* since the 1598 incident when a horse's hoof unearthed a spring. Thus, Hispano settlers eagerly embraced their own miraculous shrine reminiscent of the Spanish homeland.

The Penitentes also represented a new phenomenon in New Mexico at the time of secularization. Active in the church of Santa Cruz near Chimayó, they stored new leather whips and wooden crosses that had not yet aged at the church. Again, the recent arrivals from Durango had told the locals about penitential brotherhoods that conducted rituals in Lent and Holy Week. They passed on alabados to newly formed brotherhoods. Soon people came from as far away as Santa Fe for the dynamic Holy Week ceremonies and processions of the brotherhood. Fray Angélico argues that these new Penitente groups re-created Abraham's *hesed* in the stark New Mexico landscape, adding the new element of the Spanish Nazarite—now a life-size wooden statue with a black wig, crown of thorns, and red gown depicting Christ being led to the crucifixion. Fray Angélico masterfully describes these Holy Week rituals of the Penitentes, the townspeople, and visitors, connecting the rituals and images to biblical passages and making readers feel as if they were there. His documentary research showed that the brotherhoods did not come to New Mexico before the late eighteenth or early nineteenth century, and he therefore emphasizes details about the newness of the whips and crosses stored at the church at Santa Cruz.

Fray Angélico also revises the story of the Virgin of Guadalupe, central to the Mexican soul, but not castizo, as were many of the religious images in New Mexico. Fray Juan de Zumárraga, the first bishop of Mexico and a strong defender of the Indians, became the focus of a legend written one hundred years after his death about the appearance of the Virgin of Guadalupe. Historical documents show that on the hill of Tepeyac where the Indians worshipped Tonantzin, Christians built a chapel to honor the Our Lady of Guadalupe or the "Mother of God" about 1556 following the arrival of Zumárraga's successor. A sheepherder claimed that the Virgin of Guadalupe had miraculously cured him on the hill, and one of Fray Pedro de Gante's art pupils, Marcos, painted a picture of the Virgin that was placed in the chapel. The painting was Gothic, not Spanish or Indian, and Marcos likely patterned his image on a block print from a prayer book printed in Flanders. The feast day of the shrine was set on September 8, commemorating the nativity of the Blessed Mother. The primary pilgrims to the chapel at the time were Spaniards, and the record shows that the new bishop received a substantial income from the offerings donated. There are secular references throughout the sixteenth century to the existence of the shrine and the Spaniards' devotion to it as a site of miracles. The earliest reference states that the Virgin appeared in 1555 or 1556 when the shepherd was cured and mentions nothing about a miraculous origin of Marcos' painting.

In 1648, one hundred years after Bishop Zumárraga's death, however, a different account was published, which gave rise to the legend that has come down to our times. New tensions had developed between social and racial groupings in Mexico, and a priest from one of these groups, the criollos, published a booklet in Spanish retelling the story, now with the Virgin Mary appearing to the Indian Juan Diego in December 1531, the miraculous image on his tilma, and the roses as signs to convince Zumárraga to build a chapel for her. After this booklet was published, the shrine changed its feast day to December 12 when the miracle was said to have taken place, and the shrine's chaplain, Lasso de la Vega, published the story in a long Nahuatl poem. Fray Angélico argues that Lasso de la Vega's dramatic poem began to be interpreted as history because different social groups in New Spain could identify with the legend. Criollos identified with the name Guadalupe, the Castilian roses, and the figure of Bishop Zumárraga. Christian Indians identified with the language of the poem, the figure of Juan Diego, and the association with Tonantzin. Mestizos interpreted the aging, sallow color of the Virgin's face and its lines and features as the faces of their own daughters. Suggesting that the semiotics of audience response played a strong role in the popular acceptance of the revised legend, Fray Angélico questions the legend on several grounds, especially the fact that Bishop Zumárraga made no mention of what would have been a tremendous event in his life in his last will and testament. If such a momentous event had occurred on December 12, 1531, why was it celebrated on September 8 for over one hundred years until after 1648, Chávez asks. He compares the adherence to the new legend to the common practice of the literal interpretation of religious poems since Genesis.

If Fray Angélico combines intuition, intellect, and poetic consciousness to write revisionist history in *My Penitente Land*, he also departs from standard historical studies by including several autobiographical stories. He remembers being singled out for his ethnicity in the novitiate when the new novices were given soft cord whips to engage in symbolic self-flagellation in their cells. When the others looked dubiously at the whips, the friar in charge told them it wasn't nearly as bad as what the Penitentes in New Mexico did, glancing at Fray Angélico as he spoke. The other novices in the Midwestern novitiate knew nothing about his Hispano traditions. Yet all of the young men, including Fray Angélico, were uncomfortable with the tradition of corporeal penance and could not stop giggling as they entered their cells with the whips. They all engaged in the same self-protective strategy of whipping their mattresses instead of their backs, and the novice master ignored their disobedience. Fray Angélico notes that this practice was completely out of step with the spirit of St. Francis and was mistakenly prescribed by the Franciscan authorities in Rome. Nonetheless, he recognizes the importance of the Penitente spirit and tradition in New Mexico history and emphasizes it throughout the book.

Chávez recounts a conversation overheard as he was dressing one morning in a *pensión* in Sevilla in which the owner voiced shock that

Protestants do not approve of the crucifix or recognize the Virgin Mary as the Mother of God. Her remark, "Válgame Dios, qué barbarida[d]!" (God save me, how uncouth!) symbolizes for Fray Angélico the centrality of the image of the suffering Christ and the Blessed Mother to Spanish Catholicism.[36] For Fray Angélico, this deeply embedded belief in the Virgin Mother throughout his people's history manifests itself as he converses with and embraces a few of the original statues during his trip to Spain. When he visits the shrine of the black Virgin of Guadalupe in Extremadura, the oldest shrine to Mary in Spain, he embraces the small statue, calls her "sweetheart" and kisses her cheeks. The priests at the shrine call his actions truly *castizo*, and they attribute the same character to Fray Angélico's description of Hispanos' devotion to La Conquistadora in New Mexico.

His June 1952 trip to Spain allowed him to see firsthand the landscape of his forebears' villages, moving beyond the simulacra of the magazine and encyclopedia photographs. He compares the connections he sees between Palestine, Spain, and New Mexico to time and space collapsing, shrinking together "like a camera lens zooming in upon a scene."[37] When struck by the similarity of Spain to the New Mexico landscape, he took photographs to "assure myself there was no self-deception."[38] Everyone he showed them to upon his return thought they were scenes of northern New Mexico. Thus, Fray Angélico moves from simulacra of Spain to direct knowledge of the landscape and then again to photographic simulacra to retain what he saw and prove his theories. Surprisingly, he includes no pictures in *My Penitente Land*, relying on words and rhetorical techniques such as ekphrasis to communicate visual images.[39]

As he traveled through Extremadura, he recognized the village names from the settler lists in documents he had researched at home. The highlight of his trip was the village Valverde de Llerena where he arrived on the feast of San Antonio de Padua. His ancestor Don Pedro Gómez Durán y Chávez had come from the village in 1600, and many of the townspeople shared the Chávez name. To honor his visit, the priest suggested a second procession that evening for the feast of St. Anthony, and Fray Angélico led the candlelight procession with the statue. As an English-dominant bilingual he was usually less confident speaking in Spanish, but that evening his sermon to the townspeople flowed easily: "Since by now I had already found out that these good people's Castilian was like my own, I felt no embarrassment or hesitation as I told them of all my *extremeño* forbears and of a new homeland they had found across the world so very much like their own birthplace. In fact, I had never been so eloquent in the tongue of my fathers."[40] New Mexico and Spain shared both a landscape and a language: the Spanish of Extremadura. The word *monacillo* instead of *monaguillo* (acolyte), for instance, was used only in this area of Spain and in New Mexico.

While Fray Angélico sought to explain the history and traditions of New Mexico Hispanos to a wide audience in *My Penitente Land*, he also aimed to remind Hispanos of the precise traditions of their castizo roots, which some were forgetting. Following Unamuno's emphasis on lo castizo—that which is purely Spanish that persists in Spain despite the periods of foreign conquest—Chávez urges fellow Hispano New Mexicans not to lose the signs of their origins. Writing the book became urgent for him, he notes, before Mexican influences and American technology erased the castizo tradition and landscape altogether. Like Unamuno, Fray Angélico believes that the Spanish soul will persevere in the face of conquests and foreign influence if his people can remember their history. While his notions of cultural purity might offend some, his efforts to preserve Spanish culture in New Mexico are similar to the tenets of Chicano nationalism developing at the same time in which Chicanos fought against the attempted dilution of their cultural traditions in the American melting pot, and worked to recover their indigenous roots and set themselves off proudly as a distinct people with long traditions.

Public Intellectual

Fray Angélico's departure from active ministry in mid-1971 marked a new phase in his intellectual career in which he advanced his role as public intellectual, returning knowledge to larger sectors of society beyond small academic circles. After retiring from the Franciscan Order that had taken care of his material needs for forty-seven years, he now needed income from his writing to support himself. He arranged book contracts with advance royalty payments and sold articles to *New Mexico* magazine in addition to being named its book review editor. These small sums were not enough to support him, and he put together his social security pension, small salaries from various jobs, and gifts from friends to be able to live on his own after two years with his sister in the family home. Beyond financial exigency, however, Fray Angélico was also motivated in this new phase of his career by a deep desire to communicate knowledge to a wider public.

He had sought increasingly wider audiences throughout his Franciscan life. Already in 1925, the fifteen-year-old high school student published poetry and essays in the seminary magazine *Brown and White*, of which he became editor. In this period, he contributed poetry to his hometown newspaper, the *Santa Fe New Mexican*, and to national Catholic publications such as *St. Anthony Messenger*, *America*, and *Commonweal*. For three decades from the early 1930s on, he regularly wrote essays and reports for the *Provincial Chronicle* to document his work. The wider audience he addressed here was not only Franciscans throughout the country, but future generations who would turn to this publication for valuable historical information, as he argued in a 1959 piece urging friaries to bind issues of the journal to ensure their preservation. His essays and notes in the *Provincial Chronicle* reflect his lifelong concern with communicating accurate historical knowledge to wider audiences and his sense of his own role in the long history of Christianity.

In 1948 he published in the *Chronicle* an essay about his initial research on the history of the Church in New Mexico, announcing that he was undertaking a lengthy project to fill in the details of this general sketch. This piece had been preceded a decade earlier by "The Gold Hunters," an essay on Fray Juan de Padilla and the first Franciscans in the United States who found the gold of souls to save in Quivira when Coronado found none. Published with Fray Angélico's own drawing of the Isleta mission, the essay reached thousands of Third Order Franciscans when it appeared in their official magazine, the *Franciscan Herald*, in March 1938.

Besides publishing historical work in these nonacademic publications, Fray Angélico also wrote himself and his work into history with numerous notes and essays sent to the *Chronicle*. Particularly touching is a detailed 1947 narrative about his military service in WWII and its 1952 sequel after his tour of duty in Germany. In 1954 he signed the detailed account of his pilgrimage throughout New Mexico, in which he drove La Conquistadora to every church for the Marian Year celebrations, "By Fr. Angelico, C.C.C.C.C.," with a note explaining that the initials stand for "Chavez, Concionator, Chaffeur, Courturier, Conquistadorae."[41] Other essays document the rebuilding and murals he did at Santa Dorotea Church at Domingo in 1938, the renovation of La Conquistadora Chapel in the mid-1950s, and the remodeling of the sanctuary of St. Joseph Church in Cerrillos in 1961. A humorous 1958 contribution to the *Chronicle* ("Resurrectionist Mystery") sets the record straight on the nickname of a painting Fray Angélico did for the chapel at Oldenburg, Indiana, in the 1930s. After repainting the canvas-covered figure of the Risen Christ with jet-black hair, a beard, and a staring look, Fray Angélico commented to other friars that it looked like Haile Selassie, the emperor of Abyssinia in the news at the time because of Mussolini. In 1958 the editor of the *Chronicle* had miswritten the image's nickname as "Heile," which Chávez corrected.

Among his writings that brought history to a wider audience in the period after he left active priestly ministry is the article on the genízaros for the *Handbook of North American Indians*. He attempts to correct errors in people's understanding of the term, documenting its use since the colonial period. He argues that is has been misused in the sense of "half-breed," when in fact it refers not to racially mixed peoples, but to the ethnic intermixture of Native American tribes or nations. The genízaros were primarily women and children of Plains Indian tribes who had been captured in intertribal raids and sold to the Spaniards. Fray Angélico avoids the word *slavery* for most of the article, while clearly describing the sale and purchase of human beings for forced servitude. He argues that the Spaniards had the alleged pious purpose of raising the genízaros as Christians when they "ransomed" them during retaliatory raids, admitting that they also obtained unpaid household and ranch labor in the process. Conceding that the practice might be considered slavery in the broad sense, Chávez argues that "it was benevolent and the servitude lasted only into early adulthood, usually at marriage time."[42] The children of these marriages were the real genízaros, he notes, because they lost their parents' connection to tribal culture and followed Hispanic life patterns. Nonetheless, they were not Hispanic, mestizo, or Pueblo Indian, hence the term *genízaro* was applied to them. The term died out in official records (although some people still use it informally) after Mexican independence and the Plan de Iguala of 1822 decreeing that all peoples, no matter their racial mixture, be officially termed Mexican citizens.

Chávez's journalism and other media contributions were directed to an even wider contemporary audience. Besides a few radio and television appearances, he contributed regularly to *New Mexico* magazine, especially during the 1970s to support himself. The magazine listed its circulation at 106,245 in October 1970, as Fray Angélico started to write again for it.⁴³ While many of his essays dealt with the history of New Mexico, he frequently placed this information in wider national and international contexts. In describing the origin of the tortilla, for example, he referred readers to the bread popular among poor people of the Middle East, brought to Spain by Arabs. In an essay written in Peña Blanca before he retired from the order, he connected the word *gringo* to a sixteenth-century adaptation of the word *griego* in Spain, where numerous Greeks were immigrating to repair body armor and war armaments for the conquest of the New World. Readers not only learn about the painter El Greco, one of these immigrants, whom Fray Angélico theorizes was called El Gringo by the ordinary folks of Toledo, but that the term *gavacho* originally referred to French people from the River Gabache in the Pyrenees. Records show that as early as 1752 in New Mexico, a Santa Fe woman married to a French man was called La Gavacha, and the descendants of a Greek man who came with Oñate in 1598 gave their name to Los Griegos.⁴⁴

Chávez's contributions to *New Mexico* magazine gave readers local historical knowledge in an international context and frequently sought innovative means of drawing in readers. His 1976 narrative "New Mexico's Real Romeo and Juliet" presents historical events in 1733 New Mexico as a prose play, changing a "bare court case" into a "living human drama."⁴⁵ In a creative hybridization of literary genres, Fray Angélico draws readers into history, employing narrative suspense and the trappings of drama. In other essays such as "The Carpenter Pueblo" (1971), "The Mora Country" (1972), "Ruts of the Santa Fe Trail" (1972), "Valle de Cochiti" (1973), and "La Jornada del Muerto" (1974), he uses the genre of the tourist guide to familiarize readers with centuries of New Mexico history and to correct misconceptions. Sometimes historical knowledge from his years of religious training is brought to bear. Praising the post–Vatican II liturgical innovations put into practice in Santa Fe under Fr. Blase Shauer in the early 1970s, he shows readers that historically New Mexico has always been in the vanguard of nontraditional forms of worship. Elements of liturgy now considered traditional, such as organ music, were once viewed as the instruments of the Devil.⁴⁶

In several articles Fray Angélico includes autobiographical elements that shape his historical analysis and chosen topics. "The Carpenter Pueblo" draws on his family's tradition of carpentry to theorize about the demise of Pecos Pueblo.[47] While dense historical detail almost overwhelms the piece, the autobiographical overlay allows him insights into previously unanswered questions about the pueblo. Historians surmised that the formerly great pueblo was definitively abandoned in 1839 because Comanche raids and disease had taken their toll. He offers another explanation based on references in Church documents to most of the men in the pueblo being excellent carpenters. Himself the son and grandson of carpenters, Fray Angélico theorizes that the more reasonable explanation for the demise of the pueblo in the eighteenth century was that many families left to take carpentry jobs in other sites as new towns and churches were being built, and they remained in these places after finishing the job. Just as his family moved to San Diego where there was carpentry work for his father and uncle in 1912, then to Mora to build the school, and later to Albuquerque to build a house, so too might the Pecos carpenters have dispersed throughout the 1700s, with the remaining forty men moving to Jemez in 1839, the only other pueblo where their language was spoken.

In "The Mora Country," Fray Angélico's autobiographical overlay presents firsthand details that make the essay come alive. Having grown up in Mora shaped his choice of the article's subject, and he carefully explains the main French migration to the town with details from his personal remembrances. As he had noted earlier, the area's name did not derive from the French phrase "l'eau du mort," as many believe, because the area was named long before the French came. Rather it is from the Spanish expression "lo de Mora," meaning the land belonging to a man named Mora who claimed the area in the early eighteenth century. Although the French visited the area briefly in 1693, 1739, and 1760, the large migration of the French to Mora did not occur until 1839 when they came from Taos. He also recounts an autobiographical connection to the most famous French resident of Mora, Ceran St. Vrain, who built the town mill. Fray Angélico enables readers to see and feel the famous mill as he recalls days playing with his childhood friends "amid the white-powdered roaring machinery of the flour mill. The mill's runway by the big water wheel was a deep treasure-trove of lively native trout. When the sluices above were closed, their moist beds teemed with gasping *boquinetes*, or delicious clear-water suckers."[48] Additionally, when his parents moved to Albuquerque for his father to build a house, he remained to finish the school year, staying in the home of St. Vrain's daughter, Doña Felicitas Gallegos, whose adobe house was filled with opulent, French-style furnishings. The autobiographical details add a visuality and vibrancy to the essay.

As a large new recreational lake was being designed for the Cochiti valley, Fray Angélico documented the history of the villages of the area, some of which would disappear because of the project. He predicted that the new city of Cochiti Lake would become a large "micropolis" with ancient pre-European Indian villages at either end. Autobiographically connected to the history of the area both through his research and the many years of Franciscan ministry there, Chávez describes the terrain in minute detail, taking readers on a guided tour with a map and pictures. At the Rancho de Santa Cruz, a pre-1680 land grant on the east bank of the Rio Grande, for example, Bishop Pedro Tamarón of Durango administered Confirmation to Indians and Hispanos on a special day in June 1760—he was the first bishop to visit the area in 150 years. Nostalgically, Fray Angélico observes, "The site of El Rancho de Santa Cruz will be at the very bottom of the new lake. . . . A sort of minor Atlantis, one might say."[49]

Peña Blanca, where Fray Angélico served his first missionary assignment, began as a large homestead established by José Miguel de la Peña and was called Rancho de Peña until 1792. Then it began to be called Rancho de la Peña Blanca, to distinguish it from an area called Peña Negra across a dry arroyo. Fray Angélico includes autobiographical information about his renovations of the church in Peña Blanca in the late 1930s and early 1940s. Having "separated himself completely from the Franciscan Order and the priestly ministry,"[50] according to his contributor's note at the beginning of the magazine, he freely criticizes the "benevolent vandalism" of French secular pastors and German American Franciscans who destroyed the character of the beautiful 1869 New Mexico–style church in subsequent years. He continues,

> Over 30 years ago, the writer personally rebuilt the façade in Territorial style, with a *portal* made from the well-aged beams of a discarded Santa Fe Railway bridge at nearby

Domingo; but the beams have been painted over since, instead of being merely oiled. He was not able to restore the rest of the church by removing banal stained windows and a scrolled tin ceiling, but he did cover the interior walls with large murals. These are now a focus of curiosity, because the faces on the many human figures are those of the local people.[51]

The essay is not merely a tourist guide of the settlements and villages of the Cochiti Valley, which are about to be transformed by the recreational lake, but an effort to preserve the history of the area in a wider forum than scholarly venues. His historical research and common sense have taught him that before long, many of the material historical artifacts of the area, including his own church renovation and art, may also disappear like the New Mexico Atlantis of El Rancho de Santa Cruz at the bottom of Cochiti Lake.

Perhaps his most innovative attempts at teaching the public through entertaining, accessible writing are those essays in which his famous sense of humor predominates. In six pieces in the magazine from 1973 to 1975 he wittily personifies elements of local color such as the "adobe brick," the *buñuelo*, the sopaipilla, the chile, the tortilla, and the New Mexico state bird. Again, he connects local culture to larger international historical narratives and provides accessible lessons in etymology. Humor is also his tool of choice for correcting grammatical inconsistencies resulting from contemporary historical amnesia. The adobe that he personifies in "Lo, the Poor Adobe!" for example, is distraught not because the wall he is part of is being remodeled for a luxury hotel, but because English-speaking folks redundantly use his name to refer to the clay the brick is made from rather than the brick itself:

> "We're a very ancient family originally called *Atob*," he began. "The name itself is Arabic meaning 'sun-dried brick' and nothing else, nothing else. Our ancestry is also Egyptian, Syrian, Hebrew and Babylonian, going back more than 5,000 recorded years.
>
> "It's all right for an anglo to call himself Henry Clay or Roger Mudd if he wants to, but that's not my earthen cup of tea. It's a dirty trick, to say the least."[52]

Similarly decrying the redundancy that non–Spanish speakers employ in phrases such as the "La Fonda Inn" or the "Rio Grande River," the voice of the adobe in this essay strives to teach readers not only about expressions that "commit tautology" such as "adobe brick," but also to impart important historical and etymological knowledge many are unaware of.

In two humorous pieces building on the gender distinctions of the Spanish words *sopaipilla* and *chile*, Chávez plays freely with sexual metaphors to educate readers about the origins of words: "They must have been triplets, those three pretty blonde daughters of Doña Sopaipa of Castile who long ago came to the New World and all bearing their mother's name in diminutive form. One Miss Sopaipilla settled in Bolivia, another in Chile, and the third in New Mexico. They haven't corresponded with each other for almost 400 years, perhaps for being beautiful but dumb blondes who can't even write. But who cares, so long as they are delicious."[53] Fray Angélico notes that the New Mexican sopaipilla "swell[s] out into womanhood" when fried, and that when "her golden curves swell with honey or any kind of jelly, or just with the clean hot breath of her birth, she makes everyone drool with anticipation."[54] But before criticizing this wonderful educational essay for playing on sexist stereotypes, we should read it in the context of its companion piece on "Bonnie Prince Chile," in which, using Shakespeare, Chávez teaches people about the history and etymology of the chile through gendered metaphors in which prince chiles are married and bedded down with pretty princess tomatoes to form a delicious salsa in Mexico. "No need here [in New Mexico] of bedding me down with tomatoes or burying me in spices. Here I am loved for myself. In this way I am really Spanish here, pure *castizo*, for being taken purely for what I am."[55] As his thesis about the importance of lo castizo to New Mexico was about to be published in *My Penitente Land*, Fray Angélico focuses on the transformation of an indigenous food transplanted to an area of rich Hispano tradition in New Mexico. And, having left celibate religious life, Fray Angélico now feels more freedom to humorously develop sexual metaphors in his journalism.

In the 1974 essay "Tortilla Flat—Of Course It Is!" he reclaims his baptismal name, Manuel Chávez, as his byline to highlight his Jewish roots with the pun "Manny Chevitz." Besides teaching readers about the origin of the word *tortilla* and the connection of this bread to

FIG. 8.2. Fray Angélico Chávez, 1979, courtesy Palace of the Governors Photo Archives (NMHM/DCA), Neg. No. PA-MU-082.07.

Middle Eastern peoples and the Bible, Chávez portrays himself as a character in the story who exemplifies the goal of making knowledge accessible to the public: "A Latin scholar in balmier days, Manny still looks for any chance to show off his etymological prowess. Only that he doesn't betray himself with such big terms as had Sol with 'social commentary.'"[56] Santa Fe attorney and book collector Sol Cohen, the character reading Steinbeck's *Tortilla Flat* in the story, utters such esoteric phrases as "twisted *postfactum*." The accompanying drawing caricatures this lawyer with a social conscience. Once again with humor, Fray Angélico urges the intellectual to return knowledge to the community in a noncondescending, helpful manner, to strive to communicate and educate rather than to pontificate and show off.

A Writer Reads

Fray Angélico's seven years as book review editor for *New Mexico* magazine left a treasure trove of information about his life and intellect. Not content to follow the traditional staid format of the book review, he creatively reinvented the genre, speaking directly to readers in often poetic prose. He imaginatively arranges books singly or in groups of two or three for comparison and, constructing each "Southwestern Bookshelf" as a whole, refers readers to previous and ensuing points in the column. He is both artist and intellectual as he reads and selects books and designs and writes the column. While his chatty tone and personal anecdotes make the columns attractive to a wide audience, he engages in sophisticated wordplay and humor, presents important historical information, theorizes about the aesthetic, and articulates strong political views about contemporary American society. Although no one has systematically studied this minor form of writing in Fray Angélico's oeuvre, it is a mistake to overlook this collection of reviews of 531 books. Together they open a new window into Fray Angélico's life and thought.

What we might term Chávez's populism appears in his repeated concern about the price of the books he reviews. He advises readers of good buys and of high prices that are prohibitive for most people but perhaps within the budget of libraries. This concern for readers' pocketbooks also stems from his own new worries about money after having left the Franciscan Order. In the March–April 1973 issue, he comments that he's glad to be a reviewer and to have access to many books for free. Another sign of his populist spirit—that is, his desire to reach, serve, and meet the needs of large numbers of ordinary people—is his criticism of the academic jargon and unintelligible writing in some of the books he reviews. He admits his own difficulty understanding one art historian's language and complains, "The text . . . is in the art critic's jargon, addressed presumably to the inner circle; to the layman it can be as frustrating as is governmental bureaucratese, or the cant of modern theologians for that matter. (Remember, sirs, this review section is for the average reader.)"[57] In June 1975 he praises the clear writing of a study of Indians: "The dry bones of ethnology and archeology are here clothed with the living flesh of clear readable writing. Evidently the author had you in mind and not her colleagues."[58]

In contrast to difficult academic prose, Chávez often adopts a chatty tone and includes personal information about himself. In a 1972 issue, he writes of his great personal letdown as an artist and creator when learning from one book under review that many great artists perhaps traced photographs. He then turns his disillusion into an important theoretical insight—that nothing is ever completely original: "Inspiration in any medium is sparked by what has gone before."[59] In another review he reveals that despite his expertise on Southwest history, he learned a good deal from the introductory book on the subject.[60] Although he often openly shows his deep knowledge of history and its minute details, in this personal comment he is not afraid to tell readers that he continues to learn, even from a basic text.

In keeping with his chatty, self-revealing tone, Fray Angélico refers to autobiographical events in the reviews, helping to further our understanding of him as a person. He mentions that he selected one picture book for reviewing because it included images of Watrous and Wagon Mound, towns related to his family history. He mentions that a book on Padre Martínez would be a good idea in the November–December 1973 issue, the seed of a book that he would begin to write later and publish in 1981. To underscore a prevalent stereotype of the Southwest in a September 1975 review, he refers to his meeting with mystic Theresa Newmann in Europe in 1952, who, upon learning he was from New Mexico, commented in German that it was the land of cowboys and Indians.

Other autobiographical anecdotes reveal more significant information. He especially identifies with the autobiography of Major General Charles Corlett, for example, because of similarities between his life and the general's. Chávez reveals that he performed "a caper" during the Philippines invasion that Corlett had heard about and believed Chávez should have been awarded the Silver Star for. Now, reading Corlett's autobiography, he realizes that the general was so concerned about Chávez's lack of recognition because others had taken credit for some of Corlett's great wartime accomplishments. Fray Angélico further identifies with Corlett because he also was of small stature: "But what strikes me personally at this reading is the fact that, with all his inner toughness, General Corlett was a little man physically at least for a combat general. This too often proves a disadvantage in modern bureaucratic systems which tend to favor six-foot-ten, two-hundred-pound mediocrities."[61] Chávez subtly reveals what he himself felt as a small man serving in the army, and perhaps throughout his life.

In another significant story, he tells about his fascination in the 1920s with the illustrations in an early edition of Cather's *Death Comes for the Archbishop*. In the lead review of a new book of Harold Von Schmidt's paintings and drawings, Chávez tells of his enchantment with Von Schmidt's illustrations in Cather's classic book while he was away from the Southwest studying with German friars. At that time he wondered how an artist with "such a high-sounding Teutonic name . . . could have captured New Mexico's atmosphere so perfectly and with such charm," later learning that Von Schmidt lived in the Southwest and that Cather personally chose him to illustrate the book. Chávez even argues that perhaps the novel owed its early success to Von Schmidt. "The author's prose, I thought, was the exclusive source of the magic, until I realized that the black-and-white illustrations had very much to do with the enchantment. They were to the text what bacon is to eggs."[62] Chávez reveals his early understanding of the strong interdependence between image and text in creative writing. Von Schmidt's illustrations for Cather's novel were an important model for Chávez's drawings in his early stories published in the seminary and, shortly thereafter, in *New Mexico Triptych*.

Fray Angélico comments on many social issues in the reviews, revealing his political views and social concerns at the time. One especially predominant thread is the environment and ecology. In 1972 he comments on the "scenic backgrounds which evoke bittersweet nostalgia" in the photos in a book on logging, and the pictures of desert scenes around Lumberton that "also make one sad about indiscriminate deforestation."[63] Reviewing books on backpacking he notes, "Nowadays, smog and sundry other pollutions of land and air are driving the urban greenhorn to a shrinking wilderness which beckons with idyllic promises."[64] Although he wishes Stewart Udall's book on national wildlife refuges, seashores, and scenic rivers were thicker, that is, that there were more such national treasures, Fray Angélico praises the book and emphasizes its importance "in these times so crucial to our national landscape's future."[65] In a humorous review of *Woodall's Trailering Parks and Campgrounds*, Chávez notes that "as a devotee of Mother Nature, I decry the ever growing trailer villages marring the Western landscape with the harsh sheen of metal" but concedes that they have to be accepted as part of contemporary life "like rock music and taxes."[66] The visual pollution of trailers is as bad as rock music in his view, and both are as dreadful as taxes, he implies. A 1973 book of cartoons about air and water pollution in the West is "a much-needed gospel" that should be "proclaimed from the house-tops" and "bought in lots . . . for free distribution."[67] By 1975, he is imagining the depletion of the world's fuels and praising the

Sierra Club's "dignified" slogan: "Not blind opposition to progress, but opposition to blind progress." He praises Horgan's *Far from Cibola* as "most certainly apropos of our big Ecological Crisis."[68]

In an especially strong critique in July 1973, he urges political and economic leaders to read the somewhat dry *A Landscape for Humans* to learn "what to do and what to avoid if our beautiful land is to continue as a Landscape for Happy Human Living, and not a raped paradise for only the toughest of insects and lizards." Additionally, ordinary people "not guided by immediate profit and a to-hell-with-the-future attitude" can use the book to prepare for civic action.[69] In a 1974 critique using wordplay, he argues that not only do the Hopi suffer the pollution of electrical energy, but a new tribe he terms "The Hopeless" both experience pollution's harm and help to create it:

> The Hopeless are all of us in the West along with the rest of the country's population. More and more are the producers of electric energy irreparably ruining the landscape, while wasting and polluting its water and atmosphere on the one hand, and on the other pressing the consumer to squander the power produced in a needless display of giant neon signs and countless home gadgets. Hence, in a way, the consumer is more to blame than the producer, and our comfy world is apt to end, not with a bang but with an ampere.[70]

Despite the wordplay and humor, Chávez preaches a serious warning about ecology and lifestyle choices to his new congregation of magazine readers.

Fray Angélico also criticizes materialistic values, the "Ugly American" mentality, and the Vietnam War. Reviewing a book on archeologist Alfred V. Kidder, he comments, "In our materialistic society, the impact of the business tycoon and the *politico* is better remembered than that of the scholar."[71] In a similar vein, he complains that young people watch TV and read comic books instead of books. The book *Juan of Santo Niño* "should also be for adolescents, if there are any such left who are not already hung up on Saturday morning TV, comic books and even confession magazines."[72] He warns against the Ugly American attitude, reflecting on the strong critique of American arrogance and chauvinism in William J. Lederer and Eugene Burdick's 1958 popular novel of the same title. He invokes the concept in reviewing a volume on diversity in the Southwest, suggesting that someone also write a book on the "great Gringos" of the area, "by way of a much deserved tribute and as a means of instructing those others who are 'ugly ones' solely because of ignorance and an Archie Bunker mentality." Insisting that there are good and bad people within all ethnic groups, he frequently urges nuanced understandings of the diverse ethnic groups in the United States.[73] In 1970 he uses the Ugly American concept to describe a nineteenth-century American adventurer, James Hobbs. "Now a man who delighted in shooting Indians and Mexicans by the score with such gusto, and who regarded Catholics and Mormons as the scum of the earth, looks rather like a forerunner of the modern Ugly American, in protest against whom the so-called liberal and hippie came into being," writes Chávez, debunking the volume editor's critique of hippies and liberals.[74]

Chávez notes that contemporary Ugly American interventions such as Vietnam and Cambodia have historical precedents. Reviewing a book about General Pershing's expedition across the U.S./Mexico border after Pancho Villa's raid on Columbus, New Mexico, he notes, "The Wilson administration and the War Department don't come off so beautifully. It is Vietnam, with all its political stink, prefigured in a desert land instead of a jungle setting, and with the punitive expedition under Pershing another Cambodia adventure. Chauvinistic war hawks will very likely label all this as 'liberal propaganda,' when it is nothing else than clear, honest, straightforward reporting of the facts."[75]

Chávez is sometimes patronizing in his comments about women writers and feminists. Mentioning an irrelevant physical characteristic of Cleofas Jaramillo, he calls her a "tiny lady" and notes that the republication of her book will fill a need for people interested in old social customs, "especially . . . the ladies." The essays in the second book under review by the "gentle members" of Santa Fe's Sociedad Folklórica who are taking a Spanish class "are not bad at all. Both books should prove most welcome to the same clientele."[76] Does Chávez mean that their Spanish prose or that the content and analysis of the essays is not bad? And why would men not be interested in these books? In reviewing a biography on Pablita Velarde, he reports, "A lady writer chitchats in a style which should enthrall other ladies. . . . It's women's lib as it should be—with feminine grace."[77] Again, because the book is about a woman, Fray Angélico seems to think it will only be of interest to women. Although perhaps intended as a compliment, his insistence that feminists retain feminine grace aims to make women adhere to reductive stereotypes.

While very supportive of Native American culture and sociopolitical issues in the reviews, he insists that accurate history must replace inadequate, partial truths. A "white man's" foreword to a young Navajo's poetic vignettes overemphasizes the Navajos' Long Walk under Kit Carson, Chávez argues. "It ignores the fact that the newcomer Navajo . . . preyed heavily on the Hopi and the Zuni for generations. . . . [All] of us, no matter what our racial derivation, ought never to forget, while airing whatever grievances we might have, that our respective ancestors were not always lily-pure."[78] The implication that Navajo ancestors' exploitation of other groups justifies later exploitation of the Navajos is weak. Nonetheless, Chávez argues here for a nuanced understanding of history that questions the strong ethnic nationalism of minority groups in the 1960s and 1970s. In another review he argues, "While presenting the injustices the Indians suffered at the hands of Europeans, one need not make the other side a Compleat Ogre."[79] He praises Vine Deloria's *God Is Red* for the author's "widely informed and philosophically trained mind in both the secular and religious fields."[80] Chávez included many books on Native Americans in his seven years of book reviewing, but he humorously introduces one review in 1975 with a slight jab at militancy: "Lest Marlon Brando and a bunch of braves occupy this writer's study," he will include a book on Indians this month. He praises the book but takes issue with the repeated contention that early Indian pottery survived because it was buried with the dead until the Spanish missionaries arrived and insisted on Christian burial rites. In fact, Chávez argues, most Pueblos buried their dead secretly, and the priest sometimes blessed the grave on his next visit. "Nor were most pueblos so much Christianized that they would obey the padres' regulations of their own accord."[81] Here he uses both his own missionary experience and information from the historical records.

Chávez was especially outspoken in the reviews on Chicanos and the Chicano Movement. He objects to a 1971 sociological study because it attempts to "put all Mexican-Americans into one broad classification, as if all had an identical background."[82] He argues for retaining important historical and cultural distinctions between Hispanos and Mexican Americans. In 1975 he critiques a book for repeating an error about the early Spanish settlement of the Southwest—that Mexican Americans inhabited the entire region when the United States took over in 1846–50. In fact, only Spanish New Mexico had a sizeable Hispano population at the time, with only a sprinkling of Mexican pioneers in California, Texas, and Arizona. American Indians primarily inhabited the vast Southwest at the time, not Mexican Indians. Consequently, sociologists now studying "the Chicano question" in the entire Southwest "ought to base their contentions not on remote history, but on the constant flow of immigration from Mexico during the past hundred years or so."[83] Similarly, in a review of Jacinto Quirarte's *Mexican American Artists*, he reminds readers that only New Mexico has been inhabited by the Spanish and their descendants for 375 years and that the Spanish in the other Southwestern states "were completely swallowed up by the more recent waves of immigration from Mexico. Only the Hispanic New Mexicans, and of course the aborigines, can claim their very own territory as their continuous homeland for almost four centuries."[84] Fray Angélico repeatedly asserts the difference between New Mexico Hispanos and Chicanos and proudly emphasizes the former's uniqueness.

Occasionally, Chávez's critique is much stronger. He comments that the excellent book *Little Lion of the Southwest* by Marc Simmons "should provide a good vaccine against the Chicano Plague that has hit our countryside."[85] As a carefully researched study of the important nineteenth-century Spanish New Mexican Manuel Antonio Chávez, the book, in Fray Angélico's view, brings attention to the contributions of Hispano New Mexicans who have a distinct identity and should not be subsumed in the Chicano Movement. In another somewhat mean-spirited comment in 1976, Chávez digresses from the book under review with a discussion of proper accent marks and stress in Spanish. He complains that a popular Mexican actor is currently mispronouncing a car in an ad as "Cordóva" instead of the proper "Córdova"; "And we've heard no militant Chicano group protesting such a horrendous rape of their language and history!" Chávez remarks.[86] Although in several reviews he promotes bilingual education and children learning Spanish while they are young, and urges Chicanos to better their Spanish skills, this sarcastic remark suggests that he resents Chicano militancy. He implicitly asks, why do they protest other social issues and not the loss of their language?

In other reviews he offers milder criticism and sometimes support of the Chicano Movement. He cautions in 1975: "Not all Americanos have been as bad as the Chicanos would make them"; but he is more supportive of the movement in another review: "God knows that the ubiquitous Mexican-Americans, as self-described 'brown' citizens, . . . do have a redress coming from the so-called WASP majority in power." He can understand the anger that sometimes surfaces in the book under review and appreciates that the volume might enlighten those who are against the Chicano struggle because of ignorance. But, he adds, "In all petitions and demonstrations for civil rights under our nation's Constitution, it is the American flag that should be raised aloft, and none other."[87] He reviews only five books of Chicano fiction—all by New Mexico writers Rudolfo Anaya, Sabine Ulibarrí, Orlando Romero, and Nash Candelaria—and praises them all. In selecting only these few books from among the many new volumes of Chicano writing published at the time, Chávez shows his preference for and loyalty to New Mexico Hispano culture. In the November–December 1971 column, he praises Ulibarrí for his authentic New Mexico Spanish that is grammatically correct and urges parents to use *Tierra Amarilla* for their children's bilingual education. The first half of his review of Anaya's 1977 *Heart of Aztlán* reminds Chicanos that they are not descended from the Aztecs themselves, who remembered Aztlán as their place of origin, but rather from "the tribes the latter held in serfdom."[88] Again, Chávez pushes for accurate history rather than convenient myths.

He frequently comments on historical mistakes in books he reviews and urges historians not to judge previous historical figures through a twentieth-century lens. Instead of the "know-it-all flippancy" of one book on the American push westward, he urges writers to grasp history "through the spirit of human dignity inherent in the Great Papers of 1776."[89] He criticizes a 1963 book of folklore by Arthur L. Campa for incorrectly retelling the mystery of Padre Padilla of Isleta, which "was solved historically 16 years before this book was written." Concerned that readers often take folklore as fact, he admonishes, "Unfortunately . . . folklorists go on building their airy castles from puffs of hearsay with only a nod to historical fact if it happens to suit their purpose."[90] The historian in Fray Angélico trumps the literary figure in this review, as he complains about the dangers of folklore being understood as history. Strangely, he does not direct readers specifically to his 1947 and 1952 articles on Padre Padilla, since he refers to many of his other writings in the reviews over the years. How does this excessively subtle reference to the correct history help readers to escape the "airy castles" that he complains about?

While he highly praises Marta Weigle's 1976 book on the Penitentes, he takes her to task for still subscribing to the idea that they were part of the Franciscan Third Order. He attributes this continued error to three sophisms: (1) if the first Penitentes of Santa Cruz happened to be Third Order members, then their practices came from the Third Order; (2) "guilt by association": if the Penitentes and Franciscans use some of the same expressions, the two groups are identical; (3) "majority rule": if so many people including Church authorities believed the Penitentes derived from the Third Order, it must be true.[91] Although highly laudatory of the book overall, Fray Angélico feels compelled to pursue this key point on the origins of the Penitentes in New Mexico by expanding on his previous argument that they were not part of the Third Order.

Sometimes he is much less polite in his critique. He is particularly incensed that C. W. Ceram resurrects the anti-Spanish Black Legend in an archeological study. Noting that the writer is a German expatriate, he inverts the letters of his name to "Marek," comparing the inversion to Serutan, a laxative being marketed then that inverted the word *nature*. He ends with an especially biting attack based on the writer's nationality: "Hispanic cruelty and militarism? Does Herr Marek forget, and in our time, two World Wars and Buchenwald?"[92] In a 1974 review he quotes a passage imbued with prejudice of the Black Legend and then says that no reputable historian would waste time refuting such statements. No ethnic group in the world has been free of blame, Chávez argues, whether they were called the "Noble Savage" or the "People of God." "Man's inhumanity to man, under whatever guise, has to be considered objectively on all sides within particular contexts. . . . [T]he author forgets that, had the Spaniards been as evil as he claims they were, he would have no living Pueblos or Pueblo culture to write about."[93] Fray Angélico employs both biting remarks and reasoned arguments to persuade his audience.

Such harsh critiques are somewhat offset by a number of humorous statements throughout the reviews. Correcting a mistake about the renovations he did on the chapel at Golden in a 1975 book, he writes, "It says that in 1910 Fray Angelico Chaves [*sic*] repaired it, and that most of the structure above the foundation has been replaced. Actually, except for the side tower and the pediments which I added, the entire body of the church is the original one. That I made those changes in the year I was born is quite a marvel."[94] Fray Angélico often engages in humorous wordplay in the reviews. Comparing new editions of two books that are as different as "marble cake and a bagel," Chávez notes that "both deserve defrosting and a warmed-up welcome."[95] Blaming his irritable stomach for his inability to vouch for the recipes in a Mexican cookbook by Idella Purnell Stone, he humorously notes, "A dyspeptic like myself will have to trust the good lady's credentials which appear altogether kosher (to use an Aztec word)."[96] He has fun in a short review of a book on sheep ranching: "Much more of a big album of old and new photos and prints than a textual history of bovine bucolics. Nice for Ram fans—that is, of the woolly species that eat their own playing field."[97]

Chávez is not beyond humorously asking for remuneration for his ideas. In reviewing a work of fiction on the Pueblo Revolt, he criticizes the style, dialogue, and character development for being like a movie script: "Perhaps because of [these faults], it might be picked up by the movie people. Good luck, Señor Baca, and my ten percent if this happens."[98] In the longest of any of his reviews, he dedicates nearly a column and a half to a book on the burro. Alluding to his own allergy to cow's milk, he notes that the donkey, "or rather his dam or dame, saved my own life in early infancy, presumably because I was determined to write this encomium six decades later." Chávez takes issue with the author by humorously noting, "The burro is an ass, true, but the ass is not always a burro," and he continues with a long, detailed section on the distinctions between the two terms in the Bible.[99] With the humor he adds his personality to reviews and seeks to give readers enjoyment as they learn about books and intellectual currents.

Readers are also treated to Fray Angélico's poetic language in some reviews. "Here is a treasure trove of richly mixed historical material that serves to calk the vacant spaces ordinarily left between the bricks of important historical works, the wider gaps left between the looser masonry of history textbooks," he writes in a 1972 review.[100] He terms a Rand McNally book about the formation of the earth "a sequoia amid the world's bush of notebooks."[101] In a book of photographs, Ansel Adams "trips the camera shutters with poetry in his brow and music at his fingertips."[102]

As an artist, Fray Angélico is also very much taken by the aesthetic composition of certain books. "Outwardly, this large-size book captures the eye with its rough-cloth cover dyed in turquoise, and on it the lettering and an emblem stamped in silver. Inside, the printing on fine stock is no less captivating because of the chaste type-face surrounded by wide margins."[103] Likewise, he complains about the "drab look" of a book on New Mexico populism and the unattractive typeset forms of an anthology of New Mexico poetry.[104] He dislikes creative writing that includes political statements, such as social protest poetry, but at the same time does not care for literary modernism. He is willing to accept books with "echoes of social anger" but not "the contemporary obscene diatribe which likes to pass for poetry."[105] He makes several comments about the beauty of black-and-white photography and its superiority to color: "Most folks nowadays prefer pictures in color, long spoiled by the handy automatic camera and no less by the movies, television and the magazines; but black-and-white photography, duller perhaps for being more honest than color film exaggeration, is still the master's medium."[106] As an artist who works in both visual and verbal media, he praises May Sarton's *A World of Light*, "a word painting of residential Santa Fe more than 35 years ago." He theorizes about the interrelation of the visual and verbal arts in reviewing *The Peter Hurd Sketch Book*: "For these are ... landscape 'notes' captured in watercolor, that medium which tolerates no erasures or connections, just the opposite of a poet's or other writer's penciled jottings. Yet these brush 'jottings' surpass many a good artist's finished work. . . . [T]he artist's own lengthy and revealing introduction . . . turns out to be the soul of the book animating for the reader its physical graphic part."[107] A number of Fray Angélico's book reviews reflect his artistic concerns by focusing on the aesthetic composition of certain books, what he considers unaesthetic in both form and content, the beauty of black-and-white photography, the interrelation of the visual and verbal arts, and the necessity of art remaining separated from political concerns.

Although Fray Angélico often promoted himself and his work while in active ministry, it is surprising how often he promoted his own work in the book review section when he was editor. This included criticisms that authors had not interviewed him or used his work for their books and numerous self-reviews of his own publications in the columns. In reviewing *The Old Ones of New Mexico* by Robert Coles, he complains, "[I]n the final essay . . . a very old native priest does the talking: actually the native priests are relatively young men, and I as the oldest by far was never consulted." He complains that a local sociologist did not consult him about the first families of New Mexico and therefore made mistakes, and that the editor of a 1974 book should have consulted his research work in the 1972 *The Oroz Codex*.[108] Chávez voices such concerns many times in the seven years of reviewing.

After including in his column reviews written by *New Mexico* magazine editor Walter Briggs of his 1970 *Selected Poems* and 1973 *The Song of Francis*, Chávez wrote his own pseudo-review of *My Penitente Land* in the January 1975 issue. Pretending he is only announcing the book, he mediates his self-promotion with a hint of humor: "An advantage that a reviewer has is that he can blatantly announce his own book, and cravenly stave off bad notices in his own columns. But this is nullified by the fact that he cannot review it himself. But there is a way out when he can sneak in comments by someone like Paul Horgan." He then quotes from Horgan's glowing assessment of the book. In subsequent issues, however, he reviews all of his own new books and new editions of older works. In the "review" of the new edition of *Origins of New Mexico Families*, he recounts the history of the book's publication, its slow sales in the first years, and its new popularity as more New Mexico Hispanos became interested in tracing their family lines. In his June 1977 review of the new edition of *When the Santos Talked*, he informs readers that the New York publisher originally mistitled the book *From an Altar Screen*. Chávez announces that he was asked to write *The Lord and New Mexico* to celebrate the centenary of the Santa Fe Archdiocese in 1975. After describing the book, he claims that he includes it in his book review column because non-Catholics might want to buy it as a historical keepsake.[109] While it is strange to see a reviewer include his own books, omitting them would have been a major gap in this account of important books on the Southwest published at the time. Chávez manages gracefully to include his own books, providing further information about his own changing relationship to them. In January 1976, for example, he notes that he now wishes he had titled *The Missions of New Mexico, 1776* "New Mexico 1776," because it is not only about the missions but is also the first detailed description of New Mexico's terrain, economy, people, and customs.

Books for a Wider Audience

As we have seen, Chávez's move into the secular world in 1971 to devote full time to writing also required that he support himself financially by this intellectual work. He continued historical research but also tried to publish more accessible books that would reach wider audiences, sell well, and support his living on his own. In addition to producing new works, he sought new ways to present previously written material to increase readership.

Shortly after leaving Peña Blanca and moving into the family home, Fray Angélico met Colorado artist Judy Graese at an arts festival on the Santa Fe plaza. Her intricate artwork intrigued him, and he got the idea of republishing the short account of St. Francis' life he had written in 1964 in a new book with illustrations by Graese. In late November 1971 in response to his request, the editor of *St. Anthony Messenger* sent him a copy of the story "The Bird of Perfect Joy: A Life of St. Francis" and a translation Chávez did of St. Francis' poem "Canticle of the Sun," both previously published in the magazine. Fray Angélico had a difficult time finding a publisher and pinning Graese down to doing the art. His friend Fred Grillo wrote to Northland Press in Arizona and interested them in publishing the book. Although Chávez did not revise the earlier version of the story, he did not want to send it to the publisher without the illustrations, and by the end of April 1972, he still did not have them. He knew the importance of illustrations in the prospective book so that children and young adult readers could visualize the story, and without the illustrations, all he had was a six-page magazine story—too short for a book. Finally, in February 1973 the author and artist signed contracts and submitted the work, which was published in September 1973.[110]

Fray Angélico's persistence and patience paid off. The handsome book had a Franciscan-brown cloth cover engraved with a golden-inlaid drawing of a lute, and the book jacket showed an intricate painting of St. Francis by Graese. The color frontispiece signed by Graese in 1973 depicts the young boy Francis playing the lute with a "flower-child" woman figure holding a bird and listening to him play. The style of the illustrations, which aimed for an eleventh-century milieu, resembles the attire worn at the popular Renaissance fairs of the 1970s. They depict the key events in the life of Francis as highlighted in Chávez's narrative: the mother's encouragement of the lute rather than the sword for the boy; then Francis playing music in a tavern as a youth; departing as a warrior for the nobles of Assisi; stopping to embrace a leper and giving his horse away; kneeling in devotion before the painted cross at San Damiano Chapel; returning his father's money and removing his rich clothing; traveling the countryside to preach; and lying on the ground as he died.

Having read several biographies of the saint, Fray Angélico reduced them to key narrative images in the paintings he himself did in 1938 in the sacristy and refectory of the Peña Blanca church. These first images shaped his retelling of the story in prose in the 1965 magazine publication, but he did not impose his artistic vision from the 1930s on Graese, who depicted different scenes of the saint's life. Fray Angélico's life-size murals at Peña Blanca are a progression of images going over and around doors and walls. As we have seen, first Francis kneels before the San Damiano crucifix in his privileged clothing; the next image, painted across both angled walls of the corner, depicts Francis renouncing his comfortable life and placing his clothing at his father's feet; other images depict the official recognition of the order, the Christmas crib he designed, his vision of the Bird of Perfect Joy when he received the stigmata, the investiture of St. Clare, the sending of friars to preach in foreign lands, and his death scene.

Fray Angélico's narrative in the 1973 book begins with Francis' boyhood in Assisi, "a week of centuries ago," and enticingly recounts the key episodes in the saint's life while explaining the time period and customs for young readers.[111] His literary talents make the writing as artistic as the accompanying drawings. He builds on the motif of a glowing light that Francis sees throughout his development as he experiences intuitions or performs good deeds: "He thought that he caught a glimpse of a birdlike flash in the darkness," or after embracing the leper, "the world around lit up with the golden glow of that winged sun or burning bird which he had lost long since."[112] Although he wrote the story earlier while in active ministry, his efforts to publish it in a new form with attractive illustrations signify the continuing centrality of the spirit of St. Francis in his life, even after leaving the order, and his desire to reach wider audiences in his growing role as a public intellectual. He also hoped to generate income from the new book that he believed would sell well. Released in time for the Christmas trade, the book was promoted with book signings, including one December 7 at Rhodes in Albuquerque. In the first six months 1,571 copies sold, and after splitting the royalties with Graese, Fray Angélico received $510. In January 1974 the book went into a second printing, and he received small sums thereafter every six months through 1982.[113]

In the period after he left active ministry, Fray Angélico was fortunate to receive the caring spiritual and material support of Robert F. Sánchez, the future archbishop of Santa Fe. Sánchez contacted him and invited him to celebrate the Eucharist at his side for two or three months, which Chávez at first declined. To help him financially because he did not receive much money from *New Mexico* magazine, Sánchez spoke to the sister superior at St. Joseph's College and arranged for him to teach a class there. Knowing he needed a car to get to Albuquerque, Sánchez asked the owner of the Toyota dealership if he could help Fray Angélico out, and the owner generously provided a small car for him. For several months, Sánchez had Fray Angélico come over for lunch every Wednesday after the class at St. Joseph's on the pretense that he wanted to learn about New Mexico history. When he received the call to be archbishop of Santa Fe in 1974, he called Fray Angélico that evening and offered to pay him to write a book for the centennial of the Santa Fe Archdiocese in 1975. Chávez did so and was proud that Archbishop Sánchez gave a copy of the book to the Pope and Mother Teresa. Sánchez then appointed him archdiocesan archivist, where he worked for several years with a team of five women he called his "*compañeras*" to organize the materials that were in extreme disarray. On Christmas Eve 1976, Sánchez visited Chávez in his apartment to invite him to concelebrate midnight Mass in the cathedral, and he agreed to do so. Afterward, people swarmed around Fray Angélico with happiness, but others wrote to people in Washington to complain about Sánchez allowing him to say Mass. Nonetheless, Sánchez invited him again to concelebrate Easter Vigil Mass and urged him to begin wearing the habit again. When Chávez did so several years later, he remarked to Sánchez, "Look at me, you've taken my identity away completely! Here I am the same old friar in a habit."[114]

Chávez wrote and signed his name to the program copy for Sánchez's inauguration held in University Arena in Albuquerque on July 25, 1974. In the piece, he situated Sánchez within American and Hispano traditions: "We have been using the word 'American' with the last four prelates purposely because the latest one is likewise a genuine American by birth, nationality, and upbringing. But with his name and particular heritage, Archbishop Robert F. Sánchez brings a signal honor at long last to the oldest Catholic community by far in our great Nation."[115] Also identifying himself as both an American and an Hispano, Fray Angélico was extremely proud that, befitting the long history of Hispano Catholicism in New Mexico, an Hispano American archbishop had finally been named.

Sánchez commissioned Fray Angélico to write a booklet commemorating the centenary of the archdiocese—the 1975 *The Lord and New Mexico*. The beautiful booklet with color photographs of most of the churches in the archdiocese succinctly presents "in words and pictures" the history of the Catholic Church in New Mexico in readable style for the public.[116] The scholar summarizes four centuries of history in a few pages and explains official terms for all to understand. Opening with a panoramic view of "God's country," Fray Angélico includes his observations from *My Penitente Land* that early Spanish settlers thought it looked like the Spanish landscape of their homeland, and others who were familiar with Palestine thought it looked like the Holy Land. With a post–Vatican II ecumenical spirit, he evenhandedly delineates the various religious traditions of the area. He explains the Pueblo Indians' belief in the Great Power and the Spaniards' importation of the specific God of the Hebrew covenant, shaped by Spanish tradition. These beliefs also became elements of the land as churches were built and places named "which read like a litany."[117]

Chávez notes the establishment of the Custody of the Conversion of St. Paul in 1598, explaining that the term *custody* refers to the groups of St. Francis' followers, literally meaning a "jail" intended to keep them humble. The head is termed a "custos" or jailer rather than a prior. Friars' dwellings were called "conventos" or gathering places, and the head was a "guardian," which became our word *warden*. The Franciscan habit only officially became brown in 1898; previously it was various shades of gray according to the mixture of wools. Mexico City's Holy Gospel Province used the color blue to honor the Immaculate Conception, and this color came with the Franciscans to New Mexico. In 1850 Bishop Lamy brought French priests to the area and founded schools and hospitals staffed by the American religious orders of women and French Christian Brothers. The diocese was made an archdiocese in 1875. Presenting pictures of many of the parishes, schools, and hospitals and descriptions of the religious orders that served the archdiocese, Chávez laments the decline in religious vocations in the later 1960s and 1970s that resulted in the closing of many of these institutions. He ends with pictures of old New Mexico santos and pictures and narrative about La Conquistadora.

Chávez again functioned as a public intellectual in March 1973 when La Conquistadora was stolen from the cathedral. Interviewed in the press, he argued that the theft was worse than sacrilege because of the statue's key role in the history of New Mexico: "If someone stole the Statue of Liberty, it would be to the nation like the loss of La Conquistadora to New Mexico."[118] Chávez shared his extensive knowledge of the statue's history and connection to early New Mexico families in several public statements and articles before and after the statue was returned and the culprits arrested. Having written two books on the statue, including one in the form of La Conquistadora's autobiography, Fray Angélico was asked by a reporter what the statue might say now in an epilogue. He humorously replied, "'Help, Help! I'm being held in durance vile.'"[119] The theft and subsequent public outcry suggested to Fray Angélico that there was still a wide audience that would be interested in reading his autobiography of the statue. And perhaps with the reporter's mention of an epilogue, he decided to write one.

In 1971 Marcia Muth and Jody Ellis founded Sunstone Press in Santa Fe to publish poetry and Southwestern writers, many of whom were being overlooked by mainstream publishers. Ellis had been in Santa Fe since the 1940s and knew Fray Angélico. He approached them in 1974 about republishing the autobiography of La Conquistadora, which was out of print, arguing that many tourists would buy it. In keeping with this idea, Muth and Ellis later promoted the book by placing it in a display window at La Fonda.[120] With permission from his friend Fr. Guadalupe Rivera, the pastor of St. Anne's Parish in Santa Fe, Chávez sold the new edition outside the church after Sunday Masses. In March 1976, after Muth and Ellis sold the press to John Reardon and James Smith, Fray Angélico wrote to the press to question the recent six-month royalty report of 151 books sold, noting that he had sold 50 copies he bought himself during the month of January and bought another 25 in February. Maura Miller of Sunstone wrote back that the book had not been very popular, after initial good sales in July, August, and September.[121] Although Chávez was disappointed with the sales of the second edition, most likely because of his need to support himself, the book has sold steadily for three decades and is still in print.

A year earlier, Fray Angélico accepted a paying job with the Four Corners States' Bicentennial Commission to do a new translation of *The Domínguez-Escalante Journal of 1776*. In 1950 he had written to historian Herbert E. Bolton pointing out that Bolton's translation of the work had several errors.[122] Among them, the name "Escalante Journal" was erroneous because the friar's name was Vélez Escalante, and it was not in fact his expedition but rather one headed by Fray Francisco Atanasio Domínguez, who together with Vélez Escalante had written the journal. In the preface to his new translation, Fray Angélico laments that because of the shortage of time to publish the re-translation for the U.S. bicentennial, he was unable to consult all nine extant copies of the manuscript. Nonetheless, he made an important discovery while comparing the three manuscripts he worked with from the Newberry Library in Chicago, the Archivo General de la Nación in Mexico, and the Archivo General de Indias in Sevilla. From his years of experience reading colonial Franciscan manuscripts, he recognized the handwriting of the Newberry copy of the manuscript as that of Fray José Palacio, who was Domínguez's secretary during the New Mexico visitations earlier in 1776. This was the first copy of the document sent to Mexico shortly after the expedition. Although it was hastily done and in difficult penmanship, corrections had been made either by Palacio on his own or at Domínguez's request. The other two manuscripts were copied later by other scribes in Mexico who left sentences out, changed wording, and added phrases praising the Crown and the Spaniards. By studying the three copies together, Fray Angélico was able to clarify certain smudged or illegible words in Palacio's first copy of the original.

Chávez's scholarly skills in translating the important document were enhanced by his ethnic heritage. In the translator's note he emphasizes his ethnic identity as he frequently does in his writings: "I mainly listened to Padre Escalante (and his companions) speaking as I read the text aloud to myself. This was not only as a Spaniard or a Mexican would, but also as a twelfth-generation Hispanic New Mexican with an ear for the language of the times and the locale would."[123] Chávez also emphasizes his religious identity, noting his familiarity with ecclesiastical and Franciscan terminology, and his skills as a historian well versed in the style that the eighteenth-century friars used. He renders the document in a readable, flowing English accessible to contemporary readers. One phrase, however—"we no longer had a thing for eating supper tonight"[124]—is inflected with 1970s slang no longer in use. Fray Angélico's fine English-language sensibilities gave way to a catchy phrase temporarily in vogue at the time.

The translated narrative is a firsthand, detailed picture of the arduous journey through the beautiful and sometimes desolate wilderness and the dramatic trials the expedition suffered. For days the men tried to cross a treacherous section of the Colorado River by swimming, on rafts, and on horseback. Members of the group were sick, hungry, and suffered severe weather conditions. They killed horses at several points to feed themselves. In the high mountains, snow and winter arrived by early October, and Frs. Domínguez and Escalante made the decision to return home without reaching Monterey in California as planned. The others were adamant about continuing the course, so the padres used a lottery to convince them that God willed them to return. They named the sites they explored for religious figures, themselves, and incidents such as "La Fuente de la Guía," in honor of an Indian guide from whom they obtained information.

Despite the enormous suffering, the leaders of the expedition engaged frequently in reconnoitering suitable sites for future missions and in proselytizing to the Indians they met. They characterize most of the Indians as timid and fearful, except the "obstinate Hopi,"[125] and record the rhetorical techniques and material goods they used to persuade the Indians to convert to Christianity. Not surprisingly, the Domínguez-Escalante account portrays the padres as benevolent and the Indians as childlike and easily and almost immediately accepting of conversion. When meeting some bearded, pierced-nosed Utes on October 2, the padres preached about God's oneness, his punishment of the wicked and reward for the good, the need for baptism, and observance of divine law. "They all replied very joyfully that we must come back with other padres, that they would do whatsoever we taught them and ordered them to do," and they said that they would go to live with the Lagunas following the padres' advice.[126] The Franciscans gave some of the Indians glass beads and red ribbons to win them over, and when they discovered superstitious rituals, they threatened them with hell. Chávez's annotations call into question the quadrant measurements the expedition took of the latitude of the sites they stayed at, but he does not discuss the subjectivity of the padres' account of converting the Indians. The translation gives a strong sense of the deep religious commitment of the padres, which permeated their thought and actions. When Indians they meet insistently try to dissuade them from continuing because of the dangerous Comanches ahead, the padres argue that their God will protect them should they encounter these groups. After their guide deserts to return to his pueblo, the padres regret that they will not be able to hasten his salvation.

Fray Angélico completed his translation by summer 1975, and teams of researchers used it to re-trace the trail and campsites of the expedition. Editor Ted J. Warner used the reports of these field researchers to prepare the footnotes throughout the text, documenting where possible the present-day locations referred to in the 1776 journal. These notes make history come alive for contemporary readers by situating the campsites and geography that the expedition encountered two hundred years ago in today's locales and geography. On September 8, for example, the friars stopped at a bend with good pastures that they named Santa Delfina. The note informs readers: "Camp was located very near the junction of East Douglas and Cathedral creeks. The camp was about 2.5 miles beyond the junction of these creeks."[127] The 1976 U.S. bicentennial edition of the journal is an important collaborative effort of historians, botanists, field researchers, and the knowledgeable and talented translator Chávez. The new and richly annotated translation paid fitting homage to the expeditionary group's dedicated efforts two hundred years earlier by explicating and making accessible a key historical document that the pioneering padres had the foresight to write as they struggled in the wilderness.

As the U.S. bicentennial approached, Chávez was heartened that new editions of his works appeared. Calvin Horn republished *Origins of New Mexico Families* in July 1975, and Sunstone Press reissued the autobiography of La Conquistadora also that month with Chávez's new afterword about the 1973 kidnapping. In October 1975 the University of New Mexico reissued *Missions of New Mexico, 1776* under the auspices of the New Mexico Bicentennial Commission. Listing these reprints, Chávez added in a letter to friends Fred and Marguerite Grillo: "Am also reprinting Haniel Long's *Piñon Country* with my Introduction, for which trouble his son grants me the royalties. All these should get me a couple of hundred bucks next year."[128]

Besides the fulfillment of seeing his works come back into print, Fray Angélico was also grateful for the financial support. After a joking hint from Fray Angélico about nominating him for the "Poolitzer," Grillo nominated *My Penitente Land* for the Bancroft Prize. He received a reply in February 1975 that the deadline for 1974 books had already passed. Grillo must have also received negative news from the Pulitzer committee, because on January 15, Fray Angélico wrote him a letter of consolation beginning in Italian and playing on Grillo's name, meaning "cricket": "Ecco! Amico caríssimo, non piángare. Cantate invece come gli *grilli* nel'giardino! Yes, those poolitzers and the like have it all sewed up more than a year before. So we needn't cry or cuss, except to use a few dirty words of relief. And a million thanks to you for the pains you take on my poor behalf."[129]

After having met bibliographer Phyllis Morales at his cousin's home in Albuquerque in 1975, Chávez began to work with Morales on a comprehensive bibliography of his writings. He wrote in October that he had been ill for the past five weeks with a recurring flu and eye trouble and was quite exhausted, and he included information on the new editions of his works. Later he wrote that he had discovered some of his early publications in a cardboard box in the cellar of his late mother's home, including several written under pseudonyms that he had completely forgotten about.[130] Morales' painstaking and invaluable bibliography was published in 1980.

Fray Angélico's tremendous productivity in the five years after leaving ministry not only served to support him financially but to make key contributions to intellectual and public life in New Mexico and the Southwest. As he returned to the sanctuary of St. Francis Cathedral to concelebrate midnight Mass with Archbishop Sánchez on December 24, 1976, he no doubt celebrated his personal independence at the end of the bicentennial year as well as his Franciscan priestly heritage. As he approached his seventies, he would undertake the massive study of three beleaguered nineteenth-century New Mexico priests whom he would vindicate with an eight-hundred-page manuscript based on copious research and strong criticism of previous historical studies. This work represented what he later termed the "swan song" of his four decades of writing history, but he approached the research and writing with energy and enthusiasm in the late 1970s.

CHAPTER NINE

Twilight of the Historian

Vindicating Hispano Clergy

Truth Stalks the Archbishop

At the February 2, 1970, retreat of the national Chicano priests' organization, PADRES (Priests Associated for Religious, Educational, and Social Rights), Fray Angélico gave a speech on "Native Hispano Vocations," outlining the history of New Mexico's dearth of native priests. In its first century Santa Fe had only six hundred people and no outlying villages, so there was no sense of a need for native vocations. No one was recruited to go to the Franciscan seminary twelve hundred miles away. "I am the first since the Conquest," Chávez tells fellow Chicano priests.[1] The first native Chicano priest in the United States was his uncle seven generations removed, Santiago de Roybal. The young man went to Mexico to study for the secular priesthood and immediately after ordination in 1728 was named vicar of the bishop of Durango in Santa Fe where he presided for several decades. After his death about 1764, the population grew but fewer priests ministered to the people. Not until 1833 did the new Durango bishop,

Antonio Zubiría, visit Santa Fe and encourage several New Mexico men to journey to Durango for seminary training and ordination.

After the American takeover, the Frenchman Bishop Lamy was sent to New Mexico, but he knew nothing about local conditions. Because the native priests had been educated in Mexico, they opposed the 1862 French invasion of Mexico and therefore were anti-French. "The one they sent to them was a Frenchman! But the Irish hierarchy in Baltimore knew everything—they should not have done it this way."[2] Problems would arise in the clash of cultures after the French bishop arrived.

Also attending the retreat was Fr. Juan Romero, born in Taos and ordained a priest in the Los Angeles Archdiocese in 1964. He helped to found PADRES and served as its executive director from 1972 to early 1976. In this period he began research on the life of Padre Antonio José Martínez, *cura* de Taos, a key native priest of New Mexico who was ordained in Mexico in 1822. Using documentary sources including early biographies and a partial autobiography of Martínez in the Huntington Library, Fr. Romero published a short history of the famous priest's life, *Reluctant Dawn* (1976). In a second edition published in 2006, he notes, "Fray Angélico commended my first edition, and in an informal note to me chided, 'If I were younger, I would have beat you to it.'"[3] Fray Angélico highly praised Padre Martínez in his 1974 *My Penitente Land*, and in 1976 he began more extensive research on Martínez and two other nineteenth-century native Hispano priests who clashed with Lamy.

At this time as well, Paul Horgan completed his lengthy study of Archbishop Lamy on which he had worked for twenty years.[4] Horgan cited only three of Chávez's books in the bibliography and simply mentioned his name in the acknowledgments after John Gaw Meem's.[5] Chávez would later take issue with Horgan's uncritical presentation of documents Lamy and his associate Machebeuf wrote, which denigrated Hispano clergy of the period. He was especially appreciative, however, that after finishing the book, Horgan donated the documents he had obtained through much persistence and difficulty at Propaganda Fide in Rome (see chapter 7) to the Archives of the Archdiocese of Santa Fe where others including Fray Angélico could study them.

What we today know as three separate biographies of key nineteenth-century Hispano priests—Padres Antonio José Martínez of Taos, José Manuel Gallegos of Albuquerque, and Juan Felipe Ortiz of Santa Fe—began as a "compendious" work of over eight hundred manuscript pages entitled *Truth Stalks the Archbishop*. "If I played with [Cather's] happily conceived title, *Death Comes for the Archbishop*, it was by way of a signal warning the reader that her heroes, Lamy and his bosom friend Machebeuf, had not been quite truthful in their accounts concerning the native clergy of New Mexico," Chávez wrote in 1982. He also wished to counter Horgan's 1975 *Lamy of Santa Fe* "in which the copious writings of both Frenchmen, naively accepted as gospel truth, were used to paint the blackest picture of the New Mexico padres." Chávez's own decades of immersion in "ecclesiastical minutiae and the vagaries of hierarchy" enabled him to more critically evaluate these documents as no lay person could. Lamy and Machebeuf had in fact lied.[6]

Chávez had trouble finding a publisher for the lengthy manuscript and "by some sort of Solomonic wisdom . . . got the idea of splitting the dear infant into three books." Joining the abundant material he had gathered on the three priests with the documents Horgan made available on Lamy and Machebeuf, "the three biographies took shape simultaneously, . . . each one concentrating on the different phases of the Lamy-Machebeuf fiasco." The first, *But Time and Chance*, was published in 1981 "but in a dress which has been a pain to me as well as to the reviewers and the general reader." Despite high printing costs, he was optimistic that "the other two bairns, already full developed *in utero*, might also see the light of day."[7] Unhappy with the first book's appearance and typographical errors, Chávez hoped that its two companions would appear in good time. He thanked historian Marc Simmons in November 1981 for the praiseworthy review of the Padre Martínez book in the *Santa Fe Reporter*, noting that he had finished the lives of Gallegos and Ortiz, completing the trilogy, and hoped to have them published "one and two years from now."[8] *Très Macho—He Said* on Padre Gallegos did not appear until 1985. Early the following year Fray Angélico wrote to Fr. Thomas Steele that he would not be publishing the third volume. Calling the second volume his "swan song," he added,

> I've outgrown my history phase just as I outgrew the poetic one 40 years ago. I don't care to write and publish anymore as I approach my 76th birthday. My nephew Tom Chávez at the Museum, and who has a Ph.D. in history, plans to do

the Juan Felipe Ortiz story from my draft and notes... If I
sound pessimistic by saying that my writing phase is over, the
facts are just the opposite. I feel greatly relieved after so many
years of such work, while freed of the so-called Protestant
work ethic.[9]

Discouraged by the lengthy publication process for the second volume and facing some of the health problems that plagued him in his last decade, Fray Angélico was confident that his nephew would see to the publication of the final "bairn" in the trilogy. Coauthored by the two Chávezes, *Wake for a Fat Vicar* was published posthumously in 2004.[10]

Much more detailed and lengthy than previous accounts of the life of Padre Martínez, Fray Angélico's *But Time and Chance: The Story of Padre Martínez of Taos, 1793–1867* (1981) takes issue with the earlier narratives and the widely circulated false rumors about the priest. Chávez documents Martínez's tremendous accomplishments from his youth to the mid-1850s when he began to have grave problems with Lamy. This resulted in his excommunication and his determined continuance of priestly ministry in defiance of Lamy's orders. With adept documentary research and a critical eye, Fray Angélico contests previous writers without always naming them to re-evaluate Martínez's life. When documentation is incomplete or missing, he alerts readers that he is hypothesizing based on logic, extrapolation, and his decades of experience with priestly ministry and the practices of the Church hierarchy. His meticulous scholarly study is not as readable as more popularly written accounts, but it stands as Chávez's ultimate homage and testimony to the key nineteenth-century Hispano priest of New Mexico.

Chávez brings to the biography decades of documentary research on the Church's birth, death, and marriage records in New Mexico, along with the correspondence and official Church documents Horgan brought from Rome. He compares previous accounts of Martínez's life including the priest's own memoir, *Relación de méritos* (1838); the *Historia consisa del cura de Taos* (1861), which Chávez attributes to Vicente Ferrer Romero; Santiago Valdez's 1877 *Biografía del Rev. P. Antonio José Martínez*; and Pedro Sánchez's 1903 *Memorias sobre la vida del presbítero Don Antonio José Martínez*. He critically reads between the lines of each account and puts together pieces of the complex puzzle unearthed in the hundreds of extant documents. Although continually striving for accuracy and fairness, Fray Angélico is not the disinterested, neutral historian. He wishes to answer the negative portrayals of Martínez in Cather's *Death Comes for the Archbishop* and Horgan's *Lamy of Santa Fe*. As a pioneer native Hispano priest himself like Padres Martínez, Gallegos, and Ortiz, Chávez identifies with the vagaries they faced from the Church hierarchy. He asserts his ethnic and religious identity in approaching his subjects, arguing both that they were misunderstood and discriminated against as Hispanos and that his own priestly experience gave him a greater understanding of the nineteenth-century Church than the previous lay authors possessed.

He argues that extraordinary human beings arise only rarely and that they are aided and limited by the time and circumstances in which they live. Employing Padre Martínez's epigraph from Ecclesiastes in his 1838 memoir that "the race is not to the swift, nor the battle to the strong . . . but time and chance happeneth to them all," Chávez notes that Martínez's genius was part of a script beyond his control, and his tragic denouement "was due as much to certain grave flaws in his personality as to the quirks of history dictating the plot. Both Time and Chance, as he presaged early in his career, did have their say."[11] People have viewed Padre Martínez as either a hero or a villain or both depending on their ethnic feelings or morals. Chávez subtly reminds readers of his own ethnicity that together with his moral stance shapes his account of Padre Martínez's life.

The errors Chávez needs to correct begin with the original family name, which was misrepresented in Santiago Valdez's 1877 biography. Not checking the original Church documents as Chávez did, Martínez's foster son Valdez claimed that the future padre's baptismal certificate listed the surname of his parents and grandparents as "Martínez." In fact their name was Martín, and the Franciscan who baptized the infant made the entry as a *ministro* (missionary), not a *párroco* as Valdez claimed the document stated. Chávez reveals the possible existence of a fake birth certificate that Martínez himself may have left among his papers or Valdez may have invented. In fact, the family did not begin to use the name Martínez until thirty years later, after the new priest's return from the Durango seminary, perhaps in relation to a 1710 land grant deed made to a purported Mexican ancestor, Antonio Martínez. Assembling complicated ancestral information from colonial baptismal, marriage, and death certificates, Chávez names a number of forebears of Padre Martínez who were "a relatively superior sort in their day" and therefore contributed to the future priest's "fortuitous assemblage of genes."[12]

The precocious Antonio José Martín learned to read, write, and do sums at age five. When his family moved to Taos in 1804 where there was no school, he did ranch work while receiving private tutoring. In 1812 he married a woman with the same surname, María de la Luz Martín, who died fourteen months later in childbirth. The couple's daughter also died when she was only twelve. Meanwhile, in 1817, the young Antonio José Martín entered the diocesan seminary in Durango, both to pursue his intellectual interests and, Chávez suggests, because of his sense of the need for native clergy in New Mexico (none had been ordained since Don Santiago Roybal in 1730). Perhaps also, he wished to follow the model of the revolutionary Padre Hidalgo who fought for Mexican independence. Conceivably projecting some of his own seminary experience onto Martín, Chávez speculates that because of his ranch work, the seminarian was ganglier than the cultured, younger students from New Spain, and this may have inspired him to work harder to become first in his class and win his professors' esteem. Fray Angélico identified with Martín who journeyed to a far-off seminary as a pioneer native student and felt that he needed to prove himself in the strange new environment.

Martín was given supervisory and managerial duties in the seminary as well as a royal scholarship. He was ordained in 1822, a year before he completed theological studies, and given ministerial faculties for the entire diocese. He would later claim that these original faculties overrode Lamy's revocation of his priestly privileges in Taos. He returned to Taos because of breathing difficulties and palpitations, and proudly recorded his new name, Martínez, and his new status as Presbítero and citizen of the new country Mexico. He saw himself following in the footsteps of Presbítero José Miguel Hidalgo, the father of the Mexican independence movement, who was a prodigious scholar, exiled to a small parish, and in 1810 led exploited Indians and mestizos in revolt against Spain. The Church hierarchy publicly defrocked him, and the royal troops executed him. Like Hidalgo, throughout his life Martínez championed the poor—often giving them money and food from his personal resources—and defended the interests of Hispanos when the French hierarchy undermined them. He was elected a deputy to New Mexico's Departmental Assembly for several terms in the 1830s. He also strongly supported the Penitentes, requesting and receiving permission for sixty members to hold their services in Taos in 1831, even though because of his unfamiliarity with Franciscanism, he also confused the group with the Franciscan Third Order.

Along with his strong praise for Martínez, Chávez insists that a historian must also write about the subject's shortcomings. In 1990, in reference to the Martínez book, he told a reporter: "Tell the truth. If you have a hero, tell his faults too."[13] In addressing the rumors about Martínez having children and various people's claims after his death that he was their father, Chávez closely examines Church records to ascertain the facts. While he disapproves of the priest's personal life in this regard, he also tries to understand Martínez's motivations and behavior with regard to the baptism of his children. From the extant documents, Chávez argues that Santiago Valdez, baptized in February 1830, was in fact the illegitimate son of Martínez's brother, not the padre's son. The priest would never have baptized his own son, an egregious sin against his priesthood. Instead, he took Valdez under his wing as his foster son, later leaving him all his papers from which Valdez wrote the 1877 biography. In contrast, however, Martínez recorded guarded evidence of his paternity of other children in the baptismal records of Taos, which Chávez documents for the first time. Martínez recorded the church baptismal ceremonies for the nine-day-old George Antonio on May 1, 1831, the legitimate child of "Antonio Martínez"; the child had already been baptized by the padre's brother "in case of necessity," as if there had been an emergency. In this way, he avoided baptizing his own son, Fray Angélico contends, since the sacrament had already been administered, and he partially records his own name as the father, Antonio Martínez. He has it both ways, giving his child legitimacy, yet disguising his paternity by using only part of his name. Chávez suggests that Martínez might have hoped that some future researcher might conclude that he had a brother named Antonio, but he did not.

Padre Martínez used this same or a similar method of baptism for four more children he recorded in the register, also the children of Teodora Romero who lived next door to him and later in his house: María de la Luz in 1833; another María de la Luz in 1835 after the probable death of her older sister; María Soledad in 1842; and Vicente

Ferrer in 1844. No father is named for the last two children, but Martínez had an assistant priest baptize María Soledad, later recording the baptism in his own writing as "overlooked," and records Vicente Ferrer's baptism a day later, with the priest's youngest brother as godfather. Chávez argues that these elaborate subterfuges about baptisms, recorded names, paternity, and godparents reveal Martínez's insistence on not committing the grave sin against his priesthood of baptizing his own children. "Evidently this subterfuge seemed far less baneful to him than his own really most serious breaches of the Lord's commandment and his violation of his clerical oath of celibacy. Moreover, unlike the Franciscan padres he had known, he had not made a solemn vow of chastity, hence he could have assured himself, as a canon law hair-splitter, that his secular priest's promise of celibacy was not that binding."[14] Padre Martínez kept his secret, Chávez notes, leaving out of his will George Antonio, María de la Luz, Soledad, and Vicente Ferrer. His bequest of his papers to foster son Santiago Valdez was perhaps "a red herring to draw away attention from his clandestine real progeny," and the secret was so well kept that even Machebeuf and his other political foes did not make use of it.[15]

Chávez stays strictly with the ecclesiastical documents in delineating Padre Martínez's children. He did not pursue, for example, as did Fr. Juan Romero, conversations with Vicente Martínez, who claims to be the padre's fifth-generation grandson. Mr. Martínez lived in the house of Padre Martínez off the Taos plaza and retains one of the priest's cassocks, a chest of drawers, and a favorite painting of the Virgin. He claims his mother is a descendant of Santiago Valdez, who gave his children the Martínez surname following the instructions in Padre Martínez's will; in 1975 he named his newborn son Antonio José Martínez after the cura.[16] By ignoring popular traditions and rumors, Fray Angélico relies completely on perhaps evasive Church documents, albeit with his own educated guesses and interpretations.

Despite these personal shortcomings, Padre Martínez worked tirelessly for the poor, trained new native seminarians, published books on his printing press, and generously loaned it to others. Although he preached the ideas of Padre Hidalgo to the poor in northern New Mexico, he was unjustly accused of inciting the Chimayó rebellion in 1837 against new taxation from Santa Fe. When the rebellion spread to Taos, he urged the insurgents to put down their arms, and his own life was threatened. He accompanied Governor Armijo as chaplain in the fighting against the rebels. Nonetheless, stories persisted that he incited the insurrection, just as years later, after the 1847 Taos rebellion, writers incorrectly insisted that he was anti-American and against American institutions. Chávez attributes this to political malice and to "the combined ethnic and religious bigotry of certain ones among the newcomers—like those first newspaper editors who still looked down on their fellow citizens of Hispanic or Mexican descent, and most especially their clergy, as low-down Catholic Mexicans."[17]

Continuing the metaphor of Padre Martínez's life as a three-act tragedy, Chávez terms the arrival of Bishop Lamy in August 1851 as the beginning of "the closing third act of a play which the Muse of History had seemingly intended to be a classic tragedy from the start."[18] Chávez takes issue with previous accounts of Martínez and Lamy's relationship. Based on the misreading of a letter Martínez sent to Bishop Zubiría, "superficial writers" contend that Padre Martínez was disturbed about Lamy's arrival, Chávez argues. Even Archbishop Salpointe wrote incorrectly fifty years later that the native people and priests were suspicious of all strangers. Chávez attributes Salpointe's mistake to his non-native understanding of English and his lack of training as a historian.

In fact, when Lamy journeyed to Taos in March 1852, "he was both surprised and pleased by what he encountered there."[19] Martínez and Lamy discussed theology and canon law, and the bishop realized that the priest had an extraordinary personality. He allowed Martínez to continue educating four native students for the seminary. Despite what previous writers "have parroted from each other," the two "had become fast and mutually respected friends."[20] Even as Lamy's friend Fr. Machebeuf arbitrarily suspended native priests in the coming months and broke the seal of confession, Padre Martínez played the role of an éminence grise, advising the bishop and not attacking him.

Chávez attributes Jansenist puritanical natures to the two French prelates, because of which they believed rumors about the immoral sexual conduct of Hispano priests and viewed local Hispano traditions as sinful. In Lamy's absence and without due process, Machebeuf suspended pastor of Santa Clara Ramón Salazar and then, with Lamy's permission, waited until Padre José Manuel Gallegos of Albuquerque was away in Mexico to suspend him and take over his parish. Lamy was a fair person but was persuaded by his close friend Machebeuf to allow these suspensions of native priests without preliminary investigations.

Chávez also corrects the record on the important Christmas Pastoral Letter that Lamy issued in 1852, which many writers characterized as inciting the Hispano clergy against him. Chávez outlines the main points of the letter and shows that no native clergy took issue with it. Even its very severe provision about denying the sacraments to those who did not pay tithes was not contested until later.

When complaints arose about Machebeuf, and Padre Martínez reiterated his and other priests' requests for a hearing on their complaints, Bishop Lamy began writing to other bishops and priests in defense of his vicar, placing the blame on the native clergy. Chávez delineates the mistruths in these letters, suggesting that certain exaggerations pointed to Machebeuf's collaboration in their composition. Chávez humorously notes that Lamy's argument that Machebeuf "was kept in the confessional day and night for weeks" would make the busiest Catholic priests in missions laugh.[21] Eventually Machebeuf was brought before a Vatican tribunal, and Chávez documents that he successfully defended himself by lying about the Hispano clergy of New Mexico.

Machebeuf used in his defense a letter Padre Martínez had written four years earlier, saying that he was satisfied that Machebeuf had not broken the seal of confession and playing the role of éminence grise for Lamy, as Chávez argues. Nonetheless, Martínez betrayed his fellow native priest, ex-vicar Ortiz, in December 1853 by sending Lamy a copy of Ortiz's complaint to the Vatican so that the bishop could prepare his defense of the charges. Chávez chastises Martínez: "It is not only a shameless piece of sycophancy, but the lowest form of betrayal . . . while all during this time having acted as . . . champion, of all of his fellow native padres. In comparison, one could almost overlook his most grave breaches of celibacy many years back."[22] The letter represented the beginning of Padre Martínez's madness, Chávez argues.

In the final decade of his life, under the pseudonym José Santisteban, his mother's surname, Padre Martínez published controversial newspaper articles on religious issues that were critical of Lamy's policies. In April 1856 he wrote to Lamy requesting that Padre Ramón Medina be sent to Taos to be trained as pastor, after which he would resign. Lamy immediately moved to get rid of Martínez "by shooting him down on his own petard," Chávez argues, and sending Padre Tallarid from Spain to take over Martínez's parish.[23] There followed unanswered letters to Lamy and newspaper articles attacking the bishop's policy of denying the sacraments to those who could not pay complete tithes. Chávez argues that Martínez was pushed to the edge of madness by Tallarid's arrival—there being "a very thin membrane between genius and madness."[24] His writing obsequious letters to Lamy, which were immediately followed by newspaper attacks on foreign priests who accumulated Mass stipends and a defense of native padres under suspension, meant that Martínez had succumbed to schizophrenia, Chávez argues.

Martínez built his own private oratory because Tallarid impeded his conducting liturgies in the main church in Taos, and Martínez began saying Mass and giving sacraments there. Fray Angélico argues that this did not constitute a schismatic church because in a true schism, an individual or group breaks away from papal authority and continues recruiting followers and fighting that authority. Martínez never rejected the Pope's supreme authority, only protested that Lamy did not have the authority to suspend him. He did not split the Taos parish but only ministered to a few friends and family in the oratory. Lamy finally had Machebeuf read an order of excommunication against Martínez in Taos and recorded it where no one would see it in the Taos burial book in 1860, perhaps because he was not sure the extreme measure was appropriate. He did not notify the Vatican or any eastern bishops, so there is no record of when the excommunication actually took place.[25]

More than two thousand people attended Martínez's funeral, including three hundred members of the Penitente Brotherhood. Among the twelve honorary pallbearers were seven American names, pointing to Martínez's good relations with the Americans. While acknowledging the padre's willful pride and final dementia, Fray Angélico notes that he "still had at heart the welfare of the poor and downtrodden."[26] Concerned that in his final will and testament Martínez did not acknowledge his children with Teodora Romero or show humility after having betrayed fellow padres, Chávez wishes that Martínez would have at least used the statement common in wills of having been a sinner during his life. Although Fray Angélico does not suggest it, perhaps the dying man's words that he was at peace with himself were part of the defensive bravado he had practiced for so long in response to the attacks by Lamy and Machebeuf. Chávez notes with regret at the end of his biography that he must retract his previous statement that Padre Martínez was New Mexico's greatest son, arguing instead that "he was her major genius in his own century as well as those before and after his time." Martínez was the "most prominent player on the historical stage, both on the civil and the ecclesiastical scene" in the nineteenth century.[27] True to his role as historian, Fray Angélico tells both his hero's faults and accomplishments, delineating the major historical clash between the new French hierarchy and native priests such as Padre Martínez.

French versus Mexican: The Battle against Padre Gallegos, New Mexico's First Congressman

The cover of the second volume in the series, *Très Macho—He Said: Padre Gallegos of Albuquerque, New Mexico's First Congressman*, bears Fray Angélico's drawing of a handsome young José Manuel Gallegos with the U.S. capitol to the left and the Albuquerque church of San Felipe de Neri to the right. Through the visual and verbal signs of the cover illustration and title, Fray Angélico hopes to remedy the omissions on the other key visual representation of Gallegos—his tombstone—shown in a 1984 photograph by Robert Martin before page 55; the grave marker makes no reference to either Gallegos' priesthood or his congressional career, Fray Angélico notes in the caption. Padre Gallegos, another major victim in the battle between the French clergy and Hispano priests in the mid-nineteenth century, came to be involved as well in an ethnic battle between politically configured Mexican and Hispano ethnicities after the Mexican-American War. Because of his political status as New Mexico's first congressman, Gallegos posed the most serious threat to Vicar Machebeuf because he oversaw the formal complaint and documents against Machebeuf that the New Mexico Legislature sent to the Vatican in 1856. Despite personal and political persecution by Lamy and others, Gallegos went on to a pioneering political and business career.

Both José Manuel Gallegos and Antonio José Martínez were born in Abiquiu, where the former's father was chief magistrate in 1819. Padre Martínez would later train Gallegos for the priesthood, after which he entered the major seminary in Durango. Both families cherished their Spanish ethnicity, but the two priests also identified as Mexicans after their new country was established in 1821, and then as Americans after the U.S. takeover. Fray Angélico feels connected to native padres such as Gallegos not only because he shared their ethnicity and native priesthood, but because he and the priests had common ancestors such as Don Fernando Durán y Chaves, Gertrudis Chaves, the Roybals, and the Archevêques; he invites Hispano readers to join him in identifying with Gallegos, commenting that "so many of us Hispanic New Mexicans have the same forbears one way or another."[28] Here he engages in a similar type of identity politics to that of the Chicano Movement. From a sense of ethnic, civic, and religious pride, he writes revisionist history to document the accomplishments under adversity of previously misrepresented nineteenth-century figures such as José Manuel Gallegos.

Chávez also sharply comments that Gallegos (whose name means "Galicians") came from a long line of Castilian-Galician stockmen forebears and lost his battle with a Gallic peasant-baker's son (Machebeuf) "solely because the latter's equally hard skull happened to be much better equipped with the holy horns of hierarchy."[29] The case of Gallegos is not an isolated instance of the prejudice of "alien" priests against Hispanos in New Mexico.[30] In his own thirty-four years of active ministry, Fray Angélico had seen that English-language priests coming to New Mexico heard gossip and jokes from Anglos about the Hispano parishioners. "In their turn, some of these same priests eventually relayed such things to me in conversation, curiously forgetting for the nonce that I myself was one of those Hispanic natives."[31] These prejudices and cultural clashes worked in tandem with the outright power plays of Machebeuf to take over parishes, residences, and Church funds, often in Lamy's absence. Machebeuf rode out to meet Lamy on his return from seven months' absence in the east and, after reporting scandal about Gallegos, obtained Lamy's permission to take over his parish in Albuquerque. Church records that Chávez uncovered show that Machebeuf delayed the takeover for fifteen to twenty days until Gallegos was too far away on a journey to Mexico to protest.

Fray Angélico admits that Gallegos showed signs of "cockiness and indiscretion" when in late 1840, eight months into his priestly work in New Mexico, Governor Armijo exiled him to Abiquiu because of two militiamen's false accusation.[32] Vicar Ortiz came to Gallegos' defense, arguing that the charge had not been investigated, and then he himself was bodily threatened by one of the accusers who broke into his house. Chávez suggests that Gallegos' early trouble with Armijo perhaps related to political disputes between the two that would grow later. Gallegos worked energetically from 1841 to 1845, ministering simultaneously to three parishes. In 1843 he also became involved in politics. Chávez notes that since 1821, the secular clergy in New Mexico had also worked in politics because they were among the few educated Mexican citizens in the area. In 1843, Armijo demanded that Vicar Ortiz investigate Gallegos' participation in secret meetings at Padre Martínez's house to seek redress against the large land grants in the area, which Armijo was giving to foreigners. Gallegos served as one of the electors to choose New Mexico's deputy to the Mexican Congress and in 1844 was chosen as president of the assembly and next in line to interim governor Mariano Chaves.

Although the information was not available to Fray Angélico because he did not travel to Durango to research Bishop Zubiría's correspondence there, Fr. Thomas Steele cites extensively from the transcription of an important denunciation Padre Martínez made about Padre Gallegos in May 1844. In an attempt to prevent Gallegos from being assigned to Picuris, which Martínez claimed for himself, he denounced Gallegos for having an improper relationship with Jesusa Trujillo and flaunting it publicly. Although Chávez discusses Martínez's betrayal of Padre Ortiz, he seems to have been unaware of this denunciation of Gallegos. Steele suggests that Zubiría and Vicar Ortiz had trouble finding a place for Gallegos in the ensuing months because of Martínez's disapprovals, and they made him *cura propio* of San Felipe de Neri in Albuquerque.[33]

After his transfer there in 1845, Gallegos restored and expanded the adjacent Franciscan friary for his residence with his own funds. A watercolor sketch of the beautiful renovated dwelling by an American lieutenant reveals why Machebeuf desired to take it from Gallegos in 1852. Chávez comments that Gallegos' neatly written ministerial records for the period show that he was never away or absent during the entire seven-year period of 1845–52 at San Felipe de Neri, contrary to Machebeuf's later accusation that Gallegos was constantly away on mercenary trips. Gallegos did write in the parish register on September 21, 1852, that he had notified authorities he was leaving on a trip to Mexico and had placed his coadjutor, Padre José Luján, in charge. Luján signed entries until October 10 when Machebeuf took over the parish.

Chávez argues that Machebeuf abandoned the parish after taking over, just as he had done earlier in Peña Blanca. On December 5 he read in church a suspension of Padre Gallegos from Lamy and accused Gallegos of leading a scandalous life. Machebeuf wrote to his sister that Gallegos was one of those "Padres" who were typically Mexican in their ambition and their love of worldly pleasures and scandals; they did not deserve the French title of *père* or *curé*. "What unabashed chauvinism, one is forced to exclaim!" Chávez writes; "Had he forgotten about such worldly and ambitious fellows as Richelieu and Talleyrand, both of them high churchmen of his native soil?"[34]

Expanding on his discussion of Machebeuf's scrupulosity in the book on Padre Martínez, Chávez suggests that the vicar dominated Lamy and was attracted to him sexually although he repressed these feelings. Lamy and Machebeuf were raised in a milieu of strict French Catholic Puritanism that shaped their judgments and actions throughout life. Based on his many years in the priesthood, Chávez argues that the emphasis on chastity resulted in some clergy imagining they could never attain spiritual perfection because of sexual desires, whether heterosexual or homosexual, that they had buried in the subconscious. He argues that Machebeuf's fanatical obsession with the sins of the flesh can be traced to a latent homosexuality that first inclined him to the all-male army, then to the seminary, and ultimately to the "particular friendship" with his boyhood friend Lamy. The vicar was the domineering partner in the close friendship. Chávez cites gushy phrases in Machebeuf's letters about his special, enduring friendship with Lamy.

While Chávez notes that perhaps Gallegos did not have a true vocation and entered the seminary because he hoped to pursue a political career, Machebeuf and Lamy's treatment of the Mexican cleric was unjustified. The small business enterprise he undertook with his housekeeper Jesusa, for which he traveled to Mexico in 1852 to buy merchandise, was most likely necessary because of the Church's lack of financial support in the poor area. Chávez explains that the "pleasures of the world" such as drinking, gambling, and dancing were part of Hispanos' tradition since they had no Reformation past and were "unhampered all along by any such Puritanism."[35] Again, part of the problem between the French hierarchy and the native padres was a cultural clash.

When Padre Gallegos returned to Albuquerque at the beginning of March 1853, 950 citizens signed a letter of protest to Lamy about Machebeuf's abuses. Chávez recounts the main points of the letter that had been largely ignored by previous historians. The signatories charged that Gallegos left his parish with the oral permission of Machebeuf and provided for a replacement priest. The vicar then removed the substitute and left the parish without adequate ministry. When he did say Mass and give sermons, he threatened people with dire consequences for not paying full tithes and revealed secrets of the confessional. They asked Lamy for Gallegos' immediate reinstatement. Lamy replied that Gallegos had disobeyed his orders and left the parish without permission, and it would be difficult to rehabilitate him; the parishioners needed to give him proof about Machebeuf's alleged misdeeds before he would consider the allegations.

Shortly thereafter, having served as a local legislator for years, Gallegos attended the first Territorial Legislature in June 1853 as the representative of Bernalillo and Santa Ana counties. At the first Democratic Party convention in August, he became the party's nominee for the U.S. House of Representatives. Anglo politicians in Santa Fe terming themselves the "American Party" contested his nomination and proposed James Carr Lane instead. A dirty political campaign ensued in which the Santa Fe newspaper printed unfounded accusations against Gallegos that Chávez argues had to have come directly from Machebeuf and Lamy—for example, that Gallegos was an ex-priest suspended for immorality. Despite the negative campaign, Gallegos won by five hundred votes. Gallegos was forced to make the months-long journey to Washington alone because of dirty tricks by his political enemies. When he arrived in Santa Fe to take the stagecoach to Missouri, he was told it was sold out. He bought mules to pull his own carriage behind the stage, but he next day the mules had disappeared. He then learned that there indeed had been space on the stagecoach. He ultimately undertook the long journey privately. Although the American Party accused him of not knowing English, he enthusiastically worked with his friend and future governor David Meriwether for tutoring in the U.S. Constitution. The anti-Mexican tactics of the campaign and the refusal to allow the territory's first congressman a seat on the coach reveal the difficult path Mexicans in New Mexico faced after the U.S. takeover as they struggled for even rudimentary civil rights in the new country. Chávez reveals Gallegos' courage, persistence, and acumen despite adversities.

Further complicating the ethnic conflict was the distinction being used for political purposes between Hispanos and Mexicans in the territory. Congressman Gallegos, who became a Mexican citizen at age seven when Mexico won independence and was a native Spanish speaker, was pitted in his second campaign in 1855 against Miguel Otero who termed himself "Hispano" and spoke English fluently. Gallegos won by ninety-nine votes, and Bishop Lamy complained in a letter to Bishop Purcell of Cincinnati: "The party of padre Gallegos succeeded again and sent him to Congress. They are trying all they can to embarrass us. Besides, the old ex-vicario Ortiz has returned from Durango, and we receive from him new vexations every day.... Some of our Mexican padres are more troublesome to us than the Know-Nothings to you."[36] Otero charged that some who voted for Gallegos were not American citizens and that corrupt Mexican clergy had interfered in the election. When he challenged Gallegos' seat before Congress in July, Gallegos countered with an attack on Lamy's interference in the election and the bishop's attacks on native priests. Otero boasted of his unmixed Spanish heritage, his eastern education, and his being the first native New Mexican to address Congress in English. He connected himself to the great tradition of Spanish Franciscanism in New Mexico, distinct from the corrupt Mexican priests. These anti-Mexican statements worked together with other prevalent anti-Mexican writings at the time, and Congress unseated Gallegos. Lamy was jubilant and attributed the political victory to Providence in a letter to Rome. Fray Angélico decries the division of the Hispano population into the native landowning *ricos* drawn into the American faction of business and high finance and the "Mexican" Democratic party that fought for the common people. Although Gallegos was a businessman, he took the part of the ordinary people, Chávez argues.

In April 1856, Gallegos sent a letter from the native majority of both houses of the Territorial Legislature dated January 1 attacking Bishop Lamy for malfeasance and for treating native priests unjustly. Chávez argues that Gallegos was the principal author of the complaint and that it reveals mistaken understandings of canon law. The letter nominated Vicar Ortiz to replace Lamy as bishop. It enclosed documents relating to the complaints, including Machebeuf's breaking the seal of confession. Machebeuf was then summoned before Propaganda Fide in Rome, and he defended himself in a rambling document with lies about Gallegos and the other Mexican priests. Rome exonerated Machebeuf, following almost point-by-point the phrases he had underlined in his response. Lamy continued to complain to Bishop Purcell that the Mexican priests were encouraging people not to pay tithes and thereby cut the Church off financially.

While Gallegos was away in Congress, Machebeuf filed a lawsuit to obtain the former Franciscan convento next to San Felipe Neri Church, which Gallegos claimed Zubiría had given him and that he had extensively renovated. Chávez doubts Machebeuf's claim that Zubiría affirmed in a letter he did not give the convento to Gallegos. Fr. Thomas Steele cites a letter in the Durango archives that Zubiría wrote to Machebeuf on August 24, 1854, in which the bishop notes that he gave Gallegos oral permission to renovate the old convento and take ownership of it. Steele notes that the trial over the property ended in a hung jury and that in 1856 Gallegos sold the residence to the diocese for a large sum.

After Gallegos lost his congressional seat, he moved to Santa Fe, supported a large extended household, and engaged in business and civic activities. According to Lamy, however, the ex-priest was "trying to do all the mischief he [could]."[37] Fray Angélico counters by noting that Gallegos procured funds for a good road between Santa Fe and Taos, served as president of the Río Arriba Bridge Company, was elected to the Territorial Legislature, and served as Territorial treasurer for five years. During the Civil War, he was jailed after publicly protesting the Confederate Army's takeover of Santa Fe in 1862. President Andrew Johnson named him superintendent of Indian Affairs for a brief period in 1868. In December 1868, at age fifty-eight, he married Candelaria Montoya, who had been living in his household, and adopted her children.

Reinventing the tropes of Willa Cather's famous novel, Fray Angélico ends his biography by placing Padre Gallegos' death in counterpoint to Lamy's continually rising star. In February 1875, the Diocese of Santa Fe became an archdiocese. Gallegos died on April 21 following a stroke, after being given conditional absolution by Vicar General Pierre Eguillon. After the funeral in the cathedral, one of the largest cortèges ever held in the capital escorted his body to Rosario Cemetery, according to the newspaper. Seven weeks later on June 16 Lamy was consecrated as Santa Fe's first archbishop. Within two years, three quarters of the priests in the ecclesiastical province of Santa Fe would be French, "une petite Auvergne" as Machebeuf would boast.[38] As Lamy was consecrated, Chávez poignantly notes, "poor José Manuel Gallegos, the earliest big loser in those most uneven contests with the French team ... lay seven weeks cold underneath the clay court of his native land, while the foreign Auvergnat winners found cause for rejoicing at the clubhouse for all the victories won in years gone by."[39] In fact, Fray Angélico is suggesting, it is more important to focus on other deaths such as those of Padres Martínez and Gallegos when telling Archbishop Lamy's story—key players on the native Mexican team who lost the struggle for survival after the French "conquest."

The Vicar's Wake as Testimony

A third key nineteenth-century native priest whom Lamy and Machebeuf defamed was Fr. Juan Felipe Ortiz, from one of Santa Fe's richest land-owning families, who was probably ordained in late 1824, made pastor of Santa Fe in 1828, and in 1832 named vicar forane of Santa Fe by Bishop Zubiría of Durango. Ortiz's grand uncle, Don Antonio José Ortiz, had used his own funds to restore the parroquia of San Francisco and the chapel of San Miguel and to build Rosario Chapel in the first decade of the 1800s. After ordination, Fr. Juan Felipe Ortiz worked in several outlying missions, served as a member of the Mexican Departmental Assembly, and after passing special examinations in Durango, received the title cura propio or "irremovable pastor" of Santa Fe. Like his granduncle who had bought the property of San Miguel Mission after having restored it, Fr. Juan Felipe in 1831 purchased the Franciscan convento next to the parroquia in Santa Fe from the Diocese of Durango, a legal sale that Bishop Lamy would later contest.

Discouraged about the difficulties of publishing his trilogy on the native priests, and desiring to retire from the pressures of scholarship in his last decade, Fray Angélico gave the draft and notes for the last volume to his nephew Thomas Chávez. The latter expanded his uncle's manuscript, adding additional historical information and augmenting the footnotes to include new studies that had been done on the figures since Fray Angélico completed his work in the early 1980s. Most significantly, where Fray Angélico was reluctant to criticize the work of his friend Paul Horgan by naming him directly in the main text of the first two volumes, his new coauthor had no such trepidations. In the earlier books, Fray Angélico referred only to "contemporary authors," for example, followed by an endnote referring to Horgan's work; in contrast, his nephew cites in the main text passage after passage of errors and misreadings of documents in Horgan's famous 1975 book *Lamy of Santa Fe*. Published in 2004 after both Fray Angélico and Horgan were dead, the third volume corrects Horgan's and other writers' mistakes directly rather than subtly.

The Chávezes portray Vicar Ortiz as a calm, peaceful man who tried to avoid confrontation when disputes arose and deferred key decisions to the bishop of Durango rather than acting immediately on his own. When Padre Martínez contested his authority over Taos, Picuris, and Lo de Mora, Ortiz affirmed his jurisdiction in two letters but referred the matter to the bishop rather than insisting on an open confrontation with Martínez. Later, he sent Martínez the bishop's letter confirming his authority over all of New Mexico. After the American takeover, Vicar Ortiz was maligned in several American publications and faced a number of difficulties, including a schism that Fray Angélico detailed in a 1983 article.[40] *Wake for a Fat Vicar* contests the negative portrayals of Ortiz in the ethnocentric American accounts, arguing that although he was overweight, he was not the gambling, drinking, fat blob that some American accounts called him, but rather, he was well loved by the townspeople who would, the authors hypothesize, stop him to chat on many topics as he walked about Santa Fe. In the tumultuous times around the American takeover, he protected the interests of the Church, despite being falsely accused of participating in the revolt against Governor Bent. With much difficulty, he ended the schism of Padres Valencia and Cardenas in Belén by having Cardenas expelled. Through the many problems, he consistently kept Bishop Zubiría apprised and worked with him to solve the difficulties.

The book documents Ortiz's peaceful, good-natured personality and his loyalty during these many difficulties. The Chávezes undermine the innuendos and charges against Ortiz after Vicar Machebeuf replaced him when Bishop Lamy took over the vicariate. In one document that other writers had overlooked, Lamy praises Vicar Ortiz for journeying one hundred miles to meet his party in Tomé, so enthusiastic was Ortiz about the new bishop's arrival. Ortiz supervised the lavish preparations to celebrate Lamy's arrival, and Lamy's letters praised Ortiz's warm welcome and his generously offering his newly renovated personal residence next to the parroquia for Lamy to live in.

At the same time however, Lamy and Machebeuf wrote other letters about the sad state of the Mexican clergy and the faithful in the new vicariate. Arguing that the area needed new young priests who were "zealous and devout," Lamy criticized the native priests for only preaching once a year for a large fee. Machebeuf wrote that half of the native priests were old and without energy, and the others were "devoid of zeal and scandalous to a degree you could not imagine." This was all one could expect from "a Mexican clergy, which dreaded reform of their morals."[41] These anti-Mexican prejudices uttered only two weeks after the grand celebration of the bishop's arrival were likely the result of the lurid stories the French bishop of Galveston, Jean-Marie Odin, had told them on their journey to Santa Fe, the book argues. Additionally, questionable figures such as Judge Otero and ex-governor Vigil, who had supported the figures of the Belén schism against Vicar Ortiz, could have disparaged him to the new bishop and vicar.

The book accuses Paul Horgan of "bend[ing] the truth to put it mildly."[42] Despite evidence to the contrary, Horgan argues that the native clergy immediately distrusted Lamy as an outsider, questioned his credentials, and refused to recognize him as bishop of Santa Fe. He contends that Ortiz, who had little zeal for his duties and caused the native clergy to lose theirs, suddenly became very zealous and stubborn about the change of bishops.[43] Fray Angélico's research in the archdiocesan archives about the arrival of Bishop Lamy proves these contentions false because Vicar Ortiz generously welcomed Lamy, praised him, and gave him use of his house. Horgan also mistakenly writes that Lamy undertook the long, dangerous journey to Durango shortly after his arrival because of troubles with the native clergy. In fact, the Chávezes argue, the purpose of the trip was to try to obtain El Paso del Norte and the Mesilla Valley from Bishop Zubiría for Lamy's jurisdiction. The book shows that Ortiz accompanied Lamy to Durango to meet with Zubiría and that Cather's and Horgan's accounts of the long journey Lamy made alone are erroneous, along with "Horgan's blind insistence on having the enmity of the native clergy as the real motive."[44]

Fr. Ortiz quietly ministered to the parroquia of San Francisco that he headed under the new vicariate apostolic, avoiding involvement in the conflicts Lamy and Machebeuf were having with some native clergy. Padre Martínez and other signatories complained in a

January 1853 letter to Lamy that Machebeuf had unfairly dismissed native clergy without due process, appropriated parish funds, broken the seal of confession, and threatened people who did not pay full tithes. As laypeople sent more concerns about Machebeuf to Lamy, the bishop accused those lodging the complaints of attacking him, not his vicar. Although Ortiz was not involved in these complaints, his brother-in-law Don Tomás C. de Baca accused Machebeuf of three specific violations of confessional secrecy. Another complaint letter contained the signatures of 950 parishioners. In the middle of these troubles, Lamy devastated ex-vicar Ortiz by announcing the division of Ortiz's parish and the merging of part of it with the Castrense where the English-speaking parishioners had diminished; the bishop would take the old parroquia for himself. Fray Angélico theorizes that this severe measure "may have planted the seeds of mental disturbance" in the aging Ortiz, perhaps accelerating a kind of "advanced senile deterioration"—a similar mental change Chávez attributed to Padre Martínez's final decade.[45]

The book hypothesizes that Fr. Ortiz told Lamy that he had been appointed cura propio of the parroquia and could not be removed without due process. After Ortiz refused to accept the division of the parish and resigned, Lamy appointed his new protégé, Fr. Brun, ordained only a few months earlier, as rector of the parroquia. The Chávezes point out that in fact the parish was never divided, suggesting that perhaps telling Ortiz it would be was merely a ploy by Lamy to force the pastor out. Ortiz wrote an apologia to complain to the Vatican, but his colleague Padre Martínez, who had defended him in other venues, leaked part of the document to Lamy to curry favor with the bishop.

Sometime later in April or May 1853, Ortiz journeyed to Durango, hoping to arrange for his apologia to be forwarded to the Vatican. Although this complaint did not reach Rome, Lamy wrote numerous letters to his friends in the Church hierarchy and to Bishop Zubiría repeating the false charge that the native priests had rebelled against him.

Hurt that the bishop whom he had treated so magnanimously would take his beloved parroquia away, three years later Fr. Ortiz rescinded permission for the bishop to reside in the house he owned next to the parroquia. He also refused to sell the property back to the diocese. During a trip to France to recruit new clergy, Lamy went to Rome to ask the Vatican to settle the property dispute. There was no final resolution until Lamy purchased the convento and grounds from Ortiz's estate after his death. The Chávezes point to the enormous upkeep and renovations Ortiz made on the churches and his legally owned properties at his own expense throughout his tenure as cura propio of the parroquia. While Ortiz saw this as carrying on his long family tradition of materially supporting the Church, Lamy and Machebeuf characterized his ownership and upkeep of the properties as "typical native greed and arrogance."[46]

Fr. Ortiz returned from Durango in mid-1855, hoping to reconcile with Lamy and receive his parroquia back. Instead, the bishop suspended him after he said vesper services at San Juan at the request of his half brother Padre Eulogio Ortiz who had to be away for his parish's feast day. There followed disputes about chalices and vestments from a private chapel, which Ortiz refused to turn over because Lamy was selling or disposing of many of them, including forty dresses for the statue of Our Lady of the Rosary that had been burned. The situation deteriorated further when the New Mexico Legislature sent a letter to the Vatican condemning Bishop Lamy. Padre Ortiz was not involved in the matter, the Chávezes argue, because of various errors in the document that he would not have made. Nonetheless, the legislators nominated Ortiz as a replacement for Lamy, an office the cleric did not want since he was obsessed only with regaining his simple parroquia. Fray Angélico perhaps identified with Ortiz in this regard because three Hispano priests had nominated him to be vicar in 1971 without his knowledge. Lamy wrote to Bishop Purcell of Cincinnati that Ortiz had instigated the protest petition and proposed himself as bishop.

Playing on the perspective of death in the title of Cather's novel—a finality that often helps people to see life events in historical perspective—this volume's title, *Wake for a Fat Vicar*, points to Ortiz's vindication by the tremendous show of popular support for him at his death. After suffering a stroke, he asked for Bishop Lamy to administer the last sacraments, but the bishop perhaps was out of town since there is no record of his signature in Santa Fe until a week later. Ortiz's deathbed request and the fact that he received a Christian burial in the adobe cathedral means that his suspension had been lifted sometime previously. The priests who conducted his funeral and burial would not have done so if he had been under suspension. Ortiz died at home on January 20, 1858, and for two days and nights the public came to the house to pay their respects. The town flag was lowered to half-staff, and, the newspaper reported, the governor, legislators, and civil and military officials overflowed the church for the funeral. He was buried in the dirt floor of the adobe church, but years later during renovations of the cathedral, his remains were "unceremoniously mixed together in boxes and taken to the Rosario Cemetery north of town for what one hopes was a last internment. *Sic transit* . . . ," Fray Angélico comments at the end of the book.[47] Similarly, the Spanish-style chasubles and altar vessels that Ortiz's half sister later donated to the cathedral from his collection disappeared over the years just as Ortiz feared they would. The vestments went missing "when the rear part of the cathedral was ravaged some years ago in the name of spatial renovation," Chávez critically comments.[48] Just as the vicar's wake gave testimony to the people's love and respect for him in contrast to the lies and defamation writers have perpetuated, the Chávezes hope that their volume of revisionist history will give similar testimony and not disappear as did the vicar's remains and the material church artifacts he strove to preserve.

As an offshoot of his work on vindicating the three nineteenth-century Hispano priests, Fray Angélico published a separate account of two truly renegade Hispano priests who in fact created a schism in New Mexico during this period.[49] When the Church was still under the control of the bishop of Durango, Padre Nicolás Valencia and Fray Benigno Cárdenas broke away in Belén and Tomé. Valencia was suspended in 1848 for insubordination but refused to stop ministering in the parish at Belén, and got the local magistrate to support him over Padre Otero whom the bishop had appointed to replace him. One year later Fray Benigno Cárdenas, an apostate friar from Mexico City (a fugitive from the Franciscan Order), came to the area and, using forged papers, took possession of the church at Tomé, also with the help of the local magistrate. The bishop of Durango excommunicated him, but his decree had no effect because the area was now under U.S. jurisdiction. Ultimately, Vicar Ortiz was able to end the schism and seat the officially appointed pastors in the two towns.

Nonetheless, Valencia ingratiated himself with Machebeuf, and Lamy assigned him to San Felipe. He recanted his heresies in 1856. Thereafter he was assigned to Socorro and Jemez and finally suspended again in 1864, although reinstated two years later; and then he was suspended several more times until his death in 1885. While there was no room to tell the full stories of these renegade priests in his three-volume study, Fray Angélico believed their history was significant and published the separate article. Their cases continue the theme of "truth comes for the archbishop," as Chávez reports Lamy's support and reappointment of Valencia. Most significantly, the story of their schism reveals the interference of local civil authorities who did not respect the separation of church and state guaranteed under the new U.S. government, Chávez argues.

Final Historical Opus: Family History as New Mexico History

After five decades of historical research on New Mexico, Fray Angélico wrote his swan song in the field in the late 1980s. Although centered on the Chávezes, "a distinctive American clan of New Mexico," the

FIG 9.1. Fray Angélico Chávez's immediate family at parents' fiftieth wedding anniversary, Santa Fe, New Mexico, 1959, courtesy Palace of the Governors Photo Archives (NMHM/DCA), Neg. No. 132816.

book revisits central historical events that Fray Angélico had studied throughout his career, now with further insights. The narrative journey back to his roots is also a journey through the central historical themes, problems, and events he had written about since returning from World War II. Additionally, while documenting the Chávez roots and his pride in his New Mexico Spanish heritage, he insists on his patriotic pride as "an unhyphenated American."[50] Chávez asserts his ethnic identity in this book, at the same time insisting on his full-fledged American identity as a veteran who risked his life for his country in World War II.

The seeds of this final book began with his early research on New Mexico families in old Church records and other colonial documents, his 1952 journey to the village of his Chávez forebears in Spain, and the 1954 publication of *Origins of New Mexico Families*. When stationed at the cathedral after the war, he began researching in Church documents and colonial material that University of New Mexico historian France V. Scholes made available to him. In addition to sending him photocopied archival material from the UNM library, Professor Scholes typed up responses to Fray Angélico's queries from his own note cards he kept for years on numerous documentary sources. In January 1948 letters to Scholes, Chávez thanks him for "the Duran y Chavez references you are preparing for me" and "the typed notes on the first Pedro D. de Chavez." He laments that this ancestor's 1626 testimony did not say more about the village of Llerena and the parents of the ancestor's wife. "As you once remarked," he writes to Scholes with a document-seeker's humor, "too bad Pedro and Fernando were not hauled before the Inquisition."[51] In April 1948, Chávez published an article based on this research, "Don Fernando Durán de Chávez." He corrected and expanded this early work in the 1989 book on the Chávez clan. Fray Angélico recounts the importance of his visit to the town Valverde de Llerena in 1952 in the article "Old Guadalupe in Spain," a key travel experience that helped to shape the 1954 *Origins of New Mexico Families*, the 1974 *My Penitente Land*, and the 1989 book on the Chávez clan.

After the book on New Mexico families appeared, Chávez received a letter from Doña María Flor de Chaves, Duchess of Noblejas and head of the royal Chaves branch in Spain. He answered, noting that any noble blood had long ago disappeared in his family line. Nonetheless, the duchess sent him a hand-painted copy of the family coat of arms that he later adapted for his book seal and family reunion programs and reproduced in color on the cover of his 1989 book on the Chávezes. In July 1957 the duchess visited Santa Fe with her sister and niece. When Fray Angélico met her at the airport, she remarked to her sister on seeing the Sangre de Cristo Mountains, "Mira, Pilar, ésta es Castilla!"[52] He comments that the duchess had unwittingly nurtured the seed for his *My Penitente Land* with this observation about the similarity of the New Mexico landscape to that of Spain. The two corresponded for many years, and by putting information together, they concluded that the New Mexico Chávezes descend from a branch of a brother of one of her grandfathers in the sixteenth century. The Spanish and New Mexico branches share a common ancestor, Don Pedro Durán y Chaves from Valverde de Llerena in Extremadura, along with another important descendant, Colonel Manuel Antonio Chaves of Civil War fame, who inherited a signet ring with the five Chaves keys pictured on the coat of arms.

In 1961, as he was renovating the chapel of San Francisco at Golden and the church of St. Joseph in Cerrillos, Fray Angélico organized the first reunion of the Chávez clan in New Mexico on Memorial Day, May 30. He began on a small scale, inviting only Monsignor Alberto Chávez of Taos, Fr. Arturo Chávez of Santa Fe, four seminarians named Chávez, their families, and his to celebrate a Mass in honor of San Fernando. More Chávezes heard about the event and attended. Fray Angélico designed the program with the family coat of arms on the front and the title "Celebración anual de la fiesta de San Fernando, Rey de León y Castilla, miembro y celestial patrón de la familia Chávez." He gave the sermon and wrote a historical note on St. Ferdinand for the program. Ferdinand succeeded his father on the throne in 1230, uniting the kingdoms of León and Castile. In addition to conducting wars against the Moors, he worked for social justice by building hospitals and churches and saying that he feared the curse of one poor woman more than an army of Saracens. In Spain the Chávezes have considered San Fernando a family member on his father's side and therefore also their patron saint.

Fray Angélico's drawing of the coat of arms depicts the helmet facing right rather than straight ahead as in the painting the duchess sent Fray Angélico, with five keys drawn in the center of the shield and heraldic crosses around the border. He notes that while the original coat of arms depicts the knight's helmet facing forward, the second herald shows the helmet facing to the right for a legitimate ancestor and left for an illegitimate one.[53] For the reunion program, the helmet faces right for the legitimate lines of descent from Don Pedro Gómez Durán y Chaves, which he documents in the book.

The 1967 program includes the words of a processional for La Virgen del Valme that opened and closed the Mass in honor of San Fernando. Chávez explained the legend of Nuestra Señora del Valme, following the account of the Spanish novelist Fernán Caballero. In 1248 San Fernando set up camp at Buena Vista, three miles from Sevilla where he had a "beautiful view" of the city occupied by the Moors. He promised the Virgin Mary to whom he prayed that if victorious, he would build a chapel on the spot for the statue of the Virgin he always carried with him. His battle cry and prayer was "Valme, Señora," an old form of the expression "Válgame, Dios." For the 1981 reunion at El Rancho de las Golondrinas, the program includes an agenda and the names of officers including Fray Angélico's sister Nora Chávez who was president. Chávez spoke about his new book, *But Time and Chance*, on Padre Martínez of Taos. He also wrote a detailed account of the relation between San Fernando and the Chávez family in Spain.[54]

Fray Angélico's work on these reunions and programs, along with meeting the many Chávez descendants at the celebrations, spurred him to the write his final book on the history of the clan. He carefully documents the lines descended from Don Pedro Gómez Durán y Chaves in the colonial period and thereafter, an immense task given that the name has become as common as Smith or Jones over the years.[55] Committed to accuracy, he recounts the successes as well as the soap-operatic scandals, arguing that his family line has good and bad elements, as does any other. He expands upon and corrects information in his 1948 article "Don Fernando Durán de Cháves." In the 1948 piece he reported on complaints to the Inquisition that accused Don Pedro Durán y Chaves of taking the side of the local military government against the Franciscans. In the 1989 book, he presents more nuanced information about Don Pedro. Having arrived with the second consignment of colonists in 1600 at about age fifty, Sargento Pedro Gómez Durán y Chaves bore his mother's surname as did the other conquistadores. Now Fray Angélico reports that Don Pedro and Capitán Cristóbal Vaca wrote to the viceroy to propose that the colony be continued as a civil entity apart from the military, a "república" with a popular government rather than a kingdom. When his proposal was not accepted and El Reyno de la Nueva México was established, he assisted Governor Peralta in 1610 in founding La Villa de Santa Fe de los Españoles.[56] Now Fray Angélico is more critical of the head of the Franciscans in this period, Ordoñez, who claimed superiority over the civil ruler and had Governor Peralta kidnapped and chained. A decade later, in 1621, Pedro Durán y Chaves is supporting an "impious" governor, Don Juan de Eulate; there were three separate complaints that Durán y Chaves publicly told the Indians not to obey the friars. In 1624 he led a punitive expedition against the Jemez Pueblos who were plotting to overthrow the Spaniards, and the next year other Franciscans accused him of being an enemy of the Church. The Inquisition in Mexico City took no action against him. Durán y Chaves became an *encomendero* for Sandía and San Felipe, responsible for the material and religious well-being of the Indians in this area. His vast estancia was called El Tunque, and he and his family lived at Ranchos de Santa Ana. The grandson of Don Pedro Gómez Durán y Chaves, Don Fernando Durán y Chaves II, called the property Bernalillo after his own firstborn son.

In his 1948 article, Fray Angélico had preferred to concentrate on Don Pedro's son, Don Fernando, who had a more positive relationship with the friars. The situation with the governors had become worse than in his father's time, Fray Angélico notes in the 1989 book, and the successive governors sent from Mexico City were scoundrels who exploited the padres, the Indians, and any colonists who contested this exploitation. Don Fernando signed a complaint against Governor Rosas' abuses in 1638 and several years later was almost killed along with eight men who were executed by having their throats slit. Don Fernando was pardoned after the intercession of Fray Juan de Salas. A generation later, Don Fernando's son of the same name would term New Mexico a "miserable kingdom" because of this mass execution.

Fray Angélico traces the descendants of Don Fernando's second son, Don Fernando Durán y Chaves II, since this is the line of the family that returned to what is now New Mexico after the reconquest. Don Fernando II carried the standard of Nuestra Señora de los Remedios in both the 1692 and 1693 reentries to Santa Fe, and Fray Angélico's friend, artist José Cisneros, drew a figure with the face of Fray Angélico's father to represent this ancestor. The image in the chapter on Don Fernando II conveys the ancestor's identity semiotically through an emblem with five keys representing the family escutcheon on the figure's chest.[57] Within two years after the reconquest, Don Fernando II moved back to his former Bernalillo estancia (not the present Bernalillo but the renamed El Tunque, which was later sold to the Santa Ana Indians), and there, with his son Bernardo, he witnessed the will of Diego de Vargas, most likely at their home after de Vargas was taken ill in 1704. Fray Angélico poetically comments on the lack of record of where de Vargas was buried: instead of a monument recognizing him, "New Mexico's traditional adobe memory had swallowed up the dust and ashes of her greatest Governor and Captain-General without leaving a trace."[58]

Don Fernando II suffered a tragedy in November 1705 when his son Bernardo was accidentally killed by his cousin as Bernardo pretended to be an Indian in a prank. His father then sold his ancestral lands and moved his family to Atrisco. To explain the bizarre behavior of Don Fernando shortly before his death, Fray Angélico suggests, as he did for Padres Martínez and Ortiz, that Don Fernando had a senile preoccupation with the past and the radical changes among the younger generation of his day. In 1712 when a younger man, Juan González, was appointed *alcalde mayor* of Albuquerque, he attacked the new mayor physically, calling him "un perro mulato," "un perro Indio Griego," and saying that no Indian should be mayor. The charges against Don Fernando were eventually dropped, most likely because of political connections, and four years later by 1716 his wife was listed as a widow. Again there is no record of his burial, and Chávez imagines, "One likes to think that his beloved New Mexico did put on a show the day he died, as her adobe-flecked atmosphere and colorful features lit up the sky with the red and gold of Castile as the sun itself went down, but eventually making his dust her very adobe own without leaving a trace as in the case of his friend Don Diego de Vargas."[59]

Chávez then tells the story of Don Fernando II's seven sons and their descendants, noting in italics special achievements of many Chávezes. Francisco Xavier Chaves, for example, was the first governor of New Mexico under the new Republic of Mexico in 1822. The son of Bárbara Casilda Chaves and Vicente Ferrer Durán de Armijo was Manuel Armijo who was governor of New Mexico from 1837 to 1839 and in 1846. Armijo's sister married Jesús María Chaves, and two of their grandchildren were the famous Senator Dennis Chávez, who served in Congress from 1930 to 1962, and federal judge and New Mexico Supreme Court Justice David Chávez. At the same time, he is careful to recount throughout the book various negative figures in the Chávez clan, arguing that some episodes are like today's supposedly original soap operas. These episodes include bigamy, sexual relations with a stepdaughter, illegitimate children, wife beating, and so forth. Fray Angélico also carefully documents the family lines and stories of the wives of the first Chávezes and those of their descendants, both because they deserve equal treatment and because DNA lines are transmitted by the mothers even though their patronyms may not be Chávez. He had asked France Scholes in a January 1948 letter what the "caso" of Doña Isabel was, and his research enabled him to report on the first Don Pedro's wife, Doña Isabel de Bohórques Vaca, in the 1989 book. While the male Chávezes head every chapter, their wives are listed beneath and their stories recounted as well.

While some may choose not to read the book, fearing that it is only of interest to Chávezes, Fray Angélico deals extensively with important historical events and shows how the Chávez story is very much also the story of New Mexico. He recounts in detail the "troublous times" between the friars and the military governments, the Pueblo Revolt, the various attempts to retake the territory before 1692, the de Vargas reconquest in 1692–93, and other key events in New Mexico history. He asserts once again his argument that a mulatto, Diego Naranjo, led the Pueblo Revolt and claimed to be the representative of Pohé-Yemo, using his last book to insist once again on his controversial theory.

While the story of the Chávez clan is also the story of New Mexico, it is at the same time an important part of American history, Fray Angélico insists. He emphasizes his strong American patriotism throughout the book. The New Mexico family of Chávezes got its start in America before Jamestown and Plymouth Rock, and they became U.S. citizens before the Ellis Island immigrants. The family is also truly American because it has intermarried with Native Americans for almost four centuries. The Chávezes fought on the Union side in the Civil War and sent many to other wars for the United States. Several Chávez descendants played important roles in the U.S. government from the nineteenth century to the present. Fray Angélico argues that Don Fernando II would be proud that his "beloved homeland . . . is no longer a miserable one as an integral part of the United States of America. *This great Country of ours was only seventy years old*

(1776–1846) when, thanks be to God, we became a part of the best Nation on earth and have served her faithfully ever since."[60] While Chávez's patriotism is straightforward here, throughout the book he nuances his proud American identity as one seamlessly connected to his New Mexico Hispano ethnicity. He terms himself an "unhyphenated American" and desires that others view him and his ancestors in the same way—indisputably a crucial element of American history. As icing on the cake at the end of the book, he compares himself in this project of genealogy to the image of Don Quixote, which book Cervantes was writing as New Mexico was being first settled. And the protagonist of Graham Greene's *Monsignor Quixote* tilted at windmills like his fictional antecedent, although ecclesiastical ones, Chávez notes. Ending the book with humor he writes, "Both *Fray* Quixote and Monsignor Quixote have shared the same windmills with the original classic creation of Miguel de Cervantes."[61] While pretending that his long project was madness, Fray Angélico adds one more touch of Hispano ethnicity to the strong American identity he insists on.

Public Historian in the Final Years

We have seen that throughout his life, Chávez frequently contributed his historical and religious knowledge to larger public venues beyond the usual scholarly publications. From his early days in the seminary on, he wrote exuberant essays and stories about New Mexico to explain his specific geospace and culture to a larger audience. In addition to writing regularly for *New Mexico* magazine after leaving the order in 1971, he looked for wider publication venues not only to earn money to support himself, but also to reach more people with the wealth of historical information he had uncovered. In October 1973, for example, he wrote to Governor Bruce King to urge that the state sponsor a reprint of Domínguez's *Missions of New Mexico, 1776* as part of the upcoming national bicentennial. The book contains, he argued, information on the missions, land, and "every phase of life in New Mexico in that historic year when our beloved country was born." Because he does not have the copyright, he urges Governor King to exercise the right of eminent domain (citing the law by number) to make the book available to the people of the state, "utiliz[ing] something already made to order, and of lasting value, as a prime contribution to the Great Event of 1776 being celebrated."[62]

He believed that Domínguez's book filled an important public need for information at the bicentennial.

Chávez joined his artistic and historical skills in proposing ideas for a monument on the Santa Fe plaza and for the construction of the new capitol building completed in 1966. A drawing signed "Angélico Chávez" appeared in the *Santa Fe New Mexican* in response to a proposal for the building in the newspaper. Concerned that the main section of the building was not big enough, Chávez wrote, "Since a dome is not allowed by the Santa Fe Pueblo style, a sort of tower should rise high above the wings of the building and thus be the most prominent part of the capital city. Then too, an elevated approach to the main entrance lends appropriate dignity to an edifice of this kind.... I send you a hasty sketch."[63] His artistic vision and experience in renovating churches moved him to present his ideas for the new capitol building in a wide public forum. A larger central section of the building together with gradually elevating flagstone steps to the main entrance would give the building dignity, he argues. Planting native plants along with green lawns and trees around the building would also enhance aesthetic balance and proportion.

When La Conquistadora was stolen from the cathedral in March 1973, Chávez was interviewed as an expert on the statue. He told news outlets that it was as if the Statue of Liberty had been stolen from the people of the United States, or an even earlier artifact, the Liberty Bell—which still was not as old as the ancient statue. The theft went beyond sacrilege: "To steal something that's historic at the same time—part of the life of the people—is more than sacrilege.... A New Mexican wouldn't have done this in the past."[64] In an attempt to discourage the thieves, Fray Angélico notes that the statue is not very beautiful without the dresses: "The original carved robes were cut away at the waist. The hair was hacked away to fit a wig. There was a screw in the head for crowns.... So whoever stole it only has a piece of junk it's so mutilated. Its only value is history."

Later that year, after the statue's recovery, Chávez began a newspaper article with the eye-catching idea that for the past ninety-nine years in New Mexico, several times "Jesus has been arrested and jailed for all sorts of mayhem."[65] The article carefully documents the history of naming children Jesús in the Spanish tradition, beginning with sixteenth-century religious figures renaming themselves John of the Cross and Teresa de Jesús. By the nineteenth century, New Mexico's baptismal records show that children were increasingly named with all three names of the Holy Family—Jesús María José—but the name Jesús was never used alone. By the late nineteenth century many in a single family were named Juan de Jesús, and in order to differentiate father from son, the child's name was shortened to Jesús. Chávez explains that to this day, the name has been dissociated from the referent of Christ himself, just as has occurred with the Anglo surname Christ and the name Christine. Therefore, a person's name could be Jesús whether or not he might be an upright person or a criminal, since linguistic usage had attenuated the original referent of the person of Christ. When non-Hispano clergy came to New Mexico they viewed the Hispano naming custom as blasphemy, mistakenly reconnecting the literal referent to the signifier. Archbishops told their clergy to forbid Hispanos from baptizing their children with this name, and many pastors followed these orders, causing hard feelings among Hispanos. Chávez argues both for and against this prohibition: "What had sounded all right when everybody was Spanish began to look and sound just the opposite as New Mexico fast became a pluralistic society both ethnically and religiously." In the end, however, he asserts ethnic pride and criticizes the double standard by complaining that no one seems to object when the popular Anglo name Christine is connected to the forced resignation of an English member of Parliament.

For the 1986 centennial celebration of St. Francis Cathedral, Chávez was a member of the planning committee and designed two important visual monuments for the occasion—the new church doors and the massive altar screen. Each of these impressive artifacts embodied Fray Angélico's role as a public historian, as he brought years of research and discoveries about New Mexico history to wide sectors of the public who for generations to come would visit the cathedral in the heart of Santa Fe. The visual images he proposed and designed for the doors and the altar screen would draw local people and visitors into the history of New Mexico and the Americas, which was closely tied to Catholicism. As visual texts, they would require verbal anchoring by explanatory notes or captions to allow many viewers to understand their precise connection to the historical chronology.[66] The language Fray Angélico wrote for the design plans of both the doors and altar screen is reproduced almost exactly in a brochure that explains the images on the doors and on postcards available in the cathedral, which briefly tell the story of each saint on the altar screen. Through the designs and captions he wrote, he makes the history that the visual images begin to tell more available to a wide public.

Chávez proposed a verbal chronology along with rough sketches for sixteen bronze plaques for the new cathedral doors that would visually narrate the role of the Church in New Mexico history since 1539 with the arrival of Fray Marcos de Niza. The series ends with the dedication of the renovated cathedral in 1986 by the apostolic delegate for the centenary. The panels sculpted by Donna Quasthoff follow many of the visual images he suggested. Quasthoff paid a subtle tribute to Fray Angélico in panel 15—which commemorates the episcopal coronation of La Conquistadora in 1954 and the statue's papal coronation in 1960—by casting Fray Angélico in the background wearing his characteristic beret.[67] In designing the narrative elements that would be visually depicted on the door, Chávez carried on the centuries-old religious pedagogical tradition of teaching through visual representation. Although the bronze panels allow important history to become visually present with a permanent monumental grandeur as people enter the cathedral, the verbal text Fray Angélico wrote that is included in the brochure inside the church is an essential element of this process of historical recuperation as it anchors and explains the images in the bronze panels.[68]

In the case of the large altar screen, Fray Angélico prepared a handwritten plan with sketches entitled "REREDOS: The Saints of the Americas." Besides naming the saints who would be depicted, he wrote brief biographies of each and insisted on the clothes they should be wearing, the colors that should be used to achieve overall balance, and that the background of each panel should be yellow or gold leaf to create a sense of Byzantine splendor. He noted that the figures "should be somewhat formally stiff" so that they would bear some resemblance to New Mexico santos but not be as "primitive."[69] It had been suggested that various New Mexico artists each paint a panel of a saint, and Fray Angélico alludes to this plan in his proposal. He notes that he will be available to advise the individual artists on the correct dress and color of the ecclesiastical and secular clothing of the saints, but that the artists will be free to decide details such as arm placement and the stance of the figures. Nonetheless, he argued later that a single artist should paint all of the panels to avoid a hodgepodge, and his view eventually won out. In a 1987 newspaper article, he answered critics who protested the choice of a single artist (Robert Lentz) from outside New Mexico to paint the images. After discussions with various local painters, Chávez realized that no matter how good each separate painting by a different artist for the reredos might be, the result would be an unbalanced whole.[70]

Fray Angélico's public service extended to the visits of national and international dignitaries. In 1983, at the invitation of Stewart Udall, he gave Jacqueline Kennedy Onassis a tour of Santa Fe's important historical sites and told her about the history of Hispanos in the area. He was invited to make a presentation in La Conquistadora Chapel in the cathedral to the visiting King Carlos and Queen Sofía of Spain on September 29, 1987. In a speech prepared in Spanish, he began with a blessing for the monarchs, "Qué Dios guarde a Sus Majestades Católicas." These poor adobe walls and vigas, he noted, house the oldest representation of the Mother of God in the United States. He told the royal audience that the statue was many years in Spain before coming to the Americas because it had arabesque and baroque decorations. It was sent from the Franciscan Convento Grande in Mexico City to Santa Fe as a representation of Mary's Assumption, the patron of the parish at that time. After the reconquest, Diego de Vargas named the statue "Reyna del Reyno de la Nueva Méjico y su Villa de Santa Fe" and became head of the confraternity. Chávez's research forty years ago revealed that the statue's caretakers in every generation were the ancestors of New Mexico Hispanos, and therefore the statue was their paisana. The statue is not a miraculous Virgin, but rather connected to the land of Santa Fe, much like the Virgins of Sagrario in Toledo and of Guadalupe in Extremadura—the geographic roots of La Conquistadora's first devotees in New Mexico.

In August 1984, photographer Cynthia Farah took Fray Angélico's portrait in the kitchen of his apartment on Rio Vista Place for a project on Southwestern writers she was preparing for the El Paso Library. Four years later, after the book *Literature and Landscape* was published, Fray Angélico appeared at the book signing on November 19, 1988, along with other famous Southwestern writers included in the book. On June 21, 1992, Chávez was awarded the Oficial de la Orden de Isabel la Católica medal by José Ramón Remacha, cultural attaché to the Spanish Embassy in Washington, D.C., in honor of his contributions to Hispanic culture. Because he had returned to live in the cathedral friary, Chávez wore his Franciscan robes to receive the award.

FIG. 9.2. Fray Angélico Chávez, 1984, courtesy Cynthia Farah Haines.

FIG. 9.3. Left to right: Fray Angélico Chávez and José Ramón Remacha, June 21, 1992, History Library, Palace of the Governors, Santa Fe, New Mexico. Photo by Robert Shlaer, courtesy Palace of the Governors Photo Archives (NMHM/DCA), Neg. No. 163709.

After the ceremony held in the History Library in the Palace of the Governors in Santa Fe, he appeared with Remacha on the balcony.

Having been diagnosed with a brain tumor and a bad artery that could burst at any moment, Fray Angélico continued to contribute small bits of public history when he could.[71] In shaky and uneven handwriting, he composed a short narrative, "A Fountain Mystery," on April 25, 1994, two years before his death. He tells about a historical discovery he made in the 1950s on the cathedral parking lot that constantly needed leveling because it was built over a swamp. One summer day he helped his father build a retaining wall on the *acequia madre* to safeguard the family's front garden. On his way back to the cathedral, he saw a truck filled with dirt and a large metal object about to go to the dump. The workmen removed the object for him, and he took it to his father's garden. After cleaning off the rust, he saw a copy of the New Orleans coat of arms and concluded that the fountain had belonged to Archbishop Chapelle who had come to Baltimore from France. By 1894, "he had himself named Archbishop of Santa Fe," and only three years later "he had himself transferred to New Orleans," as he was disappointed in Santa Fe.[72] The mystery Chávez refers to is how and when the fountain had come to Santa Fe. He recalled a local tradition he had heard about a bishop building a pond to hold a fountain. When the pond dried up, workmen covered it with dirt along with the fountain. He proudly concludes that he himself rescued this historic fountain from a second burial at the city dump by bringing it that day to his father's garden at 712 Acequia Madre. Always concerned with preserving the historical record, Fray Angélico leaves a written record of the disposition of this historical artifact and his quick thinking to save it in this short narrative written with difficulty two years before his death.

✤

The life and work of Fray Angélico Chávez expand received ideas of American culture and the Hispano component that adds nuance to it. Chávez's complex formation of identity throughout his life and work marks his uniqueness as an American writer and a proud ethnic subject with a rich legacy of Hispano culture. His vast intellectual and artistic contributions help to recenter key regional and ethnic legacies within the American mainstream. At the same time, his life and work point to new conceptualizations of U.S. Latino identity, which include hybrid identity formation in the pre–Chicano Movement period in modes rooted in the particular historical periods of the twentieth century in which Chávez lived and worked.

Fray Angélico's prolific work reveals a complex sense of self as an ethnic, American, and religious subject who was at the same time a historian and artist, a creative writer and preservationist. Throughout his life, his multiply conceived identity involved cross-generic aesthetic and intellectual work and a strong emphasis on the interconnection of the verbal and visual. Performance was a central trope in his presentation of the ethnic self in both his life and work, and writing, art, church restoration, and even priestly ministry were key sites in which this ethnicity was negotiated and publicly displayed. Whether wearing a gaucho costume, brown Franciscan robes, an army uniform, or a beret, Fray Angélico insisted on accurately portraying and accounting for the rich legacy of the Hispano presence in the United States since the colonial period. His particular ethnic self was strongly intertwined with his deep Catholic spirituality—so strong a component of his identity that he left the security of his family and beloved New Mexico as a child of fourteen and died at eighty-six in the Franciscan habit. Even his nineteen-year period of separation living outside the Franciscan community involved continued writings on religious issues and participation in religious liturgies at the cathedral. He described ethnic, religious, and institutional reasons for this separation, in addition to his compelling need to write.

Chávez's life was closely connected to key periods of twentieth-century American history, each of which contributed to his identity formation—the development of Santa Fe–style architecture in the first decades, the arrival of important American writers and artists in northern New Mexico in the 1920s, the Great Depression of the 1930s, the Spanish Civil War (1936–39), World War II, the explosion of the atomic bombs, the postwar U.S. occupation of Germany, and the social upheaval of the 1960s and its aftermath, including the effects of Vatican Council II. At the same time that he was deeply connected to the key events of his age, he insisted on situating the present in history: he remedied the partial and frequently incorrect narratives in standard history books with carefully researched revisionist history that invited both scholars and the public to understand the legacy of the Spanish friars and colonists in La Nueva México.

In the period of intense historical research and writing after his return from World War II until shortly before his death, Chávez reterritorialized himself as an ethnic and religious subject by delineating the history of New Mexico, his beloved land. During his semi-exile studying for the priesthood in Ohio, Michigan, and Indiana, he had asserted his ethnicity primarily through literary and artistic self-presentation. In the second half of his life, however, he did so most often through copiously researched revisionist history. In his historical research, ministry, and church renovation he re-lived the lives of the early Franciscans whose traces he discovered in Church documents. His writing, research, and ministry led him in a sense to "become" these early friars, to understand his connection to their legacy as he read details from handwritten documents, unearthed forgotten corpses in crumbling blue robes, and envisioned unknown details of their lives through his literary imagination. He *performed* his role in history while he researched and documented it for posterity.

In the 1970s and 1980s, during his separation from active priestly ministry, he published in venues with a broader reach both to support himself and in keeping with his desire to share historical knowledge as widely as possible. In his later years, Fray Angélico took on a greater role as a public intellectual and one of the foremost experts in New Mexico history. The tireless work he engaged in throughout his life, often working through the night during the decades he was a full-time priest, and continuing this pace when he could devote himself to writing full time, resulted in a vast record of publications that situates him as the most prolific and wide-ranging U.S. Hispano writer of the twentieth century.

A product of his times, the Hispano community of northern New Mexico, and his rigorous religious formation in the Franciscan seminary, Fray Angélico antedates the militant demands for recognition in the American mainstream by Chicanos and other Latino groups in the late 1960s and beyond. His mode of asserting ethnic identity involved artistic and literary expression, church remodeling and preservation, priestly ministry to the Pueblo Indians and Hispano Catholics, and careful, persistent historical research and writing that documented the narrative of the Hispano presence in what is now the southwestern United States—a European presence predating even the arrival of the British colonizers. His constantly developing and multiply conceived identity stands in contrast to the more fixed and militant identity of the Chicano Movement period, but his contestatory and copious literary, artistic, and historical contributions also leave a key legacy by reinserting the Hispano presence in New Mexico into the master narratives of American history and culture.

Notes

Chapter One

1. Cited in Meg Sandoval, "Fray Angélico Chávez," *Denver Catholic Register*, October 3, 1990, 6.
2. Ramón Saldívar, "The Borders of Modernity: Américo Paredes's *Between Two Worlds* and the Chicano Nationalist Subject," in *The Ethnic Canon: Histories, Institutions, and Interventions*, ed. David Palumbo-Liu, 71–87 (Minneapolis: University of Minnesota Press, 1995), 71–87.
3. Interview with Fray Angélico Chávez by John Pen La Farge, August 14, 1989, Santa Fe, New Mexico, made available to me by La Farge; edited version published in John Pen La Farge, *Turn Left at the Sleeping Dog: Scripting the Santa Fe Legend, 1920–1955* (Albuquerque: University of New Mexico Press, 2001), 34–42. See also, Fray Angélico Chávez, *La Conquistadora: The Autobiography of an Ancient Statue* (Paterson, NJ: St. Anthony Guild Press, 1954), v.
4. Ellen McCracken and Mario García, interview with José Chávez, August 7, 1997, Santa Fe, New Mexico.
5. Ellen McCracken and Mario García, interview with Fabián Chávez Jr., August 21, 2000, Santa Fe, New Mexico.
6. Ellen McCracken and Mario García, interview with Chávez's sister-in-law, Bernice Chávez, August 2003, and letter from Fray Angélico Chávez to Marie Belt, June 15, 1991, Marie Belt File, Fray Angélico Chávez History Library and Photographic Archives, Santa Fe, New Mexico.
7. Ellen McCracken and Mario García, interview with Francisco Chávez, August 19, 1996, Santa Fe, New Mexico.
8. La Farge, interview with Chávez, 1989.
9. La Farge, interview with Chávez, 1989.

10. Commissioned to paint a series of large murals depicting Mayan cities for the San Diego Exposition, Carlos Vierra executed four of them in Tesuque, New Mexico, and two on-site in San Diego. See Carl Sheppard, *The Saint Francis Murals of Santa Fe: The Commission and the Artists* (Santa Fe, NM: Sunstone Press, 1989), 84–85.
11. See Elton T. Brown, *The 1916 Exposition in Black and White, San Diego, California* (Coronado, CA: Coronado School, 1916); *Catalogue of Exhibits, New Mexico Building—San Diego, 1915, Panama-California Exposition*; and *San Diego Panama-California Exposition 1915–6: Official Views*, documents available in the Fray Angélico Chávez History Library and Photographic Archives; and Sharon Rohlfsen Udall, *Santa Fe Art Colony, 1900–1942* (Santa Fe, NM: Peters Corporation, 1987), 22.
12. La Farge, interview with Chávez, 1989.
13. Ellen McCracken and Mario García, interview with Judge Antonio Chávez, August 20, 1996, Albuquerque, New Mexico. Antonio Chávez remembers his uncle Gus Sosaya, who was also working in San Diego at the exposition at the time, remarking, "The gringos liked [Fabián Chávez] because he knew how to handle the Mexican labor."
14. La Farge, interview with Chávez, and *Empire Magazine, Denver Post*, January 11, 1981.
15. La Farge, interview with Chávez; *Empire Magazine, Denver Post*, January 11, 1981; and Fray Angélico Chávez, "Fray Angelico Chavez, O.F.M." in *The Book of Catholic Authors*, ed. Walter Romig (Grosse Pointe, MI: Walter Romig, 1943), 60–62.
16. See Fray Angélico Chávez, *Chávez: A Distinctive American Clan of New Mexico* (Santa Fe, NM: W. Gannon, 1989), xiv–xv.
17. Ellen McCracken and Mario García, interview with Nora Chávez, August 13, 1996, Santa Fe, New Mexico.
18. Ellen McCracken and Mario García, interviews with Nora Chávez, August 16, 1996, and Fabián Chávez Jr., August 21, 2000, Santa Fe, New Mexico, and Fray Angélico Chávez, "The Mora Country," *New Mexico* (January–February 1972): 32–37.
19. For Chávez's description of the museum's architecture see La Farge interview. In a 1990 interview Chávez remarked, "Santa Fe was a little town then. I ran all over town. I remember when the first 'Santa Fe style' building was built, the Fine Arts Museum. Oh, I was thrilled by the sight of it." See Kate McGraw, "About to Turn 80, Poet-Priest Still Busy," *Santa Fe New Mexican*, April 8, 1990, A-4.
20. Quoted in Edna Robertson and Sarah Nestor, *Artists of the Canyons and Caminos* (Santa Fe, NM: Ancient City Press, 1976), 55.
21. La Farge, interview with Chávez, 1989.
22. Ellen McCracken and Mario García, interviews with Jaime Baca, August 17, 2000, and Erlinda Baca, August 9–10, 2001, Albuquerque, New Mexico.

23. The *Provincial Chronicle* lists the religious names of the nineteen men made novices on August 15, 1929, at Mt. Airy, all of which begin with "Friar." Manuel Chávez's religious name is listed as "Fra Angelico" ("Investiture and Profession," *Provincial Chronicle* 2, no. 1 [October 1929]: 9). Chávez changed the "Fra" to "Fray" to honor his Spanish heritage.
24. Ellen McCracken, interview with Father Bernard Gerbus, O.F.M. (fellow seminarian with Fray Angélico), March 22, 1997, Cincinnati, Ohio.
25. Fray Angélico Chávez, "Fray Angélico's Thread," *Santa Fe New Mexican*, one hundredth anniversary of daily publication issue, 1959. Chávez gave this reason for the paucity of visits home in the interview with La Farge. However, despite his memory that he did not come home for eight years after entering the novitiate, he did make brief visits home on June 2, 1933, for the installation of Rudolph Gerken as the seventh archbishop of Santa Fe and on July 5, 1934, to attend his parents' twenty-fifth wedding anniversary, returning July 14.
26. McCracken and García, interview with Nora Chávez, August 13, 1996. Younger brother Judge Antonio Chávez tells of Fray Angélico's similar role in naming him. While his mother was pregnant, Manuel wrote home from the seminary that it was strange that a family with a son studying to be a Franciscan had named none of its children for St. Anthony, the order's patron. Nicholasa Roybal heeded Manuel's subtle hint when her son was born, naming him after the saint. McCracken and García, interview with Judge Antonio Chávez, August 20, 1996.
27. McCracken and García, interview with Francisco Chávez, August 17, 1999, Santa Fe, New Mexico. Fabián Chávez Jr. recounts that his father bought ten acres on Acequia Madre adjacent to the Sosaya land. Chávez Sr. designed and built the house in territorial style after seeing a plan in the Montgomery Ward Catalogue. Later, after World War II, Fray Angélico supervised and helped his brothers build the wall in front of the house. See David Roybal, *Taking on Giants: Fabián Chávez, Jr. and New Mexico Politics* (Albuquerque: University of New Mexico Press, 2008).
28. Phyllis Morales interview with Fray Angélico Chávez, May 27, 1995, Santa Fe, New Mexico.
29. McGraw, "About to Turn 80, Poet-Priest Still Busy."
30. McGraw, "About to Turn 80, Poet-Priest Still Busy."
31. McCracken and García, interview with Nora Chávez, August 16, 1996.
32. Florence Davies, "Play Is Tribute to St. Anthony," *Detroit Mirror*, June 8, 1931.
33. Documents relating to the property at 712 Acequia Madre Street, Chávez Collection, AC 287, Folder 2: Chávez Family, Fray Angélico Chávez History Library and Photographic Archives; McCracken and García, interview with Fabián Chávez Jr., August 21, 2000, and La Farge interview with Chávez.
34. McCracken and García, interviews with Nora Chávez, August 16, 1996, and Mónica Sosaya Halford, August 18, 1998, Santa Fe, New Mexico;

Kathryn M. Córdova, "Fray Angélico Chávez: 1937 Ordination in Santa Fe, Icon a Memorable Event," *La Herencia* (Summer 2006): 27.
35. Years later, his sister-in-law Bernice Chávez discovered it in the basement of the Acequia Madre house and asked Fray Angélico if she could have it. He agreed and wrote a humorous inscription to her inside. After she donated the volume to the Fray Angélico Chávez History Library and Photographic Archives, Nasario García edited and published the work with Arte Público Press, Houston, in 2000 (McCracken and García, interview with Bernice Chávez, August 13, 2003).
36. Letter from Chávez to Provincial Ripperger, September 15, 1937, "Correspondence with the Provincial, 1937–1946," Chávez File, Archives of St. John the Baptist Province, Cincinnati, Ohio. Hereafter referred to as Franciscan Archives.
37. McCracken and García, interview with Nora Chávez, August 16, 1996.
38. Letter from Haniel Long to Father Angélico, July 18, 1938, "Letters of Interest, 1929–1940," Box 521, File XIV, Chávez Collection, Fray Angélico Chávez History Library and Photographic Archives; Ellen McCracken and Mario García, interview with Kate McGraw, August 19, 1996, Santa Fe, New Mexico.
39. In a September 15, 1937, letter to Fr. Provincial Ripperger, he notes, "Ever since I came West I've been asked to contribute to 'New Mexico,' a State publication. . . . I have sent out poems and articles to Catholic publications, but few have been accepted. I keep the St. Anthony Messenger well supplied." ("Correspondence with the Provincial, 1937–1946," Chávez File, Franciscan Archives). Two earlier poems in the magazine are "Pecos Ruins" (March 1937) and "Cross of the Martyrs" (August 1937). In the first years of his ministry at Peña Blanca, the poems he published in *New Mexico* magazine were "Clouds over Santa Clara" (January 1938), "Singing Cowboy" (March 1938), "Litany of Pueblos" (July 1938), "Sandoval Sunset" (June 1939), and "Sangre de Cristo Range" (August 1939).
40. Chávez, "Fray Angelico Chavez, O.F.M.," 60–62.
41. Letter from Chávez to Provincial Adalbert Rolfes, February 17, 1940, "Correspondence with the Provincial, 1937–1946," Franciscan Archives.
42. Chávez mentioned the autographed copy of the play in a note he wrote on a Christmas card to Fred Grillo, 1970, Chávez Collection, Box 574-#2, File 9, Fray Angélico Chávez History Library and Photographic Archives. See also Kate McGraw, "Padre or a Renaissance Man?" *Santa Fe Reporter*, October 21, 1981, 21, 26, and "About to Turn 80, Poet-Priest Still Busy."
43. In 1935 Fr. Remigius Austing was denied the right to say Mass at Santo Domingo Pueblo on the first Sunday of July and reported this to the archbishop. On July 16, 1935, Archbishop Rudolf A. Gerken placed an interdict on Santo Domingo prohibiting every religious function and ministration except for the dying.

44. Ellen McCracken and Mario García, interview with Julia Silva, August 11, 1997, Santa Fe, New Mexico.
45. May Sarton, *A World of Light: Portraits and Celebrations* (New York: Norton, 1976), 130–33, 136.
46. Chávez, letters to Provincial Rolfes and Fr. Robert Kalt, "Correspondence with the Provincial, 1937–1946," Franciscan Archives.
47. Chávez, "With Fr. Angelico in the Service," *Provincial Chronicle* (June 1947): 64–72.
48. Letter from Chávez to the Provincial, September 18, 1943, "Chaplain's Correspondence, 1942–1946," Franciscan Archives.
49. Chávez, "With Fr. Angélico in the Service," 66–67.
50. Chávez, "With Fr. Angélico in the Service," 66–67, and 77th Division reunion program, August 1987, kindly shared with me by Dr. Randolph Seligman, Albuquerque, New Mexico.
51. Chávez, "August 1944 Monthly Report of Chaplain to Military Ordinature, New York City from Guam," "Chaplain's Correspondence, 1942–1946," Franciscan Archives.
52. Chávez, "December 1944 Monthly Report of Chaplain to Military Ordinature, New York City from Philippines," "Chaplain's Correspondence, 1942–1946," Franciscan Archives.
53. Chávez, "With Fr. Angelico in the Service," 71.
54. Chávez, "With Fr. Angelico in the Service," 68.
55. Chávez, "With Fr. Angelico in the Service," 72.
56. Chávez, "With Fr. Angelico in the Service," 72.
57. He even toyed with the idea of checking into the hospital because he was losing weight as a way of speeding up his dismissal. Letter from Chávez to Provincial Mollaun, October 15, 1945, "Chaplain's Correspondence, 1942–1946," Franciscan Archives.
58. Letter from Chávez to the Provincial, August 22, 1946, "Correspondence with the Provincial, 1937–1946," Franciscan Archives.
59. Letter from Chávez to the Provincial, January 7, 1947, "Correspondence with the Provincial, 1947–1949," Franciscan Archives.
60. Letter from the Provincial to Chávez, June 2, 1947, "Correspondence with the Provincial, 1947–1949," Franciscan Archives; also, in a December 3, 1947, letter, the provincial tells Fray Angélico that the archbishop is opposed to friars attending New Mexico University.
61. Letter from Chávez to Provincial Mollaun, July 30, 1947, attachment to letter from Chávez to Mollaun, December 9, 1947, and letter from Chávez to the Provincial, March 10, 1948, "Correspondence with the Provincial, 1947–1949," Franciscan Archives; "Missions and Retreats," *Provincial Chronicle* 20, no. 2 (Winter 1948): 107.
62. Letter from Chávez to the Provincial, September 10, 1948, "Correspondence with the Provincial, 1947–1949," Franciscan Archives.
63. Letter from Chávez to the Provincial, September 10, 1948,

"Correspondence with the Provincial, 1947–1949," Franciscan Archives; Marc Simmons, "Fray Angélico Chávez: The Making of a Maverick Historian," in *Fray Angélico Chávez: Poet, Priest, and Artist*, ed. Ellen McCracken (Albuquerque: University of New Mexico Press, 2000), 11–23; letter from Chávez to Fr. John Forest, May 9, 1949, "Correspondence with *Chronicle*," Chávez File, Franciscan Archives.

64. Letters from Chávez to Fr. Forest and Provincial Mollaun, February 24, 1950, "Correspondence with *Chronicle*" and "Correspondence with Provincial, 1947–1949," Franciscan Archives.
65. Letters from Chávez to the Provincial, February 24, July 14, and October 11, 1950, "Correspondence with Provincial, 1950–1954," Franciscan Archives.
66. Letter from Chávez to the Provincial, January 2, 1947, "Correspondence with the Provincial, 1947–1949," Franciscan Archives.
67. Letter from Chávez to Fr. Forest, editor of the *Provincial Chronicle*, August 2, 1948, "Correspondence with *Chronicle*," Chávez File, Franciscan Archives.
68. La Farge interview with Chávez, 1989; In a July 24, 1950, letter to his provincial, Chávez immediately expressed his shock at reading the news in the paper, "Correspondence with Provincial, 1950–1954," Franciscan Archives.
69. Letter from the Provincial to Chávez, July 26, 1950, "Correspondence with Provincial, 1950–1954," Franciscan Archives.
70. Letter from Chávez to the Provincial, October 11, 1950, "Correspondence with Provincial, 1950–1954," Franciscan Archives.
71. Bernice Chávez recounts that she sent the archbishop a wedding invitation and was surprised that he came to the ceremony (Ellen McCracken and Mario García, interview with Bernice Chávez, August 20, 2003, Santa Fe, New Mexico). Fray Angélico wrote that "the Archbishop had finished his Mass right before and he lingered by for the wedding service in his *purpura*" (letter from Chávez to the Provincial, February 5, 1951, "Chaplain's Correspondence, 1949–1952," Franciscan Archives). No doubt the bride's invitation and the relationship of the groom to Fray Angélico both contributed to the archbishop's presence.
72. McCracken and García, interview with Bernice Chávez, August 20, 2003.
73. Letter from Chávez to the Provincial, February 13, 1951, "Chaplain's Correspondence, 1949–1952," Franciscan Archives.
74. Letter from Chávez to Chaplain (Maj. Gen.) Roy H. Parker, "Chaplain's Correspondence, 1949–1952," Franciscan Archives.
75. Letter from Chávez to the Provincial, February 1, 1952, "Chaplain's Correspondence, 1949–1952," Franciscan Archives.
76. Letter from Chávez to the Provincial, February 14, 1952, "Chaplain's Correspondence, 1949–1952," Franciscan Archives.
77. Letter from Chávez to the Provincial, February 14, 1952, "Chaplain's Correspondence, 1949–1952," Franciscan Archives.

78. Letter from Chávez to Provincial Kroger, March 3, 1952, "Chaplain's Correspondence, 1949–1952," Franciscan Archives.
79. Letter from Chávez to his parents, April 10, 1952, Nora Chávez scrapbook, Chávez Collection, Fray Angélico Chávez History Library and Photographic Archives; letter from Chávez to Provincial Kroger, April 14, 1952, "Chaplain's Correspondence, 1949–1952," Franciscan Archives; photo album, *Canticle of the Sun: Franciscan Photos Early Years*, Palace of the Governors, Photo Archives, Santa Fe, New Mexico.
80. Letter from Kroeger to MacAuley, November 12, 1952, "Jemez Pueblo, NM, San Diego, Place Files," "Letters 1949–1954," Franciscan Archives.
81. Letter from N. Scott Momaday to Ellen McCracken, January 20, 1997.
82. Letter from Kroger to Chávez, August 29, 1953, "Correspondence with Provincial, 1950–1954," Franciscan Archives.
83. Letter from Chávez to Kroger, September 12, 1953, "Correspondence with Provincial, 1950–1954," Franciscan Archives.
84. Letter from Chávez to Provincial Kroger, September 9, 1954, "Correspondence with Provincial, 1950–1954," Franciscan Archives, and "New Mexico Honors 'La Conquistadora,'" *Provincial Chronicle* 26, no. 3 (Spring 1954): 271–73.
85. Fr. Angélico, C.C.C.C.C., "Pilgrimage of La Conquistadora," *Provincial Chronicle* 27, no. 1 (1954): 29.
86. Letter from Chávez to Provincial Kroger, October 16, 1954, "Correspondence with Provincial, 1950–1954," Franciscan Archives.
87. Letters from Chávez to the Provincial, October 24 and December 15, 1954, "Correspondence with Provincial, 1950–1954," Franciscan Archives.
88. Letters from Chávez and Fr. Edgar Casey, March 15 and March 19, 1955, "Correspondence with *Chronicle*," Chávez File, Franciscan Archives.
89. "Ordinations and First Masses," *Provincial Chronicle* 27, no. 4 (Summer 1955): 310–11. Fr. Aragón recounts that it was really his "second" first Mass, because his parents had moved to Albuquerque when he entered the seminary, and he said his first Mass in their new parish. The priests in Peña Blanca invited him to say another first Mass there, and Fray Angélico came from Jemez to celebrate with the first *peñablanquero* to be ordained a Franciscan. Ellen McCracken and Mario García, interview with Fr. Aragón, August 17, 1999, Santa Fe, New Mexico.
90. Father Virgil Kaiser, a classmate of Fray Angélico's who had often invited him to his family's home during the seminary years, was later involved in a disturbing set of events. When he was pastor of St. Joseph Nazareth, he fathered two children, and to make matters worse, baptized them himself. One morning, shortly after his mother died, he left a note for the assistant pastor that he was leaving the order. He moved to Kentucky and later married the woman. After Vatican II, Fray Angélico and Fr. Leo Pheiffer talked to Kaiser about coming back to the order (McCracken, interview with Fr. Bernard Gerbus, March 22, 1997). In a July 19, 1968, letter to Chávez,

Provincial Huser told him that both Virgil and his wife had been reconciled to the Church in every way and their marriage validated. The couple had twelve children, and Fr. Huser gave them one hundred dollars at Easter one year. Fray Angélico replied on July 22 that "Virgil's rehabilitation is the best news I've had in ages! . . . Nor can we discount the intercession of his good father and mother in heaven, for they were real good Catholics. It all makes one very humbly grateful to God for His mercies, as well as preserving us in his 'easy' way of life" ("Troubled Times," Chávez File, Franciscan Archives).

91. Letter from Chávez to Fr. Casey, September 6, 1955, "Summary of Letters, 1937–1970," Chávez File, and letter from Chávez to Fr. Casey, September 7, 1955, "Correspondence with *Chronicle*," Chávez File, Franciscan Archives.

92. Simmons, "Fray Angélico Chávez: The Making of a Maverick Historian," 18.

93. Letter from Chávez to Provincial Kroger, May 23, 1955, "Jemez Pueblo letters, 1955–1960," "Jemez Pueblo, NM, San Diego, Place Files," Franciscan Archives.

94. "Summary of Letters, 1937–1970," Chávez File, Franciscan Archives.

95. Letter from Chávez to Provincial Kroger, May 25, 1956, "Correspondence with Provincial, 1955–1956," Franciscan Archives. Letter from Bynre to Chávez, July 26, 1956, Box 521, File XVII 1956–60, Chávez Collection, Fray Angélico Chávez History Library and Photographic Archives.

96. Letter from Horgan to Chávez, March 8, 1956, Box 521, File XVII 1956–60, Chávez Collection, Fray Angélico Chávez History Library and Photographic Archives.

97. Letter from Vincent Kroger to Fr. Pat MacAuley, June 5, 1956, and letter from Chávez to Provincial Kroger, June 29, 1956, "Summary of Letters, 1937–1970," Chávez File, Franciscan Archives.

98. National Council of Catholic Men, "Close-Up: Fray Angélico Chávez and Mr. Paul Horgan, August 26, 1956," transcript of broadcast, scrapbook of Nora Chávez, Fray Angélico Chávez History Library and Photographic Archives; *Provincial Chronicle* 29, no. 1 (Fall 1956): 99; and "Fr. Angelico Chávez: Missionary—Author—Poet," *Provincial Chronicle* 29, no. 2 (Winter 1957): 157–61.

99. Chávez recounts this episode in "Fr. Angélico Chávez: Missionary—Author—Poet," 160, 161.

100. Letters from Chávez to Provincial Kroger, January 16 and February 1, 1957, "Correspondence with Provincial, 1957–1970," Chávez File, Franciscan Archives.

101. Letter from Chávez to Fr. Edgar Casey, June 22, 1957, "Correspondence with *Chronicle*," Chávez File, Franciscan Archives. Among others, he specifically mentions the rector of the cathedral.

102. Letters from Chávez to the Provincial, March 5 and 26, 1957, "Correspondence with Provincial, 1957–1970," Chávez File, Franciscan Archives.

103. Letter from Chávez to Fr. Casey, July 10, 1957, "Correspondence with *Chronicle*," Chávez File, Franciscan Archives.
104. Letter from Chávez to Provincial Kroger, August 16, 1957, "Correspondence with Provincial, 1957–1970," Chávez File, Franciscan Archives.
105. Letters from Provincial Kroger to Chávez, November 21, 28, and December 9, 1957; from Chávez to the Provincial, November 25, 1957; from Provincial Kroger to Fr. Gabriel Buescher November 21, 1957; from Fr. Roger Huser to Provincial Kroger, December 7, 1957, "Correspondence with Provincial, 1957–1970," Chávez File, Franciscan Archives.
106. Letters from Chávez to the Provincial, December 31, 1957, and January 6, 1958; letter from the Provincial to Chávez, January 3, 1957, "Correspondence with Provincial, 1957–1970," Chávez File, Franciscan Archives. (Chávez likely means twenty-eight years in the habit.)
107. See letters from Chávez to the Provincial, January 25, April 1, and May 24, 1959; letter from Kroger to Chávez, January 28, 1959, "Correspondence with Provincial, 1957–1970," Chávez File, Franciscan Archives.
108. "Fr. Angelico Chávez: Missionary—Author—Poet," 157–61.
109. Letters from Chávez to the Provincial, September 15, 20, and 28, 1959, "Correspondence with Provincial, 1957–1970," Chávez File, Franciscan Archives.
110. Fray Angélico Chávez, "San Francisco De Golden," *Provincial Chronicle* 33, no. 2 (1961): 172; Thomas E. Chávez, "La Iglesia de San Francisco de Paula, or The Church at Golden," unpublished paper.
111. "New Sanctuary at Cerrillos, New Mexico," *Provincial Chronicle* 34, no. 2 (1962): 187–89.
112. Fray Angélico Chávez, "To the Sons of San Fernando Rey," speech at twenty-fifth reunion of the Chávez clan, Nora Chávez scrapbook, Chávez Collection, Fray Angélico Chávez History Library and Photographic Archives; "The Province and Beyond," *Provincial Chronicle* 33, no. 4 (Summer 1961): 507–9. The article includes a picture of new Golden church on page 509, with the caption "The White Dove of the Mountain—San Francisco Chapel, Golden, New Mexico."
113. Letter from Chávez to the Provincial, January 31, 1960, "Correspondence with Provincial, 1957–1970," Chávez File, Franciscan Archives.
114. Ellen McCracken and Mario García, interview with Marc Simmons, August 11, 1996, Cerrillos, New Mexico; Bynner's note to Chávez is in copy number 583 of *New Poems, 1960*.
115. Fr. William Faber, "Missions, Retreats, Etc. Jan-Feb-Mar 1962," *Provincial Chronicle* 34, no. 3 (Spring 1962): 366–69.
116. Fr. Miguel Baca, "Fr. Angelico Chavez, Silver Jubilarian in the Priesthood," *Provincial Chronicle* 35, no. 1 (Fall 1962): 18–21.
117. "Fray Angelico Chavez Honored," *Provincial Chronicle* 35, no. 3 (Spring 1963): 327.

118. Letter from Chávez to Casey, June 17, 1963, "Correspondence with *Chronicle*," Chávez File, Franciscan Archives.
119. Letter from Minister Provincial Sylvan R. Becker to Chávez, May 19, 1964, "Correspondence with Provincial, 1957–1970," Chávez File, Franciscan Archives. For information on the dedication of the friary, see Fr. Howard Meyer, "Holy Family Friary: Albuquerque, New Mexico," *Provincial Chronicle* 36, no. 2 (Winter 1964): 175–78.
120. Letter from Chávez to the Provincial, November 29, 1964, "Correspondence with Provincial, 1957–1970," Franciscan Archives.
121. Undated Christmas greeting card from Chávez to the Provincial and letter from Chávez to the Provincial, December 26, 1964, "Correspondence with Provincial, 1957–1970," Franciscan Archives.
122. "Franciscan Missions in the States of New Mexico, Texas, and Arizona." The paper was written in English, then translated into Latin and published in *Historia missionum, ondinis fratrum minorum, III—America septentrionalis*, Secretariatus Missionum O.F.M. (Rome: Via S. Maria Mediatrice, 25, 1968). Reference courtesy of Fr. Jack Clark Robinson.
123. *The Santa Fe Cathedral of St. Francis of Assisi*, text and format by Fray Angélico Chávez (1947; repr., Santa Fe, NM: Schifani Brothers, 1995), 56.
124. Fray Angélico, however, distanced himself from the term *Chicano* in statements and in his writing.
125. Letter from Tito Meléndez to Francis Tournier, March 26, 1971, Chávez Collection, Fray Angélico Chávez History Library and Photographic Archives.
126. Letter from Chávez to Archbishop Davis, Easter Sunday 1971, Chávez Collection, Fray Angélico Chávez History Library and Photographic Archives.
127. Letter from Provincial Roger Huser to Franciscan Minister General Constantine Koser, August 13, 1974, "Troubled Times," Chávez File, Franciscan Archives.
128. Undated letter from Chávez to Provincial Huser, sent June 30, 1971, "Troubled Times," Chávez File, Franciscan Archives.
129. Letters from Chávez to Provincial Huser, July 6, 1971; Fr. Alfred Pimple, July 19, 1971; Provincial Huser, August 3, 1971; and Fr. Andrew, Aug. 13, 1971, "Troubled Times," Chávez File, Franciscan Archives.
130. Letter from Chávez to Provincial Huser, May 31, 1972, "Troubled Times," Chávez File, Franciscan Archives.
131. Report by Roger Huser, O.F.M., minister provincial, "Santa Fe, N.M.—Cathedral Rectory (Friary)—Feb. 9, 1973," "Troubled Times," Chávez File, Franciscan Archives.
132. Letter from Fray Angélico to Provincial Huser, June 16, 1972 (see also letter to Huser, May 31, 1972) "Troubled Times," Chávez File, Franciscan Archives; letter from the Sacred Congregation of the Doctrine of the Faith to Constantine Koser, Franciscan minister general, February 20, 1975,

"Troubled Times," Chávez File, Franciscan Archives. I thank Viola Miglio for this translation from the Italian of the letter from the Congregation of the Doctrine of the Faith, addressed to Koser:

> Most reverend father: Father Angélico Chávez, consecrated priest of this Order, has requested to be dispensed from all duties deriving from his Sacred Ordination and from his Religious Profession.
>
> After careful scrutiny of all acts and documents submitted to this Sacred Jury, his request was denied, as no motivation was found that would allow for a concession of such grace, given current regulations.
>
> I take this opportunity to express my deepest admiration for you, Reverend Father, and remain very devoutly yours. [signature illegible]

133. Letter to Fred Grillo, January 14, 1972, Box 574, Files 1 and 2, Fray Angélico Chávez Collection, Fray Angélico Chávez History Library and Photographic Archives.
134. Letter from Chávez to Provincial Huser, June 30, 1972, "Troubled Times," Chávez File, Franciscan Archives.
135. Letter to Fred and Marguerite Grillo, July 12, 1974, Box 574, Files 1 and 2, Fray Angélico Chávez Collection, Fray Angélico Chávez History Library and Photographic Archives.
136. Letters from Chávez to Fred Grillo, February 2, 12, and April 30, 1972, Box 574, Files 1 and 2, Fray Angélico Chávez Collection, Fray Angélico Chávez History Library and Photographic Archives.
137. Letter from Chávez to Fred Grillo, February 12, 1972, Box 574, Files 1 and 2, Fray Angélico Chávez Collection, Fray Angélico Chávez History Library and Photographic Archives.
138. Letters from Chávez to Fred and Marguerite Grillo, February 19 and April 19, 1974, and March 31 and April 11, 1972, Box 574, Files 1 and 2, Fray Angélico Chávez Collection, Fray Angélico Chávez History Library and Photographic Archives.
139. Ellen McCracken and Mario García, interviews with Tim Burch, Emily Hughes, and Malcolm Withers, August 12, 14, and 17, 1997, Santa Fe and Raton, New Mexico.
140. Fray Angélico Chávez Collection, Fray Angélico Chávez History Library and Photographic Archives.
141. Letter from Provincial Fox to Fr. Reynaldo Rivera, July 8, 1977, "Troubled Times," Chávez File, Franciscan Archives.
142. Stewart L. Udall, "Remembering Fray Angélico Chávez," *Santa Fe New Mexican*, March 27, 1996, A-7.
143. Father Jerome Martínez y Alire quoted in Thomas E. Chávez, *An Illustrated History of New Mexico* (Niwot, CO: University Press of Colorado, 1992), 239; Thomas E. Chávez, "Memories of Fray Angélico Chávez,"

in *Fray Angélico Chávez: Poet, Priest, and Artist*, ed. Ellen McCracken (Albuquerque: University of New Mexico Press, 1999), 135–40; Ellen McCracken and Mario Garcia, interviews with Fr. Gilbert Schneider, August 6, 1998, and Jaime Baca, August 17, 2000, Albuquerque, New Mexico.

144. Ellen McCracken and Mario García, interviews with Consuelo Chávez, August 19, 1998, and Fr. Salvador Aragón, August 17, 1999, Santa Fe, New Mexico; Fr. Jack Clark Robinson, written summary of unrecorded interview with Fray Angélico Chávez, March 4, 1993.

145. McCracken and García, interviews with Nora Chávez, August 16, 1996, Francisco Chávez, August 19, 1996, and Consuelo Chávez, August 19, 1998.

Chapter Two

1. James Kraft, *Who Is Witter Bynner?: A Biography* (Albuquerque: University of New Mexico Press, 1995); T. M. Pearce, ed., *Literary America: 1903–1934: The Mary Austin Letters* (Westport, CT: Greenwood Press, 1979); and Alice Corbin Henderson, *The Turquoise Trail: An Anthology of New Mexico Poetry* (Boston: Houghton Mifflin, 1928).

2. Edna Robertson and Sarah Nestor, *Artists of the Canyons and Caminos: Santa Fe, the Early Years* (1976; repr., Santa Fe: Ancient City Press, 1996); Marta Weigle and Kyle Fiore, *Santa Fe and Taos: The Writer's Era, 1916–1941* (Santa Fe: Ancient City Press, 1994); Joseph Dispenza and Louise Turner, *Will Shuster: A Santa Fe Legend* (Santa Fe: Museum of New Mexico Press, 1989); and Elmo Baca, *Mabel's Santa Fe and Taos: Bohemian Legends (1900–1950)* (Layton, UT: Gibbs Smith, 2000).

3. See Dispenza and Turner, *Will Shuster*; Robertson and Nestor, *Artists of the Canyons and Caminos*.

4. Witter Bynner, "Alice and I," *New Mexico Quarterly Review* 19 (1949): 38.

5. See Beatrice Chauvenet, *John Gaw Meem: Pioneer in Historic Preservation* (Santa Fe: Historic Santa Fe Foundation and Museum of New Mexico Press, 1985).

6. Fellow seminarian Fr. Bernard Gerbus noted that Chávez insisted that he was Spanish and not Mexican and that he was the first one who went to the seminary from New Mexico and had to go through "this damned German culture." McCracken, interview with Fr. Bernard Gerbus, March 22, 1997.

7. Fray Angélico Chávez, "Fray Angélico Chávez, O.F.M." in *The Book of Catholic Authors*, ed. Walter Romig (Grosse Pointe, MI: Walter Romig, 1943), 61.

8. See Michel de Certeau, *The Practice of Everyday Life*, trans. Steven Rendall (Berkeley: University of California Press, 1984), 24–28.

9. McCracken and García, interview with Nora Chávez, August 16, 1996;

McCracken, interview with Fr. Bernard Gerbus, March 22, 1997; and Phyllis Morales, interview with Fray Angélico Chávez, May 27, 1995, Santa Fe, New Mexico.

10. Chávez dressed as a gaucho for fiesta both in 1926 and 1928. A newspaper article notes that he won the $7.50 first prize for his costume in 1928 ("Street Costume Prizes Given," *Santa Fe New Mexican*, September 2, 1928, 2). Other sources, including Chávez himself, date the prize to 1926. A personal photo album he had bound with the title *Chavez Canticle of the Sun: Franciscan Photos Early Years* displays a photo of Manuel in a gaucho costume with the hand-lettered caption: "Gaucho Chávez they called me in them days—Costume won First Prize, Santa Fiesta—1926." See also *Vivan las fiestas*, ed. Donna Pierce (Santa Fe: Museum of New Mexico Press, 1985), 48, for a picture of Chávez in a gaucho costume at the 1926 fiesta. Both family and personal memory may have conflated the two appearances in noting the date of the prize.

11. "Read—Then Examine the Pictures," *Brown and White* 5 (June 1929): 3.

12. Chávez could not have foreseen the future implication of his remark about the Kaiser dynasty. According to fellow seminarian Fr. Bernard Gerbus, Chávez's friend Virgil Kaiser later abruptly left his position as pastor of St. Joseph Nazareth in Cincinnati, after fathering two children and baptizing them. After leaving the priesthood, he married and ultimately had twelve children. Years later Fray Angélico and his classmate Fr. Leo Pfeiffer attempted to talk to Virgil about coming back to the priesthood but were unsuccessful. McCracken, interview with Fr. Bernard Gerbus, March 22, 1997.

13. "Thanksgiving: After Dinner," *Brown and White* 4 (December 1927): 3.

14. John Penn La Farge, interview with Fray Angélico Chávez, September 14, 1989.

15. The calendar is in the scrapbook of Nora Chávez, Fray Angélico Chávez Collection, Fray Angélico Chávez History Library and Photographic Archives, Santa Fe, New Mexico. For the pen-and-ink drawings of the old missions, see Fray Angélico Chávez, "Old Missions in New Mexico," *St. Anthony Messenger* (March 1934): 532–33. Chávez's painting *By East García* (see figure 1.7) shows striking formal similarities to Vierra's oil painting *Jemez Pueblo Mission* (ca. 1920). For a reproduction of Vierra's painting, see Robertson and Nestor, *Artists of the Canyons and Caminos*, 24.

16. Ellen McCracken and Mario García, interview with Father Godfrey Blank, O.F.M., nephew of Fr. Floribert Blank, August 7, 1997, Santa Fe, New Mexico, and McCracken, interview with Fr. Bernard Gerbus, March 22, 1997.

17. McCracken and García, interview with Fr. Godfrey Blank, August 7, 1997.

18. "Literature," *New Mexico: A Guide to the Colorful State* (New York: Hastings House, 1940), 135.

19. Manuel E. Chávez, "The Wonderland of the Americas," *Brown and White* 2 (January 1926): 1.
20. Chávez, "The Wonderland of the Americas," 3.
21. Chávez, "The Wonderland of the Americas," 3.
22. Manuel E. Chávez, "On the Heights of Eagle Cliff," *Brown and White* 3 (January 1927): 2.
23. Manuel E. Chávez, "A Desert Idyll," *Brown and White* 4 (February 1928): 5.
24. Manuel E. Chávez, "The Tesuque Pony Express," *St. Anthony Messenger* 37 (July 1929): 80.
25. Robertson and Nestor, *Artists of the Canyons and Caminos*, 36; Weigle and Fiore, *Santa Fe and Taos*, 50.
26. Manuel E. Chávez, "Romance of El Caminito," *St. Anthony Messenger* 37 (March 1930): 464.
27. Manuel. E. Chávez, "The Blasphemer," *St. Anthony Messenger* (November 1929): 265, 273.
28. Manuel E. Chávez, " My Ancestor—Don Pedro," *St. Anthony Messenger* 37 (September 1929): 170.
29. Manuel E. Chávez, "Spanish and Irish," *St. Anthony Messenger* 37 (October 1929): 215–16.
30. Manuel E. Chávez, "Old Magdalena's Friend," *St. Anthony Messenger* 37 (December 1929): 313–14.
31. Manuel E. Chávez, "Sierra Moon," *St. Anthony Messenger* 37 (February 1930): 412.
32. Chávez, "Sierra Moon," 412.
33. Chávez, "Sierra Moon," 412.
34. Fray Angélico Chávez, "Notch Twenty-One," *St. Anthony Messenger* 38 (September 1930): 170.
35. Chávez, "Sierra Moon," 411.
36. See *Official Santa Fé Fiesta Program: 1928*, Vertical File collection, Santa Fe Public Library, New Mexico.
37. See Thomas A. Sebeok, *A Sign Is Just a Sign* (Bloomington: Indiana University Press, 1991), 46.
38. Mary Austin criticized Cather for having "given her allegiance to the French blood of the Archbishop; [and having] sympathized with his desire to build a French cathedral in a Spanish town. It was a calamity to the local culture. We have never got over it" (cited in Weigle and Fiore, *Santa Fe and Taos*, 25).
39. F. Chalmers Ayers, "Guitars and Adobes," *St. Anthony Messenger* 39 (June 1931): 21.
40. Ayers, "Guitars and Adobes," 252.
41. Ayers, "Guitars and Adobes," 252.
42. Ayers, "Guitars and Adobes," 250.
43. Ilan Stavans, ed., *The Scroll and the Cross: 1,000 Years of Jewish-Hispanic Literature* (New York: Routledge, 2003).

44. Stavans, ed., *The Scroll and the Cross*, 73.
45. Stavans, ed., *The Scroll and the Cross*, 134.
46. As a mature writer, Chávez published much better informed work on Jews and Jewish biblical traditions, most notably *My Penitente Land* (1974).
47. In 1884 when the *Sodalist* was first published, it was sponsored by a six-hundred-member male sodality at St. Francis Seraph Church in Cincinnati and contained articles both in German and English reflecting the immigrant population. By the time it ceased publication in June 1938, it had broadened its readership to include Catholic secondary schools and academies and all sodalities, and its format was similar to *St. Anthony Messenger*. When Chávez's stories appeared in the *Sodalist* in 1935–37, the editor was Fr. Hyacinth Blocker. See Celestine Baumann, O.F.M., "Notes on *The Sodalist*," *Provincial Chronicle* 15 (Fall 1942): 20–25.
48. An Irish educator named Anne Jellicoe (1823–80) founded the Queen's Technical Training Institute for Women on Molesworth Street in Dublin in 1861 and Alexandra College in 1866. It is unknown if Chávez was familiar with this important Irish figure in women's education.
49. He did have two contributions under his own name in the December 1936 issue: his poem "Christmas Lullaby" appeared on the back cover and the story "Spanish Joan" inside. In a note to his bibliographer, Phyllis Morales, Chávez wrote that he did not remember why he used a pseudonym for these stories. Having discovered a copy of "Winnie the Breadwinner and Saint Anthony" under the name "Monica Lloyd" in his mother's cellar, Chávez wrote to Morales: "Lo & behold! On seeing [the] printed copy, I recognized it as my own. But why I used 'Monica Lloyd' still stumps me! Maybe [it was the] editor's idea." Letter and enclosure to Phyllis Morales from Fray Angélico Chávez, November 5, 1976, Chávez Collection, Fray Angélico Chávez History Library and Photographic Archives.
50. Angélico Chávez, "How to Make Your Own Bookplate," *Sodalist* 52 (September 1936): 14.
51. Chávez, "How to Make Your Own Bookplate," 14.
52. Angélico Chávez, "Time and Tide," *Sodalist* 51 (September 1935): 6.
53. Chávez, "Time and Tide," 7.
54. Ann Jellicoe, "Viola Comes of Age," *Sodalist* 52 (November 1936): 2.
55. The *Sodalist* reproduced a lithograph Gerald Cassidy had done for the February 1935 installment of *Guitars and Adobes* to depict Viola's Spanish dance.
56. Jellicoe, "Viola Comes of Age," 3.
57. Jellicoe, "Viola Comes of Age," 16.
58. Angélico Chávez, "Spanish Joan," *Sodalist* 53 (December 1936): 10.
59. Chávez, "Spanish Joan," 10.
60. Chávez, "Spanish Joan," 11.
61. Ann Jellicoe, "Eve of San Isidro," *Sodalist* 53 (June 1937): 13.
62. Jellicoe, "Eve of San Isidro," 13.

63. Jellicoe, "Eve of San Isidro," 16.
64. Angélico Chávez, "A Stitch in Time," *Sodalist* 2 (April 1936): 7.
65. Ann Jellicoe, "Daily Apple," *Sodalist* 52 (September 1936): 6.
66. Jellicoe, "Daily Apple," 7.
67. Angélico Chávez, "Rolling Stones," *Sodalist* 52 (July 1936): 7.
68. Angélico Chávez, "It's an Ill Wind," *Sodalist* 52 (January 1936): 6.
69. Monica Lloyd, "Winnie the Breadwinner and Saint Anthony," *Sodalist* 54 (June 1938): 8–9.
70. The high school newspaper the *Brown and White* is the first outlet for his poems, where he publishes twenty-nine; one month after graduation he begins to publish his poetry in the Franciscan national magazine *St. Anthony Messenger*.
71. McCracken and García, interview with Bernice Chávez, August 20, 2003. The exact wording of the dedication is taken from the original volume *Cantares*, which is housed in the Fray Angélico Chávez History Library and Photographic Archives.
72. "To you, my dear parents, I give and dedicate the only collection of my poetry, not for you to show to everyone, but for you to keep as a sign of my love and devotion. Manuel, August 16, 1933 (The Day of my Solemn Profession)."
73. W. E. Barrett, "Poet in a Ghost Town," *Catholic Digest* 24 (October 1960): 93–98.
74. Chávez's poem tied for first place with "A la Virgen de la Victoria" by Juan E. Romero of Taos and was printed in a pamphlet sold by the Altar Society to support the erection of the shrine for La Conquistadora in front of the cathedral for the vesper ceremony that opened the fiesta. See "Juan Romero and Manuel Chávez Are Prize Poets," *Santa Fe New Mexican*, August 30, 1928, 4.
75. Manuel Chávez, "Foreign New Mexico," *Santa Fe New Mexican*, August 3, 1928, 4.
76. Chávez, "Foreign New Mexico," 4.
77. Chávez, "Foreign New Mexico," 4.
78. In a handwritten list of publications, Chávez noted that he published "On the Alameda" in *Revista ilustrada* in 1928, and "The Archbishop's Garden" was published in the *Brown and White*, October 1928.
79. Manuel E. Chávez, "Tango," *Santa Fe New Mexican*, July 13, 1929, 2.
80. Chávez, "Tango," 2.
81. Chávez, "Tango," 2.
82. Manuel E. Chávez, "The Deserted Mission," *Brown and White* 4 (February 1928): 5, reprinted in *St. Anthony Messenger* 39 (February 1932): 394.
83. Fray Angélico Chávez, "Pecos Ruins," *St. Anthony Messenger* 41 (December 1933): 348. This poem also appeared in *New Mexico* 15 (March 1937): 25.
84. Chávez, "Pecos Ruins," 348.

85. Chávez, "Pecos Ruins," 348.
86. Fray Angélico Chávez, O.F.M., "The Church of Acoma," *St. Anthony Messenger* 41 (October 1933): 204.
87. Fray Angélico Chávez, "The Mission Guadalupe," in *Cantares: Canticles and Poems of Youth, 1925–1932*, ed. Nasario García (Houston: Arte Público Press, 2000), 17.
88. Fray Angélico Chávez, "The Song of the Padre," in *Cantares: Canticles and Poems of Youth, 1925–1932*, ed. Nasario García (Houston: Arte Público Press, 2000), 18. Since the version in *St. Anthony Messenger* is slightly different from that in *Cantares*, it is likely that the editor of the magazine made a few editorial changes here and in several other poems by Chávez. Here, the first word of the title is changed from *A* to *The*, the word *from* is added before "Letter of Fr. Serra," and quotation marks are added to Serra's phrase quoted at the end of the first and last stanzas.
89. Fray Angélico Chávez, "Fray Serra," in *Cantares: Canticles and Poems of Youth, 1925–1932*, ed. Nasario García (Houston: Arte Público Press, 2000), 20.
90. Manuel E. Chávez, "Cinquains to the Padre," *St. Anthony Messenger* 37 (July 1929): 88.
91. "Father Eligius Drowns Trying to Save Child," *Santa Fe New Mexican*, May 30, 1927, 1; "Hero-Priest, Father Eligius to Be Buried Thursday," *Santa Fe New Mexican*, May 31, 1927, 1; "Archbishop, Many Priests and 1,000 Children Attend Ernestina Chavez's Funeral," *Santa Fe New Mexican*, June 1, 1927, 6; "Thousands Pay Reverence to Memory of Hero-Priest Who Died Trying to Save Child," *Santa Fe New Mexican*, June 2, 1927, 2.
92. Manuel E. Chávez, "In Memoriam," *Santa Fe New Mexican*, June 14, 1929, 1.
93. Chávez, "In Memoriam," 1.
94. See for example, "The Hiders" and "Sonnet (Calderón)," "Wake Me the Birds," with an epigraph from Fray Luis de León's *Vida retirado*, and "Giralda."
95. Mark P. O. Morford and Robert J. Lenardon, *Classical Mythology*, 7th ed. (New York: Oxford University Press, 2003), 614–15.
96. Fray Angélico Chávez, "Cantares," in *Cantares: Canticles and Poems of Youth, 1925–1932*, ed. Nasario García (Houston: Arte Público Press, 2000), 3; Fray Angélico Chávez, "Singing Cowboy," in *Clothed with the Sun* (Santa Fe, NM: Writers' Editions, 1939), 34.
97. It is likely that Chávez composed the poem "Cantares" in late 1932 to tie together the poems he had gathered in the book. Shortly before his solemn profession as a Franciscan, it is not surprising that he would attempt to assert his religious identity over his poetic one. In contrast, "Pegasus," was most likely written earlier and focuses his concerns with the aesthetic toward classical mythology overlain with imagery of the Southwest.

98. Fray Angélico Chávez, "Pegasus," in *Cantares: Canticles and Poems of Youth, 1925–1932*, ed. Nasario García (Houston: Arte Público Press, 2000), 4.
99. Chávez, "Pegasus," 4.
100. Chávez, "A Poet's House," 5.
101. Fray Angélico Chávez, "The Rondeau," in *Cantares: Canticles and Poems of Youth, 1925–1932*, ed. Nasario García (Houston: Arte Público Press, 2000), 112.
102. Witter Bynner Collection, bMS Am 1891.28 (652), Houghton Library, Harvard University, Cambridge, Massachusetts.
103. Fray Angélico Chávez, "To Witter Bynner," in *Cantares: Canticles and Poems of Youth, 1925–1932*, ed. Nasario García (Houston: Arte Público Press, 2000), 92. Chávez would entitle his own 1931 play *The Beloved Crusader*.
104. Chávez, "To Witter Bynner," 93.
105. Manuel E. Chávez, "The Desert Artist," *St. Anthony Messenger* 37 (September 1929): 154.
106. Fray Angélico Chávez, "The Painting Poet," in *Cantares: Canticles and Poems of Youth, 1925–1932*, ed. Nasario García (Houston: Arte Público Press, 2000), 7.
107. Chávez, "The Painting Poet," 7.
108. For further study of the interrelation of the visual and verbal throughout Chávez's work, and a color reproduction of *Burros*, see Ellen McCracken, "Iconicity and Narrative in the Work of Fray Angélico Chávez: Toward the Harmonious Imagetext," in *Fray Angélico Chávez: Poet, Priest, and Artist*, ed. Ellen McCracken, 53–90 (Albuquerque: University of New Mexico Press, 2000).
109. Fray Angélico Chávez, "Calle de Amargura," *America* 56 (February 20, 1937): 476.
110. Chávez, "Calle de Amargura," 476.
111. [Fray Angélico Chávez], *The Beloved Crusader: A Historical Drama of the Life of St. Anthony of Padua, by the Friars of Duns Scotus College, Detroit, Michigan* (Cincinnati: St. Anthony Messenger, 1931). I thank Fr. Dan Anderson, O.F.M., for making the play and program available to me.
112. "A Chronological Journal of Duns Scotus College, Detroit," 1930–1933, Franciscan Archives.
113. Souvenir Program, *The Beloved* (Detroit: Duns Scotus College), 19.
114. Chávez, *The Beloved Crusader*, 32–33.
115. Chávez recounts in an interview that when he was a boy, an old French Christian brother, Brother Joseph, came from the novitiate in Las Vegas to recruit for his order. Manuel told him he wanted to become a Franciscan, and Brother Joseph told him that the Franciscans did not take Mexicans. See John Penn La Farge, "From Mora to the Mission: Fray Angélico Chávez," in *Turn Left at the Sleeping Dog* (Albuquerque: University of New Mexico Press, 2001), 39.

Chapter Three

1. Letter from John Gould Fletcher to Fray Angélico Chávez, April 3, 1949, Chávez Collection, Box 520, File II, Fray Angélico Chávez History Library and Photographic Archives, Santa Fe, New Mexico.
2. Having been given special dispensation to be ordained in the Santa Fe cathedral, he returned to Oldenburg, Indiana, to finish the last weeks of the academic year on May 15, 1937, and on June 4 went to Cincinnati until the Chapter meeting. On July 13 he was assigned to Peña Blanca (Occupation Card, Chávez File, Franciscan Archives, Cincinnati, Ohio).
3. In his 1989 book *Chávez: A Distinctive American Clan of New Mexico* (54), Fray Angélico names his ancestor in the reconquest as Alférez Real Don Fernando Durán y Chaves who carried the royal Remedios standard on horseback. He designed his ordination card before conducting extensive research on his ancestors.
4. From 1937 ordination card, Nora Chávez scrapbook, Chávez collection, Fray Angélico Chávez History Library and Photographic Archives, and Chávez File, Franciscan Archives. "Impendam et superimpendar" (2 Corinthians 12:15a) is literally translated, "I will expend (myself) and I will be exceedingly spent." The *New English Bible* translation is "I would gladly spend everything, for you—yes and spend myself to the limit." I thank the Reverends Michael McCarthy, S.J., and Francis Smith, S.J., of Santa Clara University for providing me with these translations.
5. Letter from Chávez to Provincial Ripperger, September 15, 1937, "Correspondence with the Provincial, 1937–1946," Franciscan Archives.
6. Letter from Provincial Ripperger to Chávez, October 15, 1937, "Correspondence with the Provincial, 1937–1946," Franciscan Archives.
7. Other Catholic publication venues in this period include *Spirit*, the *Franciscan, Extension, Franciscan Herald*, the *Sentinel of the Blessed Sacrament*, and the *Sign*.
8. Fray Angélico Chávez, "Cross of the Martyrs," *New Mexico* 15 (August 1937): 26.
9. Fray Angélico Chávez, "Litany of Pueblos," *New Mexico* 16 (July 1938): 24.
10. Fray Angélico Chávez, "Adventures in Cíbola," *New Mexico Sentinel*, June 12, 1938.
11. Fray Angélico Chávez, foreword to *Selected Poems: With an Apologia* (Santa Fe, NM: Press of the Territorian, 1969), np.
12. Fray Angélico Chávez, "Southwest Sunset," *New Mexico Sentinel*, June 12, 1938.
13. Fray Angélico Chávez, "Christ at the Well," *Commonweal* 27 (November 12, 1937): 66.
14. Fray Angélico Chávez, "Mulier amicta sole," *Commonweal* 27 (April 15, 1938): 689.

15. Letters from Long to Chávez, April 29 and July 18, 1938, Chávez Collection, Fray Angélico Chavez History Library and Photographic Archives. White's full name was Amelia Elizabeth White.
16. "Poets Round Up Ten of Their Number and Two Guests for Program August 6," newspaper clipping, Nora Chávez album, Chávez Collection, Fray Angélico Chávez History Library and Photographic Archives.
17. T. M. Pearce, *Alice Corbin Henderson* (Austin, TX: Steck-Vaughn, 1969), 29–31. (I thank Kathleen Campos for giving me this article.)
18. "Bynner to Read for 10th Time at 10th Poets' Roundup," *Santa Fe New Mexican*, August 4, 1939.
19. Letter from Long to Chávez, August 14, 1938, Chávez Collection, Fray Angélico Chávez History Library and Photographic Archives.
20. Fray Angélico Chávez, "A Dance at Cochiti," *New Mexico Sentinel*, October 2, 1938.
21. Fray Angélico Chávez, "Birds," *New Mexico Sentinel*, October 2, 1938.
22. Fray Angélico Chávez, "Prisoner," in *Cantares: Canticles and Poems of Youth, 1925–1932*, ed. Nasario García (Houston: Arte Público Press, 2000), 117.
23. Fray Angélico Chávez, "Ecce ancilla," *New Mexico Sentinel*, October 2, 1938.
24. Fray Angélico Chávez, "This Winter Day," *New Mexico Sentinel*, October 2, 1938.
25. Viktor Shklovsky, "Art as Technique," in *Russian Formalist Criticism: Four Essays*, trans. Lee T. Lemon and Marion J. Reis (Lincoln: University of Nebraska Press, 1965), 3–24.
26. Fray Angélico Chávez, "Sunlight," *New Mexico Sentinel*, October 2, 1938.
27. Fray Angélico Chávez, "Whose Broken Heart Is Brave," *New Mexico Sentinel*, October 2, 1938 (later published in *St. Anthony Messenger*, April 1942, and *Eleven Lady-Lyrics*, 1945).
28. Fray Angélico Chávez, "A Caballero Recalls Lamy," in *Eleven Lady-Lyrics* (Paterson, NJ: St. Anthony Guild Press, 1945), 83.
29. Chávez, "A Caballero Recalls Lamy," *New Mexico Sentinel*, December 4, 1938.
30. Letters from Wilder to Chávez, September 26, 1938, and January 9, 1939, Chávez Collection, Fray Angélico Chávez History Library and Photographic Archives.
31. Fray Angélico Chávez, "Peña Blanca," *Spirit* 5 (January 1939): 167.
32. Fray Angélico Chávez, "Grey," *Spirit* 6 (May 1939): 45.
33. A letter to Chávez from Charlie May Fletcher (December 19, 1939, Chávez Collection, Box 520, File II, Fray Angélico Chávez History Library and Photographic Archives) refers to their attending the play and dances the previous year.
34. Letter from Chávez to Provincial Maurice Ripperger, March 6, 1939, "Correspondence with the Provincial, 1937–1946," Franciscan Archives.

35. Letter from Chávez to Provincial Adalbert Rolfes, July 15, 1939, "Correspondence with the Provincial, 1937–1946," Franciscan Archives.
36. "A Report on Father Angélico's Books," sent by Chávez to Fr. John Forest McGee, editor, *Provincial Chronicle*, page 2, with accompanying letter dated April 17, 1941, "Correspondence with *Chronicle*," Chávez File, Franciscan Archives.
37. Advertisement, *St. Anthony Messenger* 47 (December 1939): 57.
38. Letter from Fletcher to Chávez, February 27, 1940, Chávez Collection, Box 520, File II, Fray Angélico Chávez History Library and Photographic Archives.
39. Fray Angélico Chávez, *Clothed with the Sun* (Santa Fe, NM: Writers' Editions, 1939).
40. Chávez, *Clothed with the Sun*, 20.
41. "A Report on Father Angelico's Books," p. 1. Letters from Wilder to Chávez, September 26, 1938, and January 9, 1939, Chávez Collection, Fray Angélico Chávez History Library and Photographic Archives.
42. Chávez, *Clothed with the Sun*, 45.
43. Chávez, *Clothed with the Sun*, 49.
44. Chávez, *Clothed with the Sun*, 14.
45. Chávez, *Clothed with the Sun*, 29, 28.
46. Chávez, *Clothed with the Sun*, 27.
47. Fray Angélico Chávez, "Carrie's Notion," *St. Anthony Messenger* 45 (June 1937): 32ff.
48. Arthur Chapman, "Beads," *St. Anthony Messenger* 45 (August 1937): 140ff.
49. Fray Angélico Chávez, "Mateo Makes Money," *St. Anthony Messenger* 45 (November 1937): 346.
50. Fray Angélico Chávez, "Honest Art," *St. Anthony Messenger* 45 (February 1938): 562–64.
51. Editorial tagline, Fray Angélico Chávez, "The Penitente Thief," *St. Anthony Messenger* 45 (April 1938): 649.
52. See "The Editor Apologizes," *St. Anthony Messenger* 46 (July 1938): 59–60.
53. Letters from Long to Chávez, April 29, August 14, and October 7, 1938, Chávez Collection, Fray Angélico Chávez History Library and Photographic Archives.
54. Letter from John Gould Fletcher to Chávez from Memphis, Tennessee, June 14, 1940, Chávez Collection, Box 520, File II, Fray Angélico Chávez History Library and Photographic Archives.
55. Chávez's entry in the Peña Blanca House Chronicle, December 4, 1939: "The mural stations of the cross in this church were completed two weeks ago after three months of labor, May, October and November. They will not be dedicated until Lent." I thank Fr. Jack Clark Robinson, O.F.M., and the Very Reverend Larry Dunham for providing me with the sections

of the Peña Blanca House Chronicle (Chronologium Domus ad BVM de Guadalupe-Petralbe, Peña Blanca) Vol. II, 1937–51, written by Chávez from 1939 to 1943, St. Michael's Friary Archives, St. Michael's, Arizona.

56. Fray Angélico Chávez, *New Mexico Triptych; Being Three Panels and Three Accounts: 1. The Angel's New Wings; 2. The Penitente Thief; 3. Hunchback Madonna*, illustrated by the author (Paterson, NJ: St. Anthony Guild Press, 1940), 14. For a current reprint of these and selected other stories by Fray Angélico, see *The Short Stories of Fray Angélico Chávez*, ed. Genaro M. Padilla (Albuquerque: University of New Mexico Press, 1987) and *Guitars and Adobes and the Uncollected Stories of Fray Angélico Chávez*, ed. Ellen McCracken (Santa Fe: Museum of New Mexico Press, 2009).

57. Chávez, *New Mexico Triptych*, 15.

58. Chávez, *New Mexico Triptych*, 17.

59. Chávez's choice for his characters of two exceptional Penitentes who are sinful was perhaps influenced by the childhood experience he recounts in *My Penitente Land* (1974) in which he and another boy teased an upright member of the brotherhood with a song about a Penitente who had stolen a cow. His mother carefully explained that although a few Penitentes were not good outside of Lent, most were honest people.

60. Chávez, *New Mexico Triptych*, 25.

61. Chávez, *New Mexico Triptych*, 35.

62. For a description of this tradition in Santa Fe in the 1920s, see Anita Gonzales Thomas, "Before the War," in *Turn Left at the Sleeping Dog: Scripting the Santa Fe Legend, 1920–1955*, ed. John Pen La Farge (Albuquerque: University of New Mexico Press, 2001), 95–96.

63. See Ellen McCracken, ed., *Fray Angélico Chávez: Poet, Priest, and Artist* (Albuquerque: University of New Mexico Press, 2000), 140, for a reproduction of this self-portrait.

64. Letter from Chávez to Provincial Maurice Ripperger, September 15, 1937, "Correspondence with the Provincial, 1937–1946," Chávez File, Franciscan Archives. He refers to the townspeople who will help with the renovation as "Mexican" to distinguish the town of Domingo Station from Santo Domingo Pueblo where he also ministered.

65. See "A Little Gem at Domingo," *Provincial Chronicle* 10 (April 1938): 93–94.

66. "A Little Gem at Domingo," 94, and Peña Blanca House Chronicle, February 6, 1938.

67. Photograph, "Interior of the Spanish Mission of St. Dorothy, Domingo, New Mexico (Peña Blanca Parish)," January 1949, "Peña Blanca Place File," Franciscan Archives. On the reverse of the 1939 photograph of the newly remodeled interior of the church, handwriting that appears to be that of Fray Angélico notes, "Interior of St. Dorothy's, Domingo, N.M. Crucifix is a home-made copy of San Damiano's crucifix made by P. Angelico Chavez, 1939." In his entry in the Peña Blanca House Chronicle, November 29,

1938, Fray Angélico writes, "Copy of San Damiano Crucifix installed and dedicated at St. Dorothy's in Domingo, . . . Vespers sung by the [Peña Blanca] choir with Fr. Eugene from Cerrillos as celebrant." Beneath the entry he drew a small image of the crucifix he had made for the chapel.

68. "About the Province," *Provincial Chronicle* 11, no. 2 (Winter 1938 [*sic*:1939]): 84.
69. Peña Blanca House Chronicle, September 1938 (no day written).
70. Peña Blanca House Chronicle, December 10, 1938.
71. "And this our life exempt from public haunt / Finds tongues in trees, books in the running brooks, / Sermons in stones and good in every thing" (*As You Like It*, act 2, scene 1). In 1927 Chávez published a poem developing Shakespeare's metaphor further in the seminary magazine: "Sermons in Stone," *Brown and White* 3 (April 1927): 3. Another seminarian quoted Shakespeare's phrase in "Apologia pro dementia nostra," an article in the same issue of the seminary magazine; it is likely that the seminarians read *As You Like It* at the time or that their teachers referred to these lines from Shakespeare. Fray Angélico termed his renovation of the church at Golden in 1961 a "sermon in stone."
72. Letter from Chávez to Provincial Rolfes, July 28, 1939, "Correspondence with the Provincial, 1937–1946," Franciscan Archives.
73. See M. Yamashita, "Fray Angélico Chávez: The Murals at Peña Blanca," *Traditions Southwest* (Spring 1991): 9–10; Harold Butcher, "Re-creating a Spanish Mission: Priest, Poet and Painter," *Travel* 80 (March 1943): 20–21; Ina Sizer Cassidy, "Fray Angélico Chávez," in "Art and Artists of New Mexico," *New Mexico* 18 (March 1940): 27, 46; Robert Huber, "Fray Angélico Chávez: 20th Century Renaissance Man," *New Mexico* 48 (March–April 1979): 18–23; Jim Newton, "Fray Angélico's Artistic Ability Reflected in Church," *Albuquerque Journal*, August 31, 1969, C1; "Young Franciscan Paints His Own Church," *St. Anthony Messenger* 47 (May 1940): 21; Ben Gallegos, "Fray Angélico as Muralist," *Santa Fe New Mexican*, July 9, 1972, 3–4; and Fabián Chávez, "Fray Angélico and the Stations of the Cross," *La Herencia* (Spring 1998): 34–35.
74. See, "Cuadros at Peña Blanca Revisited," *Provincial Chronicle* 41, no. 1B (1969–70): 118–26.
75. See letter of invitation to the Provincial Minister from Fr. Robert Kalt, O.F.M., January 5, 1940, "Peña Blanca Place File," Franciscan Archives.
76. McCracken and García, interview with Jaime Baca, August 17, 2000.
77. McCracken and García, interview with Lorenzo Armijo and Darlene Ortiz, August 6, 2002, Peña Blanca, New Mexico.
78. McCracken and García, interview with Jaime Baca, August 17, 2000.
79. Fray Angélico Chávez, "To Rebecca Dead," *Spirit* 6 (November 1939): 140. For a picture of Rebecca, see Virginia E. Quintana de Ortiz, *Tradition and Heritage: A History of the Parish of Our Lady of Guadalupe in Blanca, New Mexico* (Albuquerque, NM: LPD Press, 2007), 21.

80. See Fray Angélico's entries in the Peña Blanca House Chronicle, August 13, 14, 1940; January 16, February 13, March 12, and April 15, 1941.
81. Butcher, "Re-creating a Spanish Mission," 21.
82. Letter from Chávez to Fr. John Forest McGee, Ash Wednesday, March 1941, "Correspondence with *Chronicle*," Chávez File, Franciscan Archives. Chávez also notes that the article about the renovations in the *New Mexico Register* was wrong: "All hooey—there simply ain't no such tower!" In his March 14, 1941, reply, Fr. McGee remarks, "Received your note just too late to delete the short notice in the *Chronicle* that I culled from the *Register*. . . . Keep up your good work and make a real masterpiece of the Pena Blanca church."
83. Fray Angélico's entries in the Peña Blanca House Chronicle, September 1 and December 12, 1940.
84. Entries in the Peña Blanca House Chronicle, April 23, June 4, August 28, September 8, October 4, and November 5, 1941.
85. Chávez letter to editor of the *Provincial Chronicle*, October 23, 1941, "Correspondence with *Chronicle*," Chávez File, Franciscan Archives.
86. McCracken and García, interview with Jaime Baca, August 17, 2000. Bertille Baca, "Stories I Remember about Father Angélico Chávez," manuscript kindly shared by Bertille Baca.
87. See John L. Kessell, *The Missions of New Mexico since 1776* (Albuquerque: University of New Mexico Press, 1980), 130, fig. 115.
88. McCracken and García, interview with Mónica Sosaya Halford, August 18, 1998.
89. Jaime Baca recounted the "monos" anecdote in an interview with McCracken and García, August 17, 2000. Thomas Chávez and other family members recount that Fray Angélico was devastated after the destruction of the murals.
90. *Albuquerque Journal*, January 2, 1986.
91. Rosemary Lynch, "Pena Blanca Benediction," *Santa Fe New Mexican*, August 3, 1986.
92. Lynch, "Pena Blanca Benediction."
93. Father Jerome Martínez, cited in Michael Moquin, "The Adobe Quagmire: New Mexico's Endangered Churches," *Traditions Southwest* 1, no. 1 (Fall 1989): 24.
94. Letter from Chávez to Provincial, August 7, 1940, "Correspondence with the Provincial, 1937–1946," Franciscan Archives.
95. *Provincial Chronicle* 11, no. 2 (Winter 1938): 81.
96. Fray Angélico Chávez, "Everything to the Poor," *St. Anthony Messenger* 45 (September 1937): 208.
97. Fray Angélico Chávez, "In Our Midst," *St. Anthony Messenger* 45 (October 1937): 267.
98. Fray Angélico Chávez, "Spend and Be Spent," *St. Anthony Messenger* 45 (February 1938): 526.

99. Fray Angélico Chávez, "Social Outcasts," *St. Anthony Messenger* 46 (June 1938): 30.
100. Letters from Fr. Erbacher to Fray Angélico, November 20, 1938, and from Fr. Forest to Fr. Erbacher, October 17, 1939, Chávez File, Franciscan Archives.
101. Fr. Sebastian Erbacher, O.F.M., ed., *Seraphic Days: Franciscan Thoughts and Affections on the Principal Feasts of Our Lord and Our Lady and All the Saints of the Three Orders of the Seraph of Assisi* (Detroit, MI: Duns Scotus College, 1940), 95.
102. Erbacher, ed., *Seraphic Days*, 69.
103. "Retain Embargo, Priest Says," undated newspaper article, Nora Chávez scrapbook, Chávez Collection, Fray Angélico Chávez History Library and Photographic Archives.
104. Erbacher, ed., *Seraphic Days*, 2.
105. Erbacher, ed., *Seraphic Days*, 15.
106. Erbacher, ed., *Seraphic Days*, 73.
107. Erbacher, ed., *Seraphic Days*, 45.
108. Erbacher, ed., *Seraphic Days*, 15.
109. From its inception through May 1939 (except from September to December 1935) the column was titled "From Out of the Centuries"; thereafter the title was shortened to "Out of the Centuries." Robert Ripley's "Believe It or Not" cartoon was first published in the *New York Globe* in 1918 and became the world's longest-running syndicated newspaper cartoon. It pictured and recounted bizarre bits of information from around the world. Especially popular in the 1920s and 1930s, the cartoon inspired Fray Angélico to disseminate information on Franciscan history through a similar visual/verbal medium.
110. "Out of the Centuries," *St. Anthony Messenger*: October 1939, 53; August 1940, 57; September 1937, 237; April 1936, 688; and November 1935, 364.
111. "Out of the Centuries," *St. Anthony Messenger* 44 (January 1937): 482.
112. "From Out of the Centuries," *St. Anthony Messenger* 42 (May 1935): 738.
113. Fray Angélico Chávez, "Santo Domingo," *Provincial Chronicle* 14, no. 1 (Fall 1941): 7. The article continues in the following issue: *Provincial Chronicle* 14, no. 2 (Winter 1942): 91–98, although the date is misprinted on the issue as "Winter 1941."
114. Fray Angélico Chávez, "Santo Domingo," *Provincial Chronicle* 14, no. 1 (Fall 1941): 11–12.
115. His nephew, historian Thomas E. Chávez, completed the volume published posthumously in 2004: *Wake for a Fat Vicar: Father Juan Felipe Ortiz, Archbishop Lamy, and the New Mexican Catholic Church in the Middle of the Nineteenth Century* (Albuquerque, NM: LPD Press, 2004).
116. Fray Angélico Chávez, "Apology to a Long-Dead Priest," *Provincial Chronicle* 25, no. 1 (Fall 1952): 44.
117. Chávez, "Apology to a Long-Dead Priest," 45.

118. Letter from Chávez to Fr. John Forest, March 21, 1941, "Correspondence with the *Chronicle*," Chávez File, Franciscan Archives.
119. Chávez, "Santo Domingo," *Provincial Chronicle* 14, no. 2 (Winter 1942) 93, 97, 95–96.
120. Chávez, "Santo Domingo," *Provincial Chronicle* 14, no. 2 (Winter 1942) 93.
121. Chávez, "Santo Domingo," *Provincial Chronicle* 14, no. 2 (Winter 1942) 93.
122. Chávez, "Santo Domingo," *Provincial Chronicle* 14, no. 2 (Winter 1942) 96.
123. Chávez, "Santo Domingo," *Provincial Chronicle* 14, no. 2 (Winter 1942) 97.
124. Chávez, "Santo Domingo," *Provincial Chronicle* 14, no. 2 (Winter 1942) 93, my emphasis.
125. Chávez, "Santo Domingo," *Provincial Chronicle* 14, no. 1 (Fall 1941) 13.
126. Chávez, "Santo Domingo," *Provincial Chronicle* 14, no. 2 (Winter 1942) 97.
127. Chávez, "Santo Domingo," *Provincial Chronicle* 14, no. 2 (Winter 1942) 96.
128. "Congratulations on your re-election!" July 20, 1942, "Correspondence with the Provincial, 1937–1946," Chávez File, Franciscan Archives.
129. Letters from Chávez to Provincial Rolfes, August 12 and 19, 1942, "Correspondence with the Provincial, 1937–1946," Franciscan Archives. See also letters in the same file from Chávez to Fr. Herbert Klosterkemper, Provinical Secretary, July 29 and August 3, 1942, requesting an imprimatur from the Cincinnati archbishop and Fr. Herbert's August 6 response.
130. Letter from Fr. Jerome Hesse to Provincial Rolfes, July 28, 1940, "Correspondence with the Provincial, 1937–1946," Franciscan Archives.
131. Letter from Chávez to Archbishop Gerken, July 29, 1940, "Correspondence with the Provincial, 1937–1946," Franciscan Archives.
132. Letter from Chávez to Provincial Rolfes, July 29, 1940, "Correspondence with the Provincial, 1937–1946," Franciscan Archives.
133. Letter from Chávez to Fr. Robert Kalt, August 12, 1942, "Correspondence with the Provincial, 1937–1946," Franciscan Archives.
134. Letter from Fr. Robert Kalt to Provincial Rolfes, July 29, 1942, "Correspondence with the Provincial, 1937–1946," Franciscan Archives.
135. Letter from Wilder to Chávez, May 2, 1940, Chávez Collection, Fray Angélico Chávez History Library and Photographic Archives.

Chapter Four

1. Ellen McCracken and Mario García, interview with Eliseo Rodríguez, August 13, 2001, Santa Fe, New Mexico, and Carmen Padilla, *Eliseo Rodríguez: El Sexto Pintor* (Santa Fe: Museum of New Mexico Press, 2001).
2. Letter from Fletcher to Chávez, July 31, 1940, "Letters of John Gould Fletcher," Box 520, File II, Chávez Collection, Fray Angélico Chávez History Library and Photographic Archives.
3. Letter from Fletcher to Chávez, December 15, 1941, "Letters of John Gould Fletcher," Box 520, File II, Chávez Collection, Fray Angélico Chávez History Library and Photographic Archives.

4. Letter from Fletcher to Chávez, July 31, 1942, "Letters of John Gould Fletcher," Box 520, File II, Chávez Collection, Fray Angélico Chávez History Library and Photographic Archives.
5. Reprinted in Julia Keleher, "Los Paisanos," *New Mexico Quarterly Review* 12 (May 1942): 256. Information about the Conference on Folk Art and Literature also appears in this article.
6. Fray Angélico Chávez, "Whose Broken Heart Is Brave," *St. Anthony Messenger* 49 (April 1942): 18.
7. Fray Angélico Chávez, *Eleven Lady-Lyrics* (Paterson, NJ: St. Anthony Guild, 1945), 3. In the interest of readers' access to the poems quoted in this chapter, I cite their references from the book *Eleven Lady-Lyrics*, rather than the original magazines such as *America* or *St. Anthony Messenger*.
8. See www.raf.mod.uk/history/line1942.html
9. Chávez, *Eleven Lady-Lyrics*, 6.
10. Chávez, *Eleven Lady-Lyrics*, 6.
11. Chávez, *Eleven Lady-Lyrics*, 5.
12. Chávez, *Eleven Lady-Lyrics*, 5.
13. See Chávez, "With Fr. Angélico in the Service," *Provincial Chronicle* 19 (June 1947): 64–72.
14. Chávez, "With Fr. Angélico in the Service," 64–72, and June 12, 1943, letter from Chávez to Franciscan Provincial, "Chaplain's Correspondence, 1942–1946," Franciscan Archives.
15. Chávez, *Eleven Lady-Lyrics*, 52.
16. Chávez, *Eleven Lady-Lyrics*, 52.
17. Chávez, *Eleven Lady-Lyrics*, 53.
18. Fray Angélico Chávez, "Noche Buena," *Indian Sentinel* 23, no. 10 (December 1943): 147–51.
19. Chávez, "Noche Buena," 147.
20. Chávez, "Noche Buena," 147.
21. Chávez, "Noche Buena," 148.
22. Chávez, *Eleven Lady-Lyrics*, 25.
23. Chávez, *Eleven Lady-Lyrics*, 4.
24. Chávez, *Eleven Lady-Lyrics*, 4.
25. Chávez, "With Fr. Angélico in the Service," 67.
26. McCracken and García, interviews with Francisco Chávez, August 17 1999, and Dr. Randolph Seligman, August 12, 1999, Albuquerque; *77th Division Reunion Program*, August 1987.
27. Fray Angélico Chávez, "Good News from Guam," *St. Anthony Messenger* 52 (October 1944): 24–25.
28. Copy of report in Chávez File, "Chaplain's Correspondence, 1942–1946," Franciscan Archives. The information about the lost book outline appeared in a letter from Chávez to Provincial Mollaun, November 14, 1945, "Chaplain's Correspondence, 1942–1946," Franciscan Archives.

29. Chávez, "With Fr. Angélico in the Service," 70; letters from Chávez to Provincial, September 6 and October 2, 1944, "Chaplain's Correspondence, 1942–1946," Franciscan Archives.
30. Chávez, *Eleven Lady-Lyrics*, 13.
31. Chávez, "With Fr. Angélico in the Service," 70.
32. Chávez, "With Fr. Angélico in the Service," 71.
33. Capt. (Ch.) Angélico Chávez, "Christmas on Leyte," *St. Anthony Messenger* 52 (March 1945): 27.
34. Chávez, "Christmas on Leyte," 27, and "Monthly Report of Chaplain," December 1944, "Chaplain's Correspondence, 1942–1946," Franciscan Archives.
35. "Monthly Report of Chaplain," December 1944, and handwritten note at the bottom of "Report to Province," December 1944, "Chaplain's Correspondence, 1942–1946," Chávez File, Franciscan Archives.
36. See theworld.com/~dduncan/poetry/mothercarey.html.
37. Chávez, *Eleven Lady-Lyrics*, 49.
38. Chávez, *Eleven Lady-Lyrics*, 17.
39. Chávez, *Eleven Lady-Lyrics*, 10.
40. Chávez, *Eleven Lady-Lyrics*, 50.
41. Chávez, *Eleven Lady-Lyrics*, 50.
42. Chávez, *Eleven Lady-Lyrics*, 8.
43. Chávez, *Eleven Lady-Lyrics*, 8.
44. Fray Angélico Chávez, "God Provides for Home and Nation," *St. Anthony Messenger* 52 (January 1945): 15.
45. Letters from Chávez to Fr. Romuald, January 2 and 18, 1946, "Chaplain's Correspondence, 1942–1946," Franciscan Archives.
46. May Sarton, *A World of Light* (New York: Norton, 1976), 136.
47. Letter from Chávez to Provincial Rolfes, April 14, 1945, "Chaplain's Correspondence, 1942–1946," Franciscan Archives.
48. Letter from Chávez to Provincial Rolfes, April 27, 1945, "Chaplain's Correspondence, 1942–1946," Franciscan Archives.
49. Chávez, *Eleven Lady-Lyrics*, viii.
50. Chávez, *Eleven Lady-Lyrics*, vii.
51. Chávez, *Eleven Lady-Lyrics*, 7.
52. Chávez, *Eleven Lady-Lyrics*, 9.
53. Virgil, *The Aeneid*, trans. Robert Fitzgerald (New York: Random House, 1983), 3.
54. Chávez, *Eleven Lady-Lyrics*, 11.
55. Chávez, *Eleven Lady-Lyrics*, 11.
56. The great wars of the twentieth century have reminded others of the ancient epics. Born in the same year as Fray Angélico Chávez, poet and translator Robert Fitzgerald recounts his first complete reading of the *Aeneid* during the last months of World War II when he was stationed in the Philippines. Unlike Chávez, as a staff officer he had a "commodious Quonset hut" in

which to read by the light of a good lamp to combat his boredom. As he describes his circumstances through the optic of Virgil's poem, he notes, "The scene could not have been more imperial or more civilized," admitting, however, that "a good many young and brave on both sides were tasting the agony and abomination that the whole show came down to, in fact existed for" (Robert Fitzgerald, postscript to *The Aeneid*, by Virgil, trans. Robert Fitzgerald [New York: Random House, 1983], 414). In a completely different vein, Ambrose Bierce's poem with the same title as Fray Angélico's criticizes the association of Christianity with war and the notion "of a brass-buttoned Jesus firing guns." Fray Angélico's poem shows more affinity to Fitzgerald's thinking than that of Bierce.

57. Chávez, *Eleven Lady-Lyrics*, 12.
58. Chávez, *Eleven Lady-Lyrics*, 14.
59. According to William E. Barrett in a 1960 interview with Fray Angélico, a poem Chávez wrote when he was seventeen was published in *America*. See "Poet in a Ghost Town," *Catholic Digest*, October 1960. He notes that this poem was later included in an anthology edited by Alfred Noyes. (The poem was "Esther.")
60. In *St. Anthony Messenger*: "Lullaby" ("Christmas Lullaby," December 1932), "St. Paschal" (May 1933), "Victus" (October 1935), "Ladies of St. Francis" (May 1937), "Prayer for the Nations" (June 1937), and "Goldfish" (May 1938); in *Spirit*: "Drama of Dramas" (July 1938), "Mary" (July 1939), "Shepherds" (September 1939), "To Rebecca Dead" (November 1939), "Lyric-Lady" ("To Gerard Manley Hopkins," July 1940), "Siren Song" (September 1940), "In Extremis" (July 1944), and "Lady of Peace" (November 1944); in *Commonweal*: "Candidate" (February 16, 1940), "Cologne Epiphany" (December 25, 1942), and "Of Toads and Such" (November 10, 1944); in *Sodalist*: "For a Nun's Golden Wedding" (November 1936); and other poems published in *America*, *Extension*, *Franciscan Herald*, the *Franciscan*, *Compass*, and the *New Mexico Sentinel*.
61. Letter to Provincial Romuald Mollaun, September 10, 1945, "Correspondence with the Provincial, 1937–1946," Franciscan Archives.
62. Chávez, "With Fr. Angelico in the Service," 72, and *Program, Catholic Poetry Society of America*, April 28, 1946, Franciscan Archives.
63. Letter from Chávez to Fr. Romauld Mollaun, October 22, 1945, "Correspondence with the Provincial, 1937–1946," Franciscan Archives.
64. Letter from Chávez to "The Wise Man," December 19, 1946, "Correspondence with the *Chronicle*," Chávez File, Franciscan Archives. Fray Angélico also uses this sentence in "I Saw Her Picture," *St. Anthony Messenger* (December 1945): 22.
65. Chávez, "I Saw Her Picture," 22.
66. Fray Angélico Chávez, *The Old Faith and Old Glory: The Story of the Church in New Mexico since the American Occupation, 1846–1946* (Santa Fe, NM: Santa Fe Press, 1946), 27.

67. Chávez, *The Old Faith and Old Glory*, 33.
68. Chávez, *The Old Faith and Old Glory*, 13.
69. Chávez, *The Old Faith and Old Glory*, 30.
70. Letter from Chávez to Provincial Mollaun, September 6, 1946, "Correspondence with the Provincial, 1937–1946," Franciscan Archives.
71. Letter from Chávez to Provincial, October 2, 1946, "Correspondence with the Provincial, 1937–1946," Franciscan Archives.
72. Chávez corrects this misinformation in later editions of the cathedral booklet and elsewhere, noting that the original name was "La Villa de Santa Fe de los Españoles." The name "Villa of St. Francis of Assisi" came into use two centuries later, he notes, when the City Council chose St. Francis as the patron saint in 1823. See, Chávez, *Chávez: A Distinctive American Clan of New Mexico*, 4n3.
73. Letters from Provincial Mollaun to Chávez, November 20, 1946, and from Chávez to Mollaun, December 4, 1946, "Correspondence with the Provincial, 1937–1946," Franciscan Archives.
74. Fray Angélico Chávez, *The Cathedral of the Royal City of the Holy Faith of St. Francis* (Santa Fe, NM: Schiffani Bros., 1947), section 4, np.
75. *The Santa Fe Cathedral of St. Francis of Assisi*, text and format by Fray Angélico Chávez (1987; updated, Santa Fe: Shifani Brothers, 1995), 54. Citations are to the 1987 edition.
76. Chávez, *The Santa Fe Cathedral of St. Francis of Assisi*, 56.
77. Chávez, *The Santa Fe Cathedral of St. Francis of Assisi*, 56.
78. Letters from Chávez to Provincial Mollaun August 22 and September 19, 1946, "Correspondence with the Provincial, 1937–1946," Franciscan Archives.
79. Letter from Chávez to Provincial Mollaun, July 30, 1947, "Correspondence with the Provincial, 1947–1949," Franciscan Archives.
80. Fray Angélico Chávez, *The Single Rose: The Rose Única and Commentary of Fray Manuel de Santa Clara* (Santa Fe, NM: Los Santos Bookshop, 1948), 49.
81. Chávez, *The Single Rose*, 37.
82. Chávez, *The Single Rose*, 38.
83. Chávez, *The Single Rose*, 46.
84. Chávez, *The Single Rose*, 38, 42.
85. Chávez, *The Single Rose*, 50.
86. Chávez, *The Single Rose*, 54.
87. Chávez, *The Single Rose*, 62.
88. Chávez, *The Single Rose*, 46.
89. Chávez, *The Single Rose*, 34.

Chapter Five

1. Linguists classify Spanish/English-speaking bilinguals as Spanish dominant, English dominant, or the rare ambilingual, that is, completely fluent in both Spanish and English. Although Chávez was an English-dominant bilingual, more fluent in English than Spanish, he publicly asserted his Spanish-language competence in his early historical articles. At the same time, however, he told his Franciscan superior that he would ask a priest from Spain to check his translations of St. Leonard's *Stations of the Cross* for grammar and syntax. See letter from Chávez to Provincial, September 20, 1946, "Correspondence with the Provincial, 1937–1946," Franciscan Archives.
2. Letters from Provincial Mollaun to Chávez, November 20, 1946, and from Chávez to Mollaun, December 4, December 16, 1946, and January 2, 1947, "Correspondence with the Provincial, 1937–1946" and "Correspondence with the Provincial, 1947–1949," Franciscan Archives.
3. Letter from Chávez to Provincial Mollaun, January 7, 1947, "Correspondence with the Provincial, 1947–1949," Franciscan Archives.
4. Letter from Chávez to Provincial Mollaun, February 27, 1947, "Correspondence with the Provincial, 1947–1949," Franciscan Archives.
5. Marc Simmons, "Fray Angélico Chávez: The Making of a Maverick Historian," in *Fray Angélico Chávez: Poet, Priest, and Artist*, ed. Ellen McCracken (Albuquerque: University of New Mexico Press, 2000), 12.
6. Letter from Fr. Cletus Kistner to Provincial Mollaun, November 9, 1947, "Santa Fe Letters, 1945–1950," Santa Fe Place File, Franciscan Archives.
7. Fray Angélico Chávez, "The Gallegos *Relación* Reconsidered," *New Mexico Historical Review* 23 (January 1948): 3.
8. Chávez, "The Gallegos *Relación* Reconsidered," 11, italics in original.
9. Chávez, "The Gallegos *Relación* Reconsidered," 21.
10. Chávez, "The Gallegos *Relación* Reconsidered," 21.
11. Simmons, "Fray Angélico Chávez," 17.
12. Letter from Chávez to Provincial Mollaun, November 25, 1947, "Correspondence with the Provincial, 1947–1949," Franciscan Archives
13. Fray Angélico Chávez, "The Archibeque Story," *El Palacio* 54 (August 1947): 182.
14. A decade earlier, Fray Angélico had attributed to legend the story that Fray Juan de Padilla, the first New Mexican martyr, was buried at Isleta Pueblo in his article "The Gold Hunters" (*Franciscan Herald* 26 [March 1938]: 269), which was accompanied with his own drawing of Isleta. He argued that the first Fray Juan de Padilla, who traveled with the conquistadores seeking gold, died probably on November 30, 1554, at the hands of Indians. Nonetheless, Padilla found his own gold in the souls he was trying to convert to Christianity.
15. Fray Angélico Chávez, "The Mystery of Father Padilla," *El Palacio* (November 1947): 256.

16. Chávez, "The Mystery of Father Padilla," 267.
17. Fray Angélico Chávez, "A Sequel to the Mystery of Father Padilla," *El Palacio* 59 (December 1952): 389.
18. Letter from Chávez to Provincial, March 10, 1948, "Correspondence with the Provincial, 1947–1949," Franciscan Archives.
19. Fray Angélico Chávez, *Coronado's Friars* (Washington, DC: Academy of American Franciscan History, 1968), 86n7. Some writers continue to ignore Fray Angélico's important research on Fr. Padilla, passing on errors. See Don Bullis, "The Martyrdom of Fray Juan De Padilla," *Tradición Revista* (Summer 2005): 56–57.
20. Fray Angélico Chávez, "Don Fernando Durán de Chávez," *El Palacio* 55 (April 1948): 109. In his 1989 book *Chávez: A Distinctive American Clan of New Mexico*, Fray Angélico regularized the spelling of his ancestors' name to "Chaves" and consistently used the form "Durán y Chaves" rather than "Durán de Chávez" as he did in this early article.
21. Chávez, "Don Fernando Durán de Chávez," 116.
22. Chávez, "Don Fernando Durán de Chávez," 117.
23. Fray Angélico Chávez, "El Vicario Don Santiago Roybal," *El Palacio* 55 (August 1948): 252.
24. Letters from Chávez to Provincial Mollaun, March 18 and June 3 1948, "Correspondence with the Provincial, 1947–1949," Franciscan Archives.
25. Letter from Chávez to Provincial Mollaun, November 25, 1947, "Correspondence with the Provincial, 1947–1949," Franciscan Archives.
26. Letters from Chávez to Provincial Mollaun, December 9 and 26, 1947, "Correspondence with the Provincial, 1947–1948," Franciscan Archives.
27. Fray Angélico Chávez, "Nuestra Señora del Rosario La Conquistadora," *New Mexico Historical Review* 23 (April 1943): 94–128; continued in July 1948, 177–216.
28. Even J. Manuel Espinosa concluded his 1936 article on the statue by arguing that the present statue was not the original one brought by Governor de Vargas in 1693, since many statues of the Virgin were brought to New Mexico in the 1693 expedition, and de Vargas' will bequeaths Masses for his protector, the Holy Virgin of Remedies, not La Conquistadora. See manuscript, "The Virgin of the Reconquest of New Mexico," *Mid-America* 18 (April 1936), La Conquistadora File, No. 1, Fray Angélico Chávez History Library and Photographic Archives.
29. Simmons, "Fray Angélico Chávez," 17.
30. Chávez discovered a casual reference to the confraternity in Gómez Robledo's testimony before the Inquisition on February 13, 1664. (Fray Angélico Chávez, *Our Lady of the Conquest* [Santa Fe: Historical Society of New Mexico, 1948], 16).
31. Chávez, *Our Lady of the Conquest*, 29–30.
32. Chávez, *Our Lady of the Conquest*, 32.
33. Chávez, *Our Lady of the Conquest*, 29.

34. Letter from Chávez to Provincial Mollaun, March 10, 1948, "Correspondence with the Provincial, 1947–1948," Franciscan Archives.
35. Letter from Chávez to Provincial, August 18, 1948, and letter to Fr. Forest, editor of the *Provincial Chronicle*, August 19, 1948, "Correspondence with the *Chronicle*," Chávez File, Franciscan Archives.
36. The women in the photograph are identified in a similar photo in Kathryn M. Córdova, *Concha! Concha Ortiz y Pino, Matriarch of a 300-Year-Old New Mexico Legacy* (Santa Fe, NM: Gran Vía, 2004), 118.
37. Even the foreword, which appeared under Archbishop Byrne's name, reflected Fray Angélico's artistic talent. Chávez told his provincial that he in fact was "guilty" of the foreword. After Dr. Morley requested a foreword from the archbishop, the latter asked Fray Angélico to write it, and Morley commented to Fray Angélico, "His Excellency writes beautiful English!" See Chávez's letter to Provincial Mollaun, August 19, 1948, "Correspondence with the Provincial, 1947–1949," Franciscan Archives.
38. Fray Angélico Chávez, "The Modern Story of La Conquistadora," *Santa Fe New Mexican*, July 1, 1973.
39. Fray Angélico Chávez, "Queen of the Southwest," *St. Anthony Messenger* 55 (May 1948): 11. He also tells the provincial on March 10, 1948, that *St. Anthony Messenger* is publishing a more popular version of his lengthy research soon to appear in *New Mexico Historical Review*.
40. Larry Calloway, "Angélico Chávez Views Statue Loss," *Santa Fe New Mexican*, March 25, 1973, 1.
41. Fray Angélico Chávez, "La Conquistadora Is a Paisana," *El Palacio* (October 1950): 299.
42. Chávez, "La Conquistadora Is a Paisana," 299.
43. Chávez, "La Conquistadora Is a Paisana," 300.
44. Chávez, "La Conquistadora Is a Paisana," 306.
45. Chávez, "La Conquistadora Is a Paisana," 306n13.
46. Letter from Fr. Cletus Kistner to Provincial Mollaun, November 9, 1947, "Santa Fe Letters, 1945–1950," Santa Fe Place File, Franciscan Archives.
47. Letter from Chávez to Provincial Mollaun, December 9, 1947, "Correspondence with the Provincial, 1947–1949," Franciscan Archives.
48. Fray Angélico Chávez, "An Ancient Painting of the Assumption in the United States," *St. Anthony Messenger* 56 (May 1949): 28.
49. In 1950 Pope Pius XII declared ex cathedra the Doctrine of the Assumption.
50. Fray Angélico Chávez, "Journey's End for a Pilgrim Lady and a Family," *El Palacio* 56 (April 1949): 99–101.
51. Fray Angélico Chávez, "De Vargas' Negro Drummer," *El Palacio* 56 (May 1949): 131.
52. Chávez, "De Vargas' Negro Drummer," 133.
53. Chávez, "De Vargas' Negro Drummer," 135.
54. Fray Angélico Chávez, "The Mad Poet of Santa Cruz," *New Mexico Folklore Record* 3 (1948–49): 10.

55. Fray Angélico Chávez, "Doña Tules, Her Fame and Her Funeral," *El Palacio* 57 (August 1950): 227.
56. Chávez, "Doña Tules, Her Fame and Her Funeral," 231.
57. Fray Angélico Chávez, "Saints' Names in New Mexico Geography," *El Palacio* 56 (November 1949): 323–35; Chávez, "New Mexico Place-Names from Spanish Proper Names," *El Palacio* 56 (December 1949): 367–82; Chávez, "New Mexico Religious Place Names Other Than Those of Saints," *El Palacio* 57 (January 1950): 23–26; Chávez, "Neo-Mexicanisms in New Mexico Place-names," *El Palacio* 57 (March 1950): 67–79; and Chávez, "Aztec or Nahuatl Words in New Mexico Place-names," *El Palacio* 57 (April 1950): 109–12.
58. Letter from Chávez to Provincial Mollaun, July 14, 1950, "Correspondence with the Provincial, 1950–1954," Franciscan Archives.
59. *Santa Fe New Mexican*, May 7, 1950.
60. Fray Angélico Chávez, *Lamy Memorial* (Santa Fe, NM: Schiffani Bros., 1951), 16.
61. Chávez, *Lamy Memorial*, 21.
62. Chávez, *Lamy Memorial*, 23.
63. Chávez, *Lamy Memorial*, 24.
64. Chávez, *Lamy Memorial*, 27.
65. Chávez, *Lamy Memorial*, 27.
66. Chávez, *Lamy Memorial*, 29.
67. Chávez, *Lamy Memorial*, 88.
68. Fray Angélico listed this ghostwriting work in a letter to the provincial, November 1, 1950, "Correspondence with the Provincial, 1950–1954," Franciscan Archives.
69. See "A Milestone in Clovis," *Provincial Chronicle* 21, no. 4 (Summer 1949): 221–49. The pastor notes that in October 1947 "I drove up to Santa Fe and cornered Fr. Angélico Chávez and 'demanded lovingly' that he draw a sketch for a facade that would befit our new church-to-be. In less time than it takes to tell it, he had drawn a sketch that pleased me at once" (224).

Chapter Six

1. Letter from Chávez to Fr. Urban, September 15, 1952, "Letters 1949–1954," Jemez Pueblo, New Mexico, San Diego, Place File, Franciscan Archives.
2. Fray Angélico Chávez, "From Major to Minor," *Provincial Chronicle* 24, no. 4 (Summer 1952): 279.
3. Fray Angélico complained that the post chaplain wanted him and the others to take on extra duties at the Main Post, in addition to responsibilities for their own battalions, and that the chaplain had accused him and another priest of "sitting on our ass." On the same day he wrote another short note to the provincial: "The Post Chaplain drove up this morning in his

big Cadillac and we had it out here in my office." Fray Angélico lodged a complaint the next day with the brigadier general who sided with Chávez. In early January, he reported, "Since I talked to the General about my fracas with the Post Center crowd, nothing more has been said; The Post Chaplain talks to me but briefly, and strictly business, without looking me in the eye" (letters from Chávez to Provincial, December 19 and 20, 1950, and January 2, 1951, "Correspondence with the Provincial, 1950–1954," Chávez File, Franciscan Archives). According to his brother Francisco Chávez, Fray Angélico came to blows with two officers who came back drunk one night, swearing loudly. After yelling for them to be quiet and one of them calling him a derogatory term, Fray Angélico punched him with his fist and knocked him out (McCracken and García, interview with Francisco Chávez, August 17, 1999).

4. Ellen McCracken and Mario García, interview with Fabián Chávez, August 9, 1996, Santa Fe.
5. Chávez, "From Major to Minor," 280.
6. Chávez, "From Major to Minor," 283.
7. Chávez, "From Major to Minor," 280.
8. Chávez, "From Major to Minor," 283.
9. "The Province and Beyond," *Provincial Chronicle* 24, no. 3 (Spring 1952): 227–29.
10. Fray Angélico Chávez, "Yellow Is Yellow Is Yellow," *Homiletic and Pastoral Review* 53 (February 1953): 445.
11. Chávez, "Yellow Is Yellow Is Yellow," 446.
12. Chávez, "Yellow Is Yellow Is Yellow," 446.
13. Letters from Chávez to Fr. Casey and from Casey to Chávez, November 6 and 11, 1952, "Correspondence with the *Chronicle*," Chávez File, Franciscan Archives.
14. Fray Angélico Chávez, "Santa Fe Church and Convent Sites in the 17th and 18th Centuries," *New Mexico Historical Review* 34 (April 1949): 85–93, sketch, 84.
15. Fray Angélico Chávez, "How Old Is San Miguel," *El Palacio* 60 (April 1953): 150.
16. Chávez, "How Old Is San Miguel," 149.
17. Fray Angélico previewed his research for this article in a response sent to Monsignor Matthew Smith's column "Listening In" in the *New Mexico Register* November 23, 1951. Smith had noted in a previous column that the Christian Brothers at San Miguel now claimed that the church was built in 1541. Although Chávez had hoped to be able to prove San Miguel dated that far back, his research showed that it was not built before 1600, and most probably right after 1610 (*Provincial Chronicle* 24, no. 2 [Winter 1952]: 139–40).
18. Fray Angélico Chávez, "San José de Chama and Its Author," *El Palacio* 60 (April 1953): 154.

19. Chávez, "San José de Chama and Its Author," 157.
20. Fray Angélico Chávez, "The First Santa Fe Fiesta Council, 1712," *New Mexico Historical Review* 28 (July 1953): 183.
21. Chávez, "The First Santa Fe Fiesta Council, 1712," 190.
22. Chávez, "The First Santa Fe Fiesta Council, 1712," 191.
23. Fray Angélico Chávez, "The Kingdom of New Mexico" (Part I), *New Mexico* 31 (August 1953): 58.
24. Fray Angélico Chávez, "The Kingdom of New Mexico" (Part II), *New Mexico* 31 (September 1953): 17.
25. Chávez, "The Kingdom of New Mexico" (Part II), 42.
26. Chávez, "The Kingdom of New Mexico" (Part II), 43.
27. Letter from Kroger to Chávez, August 29, 1953, "Correspondence with the Provincial, 1950–1954," Franciscan Archives.
28. Letter from Chávez to Kroger, August 23, 1953, "Correspondence with the Provincial, 1950–1954," Franciscan Archives.
29. Letters from Chávez to Cisneros, March 10 and 14, 1953, private collection of José Cisneros, El Paso, Texas. I am extremely grateful to historian Félix D. Almaráz Jr. of San Antonio for organizing, photocopying, and sending to me sixty of Chávez's letters, cards, and drawings sent to Cisneros from 1951 to 1991.
30. Letters from Chávez to Cisneros, April 8 and 9, 1953, private collection of José Cisneros.
31. Letter from Chávez to Cisneros July 4, 1953, private collection of José Cisneros.
32. "Now that [the publisher] returned it to me, I dared to erase the Virgin's face and impose one with my own fist—maybe then it would be accepted. It came out looking very much like the Virgin, but (God save me!) my poor lines clashed horribly with your professional ones, so I have ruined that beautiful work you gave me. I trust you'll pardon my foolishness. Don't worry now that I'll do a similar stupidity with the drawings of Oñate and De Vargas!" (letter from Chávez to Cisneros, September 2, 1953, private collection of José Cisneros).
33. Letter from Chávez to Cisneros, December 30, 1954, and W. J. T. Mitchell, *Picture Theory: Essays on Verbal and Visual Representation* (Chicago: University of Chicago Press, 1994), 89n9.
34. Fray Angélico Chávez, reviews of Francis. L. Fugate, *The Spanish Heritage of the Southwest* (El Paso: Texas Western Press, 1952), in *New Mexico* (August 1953): 56; another review of the book appears in *Americas* 10 (July 1953): 99.
35. Fray Angélico Chávez, *Origins of New Mexico Families in the Spanish Colonial Period* (Santa Fe: Historical Society of New Mexico, 1954), xix.
36. Chávez, *Origins of New Mexico Families*, xix.
37. "Then I cut each name and paste it in its place, and after, I make the lines in black ink. It takes a lot of work and patience" (letter from Chávez to Cisneros, April 4, 1953, private collection of José Cisneros).

38. "The dedication was a last-minute inspiration; thus, I told the truth poetically to my Father St. Francis and at the same time a little irony toward my paisanos. With the poetic you remove or hide bitterness" (Letter from Chávez to Cisneros, December 30, 1954, private collection of José Cisneros).
39. Letters from Chávez to Cisneros, July 4 and August 3, 1953, private collection of José Cisneros.
40. Fray Angélico Chávez, *La Conquistadora: The Autobiography of an Ancient Statue* (Paterson, NJ: St. Anthony Guild Press, 1954), 30.
41. Chávez, *La Conquistadora*, 24.
42. Chávez, *La Conquistadora*, 27.
43. Chávez, *La Conquistadora*, 45.
44. Chávez, *La Conquistadora*, 97.
45. Chávez, *La Conquistadora*, 40.
46. Chávez, *La Conquistadora*, 41.
47. Letter from Chávez to Provincial Kroger, September 9, 1954, "Correspondence with the Provincial, 1950–1954," Chávez File, Franciscan Archives.
48. "New Mexico Honors 'La Conquistadora,'" *Provincial Chronicle* 26, no. 3 (Spring 1954): 271–73.
49. "The Province and Beyond," *Provincial Chronicle* 26, no. 4 (Summer 1954): 421–22.
50. Letter from Chávez to Provincial Kroger, September 9, 1954, "Correspondence with the Provincial, 1950–1954," Chávez File, Franciscan Archives.
51. Fray Angélico Chávez, "The Modern Story of La Conquistadora," *Santa Fe New Mexican*, July 1, 1973. His remark about Cardinal Spellman liking his book and agreeing to come appears in Chávez's letter to Provincial Kroger, July 17, 1954, "Correspondence with the Provincial, 1950–1954," Chávez File, Franciscan Archives.
52. Chávez, "The Modern Story of La Conquistadora."
53. Fray Angélico Chávez, "The Penitentes of New Mexico," *New Mexico Historical Review* 29 (April 1954): 97.
54. Chávez, "The Penitentes of New Mexico," 109.
55. Chávez, "The Penitentes of New Mexico," 114.
56. Chávez, "The Penitentes of New Mexico," 115n46.
57. Chávez, "The Penitentes of New Mexico," 100.
58. Chávez, "The Penitentes of New Mexico," 123.
59. Letter from Chávez to Provincial Mollaun, August 22, 1946, "Correspondence with the Provincial, 1937–1946," Chávez File, Franciscan Archives.
60. Letter from Chávez to Provincial Mollaun, November 1, 1950, "Correspondence with the Provincial, 1950–1954," Chávez File, Franciscan Archives. For an account of these negotiations, see Thomas J. Steele and

Rowena A. Rivera, *Penitente Self-Government* (Santa Fe, NM: Ancient City Press, 1985), 63–74. For additional views on the Penitentes, see Marta Weigle, *Brothers of Light, Brothers of Blood: The Penitentes of the Southwest* (Albuquerque: University of New Mexico Press, 1976), and Alberto López Pulido, *The Sacred World of the Penitentes* (Washington, DC: Smithsonian Institution Press, 2000).

61. Ellen McCracken and Mario García, interview with Roque García, August 2005, Santa Fe. An undated photograph in *Penitente Self-Government*, 72, shows Fray Angélico and Archbishop Byrne, perhaps at this Mass.

Chapter Seven

1. Fray Angélico Chávez, "Spanish Salve Sancte Pater," *Provincial Chronicle* 28, no. 1 (Fall 1955): 94–95, and "The Responsory of St. Anthony for Recitation or Singing in Spanish and English," *Provincial Chronicle* 28, no. 2 (Winter 1956): 158–60.
2. Chávez, "The Responsory of St. Anthony," 159.
3. Chávez, "The Responsory of St. Anthony," 159.
4. Fray Angélico Chávez, "Poetry and the Ten Commandments," *Spirit* 23 (November 1956): 146, 147.
5. "The Province and Beyond," *Provincial Chronicle* 30, no. 1 (Fall 1957): 100.
6. Three months later, he turned the fee over to the Jemez house fund because the subscriptions for the book on the families had reached the two-thousand-dollar mark. See letters from Chávez to Provincial Kroger, October 16 and December [15], 1954, "Correspondence with the Provincial, 1950–1954," Chávez File, Franciscan Archives.
7. Letter from Horgan to Chávez, July 1, 1954, "Letters of Interest, 1951–1955," Box 521, File XVI, Chávez Collection, Fray Angélico Chávez History Library and Photographic Archives.
8. Letter from Horgan to Chávez, November 11, 1954, "Letters of Interest, 1951–1955," Box 521, File XVI, Chávez Collection, Fray Angélico Chávez History Library and Photographic Archives.
9. Letters from Horgan to Chávez, October 11 and 25, 1955, "Letters of Interest, 1951–1955," Box 521, File XVI, Chávez Collection, Fray Angélico Chávez History Library and Photographic Archives.
10. Paul Horgan, "The Adventure of the Hundred-Year Proviso," *America*, March 23, 1991, 314.
11. Letter from Horgan to Chávez, December 11, 1952, "Letters of Interest, 1951–1955," Box 521, File XVI, Chávez Collection, Fray Angélico Chávez History Library and Photographic Archives.
12. In a letter to Chávez, March 8, 1956, Paul Horgan wrote, "But what became of your book of stories? Hal said he'd advised you to send it to Knopf. If AAK did not take it on, may I sponsor it with my publishers,

Farrar, Straus and Cudahy?" "Letters of Interest, 1956–1960," Box 521, File XVII, Chávez Collection, Fray Angélico Chávez History Library and Photographic Archives.
13. Letters from Peter Hurd to Chávez, September 14, 1956, and March 22, 1957, and from Horgan to Chávez, October 4, 1957, "Letters of Interest, 1951–1955," Box 521, File XVI, Chávez Collection, Fray Angélico Chávez History Library and Photographic Archives.
14. Fray Angélico Chávez, *From an Altar Screen: El Retablo: Tales from New Mexico* (New York: Farrar, Straus & Cudahy, 1957), 118–19.
15. A few years later he would praise the original santero art again in the foreword he wrote for José E. Espinosa's *Saints in the Valleys* (Albuquerque: University of New Mexico Press, 1960), for "their having been born out of a deep-felt spiritual need, in their creators as well as in the persons requesting them, and not from any purely commercial motive or even for art's sake alone. In this idea of hearth and heart, I am sure, lies the secret of their appeal and of their worth" (ix).
16. Chávez, *From an Altar Screen*, 119. In a review in his own book column (what he termed "an announcement") of the 1977 edition of the book, Fray Angélico describes it as follows: "Santos be praised for a reviewer's advantages! This reprint of seven fantasies of mine about as many New Mexico generations (originally mislabeled *From an Altar Screen* by New York publishers) now gets a rebirth announcement in this apter title and attractive swaddling. Needless to say, Peter Hurd's sketches continue to lend the same old charm." See "Southwestern Bookshelf," *New Mexico* (June 1977): 36.
17. Thomas J. Steele, S.J., "Wonders and Truths: The Short Stories of Fray Angélico Chávez," in *Fray Angélico Chávez: Poet, Priest, and Artist*, ed. Ellen McCracken (Albuquerque: University of New Mexico Press, 2000), 47–52.
18. Chávez, *From an Altar Screen*, 30.
19. Chávez, *From an Altar Screen*, 43.
20. Among other additions and changes to the 1954 version of the story are the sentences: "Since then the Captain had not come to see her, and she had told the Frenchman to stay away," and "Now she was lonelier than ever" (Chávez, *From an Altar Screen*, 35–36).
21. Chávez, *From an Altar Screen*, 53, added material in italics.
22. Chávez, *From an Altar Screen*, 54, added material in italics.
23. Chávez, *From an Altar Screen*, 24, 26.
24. Chávez, *From an Altar Screen*, 113.
25. Letters on file in the Franciscan Archives, Cincinnati, Ohio, reveal that both the censor and the provincial minister were troubled by Dalí's nontraditional representation of the Blessed Virgin in the painting and urged Chávez not to include the reproduction in the book. After a series of letters in which both sides attempted to secure interpretive closure over the semiotic potential of the painting, other Church officials in different stages of

the censorship process ruled in Chávez's favor in December 1957, and the imprimatur was granted shortly thereafter.
26. Letters from Chávez to Provincial Kroger, May 3, 1958, April 1 and May 24, 1959, "Correspondence with the Provincial, 1957–1970," Franciscan Archives.
27. In the new undated typescript, probably prepared in 1989, Chávez notes that he was emboldened to propose the "brazen title pairing of both artist and poet" (vi) for a new edition of the book because of the high praise A. Reynolds Morse gave the poem in his 1973 *Poetic Homage to Gala–Salvador Dalí*. Morse argued that Chávez's poem "was the first serious recognition that a message could be found in Dalí's religious art" (Chávez typescript, Chávez File, Fray Angélico Chávez History Library and Photographic Archives, vi). I submit, however, that the new title Chávez proposed in fact reveals the harmonious, noncompetitive relation Chávez felt between word and image and between his poem and Dalí's painting.
28. "The Virgin does not touch the seat of her throne, nor anything else around her; even the various parts of the classical throne and arch have air spaces in between. The central Child is also suspended in mid-air, and curiously framed in a geometric square cut through the Mother's bosom. A similar window in the Child's own breast encloses a floating piece of bread" (xiii).
29. See Christopher Masters, *Dalí* (London: Phaidon, 1995), 108.
30. See Meredith Etherington-Smith, *The Persistence of Memory: A Biography of Dalí* (New York: Random House, 1992).
31. The magazine article that helped to inspire Fray Angélico Chávez to write his *Port Lligat* poem suggests that Dalí hoped to impart the image of purity to Gala through the motif of the cuttlefish bones. See "Madonna in Mid-air," *Life*, December 18, 1950, 48–50.
32. Fray Angélico Chávez, *The Virgin of Port Lligat* (Fresno, CA: Academy Literary Guild: 1959), xv.
33. For further discussion of Dalí's transgressive imagery in the painting, see Ellen McCracken, "A Dalí-Chávez Duet: Visual and Verbal Semiosis in *The Virgin of Port Lligat*," in *Interdigitations: Essays for Irmengard Rauch*, ed. Gerald F. Carr, Wayne Harbert, and Lihua Zhang (New York: Peter Lang, 1999), 681–89.
34. Chávez notes that he came across a full-page color reproduction of the painting in *Life* magazine and tacked the page on the wall facing his cot; the painting "aroused in me a certain frenzy which, after some weeks of my staring at it, made me compose an ode crammed with images of every sort" (1989 foreword for projected new edition, Chávez File, Fray Angélico Chávez History Library and Photographic Archives).
35. Chávez, *The Virgin of Port Lligat*, xvii.
36. See Murray Krieger, *Ekphrasis: The Illusion of the Natural Sign* (Baltimore, MD: Johns Hopkins University Press, 1992), 17.
37. Chávez, *The Virgin of Port Lligat*, 39.

38. Chávez, *The Virgin of Port Lligat*, 1, 3, 37n8.
39. Chávez, *The Virgin of Port Lligat*, 29.
40. Chávez, *The Virgin of Port Lligat*, 29, 65n94.
41. Chávez, *The Virgin of Port Lligat*, 3.
42. W. J. T. Mitchell, *Picture Theory: Essays on Verbal and Visual Representation* (Chicago: University of Chicago Press, 1994), 152, 89.
43. For a different view of the novel, see Melina V. Vizcaíno, "A New Mexican Triptych: The Civil Rights Movement, the Pueblo Revolt, and Fray Angélico Chávez's *The Lady from Toledo*," in *Recovering Hispanic Religious Thought and Practice of the United States*, ed. Nicolás Kanellos (Newcastle: Cambridge Scholars Publishing, 2007), 145–64.
44. Fray Angélico Chávez, *The Lady from Toledo*, illustrated by the author (Fresno, CA: Academy Guild Press, 1960), 7.
45. Chávez, *The Lady from Toledo*, 136.
46. Chávez, *The Lady from Toledo*, 6.
47. Chávez, *The Lady from Toledo*, 6.
48. Chávez, *The Lady from Toledo*, 162.
49. Fray Angélico Chávez, "Pohé-Yemo's Representative and the Pueblo Revolt of 1680," *New Mexico Historical Review* 42, no. 2 (April 1967): 86.
50. Chávez, "Pohé-Yemo's Representative," 89.
51. Marc Simmons, "Fray Angélico Chávez: The Making of a Maverick Historian," in *Fray Angélico Chávez: Poet, Priest, and Artist*, ed. Ellen McCracken (Albuquerque: University of New Mexico Press, 2000), 21. An unidentified newspaper clipping, "Article by Franciscan Honored," refers to Fray Angélico's having won the one-hundred-dollar award for the 1967 article, Fray Angélico Chávez Collection, Box 520, File X, Fray Angélico Chávez History Library and Photographic Archives.
52. Fr. Angélico Chávez, "San Francisco De Golden, New Mexico," *Provincial Chronicle* 33, no. 2 (Winter 1961): 172.
53. Chávez, "San Francisco De Golden, New Mexico," 172.
54. Ellen McCracken and Mario García, interview with Fred Grillo, August 15, 1996, Santa Fe.
55. Chávez, "San Francisco De Golden, New Mexico," 172.
56. Quoted in Tom Chávez, "La Iglesia de San Francisco de Paula, or the Church at Golden," unpublished paper, 6.
57. Chávez, "La Iglesia de San Francisco de Paula," 7.
58. Chávez, "La Iglesia de San Francisco de Paula," 7.
59. Letter from Archbishop Robert F. Sánchez to Chávez, April 3, 1986, Chávez Collection, Box 521, File 22, Fray Angélico Chávez History Library and Photographic Archives. See also Bob Quick, "One of Life's Crowning Works," *Santa Fe New Mexican*, August 21, 1986, 9, and Tom Chávez, "La Iglesia de San Francisco de Paula," 7. Fray Angélico presented historical arguments for preserving the statue's original faded and chipped blue paint: blue became popular in the 1500s after the Spaniards discovered the dye in

the Philippines, and friars in the New World began to use it for their habits because it was the traditional color of the Blessed Virgin. Earlier, while stationed at Jemez Pueblo, Fray Angélico had similarly arranged for the restoration of the statue of Santo Toribio in the church at the nearby town of Ponderosa. See E. Boyd, "The Only Bulto of Santo Toribio," *El Palacio* 64, no. 3–4 (March–April 1957): 109–14.

60. Chávez, "San Francisco De Golden, New Mexico," 173. Many years earlier Fray Angélico had published a poem, "Sermons in Stone," in the seminary magazine the *Brown and White* 3, no. 7 (April 1927): 3. Here Chávez developed Christ's connection to the literal stones of the terrain in which he was born, lived, and died and the figurative stones such as St. Peter whom he asked to lead the Church. He emphasized the sacrality of stones, some of which "received" and "preserved" Christ's body after the crucifixion and others that are the material of altars on which "the priest doth daily lay Him." Thirty-four years later, Fray Angélico expanded this poetic meditation based on Shakespeare's phrase, "sermons in stones," to suggest that his renovation of the church at Golden would give aesthetic testimony to Christianity to passersby on the newly routed highway.

61. In a May 18, 1961, letter to Fr. Edgar Casey, Chávez notes, "I am busy remodeling the sanctuary of the Cerrillos church—knocking out a big chunk of the rear wall for a built-in reredos. It is tiring work but I love it. Hope to have it finished in a month or so. P.S. The Golden folk are now plastering the chapel, poco a poco, and the AT&SF is sending me a locomotive bell for it" (*Provincial Chronicle* 33, no. 4 [Summer 1961]: 459).

62. "New Sanctuary at Cerrillos, New Mexico," *Provincial Chronicle* 34, no. 2 (Winter 1962): 187–89.

63. "New Sanctuary at Cerrillos, New Mexico," 188. Not only did Fray Angélico wish to document his work on the church and his aesthetic intentions in staining the baldachin only slightly white for contemporary members of his Franciscan province, but for future priests as well. He expresses his fear that someday "some pastor will dab the whole thing with white enamel!" ("New Sanctuary at Cerrillos, New Mexico," 188).

64. Fray Angélico Chávez, *Archives of the Archdiocese of Santa Fe, 1678–1900* (Washington, DC: Academy of American Franciscan History, 1957).

65. Mario T. García, "Fray Angélico Chávez, Religiosity, and New Mexican Oppositional Historical Narrative," in *Fray Angélico Chávez: Poet, Priest, and Artist*, ed. Ellen McCracken (Albuquerque: University of New Mexico Press, 1999), 29.

66. "'Black Legend': Bigotry in Disguise," *New Mexico Register*, May 12, 1961; reprinted in *Provincial Chronicle* 33, no. 4 (Summer 1961): 458.

67. Subsequent references are from the article in *Good Work* 26, no. 4 (Fall 1963): 114–19.

68. Chávez, "'Black Legend,'" *Good Work*, 114.

69. Chávez, "'Black Legend,'" *Good Work*, 115.

70. Although the encyclical "Nostrae Aetate" was not promulgated until October 28, 1965, proclaiming that "the Catholic Church rejects nothing that is true and holy in [other] religions," ecumenism was widely discussed in the years preceding the encyclical.
71. Chávez, "'Black Legend,'" *Good Work*, 119.
72. Chávez, "'Black Legend,'" *Good Work*, 119.
73. Chávez, "'Black Legend,'" *Good Work*, 119.
74. Chávez to Provincial Sylvan Becker, undated Christmas card [December 1964], "Correspondence with the Provincial, 1957–1970," Chávez File, Franciscan Archives.
75. Letter from Chávez to Provincial Becker, August 8, 1965, "Correspondence with the Provincial, 1957–1970," Chávez File, Franciscan Archives.
76. Fray Angélico Chávez, "The Unique Tomb of Fathers Zárate and de la Llana in Santa Fe," *New Mexico Historical Review* 40, no. 2 (April 1965): 104.
77. Fray Angélico Chávez, "Two Holy Friars of New Mexico," *St. Anthony Messenger* (July 1965): 32.
78. Fray Angélico Chávez, "The Holy Man of Zia," *New Mexico Historical Review* 40 (October 1965): 309–17.
79. Fray Angélico Chávez, "The Organist of Heaven," *St. Anthony Messenger* (February 1966): 42–43.
80. Chávez, "The Organist of Heaven," 44.
81. Letters from Chávez to Provincial Kroger, January 25, 1959, and from Kroger to Chávez, January 28, 1959, "Correspondence with the Provincial, 1957–1970," Chávez File, Franciscan Archives.
82. Fray Angélico Chávez, *Coronado's Friars* (Washington, DC: American Academy of Franciscan History, 1968), viii.
83. Chávez, *Coronado's Friars*, 41.
84. Chávez, *Coronado's Friars*, 83.
85. Letters from Fray Angélico to Provincials Sylvan Becker and Roger Huser, August 8, 1965, and July 10, 1968, "Correspondence with the Provincial, 1957–1970" and "Angélico Chávez: Troubled Times," Chávez File, Franciscan Archives.
86. Fray Angélico Chávez, O.F.M., ed. and trans., *The Oroz Codex* (Washington, DC: Academy of American Franciscan History, 1972), v.
87. Chávez, ed. and trans., *The Oroz Codex*, xiv.
88. Chávez, ed. and trans., *The Oroz Codex*, 32.
89. Chávez, ed. and trans., *The Oroz Codex*, 19.
90. Chávez, ed. and trans., *The Oroz Codex*, 20.
91. Letters from Chávez and Blocker to Provincial Huser, February 15, 1970, and February 26, 1969, "Correspondence with the Provincial, 1957–1970" and "Angélico Chávez: Troubled Times," Chávez File, Franciscan Archives.
92. Fray Angélico Chávez, foreword to *Selected Poems: With an Apologia* (Santa Fe: Press of the Territorian, 1969), np.

Chapter Eight

1. Fray Angélico Chávez, O.F.M., "A Canticle of Gratitude," June 13, 1962, Consuelo Chávez Collection, ACC 287, Box 1, Folder 8, Fray Angélico Chávez History Library and Photographic Archives.
2. Letter from Chávez to Provincial Roger Huser, undated ("6/30/71" written on upper left corner), "Troubled Times," Angélico Chávez File, Franciscan Archives.
3. John A. Coleman, *The Evolution of Dutch Catholicism, 1958–1974* (Berkeley: University of California Press, 1978), 248.
4. See "W.A.S.V.," www.tldm.org/news5/w.a.s.v.htm.
5. Letter from Chávez to Provincial Huser, undated, "Troubled Times," Chávez File, Franciscan Archives.
6. *A New Catechism: Catholic Faith for Adults*, trans. Kevin Smyth (New York: Herder and Herder, 1967), 207.
7. For information on the Chicano use of the model of internal colonialism, see Tomás Almaguer, "Toward the Study of Chicano Colonialism," *Aztlán* 2, no. 1 (Spring 1971): 7–20, and Mario Barrera et al., "The Barrio as Internal Colony," in *People and Politics in Urban Society*, ed. Harlan Hahn (Beverly Hills, CA: Sage, 1972), 465–98.
8. Cited in Richard Edward Martínez, *Padres: The National Chicano Priest Movement* (Austin: University of Texas Press, 2005), 72. For further documentation of the concerns of PADRES, see pages 13–50 of this important study.
9. Speech published as "The Authentic Spanish New Mexican—A Question of Identity," in *Environment, People, and Culture*, vol. 1, part 2, *The Inaugural Papers* (Las Cruces, NM: New Mexico State University Press, 1971), 14–19, and as "A Look at Background of N.M. Cultures," *Albuquerque Journal*, December 18, 1970, A-5.
10. Chávez, "The Authentic Spanish New Mexican," 19.
11. Chávez, "The Authentic Spanish New Mexican," 18.
12. Chávez, "The Authentic Spanish New Mexican," 17.
13. This position on the Guadalupe story contrasts sharply with his enthusiasm for the crowning of the Virgin as "Goddess of the Americas" in his article "I Saw Her Picture," *St. Anthony Messenger* 53 (December 1945): 22, written after he accompanied Bishop Metzger of El Paso to the coronation ceremonies in Mexico City in 1945.
14. Richard S. Johnson, "'A Genius of Sorts': Respected Historian Fray Angélico Chávez Keeps Setting the Record Straight," *Empire Magazine*, *Denver Post*, January 11, 1981, 20.
15. McCracken and García, interview with Judge Antonio Chávez, August 20, 1996.
16. Fr. Jack Clark Robinson, interview with Nora Chávez; Fray Angélico Chávez letters to Fred and Marguerite Grillo, August 16, 1973, and

July 12, 1974, "Letters 1973–1974," Box 574, Files 3–4; letter from Jack D. Rittenhouse to Chávez, February 22, 1974, "Letters of Interest 1974–1979," Box 521, File 21, Fray Angélico Chávez Collection, Fray Angélico Chávez History Library and Photographic Archives.

17. Thomas J. Steele, S.J., foreword to *My Penitente Land*, by Fray Angélico Chávez (Santa Fe: Museum of New Mexico Press, 1993), v.
18. Fray Angélico Chávez, *My Penitente Land: Reflections on Spanish New Mexico* (1974; repr., Santa Fe: Museum of New Mexico Press, 1993), 123.
19. Chávez, *My Penitente Land*, 6.
20. Chávez, *My Penitente Land*, xiv.
21. Chávez, *My Penitente Land*, xiv.
22. Chávez, *My Penitente Land*, xiv.
23. Miguel de Unamuno, *Ensayos* (Madrid: Publicaciones de la Residencia de Estudiantes, 1916), 1:57–96.
24. Chávez, *My Penitente Land*, 26.
25. Unamuno, *Ensayos*, 1:81.
26. Chávez, *My Penitente Land*, 29.
27. At Mabel Luhan's request, Lawrence wrote "New Mexico" in December 1928 for *Survey Graphic*. In it he criticizes the cultural experiences of his worldwide travels as superficial: "On the superficies, horizontally, we've been everywhere and done everything, we know all about it. Yet the more we know, superficially, the less we penetrate, vertically." In New Mexico, in contrast, witnessing Native American cultural practices allowed Lawrence "to feel the old, old root of human consciousness still reaching down to depths we know nothing of" (Keith Sagar, ed., *D. H. Lawrence and New Mexico* [Salt Lake City, UT: Gibbs M. Smith, 1982], 95, 97).
28. Chávez, *My Penitente Land*, 40, 38.
29. Chávez, *My Penitente Land*, 32, 37.
30. Chávez, *My Penitente Land*, 47.
31. Chávez, *My Penitente Land*, 50.
32. Chávez, *My Penitente Land*, 64.
33. Villagrá, quoted in Chávez, *My Penitente Land*, 67.
34. Chávez, *My Penitente Land*, 191.
35. Chávez, *My Penitente Land*, 114.
36. Chávez, *My Penitente Land*, 136.
37. Chávez, *My Penitente Land*, 137.
38. Chávez, *My Penitente Land*, 138.
39. Some photographs from his trip, with his creative captions, such as "Cerro de Wagon Mound entre Granada y Anteguerra," (Wagon Mound Hill between Granada and Anteguerra) appear in his photo album *Canticle of the Sun: Franciscan Photos Early Years*, Palace of the Governors, Photo Archives, Santa Fe, New Mexico.
40. Chávez, *My Penitente Land*, 140.

41. "Pilgrimage of La Conquistadora," *Provincial Chronicle* 27, no. 1 (Fall 1954): 29.
42. Fray Angélico Chávez, "Genízaros," in *Handbook of North American Indians*, ed. William C. Sturtevant, vol. 9, *Southwest*, ed. Alfonso Ortiz (Washington, DC: Smithsonian Institution, 1979), 199.
43. "Statement of Ownership, Management and Circulation," *New Mexico* 49 (January–February 1971): 49.
44. See Fray Angélico Chávez, "Tortilla Flat—Of Course It Is!" *New Mexico* 52 (July–August 1974): 36–37, and "Gringo—It's All Greek to Me!" *New Mexico* 49 (July–August 1971): 40.
45. Fray Angélico Chávez, "New Mexico's Real Romeo and Juliet," *New Mexico* 54 (October 1976): 13.
46. Fray Angélico Chávez, "A Renaissance of Christian Heritage in New Mexico," *New Mexico* 50 (November–December 1972): 24–27.
47. Fray Angélico Chávez, "The Carpenter Pueblo," *New Mexico* 49 (September–October 1971): 26–33.
48. Fray Angélico Chávez, "The Mora Country," *New Mexico* 50 (January–February 1972): 35.
49. Fray Angélico Chávez, "Valle de Cochiti," *New Mexico* 51 (January–February 1973): 12.
50. Walter Briggs, "From Your Editors," *New Mexico* 51 (January–February 1973): 3.
51. Chávez, "Valle de Cochiti," 17.
52. Fray Angélico Chávez, "Lo, the Poor Adobe!" *New Mexico* 51 (July–August 1973): 33.
53. Fray Angélico Chávez, "A Sweet Spanish Blonde of New Mexico," *New Mexico* 52 (March–April 1974): 17.
54. Chávez, "A Sweet Spanish Blonde of New Mexico," 17.
55. Fray Angélico Chávez, "New Mexico's Bonnie Prince Chile," *New Mexico* 52 (May–June 1974): 31.
56. Manuel Chávez, "Tortilla Flat—Of Course It Is!" *New Mexico* 52 (July–August 1974): 37.
57. Fray Angélico Chávez, review of *Indian Painters and White Patrons*, by J. J. Brody, "Southwestern Bookshelf," *New Mexico* 49 (September–October 1971): 47.
58. Fray Angélico Chávez, review of *Indians of the American Southwest*, by Bertha P. Dutton, "Southwestern Bookshelf," *New Mexico* 53 (June 1975): 33.
59. Fray Angélico Chávez, review of *The Painter and the Photograph*, by Van Deren Coke, "Southwestern Bookshelf," *New Mexico* 50 (September–October 1972): 45.
60. Fray Angélico Chávez, review of *The Santa Fe Trail*, by Jack D. Rittenhouse, "Southwestern Bookshelf," *New Mexico* 49 (November–December 1971): 63.

61. Fray Angélico Chávez, review of *Cowboy Pete*, by Charles H. Corlett, "Southwestern Bookshelf," *New Mexico* 53 (January 1975): 39.
62. Fray Angélico Chávez, review of *Harold Von Schmidt Draws and Paints the Old West*, ed. Walt Reed, "Southwestern Bookshelf," *New Mexico* 51 (September–October 1973): 36.
63. Fray Angélico Chávez, review of *Logging along the Denver and Rio Grande*, by Gordon S. Chappell, "Southwestern Bookshelf," *New Mexico* 50 (May–June 1972): 46.
64. Fray Angélico Chávez, review of *Backpacking* (and others), by R. C. Rethmel, "Southwestern Bookshelf," *New Mexico* 50 (September–October 1972): 45–46.
65. Fray Angélico Chávez, review of *America's Natural Treasures*, by Stewart L. Udall, "Southwestern Bookshelf," *New Mexico* 50 (November–December 1972): 58.
66. Fray Angélico Chávez, review of *Woodall's Trailering Parks and Campgrounds*, "Southwestern Bookshelf," *New Mexico* 51 (January–February 1973): 48.
67. Fray Angélico Chávez, review of *Bill Mauldin's "Name Your Poison,"* by Bill Mauldin, "Southwestern Bookshelf," *New Mexico* 51 (November–December 1973): 32.
68. See reviews of *Railroads, An American Dream*, by Don Ball Jr., "Southwestern Bookshelf," *New Mexico* 53 (May 1975): 33; *New Mexico, Gift of the Earth*, by Russell D. Butcher, "Southwestern Bookshelf," *New Mexico* 53 (October 1975): 30; and *Far from Cibola*, by Paul Horgan, "Southwestern Bookshelf," *New Mexico* 53 (March 1975): 29.
69. Fray Angélico Chávez, review of *A Landscape for Humans*, by Peter van Dresser, "Southwestern Bookshelf," *New Mexico* 51 (July–August 1973): 43.
70. Fray Angélico Chávez, review of *Black Mesa*, by Suzanne Gordon, "Southwestern Bookshelf," *New Mexico* 52 (January–February 1974): 37.
71. Fray Angélico Chávez, review of *Alfred V. Kidder*, by Richard B. Woodbury, "Southwestern Bookshelf," *New Mexico* 52 (January–February 1974): 36.
72. Fray Angélico Chávez, review of *Juan of Santo Niño*, by Charles Ethrige Minton, "Southwestern Bookshelf," *New Mexico* 51 (November–December 1973): 32.
73. Fray Angélico Chávez, review of *Plural Society in the Southwest*, by Edward H. Spicer, "Southwestern Bookshelf," *New Mexico* 50 (November–December 1972): 56.
74. Fray Angélico Chávez, review of *Wild Life in the Far West*, by James Hobbs, "Southwestern Bookshelf," *New Mexico* 48 (November–December 1970): 64.
75. Fray Angélico Chávez, review of *The Great Pursuit*, by Herbert Molloy Mason Jr., "Southwestern Bookshelf," *New Mexico* 48 (November–December 1970): 64.

76. Fray Angélico Chávez, review of *Shadows of the Past*, by Cleofas M. Jaramillo, and *Compendio de Folklore Nuevo Mejicano*, by Sociedad Folklórica de Santa Fe, "Southwestern Bookshelf," *New Mexico* 51 (May–June 1973): 39.
77. Fray Angélico Chávez, review of *Pablita Velarde*, by Mary Carrol Nelson, "Southwestern Bookshelf," *New Mexico* 50 (January–February 1972): 52.
78. Fray Angélico Chávez, review of *Child of the Hogan*, by Ray Baldwin Louis, "Southwestern Bookshelf," *New Mexico* 54 (April 1976): 8.
79. Fray Angélico Chávez, review of *The Great Southwest*, by Elna Bakker and Richard G. Lilard, "Southwestern Bookshelf," *New Mexico* 51 (March–April 1973): 47.
80. Fray Angélico Chávez, review of *God Is Red*, by Vine Deloria, "Southwestern Bookshelf," *New Mexico* 52 (May–June 1974): 35.
81. Fray Angélico Chávez, review of *Historic Pottery of the Pueblo Indian, 1600–1880*, by Larry Frank and Francis H. Harlow, "Southwestern Bookshelf," *New Mexico* 53 (May 1975): 33.
82. Fray Angélico Chávez, review of *Mexican-Americans*, by Joan W. Moore, "Southwestern Bookshelf," *New Mexico* 49 (September–October 1971): 47.
83. Fray Angélico Chávez, review of *Mexican-Americans Tomorrow*, ed. Gus Tyler, "Southwestern Bookshelf," *New Mexico* 53 (December 1975): 39.
84. Fray Angélico Chávez, review of *Mexican American Artists*, by Francisco [sic] Quirarte, "Southwestern Bookshelf," *New Mexico* 52 (November–December 1973): 31.
85. Fray Angélico Chávez, review of *Little Lion of the Southwest*, by Marc Simmons, "Southwestern Bookshelf," *New Mexico* 51 (November–December 1973): 31.
86. Fray Angélico Chávez, review of *Ácoma, Pueblo in the Sky*, by Ward Alan Minge, "Southwestern Bookshelf," *New Mexico* 54 (September 1976): 28.
87. Fray Angélico Chávez, reviews of *The Architecture and Art of Early Hispanic Colorado*, by Robert Adams, "Southwestern Bookshelf," *New Mexico* 53 (February 1975): 34, and *Chicanos and Native Minorities*, compiled by Rudolph O. de la Garza, Anthony Kruszewski, Tomás A. Arciniega, "Southwestern Bookshelf," *New Mexico* 53 (March–April 1974): 32.
88. Fray Angélico Chávez, review of *Heart of Aztlán*, by Rudolfo A. Anaya, "Southwestern Bookshelf," *New Mexico* 55 (June 1977): 36.
89. Fray Angélico Chávez, review of *Shadow of a Continent*, by Larry L. Meyer, "Southwestern Bookshelf," *New Mexico* 54 (February 1976): 30.
90. Fray Angélico Chávez, review of *Treasure of the Sangre de Cristos*, by Arthur L. Campa, "Southwestern Bookshelf," *New Mexico* 54 (January 1976): 5.
91. Fray Angélico Chávez, review of *Brothers of Light, Brothers of Blood*, by Marta Weigle, "Southwestern Bookshelf," *New Mexico* 54 (June 1976): 21.

92. Fray Angélico Chávez, review of *The First American*, by C. W. Ceram, "Southwestern Bookshelf," *New Mexico* 50 (March–April 1972): 48.
93. Fray Angélico Chávez, review of *Pueblos, Gods, and Spaniards*, by John Upton Terrell, "Southwestern Bookshelf," *New Mexico* 52 (January–February 1974): 36.
94. Fray Angélico Chávez, review of *Ghost Towns and Mining Camps of New Mexico*, by James E. and Barbara H. Sherman, "Southwestern Bookshelf," *New Mexico* 53 (April 1975): 29.
95. Fray Angélico Chávez, review of *Behind the Mountains*, by Oliver LaFarge, and *Las Vegas and Uncle Joe*, by Milton C. Nahm, "Southwestern Bookshelf," *New Mexico* 53 (February 1975): 34.
96. Fray Angélico Chávez, review of *30 Mexican Menus*, by Idella Purnell Stone "Southwestern Bookshelf," *New Mexico* 51 (March–April 1973): 48.
97. Fray Angélico Chávez, review of *This Was Sheep Ranching, Yesterday and Today*, by Virginia Paul, "Southwestern Bookshelf," *New Mexico* 55 (June 1977): 36.
98. Fray Angélico Chávez, review of *Sound Retreat for the Conquistadores*, by John E. Baca, "Southwestern Bookshelf," *New Mexico* 52 (September–October 1974): 33.
99. Fray Angélico Chávez, review of *The Burro*, by Frank Brookshier, "Southwestern Bookshelf," *New Mexico* 52 (July–August 1974): 41.
100. Fray Angélico Chávez, review of *Maverick Tales*, by J. D. Rittenhouse, "Southwestern Bookshelf," *New Mexico* 50 (July–August 1972): 47.
101. Fray Angélico Chávez, review of *The Earth and Man*, "Southwestern Bookshelf," *New Mexico* 51 (May–June 1973): 39.
102. Fray Angélico Chávez, review of *Ansel Adams*, by Liliane De Cock, "Southwestern Bookshelf," *New Mexico* 51 (July–August 1973): 42.
103. Fray Angélico Chávez, review of *My Adventures in Zuñi*, by Frank H. Cushing, "Southwestern Bookshelf," *New Mexico* 52 (January–February 1974): 36.
104. Fray Angélico Chávez, "Southwestern Bookshelf," *New Mexico* 53 (February 1975): 34, and *New Mexico* 53 (March 1975): 29.
105. Fray Angélico Chávez, review of *Ecos Serranos*, by Lautaro Vergara, "Southwestern Bookshelf," *New Mexico* 49 (November–December 1971): 64. For his comments on the techniques of modernism in fiction, see his review of *Nambe-Year One*, by Orlando Romero, "Southwestern Bookshelf," *New Mexico* 55 (March 1977): 40.
106. Fray Angélico Chávez, review of *Enchanted Land . . . New Mexico*, by Harvey Caplin, "Southwestern Bookshelf," *New Mexico* 52 (March–April 1974): 33.
107. Fray Angélico Chávez, review of *A World of Light*, by May Sarton and *The Peter Hurd Sketch Book* by Hurd, "Southwestern Bookshelf," *New Mexico* 55 (February 1977): 41, and *New Mexico* 49 (September–October 1971): 46.
108. Fray Angélico Chávez, review of *The Old Ones of New Mexico*, by Robert Coles, "Southwestern Bookshelf," *New Mexico* 52 (May–June 1974): 34,

review of *Los primeros pobladores*, by Frances L. Swadish, "Southwestern Bookshelf," *New Mexico* 52 (July–August 1974): 42, and review of *Sixteenth Century Mexico*, ed. Munro S. Edmonson, "Southwestern Bookshelf," *New Mexico* 53 (March 1975): 29.
109. Fray Angélico Chávez, "Southwestern Bookshelf," *New Mexico* 53 (January, September, and October 1975): 38, 32, and 30.
110. Letters from Chávez to Fred Grillo, February 2, 12, and April 30, 1972, Box 574, Files 1 and 2, and letter and contract, "Northland Press—*Song of Francis*," File 6, Fray Angélico Chávez Collection, Fray Angélico Chávez History Library and Photographic Archives.
111. Fray Angélico Chávez, *The Song of Francis*, illus. Judy Graese (Flagstaff, AZ: Northland Press, 1973), 7.
112. Chávez, *The Song of Francis*, 24, 33.
113. Royalty statements and contract with Northland Press, Fray Angélico Chávez Collection, File 6, "Northland Press—*Song of Francis*," and book signing advertisement, Consuelo Chávez Collection, Fray Angélico Chávez History Library and Photographic Archives.
114. Fr. Jack Clark Robinson, O.F.M., interview with Robert Fortune Sánchez, May 24, 2008, in Robinson, "The Franciscan Friars of New Mexico: Three Borderlands Trails to Vatican II, 1957–1985" (Ph.D. dissertation, University of California, Santa Barbara, 2009). I am extremely grateful to Fr. Robinson for sharing this material with me.
115. Fray Angélico Chávez, program for Robert F. Sánchez's inauguration held in University Arena in Albuquerque on July 25, 1974, 5.
116. Fray Angélico Chávez, *The Lord and New Mexico* (Albuquerque, NM: Starline Printers, 1975), 1.
117. Chávez, *The Lord and New Mexico*, 4.
118. Larry Calloway, "Stolen Statue Had Role in History," *Albuquerque Journal*, March 25, 1973, A12.
119. Calloway, "Stolen Statue Had Role in History," A12.
120. Ellen McCracken and Mario García, interview with Marcia Muth, Jody Ellis, and Roz Eisenberg, August 13, 1997, Santa Fe.
121. Ellen McCracken and Mario García, interview with Fr. Guadalupe Rivera, August 12, 1997, Santa Fe; letters March 10 and March 15, 1976, Fray Angélico Chávez file, Sunstone Press, Santa Fe.
122. In the translator's note, Fray Angélico suggests that Bolton relied heavily on Herbert S. Auerbach's 1943 translation and reproduced several of its errors. Both Auerbach and Bolton only spot-checked their translations with the manuscript from the Newberry Library in Chicago.
123. Silvestre Vélez de Escalante, *The Domínguez-Escalante Journal: Their Expedition through Colorado, Utah, Arizona, and New Mexico in 1976*, trans. Fray Angélico Chávez, ed. Ted J. Warner (Provo, UT: Brigham Young University Press, 1976), xxi.
124. Vélez de Escalante, *The Domínguez-Escalante Journal*, 129.

125. Vélez de Escalante, *The Domínguez-Escalante Journal*, 130.
126. Vélez de Escalante, *The Domínguez-Escalante Journal*, 80.
127. Vélez de Escalante, *The Domínguez-Escalante Journal*, 49n175.
128. Letter from Chávez to Fred and Marguerite Grillo, September 10, 1975, Chávez Collection, Box 574, No. 2, File 6, Fray Angélico Chávez History Library and Photographic Archives.
129. Letter from Jemmot to Grillo, February 5, 1975, and from Chávez to Grillo, January 15, 1975, Chávez Collection, Box 574, No. 2, Files 8 and 6, Fray Angélico Chávez History Library and Photographic Archives.
130. Letters from Chávez to Morales, October 21, 1975, and November 5, 1976, Chávez Collection, Fray Angélico Chávez History Library and Photographic Archives.

Chapter Nine

1. Fray Angélico Chávez, "Native Hispano Vocations," in *Prophets Denied Honor: An Anthology of the Hispano Church in the United States*, ed. Antonio M. Stevens Arroyo, C.P. (Maryknoll, NY: Orbis Books, 1980), 79.
2. Chávez, "Native Hispano Vocations," 79.
3. Rev. Juan Romero, *Reluctant Dawn*, 2nd ed. (Palm Springs, CA: Taos Connection, 2006), 62n111.
4. Paul Horgan, *Lamy of Santa Fe: His Life and Times* (New York: Farrar, Strauss and Giroux, 1975). Horgan mentions this length of time for writing the book in a letter to Chávez, August 12, 1974, "Letters of Interest 1974–1979," Chávez Collection, Box 521, File 21, Fray Angélico Chávez History Library and Photographic Archives.
5. Horgan, *Lamy of Santa Fe*, 504.
6. Fray Angélico Chávez, "Truth Stalks the Archbishop," *Book Talk: Newsletter of the New Mexico Book League*, February 1982, 6. I thank the meticulous historian and collector Marc Simmons for providing me with this document.
7. Chávez, "Truth Stalks the Archbishop," 6.
8. Letter from Fray Angélico Chávez to Marc Simmons, November 17, 1981, private collection of Marc Simmons.
9. Letter from Fray Angélico Chávez to Fr. Thomas Steele, January 30, 1986, Chávez Collection, (uncatalogued new material, 1997) Fray Angélico Chávez History Library and Photographic Archives.
10. Thomas Chávez terms Fray Angélico "the principal author of this tome," *Wake for a Fat Vicar: Father Juan Felipe Ortiz, Archbishop Lamy, and the New Mexican Catholic Church in the Middle of the Nineteenth Century* (Albuquerque, NM: LPD Press, 2004), 167n35.
11. Fray Angélico Chávez, *But Time and Chance: The Story of Padre Martínez of Taos, 1793–1867* (Santa Fe: Sunstone Press, 1981), foreword, np.
12. Chávez, *But Time and Chance*, 16.

13. Meg Sandoval, "Fray Angélico Chávez," *Denver Catholic Register*, October 3, 1990, 6.
14. Chávez, *But Time and Chance*, 38.
15. Chávez, *But Time and Chance*, 40.
16. Romero, *Reluctant Dawn*, 30–31.
17. Chávez, *But Time and Chance*, 90.
18. Chávez, *But Time and Chance*, 92.
19. Chávez, *But Time and Chance*, 99.
20. Chávez, *But Time and Chance*, 100.
21. Chávez, *But Time and Chance*, 119.
22. Chávez, *But Time and Chance*, 121.
23. Chávez, *But Time and Chance*, 130.
24. Chávez, *But Time and Chance*, 134.
25. For arguments that this excommunication was not conducted according to canon law and is therefore invalid, see Fr. Alberto Gallegos, O.S.M., S.T.L., "Canon Law of the Church and Excommunication," in *Padre Martínez and Bishop Lamy*, ed. Ray John de Aragon (1976; repr., Santa Fe: Sunstone Press: 2006), 122–25.
26. Chávez, *But Time and Chance*, 158.
27. Chávez, *But Time and Chance*, 160.
28. Fray Angélico Chávez, *Très Macho—He Said: Padre Gallegos of Albuquerque, New Mexico's First Congressman* (Santa Fe, NM: William Gannon, 1985), 5.
29. Chávez, *Très Macho*, 6.
30. Chávez, *Très Macho*, 77.
31. Chávez, *Très Macho*, 30.
32. Chávez, *Très Macho*, 10.
33. Transcription of letter from José Martínez to Bishop Zubiría, May 28, 1844, by Mary Taylor, cited in Thomas J. Steele, S.J., "Padre Gallegos, Père Machebeuf, and the Albuquerque Rectory," in *Folk and Church in Nineteenth Century New Mexico*, ed. Thomas J. Steele (Colorado Springs: Hulbert Center for Southwest Studies/Colorado College, 1993), 58–72.
34. Chávez, *Très Macho*, 45.
35. Chávez, *Très Macho*, 46.
36. Chávez, *Très Macho*, 76.
37. Chávez, *Très Macho*, 94.
38. Chávez, *Très Macho*, 104.
39. Chávez, *Très Macho*, 105.
40. Fray Angélico Chávez, "A Nineteenth Century New Mexico Schism," *New Mexico Historical Review* 58, no. 1 (January 1983): 35–54.
41. Fray Angélico Chávez and Thomas E. Chavez, *Wake for a Fat Vicar*, 92.
42. Chávez and Chavez, *Wake for a Fat Vicar*, 98.
43. Horgan, *Lamy of Santa Fe*, 113–14, cited in Chávez, *Wake for a Fat Vicar*, 98.
44. Chávez and Chavez, *Wake for a Fat Vicar*, 106.

45. Chávez and Chávez, *Wake for a Fat Vicar*, 137.
46. Chávez and Chávez, *Wake for a Fat Vicar*, 164.
47. Chávez and Chávez, *Wake for a Fat Vicar*, 205.
48. Chávez and Chávez, *Wake for a Fat Vicar*, 205.
49. Chávez, "A Nineteenth Century New Mexico Schism," 35–54.
50. Fray Angélico Chávez, *Chávez: A Distinctive American Clan of New Mexico* (Santa Fe, NM: William Gannon, 1989), xv.
51. Marc Simmons, "Fray Angélico Chávez: The Making of a Maverick Historian," in *Fray Angélico Chávez: Poet, Priest, and Artist*, ed. Ellen McCracken, 11–23 (Albuquerque: University of New Mexico Press, 2000), 16; letters from Chávez to Scholes, January 20 and 23, 1948, private collection of Marc Simmons.
52. Chávez, *Chávez*, 10.
53. Chávez, *Chávez*, 11n8.
54. Programs for the Chávez reunions, May 30, 1967, St. John the Baptist Church, Santa Fe, and May 30, 1981, El Rancho de las Golondrinas, Chávez Collection, Box 574, No. 2, File 12 (c), Fray Angélico Chávez History Library and Photographic Archives.
55. Fray Angélico uses the metaphor of the "Smiths and Jones" in the book when recounting a period when some New Mexico Chávezes called themselves "los Chaves Mexicanos" (*Chávez*, 117) because their grandmother had come from Mexico City. Some even used *Mexicano* in their surname as Church records show. His own grandfather Eugenio Chávez proudly used the term, hoping to distinguish himself from the many other Chávezes in New Mexico, but he was mistaken about having a Mexico City ancestor, Fray Angélico notes.
56. In citing the original name of Santa Fe here, Fray Angélico also corrects his earlier rendition of the name in the 1947 booklet on the cathedral, noting that the "villa de St. Francis of Assisi" did not come into use until after 1823 when the city council chose St. Francis as the patron saint (*Chávez*, 4n3).
57. This illustration originally appeared in *Origins of New Mexico Families* (1954). Fray Angélico's correspondence with Cisneros at that time shows his role in advising his friend on historical figures to include and symbols such as this. Cisneros notes that Fray Angélico sent him a picture of his family that he used to draw the face of the figure wearing the Chávez coat of arms in this illustration (Ellen McCracken and Mario García, interview with José Cisneros, August 21, 1996, El Paso, Texas).
58. Chávez, *Chávez*, 60.
59. Chávez, *Chávez*, 66.
60. Chávez, *Chávez*, 145, original italics.
61. Chávez, *Chávez*, 146.
62. Letter from Chávez to Governor Bruce King, October 5, 1973, "Letters of Interest," Chávez Collection, Box 521, File XXI, Fray Angélico Chávez History Library and Photographic Archives.
63. Undated newspaper clipping, Consuelo Chávez Collection, Fray Angélico

Chávez History Library and Photographic Archives.
64. Quoted in Larry Calloway, "Angélico Chávez Views Statue Loss," *Santa Fe New Mexican*, March 25, 1973, 1.
65. In the *Santa Fe New Mexican*, December 2, 1973.
66. French semiotician Roland Barthes argues that because visual images are polysemous, they often undergo the process of "anchoring" whereby one of their many meanings is secured through a caption or other verbal text. See "Rhetoric of the Image," in *Image, Music, Text*, ed. and trans. Stephen Heath (New York: Hill & Wang, 1977), 32–51.
67. Ellen McCracken and Mario García, interview with Donna Quasthoff, August 18, 1998, Santa Fe, New Mexico.
68. As usually occurred with Fray Angélico's brochures and books on the cathedral and the Church in New Mexico, no authorship is attributed to him. It is important now to recognize his key role as the author of the narrative depicted on the cathedral doors.
69. Fray Angélico Chávez, "Reredos," Chávez Collection, Box 520, File 10, Fray Angélico Chávez History Library and Photographic Archives.
70. Fray Angélico Chávez, "Selecting Artist for Reredos No Easy Task," *Santa Fe New Mexican*, December 1987.
71. He mentions his condition in 1993 letters to two friends. To fellow seminary student Fr. Bernard Gerbus, he writes, "At 83 in April, I am in poor shape. First I have a *tumor* at the top of my brain. It affects my memory of persons and things. Second, I have a bad *artery* which is not operable and can burst anytime. When it does, the doctor says, I die right away" (June 19, 1993, letter made available by the late Fr. Bernard Gerbus, O.F.M., Cincinnati). On December 12 he wrote to Doris Maiorano: "My condition could be worse than yours. Brain tumor and incurable artery. It can burst at any time. Doctors said I would die this year. But here I am as Xmas arrives!" (December 12, 1993, letter made available by Mrs. Doris Maiorano, New Haven, Connecticut).
72. Fray Angélico Chávez, "A Fountain Mystery," Consuelo Chávez Collection, ACC 287, Box 1, Folder 8, Fray Angélico Chávez History Library and Photographic Archives.

Note on Sources

THE PRIMARY WORK UPON WHICH this study rests is the invaluable bibliography of Chávez's writing compiled by Phyllis Morgan (Morales). The information in this book, *Fray Angélico Chávez: A Bibliography of His Published Writings (1925–1978)* (Santa Fe, NM: Lightning Tree, 1980), allowed me to obtain copies of all of Chávez's writing, the prerequisite for writing this book. I direct readers to this key reference work for a listing of Chávez's writing through 1978, since including a bibliography of all of Chávez's work in this book would be repetitive and prohibited by space limitations.

The extensive Fray Angélico Chávez Collection at the Fray Angélico Chávez History Library, Palace of the Governors, Santa Fe, contains thousands of documents donated by Chávez, his family, friends, and acquaintances relating to his life and work. Among the material are manuscripts, correspondence, artwork, newspaper articles, military records, memorabilia, and the original book *Cantares* donated by his sister-in-law Bernice Chávez. The Consuelo Chávez Collection, donated by his niece, contains hundreds of documents collected over the years by his sister Nora Chávez. The History Library also houses invaluable collections relating to people Chávez worked with such as Witter Bynner and other members of the Santa Fe Writers Group.

The archives of the Franciscan Province of St. John the Baptist of Cincinnati houses meticulous records of almost every phase of Chávez's life, from his entry to the seminary in 1924 until the years after his departure from the order in 1971. Correspondence, artwork, manuscripts, literary texts, school records, club minutes, newspaper articles, and photographs richly document Chávez's student years and his work as a Franciscan. "A Chronological Journal of Duns Scotus College, Detroit" chronicles the daily life of students in the college's first three years when Chávez studied there. "Place Files" about individual Franciscan missions in New Mexico contain important documentation about Chávez's life and work. The archives houses the complete bound issues of the student publication the *Brown and White*, for which Chávez wrote and was editor, and bound issues of the *Provincial Chronicle*, the publication of St. John the Baptist Province. Other difficult-to-find material such as Chávez's publications in the *Sodalist* are also available in the archives.

The offices of *St. Anthony Messenger* in Cincinnati house bound issues of the entire run of the magazine.

The Santa Barbara Mission Archive Library in Santa Barbara, California, houses valuable Franciscan documents and books. Especially useful is the complete bound issues of the *Provincial Chronicle* of St. John the Baptist Province, which provides much information on friars and missionary work in New Mexico over the years of Chávez's ministry.

The Archives of the Archdiocese of Santa Fe contains documents on Chávez and his work, including newspaper articles, the minutes of the meetings on remodeling St. Francis Cathedral, the thousands of "priest cards" he created on Franciscan priests who ministered in New Mexico over three centuries, and many of his publications.

The Santa Fe Public Library houses microfilm of the newspaper the *Santa Fe New Mexican* as well as vertical files with material on topics related to Chávez's life such as the Santa Fe Fiesta and La Conquistadora.

Oral interviews and written testimony given by nearly eighty people who knew Chávez have provided invaluable information, not all of which could be included in this book. See the acknowledgments for a listing of these sources.

Index

Page numbers in italic text indicate illustrations.

Acoma, 12, 15, 68, 79, 102, 189, 194, 296, 322–23
Adams, Eleanor B., 42
anti-Communism, 32, 93–94, 107, 156–57, 269–70
anti-Semitism, 87–88
Aragón, Father Salvador, 41, 51, 63, 312
Archives of the Archdiocese of Santa Fe, 33, 41, 45, 48, 170, 294–95

Baca, Father Michael, 50, 56, 312
Barceló, Doña Tules, 84, 85, 86, 87, 89, 221–23
Black Legend, the, 297–99, 345
book reviews, by Chávez, 336–48
Boyd, E., 49, 258, 291
Bynner, Witter, 7, 9, 19, 24, 50, 66, 70, 72, 79, 99, 103, 105, 116, 117, *118*, 119, 123, 124, 130, 455
Byrne, Archbishop Edwin, 38, 40, 41, 43, 53, 181, 189, 227, 230, 256, 263

Cantares: Canticles and Poems of Youth, 22, 98–99, 102–6, 113–16, 120, 125–26, 184, 415n71, 416n88, 416n97
Cassidy, Gerald, 12, 19, 66, 72, 77–78, 84, 89, 414n55
castizo, the, 320, 325, 327, 328, 335
Cather, Willa, 6, 60, 66, 84, 85, 89, 338–39, 360, 362, 375, 378, 380, 413n38
Catholic Poetry Society of America, 31, 44, 169, 186
Cerrillos, NM, St. Joseph Church at, 5, 48, 49, 289, 290, 292–93, 297, 330, 384
Charlot, Jean, 33, 212
Chávez, Bernice (sister-in-law), 36, 98–99, 403n35, 405n71
Chávez, Consuelo (Gorski), 28–29, 31, 146, 382
Chávez, Consuelo (niece), 56, 62, 64
Chávez, Fabián, Jr., *18*, 49, 61, 233, 245, 290, 382, 402n27
Chávez, Fabián, Sr., 10, 12, 15, 18, 22,

46, 47, 54, 78, 125, 139, 382, 401n13, 402n27
Chávez, Francisco Eugenio (Gene), 18, *18*, 26, 63–64, 164–65, 382, 402n27, 433–34n3
Chávez, José, 36, 382
Chávez, Judge Antonio, 18, 318, 382, 401n13, 402n26
Chávez, Mary (niece), 18–19
Chávez, Nicolasa Roybal de, 10, *18*, 20, 22, 29, 46, 47, 54, 93, 125, 218, 245, 308, 318, 382, 402n26, 421n59
Chávez, Nora, 12, 14, 18, 22, 24, 57, 63, 64, 146, 319, 382, 385
Chávez, Senator Dennis, 49, 156, 387–88
Chávez, Thomas (nephew), 62, 153, 250, 376, 433n89, 450n10
Chávez family history, 207–8, 211, 382–89
Chicanos, the, 9, 53, 315, 316, 317, 328, 342–44, 358, 370, 397, 399, 409n124
Cisneros, José, 45, 245–47, 249, 250–52, 266, 270, 386, 452n57
Clothed with the Sun, 4, 24, 104, 117, 120, 123, 124–27
Cochiti Pueblo, 25, 33, 196; article about, 331, 333–34; poem about, 106, 119, 127; restoring church at, 26, 144
Conquistadora, La: chapel of, 3, 5, 45–46, 53, 258–59, 274, 296, 300, 307, 323–24; Chávez's writings about, 39–40, 43, 89, 209–18, 227–28, 244, 250–56, 259, 265, 272, 274, 353, 356; Cofradía of, 3, 193–95, 208, 238, 258–59, 296; coronation of, 40, 392; dresses for, 37, 230, 235–36; pilgrimage of, 40, 257–58, 257, 329; theft of, 353, 390
Corbin Henderson, Alice, 24, 66, 67, 75–76, 106, 117, *118*, 123, 124, 130, 134, 261
Coronado's Friars, 52, 302–5

Daeger, Albert (archbishop of Santa Fe), 15, 16, 23, 138, 140, 141, 189
Dalí, Salvador, 5, 46, 166, 280–83, 439n27
del Río, Dolores, 16, 70, 141, 145
Domingo Station, church renovation at, 22, *140*, 141–42, 421n64
Domínguez, Fray Francisco Atanasio, 34, 42, 215, 239, 257, 260, 295, 354–55

Domínguez-Escalante Journal, The, 354–56
drama. *See* plays
Duns Scotus College, 20, 31, 74, 89, 97, 107–9, 119, 155, 455
Dutch Catechism, the, 54–55, 313–15, 318

ekphrasis, 121, 193, 327
Eleven Lady-Lyrics, 31, 99, 117, 121, 181–84, 186, 191, 230

Fletcher, John Gould, 3, 9, 24, 28, 66, 110, 123, 124, 131, 166, 168–69, 196
Fort Bliss, TX, 31, 35, 36, 43, 56, 186, 233, 234, 235, 245
Franciscans, the, 56, 64, 75; colonial missionaries, 294–307, 329, 354–56; history of, 15–16, 32, 45–46, 158–59, 188, 189, 194, 202, 203–7, 219–20, 237, 232–33, 242, 250, 385–86; martyrs, 15, 32, 113–14; poems on, 103–4, 113–14, 125; Third Order, 32, 260, 263, 266–68, 320, 329, 345, 364
From an Altar Screen (When the Santos Talked), 273–79, 348, 438n16, 438n20

Gallegos, Padre José Manuel, 60, 66, 359, 360, 366, 369–76
gaucho costume, 7, 8, 9, 19, 77, 242, 397, 412n10
genízaros, the, 316–17, 330
Germany, tour of duty in, 37–38, 232–36, 235, 256, 321, 330
Gilpin, Laura, 39, 40, 230, 255
Golden, NM, church of San Francisco at, 5, 48–49, 289–92, *289*, 292, 345–46, 384, 422n71, 441n61
Graese, Judy, 57–58, 349, 350, 351
Grillo, Frederick, 58, 349, 356, 357
Guadalupe, Virgin of, 129, 137, 138, 139, 142, 148, 152, 187, 195, 252, 317, 318, 324, 325–26; in Spain, 38, 224, 236, 254, 327, 383, 393
Guam, 29, 174–75
Guitars and Adobes, 12, 83–90, 122, 144, 166, 284, 414n55

health problems of Fray Angélico, 1, 6, 41, 30, 33, 43, 51, 53, 54, 62–64, 175, 180, 206, 346, 361, 396, 404n57, 453n71
Hesse, Fr. Jerome, 16, 23, 37, 49, 54, 76, 141, 161, 164, 190, 425n130
history research: early articles, 203–26, 216; post-1953, 237–44; on Chávez family history, 382–89, 207–8, 211; on La Conquistadora, 209–14, 215–18, 250–56; on early friars, 32, 52, 160, 195, 202, 207, 228, 233, 253, 270, 288, 294–97, 299–307, 352, 354–56; on New Mexico families, 108, 244–51; on nineteenth-century priests, 359–82; on the Penitentes, 259–64
Horgan, Paul, 9, 40, 43, 44, 58, 60, 271–73, 348, 359, 360, 376–78, 437n12
Hurd, Peter, 266, 273, 275, 278–79, 347, 398
hymns, 266–69, 267

identity, 6, 8–10, 15, 18, 72, 81, 82, 83, 91–94, 128, 138, 139, 184, 191, 201, 207, 217–18, 306, 308, 350, 370, 396; American, 3, 6, 9, 71, 168, 184–85, 188, 189, 215, 243, 344, 352, 383, 389, 397; ethnic, 69, 70, 72, 77, 80, 91, 94, 98, 127, 184–85, 221, 316–17, 320, 343, 354, 383, 389, 397–98; hybrid, 3, 68, 91, 99, 168, 185, 190, 251–52, 294, 297, 397–98; religious, 3, 70, 80, 81, 105, 159, 190, 191, 204, 240, 298–99, 312, 354, 362, 397, 416n97

Jemez Pueblo, 42, 44, 46, 48, 154, 160, 232, 251, 256, 258, 302, 437n6; history of, 163, 207, 332, 381, 386

Kennedy Onassis, Jacqueline, 60, 393

La Conquistadora: Autobiography of an Ancient Statue, 39, 200, 217, 244, 250–56, 264, 265, 353, 356
Lady from Toledo, The, 49–50, 266, 284–89
Lamy, Archbishop Jean-Baptiste, 6, 60, 163, 188, 260, 272, 352; and Padre Gallegos, 369–76; and Padre Martínez, 359–68; and the Penitentes, 261–62; and Vicar Juan Felipe Ortiz, 376–82; in *Guitars and Adobes*, 84–89; images of, 188–89; poem about, 121–22
Lamy Memorial, 35, 214, 227–30
Lawrence, D. H., 66, 322, 444n27
Long, Haniel, 24, 66, 115, 117, *118*, 119, 123, 130
Lord and New Mexico, The, 348, 352–53

Machebeuf, Father Joseph P., 6, 60, 359–60, 365–80
Martin, Robert, 32, 33, 35, 191, 212, 230, 256, 369
Martínez, Padre Antonio José, 60, 229, 262, 295, 338, 359–69, 371, 376, 377–79, 385, 387
Metzger, Bishop Sidney, 41, 45, 186, 256, 443n13
Missions of New Mexico, 1776, 34, 40, 42, 215, 234, 256, 260, 275–76, 295, 348, 356, 389
Momaday, N. Scott, 38–39
Mora, NM, 12–13, *14*, 15, 16, 22, 76, 84, 85, 86, 92, 320, 331, 332–33
Morley, Sylvanus Griswold, 33–34, 212, 214, 432n37
Museum of Fine Arts, Santa Fe, 15, 133, 143, 145, 158, 401n19
My Penitente Land, 14, 59–60, 147, 236, 261, 316, 317, 319–28, 335, 342, 348, 352, 357, 359, 384, 414n46

Native Americans, 24, 26, 38, 76–77, 80, 85, 101–2, 104, 105, 159–63, 172, 193, 237, 242, 244, 254, 279, 286–88, 296, 297–99, 304, 321–25, 330, 342, 355–56, 387, 388, 444n27
New Mexico Triptych, 24–25, 50, 130–39, *132*, 166, 172, 185, 212, 271–72, 273, 279, 339

Old Faith and Old Glory, The, 31, 187–90, 227
ordination, 22, 51, 83, 111, *112*, 311

Origins of New Mexico Families, 5, 41, 208, 218, 240, 241, 244–51, 271, 285, 348, 383
Oroz Codex, The, 5, 52, 299, 304, 305–7, 349
Ortiz, Rebecca, 121, 123, 146–47, 422n79
Ortiz, Vicar Juan Felipe, 60, 161, 189, 359, 361, 376–81
Our Lady of the Conquest, 33–34, 209–14

PADRES, 53, 315, 316, 318, 358, 359
paintings and art work, 16, 42, 51, 65, 112, 139, 154, 189, 266, 384–85, 390; *By East García*, 18, 19, 106, 412n15; in the seminary, 16, 19, 70, 72–73, 73, 74, 77, 82, 142, 145; at Peña Blanca, 114, 115, 117, 122, 125, 131, 132, 350, 400n55; *On Acequia Madre*, 18, 20
Peña Blanca, 16, 22, 226, 333, 371; Chávez's ministry at, 27, 33–35, 41, 52, 55, 110, 165, 215, 311; demolition of church at, 62, 152–53, 294; house chronicle of, 141–42, 147–48, 160–61, 204; murals painted at, 114, 115, 117, 122, 125, 131, 132, 350, 400n55; remodeling of church at, 23–24, 142–53, 149, 150, 187, 333–34; literature about or written at, 3, 25, 122, 123, 137, 403n39
Penitentes, the, 10, 14, 32, 130, 135, 136, 137, 225, 230, 259–64, 296, 320–21, 324, 326, 345, 364, 421n59
Philippines, the, 29, 37, 168, 175–81, 177, 309, 338, 427n56
place-names in New Mexico, 223–26, 296
plays: *The Beloved*, 20, 107–9, 119, 417n103
poetry, early, 98–107; post-1937, 115–27, 166; on Writers Page, 115, 117, 119–21, 147; value of, 169; WWII period, 168, 170–72, 173–74, 175, 178–80, 181–84, 186, 195–98; last book of, 308–10
Poets' Roundups, 7, 24, 70, 104, 117–19, 118, 122, 130, 168, 429n18
Pohé-Yemó, 52–53, 286, 289, 388
pseudonyms (of Chávez), 83–84, 90–91, 94, 95, 97, 98, 127–28, 164, 357, 414n49
Pueblo Revolt, 32, 52–53, 89, 113–14, 160,
194, 207, 210, 217, 224, 228, 237, 239, 248, 253, 284, 285, 287, 297, 346, 388

Robinson, Father Jack Clark, 63, 64, 310, 411n144, 420n55, 449n114

Sánchez, Archbishop Robert, 57, 60, 61, 62, 195, 291, 351–52, 357
San Felipe de Neri church, Albuquerque, 224, 369, 371, 375, 381
San Felipe Pueblo, 26, 52, 172–73, 194
Santa Fe Cathedral of St. Francis of Assisi, The, 191–95
Santa Fe Writers Group, 4, 7, 19, 24, 70, 72, 77, 84, 89, 104, 109, 110, 116, 118, 131, 134, 139, 185, 455
Santo Domingo Pueblo, 28, 61, 129, 224, 288; history of, 154, 159–63, 186, 201, 301; interdict, 25, 403n43; Thornton Wilder and, 122
Sarton, May, 26, 66, 181, 347
Scholes, France V., 34, 42, 58, 168, 215, 230, 238, 297, 383, 388
Selected Poems with an Apologia, 53, 115, 308–10, 348
seminary schedule, 73–74
Seraphic Days, 155–58, 198
sermons, of Fray Angélico, 26, 40, 41, 42, 108, 144, 154–55, 186, 258, 441n60
Serra, Fray Junípero, 11–12, 102–3, 202, 313
Shuster, Will, 19, 24, 67, 70, 72, 118
Simmons, Marc, 42, 50, 202, 205, 210, 289, 343, 360
Single Rose, The, 26, 32–33, 127, 163–64, 165, 166, 169, 184, 195–98
Song of Francis, The, 57–58, 342, 349–51
Sosaya, Agustín (Gus), 15, 24, 149, 151
Sosaya, Mónica, 22, 402n34
Spellman, Cardinal Francis, 40, 48, 181, 186, 258, 269, 270, 279
St. Francis Cathedral, Santa Fe, 144, 192, 323–24, 413n38; booklet on, 190–95; 231, 247; Cardinal Spellman at, 40; history of, 15, 32, 52, 237–40, 396; King and Queen of Spain at, 393; renovations of, 42, 45, 49, 53, 61–62, 291, 299–301, 391–93, 453n68

St. Francis mural cycle, *114, 131, 131,*
142-43
St. Joseph Church. *See* Cerrillos, NM, St.
Joseph Church at
Stations of the Cross, at Peña Blanca, 3,
23, 25, 62, 131, 142, 144-47, *145,*
245, 273, 420n55; translation of St.
Leonard's, 31, 190, 200, 230

Third Order of St. Francis, 32, 160, 261,
262, 320

Udall, Stewart, 60-61, *61,* 393

Vatican II, 53, 54, 55, 161, 188, 195, 288,
292, 297, 298, 299, 313, 314, 319, 331,
352
Vierra, Carlos, 12, 66, 67, 72, 133, 145,
401n10
Virgin of Port Lligat, The, 5, 43, 46, 48,
99, 166, 198, 279-84, 309
visual/verbal hybridity, 10, 82, 106, 138-
39, 144, 279-84, 347, 424n109. *See also*
ekphrasis

Wagon Mound, 10-12, 38, 196, 338,
444n39
Wilder, Thornton, 9, 19, 24, 25, 66, 117,
118, 122-23, 166
World War II, 4, 11, 30, 164, 166, 167-95,
177, 271, 274, 287, 309, 383, 397,
427n56

www.ingramcontent.com/pod-product-compliance
Lightning Source LLC
Chambersburg PA
CBHW030103010526
44116CB00005B/79